WRITERS
OF THE
INDIAN DIASPORA

WRITERS
OF THE
INDIAN DIASPORA

A Bio-Bibliographical
Critical Sourcebook

EDITED BY

Emmanuel S. Nelson

Greenwood Press
Westport, Connecticut • London

Library of Congress Cataloging-in-Publication Data

Writers of the Indian Diaspora : a bio-bibliographical critical
  sourcebook / edited by Emmanuel S. Nelson.
      p.   cm.
    Includes bibliographical references and index.
    ISBN 0–313–27904–7
    1. Indic literature (English)—Foreign authors—History and
  criticism.   2. Indic literature (English)—Foreign authors—
  Bibliography. 3. Authors, Indic—Foreign countries—Biography.
  I. Nelson, Emmanuel S. (Emmanuel Sampath).
  PR9485.45.W75   1993
  820.9'891411—dc20   92–27898

British Library Cataloguing in Publication Data is available.

Library of Congress Catalog Card Number: 92–27898
ISBN: 0–313–27904–7

First published in 1993

Greenwood Press, 88 Post Road West, Westport, CT 06881
An imprint of Greenwood Publishing Group, Inc.

Printed in the United States of America

∞™

The paper used in this book complies with the
Permanent Paper Standard issued by the National
Information Standards Organization (Z39.48–1984).

10 9 8 7 6 5 4 3 2 1

Copyright Acknowledgments

The editor and the publisher gratefully acknowledge permission to reprint
excerpts from the works of Meena Alexander, including a letter to Denise Knight,
April 12, 1992; and the works of Rienzi Crusz, Kirpal Singh, and Edwin
Thumboo.

For Anand and Melvin

CONTENTS

PREFACE

The essays in this sourcebook have two central assumptions in common: first, that many of us, as members of the Indian diaspora, share a diasporic consciousness; second, that our shared sensibility—generated in part by a complex network of historical connections, spiritual affinities, and unifying cultural memories—manifests itself in varying degrees in the literary productions of our communities around the world. This volume, therefore, uses the concept of our global dispersal as a structural and thematic framework to examine the imaginative works of nearly sixty representative writers of the Indian diaspora. By applying the diasporic paradigm to study Indian literature produced outside the Indian center, this text broadens and reinforces several of the critical concepts advanced in my earlier work, *Reworlding: The Literature of the Indian Diaspora* (Greenwood Press, 1992).

A primary objective of this sourcebook is to offer reliable, thorough, and up-to-date biographical, bibliographical, and critical information on the writers. Advanced scholars will find this volume a useful research tool; however, its user-friendly style, format, and level of complexity should make it accessible to a much wider audience. Each of the entries begins with relevant biographical information on the writer, offers an interpretive summary of his/her major texts, provides an overview of the critical reception accorded his/her work, and concludes with a selected bibliography that lists, separately, the primary works and the critical sources. The introductory essay by Nalini Natarajan, which follows this preface, engages several theoretical issues that are significant in the context of Indian diasporic studies.

This sourcebook does not claim to be comprehensive in its coverage: for example, it excludes those writers of the diaspora who publish primarily in languages other than English. It does, however, include many representative writers from all geographical areas of the diaspora—from the South Pacific to South America, from the Indian Ocean islands of Mauritius and Singapore to the suburbs of New York, Johannesburg, London, and Toronto. The artists included in the study express themselves through a variety of literary forms: fiction, poetry, formal essay, travelogue, biography, and autobiography. An overwhelming majority of these writers are "Indian" in the sense that they could trace their roots to India—that vast territory carved out of the larger subcontinent in 1947. But some of the writers can be legitimately identified with Pakistan, Bangladesh, or Sri Lanka.

The authors included in this volume reflect the staggering diversity of the spectacular Indian mosaic: they represent a multitude of ethnicities, languages, and religious traditions. Some of them—such as Salman Rushdie, V. S. Naipaul, and Raja Rao—are well-established literary figures with worldwide reputations. Others—such as Shashi Tharoor and Neil Bissoondath—are young writers who are in the process of rapidly distinguishing themselves. Many emerging women writers—such as Vijay Lakshmi, Leena Dhingra, Mahadai Das, Ravinder Randhawa, Sujata Bhatt, and Sharan-Jeet Shan—have begun to engage in their works the complicated politics of their (dis)locations: their narratives carry the inscriptions of their complex perspectives—perspectives that are simultaneously shaped by their ethnicity, gender, migrancy, and postcoloniality. Their works receive considerable attention in this volume. And I have ensured the inclusion of Hanif Kureishi and Suniti Namjoshi—two gifted, daring, and uncompromisingly honest artists who give voice and visibility to those of us who are gay, lesbian, or bisexual. But all writers discussed in this volume, directly or indirectly, help define the personal and political implications of our Indianness outside the boundaries of the Indian subcontinent.

I would like to take this opportunity to thank all of the contributors for their hard work, cooperation, and professionalism. Many thanks also to Marilyn Brownstein, senior editor at Greenwood Press, for her encouragement; to Susan Stout and Pat Hazard for their meticulous secretarial assistance; and to Jane Carducci, Ann Gebhard, and Denise Knight for their support and friendship.

Emmanuel S. Nelson

INTRODUCTION: READING DIASPORA

Nalini Natarajan

The phenomenon of diasporic populations is by no means new, but its scale in the twentieth century is dramatic. The nature of contemporary diasporic experiences—given the unprecedented global reach of technology and media—is also significantly more complex and ambivalent than the earlier ones. As cultural theorists such as Arjun Appadurai and Anthony Smith have pointed out, large communications networks erode national boundaries even as they promote intense interaction between members of diasporic communities: diasporic communities remain local and provincial even as they acquire transnational characteristics (Appadurai 1–24; Smith 171–93). In the new world order, the homeland becomes at once remote (due to widespread migration) and accessible (due to electronic and satellite communications). Consequently, the contemporary episteme—or the way of knowing the world—is ruled not by experience but by images—images that by their sheer proliferation and scope have become more real than anyone could have anticipated even a few decades ago. Transmitted across space and time through electronic networks, fax machines, and video screens, these images play a crucial role in diasporic subjectivities.

The impact of these images unites, in video channels for Indian diasporic viewers, for example, the sartorial, culinary, literary, cinematic, and religious. They combine memory, experience, and desire in suggestive ways, juxtaposing images of Hindu (the cultural majority of India's many communities) mythology, for instance, with consumerist advertising. For example, a video of a recent Hindi movie would carry advertisements of the popular epic the *Mahabharata* serialized on TV in India and Britain, along with a series of advertisements for all of the clothes, foods, spices, even Indian kitchen gadgets catering to affluent South Asian immigrants in diaspora. The images have the effect of linking and juxtaposing across space and time new subjectivities; thus consumer, ancient Hindu, modern cosmopolitan—all of these are suggested by the typical videotape viewed by hundreds of thousands of Indians abroad. It is significant that such simultaneous viewing of the epic creates imagined communities on an unprecedented scale. Hindu religious lore has traditionally been transmitted on a regional, local, and familial basis; the proliferation of tales within the epics lends itself to different interpretations and renditions, defeating hegemonic impulses. But in the Indian diaspora, consumerism and fundamentalism can form a strange alliance through the subjectivities created by such viewing. It is important to note, however, that these diasporic images are at once conservative and subversive: within the metropolitan context they could interrupt the hegemony of cable TV, but they reinforce the hegemonies of religion, caste, and class within the diasporic community.

It is within these new global cultural conditions that I locate this introductory piece to the collection of essays that follow. How are subjectivities formed, and how may they be known, in the diasporic Imaginary? Because the circumstances surrounding diasporic movements from the Indian subcontinent are so various, generalizations can only be made with caution. Movements of trade, labor, and emigrant intelligentsia (euphemistically known as the "brain drain") comprise the three major blocs. The writers in this volume, while largely of middle-class backgrounds, are regionally diverse, representing the region's many communities and religions. They also convey the wide reach of Indian diasporic movements—encompassing, as Arthur Helweg's study notes, 136 countries and comprising over 11 million people (Helweg 103).

At the outset, a conceptual distinction may be in order: of Indians in diaspora as knowers and as known, as subjects and objects of epistemes. In managing knowledge, as Foucault has shown us, one of the most effective ways of holding together disparate images is that of nomenclature. Thus domestic workers in Kuwait and Saudi Arabia, software technologists in the United States, retail store owners or sugarcane workers in the Caribbean are part of the medley of signifiers denoted by the single signifier "Indian diaspora."

While acknowledging the heterogeneity underlying the term, an organized study of "Indian" diaspora, such as this volume, is necessary and responds to new interest in different formations within the academy. Epistemologically, the term avoids some conceptual problems in categorizing knowledge but has its own traps. On the one hand, it is a less reactive term than "Third World" and more specific than "postcolonial." By making the region of origin the basis for analysis, we avoid the homogenization of diverse cultures and regions as "postcolonial," a term that gives undue emphasis to the end of official colonialism as a point of demarcation (see Ahmad 117–35). The term "Indian diaspora" acknowledges the difference among large blocs that are otherwise lumped together as others—such as Indian, African, Chinese, and Caribbean—while being rightly demarcated as a field separate from literature produced within India.

But the term "Indian" can also indicate an unproblematized category subject to the fallacies of essentialism and homogenization. An essentialist notion of "Indianness" derives from and reflects both colonialist and nationalist discourses. Within European discourse, India is a site for the exotic, the undiscovered at least since the times of Columbus who named everything unknown "India." Second, the notion of "India" owes its being to the ideologies of "nationalism" that are both a challenge to and a reflection of Eurocentric notions. Here countercolonial "India" is as fixed and unchanging as European versions of it.

I have thus far stressed the need to question the supposed unity offered by a national identity. The term "diaspora" can be similarly problematized. Diaspora has been conceptualized as comprising the middle stage within a narrative of cultural history that includes a Golden Past (the true beginning before the scattering), a present, middle stage (symbolized by the diaspora) of "a chosen remnant" and a prophecized future. This version of diaspora, in William Spanos's account, infuses diverse narratives from Virgil to Cotton Mather as an instance of "the speculative and assimilative itinerary of imperial power" (Spanos 26). Diasporic ideologies can thus be implicated in the cultural processes that reinforce patriarchy, class structure, and ethnic divisiveness.

India itself has a history of diasporic groups that turned into imperial powers. Cultural processes such as the Brahmanization of the subcontinent and its institutionalizing as caste could be read as conforming to the ideology of the "Saving Remnant." So too the Islamic empires established in the subcontinent following the Arab conquests. When diasporic cultures acquire power in the new context, rigid class systems, linguistic hierarchies, and civil discrimination against members of minority or politically weaker groups become institutionalized. There is evidence in Indian society both for stratification following diasporic settlements and for a high level of tolerance for diversity as a result of the unsettling of the dominant cultural hegemonies following political conquest by new forces.

If elite diasporic experience within Indian history can be read as a strand in imperialist narrative, subaltern diasporic movements forced by colonial circumstances (indentured labor) or postcolonial realities (workers' migrations) can, at the moment of dispossession and wandering, interrupt the monologic discourses of metropolitan, formerly colonial power structures. Homi Bhabha characterizes the discourse of the wandering peoples of the diaspora as marking a "shifting boundary that alienates the frontiers of the modern nation" (Bhabha 291). While such diasporic experience may deconstruct and challenge the unisonance of the modern Western nation, it may equally foster other kinds of unisonance—cultural nationalisms, for instance. It can suggest one hegemony while deconstructing another. This simultaneous process is represented in many of the authors written of in this volume.

It may be fair to say, then, that the conceptual area marked by the term "Indian diaspora" is not inherently central or marginal, radical or conservative. A similar relativity must be pointed out in the transformations in diaspora that communities go through. Assimilation, Indianization, Creolization (a term used for Indian assimilation in the Caribbean), Africanization are far from being semiotically clear processes, and seem to be read differently in different contexts. Thus while the lack of a "strong" Indian cultural identity in the Creole cultures of the Caribbean is deemed to be destructive in some accounts of the Caribbean Indian diaspora (Tinker, quoted in Helweg 109), writers such as Samuel Selvon and M. G. Vassanji stress the harmful effects of resisting Creolization and Africanization. Other ambivalences arise due often to the middleman role played by Indian communities in the British colonial territories outside India (Helweg 103–29). In the process of embourgeoisment in the colonial/metropolitan cultures, the Indian communities have often internalized racist hierarchical divisions imposed by colonialism. A good number of diasporic Indians living in Western countries, for example, seek at least partial assimilation to bolster their socioeconomic status; however, a large percentage of diasporic Indians residing in places such as Fiji, Kenya, and the Caribbean resist or even reject assimilation because of their sense of cultural superiority over the indigenous peoples.

Given the relativity of the Indian diasporic experience, what are the emerging subjectivities in the diasporic condition? This volume gives voice to those subjectivities expressed through literary discourse. Creative writers are a section of the diaspora that can represent the fluctuation between centrifugal and centripetal, between center and margin, assimilation and subversion., In the distinction between subject and object, or knower and known, the writer occupies a rather ambivalent place. Literary works are a major source of knowledge about the diaspora, making them the objects of metropolitan interest. Yet as privileged informants for the metropolitan audience, the writers are distinct from those they write about. Typically they have led cosmopolitan lives. Often, they have received acclaimed awards, held prestigious academic appointments. While they may write of conditions in diaspora, often they may not write for diasporic readers. But, as the entries in this volume show, many Indian diasporic writers vigorously interrogate the terms of their Indianness, revealing its heterogeneity and examining their alienation from their own communities—as women writers do, for instance.

This raises the question of individual versus collective subjectivities. In a recent article, Nancy Hartsock claims that those in liminal positions—women, postcolonials, ethnic minorities—are capable of challenging Western epistemes because their perspectives are "situated," i.e., clearly partisan, and therefore social and collective. While the experience of difference can reinforce the cognitive edge Hartsock discusses, the relation of diasporic writer to diasporic constituency is by no means as one of simple identification. Is the diasporic self communal or individual, elite or liminal, conservative or counterhegemonic? We have seen that public subjectivities—consumerist, fundamentalist, nationalist—can result in the marginalization of the poor, the weak, the minority, the different. This is where considerations of multiple subjectivities are useful.

It seems to me that the interrogation of a unified "Indian" identity occurs in Indian diasporic writing, and it is reflected in the deep ambivalence about collectivity and community. I want to read this not as the liberal individualist effort of nineteenth-century European discourse, but rather as a reflection of the multiple subjectivities that characterize our current global dispersions and experienced realities. Many of us are required to reconcile many cultural selves. The effort by cultural power centers within the family or diasporic community to impose or valorize homogeneity can often be painful and suppress difference. While unsettling metropolitan complacency about the irrelevance of other cultures, these representations interrogate the complacency, materialism, reactionary attitudes to gender and sexuality *within* the South Asian diasporic communities. For example, travel to India convinces Bahadur Tejani of his alienation from middle-class Indians, and Peter Nazareth realizes the imaginary myths of origin that middle-class Goans construct around themselves. Ravinder Randhawa, Leena Dhingra, Suniti Namjoshi, and Mahadai Das have highlighted gender as a site for the drama of the diasporic. Instead of being the unproblematized guardians of culture who resist brutalization, à la Draupadi in the *Mahabharata* and Sita in the *Ramayana*, now women reflect all the contradictions that their diasporic experience forces on them. In Hanif Kuereshi's and Suniti Namjoshi's work, expression is given to those formerly silent voices of counterhegemonic sexualities—those of South Asian gay men and lesbians.

In three texts by the most prolific writers of the Indian diaspora—V. S. Naipaul's *House for Mr. Biswas*, Salman Rushdie's *Satanic Verses*, and Bharati Mukherjee's *Jasmine*—the insertion of private subjectivities into communal values is represented in the sections that deal with Hanuman House (the Tulsi home in Naipaul's Trinidadl), Shaandaar Cafe in London, and the Indian neighborhood in Flushing, Queens, respectively.

On one level, the protagonists represent recognizable cultural stereotypes exemplifying the history of the relations between the subcontinent and the West: brown sahib, anglophile, exotic adventuress. Thus, Biswas' alienation is symptomatic of that of Thomas Macaulay's "brown" Englishmen, schooled by colonial pedagogy to be completely out of synchrony with the desperate attempts at cultural self-perpetuation carried on by the Tulsis. In *Satanic Verses* Saladdin Chamcha is Rushdie's caricatured version of the anglicized Asian immigrant in England, fatally divided between cultures. Mukherjee's Jasmine decides, as her author recommended in the 1989 front-page article in the *New York Times Book Review*, to exploit her Indianness as a metaphor for the ability to adapt. Being Indian, in *Jasmine*, is not to be in despair or confused; rather, it is to adapt to the tremendous potential for evil, for exploiting gullibility in a naive country like the United States.

In each text, the single protagonist arrives in the Indian stronghold with the need, if not the desire, for community. Biswas' note to the Tulsis' daughter Shama results in an immediate marriage: behind the comic absurdity of the situation is Biswas' need to find "a house," a sense of place in a world where Brahmanism and poverty confuse his childhood. Jyoti Vijh (*Jasmine*), an illegal alien from terrorist-torn Punjab, desires security. Saladdin Chamcha (*Satanic Verses*), transformed into a goat by the power of invective of a racist society (he becomes a "Paki Billy"), finds in the Shaandaar Cafe a community that will still consider him normal. Behind the customary grand narratives of displacement, nostalgia, and loss are the micronarratives within diasporic communities. In these cities visible but unseen, the bizarre narrative of the picaresque diaspore interrupts a representation of ordinary life within a diasporic community.

That this "community" is in all three cases no more than a single family is suggestive of the relation to public and private in Indian diasporic communities. Distance from the home culture and the invisibility of that culture in the country of adoption create a situation where the family becomes the chief vehicle for cultural transmission.

The hospitality and kindness of both Masterji's family in Queens and the Sufyan family in London are accurate cultural representations. It also explains the appeal of ethnic communities to individuals facing the stresses of immigrant life. But equally the narrative insertion of the private subjectivity into the family/community perspective demonstrates the strains in diasporic cultures. For example, the strain manifests itself in masculine diasporic anxiety and in women's withdrawal from reality into the escape offered by film. It is noteworthy that in all three communities, masculine anxiety forms a discernible strand. Masterji sorts hair for a living, a demeaning occupation for a once respected professor; Sufyan is no more than a waiter in Shaandaar Cafe; and Biswas is the weakest member in a community dominated by women. Meanwhile, the women are represented as living in a make-believe world. The outdated rituals of the Tulsi women are, in the later novels, replaced by women's obsession with the VCR. Masterji's wife watches Hindi movies on video. For Mrs. Sufyan, too, chief architect of the Shaandaar Cafe's success though she is, the real world is that of Hindi movies, the VCR, and the Hindi movie magazine. The home she longs for is the subcontinent represented on film, a construct of postindependence India inscribing escapist messages. The subtextual inscription of male anxiety and female escapism is contained within the comic form in all three works, but it may be a cultural perception that merits attention and has implications for an understanding of the Indian diaspora.

In the current global network of interrelations, diasporic attitudes can reverberate back to the region of origin. The diasporic situation of comparative financial prosperity and cultural anxiety can determine the nature of its influence in the unstable politics within the subcontinent. Critics stress the potential for subversion in liminal populations, in the awareness of their own relativity. I would urge the necessity for attention also to the insecurities of the liminal, in their position between two worlds. On the other hand, the transnational potential of diasporic populations can go a long way toward interrupting the monologic discourses of contemporary nation-states. This book is an invaluable resource to understanding this process in the Indian case and facilitating it. In introducing readers to the multiple subjectivities that arise in conditions of diaspora, a work such as this can provide a useful antidote to the reductive processes of homogenization at work everywhere around us today.

WORKS CITED

Ahmad, Aijaz. "Jameson's Rhetoric of Otherness and the National Allegory." *Social Text* 17 (1987): 3–27.

Appadurai, Arjun. "Disjuncture and Difference in the Global Economy." *Public Culture* 2 (Spring 1990): 1–24.

Bhabha, Homi. "Dissemination: Time, Narrative and the Margins of the Modern Nation." *Nation and Narration.* Ed. Homi Bhabha. London: Routledge, 1990. 291–322.

Hartsock, Nancy. "Postmodernism and Political Change." *Cultural Critique* (1990): 15–33.

Helweg, Arthur. "Indian Diaspora: Influences on International Relations." *Modern Diasporas in International Politics.* Ed. Gabriel Sheffer. New York: St. Martin's Press, 1986. 103–29.

Smith, Anthony. "Towards a Global Culture." *Global Culture.* Ed. Mike Featherstone. London: Sage, 1990. 171–93.

Spanos, William. "The Uses and Abuses of Certainty: A Caviling Overture." *Boundary* 2:12 (Spring 1984): 17–28.

MEENA ALEXANDER (1951–   )
Denise Knight

BIOGRAPHY

In an interview published in *Dispatch*, the journal of the Center for American Culture Studies (Columbia University, City University of New York [CUNY], 1988), Meena Alexander reflects upon her connection with south-west India: "I carry that world around with me. Sometimes I find myself sitting on the Upper West Side on 113th Street [in New York City] and writing poems that are rooted in this soil and this landscape, in a village in South India. It's as if by doing this I can reconstitute what is critical for me and nourish myself" (23).

Born on February 17, 1951, in Allahabad, India, to George and Mary Alexander, Meena Alexander was the eldest of three children. Her father, an employee of the Indian government, was sent to North Africa when Alexander was five, and as a result, her childhood was split between two vastly disparate worlds. She would spend six months at a time on each continent, but her identity remained firmly anchored in India, in large part because of the influence of her extended family. While her mother, whom Alexander describes as a quiet woman, was a traditionalist whose world centered around domestic responsibilities and religious rituals, her grand-parents, and her maternal grandfather in particular, played the most sig-nificant part in shaping her emerging ideological awareness and in sharpening her political acuity. In interviews, Alexander frequently discusses her grandfather's role in the awakening of her cultural sophistication. "I think of myself [growing up] as someone who was thrown ferociously into a new India. . . . My grandfather was a great idealist who really believed that there was a new India waiting, a new world based on issues like land reform and equality for all people. . . . [Through him] I had this extraordinary world available to me" (23–24).

An exceptionally precocious child, Alexander fully explored that "extraordinary world," entering the University of Khartoum at the age of thirteen. Significantly, it was her grandfather who taught Alexander to read; ironically, it was also he who was responsible for much of the feminism that characterizes Alexander's writing. "I was brought up by my grandfather and I never wanted to study any of the feminine arts like cooking and sewing and so forth which my other grandmother, ... my father's mother, thought was appropriate. So I was always running away" (23).

By the time she was fifteen, Alexander's poems, which she wrote as a way "to piece together some of the experiences [of social change]," were being translated into Arabic and published in Sudanese newspapers. When Alexander was eighteen, the University of Nottingham, in England, awarded her a scholarship to pursue her Ph.D. Her years in England, however, left Alexander with a profound sense of displacement, an experience that adversely affected her poetic creativity. "[In the] British culture, ... I always felt that what I really was, was being left out as an Indian woman and also as someone ... from the Third World. ... I couldn't have survived in England. And not because of anything in other people; I felt that I had to go back to India" (25).

After finishing her doctoral thesis on construction of self-identity in the early English Romantic poets, Alexander returned to India, at the age of twenty-two. Part of her purpose in returning was to reclaim and to preserve her Indian identity. From 1974 until 1979, she lectured in English at various Indian universities, including the University of Delhi, Jawaharlal Nehru University, and the University of Hyderabad. Within two years after she returned to India, her first volume of poetry, *The Bird's Bright Ring*, was published. In 1979, however, she left India for New York where she arrived newly married and pregnant. Reminiscent of her move to England, the now-familiar sense of displacement was amplified by a profound sense of loss. That loss was, fortunately, remediated when Alexander realized that her immersion into the frenetic pulse of New York City could actually fuel her creative imagination. "[New York] is a world of people like me. All shapes and substances here. ... It is a great city, with an enormous energy of life. And that attracts me as an Indian, because I also come from a place teeming with life" (25).

Since her arrival in the United States, Alexander has simultaneously juggled careers in writing and in teaching. Originally hired as an assistant professor of English at Fordham University in the Bronx in 1980, Alexander accepted a visiting assistant professorship at the University of Minnesota, Twin Cities in the summer of 1981. In 1988, she held the prestigious post of writer-in-residence at the Center for American Culture Studies at Columbia University. At present, she is an associate professor of English and creative writing at Hunter College and the Graduate Center, CUNY. She also teaches in the Writing Program at Columbia University.

Alexander currently resides in New York City with her husband, David Lelyveld, and two children, a son, Adam Kuruvilla, and a daughter, Svati Mariam.

MAJOR WORKS AND THEMES

Alexander's poems have appeared in a variety of American and international journals including *Critical Quarterly*, *Chandrabhaga*, *Chelsea*, *Denver Quarterly*, and the *Massachusetts Review*, and in numerous anthologies. She has also published separate volumes of poetry including *Stone Roots*, *House of a Thousand Doors*, and *The Storm, A Poem in Five Parts*. Among her earliest published works were poems that emerged as she struggled to define her feminism in a culture where "a wife is somebody who walks ten steps behind" (25). Yet images of women and the female experience abound in Alexander's poetry and in her latest work, *Nampally Road*, a short novel set entirely in India. The female experience, indeed, is at the center of much of Alexander's published work. "I never thought of myself as a feminist as such, but I guess that's a root from which my writing comes" (23).

The feminine images in Alexander's work tend to center around strong and independent women who defy culturally imposed conventions as they strive to discover and make heard their voices. More often than not, that "discovery" does not occur in an epiphanic flash; on the contrary, it involves a gentle emergence—an evolution—a sense of growth that is often as gratifying as it is frightening.

Although she has been writing professionally for many years, it is actually her 1988 collection of poems, *House of a Thousand Doors*, that Alexander sees as a kind of genetic benchmark in her writing. It is not until *House* that the empowerment of awareness, so distinctive in her writing, begins to consciously emerge. Once again, Alexander has drawn on the influence of family in order to create an artistic vision: "The grandmother figure in [*House*] is drawn from memory and dream, she stands as a power permitting me to speak in an alien landscape" (*Contemporary Poets*, St. James Press, 1991). The older woman, in fact, often holds a prominent position in Alexander's work. In the poem "Grandmother's Mirror," for example, the old, physically broken grandmother, with keen wisdom and insight, silently inspires the speaker in her contemplation of life: "Awed at her ruined back / we crouched, whispering like silk / Tucked to her waist / it fled downwards in points / like waves in other worldly paintings / riveted to her walls." And in *Nampally Road*, the kindly and older woman doctor, Durgabai, whom the protagonist, Mira, affectionately addresses as "Little Mother," is instrumental in the awakening and cultivation of Mira's values.

Alexander's feminism, and the diasporic consciousness that characterizes much of her writing, is deeply rooted in India and in her childhood travels:

[E]ach [Indian] writer surely has her or his way of being "othered" both literally and symbolically in being cut from India, and for me this cutting from started in earliest childhood with my travels back and forth between continents. I think it is this consciousness of being cut from, or being set apart from, in my own particular version of dislocation that has permitted me to depict [in *Nampally Road*], indeed to frame within the context of political turmoil, the sorts of colonial education that still survive in India. (Correspondence with Meena Alexander, April 12, 1991)

While the diasporic consciousness is present in several of Alexander's poems ("June 1977" and "Indian Elegy" in *Stone Roots, I Root My Name*, and "City Street," for example), it is a prominent feature of *Nampally Road*, her most substantial work to date. Alexander's voice in the novel is powerfully evocative. Her language both caresses and shocks; her words are rich and sensual, capturing an unusually broad emotional range from the basest instinct for survival to an almost ethereal celebration of love. Her pages resonate with the sights and sounds indigenous to India: the colorful landscape is characterized by lotus ponds, neem and peepul trees, magnolias, street merchants, and women adorned in saris. The peace and serenity of this contemporary India, is, however, quickly eclipsed by the infiltration of government troops.

Based in part on historical fact, and in part on Alexander's own experiences, the story is told by Mira Kannadical, an English instructor at a local college who has returned to Hyderabad, India, after studying abroad in England. The novel chronicles Mira's attempts to assimilate the various changes in her homeland as she views the bloody consequences of civil unrest. Mira struggles to define herself and her heritage:

As for the Indian past, what was it to me? Sometimes I felt it was a motley collection of events that rose in my mind, rather like those bleached stones in the abandoned graveyard the boy picked his way through. I had no clear picture of what unified it all, what our history might mean. We were in it, all together, that's all I knew. And there was no way out. (*Nampally Road* 28)

As the novel opens, Mira and her lover, Ramu, sit tensely in a cafe on Nampally Road and watch in horror as the government's Every Ready corps brutally attack a group of orange sellers, who are about to launch a peaceful demonstration denouncing the latest tax increase. Mira's quiet but sheltered world at the university is shattered by the senseless violence against the unarmed civilians.

In the first several chapters, Mira reconstructs her years in England, her decision to teach in Hyderabad, her bond with Durgabai (Little Mother), the importance of her writing, and her growing affection for Ramu. Midway through the novel, the community is newly rocked by the gang rape of a peasant woman, Rameeza Be, and by her attackers' savage murder of her husband. After Rameeza Be is imprisoned by the drunken policemen who committed the rape, members of the community storm the police station, free the badly injured woman, and burn down the building. With the contamination of her idealism, Mira turns to Durgabai, initially for emotional refuge, but later to seek guidance in her attempts to assimilate this new experience—this "poetics of dislocation":

I closed my eyes to listen better. I loved her voice. It wove the world together. It made a past. Listening to her, I lost the bitter sense I often had of being evicted, of being thrust out of a place in which lives had meanings and stories accreted and grew. The present was flat and sharp and broken into pieces. There was tear gas in the present and a woman's terrible cry still hovering over a burnt out police station. (69)

It is finally through exploring the sense of "eviction" that Mira is able to make connections about her place in the world—as an Indian, as a woman, as a feminist.

Alexander continues her exploration of diasporic themes in two works-in-progress—in her forthcoming autobiography *Fault Lines*, and in a volume of short poems, which bring together "the two landscapes" of her life—that of rural Kerala in India, and that of Manhattan: chaotic and crowded. The tension between the old and the new, and the constant crossing over disparate borders, will continue to inspire her writing. "I always wanted to write as far back as I can remember," she says. "There were always rhythms in my head, images. I sank through them even as a child. I felt the wonderful possibility of saying something secret and intimate. Writing for me has always been a way of thinking further, of losing the edge of fear" (*India Currents* 19).

CRITICAL RECEPTION

Most of the criticism of Alexander's writing has been overwhelmingly positive. Reviewers often cite its lyrical quality as the most distinctive feature of her work. In his 1988 review of *House of a Thousand Doors*, Bruce King writes, "Alexander is a serious, difficult writer and has reached a stage in her career when critics should begin paying her attention, whether as a feminist, an Indian, an internationalist, or as part of the multi-ethnic literature now being produced in the United States" (379–80). King cites Alexander's use of consistent themes, images, symbols, and obsessions "as an expression of a self-contained private emotional world" (379). He also discusses the biographical dimensions of the poetry, citing the influence of Alexander's two grandmothers on her poetic consciousness.

Most of the recent criticism of Alexander, however, focuses on *Nampally Road*. As Luis H. Francia reports in the *Village Voice*, which featured *Nampally Road* as an "Editor's Choice," Alexander's "short, lyrical first novel...with its restless crowds, cinemas, shops, temples, mango sellers, cobblers, cafes, and bars,...becomes a metaphor for contemporary India. ...Her lyrical narrative has the eloquent economy that marks her best poetry" (74). *The Los Angeles Times* praises the novel's "refreshingly modest quality...that moves one to respect its honesty." And *Publisher's Weekly* promises that "readers will enjoy the details of the Indian setting."

BIBLIOGRAPHY

Works by Meena Alexander

The Bird's Bright Ring. Calcutta: Writers Workshop, 1976.
I Root My Name. Calcutta: United Writers, 1977.
In the Middle Earth. New Delhi: Enact, 1977.
Without Place. Calcutta: Writers Workshop, 1977.
The Poetic Self: Towards a Phenomenology of Romanticism. New Delhi: Arnold-Heinemann, 1979.
Stone Roots. New Delhi: Arnold-Heinemann, 1980.
House of a Thousand Doors. Washington, D.C.: Three Continents Press, 1988.
The Storm: A Poem in Five Parts. New York: Red Dust Press, 1989.
Women in Romanticism: Mary Wollstonecraft, Dorothy Wordsworth, Mary Shelley. London: Macmillan, 1989.
Night-Scene, The Garden. New York: Red Dust Press, 1991.
Nampally Road. San Francisco: Mercury House, 1991.
Fault Lines. New York: Feminist Press, 1992.

Studies of Meena Alexander

Assisi, Francis. "Humane Feminism Incites Poet Meena Alexander." *India West* (Feb. 15, 1991): 1, 44.
Divakaruni, Chitra. "Living in a Pregnant Time: Meena Alexander Discusses Feminism, Literature, Decolonization." *India Currents* (May 1991): 19, 58.
Downing, Ben. Review of *The Storm. Voice Literary Supplement* 84 (April 1990): 18.
Francia, Luis H. Review of *Nampally Road. Village Voice* 13 (March 26, 1991): 74.
Helleckson, Diane. "Red-Skirted Soul." *Hungry Mind Review* (Spring 1991): 40.
"Interview with Meena Alexander." *Dispatch*, Center for American Culture Studies, Columbia University (Spring 1988): 23–26.
Jain, Madhu. "Coming Home: An Expatriot's Lyrical Debut." *India Today* (May 15, 1991): 167.
King, Bruce. Review of *House of a Thousand Doors. World Literature Written in English* 28:2 (1988): 379–80.
Perry, John Oliver. "Exiled by a Woman's Body: Substantial Phenomena in a Poetry of Meena Alexander." *Journal of South Asian Literature* 12 (Winter/Spring 1986): 1–10.
———. "The Inward Body: Meena Alexander's Feminist Strategies of Poetry."

Feminism and Literature. Ed. K. Radha. Trivandrum: Kerala University, 1987. 86–99.

Rustomji, Roshni. Review of *House of a Thousand Doors*. *New Letters Review of Books* (Winter 1990): 15.

Schwartz, Leonard. Review of *The Storm*. *Poetry Project* 137 (April/May 1990): 4–5.

Tharu, Susie. "A Conversation with Meena Alexander." *Chandrabhaga* 7 (Summer 1982): 69–74.

Viswanathan, S. "The Dialect of the Tribe: Poetic Talents and Poetic License." *Contemporary Indian English Verse: An Evaluation*. Ed. Chirantan Kulshrestha. New Delhi: Arnold-Heinemann, 1980. 122–30.

AGHA SHAHID ALI (1949–   )
Lawrence D. Needham

BIOGRAPHY

For Agha Shahid Ali, migration is almost second nature. Born in Delhi, India, Ali grew up in Kashmir, shuttling between Srinigar, Jammu, and the Indian capital. The son of two educators who traveled within India and abroad, Ali was the beneficiary of a diverse cultural heritage that incorporated Muslim, Hindu, and Western traditions; he sees himself and his work as the synthesis of these variegated roots, as the product of multiple geographical and textual locations, which include the Koran, Shakespeare, Milton, Sufi mystics, Ghalib, Faiz, and Marx. Reflecting this hybridity, his poems thematize change, transition, fluidity and, taken as whole, stage a rich contestation of voices.

In 1961, Ali came to the United States for the first time, living for three years in Muncie, Indiana, while his father completed his Ph.D. In addition to discovering the sock-hop, American football, and rock and roll in "exile," Ali came to a strong sense of his familial and cultural resources as he dealt with separation and partial estrangement. Though writing from age ten, Ali credits his experiences as a young teen in America with crystallizing his sense of himself as a poet.

Returning to the subcontinent, Ali earned his B.A. in English from the University of Kashmir (1968) and an M.A. in English from the University of Delhi (1970). From 1970–1975 he lectured at Hindu College, the University of Delhi, publishing his first book of poetry, *Bone-Sculpture*, in 1972. His second book of poetry, *In Memory of Begum Akhtar* (1979), appeared while Ali was writing and studying in the States, where, in 1984, he received his Ph.D. in English from the Pennsylvania State University. Subsequently, his dissertation on Eliot was published as *T. S. Eliot as Editor* (1986). *The Half-Inch Himalayas* appeared a year later in 1987.

Ali's return to the United States coincided with his efforts to bring to

American audiences the ghazals of the great Urdu poet, Faiz Ahmed Faiz. His work involved translations of Faiz, published recently in the beautifully produced *The Rebel's Silhouette* (1991). Ali's latest collection of poetry, *A Nostalgist's Map of America* (1991), displays some of the marks of his work as a translator. The recipient of many poetry fellowships and awards, Ali currently teaches creative writing and English literature at Hamilton College, Clinton, NY.

Most recently, Ali has returned from a year's stay in India, during which time he visited Kashmir. Haunted, as always, by what has passed or what won't be, he nonetheless returns with visions of what might be for his embattled "home." His "translations" of the Kashmiri situation are the basis for his most recent poetry and possibly a book.

MAJOR WORKS AND THEMES

Ali's first volume of poetry, *Bone-Sculpture*, depicts a world beyond redemption, consigned to material corruption and a legacy of bones and dust. Wandering through graveyards and blasted landscapes, the poet participates in a nightmarish ritual of dead men, as he mimes the strong poetic voices of Eliot and Shelley, yet struggles to free himself from their influence. The volume ends with the poet's release from exhausted language when, in "Notes for the Unabandoned Stranger," the speaker is revealed erasing language from dead stones, the markers he himself had erected among the mosaic of graves of a modern wasteland. This too neat ending raises suspicions that the poet is whistling past the graveyard, that the casting out of spirits is not so easily achieved. Thus, whereas in "Bones," he argues the futility of searching for forgotten ancestors, in "Cremation," he confronts the "stubborn" dead whose bones refuse to burn.

The perfunctory nature of some poems in *Bone-Sculpture* is, at times, the result of literary posturing and self-protective masking, which allow the poet to speak of loss and separation without revealing the particulars of his history and the wellsprings of his feelings. With *In Memory of Begum Akhtar*, Ali reveals to his audience glimpses of a past that explain, in part, his preoccupation with death, separation, and loss. Modernist brooding takes on a local flavor and actuality when, in "Note Autobiographical—1" and "Note Autobiographical—2," he creates his own version of the Death of God and Tradition in reflecting on the story of shoes stolen at a mosque. The theft of shoes at the mosque is only a convenient occasion for the poet's apostasy; it crystallizes for him a growing sense of the irrelevance of God, who fails to answer his concerns and questions.

The turn from God marks a turn to poetry; *In Memory of Begum Akhtar* records the poet's encounter with, and immersion in, the Urdu poetic tradition, specifically the ghazals of Ghalib, Mir, and Faiz, circulated as lifeblood through the performances of Begum Akhtar. At the same time, *In*

Memory records the poet's growing discomfiture with the English language, in "Introducing" and especially in "The Editor Revisited." A comparison with the earlier "Dear Editor" from *Bone-Sculpture* shows how far the poet has come with his second volume. Though both poems draw upon the familiar Indo-Anglian topos of English as the language of alienation, "Dear Editor" casually and facilely presents the thematic, whereas "The Editor Revisited" identifies the poet's location between two cultures, recognizes the political implications of that position, and registers the lived consequences of alienation. To the extent that the poet emerges as a living presence, or voice in *In Memory*, he certainly is right to introduce himself (in "Introducing") for the first time as a poet. Unmasked, he establishes a poetic identity, and in confronting the power of time and the force of history, he discovers a poetic vocation: to memorialize.

What is experienced as lost—the dead, poetic power, tradition—merely goes underground to resurface in *The Half-Inch Himalayas*, a remarkable volume recording Agha Shahid Ali's efforts to reclaim the past without being bound by it. It works through the problematics of exile and documents an important stage in the journey of one writer of the Indian diaspora. In this volume, loss has a local habitation and a name—India, Kashmir, the Ali Klan—and there seems to be some urgency that the poet come to terms with it. The condition creating this urgency is exile, only this time, actual physical separation from the subcontinent. Separation from the beloved is both deprivation and opportunity in these poems; the poet suffers in exile, to be sure, but gains in self-knowledge and command.

The price of exile, reckoned in loneliness and anxiety, is set down in several moving poems. "A Call" records the speaker's isolation and emptiness, as well as his childlike fear that he will be supplanted in the affections of his parents by the cold moon of Kashmir. "Houses" reverses the perspective; solicitous of his family's welfare back home, the speaker expresses the anxious concern of a parent worrying about absent children. In its reversal of roles, the poem records both the need for attachment and the desire to change the terms of relationship and influence; exile is the necessary condition for both.

In their absence, the members of the poet's family are present to his memory; despite longing, however, he safeguards against nostalgia by refusing to sentimentalize the past. Nostalgia for an "authentic" time (the "real" past) or an "authentic" place (the "real" India) eventuates in a frame of mind that not only does violence to history, but ultimately diminishes the value and uses of memory, Ali's primary resource and subject in *The Half-Inch Himalayas*. One of his chief objects of *The Half-Inch Himalayas* is, in fact, to avoid the frozen embrace of the past through exercising and emphasizing the re-creative powers of memory. In this volume, Ali seems to be looking not for the "real" past, but a "usable" past, the kind represented in "Snowmen." Recognizing as his forebear a man of Himalayan snow who brought to Kashmir an inheritance of whale bones, the poet claims a legacy of change and transition. Exile is in his bones, and the poem serves as a justification for his current exiled condition. Re-creating the past, providing his own version of it, is thus enabling, unburdening him of generations of snowmen on his back who would press him into winter. At the same time, the past is the necessary ground for change; the poet rides into spring on the melting shoulders of the snowmen.

In *The Half-Inch Himalayas*, Faiz Ahmed Faiz provides the strong set of shoulders on which Ali stands as he extends his range of vision. The turn from Ghalib in earlier poems to Faiz in later poems is a telling shift, signaling Ali's growing historical and political consciousness. "A Butcher," though not overtly political, discloses the inability of language to sustain a momentary bond between two strangers, who, though sharing a line from Ghalib, are irrevocably divided along class lines. "After Seeing Kozintsev's King Lear in Delhi" finds parallels in the careers of Lear and Zafar, the poet and emperor led by British soldiers through the streets of Delhi to watch his sons hang. "Dacca Gauzes" notes the passing of the art of making gauzes after the British amputated the hands of Bengali weavers. To a great extent, the poem's effect is due to its use of contrast, specifically, the rich, poetic evocation of exquisite gauzes set against the blunt description of horrific, violent acts.

The sublime moments of *The Half-Inch Himalayas* have no counterpart in Ali's next collection of poems, *A Walk Through the Yellow Pages*. Witty, inventive, sometimes bordering on the ridiculous, this volume depicts a world of failed connections and exhausted language, in short, the contemporary American wasteland. Much of *A Walk Through the Yellow Pages* can be understood in this way; the poet discovers dead script—language processed mechanically and rendered insensible by dull repetition, language abandoned to the streets and bathroom stalls—and recovers it for vital use. He brings considerable linguistic talent to this project and, at the same time, discovers new resources, as high culture abuts popular culture in the form of advertising copy, bathroom graffiti, restaurant menus, and fairy tales. As he explores the potentialities of language, he also meditates on its limitations and shortcomings. For example, "Bell Telephone Hours," structured around ad copy, demonstrates how fabricated language, circulated through mass media and processed for profit, walls off experience and obstructs genuine connectedness. "Language Games" holds out the promise of language as refuge, lifeboat, or asylum, but shows it as a vehicle of estrangement. And his fractured fairy tales show the violence at the heart of language practice, how words are used to silence and exclude. As *The Half-Inch Himalayas* interrogate beginnings, these poems interrogate endings and closure, most simply by refashioning tales, making the "true" or "official" story one among many.

Characterized by arrivals and departures, crossings and recrossings, Ali's latest book, *A Nostalgist's Map of America*, manifestly evidences the poet's diasporic consciousness. As a writer "in search of evanescence" (the revealing title of one of his poems), Ali reclaims the voices of life's victims in painful awareness of the enormity, even futility of his task. As always, Ali is the chronicler of loss, and *The Nostalgist's Map of America* returns to the source of his poetic power. For example, the title poem, "A Nostalgist's Map of America," depicts how language fails to take the measure of suffering and is powerless, even false, before the death of a friend dying of AIDS. "Crucifixion" witnesses the death of religion, as a driver enters and leaves a timbered forest, oblivious to the futile attempts of Penitentes to incarnate a God. Yet, despite seeing life as in a rearview mirror as he hurtles by, Ali bravely memorializes the stories of the forgotten and vanished, be they the copper miners of Bisbee or the political prisoners of Chile.

A *Nostalgist's Map* weaves into an integrated whole strands of stories from diverse historical, political, and cultural contexts. It is, then, a successful act of translation, for which Ali is uniquely qualified. His retelling of the story of Majnoon and Laila in "From Another Desert" is an obvious example of cultural translation that hauntingly evokes the volume's thematic of his search for the Beloved. Yet, it is "Snow on the Desert," a poem of startling juxtapositions and stunning contrasts, that best integrates diverse cultural materials. An example of successful hybridization, which can be a resource and strength for a poet of the Indian diaspora, "Snow on the Desert" treats of change and transition when past and present collide as the poet recalls the long-silenced voice of Begum Akhtar while driving through the fogbound Arizona desert.

CRITICAL RECEPTION

Agha Shahid Ali slowly is achieving critical recognition, which is certain to increase with the publication of *A Nostalgist's Map of America* (1991) by Norton. (Some of his earlier books have not been readily accessible for commentary.) *Bone-Sculpture* and, to a lesser extent, *In Memory of Begum Akhtar*, have been viewed as journeywork on the way to his recent poetry. To date, most critical attention has been given *The Half-Inch Himalayas*. Stylistically, critics have remarked on the craft of the volume, some discovering the influence of Urdu poetry in his rich, evocative imagery, others the legacy of surrealism in his dream visions. Certainly Ali produces brilliant effects by juxtaposing the startling image with a pared down, understated line. Thematically, all comment on Ali's poignant evocation of loss, which they attribute to his exiled condition as a writer of the Indian diaspora.

What one critic says of *A Walk Through the Yellow Pages* holds for all his poetry: Ali's books "have their source in problems of growing up, leaving home, being a migrant, and the meeting of cultures" (King 13). That collision of worlds promises to be the subject of future criticism on a poet who looks to "reinvent the language" and "breathe something rich and strange into English" (quoted in King 12), and who increasingly searches for what can be gained, not lost, in acts of cross-cultural translation.

BIBLIOGRAPHY

Works by Agha Shahid Ali

Bone-Sculpture. Calcutta: Writers Workshop, 1972.
In Memory of Begum Akhtar. Calcutta: Writers Workshop, 1979.
T. S. Eliot as Editor. Ann Arbor: University of Michigan Research Press, 1986.
The Half-Inch Himalayas. Middletown, Conn.: Wesleyan University Press, 1987.
A Walk Through the Yellow Pages. Tucson: Sun/Gemini Press, 1987.
"Dismantling Some Silences." *Poetry East* 27 (Spring 1989): 5–10.
"*The Satanic Verses*: A Secular Muslim's Response." *Yale Journal of Criticism* 4 (Number 1, 1990): 295–300.
"The True Subject: The Poetry of Faiz Ahmed Faiz." *Grand Street* 9 (Winter 1990): 129–38.
The Rebel's Silhouette/Faiz Ahmed Faiz. Translated by Agha Shahid Ali. Salt Lake City: Gibbs Smith, Publisher, Peregrine Smith Books, 1991.
A Nostalgist's Map of America. New York: W. W. Norton, 1991.

Studies of Agha Shahid Ali

Bhaskaran, Nandini. "Haunted By Loss." *Sunday Review (Times of India)* (April 28, 1991): 7, cols. 1–8.
King, Bruce. "Agha Shahid Ali." *Contemporary Poets*. Ed. Tracy Chevalier. 5th ed. Chicago: St. James Press, 1991.
Needham, Lawrence. " 'The Sorrows of a Broken Time': Agha Shahid Ali and the Poetry of Loss and Recovery." *Reworlding: The Literature of the Indian Diaspora*. Ed. Emmanuel Nelson. Westport, Conn.: Greenwood Press, 1992. 63–76.
Ratner, Rochelle. Review of *The Half-Inch Himalayas*, by Agha Shahid Ali. *Library Journal* 112 (May 1, 1987): 71.

DEEPCHAND C. BEEHARRY
(1927–   )
Srimati Mukherjee and David Racker

BIOGRAPHY

Born in Floreal, Mauritius, Deepchand Beeharry grew up to study languages at the Royal College, Curepipe, in Mauritius. Following a period of teaching, Beeharry proceeded to take a master's in English from Viswa Bharati (the experimental university founded by Rabindranath Tagore) in India. He was on a Government of India Scholarship while pursuing the master's degree. In India, Beeharry traveled extensively, and on his return to Mauritius in 1954, devoted himself to journalism and, once again, to teaching. Five years elapsed before he left to join the Middle Temple in London where he was called to the bar in 1962. Beeharry's visit to the West was marked, as was his stay in India, by considerable touring, this time of the European Continent, and it would not be amiss to mention here Beeharry's corresponding propensity for frequent depiction of travel in his writings. Beeharry's return to Mauritius saw him practicing at the local bar till the time he joined the Civil Service in 1965. He served as Road Transport Commissioner for Mauritius till the midseventies, when he resigned from the position to devote himself more completely to the service of his countrymen. Despite a reasonably crowded academic and professional career, Beeharry has to his credit a number of creative works, has the linguistic versatility that equips him to write in English, French, and Hindi, and is the recipient of a literary award from the British Council. His works include *Never Good Bye* (1965), *A Touch of Happiness* (1966), *That Others Might Live* (1976), *The Road Ahead* (1976), *Three Women and a President* (1979), and *The Heart and Soul* (1983).

MAJOR WORKS AND THEMES

In *Never Good Bye* (1965), Beeharry voices a number of concerns that are to assume reiterative thematic dimensions in his later literary career. These concerns, partly socioeconomic, manifest themselves in the protagonist Ashim's anxiety (even as an adolescent) with the unmitigated oppression of Mauritian workers and his attempts (as an adult) to redress social imbalance in whatever scant ways possible. Virtually unqualified resistance to interracial relationships is another concern that emerges in this work, a stance Beeharry relates in subsequent books to the divisive nature of the Mauritian social infrastructure. *Never Good Bye* is also interesting in that it makes reference to the harrowing sea crossing made by some of the first Indian immigrants to Mauritius and the subsequent inequity they had to endure. However, characteristic of the oeuvre of a writer who inherits a diasporic consciousness, *Never Good Bye* depicts the dialectic of an inalienable emulation of features of the lost motherland (India) and a synchronic love for the new land (Mauritius).

A Touch of Happiness (1966) affirms that for the descendants of immigrants who have moved to Mauritius from India, the bonding is with Mauritius and not India. This tie emerges as the central sentiment of Dr. Bipin Bali's (the protagonist's) thought that "he could never love any other place more than the land where he was born, where his ancestors had turned night into day and day into night to secure for themselves a place in the sun" (2). However, the descendants of Indian migrants in Mauritius are largely compelled to operate within an ideological nexus that is transparently close to India. At Bipin's return from England, for instance, his mother and sisters welcome him with a "*thali* [plate] full of incense and cubes of camphor burning" (3). At a *sabha*/meeting Bipin attends in Mauritius, the prayers in Sanskrit resonate for him with the music of the waters of the Ganges "as they flew down along the corridor of the centuries reverberating with the holy call of the conk shell within the walls of the temples built on the riverside" (38). The immediacy of this pictorial and emotional evocation of India bespeaks a collective empathy in much of the Indian race, especially interesting in Bipin's case as he was not born in India and retains hardly any explicit ties with that country.

Further, Bipin derives emotional sustenance from native Indian myths. The tales associated with the Indian festival Diwali, orally repeated by Bipin's father in Mauritius, remain entrenched in Bipin's mental repository of things Indian. The symbolic significance of one of these tales (which addresses Diwali as the commemoration of the Indian hero Rama's return from exile, as a signification of the victory of light over darkness) is transferred to Bipin's own experiences at the close of the novel. Bipin feels that his alienated status in Mauritius is overcome after a year when Karen, his lover, comes to him on Diwali night. Thus, it is a matrix of Indian tales that Bipin draws from for situational parallels.

However, if the appeal of Mauritius is incumbent upon reenactments of Indian rituals and fortification through Indian myths, there is a fraudulent quality in the emotion sustained for Mauritius. Yet, hearteningly, this does not hold completely true for Bipin, who eschews an unquestioned conformity to Indian ways, attempting a realistic assessment of sociopolitical crises in Mauritius. He is even derisive of Mauritian society in areas where it exhibits negative influences from Indian culture. Mauritius shares the volubility of Indian society with unfortunate consequences, and Bipin feels that "gossip and old wives' tales seem to be the favorite pastime of this place" (6). He also believes Mauritian society to be pervaded by a sharp sense of hierarchy, another feature characteristic of India, and is troubled by the social compartmentalizations that compel the Mauritians to "still think in terms of class and community" (30). Perhaps what perturbs Bipin most acutely, particularly because he is a doctor, are the largely inadequate hospital conditions in Mauritius and the pattern he can decipher in the recurrent ailments of his patients. Generally springing from malnutrition, anemia, unhygienic conditions, or the repeated pregnancies of the women patients, these medical problems are ominously characteristic of the Third World. The graphic depiction of these maladies enables Beeharry to bring to his reader some sense of the state of being underprivileged in an underdeveloped country.

That Others Might Live (1976) shifts in time to the late nineteenth century to capture the rigors and triumphs of migrant Indian workers in Mauritius. The graphic presentation of one of the voyages made by a group of Indian migrants argues an indisputable verisimilitude in Beeharry. What evidently stands out are the on-board atrocities perpetrated by the British colonials on the Indian passengers who are reduced, in the minds of their racist crew members, to a horde of savages to be conveniently exploited. Beeharry recounts the random deaths that result from the inability of the crew to comprehend the languages of those passengers stricken by contagious diseases. The linguistic hiatus coupled with a cultural difference culminates in the arbitrary suppression of the few traditions (such as recitations from *The Ramayana*) the passengers are able to perpetuate. This nightmare journey figures as the first of a series of abusive, culturally stifling situations to be endured by the Indian diaspora in Mauritius. Several of the Indian migrants, lured to Mauritius to revive the sugarcane industry that was on the verge of collapse with the abolition of slavery, suffered what Beeharry presents as a double betrayal. Not only was their exploitation by the colonizers in sharp contrast to the dreams promised them, but the colonizers ruthlessly exploited the labor that kept their industry alive.

The delineation of the underprivileged in the Third World, seen in *A*

Touch of Happiness, assumes a more significant dimension in *The Road Ahead* (1976), in which Beeharry clearly appropriates to himself the role of speaker for the downtrodden. In an introductory section of this book entitled "Why Do I Write?," Beeharry defines the writer in developing countries as "the champion of human rights and the voice of the dumb and powerless masses" (2). Beeharry's concern with the repressed or the denied rights of the less privileged manifests itself in the title play, *The Road Ahead*, and in stories such as "The Pen and the Sword," "When the Rains Came," and "Night Duty." "The Pen and the Sword" is concurrently a documentation of Beeharry's diasporic consciousness (as the descendant of a migrant Indian), for it reflects the attitude of the economically well-placed Europeans in Mauritius to the working-class Indian immigrants. The European protagonist, Evariste's father, is seriously disturbed that his son has adopted some of the mannerisms of his Indian playmates.

That the greater part of the story focuses, however, on Evariste's concern with discriminatory social issues clearly indicates where Beeharry's sympathies lie. Evariste, the protagonist, shows a marked sense of guilt at his Indian playmate Chando's life of deprivation and his involuntary addressing of Evariste as his superior. As a mature teacher in later years, Evariste addresses with his students the corroding social machinery of Mauritius, beset with problems of discrimination. His championing of the rights of the proletariat, a stance that estranges him from kin and friends, is carried through till the end of the story when he accepts the subeditorship of a newspaper put out by a workers' union for which his childhood friend, Chando, serves as the secretary.

Beeharry's anxiety for the proletariat is evidenced also in "When the Rains Came," a story in which Prem, a laborer, inadvertently learns about the weapons his friend Maurice (a second laborer) is coerced into keeping in his house. Compelled by his foreman to do this, Maurice exposes himself to the risk of being captured by the police and implicated as the scapegoat. That in the event of such a circumstance, the possibility of compensation from the foreman is well near absent is indicated when the foreman remains unmoved by Maurice's plea of helping his family get to a refugee center on a cyclonic night. In its last pages, this story dramatizes the loss of Maurice's house and possessions to the fury of the cyclone. Through one of Prem's final questions to Maurice—"Why did not the foreman give you a lift to the refugee centre?" (8)—as well as Prem's according of shelter to Maurice's family, Beeharry clearly underlines an empathy and solidarity within the proletariat, a solidarity that could become a strength in the face of arbitrary right-wing oppression.

"Night Duty," a third story in this collection, figures as another sympathetic depiction of the oppressed, this time of the village prostitute Sonia who, the Village Council believes, should leave as she is guilty of "corrupting" the "youths." Armand, Sonia's former lover, designated, in this case, as the spokesman of the Village Council arrives at Sonia's house to coerce her into leaving, the desired departure of course involving Sonia's abandoning of her house and land. The initial movement in this story, that of a social body (represented by a man), supposedly upholding respectability, working toward the expulsion of a woman already marginalized, is obvious enough. Yet Beeharry undercuts this movement with sharp irony as the story holds indications that Armand's earlier rejection of Sonia might have culminated in her current status (or lack thereof). Sonia's challenge to Armand to resign from the Village Council and uphold her rights against the demands of the councillors is not met by her ex-lover. The defense of the marginalized against a well-entrenched, authoritative social body proves impossible for Armand. Yet the second movement in the story shows Sonia rising to precisely such a challenge when she shelters a fugitive, fleeing from the local police. Ironically once again, the fugitive's response to the discovery of Sonia's profession is a stereotypical one of horrified rejection, indicating an intractable refusal to probe the causes that might have led to her choice of profession. He leaves, avoiding having to eat at her house. However, the fugitive's voluntary return to Sonia's house at the end of the story underscores the woman's triumph, a triumph further accentuated as Sonia's door remains resolutely shut after the fugitive's repeated knocking. Through this story, especially in Sonia's refusal to relinquish her home, and at its close then, Beeharry depicts the marginalized as capable of refuting and reacting against the threat of ostracism posed it.

Idi Amin's mass expulsion of diasporic Indians from Uganda in 1972 becomes the initial push that sets in motion the plot of Beeharry's next novel, a spy thriller entitled *Three Women and a President* (1979). The novel is a fictional account of a plot by a militant organization of expelled Ugandan Indians, the League for the Defence of Indians Overseas, to assassinate Amin at the meeting of the Organization of African Unity in Mauritius in 1977. The Indian government, fearing the massacre of innocent Indians in Africa in the wake of such an assassination, sends its secret agent Ajay Sinha, also known as XXX 13, to Mauritius in order to intercept the assassins and their South African accomplices. With the help of the local police, Sinha foils the attempt on Amin's life. *Three Women and a President* derives its motivation from the real resentment of Indians and Africans against Amin and the worries among African Indians that other African leaders might follow Amin's lead.

With *The Heart and Soul* (1983), Beeharry places the themes of his first two novels within the larger context of British and Mauritian colonial relations. The novel, set in London during the time of Mauritius's coming independence, tells the story of Rishi, an Indo-Mauritian student horrified both by the corruption, nepotism, and political and racial quarrelling of his native country and by the racism, violence, materialism, and economic exploitation of immigrants in Britain. Alienated by his cramped living conditions, the cold weather of London, and the hostility directed at him as a colored immigrant to Britain, Rishi yearns for the tropical climate of Mauritius and finds solace in the letters from his German ex-girlfriend Zeita, who has gone to India to find spiritual regeneration. It is Zeita's example of spiritual harmony achieved through Hindu philosophy and practice that determines Rishi's decision to return to Mauritius intent on working for the same harmony in the land of his birth. *The Heart and Soul* ends with Rishi embracing the philosophy of his Indian ancestors with its emphasis not, like the West's, on mastering the universe through technical innovation but on mastering the heart and soul of man.

CRITICAL RECEPTION

According to Michel Fabre, "almost no critical study has been devoted to contemporary Mauritian literature in English" let alone to the works of Beeharry (135). Indeed, Fabre's survey article, "Mauritian Voices: A Panorama of Contemporary Creative Writing in English," is, along with Danielle Quet's addendum in 1984, the most comprehensive criticism of Beeharry's work. In addition to Fabre and Quet, however, there is the work of Angela Smith, who discusses Beeharry's play *The Road Ahead* and offers general remarks on Beeharry's fiction. Both Fabre and Smith find *The Road Ahead* overly didactic, but while Smith says that such "flat didacticism" is also typical of Beeharry's fiction, Fabre only notes an intrusive didacticism in *That Others Might Live*. Smith finds that Beeharry possesses a "naive and rather patronizing idealism" that produces "schematic works which reduce complex human problems to a simple question of goodies and baddies" (74), but Quet finds that in *The Heart and Soul*, at least, Beeharry fulfills his task "to create 'literature with a social purpose with a message of love and fellowship' "(310). Fabre offers synopses of all of Beeharry's works up to and including *Three Women and a President*, but his criticism focuses only on *Three Women*, *That Others Might Live*, and *The Road Ahead*. Despite "a few technical flaws" and an "overly didactic explanation of the working of historical forces," *That Others Might Live*, says Fabre, "makes interesting reading" (129):

Beyond the sometimes melodramatically interwoven fates of the major characters, Beeharry evokes beautifully the rituals and rhythms of labour in the cane fields, the heated atmosphere of political contest and labour strife, and especially the changing landscape as villages and cities spread over the island. (129–30)

The novel is "optimistic" and makes "credible heroes out of humble people" (130). *The Road Ahead*, on the other hand, "lacks action" (132), and *Three Women and a President* is "seriously weakened by ... contrived suspense and clumsy eroticism" (131). However, with its "numerous allusions to

Mauritius' position at the heart of the Indian Ocean and of international political intrigue," *Three Women and a President*, says Fabre, provides "perceptive comments on the function of popular fiction in such a context" (131). In her "further remarks" on Mauritian literature, Quet discusses *The Heart and Soul*. Beeharry's fifth novel, she says, is a "mature work" that "forcefully conveys the terrible solitude of the coloured immigrant in an indifferent or racist environment, the permanent sense of guilt linked to an irresistible feeling of desire and admiration for those who reject him" (310).

BIBLIOGRAPHY

Works by Deepchand Beeharry

Never Good Bye. Port Louis: Editions Nationales, 1965.
A Touch of Happiness. Port Louis: Editions Nationales, 1966.
That Others Might Live. New Delhi: Orient, 1976.
The Road Ahead. Port Louis: Ashley, 1976.
Three Women and a President. New Delhi: Orient, 1979.
The Heart and Soul. Port Louis: Swan, 1983.

Studies of Deepchand Beeharry

Review of *Never Good Bye*. *Asia and Africa Review* 7:109 (1967): 18.
Fabre, Michel. "Mauritian Voices: A Panorama of Contemporary Creative Writing in English." *World Literature Written in English* 19 (1980): 121–37.
Quet, Danielle. "Mauritian Voices: A Panorama of Contemporary Creative Writing in English (Part Two)." *World Literature Written in English* 23 (1984): 303–12.
Smith, Angela. "Mauritian Literature in English." *The Writing of East and Central Africa*. Ed. G. D. Killam. London: Heinemann, 1984. 70–81.

SUJATA BHATT (1956–   )

Vara Neverow-Turk

BIOGRAPHY

Sujata Bhatt was born on May 5, 1956, in Ahmedabad, India. When she was twelve, her parents moved to the United States. Having been born and raised in India and having spent her adolescence and early adulthood in the United States, Bhatt is bicultural by birth and upbringing and is tricultural by marriage. Her husband, Michael Augustin, is a German writer and radio editor/producer whom she met at the University of Iowa while working on her M.F.A. Bhatt and Augustin, with their two-year-old daughter, Jenny Mira, live in Bremen, Germany, where Bhatt works as a free-lance writer and is translating Gujarati poetry into English.

Bhatt's father, Dr. Pravin N. Bhatt, who is trained in Ayurvedic as well as Western medicine, completed his degrees in the United States and returned to India, where he worked in public health. However, government bureaucracy frustrated his attempts to deal with the diseases that accompany poverty, and he considered going into private practice. When he was offered a research position at Yale in comparative medicine and virology, he accepted, and the family moved to the United States in 1968. Bhatt's mother, Indu Pathak Bhatt, studied economics and history in India and was the only woman in her graduating class. Until recently, she worked as a laboratory technician at Yale.

In her poetry Bhatt evokes the day-to-day realities of life in America, Europe, and India. She demonstrates an extraordinary ability to re-create the richly sensual smells, tastes, textures, and colors of her South Asian childhood world in many of her poems, both in *Brunizem* (1988), her first published volume, and in *Monkey Shadows* (1991), her second collection. Writing of lizards, pregnant goats, water buffalos, leopards, cobras, elephants, funeral pyres, marigolds, cow dung, tulsi leaves, mango trees, warm *chapatis*, the red and gold of chilis and tumeric, the explosive flavor of garlic, *ghee*, and henna, Bhatt offers her reader access to the most quotidian ordinariness of this world. "Go to Ahmedabad," a poem in the *Brunizem* collection, reveals the ironic ache of Bhatt's enduring love of a place and its people and her revulsion for its pervasive poverty and degradation.

As it says on the back of the book, the title *Brunizem* "refers to the dark brown prairie soil of a kind found in Asia, Europe and North America, the three very different worlds of Sujata Bhatt's imagination." This esoteric term, a French-Russian compound, epitomizes Bhatt's complex linkage of sensual, erotic, earthy elements and highly specialized information (for example, one poem is titled "Muliebrity," an obscure term for womanhood [OED]). Aptly, as Bhatt stated in the personal interview on which much of this article is based, her poems reflect "the tensions and paradoxes of life," tensions and paradoxes that her poems hold in a precarious balance of resolution.

In her second volume, *Monkey Shadows*, Bhatt continues to fuse cultures and perspectives, writing with sensitive comprehension of other species. As the title predicts, many poems are about monkeys. The first poem in the collection, "The Langur Coloured Night," evokes the exquisite wildness of the animal's "cry" as voiced "truth." The second poem, "The Stare," balances "human child" and "monkey child" in a steady gaze, each creature too innocent to understand the gulf between them.

Elephants too are important in this collection of poems. "A Different Way to Dance" ends with a child's sad reflection on the tale of Parvati, Ganesh, and Shiva. Ganesh, the elephant-headed god, was not always so. Shiva, his father, in a moment of wrath, beheaded his own son and then, in compunction, slaughtered an elephant and gave the elephant's head to Ganesh. The speaker in the poem cannot stop herself from compulsively thinking about the "rotting carcass" of the headless elephant and, in the concluding stanzas, imagines the ritual mourning dance of the elephant's family, a dance that is never spoken of in human circles. The subsequent poem, "What Happened to the Elephant," continues the meditation.

Bhatt began writing poetry when she was only eight years old, but given the scientific orientation of her family, it is no wonder that as an undergraduate at Goucher College, Maryland, she initially chose a premed science major before changing to a literature and philosophy emphasis. However, Bhatt has two maternal uncles who were poets and her paternal grandfather was also a writer. Thus, her choice to matriculate for the M.F.A. at Iowa was simply an acknowledgment that her strongest talent was for writing poetry rather than doing science or scholarship.

As Bhatt points out, her family has always emphasized intellectual pursuits over affluence and has never made the traditional distinction in education between girls and boys. Many of Bhatt's poems focus with gentle yet sometimes shocking intensity on female experiences, including sexuality; however, when asked if she is a feminist, Bhatt simply replies that she believes that women and men should have the same options and opportunities in life.

When asked about literary influences, Bhatt identifies the poet Eleanor Wilner, one of her professors from Groucher, as her mentor (the poem "Metamorphoses II: A Dream" is dedicated to her). Bhatt also acknowledges her indebtedness to a mosaic of authors ranging from poets to novelists: T. S. Eliot and George Eliot, Yeats, Tagore, Neruda, Lorca, Plath, Woolf, Levertov, and Ferlinghetti are just a sampling of her many influences. Although most of the writers she names are in the Western literary tradition, she says they all "trigger Indian memories."

MAJOR WORKS AND THEMES

Brunizem, which was first accepted for publication in 1986, is the cumulated work of ten years. Mostly it consists of poems written while Bhatt was at Goucher and Iowa and includes the material Bhatt submitted for her M.F.A. thesis. The poems are thematically rather than chronologically organized. Bhatt says that she often writes about "the things I want to get out of my mind—to clear my head," or, conversely, so she can "keep a memory or celebrate an event." Divided into three sections, "The First Disciple," "A Different History," and "Eurydice Speaks," the sequence of the collection corresponds to Bhatt's successive cultural contexts and foregrounds what Bhatt terms her "blended identity." One of her poems, "What Is Worth Knowing?," values the ways that different cultures produce different ways of interacting with reality.

Bhatt's first language is Gujarati, and though she writes in English, she uses Gujarati in her poems to celebrate her cultural heritage. As Ranjana Ash notes, Bhatt maintained her fluency by a sustained act of will, for, as she says in an autobiographical essay, she was reduced to "reading the dictionary." Thus, the poem titles "(Udaylee)" and "(Shérdi)" in the first section of *Brunizem* are parenthetical transliterations of Gujarati characters and for concepts unavailable in English. "Search for My Tongue," in the second section of the book, directly addresses the painful politics of interweaving the two languages, highlighting both the disorientation and the divided loyalties of bicultural existence. "The Undertow," which traces the echoes of the word "dog" through its many transformations, is more than trilingual in its attempt to reconcile the psycholinguistic rift. "Well, Well, Well," the last poem in the collection, rings changes on the word "witch" and problematizes the very function of language as she frantically searches for suitable diction.

Bhatt cherishes both her Indian family values and her American self-confidence but admits that she feels alienated living in Germany. She is not totally fluent in the language and says that the atmosphere of the country makes her feel "suffocated." However, she enjoys her occasional visits to England and Holland, cultures that "tolerate eccentricity."

According to Bhatt, *Brunizem* is a collection of "young poems." Many deal with issues related to growing up (the memories of India, the excitement of awakening sexuality) or with the poet's nuanced sensitivity to the delights of the physical world, the recording of delicate, ephemeral moments, whether pleasurable or otherwise. Contrasting the Indian ritual of cremation with traditional Western burial customs, the speaker says that gravestones make her take note of trees, which she subtly associates with the scented fuel of the pyre. "At the Marketplace" is an exquisite fusion of vivid sensations, the taste of raw fish, the love-bruises that metamorphose into "purple sea horses." The poems "Menu" and "Another Act for the Lübecker Totentanz" are almost pure sensation, lovely, decadent whorls of language. Other poems, like "Written after Hearing of the Soviet Invasion of Afghanistan" and "3 November 1984" engage with the consequences of contemporary political turmoil—the horrors of Soviet napalm and the "haemorrhageing trains" of the Sikh and Hindu massacres. One critic contends that "the energy of the writing declines into diffuseness" in these poems (Welch 18), but the dissociated, distanced tone of the poems actually accentuates the reader's sense of the speaker's helpless distress over events occurring far away and out of her control.

Monkey Shadows, divided like *Brunizem* into three sections, continues many of the themes of *Brunizem* but shifts away from the strongly sexual aspect of the earlier collection to a more political and scientific emphasis. However, the poem "White Asparagus," which deals with the sexuality of a pregnant woman, suggests that these elements will reappear in later work. The poetic style of *Monkey Shadows* evidences deliberate experiments with the rhythm of reiteration. As mentioned, the new collection is also more overtly political, but the confrontational quality typical of political discourse is absent in Bhatt's work. Her political stance is entirely personal, a gesture of sorrow and dismay rather than anger in poems like "18 Mozartstrasse" and "Wine from Bordeaux," the first a meditation on the trauma of Hitler's Germany, the second on the aftermath of Chernobyl. "What Does One Write When the World Starts to Disappear," the final poem in *Monkey Shadows*, imagines sadly a posthuman world littered and inhabited only by "a few lizards."

CRITICAL RECEPTION

Bhatt's first volume of poems has received unequivocal international praise from reviewers, and there is little doubt that her second collection will be received with similar enthusiasm. She has been awarded a number of poetry prizes in the United Kingdom including a Cholmondeley Award (1991), the Commonwealth Poetry Prize for Asia (1989), and the Alice

Hunt Bartlett Prize (1988). Further, she has just been chosen as a recipient of the Poetry Book Society Recommendation for *Monkey Shadows*. Vinay Dharwadker states emphatically that *Brunizlem* is "the best first volume by an Indian-English poet to appear since the 1970s" and further that it is "certainly the best book of poems in English by an Indian woman so far" (78–79). John Welch remarks that "this is an exciting first collection" (18). Shirley Geok-lin Lim enthusiastically declares, "I salute the appearance of a sister poet" (93). Reviewing the work for teachers, Michael Bennett calls *Brunizem* "a super collection" (3).

Bhatt's public readings of her work are greeted with similar delight. For example, Ted Walker remarks that her poems are "[t]ruly innovative but entirely unpretentious . . . well-wrought, impassioned, . . . non-folksy" and describes Bhatt herself very accurately as "one to watch," "quiet and modest and dignified and laughing" (23). With slight variations in terminology, virtually every reviewer notes that Bhatt's work is "fresh" and, of course, all comment on the multicultural, multilingual tensions of the collection. As Pearse Hutchinson remarks, "[t]his poet's voice is very definitely, unmistakably, a woman's voice. And full of wisdom" (26). As Lim observes, "Each of her poems is evidence of a deeply cosmopolitan imagination, one well travelled and richly stocked with books, images, and learning, fearlessly sexual and intellectual, yet finally and altogether having her being in the immediate physical life" (93). Her compassionate imagination transforms erudition into enduring wisdom.

BIBLIOGRAPHY

Works by Sujata Bhatt

Brunizem. New York and Manchester: Carcanet, 1988.
Monkey Shadows. Toronto: Carcanet, 1991.

Studies of Sujata Bhatt

Ash, Ranjana. "Sujata Bhatt: Speaking in Tongues." *Bazaar: South Asian Arts Magazine* 15 (1990): 14–15.
Bennett, Michael. Review of *Brunizem*. *N.A.T.E. News* (Summer 1988): 3.
Dharwadker, Vinay. "The Poems of Sujata Bhatt Are Such." *Arc* (Autumn 1990): 78–81.
Hutchinson, Pearse. "Tagairt." *RTE Guide* (Jan. 5, 1990): 26.
Lim, Shirley Geok-lin. Review of *Brunizem*. *Calyx* (Summer 1990): 92–93.
Walker, Ted. "Poetry: In Toronto." *London Magazine* (October/November 1990): 23.
Welch, John. "South Asian Voices." *Poetry Review* 78:1 (Spring 1988): 18.

NEIL BISSOONDATH
(1955–   )
Victor J. Ramraj

BIOGRAPHY

Neil Bissoondath is one of several Caribbean writers who felt that they could achieve their literary potential only by leaving their native lands for the metropolitan centers of Europe and North America. While the previous generation of writers, such as V. S. Naipaul and Samuel Selvon, migrated to Britain, Bissoondath and other Indo-Caribbean writers of his generation, following in the footsteps of the Trinidadian novelist Ismith Khan, preferred to make North America their adopted home. It was in fact V. S. Naipaul, Bissoondath's uncle, who advised him that there was not much future for Caribbean immigrants to Britain, suggesting Canada instead. Bissoondath has been living in Canada since 1973 and is considered by the literary world as both a Trinidadian and a Canadian writer.

The son of Sati (née Naipaul) and Crisen Bissoondath, he was born on April 19, 1955, in Trinidad, West Indies, where he lived until the age of eighteen. After his high school education at St. Mary's College, he left Trinidad in 1973 to attend York University, Toronto. In 1977, he earned a B.A. in French, and began teaching French and English at the Inlingua School of Language. Between 1980 and 1985, he taught at the Language Workshop, Toronto. Bissoondath has never regretted his decision to migrate to Canada, but the aspect of the immigrants' experiences in Toronto that absorbs him in his fiction, particularly his most recent stories, is the unrelenting feelings of alienation and marginality.

Bissoondath's first volume is *Digging Up the Mountains* (1986), a collection of fourteen short stories, most of which had been published before in such journals as *Saturday Night* and broadcast on the CBC literary program *Anthology*. This volume was shortlisted for the City of Toronto Book Awards. "Dancing," one of the short stories, won the McClelland and Stewart Award for Fiction and the National Magazine Award in 1986.

A Casual Brutality (1988) was shortlisted for the Trillium Award and the
W. H. Smith (Canada) First Novel Award. His third and latest book, *On
the Eve of Uncertain Tomorrows* (1990), is a collection of ten stories, most
of which are about immigrants, refugees, and wanderers.

MAJOR WORKS AND THEMES

Bissoondath's fiction to date is almost exclusively concerned with the
experiences of immigrants, refugees, nomads, and wanderers. Bissoondath
would appear to agree with his protagonist in "Veins Visible" that "everybody's a refugee, everybody's running from one thing or another" (*Mountains* 222). His narratives seldom if ever are about the excitement of new
beginnings or the satisfaction of achievements. His protagonists experience
feelings of marginality, of insecurity and homelessness, of impermanence
and loss of bearings. Ramgoolam, the aged protagonist of the short story
"Security," is a characteristic Bissoondath migrant-protagonist. Having es-
caped the political turmoil in his Caribbean island to be with his sons in
Canada, he discovers to his dismay that they are now "Canadian to the
point of strangeness" and he spends "endless stretches of being alone"
(*Tomorrows* 87). In another story, a similarly unhappy West Indian immigrant returns to his island home because he needs "more from his life . . .
something indefinable that came from his familiarity with the island" (*Tomorrows* 211–12).

This West Indian immigrant, from the story "The Power of Reason," is
an Afro- not an Indo-Caribbean, and he illustrates Bissoondath's inclusive
concern not with the immigrant experience of his own racial, ethnic, or
national group, but with the immigrant experience at large. Bissoondath
does focus in *A Casual Brutality* on the Indo-Caribbean societies in Trinidad
and Toronto, but in his other fictional pieces he relates the immigrant life
of protagonists with various backgrounds. Of the fourteen stories in *Digging
Up the Mountains*, only three could be seen as having a specific focus on
Indo-Caribbean migrants: "Digging Up the Mountains," "Insecurity," and
"Christmas Lunch." In *On the Eve of Uncertain Tomorrows*, there are just
two: "Security" and "Kira and Anya." The others provide such perspectives
as those of a Japanese girl in Toronto struggling with her constricting traditional upbringing in "The Cage," of a white Canadian expatriate teaching
in Trinidad in "An Arrangement of Shadows," of a white Canadian tourist
adrift in Spain in "Continental Drift," of a black West Indian returning to
his island in "There Are a Lot of Ways to Die," and of an ethnically
undefined migrant medical doctor in Toronto awaiting a wife he has not
seen for twenty-two years in "Man as Plaything, Life as Mockery."

Bissoondath characteristically tends to avoid providing temporal, spatial,
national, or racial specificities. In "Man as Plaything, Life as Mockery,"
for instance, all we know of the protagonist is that twenty-two years earlier

he fled a brutal civil war in his country, which could be anywhere in Eastern Europe or even Asia or Latin America. His appearance—"square, pudgy, with inexpressive eyes... hair so thinned that in the muted light he looked bald" (*Mountains* 174)—individualizes him but provides no clue to his ethnic or racial identity. In the title story of *On the Eve of Uncertain Tomorrows*, the two protagonists desperately seeking refugee status in Canada are identified simply as victims of torture from an unspecified Latin American country. It would appear that Bissoondath—flying in the teeth of the postcolonial and postmodern theorists who demand of postcolonial writers an emphasis on separate identities and differences—consciously constructs his fiction without specific details of nationality and ethnicity to underscore the commonness and universality of the emotional and spiritual disruption of migrants and refugees.

Bissoondath's indifference to specificities does encourage his readers to acknowledge the common human bonds, but at the same time this diminution of details tends now and again to temper the animation of his character portraits, the immediacy of his narratives, and the authenticity of his settings. His focus on the generic in the immigrants' or interlopers' experiences renders inauthentic his characterizations in sections of such stories as "The Cage," "The Arctic Landscape High above the Equator," and "Goodnight, Mr. Slade."

Though the temporal and spatial backdrops of many of his stories remain blurred, the immediate circumambient setting is created with an eye to graphic details. But these details do more than just create the setting. Like Hemingway, whose pared style Bissoondath adopts, he conveys inner experiences through external particulars. Since his characters are not always psychologically attuned to their own complex feelings and motivations, this technique as a rule works well. In "Cracks and Keyholes," for instance, the state of mind of the protagonist, an impoverished black Caribbean immigrant employed as a dishwasher in a Toronto strip joint, is brilliantly evoked through description of the Christmas decorations on Yonge Street: "I realize it have few things more depressin' in this world than decorations that doesn't decorate: and them decorations across Yonge Street, old and wet and limp and mash-up, ain't have it in them to decorate" (*Tomorrows* 148–49). The emphasis on externals, however, can be overdone as in "Kira and Anya." The narrator's concentration on external matters in this story suggests individuals observed impersonally by a video camera; this camera eye fails to animate the characterization.

In a few of his early stories, Bissoondath exhibits a disturbingly supercilious tone in his treatment of some immigrants, as in "Christmas Lunch," a story narrated by a severely judgmental narrator who sets himself up as the mocking observer of a group of Indo-Caribbean immigrants at a Christmas get-together. A similar sardonic tone informs "The Revolutionary," a caricature of a student radical bent on returning to his West Indian island as its deliverer. Bissoondath's treatment of this character can be compared with his much more tolerant and understanding portrait of the protagonist of "There Are a Lot of Ways to Die," who returns to help his island only to be disillusioned. The sardonic voice seldom if ever reappears in the later volume of stories. Here, the author is never too distant from his characters to perceive them without tolerance and understanding and conversely is never too close to depict them quaintly or sentimentally.

The immigrant as an unanchored individual uncertain of his tomorrows features prominently also in Bissoondath's novel, *A Casual Brutality*. The protagonist Raj, a medical doctor, returns to his island of Casaquemada, a fictional version of Trinidad, after living several years in Canada. Dissatisfied and unfulfilled in Canada, he yearns, like the West Indian immigrants of Bissoondath's stories, for the familiarity of his native land. His return coincides with the island's economic slump and consequent political turmoil. A strength of the novel is its evocation of the mood of violence and corruption and its portrait of numerous secondary characters involved in the social and political conflicts.

Raj's white Canadian wife, Jan, accompanies him on his return to his island. Bissoondath's depiction of the relationship between them is not as successful as that of the social and political ambience of the island primarily because she fails to come alive. Bissoondath does not pay sufficient attention to her reluctance to leave Canada and her inability to accommodate herself to Casaquemada. She remains the stock expatriate. Their meeting and early relationship are contrived: Raj meets her in a striptease bar where she is working her way through college as a waitress; they get married primarily because she becomes pregnant. One of Raj's motivations for returning to Casaquemada is that he wants his son to grow up knowing his father's heritage, but scenes of this aspect of his personal relationship also are submerged beneath Bissoondath's sociopolitical interests in the novel.

The experience of the East Indians in the Caribbean as diaspora figures with no permanent anchorage is the dominant authorial concern. Bissoondath parallels Raj's sense of not belonging anywhere with that of his Indo-Caribbean people. He describes as "a melancholy epic" the East Indians' journey from India to Trinidad 150 years ago. In the current political turmoil, augmented by racial strife between the Afro- and Indo-Caribbean residents, Raj's friends and relatives see themselves as "the Jews of the Caribbean" (196), threatened with upheaval. Raj's return to Canada at the end of the novel (after the brutal political murder of his wife and son) is described in terms of his ancestors' placelessness: "What began so long ago as a flight from a dusty and decrepit village in India brings me now to a flight on a jet [to Canada]" (377). But if Canada is a haven from the violence of his island, it is not home. Raj recalls as a student in Toronto befriending an old man who fled the political oppression of the East Indians in Guyana and now works illegally in Canada. When Raj asks him if he will ever return to Guyana, the old man repeats the word "home" as if, Raj observes, it were "a word alien to him, a word without meaning." Raj sees a kindred spirit in this Indo-Caribbean compatriot who is "hopelessly adrift" (233). The novel concludes with Raj lamenting his and his people's state of being perpetually on the move, prophetically and liturgically saying: "So it has been. So it is. So it will remain" (378).

CRITICAL RECEPTION

Still early in his career and with his first volume published just seven years ago, Bissoondath has received little extended critical attention, but there have been a substantial number of reviews of his books in many prestigious magazines and journals. Most have been favorable and have recognized him as a very important talent from the publication of his first book *Digging Up the Mountains*. Though many reviewers point to his insightful and sensitive depiction of the dispossessed and displaced, they acknowledge that occasionally he can be cold and detached. Bissoondath's relationship with V. S. Naipaul inevitably raised for reviewers of his first book the question of the anxiety of influence. His pessimistic outlook, his sense of placelessness, and his diagnostic tone were perceived as Naipaulesque. Though his novel, *A Casual Brutality*, was positively reviewed, there were complaints about the unfocused, sluggish nature of the narrative and the deliberate striving for the literary that at times appears portentous and sententious. As the *Spectator* reviewer says, when "Bissoondath forgets he is writing 'literature' he is a very good writer indeed" (Lezard 36). The *Times Literary Supplement (London)* is representative of the reviews of Bissoondath's latest volume, *On the Eve of Uncertain Tomorrows*, when it notes that there are stories in it that do not work well but on the whole the author "has kept the amazing promise he made with that first remarkable novel" (Kanga 1271).

BIBLIOGRAPHY

Works by Neil Bissoondath

Digging Up the Mountains. Toronto: Macmillan of Canada, 1986.
A Casual Brutality. Toronto: Macmillan of Canada, 1988.
On the Eve of Uncertain Tomorrows. Toronto: Macmillan of Canada, 1990.

Studies of Neil Bissoondath

Gorra, Michael. Review of *Digging Up the Mountains*. *Hudson Review* 40 (Spring 1987): 139.
Kanga, Firdaus. Review of *On the Eve of Uncertain Tomorrows*. *Times Literary Supplement (London)* (Nov. 23, 1990): 1271.

Keneally, Thomas. Review of *A Casual Brutality*. *New York Times Book Review* (Feb. 26, 1989): 14.

Kureishi, Hanif. Review of *A Casual Brutality*. *New Statesman* (Sept. 16, 1988): 42.

Lezard, Nicholas. Review of *A Casual Brutality*. *Spectator* (Dec. 10, 1988): 36.

Maja-Pearce, Adewale. Review of *Digging Up the Mountains*. *Times Literary Supplement (London)* (June 6, 1986): 623.

Panabaker, James. Review of *A Casual Brutality*. *Queen's Quarterly* 96 (Winter 1989): 956.

Ramraj, Victor. "Still Arriving: The Assimilationist Indo-Caribbean Experience of Marginality." *Reworlding: The Literature of the Indian Diaspora*. Ed. Emmanuel S. Nelson. Westport, Conn.: Greenwood Press, 1992. 77–85.

Stephen, Jaci. Review of *Digging Up the Mountains*. *Times Educational Supplement* (July 18, 1986): 822.

Summers, Merna. Review of *On the Eve of Uncertain Tomorrows*. *Books in Canada* 19 (Oct., 1990): 35.

SASTHI BRATA (1939–   )
Chaman L. Sahni

BIOGRAPHY

Sasthi Brata [Chakravarti] was born in 1939 into a well-to-do Bengali Brahmin family in Calcutta. The fourteenth child of his aging parents, he received their lavish affection during his early childhood. His mother was a selfless, traditional Hindu woman, rooted in religious ritual and ceremony. His father was a self-made, successful businessman who admired the Western system of education. In his eleventh year, therefore, young Sasthi was sent away to an English-language Christian school known for its stern, puritanical discipline, bigotry, and intolerance. In his autobiography, *My God Died Young*, he recalls, in great detail, "the fire-eating ethic of Wesleyan asceticism, with its corollaries of sneaking, back-biting and monastic in-fighting" (66). The twin pressures of an orthodox Brahmin family and a nonconformist schooling created a lasting conflict in Brata's mind—a conflict that appears again and again in his writings.

After passing the college entrance examination under the aegis of Cambridge University, he joined Presidency College, Calcutta, from which he graduated in 1959 with a major in physics. At college, he had the misfortune of falling in love with a girl for whom her father had already arranged a husband, thirteen years her senior. This incident seemed to crystallize young Brata's vague feelings of rebellion against an authoritarian society where "fathers are always right, elder brothers wise, the senior men always more preferable" (*My God Died Young* 182). In 1961, he therefore decided to turn away from his affluent and orthodox family and left India for Europe. "Since then," he writes in the author's note to *India: Labyrinths in the Lotus Land*, "I have lived as a voluntary exile from the land of my birth in various different cities of the world" (7). He now lives in London with his family. Over the past three decades, his journalistic assignments have frequently taken him back to his homeland, and for some time now he has been regularly writing a column, "The London Notebook," for the Calcutta-based paper, the *Statesman*. "I cannot disown my past," he writes in *My God Died Young*, "my father and my mother, those generations of pious Brahmins who are my ancestors, the placid submissive way they lived their lives. All those aeons of static decay lie hidden somewhere within me. In some doomed crevice of my mind they will remain, perhaps till I die" (107).

MAJOR WORKS AND THEMES

A controversial writer and journalist, Brata has so far published six books, four of which are novels. He rose to fame with the publication of his autobiography, *My God Died Young*, in 1967. Saturated with the author's diasporic consciousness, the book deals with the theme of alienation suffered by westernized Indians like him who find the ethos of their mother country alien to their way of thought, but who also cannot feel at home in their adopted country. "The deepest tragedy of British rule in India," he writes, "is that it succeeded in producing individuals like me who can neither feel an identity with their own people nor accept the glare, the steel-muscle concept of human life as it exists in America and which seems slowly to be gripping the whole of the West" (229). As a result, he feels like a man without a country.

In his quest for self-discovery, he reveals, with remarkable candor and insight, the story of his early upbringing in a traditional Brahmin family and the way it conflicted with his repressive Christian schooling. He also gives memorable descriptions of his life at Presidency College, Calcutta, his dabbling with communist politics, his intense love affair with a girl whom he could not marry, his unsuccessful search for a prospective bride in the traditional Hindu manner, and finally his decision to leave his country. Each episode serves as a catalyst to ferment his anger at and rebellion against the Indian social setup, which he finds to be "repulsive" and "authoritarian," based on "submission, superstition, and prejudice." "Hence I disown the country of my birth," he declares in the concluding chapter of the book (228–29). He feels, however, equally alienated in his adopted country. As he puts it,

How does one explain the whole business of alienation in a few short sentences; the sheer tearing pain of not being able to belong to the very place where one wants to send down roots? This side of the twentieth century we have seen refugees galore, leaving behind them a wild trail of heroism and tenacious nationalism. But what does one do about those non-Jews who were not persecuted, those non-politicals who were not threatened with arrest; those voluntary exiles who were born in a home they found foreign and came to a land which shocked and unsettled them? (229)

Brata's first novel, *Confessions of an Indian Woman Eater* (1971), written in the picaresque mode, belongs to the erotica. It vividly describes the sexual fantasies and conquests of its first-person narrator, Amit Ray, who decides, like the author, to leave his comfortable home in Calcutta as a symbolic gesture to jerk his "life out of its predestined grooves" (3). His first stop is Delhi, where he works for a time as a shoeshine boy and later as a reporter for the *Statesman*. His assignments as a reporter take him to Rome, London, Paris, Copenhagen, and back to London. His European sojourn is heavily punctuated with overdoses of alcohol and sexual encounters, as if with a vengeance against his repressive and puritanical upbringing. He seems to subscribe to the view of a Hampstead ideologue whom he describes at great length in the novel: "We should desanctify sex, make love on park benches and buses, wherever and whenever we feel like it. Strip it of that damn thing called 'mystery' " (267).

Despite its preoccupation with lurid sexuality, the novel reflects the major theme of Brata's works: the rebel-hero's leaving home and going abroad as a defiant gesture against an orthodox and authoritarian society. This theme is developed with existential overtones. The narrator has read Camus, and he discusses existentialism with the Hampstead intellectuals. But his sense of displacement always haunts him. "The world I describe," he remarks, "is not London, it is not even Hampstead. It is a world of fringers like myself who have no home, mostly through choice, partly by compulsion" (271).

Brata's third novel, *She & He*, deals with an aspiring young writer, Zamir Ishmael—an Algerian immigrant in England, born of an Arab father and a French mother—who leads a Bohemian life in Hampstead, London. The novel dramatizes the conflict between love and desire. Zamir is in love with Sally, but he constantly desires and has a physical relationship with Cinderalla, a married woman. Marriage and settlement in life hold basic repulsions for him. The novel does not indicate whether his repulsion for a settled life has something to do with his exilic sensibility. The love story is told retrospectively by two narrators, She and He, i.e., Sally and Zamir, but their respective styles show hardly any distinction between the female and the male sensibilities. "I wrote this book," Brata says in the author's note, "during the summer of 1965 in seventeen days flat, being fed all the time on whiskey, dexedrine and steak, by a delicious American girl with whom I was very much in love."

Brata's next novel, *A Search for Home* (1975), written in an autobiographical vein, recaptures the themes of homelessness and revolt against traditional Indian society. Its protagonist, traumatized by the conflict between his native Indian culture and that of his adopted country, England, is described as a man "in perpetual suspension,... a medium at home in neither world. A mere go-between" (147). "In an exact sense Esbee [Sasthi Brata] was a man without a country, there was no place he could call his own, no nation or cause to which he could pledge his unswerving loyalty" (146).

The novel is divided into five sections, each using a different narrative form. The first section, titled "A Search for Home," is in the form of a monologue addressed to the speaker's dead wife. In it the speaker recalls his return to Calcutta after a two-year stay in Europe, his arranged marriage to a shy sixteen-year-old girl, his wife's dutiful role in a traditional Bengali household, her pregnancy, and finally her miscarriage by slipping in the bathroom and her subsequent death in the hospital. The second section, called "Whispers of Immortality," complements and sometimes repeats the family background given in Brata's autobiography. The third section, "The Trial," resumes the autobiographical vein and describes the elaborate Hindu rituals connected with the mother's death ceremony. The fourth part, "Letter to My Father," signed by the author in his own name, Sasthi Brata, uses the epistolary method to reassess his father's achievement in a traditional Bengali society. The last section, called "The Condemned Playground," dramatically describes Esbee's return to Calcutta with his British wife and children, his nostalgic trip back to his alma mater, Presidency College, his remembrance of things past, including his love for a girl called Apu, and his conversation with his former professor of physics. After a while Esbee realizes the predicament of an exile returning to his country: "The exile is always under attack from both sides. Branded a traitor in the country of his birth, he is treated as an officious nuisance when he starts complaining about conditions in his host country" (145). At the end, the Indo-Anglian in Esbee feels that "rising tide of resentment within him," and he hates "the sore-ridden putrefying face of the society around him" (145).

Brata's last novel, *The Sensuous Guru: The Making of a Mystic President*, published in 1980, no longer reflects the attitude of an angry young man lashing out at the authoritarian and conservative value system of Indian society. Set in the United States, it is best described in the author's note as "a Bacchanalian dream," filled with "grotesque fantasies in a twisted mind coming down from a bad acid trip." Graphically erotic and hilarious, the novel is a satire on the permissiveness of American society and its craze for Indian Yoga and mysticism. It also gives an intimate portrayal of contemporary literary and political life in America, as viewed by an outsider. A young Brahmin, Ram Chukker, who poses as an Indian guru in New York, initiates his American female disciples into the mysteries not only of Yoga but also of sexuality. Promoted by a lesbian friend, Evelyn Louise Teller, he succeeds in winning not only the Pulitzer Prize and the Nobel Peace Prize, but also the highest political office of the president of the United States. Evelyn, whom he later marries, is also elected the first woman vice-president of the United States. Two years later, the vice-president (and First Lady), driving back from Martha's Vineyard, meets with an accident in which the president, who was in the side seat of the car, is drowned in the river near

Chappaquiddick. Thus, by an extraordinary chain of events, Evelyn Louise Teller Chukker is sworn in as the first woman president of the United States.

That the novel is a satire on American civilization is evident from these ironical comments of the narrator:

It is our privilege to inform our readers that such an event could not have occurred anywhere else in the world. If the Press were not so free and the media so accessibly amenable, if majority opinion was not so widely revered, if literary standards were not so democratically set, and above all, if men and women were not so deeply moved by the perennials of human life, instead of ephemeral fashion, then Ram Chukker, with his humble beginning in a "Lower East Side dump" and a single ad in The Village Voice, could have neither become a guru nor the Head of the Union. (222)

In his latest book, *India: Labyrinths in the Lotus Land* (1985), Brata takes the reader on a cultural, historical, political, religious, and sociological tour of India. As he puts it, "In this book, both as a native son and as an exile in a foreign land, I have tried to show why India, in all its myriad aspects of despair and splendor, of destitution and opulence, of majestic modernity and primitive superstition, may yet be an Oriental sphinx whose secrets can and should be locked" (9). The narrative is interspersed with personal experiences, reminiscences, and autobiographical episodes, which sets the book apart from other travel guides to India, but as one reviewer points out, "the only quibble is that Brata has a disconcerting habit of making smart-alecky asides that spoil the objectivity of his tale" (*Kirkus Reviews*, 685).

CRITICAL RECEPTION

Though three of Brata's books, *My God Died Young, Search for Home,* and *India: Labyrinths in the Lotus Land,* have been widely reviewed on both sides of the Atlantic, he has not received any detailed critical attention. Some of the reasons for this neglect become obvious from the reviews. He has been praised for his talent, wit, style, and lacerating honesty, but his works suffer from attitudinizing and lack of organization. One reviewer of *My God Died Young* recognizes Brata's "undeniable literary gift," but suspects "that he is assuming an angry posture just to be in the forefront of western fashion, that his rebellious nature is mainly due to an exceptionally strong sexual urge which he found he had to 'go foreign' fully to express" ("Angry" 879). Another reviewer states that "Mr. Brata has developed his descriptive skills to a high level, but he has not yet developed a self-analytical tool which allows him to cut through pretension, pomposity, and the sophomoric urge to shock and impress" (Gropman 9). Similarly, his book on India has received mixed reviews. Una Chaudhuri finds the book "deeply flawed in both conception and execution" (650). John F. Riddick thinks that "for the most part . . . this journalistic offering is overly simplistic and poorly organized" (107). Stella Sandahl decries the misinformation and the "glaring factual errors" that the book contains (28).

The literary merit of Brata's works may be questionable, but as a writer of the Indian diaspora, he deserves an unequivocal recognition. He is in the vanguard of the new generation of the postindependence Indian writers who suffer from an acute sense of alienation and expose the shams and hypocrisy of a tradition-bound society. The lines from Thomas Mann that Brata chose as an epigraph to the last section of *A Search for Home* most appropriately express his exilic awareness: "I stand between two worlds. I am at home in neither, and I suffer in consequence" (119).

BIBLIOGRAPHY

Works by Sasthi Brata

My God Died Young. New Delhi: Orient Paperbacks, 1967; New York: Harper; London: Hutchinson, 1968.
Confessions of an Indian Woman Eater. London: Hutchinson, 1971.
She & He. New Delhi: Orient Paperbacks, 1973.
Traitor to India: A Search for Home. New Delhi: Orient Paperbacks, 1975; London: Paul Elck, 1976.
The Sensuous Guru: The Making of a Mystic President. New Delhi: Sterling, 1980.
India: Labyrinths in the Lotus Land. New York: Morrow, 1985.

Studies of Sasthi Brata

"Angry Young Brahmin." Review of *My God Died Young. Times Literary Supplement* (Aug. 15, 1968): 879.
Chaudhuri, Una. Review of *India: Labyrinths in the Lotus Land. Commonweal* (Nov. 15, 1985): 651–52.
Dimock, Edward C. Review of *My God Died Young. Journal of Asian Studies* 28 (1969): 874.
Gropman, Donald. "Young, Fierce, and a Stranger Everywhere." Review of *My God Died Young. Christian Science Monitor* (Dec. 12, 1968): 9.
Hertz, Eleanor W. Review of *India: Labyrinths in the Lotus Land. Best Sellers* 45 (1985): 350.
Leitch, David. Review of *Traitor to India: A Search for Home. New Statesman* (July 2, 1976): 24.
Pritchett, V. S. Review of *My God Died Young. New Statesman* (Sept. 20, 1968): 352.
Reichek, Morton A. "Deciphering the Mysteries of a Turbulent Land." Review of *India: Labyrinths in the Lotus Land. Business Week* (Sept. 23, 1985): 12, 16.

Review of *Confessions of an Indian Woman Eater*. *Times Literary Supplement* (June 25, 1971): 726.

Review of *India: Labyrinths in the Lotus Land*. *Kirkus Reviews* 53 (1985): 685.

Review of *My God Died Young*. *Kirkus Reviews* 36 (1968): 853.

Review of *My God Died Young*. *New York Times Book Review* (Oct. 20, 1968): 50–51.

Review of *Traitor to India: A Search for Home*. *New Yorker* (Mar. 7, 1977): 120.

Riddick, John F. Review of *India: Labyrinths in the Lotus Land*. *Library Journal* (Oct. 1, 1985): 107.

Sandahl, Stella. Review of *India: Labyrinths in the Lotus Land*. *Books in Canada* 15 (1986): 28.

NIRAD CHANDRA CHAUDHURI (1897–   )

Fakrul Alam

BIOGRAPHY

Nirad C. Chaudhuri was born on November 23, 1897, in Kishoreganj, a town in what was then Bengal and is now Bangladesh. In 1910 the family moved to Calcutta, where the education begun at home and continued in a small-town primary school. Chaudhuri distinguished himself in his undergraduate studies, securing the first rank in his B.A. (honors) examination in history at Calcutta University. However, he seemed to have had a case of nerves during his M.A. examination, and left university without bagging this degree. From 1921 to 1941 he remained in Calcutta, surviving long periods of unemployment, and drifting from job to job. But while in Calcutta he began to make a name for himself as a literary journalist who wrote both in Bengali and English. In 1942 Chaudhuri migrated to Delhi, where he had been offered a position as a broadcaster in All India Radio. In 1947 he began work on his first book, *The Autobiography of an Unknown Indian*, and managed to have it published in England in 1951. The book made him famous, and he was invited to visit the country in 1955 by the British Broadcasting Corporation. *A Passage to England* (1959), Chaudhuri's second major publication and a paean to what he calls "Timeless England," is the fruit of that five-week trip. His third book, *The Continent of Circe, Being an Essay on the Peoples of India* (1965), is a highly idiosyncratic view of Indian history and civilization.

Chaudhuri retired from his job in 1952 but continued to support himself and his family in Delhi through his writing. Two books from this period of his life are *The Intellectual in India* (1967) and *To Live or Not to Live!* (1970). These are essentially minor works and were published in India and designed to offer Indians advice on how to live happily in their country. Although these books were never reprinted in the West, the reputation he had made there through his first three books, as a man of original views, formidable learning, and many-sided interests, led to an invitation from the family of the famous Indologist Max Muller to write a biography of him. Since all of Muller's papers are in the Bodleian library, Chaudhuri had to come to Oxford in 1970. When he finished this book, the publishing firm of Bannie and Jenkins asked him to do a biography of Robert Clive, the founder of the British Empire in India. This was published as *Clive of India* in 1975. Another commissioned work, *Hinduism, A Religion to Live By* (1979), bears testimony to his interest in the religion. By the end of the seventies, however, Chaudhuri was running short of funds and was about to return to India. But an advance from Chatto and Windus to write a sequel to his still popular *Autobiography* ensured that he remained in England. Chuadhuri began work on this book in the spring of 1979 and had it published in 1987 as *Thy Hand, Great Anarch! India, 1921–1952*. He was ninety years old then but continues to write and publish books and essays even now. It must be pointed out, though, that his most recent works have been in Bengali and have been published only in India.

MAJOR WORKS AND THEMES

At one point in *Thy Hand, Great Anarch!* Chaudhuri offers this list of his major ideas: "The nature of ancient and modern Indian Culture; Bengali life and culture, the future of the Bengali people; Hindu-Muslim relations in India; nature of Indian nationalism and finally, Indo-British relations" (393). Earlier on in the book he had identified as the chief theme of all his writings "The impact of western life and civilization" on Indians and "the interaction between the two cultures of which I was a product like thousands of others" (143). All of his works deal with these ideas and this major theme in one way or the other, but it is in the *Autobiography*, still his best-known book, and *Thy Hand, Great Anarch!*, the culminating work of his career, that he handles them most impressively. This essay will thus consider only these two books in any detail.

The Autobiography of an Unknown Indian can be read on many levels, but it is very much the story of Chaudhuri's life till his twenty-fifth year written from the perspective of a fifty-year-old man who has organized his work around certain themes and places and who has thought at length about its significance and representative quality. The *Autobiography* thus begins with a record of the life lived by people in small-town and rural Bengal. He presents this life with great sensitivity and a sharp eye for detail, for he has no doubt that religious and literary traditions, as well as the landscape and seasonal rhythms, have shaped his consciousness.

In the next part of the *Autobiography*, Chaudhuri offers us affectionate portraits of his parents and traces the way they have shaped his life. His father was not merely a small-town lawyer but a cultured man whose liberal humanism became paradigmatic for his sons. Imbued with the reformist zeal of his generation of educated Bengalis, he gave his children an early taste of a rational, enlightened, and improving culture. Unlike his father, Chaudhuri's mother knew no English, but she too influenced him intellectually, introducing him to, among others, Shakespeare whom she had read in Bengali translation.

Significantly, Chaudhuri includes in the first half of the *Autobiography*, where he emphasizes the formative influences on his personality, a chapter on England. This may seem at first glance a quirky decision, but it is very much to his point that England and English culture were also part of his heritage. As the case of his parents testifies, not a few individuals in Bengal had been molded by the Western values that found their way into the Eastern civilization. Whether in remote Kishoreganj or in the imperial city of Calcutta, educated Indians would not escape the energizing influence of Western civilization. To these Indians it did not matter that Englishmen in flesh could be very arrogant and disagreeable; what was material was the ideas transmitted through European history and literature of a humane, dynamic, and reformatory world.

Consequently, a central chapter of the *Autobiography*, and indeed a major theme in everything Chaudhuri has written till now, is devoted to the praise of the hybrid culture that was formed when contact with the best in English civilization invigorated the Bengali mind in the nineteenth century. This chapter, titled "Torch Race of the Indian Renaissance," describes the rebirth of learning and the splendid efflorescence in Bengali literature that began with the founding of Calcutta's Hindu College in 1817 and created such major writers/intellectuals as Rammohan Roy, Michael Madhusudan Dutt, Bankim Chandra Chatterji, and Rabindranath Tagore. Even Hinduism, stagnant for centuries, was vitalized by the contact with Western learning. This is how Chaudhuri sums up what he considers to the be the golden age of modern Indian history: never before had the Hindu middle class "showed greater probity in public and private affairs, attained greater happiness in family and personal life, [seen] greater fulfillment of cultural aspirations, and put forth greater creativeness in every field than the fifty years between 1860 and 1910" (217).

But if the *Autobiography* is a celebration of the Bengali Renaissance of the nineteenth century, it is also a lament for a period that has passed away. Chaudhuri leaves his readers with the impression that he is the product of a last flowering of a unique culture. As far as he can tell, "all that we have learnt, all that we have acquired, and all that we have prized is threatened with extinction" (127). The snake in the garden that has made a fall inevitable was nationalism, itself a product of the revolutionary ideals propagated by Renaissance culture. Also, resurgent dogmatic Hinduism and mindless mob action were fanning the flames of hatred for the British Empire and leading to ugly Hindu-Muslim confrontations. Suddenly, everything that had been achieved by the British Empire—high civilization, stability, and progress—seemed threatened.

Up to this point of the *Autobiography*, Chaudhuri not only writes the story of an unknown Indian but implicitly hints at the representative quality of his experience. At one with the ideals propagated by the major figures of the Indian Renaissance, in sympathy even with the first stirrings of nationalism in turn-of-the-century India, Chaudhuri had felt integrated with the cultural life he had experienced as a child. But the passing away of that culture, significantly coinciding with his arrival in Calcutta as a fourteen-year-old, was the beginning of a growing alienation from his contemporaries. Paradise had been lost with the move away from Kishoreganj: "Once torn up from my natural habitat I became liberated from the habitat altogether; my environment and I began to fall apart, and in the end the environment became wholly external" (257–58).

This is the moment when the diasporic consciousness in Chaudhuri first began to assert itself—events were happening now that would ultimately lead him to choose a life of exile away from Bengal. Chaudhuri felt that he was witnessing in his Calcutta years a major catastrophe: the "degradation of Bengal... which [was], of course, part of the larger process of the re-barbarization of the whole of India," which began in the second decade of the twentieth century and which, as far as Chaudhuri is concerned, continues till the present (1983). This is the key theme of the second part of the *Autobiography*, the dominant idea of its sequel, *Thy Hand, Great Anarch!*, and the leitmotif of *The Continent of Circe*: India was committing cultural *hara-kiri* (suicide) and undergoing "a phase of unrelieved decay" (127) by withdrawing from the Empire and the culture it had created. In his comments on these distressing developments here and elsewhere in his works, Chaudhuri's tone becomes either shrill and denunciatory or exasperated and despairing. He is not capable of remaining indifferent to the scene before him and is convinced that he was fated to play the role of a Cassandra whose prophetic utterances would not be heeded.

Chaudhuri's experience of Calcutta, however, was not entirely a negative one. The *Autobiography*, like the subsequent works, could have been written only by a man of extraordinary learning; in places it even reads like a *bildungsroman*, and in the course of it Chaudhuri emerges as a bibliophile, an aesthete, a linguist, and a young man who discovers that writing is in his bones; all of these aspects of this unusual man and apprentice-writer were nurtured by Calcutta's unique cultural and educational institutions.

Perhaps the branch of learning that most attracted the young seeker after universal knowledge in these years is history, and history and historiography have continued to be Chaudhuri's primary loves. Not surprisingly, then, the two autobiographical volumes and *The Continent of Circe* are works of the historical imagination (his detractors will say that there is more

imagination in them than history). Drawing on a historiography compounded from Actonian ideals of objectivity, Darwinian principles of evolutionary biology, and Spenglerian postulates about the decline of
civilizations, Chaudhuri concludes that contemporary Indian civilization is
in irreversible decline: "Although I do believe that individual Indians will
be born who will be capable of making notable contributions to the world
civilization of the future, collectively, we shall never again achieve anything
like the greatness and individuality of the Hindu civilization" (499–500).

The stance Chaudhuri takes toward Indian nationalism, contemporary
politics, and culture in India, and the regret he everywhere expresses about
the impoverishment of the Indian sensibility after its retreat from Western
civilization and rejection of the British Empire, have also led to his alienation
from his fellow Indians: "In formulating my conception of history . . . I was
erecting a barrier of intellectual isolation which was to become more and
more impenetrable with years" (347). Not travel or emigration but cultivation of knowledge had uprooted him: "my intellect has indeed at last
emancipated itself from my country" (461). As for his countrymen, they
would treat him as a pariah for his views, even though he himself felt that
he always kept them and their interest in sight.

In *Thy Hand, Great Anarch! India, 1921–1952*, the massive sequel of
the *Autobiography* and the essential complement to the first book, Chaudhuri continues to tell the story of his life while adopting a universal perspective on India's past and future. This volume is, among other things, a
record of his working life. He begins it with a description of his years as a
clerk in a military accounts department of the government of India who
has taken the job only to support himself till he is able to write a great
historical work. It narrates his boredom with the job and his life after he
quit it, when he had to endure humiliation as an unemployed university
graduate in Calcutta. Chaudhuri is, as before, writing a sort of *Künstler-
roman*, for he describes his career as a literary critic, editor, and literary
journalist who eventually gets to write the *Autobiography*. Also, he offers
sketches of his friends and family members and dwells on his personal
relationships at some length.

Chaudhuri, however, has designed *Thy Hand, Great Anarch!* to be very
much like its predecessor in that it is more than the story of one man and
very much the account of an epoch in Indian history. The book, in fact, is
a detailed picture of the society in which Chaudhuri lived from youth to
middle age and a record of his thoughts and feelings about the public and
historical events through which he has passed. Because Chaudhuri emerged
as a publicist in this period and because he did stints in the thirties and
forties as an editor for the official journal of the Calcutta Corporation and
as the private secretary of a leading politician of Bengal, he would like his
readers to believe that he is in a fit position to comment incisively on the
politics and public figures of the period.

The title of *Thy Hand, Great Anarch!*, from the concluding section of Alexander Pope's *Dunciad*, orients us to the basic thesis of the volume: India from 1921 to 1952 was a country sliding steadily into chaos. The decline and fall of the British Empire in India, the decay of the culture created in Bengal when European civilization revitalized a hitherto moribund people, and the passing away of a generation of men who had become the torchbearers of humanistic values ensured that the forces of anarchy would have a field day in modern India. Chaudhuri, surveying the political and cultural wasteland that he thinks India is becoming, is shown foresuffering it all like Tiresias, or giving vent to prophecies of impending disaster like Cassandra, or uttering Jeremiah-like imprecations only to bring on himself the wrath of his countrymen. Chaudhuri's anger at what went on in India from the 1920s to independence is also directed at the British; he feels that they too were culpable for they had abdicated their imperial role prematurely. As far as he is concerned, the nation that had aroused India from stupor for a while was itself suffering from exhaustion and enervation by the end of World War II.

Thy Hand, Great Anarch! is thus full of apocalyptic pronouncements. At the same time, it chronicles Chaudhuri's own attempts to "pass through an age of decadence without being touched by it" (xxiii). The alienation from his own kind that was incipient in the first book becomes, by the end of the second, total. By the 1930s, Chaudhuri, convinced that Bengalis had relinquished their roles as standard-bearers of Indian civilization, had begun to look for a way out of Calcutta. As he puts it, "I was convinced that my people had no future, and I was not prepared to share their fate" (655). North India seemed to be logical place to go then, for to all appearances the "Hindu speaking people of that region had more vitality and therefore promise" (xxiv). Consequently, Chaudhuri moved himself and his family to Delhi, where he worked as a military analyst for the overseas service of All India Radio from 1942 to 1952. The anarchy let loose during partition and his experience of Delhi life in the forties persuaded him, however, that North India offered him no better an alternative than Bengal. At the end of the volume, then, Chaudhuri is contemplating the ultimate diasporic move—the possibility of leaving his country forever for England. Only his fear that his children will lose all connection with Indian culture and traditions prevents him from moving at this time. It is clear throughout the book though that he made the move afterwards, for Chaudhuri assumes habitually the tone of a prophet in exile who must warn the people who stayed behind of the dangers they were courting through their unexamined lives. Surveying his peregrinations from his home in Oxford, he concludes: "My life has always moved West, and once it has done so its direction has never been reversed" (683).

Although Chaudhuri seems destined to live in England for the rest of his life, he never forgets his status as an extraterritorial writer. He knew even when he left Calcutta for Delhi that "to be uprooted was to be for ever on the road" (203). As an expatriate, he sustains himself by reliving constantly in his memory the beauty of the landscape of his native Bengal. So conscious of his difference from other Bengalis who live overseas, he knows that he is one with them in his feelings about the Bengali diaspora, for Bengalis in exile "never forget their Zion in Calcutta" (399). The city is his Jerusalem even when, or precisely because, Calcuttans attacked him, as they did the greatest Bengali of all times, Rabindranath Tagore, and he feels like saying then: " 'O Jerusalem, Jerusalem, *thou* that killest the prophet, and stonest them which are sent to thee, how often would I have gathered thine children together, and ye would not' " (665–66).

The *Autobiography* and *Thy Hand, Great Anarch!* thus reveal a complex and fascinating man. Chaudhuri appears in these two volumes in many, and often seemingly, contradictory roles: an Anglophile and Francophile who is also passionately committed to Bengali culture; a prude and puritan who can also be romantic, reckless, extravagant, and even an "incorrigible Micawberian" (*Thy Hand*, 886); a truth sayer who is also incredibly Quixotic. He disdains academics because they pretend to detachment, but he is proud of his scholarship, analytical powers, and ability to survey everyday events dispassionately.

He assumes various guises in telling the story of his life and people: he is an ideologue, a scholar-gipsy, a controversialist, a dandy and a cultural snob, and an *engagé*, who involves himself "in every aspect of political, social, and cultural life almost all over the world" (141). An unabashed egotist, he sees himself in men like Voltaire or Tagore. Antidemocratic, he can still claim to be cosmopolitan, someone who can remain "a Bengali, an Indian, an Englishman, while being a citizen of the world" (534). Always, his delight in life, his will to live, and *jeu d'esprit* balance his jeremiads, his laments, and his moments of pique. A consummate stylist, he has shaped the two autobiographical volumes into highly readable works of art. In the last analysis, each of these volumes is, like their creator, *sui generis*.

CRITICAL RECEPTION

Nirad Chaudhuri has always had a small but devoted following in the West, while in India he has till recently been viewed more as a controversialist and a jaundiced writer on Indian history and culture than as an objective and impartial analyst of his country's civilization and progress. His first book ensured, however, that he could not remain an unknown Indian after its publication. The work, in fact, has assumed the status of a minor classic and is one of the canonical texts of Indian English literature. Chaudhuri himself has a chapter on the reception of his *Autobiography* in *Thy Hand, Great Anarch!*, where he contrasts the mostly favorable English reviews with consistently hostile Indian reactions to it when it was published.

As time has passed, though, even Indians have begun to appreciate the *Autobiography* for its rich evocation of a world that has gone by and its impressive style, while a consensus has developed that it is the one great Indian book to deal with the outcome of the Indo-English encounter. Thus Sudesh Mishra, an Indian student of Chaudhuri's work, declares: "That Chaudhuri's book is a masterpiece is unquestionable" (7).

The *Autobiography* established the pattern of the reception of Chaudhuri's subsequent books for the next three decades: in the West he would be praised and have something of a cult following, while in India he would be rebuked and rejected. About *A Passage to England*, William Walsh, an English critic who has always championed Chaudhuri, observes: "It is a graceful, unusual travel book but slight by the standards of the *Autobiography*" (45). Chaudhuri's third book, *The Continent of Circe*, won him the Duff Memorial Prize in 1967 but has, typically, exasperated even those Indians who could see some good in him. Thus, C. P. Verghese, the author of the only full-length study of Chaudhuri in print, finds this volume "not an objective analysis or appraisement of the history of a nation but a formidable attack on all things Indian" and "a diatribe" against the Hindus erected on the basis of a suspect historiography.

Chaudhuri's critical fortunes seem to have reached a plateau in the sixties and seventies despite the books he steadily published during this period. However, there has been a revival of interest in him in the last decade and full-scale revaluations after the publication of *Thy Hand, Great Anarch!* To Edward Shils, writing in the *American Scholar*, Chaudhuri's reputation has peaked with this work; it confirms, and gives further evidence, that "he is a stylist of the first order, a scholar of great intelligence, learning, and subtlety and a courageous, wise, and honest man" (550). A flurry of articles and reviews greeted *Thy Hand, Great Anarch!*, and the author received an honorary D.Phil. from the University of Oxford in 1990. Even in India, a new generation of scholars and writers have applauded the book and have started to reappraise his oeuvre with greater understanding. As for Chaudhuri himself, he has utilized his most recent essays and studies in Bengali to explain his stance to his countrymen. Chaudhuri continues to live in exile in England, a leading figure of the India diaspora who will not and cannot sever his connections with his homeland.

BIBLIOGRAPHY

Works by Nirad Chaudhuri

The Autobiography of an Unknown Indian. 1951; rpt., Reading, Mass.: Addison-Wesley, 1989.

A Passage to England. New York: St. Martin's Press, 1959.

The Continent of Circe, Being an Essay on the Peoples of India. 1965; rpt., New York: Oxford University Press, 1967.

The Intellectual in India. Delhi: Vir Publishing House, 1967.

To Live or Not to Live! An Essay on Living Happily with Others. Delhi: Hind Pocket Books, 1970.

"Universal Darkness." *London Magazine* n.s., 1:3 (Aug.–Sept. 1971): 64–75.

"Kipling." *Rudyard Kipling: The Man, His Work, and His World.* Ed. John Gross. London: Weidenfeld & Nicolson, 1972.

Scholar Extraordinary: The Life of Professor the Right Honourable Freidrich Max Muller, P.C. New York: Oxford University Press, 1974.

Clive of India: A Political and Psychological Essay. London: Barrie & Jenkins, 1975.

Culture in the Vanity Bag: Being an Essay on Clothing and Adornment in Passing and Abiding India. Delhi: Jaico, 1976.

Hinduism: A Religion to Live By. Oxford: Oxford University Press, 1979.

Thy Hand, Great Anarch! India, 1921–1952. 1987; rpt., Reading, Mass.: Addison-Wesley, 1988.

Studies of Nirad Chaudhuri

Fallowell, Duncan. "Nirad C. Chaudhuri: At Home in Oxford." *American Scholar* (Spring 1991): 242–46.

Mishra, Sudesh. "The Two Chaudhuris: Historical Witness and Pseudo-Historian." *Journal of Commonwealth Literature* 23:1 (1988): 7–15.

Roy Choudhuri, Tapan. Review of *Thy Hand, Great Anarch! Times Literary Supplement* 27 (Dec. 3, 1987): 1311.

Shils, Edward. "Citizen of the World: Nirad C. Chaudhuri." *American Scholar* (Autumn 1988): 549–72.

Verghese, C. P. *Nirad C. Chaudhuri.* New York: Humanities Press, 1973.

Walsh, William. *Indian Literature in English.* New York: Longman, 1990. 2–4, 45–53, 204.

SAROS COWASJEE (1931–)
Barry Fruchter

BIOGRAPHY

Saros Cowasjee was born on July 12, 1931, in Secundabad, Deccan, India, the son of Dara and Meher (Bharucha) Cowasjee. He received his B.A. in 1951 from St. John's College, Agra, and his M.A. in 1955 from Agra University. A lecturer in English at Agra from 1955 to 1957, he subsequently went to Britain, where he received the Ph.D. from Leeds in 1960. Since 1963, he has served on the faculty of English at the University of Regina, Saskatchewan. He received Canada Council and Social Sciences and Humanities Research Council leave fellowships in 1968–69, 1974–75, 1978–79, and 1986–87; Canada Council research grants in 1970–71 and 1974–75; and a President's Research Fund grant in 1974–75.

In published interviews, Cowasjee disclaims any particular authorial "nationality." A Canadian citizen, he is more widely read in Britain and India than in Canada. He told O. P. Mathur that "to be noticed in Canada one has to be an aggressive salesman—as aggressive as a Jehovah Witness, and as prepared to take insults and get the door shut in one's face" (22). His fiction reflects this feeling of being shut out, the vantage point of an Indian exile who must continually justify himself.

Besides critical and editorial work, Cowasjee's writings consist of two novels, *Goodbye to Elsa* (1974) and *Suffer Little Children* (1982), and two books of short stories, *Stories and Sketches* (1970) and *Nude Therapy and Other Stories* (1978). Saros Cowasjee has indicated that he plans a third novel featuring the return of his hero, Tristan Elliott, to India.

MAJOR WORKS AND THEMES

Saros Cowasjee's short stories embody the experience of a long-term resident of the Indian diaspora. Their venue ranges from Canada to Britain to India, with glances at the Middle East, Burma, and Europe. Moreover, his narrators are painfully conscious of exile (even "at home" in newly independent India) yet all the more intent on plunging into the milieus in which they find themselves. *Nude Therapy*, his second collection, consists of a dozen stories, most of which take place in an anxious, threatening India of the 1940s or 1950s. The few exceptions include the title story (later incorporated, with slight changes, as the first chapter of *Suffer Little Children*), "A Short Story," and "Staff Only." The first two are set in Canada, the third in Britain. Of the Indian stories, one of the more powerful is "His Father's Medals" (reprinted from the earlier collection). Ramu, sweeper of Thakur Madan Singh's compound, cherishes three British medals awarded his father for cleaning army latrines during the Burma campaign. Hiding these treasures upon his emaciated person, Ramu cheerfully goes about following his father's footsteps—cleaning the latrines of the ruling class. Because he is an Untouchable he has lost his true love, Kamala, to another but determines to win her favor by buying her some silver anklets. When he can offer the merchant only two rupees, Ramu is denounced for his presumption; his love is traduced as a whore. In a rage, he runs off with the anklets, only to be stopped by the police, who confiscate his father's medals, deeming them too good for the likes of him. Ignoring his pleas, they lead him away to a terrible beating.

The one British story is lighter stuff, but not without its dark side. The idealistic Hank faces crises both in his university department and at home. He may be turned down for tenure because he refuses to lock the door of the "Staff Only" lavatory after use; he may lose Judy if he fails to get tenure. His plan to get around his rival for the chairman's ear backfires when he accidentally locks Martyn, the chair, in the bathroom instead of Grigson, the rival. Perhaps an Anglo-Indian, Hank is the same sort of hapless and hopeless character as those in the Indian stories.

Like the short stories, Cowasjee's two novels, *Goodbye to Elsa* and *Suffer Little Children*, ring a series of changes on the agonies of the racially mixed, the foreigner (particularly the Indian, of course), the intellectual, the sexually frustrated, the mad. What rescues this litany of isolation from total grimness is wit. The two novels present the extended confession-autobiography of Tristan Elliott, an Anglo-Indian whose pursuit of truth, justice, and perfect love has landed him in the unlikely sanctuary of Erigon University. To some degree his testament, like that of his Anglo-American namesake, is a series of fragments that reveal his agonizing dislocation.

As we learn in *Goodbye to Elsa* (and again in a synopsis during a dinner conversation in *Suffer Little Children*), Tristan is Indian-born, son of an Indian mother and a British father later lost in a wartime airplane crash. After Nellie, his first, ideal love, loses both legs in a train accident, creating in Tristan a lifelong need to find her legs in another woman, Tristan takes ship for Britain and a degree in medieval history at Leeds. Partly as a result of his isolation he meets Heather, a British girl who becomes his first "real" lover. Rejected by Heather in favor of a Syrian, he falls in with Elsa, a fat German girl working in England, quickly marries her, and accepts the Canadian teaching post. Shortly after their son's birth, Tristan becomes estranged from the stolid, 180-pound Elsa; simultaneously, he loses an eye and, upon leaving the hospital, deserts Elsa with the intention of committing suicide so she can collect his insurance. He moves to an isolated house near Corwind, a small town not far from Erigon. Ordering supplies from the general store leads him to meet Marie, the storekeeper's daughter, and eventually to become so obsessed that he drives her back into the arms of an old boyfriend. In despair, Tristan lures Marion, Marie's twin sister, to his house, where he attempts to shoot her in a mad effort to "destroy the womb" and end his cycle of pain. As the novel ends, Tristan has been confined to a mental hospital.

The tale is at once picaresque and Candidean. Indian "intellectuals" come in for particular scourging: alone in Leeds, Tristan is taken under the sleazy wing of one Mr. Dayal, president of the Indian Association and amateur pimp of local English girls. When Dayal's pompous babu-English letter to association members is answered by an even more ridiculous letter, obviously parodying the style, signed with Tristan's name, Tristan is abruptly though ceremoniously expelled from the organization. By far the largest group of whipping boys is the Canadians; they are presented as both ordinary and eccentric, Peabody being their chief representative. His chief claim to fame is his book *Divorce Poems*, privately printed. When he sends the poems out along with prose paraphrases, the little magazines publish the paraphrases and reject the poems.

But the heart of Cowasjee's satirical project is sexual politics. In *Goodbye to Elsa*, in the story "Nude Therapy," but far more in the novel *Suffer Little Children*, he focuses on the feminist movement of the 1970s. As lover of Maura (the Evemy of "Nude Therapy"), the "liberated" housewife whom Tristan meets at Julien Wolfe's nude therapy marathon, he agrees to support her feminist principles sexually, financially, and morally. Their lovemaking usually takes the form of Maura's mounting Tristan, a morally acceptable but physically unsuccessful position. At a meeting Tristan has helped publicize, he is the only male to rise to the challenge of Roxanne, an alluring and tough leader of SCUM (the Society for Cutting Up Men); for his pains he finds himself karate-chopped and flung onto the floor. Eventually he loses Maura to Martell, a mad painter, and transfers his affections to Maura's little daughter Clare, to whom he has given suck, sweetening his nipples with jam. Deprived of Clare at her mother's insistence, Tristan leads a mothers-and-children movement relying on both biblical homily and ersatz Spockery. Finally, his teaching position in jeopardy as a result of this crusade, Tristan carries out the "rescue" of Clare from her mother's shopping cart. He plans to secure safe passage to India to raise her as a holy woman on the banks of the Ganges. His schemes are defeated by Sandy, Maura's young babysitter, an even greater martial arts expert than Roxanne. Under guard at the mental hospital, he lives in the hope that the "kidnappers" (the plainclothesmen who grabbed him) will be brought to justice.

Cowasjee's fiction, then, reflects a hilarious but often deeply pathetic view of the Anglo-Canadian section of the Indian diaspora in the 1960s and 70s. He recognizes the urge of the Western world—not only procreant but messiah-hungry. His extended satire of 1960s culture supplies both wants in the person of a "perfect" Indian intellectual in exile—the logical and insane extension of the world into which he has entered.

CRITICAL RECEPTION

Critical response to Cowasjee's fiction has so far consisted of reviews and sections of longer studies rather than book-length treatments of the novels and stories. The reception of *Goodbye to Elsa* is representative. The novel has elicited general praise for its satirical "revelations" about British and Canadian racism, Indian pretension, the academic scene, and, above all, sexual mores. G. P. Sharma notes Cowasjee's evenhandedness in approach to the problems of Indian diasporic identity: "The novel ... deals with the problem of identity of this Anglo-Indian community, both in post-independence India and in Britain, besides portraying British prejudice against Indians in general. Like Dilip Hiro, Cowasjee too is objective and dispassionate in discussing the shortcomings of Indians in Britain, and the attitudes of the Britishers towards them" (324). Both British and Canadian reviewers appreciate the academic satire. Many, however, have observed that the book is not, at root, comic, reflecting instead the pain of the alienated spirit attempting to win love through sex. Some, like the reviewer in the *Times Literary Supplement*, see the novelist as overreaching himself in an attempt to transfigure the comic hero ("Carnal" 282). But perhaps the most perceptive reviewer of *Elsa* has been Cowasjee himself, who noted that one does not need a plot to begin a novel: "When I began *Goodbye to Elsa*, all I had in mind was that mine will be a story of persecution. . . . But as the story progressed, the comedy of life broke through . . . " (23).

BIBLIOGRAPHY

Works by Saros Cowasjee

Goodbye to Elsa (novel). London: The Bodley Head, 1974; Toronto: New Press, 1974; Toronto: Paperjacks, 1975; New Delhi: Orient Paperbacks, 1975.
Stories and Sketches (short stories). Calcutta: Writers Workshop, 1970.
Nude Therapy and Other Stories (short stories). New Delhi: Orient Paperbacks, 1978; Ottawa: Borealis Press, 1980.

The Last of the Maharajas (screenplay based on Mulk Raj Anand's *Private Life of an Indian Prince*). Calcutta: Writers Workshop, 1980.

Suffer Little Children (novel). New Delhi: Allied Publishers Limited, 1982.

Studies of Saros Cowasjee

Blythe, Ronald. Review of *Goodbye to Elsa*. *Listener* (March 21, 1974): 381.

"Carnal Bogy" Review of *Goodbye to Elsa*. *Times Literary Supplement* (March 22, 1974): 282.

Mathur, O. P. "An Interview with Saros Cowasjee." *Journal of Indian Writing in English* 15:2 (July 1987): 21–25.

Seiferling, Mary. "For a Writer, Home Is Perhaps the Most Isolated Place." *Insight* (Feb. 1981): 18–19.

Sharma, D. R. "An Interview with Saros Cowasjee." *Imprint* (April 1978): 51–53.

Sharma, G. P. *Nationalism in Indian Fiction*. New Delhi: Sterling, 1978.

RIENZI CRUSZ (1925–   )
Uma Parameswaran

BIOGRAPHY

Rienzi Crusz was born on October 17, 1925, in Colombo, the capital of Ceylon (now Sri Lanka). He is a librarian at the University of Waterloo in Canada; he is the author of five volumes of poetry—*Flesh and Thorn* (1974), *Elephant and Ice* (1980), *Singing Against the Wind* (1985), *A Time for Loving* (1986), and *Still Close to the Raven (1989)*, hereafter cited as *FT*, *EI*, *SAW*, *TL*, and *SCR* respectively.

In an interview I had with him in 1989, he talked about early influences on his poetic growth. His father was a mathematics instructor who, as Crusz says in a poem addressed to him, "chased the ultimate equation" ("Elegy," *TL*) seeking that intangible something that linked heaven and earth. This conjugation of seeming polarities is evident in all his poetry and is apparent in his choice of titles. It was perhaps from his father that Crusz developed a love for precision and symmetry in structure that permeate his poetic craftsmanship. His mother, Cleta Marcellina Nora Serpanchy, was an efficient homemaker, a devoted mother who "fed, hectored and sacrificed all she had" for her eight children (1989 interview).

Crusz traces his burgher lineage to A.D. 1515 when "A Portuguese captain holds / the soft brown hand of my Sinhala mother" (*TL* 69). Other early influences came from his Roman Catholic background of Sunday services, psalm singing, and Bible reading. Shakespeare, Milton, and the Bible formed a trinity whose stamp he has borne (proudly) all his life (1989 interview). In an unpublished talk to high school students, Crusz refers to his memory of standing at his older brother's room, listening enthralled to a recitation of Francis Thompson's *The Hound of Heaven,* and the unforgettable experience of going to Shakespeare movies—*Romeo and Juliet,* starring Norma Shearer; *Hamlet,* starring Laurence Olivier; and *Julius Caesar,* starring John Gielgud. The sonorous majesty of the King James Bible, the gentle philo-

sophizing of Shakespeare, and the lush vegetation of Colombo have left
their indelible mark on Crusz's poetic diction even where the subject matter
concerns everyday, contemporary Canada. Another memory that he treasures is spending his holidays on the beaches and ditches of Galle Face
Green, living on the same street as Pablo Neruda, who was Chilean ambassador to Ceylon at the time.

In 1948, Crusz graduated with an honors degree in history and joined
St. Joseph's College, Colombo, as lecturer. In 1951, while working at the
Central Bank, he went to London on a Colombo Plan scholarship to study
library science. He came to his bank job in 1953 and continued there until
1965. Between 1962 and 1965 he held two jobs, the other as visiting lecturer
in history at Aquinas University. In 1965 he left Sri Lanka for Canada, got
a library science degree in 1966 from the University of Toronto, was appointed reference librarian at the University of Waterloo in 1969, and has
lived there ever since.

Rienzi Crusz had married and between 1956 and 1964 he and his first
wife had three children—Daphne, John, and Maria. She left him for another
man when the youngest child was little more than a year old. Crusz brought
up his children in Canada, supplementing his scholarship money with as
many jobs as he could handle at one time. He is now married to Ann, also
from Sri Lanka, and they have a son, Michael, who was born in 1979.

MAJOR WORKS AND THEMES

The typical persona in each of the five volumes of poetry is closely identified with Crusz himself. The voice of the persona is more powerful in the
first two books because the experience of betrayal in *Flesh and Thorn* (1974)
and of transplantation in *Elephant and Ice* (1980) are soul-stirring experiences. *Singing Against the Wind* (1985) brings together the energy of his
early phase with the maturity of age. His last two volumes—*A Time for
Loving* and *Still Close to the Raven*—are as well crafted as the first three,
perhaps even more so, but the passion of life has given place to more
mundane pleasures, the antics of his son, the idiosyncrasies of his wife,
images of consumerism, in short, the Canadianization of an immigrant
sensibility. Though the sensibility is metamorphosed, both he and the reader
are always aware of a diaspora, and his imagery continues to be a marvellous
conjugation of Canadian and Sri Lankan landscapes, of the elephant and
woodapple dreams on the banks of the Mahaveli mingle with the snowbanks
of this "marshmallow land."

Flesh and Thorn is a collection of twenty-four discrete poems that nevertheless have a narrative sequence of the persona's broken marriage and
emigration to a new land. There are intense images of loss; one is an in-
triguing handling of the traditional river-as-beneficent image: the speaker
is like a water creature held down in bed by a river while the river herself

is chasing "the deep sea current." Images of the sea abound, naturally, in this volume where events take place against an island setting. The speaker leaves the island one June day; the ship sails away and the smell of frangipani (red jasmine) fades; the fluid horizon shifts and "the healing sun / sealed the haemophiliac flow." Six years later, in Canada, his son is an adept skater on ice but in his racial memory, he hears "the woodapple fall." As elsewhere, Crusz shows both sides of immigration and expatriation. The boy will never actually smell the rich fragrance of red jambu, but he is also free of "your history's pain."

The first poem, "How does one reach the sweet kernel?," is an accomplished piece of poetic composition. Though it describes the process and experience of love, like many other poems in this sequence it might also be taken as a metaphor of Crusz's own poetic process. The first stanza describes the husking of a coconut by a Ceylonese farmer. The image of the coconut being pierced on an upright crowbar, the shell being cut in two by a machete, and the kernel opening out shows physical force as a natural and right way of reaching the sweet kernel. The third stanza is short. It describes another sort of love, genteel, tentative, the eating of a plum, a process that the persona obviously finds repugnant. As analogy, the poetic process of handling words just right and bringing the machete down with confident precision is central to Crusz's craft. Coconut and plum signify not only two types of lovemaking and two types of poem making but in the context of the total canon, the two homelands of Sri Lanka and Canada. Life in Canada is soft pulp, like a plum, and the hard seed needs only to be spit out, not conquered. Metaphors should not be driven too far, perhaps, but it is tempting to say that it might be symbolic of the hard core of betrayal or racism that one cannot break and so spits out as though it did not matter. The betrayal poems in *Flesh and Thorn*, along with Virgil Burnett's powerful drawings, make this a remarkable first volume of poetry.

Elephant and Ice (1980), a collection of thirty-eight poems of which thirty are new, continues the Sun-Man persona that had been created in *Flesh and Thorn*. He is given an antithetical persona, the Winter Man; together they form one of the countless antithetical pairs one sees in Crusz's poetry that signify his native land and his adopted land.

Singing Against the Wind (1985) is a collection of 34 poems of which 28 are new. The immigrant theme is as forcefully present as in *Elephant*, but instead of one-sided personal displacement, there is an awareness of the pressure being exerted by others. In "Freshcut Flowers," for example, the roses are arranged according to the cutter's sense of symmetry, given water and aspirin by the housewife Grace, but they are dying. In "A Door Ajar" he says, "I must come up / for air." Canada is sea, without life-sustaining oxygen. So he visits Paradise and finds "Dark Antonyms," the realities of an island blanched and bloodied by internal strife and burgeoning corruption because of politics, new consumerism, and international markets.

"When Adam first touched God" brings the immigrant cycle to a typical Canadian pattern—of recognition that Canada is home and that "Here on undivided ground / we'll fashion our own mythologies."

A Time for Loving (1986) could be said to have Crusz's best selections. It also contains six new poems. *Still Close to the Raven* has several beautiful poems; some of Crusz's best pieces are about poetics; the epigraphs he chooses for different sections in various volumes are always very moving, and encapsulate not only the poems in each section but summarize Crusz's poetic credo.

Rienzi Crusz had traveled far and has carefully re-collected those other beginnings that come full circle as he accepts the inevitable sense of loss.

CRITICAL RECEPTION

Rienzi Crusz is a Canadian poet who deserves to have more critical attention than he has. All his books have been reviewed by major Canadian journals, but there are very few analytical articles on his poetics and works. Irving Layton has been his first and best known critic, and his comments are in various notes that are now part of the Crusz archives at the University of Waterloo. Layton saw Crusz's poem on how boring it was to work as a cataloguer and encouraged him to keep writing. Their correspondence shows Layton's enthusiastic response to Crusz's gentle satire on the WASP values that dictate the manicured lawns of suburbia.

Arun P. Mukherjee has published articles on Crusz. She praises him for his awareness of racism in Canada: "he wears his otherness on his shoulder" (90); his response to racism is "couched in understatements," "even when a scream might seem a more appropriate response" (43). Reshard Gool is another perceptive critic who, like Arun Mukherjee, warns the reader against seeing only the surface contrasts between "elephant" and "ice" and missing out on the "marvellous" craftsmanship of his poetry (38). Judith Miller, in a paper under preparation titled "Archangel and Charlie's Angel: The Poems of Rienzi Crusz," traces "the language of oral poetry and of the King James version of the Bible." I am currently working on a full-length study of Rienzi Crusz for Toronto South Asian Review Books (TSAR Books).

BIBLIOGRAPHY

Works by Rienzi Crusz

Flesh and Thorn. Stratford, Ont.: Pasdeloup Press, 1974.
Elephant and Ice. Erin, Ont.: Porcupine's Quill, 1980.
Singing Against the Wind. Erin, Ont.: Porcupine's Quill, 1985.
A Time for Loving. Toronto: TSAR Books, 1986.
Still Close to the Raven. Toronto: TSAR Books, 1989.

Studies of Rienzi Crusz

Gool, Reshard. "Back in Touch: Rienzi Crusz's Poetry." *Toronto South Asian Review* 2:1 (Spring 1983): 38.

Mukherjee, Arun. "Songs of an Immigrant: The Poetry of Rienzi Crusz." *Currents: Readings in Race Relations* 4:1 (1987): 19–21.

———. *Towards an Aesthetic of Opposition: Essays on Literature, Criticism, and Cultural Imperialism.* Stratford, Ontario: Williams Wallace, 1980. (See chapters 5 and 6.)

CYRIL DABYDEEN (1945–   )
Srilata Mukherjee

BIOGRAPHY

Cyril Dabydeen has a vague sense, from his early years, that he was destined to be a writer. Born in the town of Canje, Guyana, Dabydeen grew up in the house of his maternal grandmother. He began reading major British, American, and Caribbean writers as an adolescent. In 1964, he won the Sandbach Parker Gold Medal, Guyana's highest poetry award.

Dabydeen moved to Canada in 1970. He obtained master's degrees in English and public administration from Queen's University. Dabydeen lives with his wife and daughter in Ottawa. He teaches English at the University of Ottawa, is an advisor to the Mayor's Race Relations Committee and a national coordinator of the Federation of Canadian Municipalities.

The Poet Laureate of Ottawa from 1984 to 1987, Dabydeen has published eight volumes of poetry, two collections of short stories, and two short novels. He has contributed to several literary magazines and anthologies and has edited *A Shapely Fire*, an anthology of Caribbean-Canadian writing. A writer with a strong social consciousness, Dabydeen feels that fiction gives him more latitude than poetry. He is currently working on two collections of short stories and longer narratives. Keenly interested in his South Asian origins, Dabydeen is also editing an anthology of South Asian–Canadian writing.

MAJOR WORKS AND THEMES

Distances (1977) opens with a house on fire, an image of the loss of habitation. The positioning of "Poet Speaks to the House" at the beginning of the collection is appropriate, for it turns on a dialogic encounter between the poet and the burning house. This discourse dramatizes some of the central concerns of Dabydeen's work, which consistently addresses the implications of dispossession, both ancestral and personal. Rootlessness is not presented as a universal predicament in Dabydeen; it is intractable *because* it is particularized. In "After the Rain," there is an almost voyeuristic observation of roots "needling down" into the natural world, an observation prompted by the speaker's "famished" rootlessness. That sense of sterility, which characterizes the displaced poetic voice, occasionally conjures up alternative visions of rooted fertility. The fat men, whose productivity takes on mythic dimensions ("The Fat Men"), are significantly housed in the poem by the porch that frames them. These men do not wander but "sit still" and ultimately come to represent habitation themselves, becoming "as houses." Though poems such as "Ways of Overcoming Loneliness" express the aloneness and ennui of the uprooted immigrant, the land from which the poetic persona has emigrated is not romanticized. Pungency, rottenness, and dismemberment mark the tropical scene in "Maestro," while economic tensions enter it in "Fruit, of the Earth." Hence, the personal experience of the poetic "I" necessitates movement; the poem that moves like the nomad in "Neighbours" becomes a metonymy for him in search of a utopia where roots can take.

Dabydeen's diasporic consciousness finds fuller expression in *Goatsong*, published in the same year as *Distances*. For Dabydeen, the diaspora is a reiterative experience: the movement of his ancestors from India to Guyana is, in a sense, reenacted by his own immigration to Canada. The speaker sees his immigrant condition as explicitly analogous to that of his indentured ancestry in "Letter." Consequently, "Grosse Ile," in which the immigrant's anticipation of "a new life" is reversed by literal death, or "Encounter," which exposes the false promise of a new world, is systematically divested of temporal and local referents. Movement, then, is recognized as a continuum; it is not surprising that many of these poems speak of turning ("Encounter") or returning ("Sun Fever"), traveling ("Seed," "Patient & Others"), or walking ("Winter," "Citizenship"). Separation, the inevitable corollary of movement, is another leitmotif; its centrality is signified by, for example, the placing of a single word "apart" preceded by a caesura in the final line of "Patient & Others." Though the speaker acknowledges itinerancy as his predicament, he refuses to accept it placidly. There is a melodramatic conception of himself as part of a people doomed to centuries of fugitiveness, complemented by a screeching indictment of divine (in)justice in "History." *Goatsong* concludes with an indirect prayer for voice ("Anthem"), the only weapon the poetic "I" has to avenge the oppression of his tribe.

The blatant self-pity at having been uprooted, which recurs in the early volumes, is replaced by a mature conviction that the homeland may be internalized in certain poems of *This Planet Earth* (1979) such as "We Are the Country." Moreover, history is personalized by an implicit paralleling of the colonizer/exploiter with the father figure (cf. "When They Came" and "Sacrament") and a mythicizing of maternal suffering so that it resonates that of the colonized/exploited (e.g., "A Mother's Life"). The poet's diasporic consciousness becomes more expansive here as, instead of revelling in his exclusive otherness, he begins to include numerous marginalized figures in his poetic world. Depicting the factory laborer ("Mute Song"), the prisoner ("Reform"), or the raped woman ("They Call This Planet Earth") with tacit sympathy, the poetic voice attempts a synthesis of the self with other "others." However, Dabydeen resists amalgamation with mainstream Canadian culture, for his distinct historical past is the source of his disruptive poetics ("Brazil"). Yet how potently *can* poetry disrupt? There is in Dabydeen a sense of the inadequacy of the logos to echo the outrage of political oppression. The use of the word "galley" in the concluding line of "Atlantic Song" is deliberately slippery; carrying associations of the ship rowed by slaves and the printer's device, it suggests that the experience of writing may become as oppressive as that of being enslaved.

Dabydeen's diasporic consciousness expresses itself through multiple explorations of the immigrant condition in the short stories of *Still Close to the Island* (1980) and *To Monkey Jungle* (1988). Though a few of these stories comprise vignettes of Caribbean life, most of them have Canada or the United States as their setting. Rather different in tone are the two short novels set exclusively in Guyana.

The Wizard Swami (1989) traces the adventures of Devan, an Indian who lives in rural Guyana. Avidly reading Hindu scriptures and talking to villagers about them, Devan gains prominence as a preacher and moves to urban areas. Ultimately, he has certain misadventures in Georgetown that effect his return to his village and family. Most of the adults in this novel are second-generation immigrants, children of Indian indentured laborers. There is in many of them the desire to reaffirm the centrality of Hinduism in their lives. However, their actions reflect a divorce from Hinduism: the avaricious Devan does not shun "the materialistic way" (33), Bhairam hopes his children settle in Anglo-American milieus, and Sarwan Singh politicizes religion. While the narrative presents this disjunction between desire and action with comic irony, it investigates whether a strict adherence to Hinduism is feasible in a multicultural environment. Distanced by space and time from India, the author can objectify Hinduism as a religion that may become life-denying or fanatical at times. What faith then, if any, can these figures embrace? An authorial desire for a faith that fuses all religions is implied through Devan's meditations about "the Creator of the World" (128), Gocolram's vision of Hindus, Christians, and Muslims praying in one temple (138), or the triumph of the Syndicate comprising members of all sects. An explicit voicing of such desire is evaded, for the author is himself caught between two worlds, a Hindu India and a more cosmopolitan Guyana. The lack of religious stability focused in this novel bespeaks a general sense of instability in the lives of the displaced Indians. The narrative significantly opens with a vision of moving houses, traces the actions of a protagonist who moves from place to place, repeatedly evokes the image of a moving ship and closes with the vision of a moving platform. The textual enactment of disorientation and a subtextual cry for orientation make *The Wizard Swami* a compelling product of Dabydeen's diasporic consciousness.

Dark Swirl (1989) is dominated by the (imagined) presence of a leviathan/ "massacouraman" in the creek of a Guyanese village. The novel has three central figures: the adolescent boy Josh, who first "sees" the mighty creature; his father Ghulam, who has a similar experience soon after; and a white scientist (the "stranger") who collects specimens from the creek and is very curious about the monster. Memories of indenture cause the Indian villagers to associate the stranger with the white colonizer and regard him with antagonism. Initially intimidated by the idea of the "massacouraman," they ultimately wish to claim it as their own, for it gives them a sense of power over the white man. The stranger's desire to capture the creature and his final identification with it indicate his colonialist instincts. Yet such instincts are present even in the colonized; at one point, Ghulam conceives of the "massacouraman" as left behind by the Arawaks to protect their coastland from the whites *and* "people like themselves" (54). In this complex power game played out on non-native territory between the white exile and the displaced Indians, the white man ceases to be a mere oppressor; he becomes a rival claimant for a place. Binary oppositions between colonizer and colonized are made to collapse in a threateningly fluid narrative. Just as the thinly disguised political hostility between the white man and the villagers is imaged in the literal darkness that envelops his meetings with Ghulam, the sympathetic ties between the stranger and Josh are highlighted by Ghulam's vision of the pair walking through "dazzling light" (62). This bonding, based on a shared sense of elemental spirituality, becomes a textual wish fulfillment, a desire to eradicate dark historical facts in determining relationships. However, the narrative underscores the vanity of such desires to dehistoricize history; the bonding is abruptly terminated with the disappearance of the white man. Like Ghulam, the reader is finally left with nothing but the enduring memory of "a nether place" (92), a symbol of displacement.

Selected poems from the early volumes, as well as from *Heart's Frame* (1979), *Elephants Make Good Stepladders* (1982), and *Islands Lovelier Than a Vision* (1986), are brought together in *Coastland* (1989). Comprising some of Dabydeen's best poetry, *Coastland* explores the enigma of origins. The symbolic ship that cannot be dislodged from the (Guyanese) horizon for more than "a hundred years" ("The Forest") metaphorizes the externality of the poetic persons and signals that the indentured cannot become indigenous. "Black Dust" treats the impossibility of belonging with sinister humor till the blackness of its title swells and fills the text. That the speaker is unable to belong even to the land of ancestral origin is manifest in apparently brighter poems such as "Elephants Make Good Stepladders." Here the childlike vision of India works as a rhetorical pointer to his sense of alienation from it. Since the poetic persona cannot belong entirely to any one location ("Two Kinds of Frenzy," "Seafarer"), there is often a blurring of geographical demarcation and a mystification of place in *Coastland*. The speaker conceives of himself on the back of an elephant in the Canadian winter ("Marina") or describes tropical "black beauties" even as he speaks of temperate landscapes ("Autumn Tides"). Yet such poems do not convey a holistic conception of place but a keen sense of fragmentation that manifests itself paradoxically in visions of holism. "Foreign Legions" takes on a surrealistic quality as the poetic "I" ultimately submerges himself in a dream world that holds the promise of rebirth.

CRITICAL RECEPTION

Early reviewers of Dabydeen's poetry overlook or criticize his historical/political incisiveness. D. Precosky discusses *Heart's Frame* in terms of emotional generality; Michael Hurley offers a universalist analysis of the images in *This Planet Earth*. Ron Miles critiques "obvious observations" (138) about oppression in *Goatsong*, and Patricia Keeney Smith considers Dabydeen's "talent more critical than creative" (189) in *Elephants Make Good Stepladders*. Arun Mukherjee points out the inadequacy of such readings in her engaging comparison of the poetry of Michael Ondaatje and Dabydeen, both Third World writers who immigrated to Canada. She indicts Ondaatje for obscuring political realities by taking a universalist stance and shows, by contrast, how the subversive strength of Dabydeen's poetry derives from its concrete political context. Such poetry, "an encounter with history and hence with otherness" (65), is a powerful expression of the colonial situation.

Coastland has received some critical acclaim. Jeremy Poynting calls Dabydeen "truly a poet of the New World" (10) and traces a sophisticated "movement from a dualistic to a dialectic imagination" (8) in this volume. He praises its complex perspectives, varied voices, and movements between the literal and the ironic. Again, Stephen Breslow elaborates on Dabydeen's mastery of description.

There has been very little critical response to Dabydeen's fiction. In reviewing *To Monkey Jungle* and *The Wizard Swami*, Peter Nazareth comments on the author's thematic interest in immigrants with a colonial past, as well as on the dreamlike quality pervading his works and inviting search for deep meaning.

BIBLIOGRAPHY

Works by Cyril Dabydeen

Poems in Recession. Georgetown, Guyana: Sadeck, 1972.
Distances. n.p.: Fiddlehead, 1977.
Goatsong. Ottawa: Mosaic, 1977.
Heart's Frame. Cornwall, Ontario: Vesta, 1979.
This Planet Earth. Ottawa: Borealis, 1979.
Still Close to the Island. Ottawa: Commoner's Publishing, 1980.
Elephants Make Good Stepladders. London, Ontario: Third Eye, 1982.
Islands Lovelier Than a Vision. Leeds: Peepal Tree, 1986.
Ed. *A Shapely Fire.* Oakville: Mosaic, 1987.
To Monkey Jungle. London, Ontario: Third Eye, 1988.
Coastland. Oakville: Mosaic, 1989.
Dark Swirl. Leeds: Peepal Tree, 1989.
The Wizard Swami. Leeds: Peepal Tree, 1989.

Studies of Cyril Dabydeen

Breslow, Stephen. Review of *Coastland. World Literature Today* 64:4 (1990): 684.
Hurley, Michael. Review of *This Planet Earth. Canadian Literature* 89 (Summer 1981): 167.
Miles, Ron. Review of *Goatsong. Canadian Literature* 81 (Summer 1979): 138.
Mukherjee, Arun P. "The Poetry of Michael Ondaatje and Cyril Dabydeen: Two Responses to Otherness." *Journal of Commonwealth Literature* 20:1 (1985): 49–67.
Nazareth, Peter. Review of *To Monkey Jungle. World Literature Today* 63:3 (1989): 523.
———. Review of *The Wizard Swami. World Literature Today* 60:4 (1986): 679.
Poynting, Jeremy. Introduction. *Coastland.* By Cyril Dabydeen. Oakville: Mosaic, 1989.
Precosky, D. Review of *Heart's Frame. Canadian Literature* 87 (Winter 1980): 143–44.
Smith, Patricia Keeney. Review of *Elephants Make Good Stepladders. Quarry Magazine* 34:2 (1985): 89–90.

DAVID DABYDEEN (1955–   )
Daizal R. Samad

BIOGRAPHY

David Dabydeen was born on a sugar plantation in Berbice, Guyana, in December 1955. He emigrated to England when he was twelve, and "grew up in the care of local authorities because his parents were divorced" (Interview with Wolfgang Binder 70); he read English at Cambridge and London universities, obtaining his doctorate in 1982. Dabydeen's experience as a West Indian immigrant in England informs both his scholarship and his poetry. Dabydeen is of South Asian extraction, a fact of which he was ashamed—foreign dress, food, and language were seen as the signals of inferiority. The replacement of that sense of humiliation with one of pride was a painstaking process of intellectual and artistic maturation.

Dabydeen's sense of cultural/racial isolation and inferiority served to compound and was a consequence of his being a product of historical and contemporaneous violence. He has been sensitized and marked by the racial violence of the early 1960s in Guyana that resulted in "massacres between the Indians and the Blacks" (Interview 67). Dabydeen is deeply aware of the heterogeneous nature of his culture and psyche; but there remains a fracture between his sense of being "black" and the meaning of blackness in the context of his "Asian-Caribbean" heritage and the violence which ruptured Guyana. (*Black* is used in this essay as an inclusive signifier for all people of color.)

Thus far, Dabydeen has dedicated his scholarly life to working with other black scholars (and scholars of black studies) to bring black peoples into focus, to give them voice. He insists that "*any* scholarship relating to black people should not be divorced from consideration of contemporary racist realities, and should not be separated from the struggles to combat such racism" (Preface to *The Black Presence in English Literature*, viii). To this end, a conference was held in Wolverhampton, England, in December 1982.

The choice of setting represented a deliberate attempt at yoking scholarship with traumatic social occurrence. As Dabydeen points out, it was in Wolverhampton that Enoch Powell made impassioned xenophobic speeches that triggered a rash of racist sentiment in the 1960s and after.

The papers that are compiled in *The Black Presence in English Literature* (1985), edited by David Dabydeen, are "concerned with locating literary texts within social and historical contexts, and within popular and scientific ideas" (Preface ix). Black peoples' literary and scholarly activity must be integrated into every level of educational curricula if they are to be treated as less than invisible. Black presence and voice are not only manifest in writers like Chinua Achebe, George Lamming, V. S. Naipaul, and Wole Soyinka; Dabydeen insists that the theme of blackness is prevalent in traditional works since the literature is "rooted in a culture characterised by a history of conquest, colonisation and imperialism" (Preface ix).

Dabydeen, by work and example, indicts those educational institutions that refuse or neglect to include black studies in their curricula. This ethnocentricity and the inability or refusal of teachers to acknowledge black or multicultural presences are signals of a potent residue of racism in education. The consequence is exclusion and bitterness, and violence is the inevitable reward.

MAJOR WORKS AND THEMES

In his first scholarly book, *Hogarth's Blacks: Images of Blacks in Eighteenth Century English Art* (1987), Dabydeen demonstrates that black people, rendered politically impotent and socially invisible, were in fact brought into visual scope on the canvas of William Hogarth. Dabydeen's point is that Hogarth, although remaining true to the sociohistorical truth that prevailed in the eighteenth century (blacks remain marginalized, diminished, and backgrounded), attempted to move black subjects from invisibility to visibility, from muteness to the realization of an inner voice. There is a recognition that they too have a perspective.

Despite being relegated to the role of the subhuman and submissive, despite being juxtaposed with animals, Hogarth's blacks maintain an inner dignity that impugns the moral decay of the whites. According to Dabydeen, Hogarth's intention was to use blacks to satirize the English upper classes, especially. Also, Dabydeen suggests that Hogarth aligns blacks with other victims of commercialism and colonialism; the former were sometimes participants in the rituals of the English peasantry. Dabydeen holds that if Hogarth's satirical intentions are missed, then the painter "can be deemed to have reflected or reinforced racism among his white contemporaries" (*Hogarth's Blacks* 113). In this book, Dabydeen has reread creatively Hogarth's dramatic narrative: the eighteenth-century painter brings black people into the picture; the twentieth-century scholar brings them into focus.

David Dabydeen's *Hogarth, Walpole and Commercial Britain* (1985) is noticeably an extension of *Hogarth's Blacks*. He examines much of the same material only with an inverted focus; he posits that Hogarth's moralistic message covers a deeper political intention: exposing the nobility and reprimanding the government. The painter's portrayal of the aristocrat as upright citizen and the commoner as the collapsed and crime-ridden is profoundly satirical. The criminal activity of the latter is a consequence of and a response to the commercial avarice, political corruption, and moral decay of the former. *Hogarth, Walpole and Commercial Britain* is another important work; however, it is weakened considerably because Dabydeen repeats almost verbatim some of the themes examined in *Hogarth's Blacks*.

David Dabydeen's various roles as agitator, poet, and scholar appear to converge in his first collection of poems, *Slave Song* (1984), winner of the 1984 Commonwealth Poetry Prize and the Quiller-Couch Prize at Cambridge. *Slave Song* is "largely concerned with an exploration of the erotic energies of the colonial experience, ranging from a corrosive to a lyrical sexuality" ("Introduction to *Slave Song*" 34).

The collection is important and fascinating for several reasons. Dabydeen assumes simultaneously various masks: he is poet, critic, translator, and social commentator. The poet captures the abrupt rhythms and raw substance of peasant life in Guyana (and in the West Indies generally). By writing in Guyana Creole, Dabydeen allows the language to be authentically part and product of historical and contemporaneous experience. Like Derek Walcott's "What the Twilight Says," the "Introduction to *Slave Song*" is important in itself; Dabydeen writes:

The language is angry, crude, energetic. The canecutter chopping away at the crops bursts out in a spate of obscene words, a natural gush from the gut, like fresh faeces. It's hard to put two words together in Creole without swearing. Words are spat out from the mouth like live squibs, not pronounced with elocution.... (36)

The poet uses the "brokenness" of the language to envelop and convey the "broken and suffering" Guyanese peasantry and their antecedents from Africa and India. However, *Slave Song* does not emit self-pitying wails of pain. The employment of Creole is a caveat of the poet's celebration and defiance:

To write in creole was to validate the experience of black people against the contempt and dehumanizing dismissal of white people. Celebration of blackness necessitated celebration of black language, for how could a black writer be true to his blackness using the language of his/her colonial master? ("On Not Being Milton" 189)

In anticipation of the "summary dismissal or parody" by white critics, Dabydeen "clothed the creole poems in an elaborate set of 'notes' and 'translations' as an act of counter-parody" ("On Not Being Milton" 182). The formality of these notes and "translations"—their anthropological/literary nature—originates in Dabydeen's role as scholar. Mark McWatt has pointed to the "ironic tensions created by the purity of the native voice and the 'purity' of the scholarly mask that presented it . . . ; the whole apparatus of notes and translations seemed to contain the great energy of the voices and that great surge of animosity . . . directed primarily at their English audience" (86).

Dabydeen assumes the posture of the critic and so becomes the audience of his own poetry. The poet supports and subverts the scholar; and because of this creative/critical self-sufficiency, he renders irrelevant the white audience even as he targets them.

The experiences that Dabydeen seeks to capture and articulate are no longer subject to the astringencies of formal English or rules of literary propriety; the images and rhythms (fractured and lyrical) in "Song of the Creole Gang Women" function outside of conventional English language and experience. The voices of the women recount the omnipresence of the white colonizer—specifically the British Company, Bookers. Even the things most cherished and private are subject to ownership and abuse: children and sexual organs. Life is a grinding ritual of work, pain, and longing.

In "The Canecutters' Song" and "Slave Song" Dabydeen dramatizes the historical/cultural longing of the canecutter for that which he perceives to be pure, spiritual, adorned, adorable, unachievable—qualities embodied in the white woman. This longing becomes fleshly lust for white skin and blondness; both desires are equally futile, and this futility generates a dream-desire to subjugate, despoil, and rape. The victim of humiliation and degradation dreams his revenge against the white master by possessing the pampered and protected white mistress. One aspect of the dream is that she *wants* to be possessed: in "Nightmare" she dreams of being raped and is aroused sexually by it. All are consumed by perverse colonialism.

The bitter fruits of British colonialism were reaped in the 1963–64 racial conflicts in Guyana: rape and murder. "For Mala" depicts the grotesque drama of the oppressed turning upon themselves in cannibal conspiracy with the oppressor. The land itself is contaminated and its yield is no longer a source of nourishment; fruits like five-fingers, starapples, and pumpkins are used to record mutilation and murder.

There are times in *Slave Song* when Dabydeen relies too heavily on the commentary and "translation." In the ironically named "Guyana Pastoral," his note that "the rape and murder of a young girl, told in hard, brutal rhythms, signify the violent aspect of Guyanese existence" (49) is not borne out by the poem itself. The commentary is more vivid than the poem. Moreover, the "translation" carries better than the lines of the poem the burdens implied in rape.

Slave Song exposes in stark fashion the tragic realities of Guyanese history and the monstrous circumstances that result. At points in the collection, Dabydeen's regret at wasted lives, beaten and broken bodies, enfeebled minds is so touching that the reader aches for a people's distress. At times in *Slave Song*, there is hope and laughter even in the teeth of racial strife and economic despair: hope in spite of suffocating futility.

David Dabydeen's second book of poems, *Coolie Odyssey* (1988), retraces the movement of indentured laborers from India to Guyana and the further, related diaspora of Guyanese to England. Like all West Indians, the Indo-Guyanese is afflicted by fragmentation and homelessness. Life in Guyana is existence in the mud, between the ideal territory of memory (India) and those sublime worlds where dreams come true—England and North America. But these cultural and economic "havens" are found to offer nothing but further alienation and disillusionment.

The underlying quest in *Coolie Odyssey* is for a myth to encompass the journeys, for a humility and honesty of perception to capture it, and for a language that reverberates with loss but that echoes hope. The rendering is complicated in this poem because the poetic consciousness and expression are aspects of the evolutionary processes that produce them; the poet's genesis is the people's history, and the language must offer a coincidental application. However, while the poet seeks to validate the experiences of his antecedents, *they* do not see their stories as worthy. As Ma tells the poet, the words that we would use are too insubstantial to bear the cargo of their history. Ma and others of her generation in *Coolie Odyssey* are aware that the children who leave and return for vacation or for weddings or funerals with mere academic knowledge are most susceptible to romanticizing the hardships endured by their forebears.

In *Coolie Odyssey*, David Dabydeen returns to the devastating results of racial violence in Guyana. The desperate longing for whiteness (especially the white woman) rages on; and the white woman, especially, tries to plunder "native" sexuality, stories, and craft. Dabydeen also refers to recent political despotism suffered by Guyanese and to two of the heroes that bring relief to the people—Rohan Kanhai, one of the world's great batsmen; and the murdered Dr. Walter Rodney, one of Guyana's great political leaders and scholars.

The language in *Coolie Odyssey* does not approximate the basilectal Creole used in *Slave Song*; nonetheless, the rhythms are West Indian, and the images are as stark and as memorable as those of the first collection.

David Dabydeen's *The Intended* (1991) is an autobiographical novel in which the narrator recalls his boyhood in a Guyanese village. It traces the flight from Guyana to England. Once there, old longings are compounded by new desires, old homelessness by new rootlessness and alienation. The West Indian remains the eternal immigrant. Dabydeen displays the permanence of the biases that have been bequeathed to rather than experienced by people of the narrator's generation. There is, consequently, a greater blindness to and deeper stupidity about racial/religious prejudice. In England, the narrator is still afflicted by Hindu/Muslim suspicions that prevail in Guyana but have their roots in the violence leading up to the India-Pakistan split. Once again, as in *Slave Song* and *Coolie Odyssey*, Dabydeen recalls the cultivated racial division between Indo- and Afro-Guyanese. The life of the Guyanese peasantry is painted with cruel precision: it is raw, crude, violent, demanding, and futile.

In England, the narrator is plagued by a deep sense of shame: language, dress, food, and clothing are all reasons for humiliation and self-loathing. This is painfully dramatized when Nasim, one of the narrator's friends, is chased by a gang of whites into the path of a car and is hurt seriously. In the hospital, he "looked small and lost, like pictures of hungry Third World children we saw on television" (14). The narrator's response is shame and anger *at* the victim: "I hated him. A strange desire to hurt him, to kick him, overcame me" (14). This abhorrence of vulnerable, wounded self and others finds expression in his deep desire for acceptance through conformity or for invisibility and dumbness.

This novel is not structurally sophisticated; at times it is almost clumsy. However, Dabydeen's *The Intended* is urgent, intense, and honest. These are qualities that inform both Dabydeen's scholarship and his art. To read his work is to read our own discomfort and anguish. David Dabydeen startles us out of our self-composure.

CRITICAL RECEPTION

Hogarth's Blacks has generated considerable interest in the scholarly world. Michael Cooke stipulates that Dabydeen "incontrovertibly established that the black was a habitual, not an accidental figure for Hogarth, and a continual attraction for the eighteenth century artist"; he writes also of the "intensity of Dabydeen's focus and conviction" (226). Roy Porter testifies that Dabydeen's research is "invigorating, his interpenetration powerful and his judgement secure" (998). However, although mostly positive in their comments, many reviewers of Dabydeen's two scholarly books accuse him of "over-reading," of flying too conspicuous a political flag.

Dabydeen's *Slave Song* and *Coolie Odyssey* are deserving of the praise they have been given. Mark McWatt concludes his review: "David Dabydeen has made an important contribution to the knowledge and self-knowledge not only to the descendants of indentured Indians but to all West Indians struggling to make themselves new" (90). Benita Parry, who has written the only full-length article on David Dabydeen's poetry, is impressed by his "radical political poetry" and by his "rewriting of the west's master narrative that addresses the post-colonial condition" (13). Nonetheless, she has reservations about Dabydeen's canecutters' "fantasies of abusing and mutilating the white woman" (6). She suggests also that the "difficulty" of the Creole "makes the reception of *Slave Song* self-limiting amongst a diversified poetry readership" (13). Wrought from the hurt of things, the language is difficult; it is also defiant, disconcerting and, at times, tender.

BIBLIOGRAPHY

Works by David Dabydeen

Slave Song. Arhus, Denmark: Dungaroo Press, 1984.

Ed. *The Black Presence in English Literature*. Manchester: Manchester University Press, 1985.

"On Writing *Slave Song*." *Commonwealth Essays and Studies* 8:2 (Spring 1986): 46–48.

"Art of Darkness: High Culture Based on Black Slavery." *Listener* (Sept. 24, 1987): 14–15.

Hogarth, Walpole and Commercial Britain. London: Hansib, 1985.

Hogarth's Blacks: Images of Blacks in Eighteenth Century English Art. Athens, Georgia: University of Georgia Press, 1987.

"Selected Themes in West Indian Literature: An Annotated Bibliography." With Nana Wilson-Tagoe. *Third World Quarterly* 9 (July 1987): 921–60.

Coolie Odyssey. London: Hansib, 1988.

"Man to Pan." *New Statesman and Society* (Aug. 26, 1988): 40–41.

"*Coolie Odyssey* and *Two Cultures*." *Landfall* 43:2 (June 1989): 153–59.

Interview with Wolfgang Binder. *Journal of West Indian Literature* 3:2 (Sept. 1989): 67–80.

"On Not Being Milton: Nigger Talk in England Today." *Landfall* 43 (June 1989): 180–91.

"Introduction to *Slave Song*." *Literary Review* 34:1 (Fall 1990): 32–38.

The Intended. London: Secker and Warburg, 1991.

Studies of David Dabydeen

Cooke, Michael G. Review of *Hogarth's Blacks: Images of Blacks in Eighteenth Century English Art*, by David Dabydeen, and *Surprizing Narrative: Olaudah Equiano and the Beginnings of Black Autobiography*, by Angelo Costanzo. *Eighteenth-Century Studies* 22:1 (Fall 1988): 225–28.

Gerrard, Nicci. Review of *The Intended*. *Observer* (Feb. 17, 1991): 59.

Review of *Hogarth's Blacks: Images of Blacks in Eighteenth Century English Art*. *History Today* 38 (Nov. 1988): 57.

Johnson, L. A. Review of *The Black Presence in English Literature*, ed. by David Dabydeen. *Choice* 23 (July 1986): 1672.

Lichtenstein, Leonie. Review of *A Reader's Guide to West Indian and Black British Literature*, by David Dabydeen and Nana Wilson-Tagoe. *Times Educational Supplement* (Apr. 15, 1988): 23.

McWatt, Mark. Review of *Coolie Odyssey*. *Journal of West Indian Indian Literature* 3:2 (Sept. 1989): 86–90.

Matthews, R. T. Review of *Hogarth's Blacks: Images of Blacks in Eighteenth Century English Art*. *Choice* 25:8 (April 1988): 1228.

Nayar, Radhakrishnan. Review of *The Black Presence in English Literature*, ed. by David Dabydeen. *Times Literary Supplement* (Mar. 8, 1991): 29.

Nettell, Stephanie. Review of *The Black Presence in English Literature*, ed. by David Dabydeen. *Times Educational Supplement* (Dec. 6, 1985): 18.

Parry, Benita. "Between Creole and Cambridge English: The Poetry of David Dabydeen." *Kunapipi* 10:3 (1988–89): 1–14.

Paulson, Ronald. Review of *Hogarth, Walpole and Commercial Britain*. *Eighteenth-Century Studies* 22:1 (Fall 1988): 90–95.

Porter, Roy. Review of *Hogarth's Blacks: Images of Blacks in Eighteenth Century English Art*. *Times Literary Supplement* (Sept. 13, 1985): 998–99.

Reynolds, Zelda. Review of *A Handbook for Teaching Caribbean Literature*. *Times Educational Supplement* (Aug. 26, 1988): 18.

Senn, Werner. "Speaking the Silence: Contemporary Poems on Paintings." *Word and Image: A Journal of Verbal/Visual Enquiry* 5:2 (April–June 1989): 181–97.

MAHADAI DAS (1956–   )
Denise deCaires Narain

BIOGRAPHY

Mahadai Das was born and grew up in Guyana. She studied economics at the University of Guyana, where she was also involved with the Cultural Action Team; she performed in various theater workshops and coproduced and presented the "Poetry on the Air" series with Al Creighton. Between 1974 and 1976 Mahadai Das was an active member of the Guyana National Service, where she served in the hinterland camp at Kimbia. At a time when many viewed the introduction of national service with some alarm (particularly for "respectable" young women), Mahadai Das caused some controversy among the Indo-Guyanese community when she decided to appear for her crowning as Deepvali beauty queen in the dark green, paramilitary uniform of the Guyana National Service (GNS). Das was very active in the Cultural Division of the GNS, and this dedicated nationalism is recorded in her first published volume of poetry. She was also a member of the Messenger group, which was involved in exploring and publicizing the cultural traditions of Guyana's large Indian population; she participated as a dancer and as a singer in the productions of this group. In the early 1980s, Das left Guyana to study philosophy at the University of Chicago, but her academic career was interrupted by severe illness and she was forced to return to Guyana, where she now lives.

MAJOR WORKS AND THEMES

Mahadai Das has published three volumes of poetry to date: *I Want To Be a Poetess of My People*, *My Finer Steel Will Grow*, and *Bones* and has had her work published regularly in various journals and newspapers including *Kyk-Over-Al*, *Kaie*, *Stabroek News* (Guyana); in *Wasafiri* (England); and in an anthology of Caribbean women's poetry, *Creation Fire*, recently published in Toronto. Das's three volumes are very interesting to explore in relation to notions of "exile" and "diasporic consciousness," for she moves from evoking a strong sense of rootedness in Guyana's land/ peoplescape, in her first volume, to exploring her own, literal exile in the second volume, and in her most recent volume, she contemplates what may be best described as "psychic exile." The disillusionment with nationalist politics in the "co-operative republic of Guyana" is striking in Das's work partly because her commitment to the ideals of the republic was so passionate early on in the postindependence period and so influential in shaping her poetic identity.

As indicated above, Das's poetic identity in her first volume, *I Want To Be a Poetess of My People*, is a militantly nationalist one, and many of the poems celebrate the beauty of Guyana's large hinterland and the role of the Young Pioneers of the GNS in harnessing the rich resources of this luxuriant jungle. The poems are energetic in their celebration of all things Guyanese and are very much in keeping with the euphoric mood of the newly independent nation. Men and women working the land are also praised, but special praise is reserved for Linden Forbes Burnham (then leader of the ruling party, the People's National Congress [PNC]), who is seen as a savior of the people in a weak poem interesting only in relation to the poems in her second volume in which this leader has become a corrupt, power-hungry tyrant. Many of the poems in this first volume are similarly limited by the assertion of a simple notion of nationalism. This declamatory tone is most evident in the poem "Militant," where the poet seems to rely on her patriotic fervor to forge her role as poet.

What is interesting about these attempts to represent or "give birth" to the body politic in poetic form is that there is a tension between its nationalist *content* and its Eurocentric *form*: "Standard English" is used throughout and there are many examples of anachronistic "poeticisms" (such as *'twixt* and *o'er*), and Das has a penchant here for long, unwieldy, rather self-consciously poetic titles. One could argue that Das is in a state of exile within the Eurocentric literary forms she uses even as she articulates a nationalist consciousness; she is a "linguistic squatter," to use the phrase of the Trinidadian poet Marlene Nourbese Philip. Interestingly, one of the most accomplished and memorable poems of the volume deals explicitly with the notion of exile and diaspora; in "They Came in Ships," Das painstakingly charts the journey to Guyana of the Indian indentured workers. She gives voice to the history of those workers who "came in droves like cattle" to work on the plantations and whose miserable living and working conditions had seldom been represented in the literature of the region.

In Das's second volume of poetry, not only does the title itself, *My Finer Steel Will Grow*, point to a change in mood from enthusiasm to endurance, but the publishing details, a Samisdat publication, signify that it is a "dissident" text; it is also prefaced by Das's explanation that she is *not* using a pseudonym because "the Guyanese government is concentrating on gunning down dissidents at home...." In the wake of Walter Rodney's assassination and the crackdown on the opposition party, the Working People's Alliance, Das (like many others involved in opposition politics) left Guyana, and her second volume of poetry was published in the United States. Here the imagery throughout is much more covert and the poet's voice much less stridently declamatory and public than in her previous work. Now the poet is in a "literal" state of exile but there is a sense of unease too about who the poet can speak on behalf *of* and *to*, and the poetic voice here is more introvert, secretive, and circular. Instead of the green fecundity of Guyana's jungles, Das presents images of a diseased body politic whose ruler is corrupt and where even the elements are hostile, so that the speaker is "Unarmed against the sky" and the "guerilla air"; the geography of the body that the poet now articulates is not that of the nation but of her own bedraggled self. Instead of the robust images of workers plowing the soil, Das now presents images of naked, vulnerable, spear-carrying individuals, thus drawing on images that evoke Guyana's most politically unempowered ethnic group, the Amerindian population. Where, earlier, Das energetically claimed her right to *sing* for her nation, she talks now almost secretively. Most of the poems in this volume are untitled which, again, suggests a loss of the confident purpose of her first volume, and most of the poems, covertly or explicitly, focus on a sense of profound disappointment in nationalist politics as espoused by the ruling PNC and its bogus leader. There is a sad irony in the fact that where her first volume ends with a poem celebrating the visionary leadership of Burnham, this second volume concludes by proclaiming the need for a revolution to overthrow him. In *Bones*, Das's third volume of poetry, the poet increasingly explores a psychic rather than geographic landscape; this solipsism can, perhaps, be linked to the effects of living in exile—an exile that, given the expressions of secure identity and community in her early work, appears particularly displacing and dislocating for the poet. There is no easy narrative (either pronationalist or antidictatorship) in any of the poems in *Bones*; instead these fragmented and secretive poems jangle dissonantly, speaking of fragmentation and "unbelonging." There is a focus, now, on the pain and difficulty of *voicing* the poems themselves, and this pain is increasingly associated with the experience of being a woman poet. In "Unborn Children," Das mourns the undecorated language of poems not yet created whereas, in "Secrets," she describes poems as stealthy bombs that have not yet exploded. In the very first poem in the collection, "Sonnet to a Broom," the poet explores the domestic image of sweeping as metaphor for writing. In "Bones," the title poem of this collection, Das's use of the closet as a central image points to the way the broad horizon of the luxurious jungles of her early Guyana poems have shrunk and a new, more intimate space is explored; the bones in this poem are vulgar adornments that hang alongside the more conventional paraphernalia of femininity (prom dresses, red pumps, veils, and petticoats). The speaker, in stressing that the bones have no desire to remain in the closet and that their story should be examined, recalls Charlotte Brontë's demonized "madwoman" in the attic and Jean Rhys's attempts to recuperate her; Das defers the process of asserting the voice of *her* "skeleton in the cupboard," pointing instead to what their sounds *might* sound/look like—"helium balloon forever." In another poem, "Pain," the speaker's sense of isolation is poignantly evoked in the image of pain as "a giant parade less one pair of eyes."

In "If I came to India," the poet throws up a series of questions about the possibility of finding roots for a secure identity but comes to no easy conclusions. But it is in the long poem in nine parts, "For Marie de Borges," in which the isolation and the diasporic consciousness of the speaker is most fully explored. Here, exiled from home, the speaker is a cow roaming the streets of the metropolis in search of work, like a phantom or a ghost. The poem relentlessly charts the way in which the city and its capitalist rulers dehumanize and exploit the speaker whose body is represented as the sum of its functioning components. The speaker in this poem articulates an identity that evokes images of women, but particularly Third World women who provide cheap labor whenever/wherever capital needs it. This notion of being constantly on the move in search of work is one that is central, historically, to notions of diasporic experience (for both men and women, of course, but here Das focuses on its effect on women).

Similarly, when Das explores notions of poetic identity and poetic agendas in this volume, it is with a particular stress on the implications for her as a *woman* poet. Where in her first volume Das embraces the role of a female poet, she now challenges the limiting expectations that this role involves. It is perhaps this sense of deliberately countering dominant narratives of feminine roles that offers an uneasy focus to this volume. In "The Growing Tip," with which the volume concludes, Das embraces the increasing sense of isolation and displacement that the preceding poems catalog and uses this sense of dislocation and *difference* to assert her own poetic identity. First she outlines the kind of decorous expectations that publishers and readers have of a poetess. But those delicate expectations are shattered by the juxtaposition of her own monstrous creations. The editors view the manuscript as a monstrosity, and it is this "monstrous" identity that Das embraces as a strategy for empowerment: the nationalist "poetess" of Das's first volume has been sloughed off to reveal a powerful, monster woman poet's body—and a distinctive voice.

CRITICAL RECEPTION

Since Mahadai Das's first two volumes of poetry are not easily available and her third volume is a fairly recent publication, her work has not received much critical attention. I have reviewed *Bones* in *Wasafiri*, where I praise the distinctive "spareness" of Das's work in this volume and the way she creates a "strangely disconcerting effect" in many of the poems, presenting images that "jangle dissonantly." Attention is drawn to the focus in *Bones* on exploring and challenging limiting definitions of woman and to the way the poet refuses the conventionally decorous role prescribed for women poets and embraces, instead, a poetic identity that is powerful *and* monstrous.

BIBLIOGRAPHY

Works by Mahadai Das

I Want To Be a Poetess of My People. Georgetown: Guyana National Service Publishing Center, 1976.
My Finer Steel Will Grow. Monroe, Conn: Samisdat, 1982.
Bones. Leeds: Peepal Tree Press, 1988.

Studies of Mahadai Das

deCaires Narain, Denise. Review of *Bones*. *Wasafiri* (Spring 1990): 32–33.
Poynting, Jeremy. "Literature and Cultural Pluralism: East Indians in the Caribbean." Diss., University of Leeds, 1985. See 538–545 for a discussion of Das's work.

ANITA DESAI (1937–   )
Hena Ahmad

BIOGRAPHY

Anita Desai was born on June 24, 1937, in Mussoorie, India. Her father was D. N. Mazumdar, a Bengali businessman, and her mother, Toni Nime, a German. Since she grew up in India and did most of her writing there, one may wonder at her inclusion among Indian diasporic writers. This inclusion, however, can be justified in that she views India from a distance, as it were, an element basic to the diasporic sensibility. Two of her novels deal specifically with the predicament of immigrants: Indians in Britain in *Bye-Bye, Blackbird* (1971) and Germans in India in *Baumgartner's Bombay* (1988). As she has said in an interview, she can look at India with a "certain detachment," which "certainly comes from [her] mother." "I feel about India as an Indian, but I suppose I think about it as an outsider" (Bliss 522).

Though Desai grew up with English, German, and Hindi, English was the first language she learned to read and write at Queen Mary's Higher Secondary School in New Delhi. Hence, when she began writing, at the age of seven, it was in English. "We spoke German at home, it was the language in which I learned nursery rhymes and fairy tales. We spoke Hindi to all our friends and neighbors. I learned English when I went to school" (Ferrell 3). Desai went on to earn her B.A. in English literature (1957) from Miranda House, an elite college of Delhi University.

Soon after receiving her B.A., Desai worked for a year at the Max Mueller Bhavan in Calcutta before getting married in 1958 to Ashvin Desai, an executive. She has four grown children. She was a visiting fellow at Girton College, Cambridge University, in 1986. In 1987–89 she taught at Smith College. Since then she has been the Purington Professor of English at Mount Holyoke College, where she teaches creative writing for one semester, spending the rest of her time in India.

Desai's first publication was a story in an American children's magazine. She has published twelve books of fiction and numerous essays, reviews, and articles. Except for *Games at Twilight* (1978), a collection of stories, the rest of her books are novels, three of them for children: *The Peacock Garden* (1974), *Cat on a Houseboat* (1976), and *The Village by the Sea* (1982).

MAJOR WORKS AND THEMES

Desai describes the major theme of all her fiction as "the terror of facing, single-handed, the ferocious assaults of existence" (Libert 47). She is concerned with the psychology of individuals who are trapped by society, as depicted in her earlier novels, *Cry, The Peacock*, *Voices in the City*, *Where Shall We Go This Summer?*, and *Fire on the Mountain*, which explore the interior selves of women oppressed by their marriages. She deals with the individual who is not part of the mainstream and, as in *Baumgartner's Bombay*, explores the misfit, the lonely outsider, who does not belong, a theme that, in a sense, forms the essence of Desai's fiction.

Cry, The Peacock (1963), her first novel, traces a passionate young woman's degeneration into insanity. Maya, childless and trapped in a joyless marriage to Gautama, an older man, fails to communicate her emotional needs to him. Desai skillfully transforms the physical landscape into a psychic one that reflects Maya's increasingly distraught mind. The lyrical, poetic style, reminiscent of Virginia Woolf, mirrors Maya's complex inner self. The hot weather closely parallels Maya's dry, joyless marriage; the havoc that nature, in the form of perpetual heat and dust followed by monsoon rains, wreaks on the environment symbolizes her violent reaction. As Maya is driven to despair, her suppressed passions erupt like the monsoon storms when she kills her husband and commits suicide.

Voices in the City (1965), which followed *Cry, The Peacock*, depicts the nihilistic influence that Calcutta, personified as Kali, who is both goddess and demon, both the Universal Mother and the Goddess of Death, has on three siblings, Nirode, Monisha, and Amla. The siblings' mother too, like the city, symbolizes Kali, and the novel shows how the mother and the city, demonized as symbols of Kali, unleash their evil power, which culminates in Monisha's suicide. Desai reinforces the evil effect of the city by showing that Amla, who has not been there long enough for the city to work its evil spell on her, does not succumb to the negative and self-defeating attitude that the city generates in her sister and brother. Amla apprehends that Calcutta, the "monster" city, had "captured and enchanted—or disenchanted" her sister and brother.

Bye-Bye, Blackbird (1971), Desai's third novel, is set in London and deals with problems confronted by Indian immigrants. It juxtaposes two friends, Adit Sen, well settled and culturally assimilated, who still feels alienated and finally returns to India, and Dev, who, despite the blatant racial prejudice he encounters, decides to stay on because he wants to live in the land of the Romantic poets. Desai sensitively portrays the psychological effects on Sarah, Adit's Anglo-Saxon wife, of her marriage. Sarah, in her effort to acculturate herself to her husband's way of life, grows virtually alienated from her own people. Desai thus presents both Adit's and Sarah's points of view—if Adit's feeling of alienation in Britain leads him to return to India, Sarah's desire to assimilate Indian culture means leaving a part of her identity behind when she embarks on the sea voyage to India.

Where Shall We Go This Summer? (1975), like *Cry, The Peacock* and *Voices in the City*, portrays an oppressed married woman but is different because Sita, unlike Maya and Monisha, is a middle-aged mother who does not commit suicide but resignedly accepts her life. An unhappy twenty-year marriage explains why another pregnancy brings not joy but despair. Named after the Hindu mythological ideal of womanhood, the wife of Lord Rama, Sita seeks refuge on a forsaken island where she goes for the summer with two of her four children. The derelict house, the barren surroundings, and memories of a childhood spent on the island with a basically selfish father provide no relief. She realizes that she cannot escape reality and returns to an indifferent husband and a meaningless existence. Though Desai recognizes Sita's inability to alter her condition, we get the impression that Sita also contributes somehow to her predicament by accepting, though reluctantly, a life devoid of joy.

Fire on the Mountain (1977) goes beyond *Where Shall We Go This Summer?* in presenting, instead of a weary middle-aged mother, an unhappy great-grandmother. It portrays Nanda Kaul who, after her unfaithful husband's death, retires to Carignano, an isolated house on a quiet mountain ridge in Kasauli. The novel examines her attitudes toward her great-granddaughter, Raka, and her old friend Ila Das, both of whom she considers intrusions into her privacy when she wants nothing more from life than to be left alone. The novel, for which Desai's model was Japanese poetry, is more like a play, with its three parts, "Nanda Kaul at Carignano," "Raka comes to Carignano," and "Ila Das leaves Carignano." Desai recognizes that Nanda's present aloof self is a result of her bitter past and, in this light, examines her relationships with Raka and Ila, thus exploring and analyzing Nanda's interior self.

Games at Twilight (1978) contains eleven short stories that invest everyday events in the lives of ordinary people with significance. They include characters as diverse as a private tutor frustrated by his job and the poverty that leaves him no option; a doctor zealous in his duty but unfeeling toward his old and sick father; a boy preparing for his high-school exam, transformed by a vision of love; a man with no job, homeless and starved, revered as a guru; and a cranky, asthmatic husband soothed by the sight of a flock of pigeons one dawn in the Delhi summer. The stories portray meaningful moments that add up to life's experiences, as the one that lends its title to the book, in which a child realizes his insignificance when no one misses him long after a game of hide-and-seek is over and his subsequent appearance causes no surprise.

Clear Light of Day (1980), which followed *Fire on the Mountain*, presents Bim who, like Nanda, is a strong female protagonist. This novel, however, is unusual because Bim is not married, a fact that sets it apart from Desai's earlier work. *Clear Light of Day* is the story of Bim from whose perspective we see the breakup of her family. The novel chronicles her family's history and portrays the effect on it of India's partition, which also symbolizes their disintegration. Her brother Raja and sister Tara leave the family nest, and Bim is left to look after her retarded brother Baba, run the family home, and see to what's left of her father's business. What makes this novel even more unusual than Bim's spinsterhood is her juxtaposition with her married sister, Tara, an aspect of which Desai takes advantage by making both Bim and Tara recount one identical period in their family history each from her point of view, related in two of the novel's four parts. Though the separate pictures allow the reader a balanced view, they do not polarize the sisters into clearly demarcated opposites. Tara leads a normal and socially successful life, in the conventional sense, and seems happier, at least superficially, than Bim, whose portrayal as an embittered yet triumphant woman who controls her own life, reflects the narrator's objective yet somewhat ambivalent attitude toward her.

The Village by the Sea (1982), though classified under children's literature, is equally enlightening and enjoyable as adult fiction. Though the novel can be perceived in the genre of a Hansel and Gretel story, with a fairy-tale ending, it is a grim comment on the life of the village poor. Reminiscent somewhat of Kamala Markandaya's *Nectar in a Sieve* in that it deals with the coming of industrialization to a village, it presents the hardship of a village family fallen on bad days because of the alcoholism of the father and portrays the acts of the courageous children, Hari and Lila, who set about turning the tide in the family's favor.

Desai, in her latest two novels, departs from her norm by presenting male protagonists (the only earlier exception being *Bye-Bye, Blackbird*). However, *In Custody* and *Baumgartner's Bombay* are thematically similar to the earlier work in that the male anti-heroes, like the women in the previous novels, are victims—though of society, not of domestic oppression.

Deven, the gullible protagonist of *In Custody*, who loves Urdu and particularly Urdu poetry, teaches Hindi, for which he has no great love, to support his wife and son. One of the faceless who comprise life's unremarkable casualties, Deven often leaves the reader with no pity but irritation at his gullibility. Yet Desai successfully evokes a sense of pathos for Deven's predicament. Duped by an old college classmate, Murad, an editor who manages to convince him to interview an old Urdu poet for his magazine, Deven is roped into the act because of the chance to interview the greatest living Urdu poet. Deven's attempts to gain an interview with Nur and the subsequent pitfalls in getting a story arouse both frustration and pathos. The reader watches helplessly as Deven, without fail, makes a fool of himself again and yet again, and finally manages, through a series of disastrous events, to become so entangled in Nur's messy life that he somehow becomes the custodian of both Nur and his poetry.

Baumgartner's Bombay is Desai's masterpiece. This superbly crafted novel is written from the outsider's point of view—Hugo Baumgartner, the protagonist, is an outsider in India. Baumgartner is an immigrant, alienated from society, and one of society's losers. Yet the reader is left with a sense of the futility and poignancy of Baumgartner's life, the life of a man who, like Kamala Markandaya's protagonist in *The Nowhere Man*, belongs nowhere. A representative of the "human race, of displaced and dispossessed people and tribes all over the world" (Bliss 527), he comes to India (just before World War II) to seek refuge but instead, ironically, meets his fate when after fifty years in India he is killed by a German drug addict. Anita Desai sees Baumgartner's suffering as typical of the human condition. She thinks of him as somebody who "has no control over his life" (Bliss 527). Like Deven, Baumgartner too is one of life's casualties. However, his predicament is compounded by the fact that he is an immigrant who fails to belong—a pathetic specimen of mankind, pitiful in his poverty. He is one of those for whom Desai perforce evokes the tribute of far more than a passing high.

CRITICAL RECEPTION

Desai, whose fiction forms an essential part of almost every critique on Indian writing in English, has won widespread critical and literary acclaim both in India and in the West. Critics compare her to Anton Chekhov, find echoes of Virginia Woolf in her novels, and universally acknowledge the psychological aspect of her fiction, using "stream of consciousness" or "feminine consciousness" to describe it. Another aspect of her fiction that critics note is the subordination of plot and theme, symbolism and imagery, language, form, and structure, to character development. Though some suspect that her love of words and their sheer lyrical and poetic magic supersedes the characters, others observe the relentless quality of her prose, which helps to maintain the tension that perfectly suits her tragic vision and existentialist view of life.

Critics universally praise Desai for the effective use of the stream-of-consciousness technique in *Cry, The Peacock* and acknowledge it to be, of all her novels, the most poetic and lyrical, a quality that has invited both praise and criticism. K. R. Srinivasa Iyengar reflects their views when he lauds her style as "supple and suggestive enough to convey the fever and fretfulness" of the protagonist, the "feelings and emotions" reflected in the "language, syntax and imagery," but complains that the reader may feel that the prose texture, rather than reflecting the mood of the character, is often a consequence of the author's "excessive cerebration" (464–65). Darshan Singh Maini calls it the "most poetic and evocative Indo-Anglian novel," but qualifies his praise by noting that if "it falls short of greatness, it's because the dramatic story is not potent and varied enough to carry the burden of sustained lyricism" (217).

Critical studies of *Voices in the City* reflect its various themes in offering different viewpoints. While A. V. Krishna Rao sees it as a symbolic novel in which Desai successfully dramatizes "the individual human relationships against the backdrop of a cosmopolitan consciousness" (178), in Ramesh K. Srivastava's view this novel emphasizes the aesthetic over the material values as it explores the predicament of artists in search of a vision (88, 95). From another perspective, Usha Bande connects Nirode's self-defeating attitude to his unsatisfactory relationships with his parents and praises Desai's ability to grasp the effects of an unhappy childhood in shaping negative adult attitudes (74), while Maini, critical of Nirode's exaggeration as the cynical and rebellious anti-hero, sees "something hollow, something phoney about [Nirode's] protestations and diatribes" (222).

Critical responses to *Bye-Bye, Blackbird* largely focus on the novel's theme of immigration and alienation and, though critical of Desai for resorting to stereotypical immigrant portraits, praise her portrayal of Sarah as the traumatized wife whose marriage increasingly alienates her from her community. Maini's view can be taken to be representative as he praises Desai for her "natural poetic and chromatic qualities" in evoking the "sights and sounds" of London and for the descriptions of the "fabled English countryside," which, however, he values more for the "rich Keatsian descriptions than for their dramatic intent" (225–26). He criticizes the superficially drawn characters who represent stereotypical immigrants and faults Desai for manipulating rather than dramatizing their actions.

Most critical studies of *Where Shall We Go This Summer?* perceive Sita as a disenchanted married woman who, after a period of existential despair, realizes that there can be no escape from reality and accepts her life. Bande finds in Sita's reconciliation to her life's reality a "defeat of individuality" but also "maturity of perception achieved by both Sita and her creator" (105, 119). Maini recognizes in Sita a lonely wife and mother who experiences feelings of extreme emptiness and existential despair. While praising the "moments of lyric beauty and intensity," he faults Desai for being "somehow unable to invent events and episodes that may bring out the dramatic potential of her *données*" (229). The "paucity of social detail," he says, "leaves the book a flawed poem" (227).

What seems to have attracted the most attention of critics in *Fire on the Mountain* is its symbolic imagery which, Asnani emphasizes, "deftly highlights Nanda's longing for seclusion," noting how a "charred tree-trunk in the forest" becomes a metaphor for Nanda's "desire for absolute stillness" (150). Malashri Lal examines the novel, from a sociological perspective, as a "fictional rendering of feminist attitudes in India" (224) and connects Nanda Kaul's and Ila Das's upbringing and education to social history. Jasbig Jain's view of this novel as the "conflict between the need to withdraw in order to preserve one's wholeness and sanity and the need to be involved in the painful process of life" (38), corresponds to the view of Bande who finds that Nanda Kaul is unaware of the "split in her personality caused by the desire of the self to recoil from all contact and yet attempt to reach out to the other" (190).

While most critics have praised the stories in Desai's collection *Games at Twilight: And Other Stories*, a few have been critical. Widely praised for conveying human insight in clear and simple prose, they have been aptly described, by Alice Adams, as "beautifully crafted, deceptively simple" stories, which give the reader "some sharp and astonishing glimpses" of the "human heart" (12). Some harsh criticism of *Games at Twilight* is found in Shiv K. Kumar, who explains why Desai "fails to engage the reader's interest." He faults her "overzealous concern with the medium of communication, regardless of the nature of experience embodied in each story," and criticizes the "laboured prose" which seldom offers the reader "any real climactic moment of suspense or stimulation" (203–4).

Critical studies of *Clear Light of Day* include analyses ranging from its use of imagery and analogy to the family's disintegration and reconciliation, from the conflict between independence and solitude on the one hand and attachment and the need to connect on the other. Madhusudan Prasad, praising the use of "domestic" imagery to evoke atmosphere and mood in *Clear Light of Day*, refers to the "feeling of stagnation... reigning in the old, unchanged house... [which is] evoked in the novel through the metaphor of a scummy pond" (75). From another viewpoint, Richard Cronin sees in Bim's forgiveness of Raja "no national implications, for *Clear Light of Day* determinedly refuses allegory," but acknowledges that in the novel's last scene Bim's and India's "fragmented cultural heritage" become one when a Hindu sings a song written by Pakistan's national poet, Iqbal, to which Bim responds with a line from T. S. Eliot (55). Meredith Marsh finds echoes of E. M. Forster and sees in Desai's depiction of individuation a reply to Forster's warning of the loneliness of independence. He suggests that Desai, like Forster, "admires the transcendent religious impulse" that brings detachment, which, however, conflicts with the urge to connect. However, he criticizes Desai for devoting "too much painstaking prose to landscape and recovery and too little to the complex adults she has invented and the changes they work between them" (40).

Praised largely for its authentic portrayal of Indian village life and for the "hypnotic vividness" of its prose, *The Village by the Sea* has been criticized for the artistic discrepancy between the sophisticated narrator and the village characters. Cronin, for example, finds that throughout the novel Desai's prose "places a barrier between the reader and the characters" (46). He questions whether a village girl like Lila, troubled by her family's poverty, would be "quite so ... sensitive to a cock-pheasant and a pigeon" (46) and argues that though Hari is the "central character" he is "observed, seen from the outside. It is Sayyid Ali who is in close proximity to the novelist" (48).

In Custody has been praised for its portrayal of Deven as a gullible man. While some critics find him both comic and poignant, and others both exasperating and admirable, he has invited some criticism too. William Walsh concedes that Desai invests Deven with "human value and interest," which "with such a dreary, feeble spirit as Deven is evidence of a rare gift for creating something completely authentic and true" (112), but finds that Desai's novel "fails through the lack of a ... complexity essential in a novel so firmly based on a single character" (113). While John Gross remarks that Desai "avoids either farce or easy pathos; she sympathizes with [Deven's] plight, and at the same time remains clear-sighted about his weaknesses" (28C), Sebastian Faulks sees the novel as a "prolonged comedy of exasperation" that sometimes "strain[s] towards allegory" because Deven at times appears to be a "mere embodiment of goodness" (26).

What seems to have aroused the curiosity of critics most about *Baumgartner's Bombay* is its subject: a German refugee in India. Desai explains that her longtime desire to include the German part of her heritage in her work prompted her to write a novel about a German in Bombay (Libert). Another motivating factor behind Baumgartner's creation lies in the fact that the element she "most sympathize[s] with is the one of being an outsider" (Bliss 521). Most critics comment on these aspects of the novel; Sarah Ferrell finds that Desai's "concern about foreignness and dividedness ... lies at the heart of the novel" (3); and Shirley Chew maintains it was "inevitable" that Desai should bring together the two strands of her heritage, Indian and German. The subject has "strong claims on her imagination: the role of the outsider, whether it is a person marginalized by society, or one who opts to live life on the periphery" (787). A historical analysis of *Baumgartner's Bombay* is provided by Judie Newman, who maintains that Desai, in this novel, "interrogate[s] the relation of discourse to history, the language of the interior to that of the outer world." Newman examines the "intertextual device" employed in the novel, "letters, literary references, songs, nursery rhymes and travellers' tales," to analyze the relationship of literature to history, and finds that history, for Desai, is not "a silenced story, but neither can it be ... rewritten at random" (37–46).

SELECTED BIBLIOGRAPHY

Works by Anita Desai

Cry, The Peacock. London: Peter Owen, 1963; New Delhi: Orient Paperbacks, 1980.

Voices in the City. London: Peter Owen, 1965; New Delhi: Orient Paperbacks, 1982.

Bye-Bye, Blackbird. Delhi: Hind Pocket Books, 1971.
The Peacock Garden. Bombay: India Book House Education Trust, 1974. (juvenile)
Where Shall We Go This Summer? Delhi: Vikas Publishing House, 1975; Delhi: Orient Paperbacks, 1982.
Cat on a Houseboat. Bombay: Orient Longman, 1976. (juvenile)
Fire on the Mountain. London: Heinemann, 1977.
Games at Twilight: And Other Stories. Harmondsworth: Penguin, 1978. (short stories)
Clear Light of Day. London: Penguin, 1980.
The Village by the Sea. London: Heinemann, 1982. (juvenile)
In Custody. London: Penguin, 1984.
Baumgartner's Bombay. New York: Alfred A. Knopf, 1988.

Studies of Anita Desai

Adams, Alice. Review of *Games at Twilight: And Other Stories*. *New York Times Book Review* (June 22, 1980): 12.

Asnani, Shyam M. *Critical Response to Indian English Fiction*. Delhi: Mittal Publications, 1985.

Bande, Usha. *The Novels of Anita Desai: A Study in Character and Conflict*. New Delhi: Prestige Books, 1988.

Bliss, Corinne Demas. "Against the Current: A Conversation with Anita Desai." *Massachusetts Review* 29:3 (Fall 1988): 521–37.

Chew, Shirley. "Life on the Periphery." Review of *Baumgartner's Bombay*. *Times Literary Supplement* (July 15–21, 1988): 787.

Cronin, Richard. *Imagining India*. New York: St. Martin's Press, 1989. 45–58.

Faulks, Sebastian. "Straining Towards Allegory." Review of *In Custody. Books and Bookmen* 350 (Nov. 1984): 26.

Ferrell, Sarah. "A Banquet of Languages." Review of *Baumgartner's Bombay. New York Times Book Review* (April 9, 1989): 3.

Gross, John. Review of *In Custody. New York Times* (Feb. 22, 1985): 28C.

Iyengar, K. R. Srinivasa. *Indian Writing in English*. 2nd ed. Bombay: Asia Publishing House, 1973.

Jain, Jasbir. "Anita Desai." *Indian English Novelists*. Ed. Madusudhan Prasad. New Delhi: Sterling Publishers, 1982. 23–50.

Kumar, Shiv K. "Desai's *Games at Twilight*: A View." *Perspectives on Anita Desai*. Ed. Ramesh K. Srivastava. Ghaziabad: Vimal Prakashan, 1984. 203–07.

Lal, Malashri. "Anita Desai: *Fire on the Mountain*." *Major Indian Novels: An Evaluation*. Ed. N. S. Pradhan. New Jersey: Humanities Press, 1986. 242–62.

Libert, Florence. "An Interview with Anita Desai, 1 August 1989. Cambridge. England." *World Literature Written in English* 30:1 (1990): 47–55.

Maini, Darshan Singh. "The Achievement of Anita Desai." *Indo-English Literature: A Collection of Critical Essays*. Ed. K. K. Sharma. Atlantic Highlands, N.J.: Humanities Press, 1982. 215–30.

Marsh, Meredith. "The Ambiguities of Independence." Review of *Clear Light of Day. New Republic* (Feb. 21, 1981): 39–40.

Newman, Judie. "History and Letters: Anita Desai's *Baumgartner's Bombay*." *World Literature Written in English* 30:1 (1990): 37–46.

Prasad, Madhusudan. "The Novels of Anita Desai." Ramesh K. Srivastava. *Perspectives on Anita Desai*: Ghaziabad: Vimal Prakash, 1984. 54–77.

Rao, Krishna A. V. "*Voices in the City*: A Study." *Perspectives on Anita Desai*. Ed. Ramesh K. Srivastava. Ghaziabad: Vimal Prakashan, 1984. 162–78.

Srivastava, Ramesh K. "Artist in Voices in the City." *The Fiction of Anita Desai*. New Delhi: Bahri Publications, 1989. 88–95.

Walsh, William. *Indian Literature in English*. London: Longman, 1990.

G. V. DESANI (1909–   )

A. L. McLeod

BIOGRAPHY

Inexplicably, there is little biographical material available on Govindas Vishnoodas Desani, and he does not respond to requests for information to supplement the meager details that he has seen fit to make known over the years, either in conversation or in publishers' handouts. In an advertisement for *All About Mr. Hatterr* that was issued by Francis Aldor, the publisher, we are offered numerous snippets from readers' comments and an exhaustive list of places at which Desani has spoken, but just the following biographical matter: "G. V. Desani, Indian journalist and broadcaster. Formerly, correspondent of the *Times of India*, Reuters and the Associated Press, lecturer on the antiquity of Rajputana, at Delhi, Ajmer, and Central India Colleges, for the Bombay, Baroda and Central India Railway." However, it is known that Desani was born on July 8, 1909, in Nairobi, Kenya, to Vishnoodas Manghirmal and Rukmani (Chabria) Desani and was educated privately.

In 1926 Desani migrated to Britain and became a correspondent for the several media listed above, beginning in 1928 and extending through 1945, though interrupted by his lecturing appointment with the Bombay, Baroda, and Central India Railway in the late 1930s. During World War II, he was employed as a lecturer by the Imperial Institute, the Royal Empire Society, the Council for Adult Education in the British Armed Services, and the London and Wiltshire County Councils as well as the British Broadcasting Corporation. As the advertisement issued by Aldor notes, "It is as a personality and a speaker that Desani has made his reputation in Britain." A dozen excerpts from testimonials and reviews remark upon "a voice singular in its beauty," upon his speed of utterance ("I have never heard any language spoken with such speed yet perfect clarity"), and upon his clear exposition of subject-matter ("I knew more of Indian thought"). Desani's audiences were quite diverse (in hospitals, prisons, resettlement units, armed services bases, Rotary Clubs, munitions canteens) and were located throughout the United Kingdom: Liverpool, Manchester, Southampton, Bath, Ayre, and Plymouth.

In 1952 Desani returned to South Asia and lived in Buddhist monasteries and Hindu ashrams until 1966, though he spent some time during 1960 in Burma pursuing religious knowledge. However, this period was not one of total devotion to the life of study and isolation: he contributed a column, "Very High and Very Low," to the *Illustrated Weekly of India* (Bombay) from 1962 to 1968, in which journal he published also a dozen short stories (four of the stories also appeared in *Noble Savage, Hindu Review*, and *Transatlantic Review*). These he is at present editing while also preparing an edition of his diaries, 1950–60.

Desani was appointed as a Fulbright-Hays lecturer in philosophy during 1968 and joined the Department of Philosophy at the University of Texas in Austin the following year; upon his retirement in 1979 (the year that he took out U.S. citizenship), he became emeritus professor. During the summers of 1979 and 1981 he taught at Boston University. Desani now lives comfortably in Austin in a house richly furnished with Indian artifacts.

MAJOR WORKS AND THEMES

While any discussion of Desani's writing inevitably must focus on his one major work, *All About Mr. Hatterr*, some indications of his themes, techniques, and point of view can be garnered from his earlier publications and intentions. Although he made, apparently, quite an impression on his audiences, Desani never published any of his speeches to British audiences. In fact, the prospectus for *All About Mr. Hatterr* states that "though a nonpolitical speaker, he often criticised the Government policy towards India, and he was given the fullest liberty of comment"—presumably the Ministry of Information in London exercised little or no supervision or censorship of his speech texts. There is no evidence of where the author stood on the vital matters of Indian-British relations during the tumultuous preindependence era.

However, the prospectus does allude to two prepared talks by Desani; the first is "an erudite paper on Pantanjali's *Yoga Philosophy*, read at the invitation of the Oxford Majlis at Rhodes House, Oxford (out of print), " and the other is *India Invites*, a paper read at New College, Oxford, on July 15, 1941. The first, a straightforward exposition, is less relevant to a study of Desani's themes than the second, which was a response to the invitation to comment on the question, "How can India and Britain be better introduced to each other's cultural productions and ideas?"

In this sixteen-page fascicule Desani offers a general semantics position that one cannot speak in generalizations about India or Indians, lists a number of supposed Indian claims ("the world's most decorative and beautiful women"; "the credit of inventing the zero symbol"; "the most graceful dress"; the invention of accountancy; and boys who "are well-behaved; and their modesty is proverbial"), and proposes that "in my country you will meet profound philosophers and enterprising men who might not hesitate to condense the entire human metaphysical and theological speculation in the concept: 'Thank God everyone is a liar.' " But he also stresses that love, war, and revenge are prominent Indian traits: people will "invite you out, waylay you, and take you to their homes as their victims." After stating that he spent "months of aimless wandering up and down the country in a mood of resignation" that did not bring him peace, he settled for a time at Sarnath, where "at the Ispatana, an ancestor, Prince Sidharta the Buddha, preached his first sermon." Then, after a long praise for the Hindu desire to spend the last twenty-five years of life in contemplation—especially in the Himalayas and on the banks of the Ganges—he observes, "Ideas, if they are not lived, are mere playthings." Before concluding that his remarks have not answered the question that he was invited to answer, he confesses, "A person like myself, half of whose time is spent in finding short-cuts and easy escapes out of trouble," may well ask such questions as why effort is necessary for achievement and why one must be subject to the law of causation. The pamphlet has some sections of truly poetic prose, but it is diffuse, does not face the question, and proposes (especially through anecdotes and illustrations) that East and West are interdependent, even though India, "the mother benevolent," has denied reality to knowledge acquired through the senses—a fundamental tenet of Western philosophy. Indian ideas he calls "my property, my racial inheritance, my national right."

The *Bookseller* for March 6, 1948, announced the imminent publication of a biography of Mahatma Gandhi by G. V. Desani. It was to be "the first complete life of one of the greatest figures of our time...written by an 'insider' without prejudice, with access to sources and personalities untapped during Gandhi's lifetime. The most comprehensive study of India's greatest man, it explains the Indian scene and thought as never explained before." One wonders how Desani, living the busy life of a London journalist and subsequently the eremitical existence of a Buddhist monk, could have had access to sources and "personalities" (not officials or individuals) not available to others; and it would be difficult for an "insider" to be disinterested, surely. However, the book was never published.

Also advertised for publication in 1948 was *Hali*, a playlet of almost twenty pages that carries a long subtitle: "The story of his Passion and of his vision of Good and Evil and something beyond them both: told by his God Raha, his mother Mira, his dearly loved Rooh, the ominous spirit Bhava, Maya (who befriended him), and Magician, and himself." There is a prologue and an epilogue. Commenting on this brief prose poem, T. S. Eliot called it "a striking and unusual piece of work... often the imagery is terrifyingly effective.... *Hali* is not likely to appeal quickly to the taste of many readers." The piece, written in a quite exalted style (exclamations, apostrophes, archaisms, and imperatives are liberally included), attempts to take the measure of man—to explore the concepts of Indian philosophy— in search of the ideal. In this it is a companion piece to *All About H. Hatterr*. The youthful eponym experiences fear, defeat, and sadness only to develop a pristine love for mankind—for the god of love made manifest in mankind. "No drums, no dirge for Hali," he says, "for if there be things of love, the things of beauty, I seek them, I seek them still! Say to my brothers and say to my sisters, all things of love and all things of beauty are theirs, theirs to be" (19).

Whereas *Hali* states a philosophy of grief, of attachment, of love, *Hatterr* offers an antithetical one. One expounds selflessness; the other expounds selfishness as the universal goal. One can understand, then, why *Hatterr* has often been viewed as the precise opposite of *Hali* in its philosophical thrust.

Hatterr consults seven sages (of Calcutta, Rangoon, Madras, Bombay, Delhi, Mogalsarai-Varanasi, and All-India); to each he offers a question: Has man a chance? Is woman worth it? Is youth a desirable age? Why do some succeed without effort? Why does evil seem to triumph? Is there anything in the concept of fate? What is the future of humanity? Clearly, all these age-old conundrums are not subject to simple answers; but Hatterr does get some pseudo-wisdom: "Be suspicious . . . dispell credible illusions"; "one man's losses are another's gains"; "appearance and disguise always wins"; "abscond from charlatans and deceivers"; and finally, "Carry on." This he does when he acknowledges that life is a constant battle between opposites, an eternal dialectic, and exclaims, "I am not fed up with life!"

The early acclaim that Desani received for his speaking is reflected in the use of the rhetorical mode in his subsequent writing; his study of philosophy clearly dictated the dialectical approach to major questions of life that perplex Hatterr; the absurdity of existence seems to have suggested the surface absurdity of Hatterr's language, and his biological union of Orient and Occident suggests that in carrying on, he will have to find a compromise between the realistic and the mystic, between East and West, between the interests of self and other. One wonders whether *Hali*, which followed *Hatterr* by two years, was Desani's momentary second thought about life's meaning; but *Hatterr*'s themes seem to have prevailed with the author.

The short stories that Desani contributed from 1957 to 1967 to the *Illustrated Weekly of India*, a popular Bombay journal, share, in many respects, the creative vision of both *Hali* and *All About H. Hatterr*, though they are less original examples of their genre, inclining nonetheless to the satiric and (as in the case of "Mephisto's Daughter" and "With Malice Aforethought") surreal or fantastic. "The Last Long Letter" is in many ways the best of these brief pieces: it may be read as an allegory of Good and Evil—perhaps the theme that most often occupies Desani's thought. In this story a young suicide wills his soul to its origin, believing that an ineffable void will ensue and that that, in turn, will give way to enlightenment. It may be read as a search for truth and an understanding of the mysteries of existence—or of the paradoxes of life. Any sustained study of Desani's short fictions will have to be suspended until he issues them in a collected and edited form.

All About H. Hatterr was published during the period when the allegorical novel and the satirical mode were enjoying a revivification in England. It was greeted by elaborate praises from some well-regarded writers and critics, such as T. S. Eliot and C.E.M. Joad, but it failed to gain any popularity outside a small coterie of enthusiasts. The reasons are several: Desani insisted that the book is "a study of Man and of Untutored Mind generally," thus inviting readers to consider it as a modern *Everyman* or perhaps a *Faust*; its language is nonliterary and (though supposedly the product of a self-taught "grotesque autodidact") inconsistent in grammar, syntax, and idiom—among other things; the structure, though obviously arranged around seven sages' counsel, is neither increasingly complex nor progressively more intricate; the characterization is deficient in that the reader never really knows the finer traits of Hatterr, who remains elusive and somewhat poltroonish; the dialogue is lacking in verisimilitude. Some readers—intending praise—have likened the language to that of *Finnegans Wake*, but it is a pale similarity and devoid of the Joycean insights, puns, and conflations.

CRITICAL RECEPTION

Desani has chosen to be a professional Indian rather than a professional writer, and his success as a speaker during World War II was in large measure attributable to his origin. Though a number of British readers and some critics of renown spoke highly of his work upon publication, his books were initially momentary successes and essentially faded from notice for over a generation. In his highly esteemed *Indian Writing in English* (1960), Professor K. R. Srinivasa Iyengar devotes just five lines out of 600 pages to Desani; he writes of *Hatterr* that it "is obviously a Joycean exercise in seeming incoherence and total comprehension, and its protagonist ... as he moves through life ... accumulates a variety of impressions and even formulates a philosophy of his own" (340). Anthony Burgess, in his Introduction to the 1970 edition, notes that the book "became a coterie pleasure" for many years and speaks of its language as "a sort of creative chaos ... gloriously impure" (ii). Perry Westbrook believes the book is "one of our century's major contributions to the literature of the absurd" (235), while S. C. Harrex, discussing Desani's "bizarre imagination" as applied to the question of "the cultural relevance of the English literary tradition to modern India," offers the thesis that beneath the surface of the novel, "complex issues are seriously alluded to" (74), and that the work is "a dramatic overt gesture" (78). D. M. Burjonjee believes that Desani has managed to "synthesize, through the dialectic of his persona, the Indian and Western traditions into a new totality," making *Hatterr* a dialogue-novel that is "a landmark in Indo-Anglian literature" (191). (His study, the most detailed to date, is commendable for its comprehensiveness though not wholly persuasive in its conclusion.) Ronald Blaber and Marvin Gilman, who state that *Hatterr* "verges on the unreadable," nonetheless conclude that it "is the comedic-picaresque *par excellence*"—particularly because of the sisyphean rhythm of the protagonist's life and because, as he says, "All improbables are probable in India" (94).

BIBLIOGRAPHY

Works by G. V. Desani

India Invites: A Paper Read at New College, Oxford, on July 15, 1941. Chiswick, Privately printed, 1941 (?).
All About Mr. Hatterr: A Gesture. London: Aldor, 1948. As *All About H. Hatterr: A Gesture.* London: Saturn, 1950; rev. ed. New York: Farrar, Straus, 1951; rev. ed. London: Bodley Head and New York: Farrar, Straus and Giroux, 1970; rev. ed. New York: Lancer, 1972. Rev. ed., as *All About H. Hatterr: A Novel.* Harmondsworth: Penguin, 1972.
Hali. London: Saturn, 1950; rev. ed. Calcutta: Writers Workshop, 1967.
Mainly Concerning Kama and Her Immortal Lord. New Delhi: Indian Council on Cultural Relations, 1973.

Studies of G. V. Desani

Blaber, Ronald. "The Contemporary Picaresque Novel: Desani and Oakley." In *Comic Relations: Studies in the Comic, Satire, and Parody.* Ed. Pavel Petr, David Roberts, and Philip Thomson. Frankfurt-am-Main: Peter Lang, 1985. 116–24.
———, and Marvin Gilman. "Gestures and Suspicions: Indian Readings. *All About H. Hatterr.*" In *Roguery: The Picaresque Tradition in Australian, Canadian, and Indian Fiction.* Springwood, N.S.W., Australia: Butterfly, 1990. 84–94.
Burgess, Anthony. Introduction. *All About H. Hatterr.* New York: Farrar, Straus, and Giroux, 1970. i–v.
Burjonjee, D. M. "The Dialogue in G. V. Desani's *All About H. Hatterr.*" *WLWE (World Literature Written in English)* 13:2 (November 1974): 191–224.
Goers, Peter. "King's English: Whole Language and G. V. Desani's *All About H. Hatterr.*" *New Literature Review* 4 (1977): 30–40.
Harrex, S. C. "G. V. Desani: Mad Hatterr Sage." *Miscellany* 92 (1979): 11–48.
———. "The Novel as Gesture" (On *All About H. Hatterr*). In *Awakened Conscience: Studies in Commonwealth Literature.* Ed. C. D. Narasimhaiah. New Delhi: Sterling, 1978. 73–83.
Naik, M. K. "Colonial Experience in *All About H. Hatterr.*" *Commonwealth Novel in English* 1 (1982): 57–75.

————. "The Method in the Madness: A Thematic Analysis of *All About H. Hatterr.*" *Journal of Indian Writing in English* 13: (1985): 1–14.

Raghavacharyulu, D.V.K. "The Counterfeit Hero: Desani's Hatterr and Naipaul's Ralph Singh." In *The Critical Response*. Madras: Macmillan India, 1980. 31–40.

Russell, Peter, and Khushwant Singh. *A Note on G. V. Desani's "All About H. Hatterr" and "Kali."* London: Szeben, 1952.

Westbrook, Peter D. "G. V. Desani." *Contemporary Novelists*. Ed. D. L. Kirkpatrick. 4th ed. New York: St. Martin's Press, 1986. 235–36.

LEENA DHINGRA (1942–   )
Jogamaya Bayer

BIOGRAPHY

Leena Dhingra, who was born in India, left her native country in her childhood. After the partition of India into India and Pakistan in 1947, her family became uprooted; their home, which was in the Pakistani part, was lost to them. During her schooling she moved between India, France, Switzerland, and England. For Dhingra this meant a life split between Asia and Europe. After receiving a diploma in drama in 1962, she worked for two years in the theaters in England and France, then for a year as a publicity and public relations officer in Brussels, where she took a certificate in film editing. From 1967 to 1990 she worked in and around the film business in the United Kingdom and in India. She was a founder member of the Workers' Film Association, which is now based in Manchester. During these years, Dhingra also studied for a degree in education in London and worked as a teacher. From 1988 onwards she concentrated on her writing, and was a coordinator of the London-based Asian Women Writers' Collective, an organization that encourages writing through reading and regular workshops. Dhingra has done writer residencies in schools and colleges all over the United Kingdom, organized by projects such as the Regional Arts Associations and the Arts Education for Multicultural Society. At present she is preparing for a master's in creative writing at the University of East Anglia.

Dhingra has contributed one essay, "Breaking Out of the Labels," to the anthology *Watchers and Seekers* (1987), and three short stories, "The Girl Who Couldn't See Herself," "The Debt" and "Right of Way," to the anthology *Right of Way*, published in 1988 by the Women's Press. A number of her articles and stories have appeared in magazines both in the United Kingdom and in India. In 1988, Dhingra's novel *Amritvela* was published. At the moment she is working on television scripts as well as on a novel about her forebears at the turn of the century.

MAJOR WORKS AND THEMES

Dhingra's works thematize cultural displacement, isolation, and exile. In her work different cultures come together without becoming properly integrated, which leads to a sense of loss and the fragmentation of one's self. However, this loss and disintegration are not just a personal matter. It is at least partly imbided from her family, which lost its city and home during the partition of India. The disintegration creates a psychic condition of rootlessness that leads to what she calls an "identity of no identity," but also a special kind of freedom, the freedom to move on. The feeling of being a refugee is ever present in her mind. In the essay "Breaking Out of the Labels" she writes about this feeling—"the three pillars of my identity: of being Indian, free and a refugee" (*Watchers and Seekers* 104). The everyday experience of racism in exile enforces the feeling of being uprooted. Only when Dhingra goes beyond the stage of "label-fitting," using terms such as "black," "ethnic minority" and so on, and becomes confident in her dignity can she confront the alien culture. In other words, until a person forges an authentic identity, she cannot know her role in society. Establishment of a valid identity is the topic of Dhingra's story "The Girl Who Couldn't See Herself": "Once upon a time there was a girl who couldn't see herself very clearly, and so she kept stumbling and losing herself all the time. For since she couldn't see herself, she didn't know what she was, or where she fitted in, or how she should behave" (*Right of Way* 29). Because the girl could see only a blur when looking at herself in the mirror, she could not constitute her self. So she decided to ask other people who and what she was. One day after a man pointed out to her that she had a beautiful smile, she was able to see this smile in the mirror, and because she recognized it as a beautiful smile, she could then see her whole self in the mirror. The identity of the girl, then, is established through something external, namely through the positive response of the man. This process could be regarded as a metaphor for the situation of the immigrant women who strive for their identity, which cannot be found without a positive response from the environment.

Disillusionment in not being able to find any sustaining ideals in one's search for a historical heritage is a recurring theme in Dhingra's writing. Loss of ideals promotes alienation. The short story "The Debt" is about this disillusionment with the absence of ideals that the protagonist recognizes in her search for her roots. Here the protagonist, a young immigrant woman in the United Kingdom, returns to India in order to work for the rural development. In the course of this work, she comes to know that she would have to work for a film company that makes educational films for tribal groups who would be resettled because of the construction of a large reactor. As she did not expect this kind of rural "development," which is done at the expense of a marginal group, she gives up her intention to work for the project. The theme of desire to belong is woven through the story. She wishes to belong to India, but to an India that has cherished the principles of Gandhi, and this absence of ideals alienates her.

Her first novel, *Amritvela*, elaborates on this theme. The novel is about the homecoming of a young Indian woman, Meera, who was taken to England by her parents when she was a child and was brought up there. She is now married to an Englishman and has a young daughter. Her husband has been promoted to a new job and must move to another town; therefore, they must live separately for the time being. She feels isolated in England, and decides to visit India in order to explore the possibility of returning with her daughter and starting a new life there. The novel depicts her experiences in India, her disillusionment, the discovery of her roots in the cultural heritage, and her final return to England. The title of the novel, which means "the time of nectar," the time just before dawn when the sun has risen but cannot as yet be seen, bears a symbolic relation to its content. It lends the novel an optimistic tone that reappears especially toward the end. The title is a premonition not simply of the experience of the root-lessness of the protagonist, but also of the discovery of perspectives that this symbol contains. A close look at the culture of the novel shows that it can be characterized as circular, episodic, and digressive. The most conspicuous element of the novel is its extensive use of interspersed stories, which conveys to the novel a digressional form. Dhingra uses epic myths, local legends, and stories with didactic elements. The mythological stories have been taken from the Indian epics, the *Ramayana* and the *Mahabharata*. The structure of the novel, as also its theme, reveals the culturally hybridized sensibility of the author.

Right at the beginning of the novel, Meera expresses her feelings in the following way: "I feel myself to be suspended between two cultures, then this is where I belong, the halfway mark. Here in the middle of nowhere, up in the atmosphere, is my space—the halfway point between East and West" (*Amritvela* 1). It is through this desire to belong to one world or the other—or to both—that the novelist enters into a dialogue with her society. In this novel, it is the sense of isolation and cultural displacement that makes the protagonist look for her roots in India. What she finds, however, is not the idealistic India of Gandhi and the freedom fighters, but a country adrift without any moral direction.

The search for one's historical and cultural inheritance is again going to be central to Dhingra's forthcoming novel, which is about her great uncle, a revolutionary nationalist who was executed in the United Kingdom in 1909 at the age of twenty-four. His body was exhumed and returned to India in 1976. This exhumation becomes the defining metaphor for the whole book. Dhingra's attempt to unravel the resonance of the past is part of the interpretation of history as a dominant life-forming force of the emigrant.

CRITICAL RECEPTION

Dhingra's novel *Amritvela* has been favorably received in the literary world. According to Vineeta Gupta, she is a gifted writer who sensitively and distinctively deals with the cultural problems of an Asian woman living in the Western world (21). Though Jasmin Kureishi misses something in the plot and finds that the characters are not developed enough, she also thinks that for those who are caught between two cultures it "will strike a poignant cord" (12). Sharbani Basu categorizes Dhingra among those Asian women novelists whose works reflect their immigrant experiences and have created a new literary genre. Their themes are often similar: "the alienation in the country one has adopted, rejection by the country one has left behind" (76). In another review, Shahrukh Husain considers *Amritvela* "an elegant novel, diary-like in the arrangement of its content and emulating in its tempo the unhurried, fatalistic rhythms of India" (172). For Pratap Chatterjee, Dhingra's simple style reminds one of R. K. Narayan, and yet it is different from Narayan's. For him the novel *Amritvela* draws on the autobiographical elements of Dhingra, for whom "to travel back to one's roots is not always pleasant or predictable" (18). In Chatterjee's view, she has accepted the hybridity of her identity: both Indian and English.

BIBLIOGRAPHY

Works by Leena Dhingra

"Breaking Out of the Labels." *Watchers and Seekers: Creative Writing by Black Women in Britain*. Ed. Rhonda Cobham and Merle Collins. London: Women's Press, 1987.
Amritvela. London: Women's Press, 1988.
"The Girl Who Couldn't See Herself." *Right of Way*. Ed. Asian Women Writers' Workshop. London: Women's Press, 1988. 29–31.
"The Debt." *Right of Way*. Ed. Asian Women Writers' Workshop. London: Women's Press, 1988. 46–57.
"Right of Way." *Right of Way*. Ed. Asian Women Writers' Workshop. London: Women's Press, 1988. 146–48.

Studies of Leena Dhingra

Basu, Sharbani. "The Native Writes Back." *Sunday* 8 (Oct. 14, 1989): 76–77.
Chatterjee, Pratap. "Between England and India." *Asian Herald* 26 (April 26–May 2, 1988): 18.
Gupta, Vineeta. "Asian Women Take Up Their Pens." *An Indian Bookworm's Journal* (Summer 1988): 21.
Husain, Shahrukh. "Passive Disorientation: Indo-Anglian Journeys." *Third World Quarterly* 11:2 (1989): 169–75.
Kureishi, Jasmin. Review of *Amritvela*. *Spare Rib* 192 (June 1988): 12.

FARRUKH DHONDY (1944–   )
Jane Carducci

BIOGRAPHY

Farrukh Dhondy was born in Poona, India, in 1944. He came from a bourgeois family; Dhondy says, "My Dad was an army engineer—I had to be a professional. My Mom was a traditional Indian parent too, except that she read a lot of English novels" (Groen 11). As a boy, Dhondy was a rebel, and in an interview with Andrew Robinson (1985) he described his friends during his childhood as "bad hats." They were "streetwise," and Dhondy categorized himself "at the polite end of street-wiseness" (15). Many of these associates were later characterized in Dhondy's stories. He loved to read. But, Dhondy recalls, "We read with absolutely no critical understanding. We would read Thomas Hardy and Marie Corelli with exactly the same attention as if they were both masterpieces" (Robinson 15).

Dhondy was educated at Bishops School in Poona; then from 1959 to 1963 he attended Wadia College where he earned his B.S. in physics and math. Offered a scholarship to study abroad, Dhondy chose Cambridge, he says, because he liked E. M. Forster's description of it and had read *Jude the Obscure*. At this point his contact with Britain was entirely literary. He began his studies at Cambridge in physics and then changed his major, earning a B.A. in English in 1967. "I decided that the Second Law of Thermodynamics was less important to me than trying to write like Lawrence Durrell" (Groen C11).

After Cambridge, Dhondy attended Leicester University earning his M.A. (1969) in English and American literature. He had a special interest in Kipling, commenting, "This was the late 60s. I was very firmly part of that left-wing movement, but I wanted to bring to it some fresh ideas. One of these was that Kipling was not such a reactionary as people thought" (Robinson 15).

While in Leicester, he was recruited by the Indian Workers Association to organize their publications, cultural activities, and political and social events. In London he taught English at the Henry Thornton Comprehensive School, and became an activist in the East End, experiencing the tough conditions that influenced his *Come to Mecca* collection of stories. From 1974 to 1980 he was head of the English Department at Archbishop Ramsey's School, Lambeth, London.

Besides being a teacher, Dhondy has also been an active writer. From 1965 to 1984 he wrote about multicultural issues for such journals as the *Times Educational Supplement*, the *Guardian*, the *Listener*, and *Time Out*; he also wrote a weekly column and feature articles for several Indian journals. For the last fifteen years, Dhondy has published several books of fiction classified as "multicultural literature." Between 1974 and 1980 he was also involved in the *Race Today* Journal Collective writing pamphlets on subjects ranging from education to reggae music. In 1979 he began his career as a playwright, joining the Black Theatre Co-operative; five of his plays were produced at the Arts Theatre and at Cottesloe. In 1983, Central TV agreed to a Sunday multicultural magazine program, "Here and Now." Dhondy wrote the first drama series, consisting of six stories of British Asian life across different generations. Currently, Dhondy is commissioning editor for Multicultural Programmes at Channel 4 television. In 1985 Channel 4 broadcast Dhondy's own comedy series, "Tandoori Nights" (commissioned before Dhondy's appointment), a program about the rivalry between two Indian restaurants called the Jewel in the Crown and the Far Pavilion.

Dhondy is also in charge of the Black Current Affairs Programme at BBC. He feels he has pioneered a new kind of documentary from India, Africa, and the West Indies; he wants to educate the local Asian and British citizens about these countries: "What India was and is like, their parents' country" (Mathai 13). Dhondy adds, "I don't want to make tourism. I don't want to make apology. I don't want to make anthropology. I want to get some aspects of the real life" (Mathai 13).

MAJOR WORKS AND THEMES

Prabhu Guptara, in his book *Black British Literature*, clearly defines black British writers. He says, "Being 'black' is a matter of visibility, with social and political consequences. Being a writer is a matter of culture. Being 'British' is a matter, not of culture, but of what passport you carry" (14). Guptara defends this notion by citing the 1981 Nationality Act, which clarifies who is and who is not British. "No one can be British and not be entitled to hold a British passport; no one can hold a British passport and claim that he or she is not British" (15). In other words, Guptara claims "black Britons" are people of non-European origin who are entitled to hold a British passport and show some substantial commitment to Britain (e.g., they have lived a large part of their lives there).

Clearly, Guptara's definition is controversial; for example, Chinese immigrants holding British passports would resent being defined as "black Britons." Further, Guptara's critics argue that he is ignoring the cultural and psychological matrix from which these literary works grow. He points out, however, that these writers have been formed by a colonial matrix, one so strong, in fact, that they are drawn to Britain for financial reasons and are eager to enter the literary circles that will recognize the value of their work.

As a writer, Dhondy feels his task is one of self-criticism and deep examination—not simply self-congratulation. He adds, "The purpose of writing is to find out who you are, personally and collectively" (Groen C12). In the multiracial British society and in keeping with the diasporic consciousness, Dhondy sees his own role as a catalyst to help bring about assimilation of and understanding between varied and highly divergent groups and traditions (Mathai 11).

True to his own mission, Dhondy has written many short stories about multiethnic Britain. His audience in his earlier works is older adolescents. *East End at Your Feet* (1976) is a collection of six stories about London teenagers, Asian and white. *Come to Mecca* (1978) is another collection of subtle and witty short stories. In the title story, Bengali youths go on strike against a wage-cut; their cause is taken up by a radical white girl, Betty. The organizer of the strike, Shahid, falls in love with her. He discovers that he has misinterpreted her intentions; she sees him merely as a token of his race, not as an individual. With his usual economy, Dhondy makes it clear that Betty is as exploitative of Shahid as is his greedy employer. Dhondy's next work, *Siege of Babylon* (1978), is based on a true story about the Spaghetti House Siege: after a failed robbery, black youths hold four hostages and consider the political and personal alternatives open to them. In *Poona Company* (1980), about Dhondy's childhood in India, the reader enjoys the busy atmosphere of the Chowk, the Poona bazaar, and the eccentricity of the English public school that Dhondy attended. *Trip Trap* (1982) is another entertaining collection of short stories for teenagers and adults.

In 1980 Dhondy began writing plays, all produced in London. Most notable were "Romance, Romance" and "The Bride," published in 1985 and originally shown on BBC2. Dhondy received the Samuel Beckett Award in 1983 for "Romance, Romance," a play based on real-life characters. In the tradition of the diaspora, this playscript addresses the Asian experience in England. Using humor and acute observation, Dhondy explores multiethnic themes, the parent-child conflict, the quest for personal identity, and the balance between freedom and responsibility. More specifically, "Romance, Romance" falls into the category of what critic Tim Youngs calls an arranged marriage play. This genre usually portrays the brides as passive victims, but Dhondy creates his heroine, Satinder, as a powerful university student. Chaddha, her father—the Asian capitalist—wants her to marry conservative businessman Bunny Singh. She, of course, protests. In a conciliatory gesture, Chaddha invites Satinder to perform at his gala, and she discovers that Bunny Singh will be in the audience. She embarrasses her father by wearing a skimpy dress and flirting with the audience. Chaddha is angry, but Bunny recognizes talent when he sees it and offers her a movie deal rather than a proposal. Satinder's father finally softens, and the play ends with an "exploratory reconciliation." Dhondy again presents the diasporic idea of mixed cultures here: an Asian capitalist bound to old marriage traditions and, as Youngs notes, Chaddha's daughter, whose "source of independence is the white dominated institution in the shape of the university she attends" (15).

Dhondy's most ambitious work in the tradition of the diasporic consciousness is *Bombay Duck* (1990). In this novel we clearly see Dhondy's role as catalyst between varied and highly divergent groups and traditions. Working within different multiethnic frameworks, Dhondy again deals with the conflicts between men and women, the old and the young, white and black. For example, in exploring the conflict between men and women, Dhondy presents one traditional view about women: "Even if Othello was wrong about Desdemona when he killed her, he would have been right about her sooner or later, had he let her live" (193). Dhondy also explores generational tensions when he tells about two brothers who were thrown out of the house when they were teenagers. The woman their father married tried to convert one of the brothers, and he would send her postcards of the occult to make her believe he had turned devil worshipper. In addition, Dhondy shows his familiarity with the problem of racism in a multiethnic country. During an interview, Ali, the black protagonist in part one, is asked how he became an actor. We find out that Ali had been a bus conductor, and on one of his shifts, a man called him "nigger." Ali walked off the job. The next day his boss told him he should have asked for assistance. Ali replied, "Listen, man, I been calling for assistance for the past three hundred years. Nobody came" (41).

By using humorous and understated examples like these and by adding more serious plots, Dhondy explores various multicultural settings in *Bombay Duck*: the journeys, adventures, decisions, and consequences of the characters. Dhondy says that this novel is about "things not being what they seem" (Groen C12). Through his use of humor and his own acceptance of and experience with the multicultural setting, Dhondy seems to agree with Zoroaster: good and evil can coexist, equally balanced. This duality is a natural part of the multiethnic world; we all encounter different struggles, prejudices, and quests. But we find that the title "Bombay Duck" is a corrupted spelling of "Bombay Dak," which is dried, stinking fish. Dhondy comments on this title, "You ask for Bombay duck in a restaurant and what you get is filthy, stinking, dried fish. The book deals with cross-cultural misunderstandings" (Groen C12). At the end of the novel, Dhondy reiterates his theme:

The breezes float in from Africa, but there isn't the scent of a great continent upon them, or the lonely odour of the sly sea, there's only the corrupt smell of Bombay Duck drying on the sands, just a few hundred yards away (316).

CRITICAL RECEPTION

Two of Dhondy's works have been especially well received. *East End at Your Feet* l(1976) and *Come to Mecca* (1978), both collections of short stories, have each won the Children's Rights Workshop Other Award. The latter also won the Collins/Fontana Books for Multi-Ethnic Britain Competition and has been extremely popular and reprinted many times. The title story in *Come to Mecca* is typical of Dhondy in its range and economy. Critic Neil Philip feels Dhondy's message here is conveyed with "great subtlety and restraint" and "a refreshing humour" (287). In *Siege of Babylon*, Dhondy finds no reason to smile. Again Philip comments, "His depiction of the suppressed violence underlying the aimless, frustrated lives of his characters is entirely convincing. . . . In the end the only moral is that of all Dhondy's writing: 'Language is identity' " (1987). Finally, Philip calls these works "an accurate and incisive recorder of cafe and street life in multi-cultural Britain" (287). Philip goes on to say that Dhondy expresses racial differences without being strident or simplistic—he is completely unself-conscious. Dhondy has an acute ear for dialogue and lets the reader eavesdrop on the characters. Philip feels, however, that Dhondy's real strength is his gift for construction, "shaping his stories as a series of interrelated scenes rather than a steady progression to a climax" (287).

Philip notes that the teasing relationship Dhondy establishes with the reader in previous works degenerates into sterile formal games and narrative twists in *Trip Trap* (1982). Prabhu Guptara describes *Trip Trap* as gripping and well-told, but agrees with Philip that the book is flawed. Guptara feels *Trip Trap* presents a weakening of Dhondy's earlier ideologies—or, Guptara says, perhaps Dhondy seeks to go beyond them.

Philip observes that *Poona Company*, drawing on Dhondy's childhood experiences, is Dhondy's best book. It is intelligent and strictly disciplined. In a laconic style with vivid force, Dhondy lets the reader enjoy the Poona bazaar and feel the stiff parody of an English public school (287).

Concerning Dhondy's playscripts, Zia Mohyeddin, who has acted some of Dhondy's best characters, says that Dhondy brings "into play his experience as a social worker, community worker and teacher. His portrayals are exceedingly good, especially those in Brick Lane, which has been his habitat" (Robinson 115). Mohyeddin feels Dhondy's political ideas may interfere with his writing. "I think he believes very strongly in certain things—perhaps that justice can only be done if the conservatives of this world are not there. Sometimes he projects this commitment into 'low life,' as though truth lies solidly on their side" (Robinson 14–15). Andrew Robinson comments that Dhondy seems "to be split between a desire to write about Asians in Britain and Indians in India, but is acutely aware of the difficulties of continuing to do the latter, living in Britain" (15). Dhondy admits, however, that he knows little about the Indian peasantry, and guards against being "in the Indian sense, a behalfist" (Robinson 15).

Jeremy Isaacs, the chief executive of Channel 4, particularly admires Dhondy's short stories about Indian life. He feels Dhondy's variety of influences offers a strong foundation for Channel 4's commitment to multiculturalism. He says, "The great advantage of people like Farrukh is that he is a creator in his own right and doesn't think in categories" (Robinson 15). Isaacs continues to say that as a writer Dhondy is neither simplistic nor single-minded.

Dhondy, then, is a successful catalyst in helping to assimilate varied cultures. He participates fully when he produces multicultural material, trying to offer real-life characters and situations. He does not want simply to offer positive images; he wants to "get it right." He says, "What TV needs is good writers, not politically correct writers. You need the entire sorrow of the world, you need an observed comment on the human circus" (Groen C12).

BIBLIOGRAPHY

Works by Farrukh Dhondy

East End at Your Feet. London: Macmillan, 1976. (fiction)
Come to Mecca and Other Stories. London: Collins, 1978. (fiction)
Siege of Babylon. London: Macmillan, 1978. (fiction)
Maids the Mad Shooter. 1979. (television play)
Being Is Believing. 1980. (television play)
Mama Dragon. Produced in London, 1980. (play)
Poona Company. London: Gollancz, 1980. (fiction)
Shapesters. Produced in London, 1981. (play)
Kipling Sahib. Produced in London, 1982. (play)
Trip Trap. London: Gollancz, 1982. (fiction)
Trojans. Adaptation of a play by Euripides. Produced in London, 1982. (play)
Moves. Fortnightly commentary, 1982–83, 1983–84. (television play)
No Problem series. 1982–83, 1983–84. (television play)
The Bride. 1983. (television play)
Come to Mecca. 1983. (television play)
Dear Manju. 1983. (television play)
Good at Art. 1983. (television play)
Romance, Romance. 1983. (television play)

A Change for Darwin. 1984. (television play)
The Empress and the Munshi. 1984. (television play)
Munshi. Monologue for Indian actor. 1984. (television play)
Romance, Romance; and The Bride. London: Faber, 1985. (play)
Tandoori Nights series. 1985. (television play)
All the Fun of the Fair. With John McGrath and others. Produced in London, 1986.
    (play)
Film, Film, Film. Produced in London, 1986. (play)
King of the Ghetto. 1986. (television play)
To Turn a Blind Eye. 1986. (television play)
Vigilantes. Produced in London, 1985. London: Hobo, 1988. (play)
Bombay Duck. London: Cape, 1990. (fiction)

Studies of Farrukh Dhondy

Carpenter, Humphrey, and Mari Prichard. *The Oxford Companion to Children's
    Literature*. New York: Oxford University Press, 1984. 148.
East End at Your Feet. *Literary Review* 34 (Fall 1990): 52–61.
Groen, Rick. Interview with Farrukh Dhondy. "Rethinking 'Minority' TV." *Globe
    and Mail*, April 24, 1990: C11–12.
Guptara, Prabhu. *Black British Literature: An Annotated Bibliography*. Sydney:
    Dangaroo, 1986.
Mathai, Sujatha. Interview with Farrukh Dhondy. *Indian Pen* 48 (1987): 11–15.
Mohamed, Khalid. "We're No Angels." Interview with Farrukh Dhondy. *Sunday
    Times of India*, October 2, 1990: B9.
Philip, Neil. "Farrukh Dhondy." *Twentieth-Century Children's Literature*. Ed. Tracy
    Chevalier. Chicago: St. James Press, 1989. 286–87.
Philip, Neil. Review of *Poona Company*. *Literary Review* 25 (Winter 1981): 287.
Robinson, Andrew. "Boys from the Currystuff." Interview with Farrukh Dhondy.
    Sight and Sound 55 (Winter 1985–86): 14–18.
Review of *Vigilantes*. *Plays and Players* 378–31 (Mar. 1985): 33.
Youngs, Tim. "Morality and Ideology: The Arranged Marriage in Contemporary
    British-Asian Drama." *Wasafiri* 9 (Winter 1988–89): 3–6.

INDIRA GANESAN (1960–   )

Marilou Briggs Wright

BIOGRAPHY

Indira Ganesan's first novel, *The Journey*, was published by Alfred Knopf in 1990, when she was only twenty-nine years old. Ganesan was born on November 5, 1960, in Srirangam, Tamil Nadu, and moved with her family to the United States just in time to enter elementary school in Rockland County, New York, and to be shaped in part by a new culture. Her degree from Vassar College is in English, and she did graduate work at the Writer's Workshop at the University of Iowa. Since then, she has attended the MacDowell Colony and the Fine Arts Work Center in Provincetown, Massachusetts. But she remembers those first five years in India and subsequent returns, including one year of undergraduate work at Stella Maris College in Madras, India. In a telephone interview, she discussed the ways in which her imagination was formed by Hinduism and by the mythology of India. Although she writes for a general audience, Indira Ganesan identifies herself as a part of the immigrant tradition and as a woman of color writing in a culture not entirely her own. The writers she most admires, such as Toni Morrison, Zora Neale Hurston, and Maxine Hong Kingston, share aspects of Ganesan's double perspective of ethnicity and gender and, in addition, she believes, have "the gift for music in their words." She admires, too, the work of Salman Rushdie, Padma Perera, and Amitav Ghosh and appreciates the rhymed metered verse of Vikram Seth. Among writers with whom she has less obvious bases for identification, she feels particular affinity for the Jewish writers Isaac Singer and Philip Roth, "Perhaps," she says "because of their fierce devotion to religion or to their struggle with the questions of religion. Hinduism is in its way as stern as Judaism" (telephone interview with Marilou Wright, May 8, 1991).

MAJOR WORKS AND THEMES

Ganesan has chosen as protagonist for her first novel, *The Journey*, a young Indian woman who has been living in America for nine years. Nineteen-year-old Renu Krishnan, whose loss of a beloved "twin" cousin in India prompts her return to the country of her birth, finds no succor in either culture and is plunged into despair. *The Journey* is concerned with the disjuncture between the power and truths represented by Hinduism and the mythology of India on the one hand and, on the other hand, the less magical, less religious, and perhaps more sterile life associated with America and propounded by Renu's father. Neither culture has the power to rescue Renu from her generalized angst and confusion as she grieves for her dead cousin, Rajesh. She suffers and cannot be comforted. Throughout the novel Renu moves passively through her depression, away from the life-giving choices offered her either by continuing in the midst of her warm, extended Indian family or returning to a more solitary life in America. Instead of doing either, she chooses the lassitude and probable death implied in the ambiguous ending of *The Journey*.

Renu Krishnan is Indian by birth but, with her academic parents and younger sister, Meenakshi (Americanized to "Manx"), moves to America and uncomfortably accommodates herself to the life of an American schoolgirl. Her earliest memories are of India and of visits to Grandfather Das's home, Nirmila Nivasam. And through the years it was there that she was periodically reunited with her "twin" male cousin, Rajesh. Renu's mother, Rukmani, and Rajesh's mother, Chitra, sisters, discovered that they had conceived on the same day, and they delivered their babies, simultaneously, while holding each other's hands. Renu and Rajesh, therefore, have a special bond: he is confident, protective, funny, and wise; even separated by an ocean, Renu feels more secure in a world inhabited by Rajesh.

The imaginative power of myth figures strongly in Renu's early consciousness. The summer Renu and Rajesh turn ten, they accidentally shoot a monkey in the garden of Nirmila Nivasam. They are convinced that they have killed an emissary of the gods—perhaps even Hanuman, the god itself— and that there will be a price exacted. Although these are the fears of ten-year-olds, the sense that she owes the gods for her transgression stays with Renu over the years: "whenever she slipped into the American way of life, when she stopped wearing the red tikka on her forehead, when she stopped going to temple, she could not free herself of the idea that the gods were still hunting her, that they were waiting to seek retribution" (14).

And now as the novel opens, the worst has happened. Rajesh has been killed. Word has reached the Krishnans in America that the train on which he was riding from Madhupur to Choimbatore has slipped from the tracks on an unsteady rainswept bridge and fallen into the waters below. The first sentence of the novel prepares us for the ambiguous ending by suggesting that a fearful symmetry is in control: "The women of her mother's village say that if one twin dies by water, the other will die by fire" (1). Renu's mother and aunts fear for her: "Rukmani knew that the gods were greedy, and if they were due two, they would not rest easy with one" (31).

This is not the first death Renu has experienced. Her father died when Renu was fifteen—four years before the novel begins. It was he who had chosen this new American culture for them, and so the family expected that the widowed Rukmani would immediately return to her native island of Pi to raise the daughters. Perhaps out of respect for her husband's wishes, Rukmani remains in America, but their lives change: they gradually abandon the Western ways that he had encouraged them to adopt and begin to follow the customs of the old country.

Rukmani and her daughters must return to the island of Pi for Rajesh's cremation. Even though the cremation has been completed before they arrive, they stay on to mourn with the family. At Nirmila Nivasam Rukmani immediately begins to throw off the last vestiges of her uneasy assimilation into American culture and comes home to her own.

Rajesh's death affects Renu beyond reason. She grows increasingly introverted, anxious, and frightened. In America she had lain awake at night thinking of spiders and snakes and of villains climbing the fire escape; here at Nirmila Nivasam she dreams of three giantesses who gather near her bed, place stones in their mouths, and swallow. She becomes obsessive, washing her clothes daily, but "nothing she did could get rid of that smell of death" (24). Finally on the feast day, thirteen days after Rajesh's death, Renu goes deep into the garden to scream and scream and then to collapse. During her physical recuperation she becomes increasingly withdrawn and addicted to melancholy. She is, one might reason, suffering from the guilt survivors feel and from a wholly natural sense of loss of this cousin-closer-than-brother; but she may also assume that her own death draws close. Renu is exiled from the America that was never entirely hers, bewildered by the India of her mother, and bereft of the cousin who had helped her make sense of the two worlds.

After her father's death, Renu had turned inward to her family, inventing excuses in high school and later in commuter college to avoid the socializing of young people. Now with Rajesh's death, the turn is more inward still, shutting out the fluttering hands and whispered concerns of her mother and aunts. Rukmani's solution to force Renu out of her melancholy is to find her a husband, and Renu does not resist. Renu, assuming that she might die soon, is resigned to such matrimonial plans.

The fifteen-year-old Manx approaches relationships with men much more aggressively. Partly from boredom, partly because she misses all things American, Manx makes friends with Freddie Flat, an itinerant American hippie, who is in love with all things Indian. The balding, benign Freddie seems harmless, and so Manx and Renu are permitted unusual freedom to spend time with him. It is at Freddie's apartment that Renu relates the story of their Spanish Aunt Alphonsa, with whom she feels an emotional bond. The first of the three sections of *The Journey* ends with the story of Alphonsa and of the journey of Rukmani's brother, Adda Krishnamurthi. Adda had set out many years ago with two purposes: to find hair ointment that would stop his fair from falling out and to go to Europe to discover the root of his island's problem. "He wanted to know why a man would leave Europe to enslave another country" (61). Adda finds himself in Spain in love with Alphonsa, the brilliant mathematician daughter of a friend he has made on his journey. They get married. Ironically, Alphonsa and Adda are forced to return to Pi because, Alphonsa's father explains, "You can't marry here. No citizen would rest knowing a brown man sweeps a white woman into his arms at night" (65). But Adda's family has its own biases. Alphonsa is not Indian and not made welcome at Nirmila Nivasam. Adda's sisters shun her, and she grows quiet and withdrawn, speaking only to her husband and his best friend and co-revolutionary, Amir. Finally, Alphonsa goes away to a Catholic retreat in the hills and inexplicably dies there.

Although Pi is an admittedly imaginary island floating in the Bay of Bengal and named for Prospero's Island in *The Tempest*, Adda and Amir participate in the real political struggles of the twentieth century and in the independence movement. The second section of the three-part structure begins with a broadly comic description of "Highway Amir," Adda's best friend. Amir, the founder of the Free Island Party, concocts plots that never quite come off and is left in the dust of history when moderates gain control of Pi after India's independence.

Now subdued and middle-aged, Amir is a master carver of umbrella handles in the town of Cosu. The handle carvings (including a special group of erotica) absorb some of Amir's creative urges, and his political urges are fulfilled by trying to indoctrinate his foundling son Kish who came to him at ten years old. Nine years after appearing on Amir's doorstep, Kish leaves Cosu. He has been a fine student, but on the night before the scholarship examination, he leaves Amir a note saying that he is going to look for an oil that will help hair grow. The same magic oil that Adda sought now draws Kish away from Amir. When Kish goes to Madhupur, he lands in jail and sends for Amir's friend, Adda, to bail him out. Adda takes him to Nirmila Nivasam where the nineteen-year-old Kish makes friends with Renu and Manx.

After becoming comfortable with the family, Kish proposes that he and Freddie, Renu, and Manx go on a journey to Trippi, a town on Pi famous for magicians and psychics. On the trip Renu begins "seeing" Rajesh. When they arrive in Trippi, Renu again has a vision of Rajesh. The travelers visit Marya the Seer, to whom Renu confesses, "I see the dead." Renu's mood blackens in Trippi, and she fears there will be no relief. Kish leads the group to Cosu. On the way they see a remarkable demonstration of hair-growth oil, Vitagrowth. They buy it, but it is a sham and does not work on Freddie's balding head. The journey is a failure. Marya the Seer has no answers to Renu's existential questions and Vitagrowth is just so much snake oil.

At Cosu Amir entertains the young people with stories of himself and Adda as boys, but he does not tell of the events that drove them apart and drove Alphonsa to a convent. It is Amir's henchman, Konga, who tells Renu that Amir was in love with the "Spanish slut" Alphonsa. She went to the convent, he says, to conceal her pregnancy. After she left, Amir behaved wildly, even for a revolutionary, trying to get himself killed, but he only managed to land in jail, and Adda bailed him our. Before Alphonsa committed suicide, she told Konga that Adda was her baby's father, but she wanted Amir to have the child. Kish is Renu's cousin.

Now Renu bears the burden of truth. The secrets of identity and parentage seem to her profound. She yearns for Rajesh to help her decide what to do. When she walks on the beach in solitude, she is drawn to the light of an oil drum, probably left there by a hot chestnut seller. "Sati" she thinks and sees Rajesh seated in the fire. "The fire called," and "she embraced the warm metal of the drum" (158). Then in succession the three giantesses, Marya the Seer, Mirazi Light of the World, and Alphonsa appear and pull stones from their pockets.

As the third and final section of the novel opens, Renu finally tells Kish about his parentage and is surprised that he has already guessed and doesn't particularly care. What has seemed so important to Renu is barely of interest to Kish, and Renu grows more troubled, more confused. What is important, what is true, what matters? Freddie explains that life is not like mathematics, that life is devoid of logic. But Freddie's credentials as a philosopher are somewhat suspect. After being failed by the Maharishi and the Beatles, Freddie now follows about an exotic woman born of Indian parents in Brooklyn, whom he calls "Mirazi, Light of the World." He hopes only for a glimpse of her now and then. When Renu questions his pursuit as a reason for being, Freddie explains that sooner or later everyone has "to create an absolute" (168).

Renu needs to act, even if there are no givens, and her decision is to return to America in spite of the fact that Rukmani will stay with her family on Pi. Rukmani and her sister go off to the festival marking the opening of a rickety new bridge to India, but Renu does not join them. Instead, she returns to the beach and to the fire. Renu feels that the stone-swallowing women from her dreams are beckoning her on. The authorial voice states, "[W]e have been told that it is important and correct to feel the earth beneath, even while flight is in our hearts. Weightless travel, metaphorical soul soaring, a shedding of swallowed stones, a mobility that can hold the keys of the universe" (173–74). The final sentence of the novel, "Renu Krishnan stood on the beach on the island of Pi, ready for her journey," suggests that Renu, standing by the fire, will fulfill the prediction of that first sentence of the book, "The women of her mother's village say that if one twin dies by water, the other will die by fire."

That symmetry of *The Journey* seems facile and is not the strongest part of this novel. The magic world of Pi created by Ganesan is never without ties to the real world, and the novel must "work" in both worlds. In the real world, Renu is a young woman coping with clinical depression, but the cause, her relationship with Rajesh, is not adequately developed. Marya the Seer asks Renu why she is preoccupied with death. Renu cannot explain. The reader assumes that Renu grieves for a presence that was part of herself, her twin who remained in India and who bridges the space between. Renu, never completely a part of America and now disconnected from her Indian family, faced with an arranged marriage, confused by the strange mixtures of Aunt Bala's superstition and her father's insistence on a world based on rational principles, seeks givens. Freddie, the ersatz philosopher, tells her that the only givens are life and death. When life is not all that attractive and when Rajesh is gone, the ending of the book seems to imply that Renu chooses death. It is, of course, possible to read the final pages of the book in a life-affirming way—that Renu is preparing for a return to America and rejecting the escape and metaphorical flight offered by the burning oil drum and Sati. But death is attractive, too. There is, after all, Vishnu's Dream.

The facts of the plot seem tired and grim—another adolescent suicide based on the uncertainty of the world and a personal loss. But this novel is much more, and the portentousness of the plot is relieved by bright comic touches. Some of the ironic juxtapositions are jarring. Renu Krishnan's internal journey through a serious mental illness is toward a "given," and the travel the young people undertake to Trippi for enlightenment is a quest for hair growth oil. These characters undertake a difficult journey, preferably for the ultimate, sacred key to truth, but, failing that, for any old profane key at all.

One of the reasons that Indira Ganesan chose to set her novel on the island of Pi is, she says, "I had to create an island where my rules would apply" (telephone interview with Marilou Wright, May 8, 1991). She had thought of Shakespeare's *The Tempest* and the notion of characters who go to an island and are transformed. The travels of Renu both to India and then on the internal journey to Trippi are transforming. "Travel," according to Ganesan, "has consequences. It is a significant kind of education. Since most cultures restrict the mobility of women, they are deprived of this special kind of education" (telephone interview). The fact that Renu's journeys across the ocean and within the island of Pi have no good consequences for her makes them no less transforming.

What makes *The Journey* worth the trip is Ganesan's wonderful grace with language. The prose is rich and nuanced. Ganesan often achieves the music she so admires in others. She moves easily, if sometimes abruptly, between sensitive descriptions of Renu's wretchedness and parodic descriptions of Amir's quixotic adventures. She manages to make the romance between Alphonsa and Adda at once both tragic and absurd. Her touch is always deft and her humor gentle. Contrary to Grandfather Das's prediction that the island of Pi is sinking, and despite the fact that the new bridge seems a rickety disaster waiting to happen, this Pi does not sink and, in fact, is the setting of Ganesan's next novel, her as yet untitled work in progress.

CRITICAL RECEPTION

The Journey has been the subject of several brief but favorable reviews. Mark Dery, for example, in the *New York Times Book Review*, praises Ganesan's image-making and the "wry sense of humor that prevents her story from collapsing under its own weight" (26). Polly Shulman writes in the *Village Voice* that Ganesan "treats her characters'... spiritual antics with a sense of humor, saving the book from solemnity. The world she creates is plausibly, and increasingly fabulist" (73). The *New Yorker* review comments: "The book occasionally has the haphazard feel of a first novel, but Ms. Ganesan... writes nimble prose that promises good things to come" (108). *Publishers Weekly* qualifies its praise somewhat: "While the charm of the writing and observations about East and West engage the reader, Renu's story drifts into an arbitrary half-resolution" (52).

BIBLIOGRAPHY

Works by Indira Ganesan

The Journey. New York: Alfred A. Knopf, 1990.
"The Wedding" (short story). *Seventeen* 48 (Feb. 1989): 110–11.

Studies of Indira Ganesan

Review of *The Journey. Booklist* 86 (May 15, 1990): 1778.
Review of *The Journey. Los Angeles Times Book Review* (July 8, 1990): 3.
Review of *The Journey. New Yorker* 66 (Sept. 1990): 108.
Review of *The Journey. Publishers Weekly* 237 (April 27, 1990): 52.
Dery, Mark. Review of *The Journey. New York Times Book Review* 95 (Sept. 1990): 26.
Shulman, Polly. Review of *The Journey. Village Voice* 35 (July 13, 1990): 73.

SUDHIN N. GHOSE (1899–1965)
C. Vijayasree

BIOGRAPHY

Sudhin Ghose was born on July 30, 1899, at Burdwan, a small town in West Bengal, India. As the only son of Sir Bipin Bihari, a judge of the Calcutta High Court, he had all the advantages of growing up in a cultured Bengali family: secure childhood, good education, firm roots in tradition, the heritage of a rich family library, and an academic bent of mind. After graduating in science from the University of Calcutta, he went to Europe for higher studies. He took his Litt.D. from the University of Strasbourg. Journalism was one of his favorite hobbies, and he published a number of articles in magazines such as the *Aryan Path*, *The Envoy*, and *The Observer*. Ghose took a series of newspaper jobs even while he was a research scholar: he was the foreign correspondent for *The Hindu* in Geneva and Switzerland from 1923 to 1931, and associate editor of *World's Youth* for about three years. Ghose's various professional appointments kept him out of India for more than twenty-five years. He was on the staff of the Information Section of the League of Nations Secretariat at Geneva for nine years. Later he moved to England where he lectured at various institutes for adult education. This long exile did not alienate him from the culture in which he was born. Ghose's work reveals his profound knowledge of Indian epics, legends, myth, and philosophy and his deep reverence for the Indian tradition. He returned to India briefly when he worked as a visiting professor at Visvabharathi University. This homecoming was not a particularly pleasant experience for him since he got entangled in a clash with students. He went back to England and died of a heart attack in 1965.

His long and successful association with editorial work must have prompted Ghose to try his hand at creative writing. His first published work, titled *Colours of a Great City*, made little impact. His career as a creative writer actually began with the publication of his first novel, *And*

Gazelles Leaping, in 1949, by which time he was already fifty. He published three more novels in quick succession: *Cradle of the Clouds* (1951), *The Vermilion Boat* (1953), and *The Flame of the Forest* (1955), and found for himself a secure place among the Indian novelists in English.

The first thing that strikes the reader of Ghose is the pictorial illustrations found in his works. Several white-on-black drawings are provided to illustrate certain key incidents of the story. The reader then discovers that he/she is reading a peculiar novel where logical and chronological progression is deliberately dispensed with; the central character is nameless; all the other characters too are a mere crowd of humanity; the setting is panoramic, covering human, divine, and animal realms; and the narration continually oscillates between reality and fantasy. The immediate impact of this, undoubtedly, is bewilderment. A serious reader, however, would soon realize that this confusion demolishes the conventional patterns in and responses to fiction writing and reading and suggests possibilities of new modes of approaching fiction and reality contained therein.

MAJOR WORKS AND THEMES

The four novels of Ghose can be read as one long epic unfolding the protagonist's quest for self-realization. Nowhere is it mentioned that these novels form a tetralogy, but the presence of a common central character knits them together. The events described cover over twenty years of his life. The first novel, *And Gazelles Leaping*, recounts the childhood days of the protagonist spent in the idyllic retreat of Mr. Svenska's kindergarten on the outskirts of Calcutta among a set of happy friends and their helpful pets. Through a series of intense emotional experiences the boy learns that freedom from fear is the first step toward happiness. His education culminates in his apprehension of the power of beauty; Ghose makes the mythical character, Urvashi, the celestial danseuse, the symbol of sublime beauty. The novel ends with the protagonist's realization that the quest for Urvashi, the search for beauty, "is the main purpose of human life" (*And Gazelles Leaping*, 226).

In *Cradle of the Clouds* the protagonist, an adolescent by now, comes under the influence of the village punditji and the schoolmaster and is constantly torn between the forces of tradition and modernity. The ritual of the plowing ceremony, or *halakarshana*, provides the context for the resolution of the protagonist's conflict. On this occasion, the women in drought-stricken areas go in a procession naked, drawing the plow and praying for rain. Such an act of self-sacrifice, the villagers believe, shall appease gods. The protagonist is chosen to lead this sacred procession as a representative of Balaram, the mythical farmer king. While the boy discharges his duty with unswerving devotion, the master mars the atmosphere of worship by slinging insults at the women participating in the ritual. The boy chastizes the master with a staff. Evil punished thus, rain pours down vindicating the faith. The protagonist realizes that there is a greater truth and wisdom than what education can give. He moves out in search of the cradle of clouds, "the symbolic seat of sapience" (*Cradle of the Clouds*, 304).

The scenario shifts to Calcutta in the last two novels, *The Vermilion Boat* and *The Flame of the Forest*. The protagonist here is like Stephen Dedalus stepping into the world of experience. The central symbol in the former is the vermilion boat. It is a toy boat the protagonist gets as a gift in his childhood. The first time he sets it to sail in the sandalwood tank, he encounters a dangerous experience: he is caught by the venomous water snakes. This signifies the hazards associated with the launching of the vermilion boat. Later on, he sails a vermilion boat to release his pet porpoise into water as a part of the ritual organized in honor of Manasa, the goddess of wisdom. The boat breaks up in the storm, but his pet, Sisi Magar, brings him back to the shore. He is delivered into the hands of Roma, his Anglo-Indian girlfriend, in whose love he finds release. This magic rescue reaffirms the benevolence of the goddess Manasa. Manasa is the active feminine principle, and in her worship holiness and joyousness are inseparably blended. The vermilion boat becomes the protagonist's instrument to apprehend this philosophy of love. He now understands the import of the Upanishadic saying: "Even things you do after the flesh are spiritual."

In *The Flame of the Forest* Balaram moves a step forward in his spiritual journey when he finds a guru in Myna the *Kirtani* (one who seeks love's consecration through song and dance). Fleeing from the evil, corruption, and hatred of the adult world around, Balaram joins Myna on her pilgrimage to the Himalayas. This retreat, as the novel clearly suggests, is a part of his preparation to return to life with a greater inner strength. The protagonist's quest in Ghose's tetralogy reflects the eternal spiritual pilgrimage of all mankind, though in its nature and direction it is authentically Indian. The quest doesn't end in self-realization, but it closes with the discovery of a guru, or spiritual mentor. However, in Ghose's work the metaphysical moorings remain the substratum while the superstructure contains elements as varied as gross absurdity and stock realism, allegory and tautology, reason and unreason, logic and fantasy, thought and dream.

Ghose was one of the earliest Indian novelists in English to experiment with the fictional form. He draws models from the indigenous narrative paradigms. His novels bear close structural resemblances to the fable literature of India as exemplified in Sanskrit prose works like *Panchatantra* and *Hitopadesa*: there is one primary story or frame tale that encloses several boxed tales forming what is popularly known as "a chinese nest of stories." As in the *Panchatantra* stories, the human and the animal realms merge in Ghose's work; characters are archetypal, the work offers an allegorical interpretation of experience and the stories are didactic while being delightfully entertaining.

Another important aspect of Ghose's art is his creative use of myths. In fact, his mode of perception itself is mythical. Often in Ghose, contemporary reality falls in perspective in terms of some ancient myth. For instance, in *Cradle of the Clouds* the myth behind the plowing ceremony becomes the informing structural principle in the story. In *The Vermilion Boat*, the myth of Manasa dramatizes an ontological viewpoint and projects the feminine principle as an active agent of self-transformation. In *The Flame of the Forest* the myth of Nahusha provides the parallel for the devious exploits of the corrupt politician Ek Number. Thus myth becomes Ghose's primary instrument to negotiate reality and perceive the meaning of existence.

Ghose's style of storytelling is digressional. His narrator often leaves the thread of narration to recall some incident from his recent past, to narrate the legendary history of some place, to relate some mythological story, to recount an interesting anecdote, or to recite a song he heard some time ago. This deliberate fragmentation of the spatio-temporal structure places his novels in the Indian *Puranic* tradition rather than in the Western genre of autobiography. The many *upkathas*, or subsidiary stories, introduced into the basic story line release the reader from a time-space stasis into a mythical continuum.

The similarity with the *puranas* is not confined to Ghose's technique alone, but extends to his vision of life as well. The fundamental narrative paradigm of any culture is a product of its ontology. In the Hindu ontological view, the world is marked by a basic tension between the empirically real and pluralistic existence and the spiritually true and unified consciousness. The human experience, therefore, cannot be analyzed in terms of binary oppositions but must be viewed as essentially paradoxical. The Indian *purana* incidentally means "old yet new" and suggests the capacity of this form to contain contradictions. Ghose, using the Indian narrative modes, communicates a world view that is authentically Indian. Despite his physical separation from India, he remains firmly grounded in Indian ethos.

CRITICAL RECEPTION

Sudhin Ghose's work has not received the critical attention it deserves. Srinivas Iyengar in his pioneering work, *Indian Writing in English*, describes Ghose's work as "fantasy with an undercurrent of serious intention" (481). But this undercurrent seems to have missed the attention of later critics. Ghose's works were either placed in the category of "biography" or dismissed as "fantasy tales." David McCutchion is one of the earliest critics to have devoted some attention to Ghose. He has a whole chapter on Sudhin Ghose in his survey, *Indian Writing in English*. Most of it is a fond recollection of his own personal association with the novelist. Here McCutchion concludes: "His [Ghose's] mind could not keep a clear hold on reality, and all is distorted and overwrought by his runaway imagination" (113). If Ghose's work is judged by the criteria employed in appraising works of documentary realism, his imagination is sure to appear "bizarre." Fantasy here, in fact, is a device used by the novelist to view reality from an unconventional perspective. Meenakshi Mukherjee, in her article "The Tractor and the Plough," offers a perceptive analysis of Ghose's work highlighting the mythical patterns in these novels. Ghose's creative use of myth has impressed critics and other creative writers too. Anita Desai describes Sudhin Ghose's quartet as "a charming attempt to clothe the Indian myth and legends in the modern dress lent it by the English Language" (68). Shyamala Narayan's *Sudhin Ghose*, published in 1973, is the only full-length study of Ghose to date. It offers a comprehensive account of Ghose's themes and techniques.

Ghose may not be a major writer in terms of prolificity of output or extent of readership. But he is undoubtedly an important writer as one of the earliest experimentalists in Indian fiction and hence as a precursor of the new generation of Indian novelists writing today, such as Salman Rushdie, Vikram Seth, and Amitav Ghosh.

BIBLIOGRAPHY

Works by Sudhin Ghose

The Colours of a Great City: Two Playlets ("The Defaulters" and "And Pippa Dances"). London: C. W. Daniel, 1924.

Rossetti and Contemporary Criticism. London: Bowes, 1928.

Post-War Europe: 1918–1937. University Extension Lecture. Calcutta: University of Calcutta, 1939.

And Gazelles Leaping. London: Michael Joseph, 1948: New York: Macmillan, 1953.

Cradle of the Clouds. London: Michael Joseph, 1951: New York: Macmillan, 1953.

The Vermilion Boat. London: Michael Joseph, 1953; New York: Macmillan, 1955.

The Flame of the Forest. London: Michael Joseph, 1955; New York: Macmillan, 1955.

Folk Tales and Fairy Stories from India. London: Golden Cockerel Press, 1961; New York: A. S. Barnes, 1964.

Folk Tales and Fairy Stories from Farther India. London: Thomas Yoseloff, 1966; New York: A. S. Barnes, 1966.

Studies of Sudhin Ghose

Bey, Hamdi. "A Look at Indo-Anglian Fiction." *Thought* 20:52 (Dec. 13, 1969): 18–19.

Ghoshal, Hiranmony. "An Indian Tetralogy: Four Novels of Sudhin Ghose." *Books Abroad* 30 (1956): 284–86.

Iyengar, K. R. Srinivas. *Indian Writing in English*. Bombay: Asia Publishing House, 1962.

McCutchion, David. *Indian Writing in English: Critical Essays*. Calcutta: Writers Workshop, 1969.

Mukherjee, Meenakshi. "The Tractor and the Plough: The Contrasted Visions of Sudhin Ghose and Mulk Raj Anand." *Indian Literature* 31:1 (1970): 88–101.

Narayan, A. Shyamala. "Reality and Fantasy in the Novels of Sudhin Ghose." *Aspects of Indian Writing in English*. Ed. M. K. Naik. New Delhi: Macmillan, 1979: 162–71.

———. *Sudhin N. Ghose*. New Delhi: Arnold Heinemann India, 1973.

———. "Sudhin Ghose." *Perspectives on Indian Fiction in English*. Ed. M. K. Naik. New Delhi: Abhinav Publications, 1986: 93–103.

ZULFIKAR GHOSE (1935–   )
Chelva Kanaganayakam

BIOGRAPHY

Zulfikar Ghose was born on March 13, 1935, in Sialkot (a city in East Punjab, which became part of West Pakistan after the partition of India in 1947), and he spent his first seven years in the midst of an extended family, in relatively prosperous circumstances. Ghose remembers the city as one untouched by modernization and its people as a rural and organic community. In 1942 Ghose moved with his family to Bombay, a vast, metropolitan, and predominantly Hindu city, and for the next ten years was to live in this city that instilled in him a strong sense of belonging and, as a Muslim among Hindus, an equally strong sense of being an outsider. These ten years coincided with the last years of the British Raj, and Ghose witnessed the growing animosity between the Hindus and Muslims. Commenting on the violence of the years preceding the partition, Ghose observes that "lorries, collecting dead bodies, would pass by the streets as though they were collecting garbage cans" (*Confessions*, 31).

In 1952, Ghose left Bombay and sailed to England. For him this meant a double exile, the predicament of departing from a land in which he was an outsider and emigrating to one in which he was an alien. The next seventeen years—from 1952 to 1969—were spent in England. He studied at Sloane School, Chelsea, and graduated from the University of Keele in 1959. During his final year as an undergraduate he edited an anthology called *Universities' Poetry*. He then worked as a reporter for the *Observer* and wrote reviews for the *Western Daily Press*, the *Guardian*, and the *Times Literary Supplement*. From 1964 to 1969 he worked as a teacher at a secondary school in Ealing. During these years one of his closest friends was the British writer B. S. Johnson, with whom he collaborated on a book of short stories entitled *Statement against Corpses*. He also brought out two collections of poems, *The Loss of India* (1964) and *Jets from Orange* (1967), and two novels, *The Contradictions* (1966) and *The Murder of Aziz Khan* (1967).

In 1969 he moved to Texas to take up a teaching appointment at the University of Texas, and for the last twenty-two years he and his wife, Helena de la Fontaine, have lived in Austin, Texas. During these years he has published eight novels, two volumes of poetry, two critical works, and several uncollected essays, short stories, and poems.

MAJOR WORKS AND THEMES

In a recent essay that appeared in the *Toronto South Asian Review* Zulfikar Ghose describes the exhilaration of visiting Pakistan after twenty-eight years. That the essay is entitled "Going Home" is not without a measure of significance, for it points to the ironies and ambiguities that one constantly encounters in Ghose's writing. Although in recent years, Ghose has often been described as a Pakistani writer by critics, one remembers that the Sialkot in which Ghose was born was then a part of India as was the Bombay in which he grew up. To make this assertion is not to engage in a futile debate about where Ghose belongs so much as to point out that the notion of "home," dependent on historical circumstance, the experience of colonialism, and the vicissitudes of nationalism, is essentially problematic in relation to "native-alien" writers like Ghose. The space it occupies eludes easy definition and remains obsessive, for it goes beyond landscape to become emblematic of a larger preoccupation with notions of self and identity.

In the same essay, Ghose speaks of his ongoing quest and his feeling of contentment in the landscape of Pakistan. He claims that "there are moments in our lives when we can hear the soul whisper its contentment that the long torment of being has been stilled as last" ("Going Home" 15), and that is achieved in Taxila. The sense of oneness derives, however, not from what is perceived so much as what lies below the surface and requires the participation of the imagination for completion. At the Peshawar museum, looking at the austere and incomplete statue of the fasting Buddha, the writer has intimations of completeness and wholeness. Says Ghose, "Reality can be composed of absent things, the unseen blazes in our minds with a shocking vividness" ("Going Home" 15).

The merging of the metonymic and the metaphoric, the referential and the fictive, constitutes a part of the complexity that characterizes Ghose's writing and makes him one of the most accomplished and experimental of contemporary postcolonial writers. Ghose's constant experiments with form and language, his movement from the mimesis of his early works to the magic realism of his more recent novels, and his refusal to be circumscribed by traditional taxonomies need to be seen as an ongoing preoccupation with the limitations of language and with the predicament of living on the margins.

While it is profitable to see Ghose in relation to experimental and counterrealistic writers like G. V. Desani and Salman Rushdie, one also needs to be aware of crucial differences that distinguish Ghose from the rest. While Rushdie is consistently nonrealistic, his fiction constantly alludes to political and social realities that, because they are identifiable as Indian or Pakistani, provide a sense of reference. Ghose's writing, for the most part, jettisons such signposting and moves away from the subcontinent to London, Brazil, Texas, and South America; the mimetic is often made problematic by the narrative modes, which range from stream-of-consciousness to picaresque, metafiction, and fantasy. Continuities thus become more difficult to detect, and Ghose succeeds in subverting the expectations of the readers by projecting fictive worlds that assert the predicament of "liminality" (Homi Bhabha's term) without being trapped in essentialisms.

In some respects, his early works, which include the collection of poems entitled *The Loss of India*, the collection of short stories (written together with B. S. Johnson) called *Statement against Corpses*, and the two novels *The Contradictions* and *The Murder of Aziz Khan* are the most easily identifiable as Indo-Pakistani writing. Issues of history, colonialism, identity, and language find expression through mimetic forms. *The Murder of Aziz Khan*, for instance, is a particularly impressive work that combines the formal demands of the realistic mode with a complex internal structure that enables the author to explore the experience of exile against a verifiable backdrop. Its realism and its sequentiality are its strength and weakness, for while the novel provides a strong sense of verisimilitude, it also remains predictable, formulaic, and conventional. In fact the constant interruptions, the flashbacks, the repetitions and shifts of perspective that one perceives in *The Murder of Aziz Khan* point to an awareness of the dangers inherent in a form that, in the process of implying a particular ontology, limits the portrayal of the postcolonial experience. This phase teaches the author the value of sequentiality, and of creating a strikingly referential surface, but it also alerts him to the limitations of the mode.

It is thus hardly surprising that his next work, *Crump's Terms* (completed in 1968 and published in 1975), moves away from the mimesis of his early phase to a form of stream of consciousness in order to explore the lives of Crump, a disillusioned and lonely teacher in London, and his ex-wife, Frieda. The locale is London and Europe, the context is the 1960s, the central character is British, and the form, with its constant repetitions, disruption of linearity, and dense layer of intertextual references, is a variant of stream of consciousness. Both Crump and Frieda are marginalized figures, the former, as the title of the novel implies, with a craving to impose order in his classroom and in his life, and the latter, having left Germany to avoid persecution, seeking to allay the despondency of homelessness. Thematic continuities persist while the form is more experimental. Free from the realism of the earlier work, this novel succeeds in asserting alienation as a state of mind. Ghose thought of the novel as an important achievement, one that suggested a direction he ought to be taking, but given the lukewarm reception given to the novel by readers, it is not surprising that he wrote his next work, the Brazilian trilogy, in a manner in which a nonrealistic, picaresque mode coexists with metonymic underpinning.

The Brazilian trilogy chronicles three centuries of Brazilian history, told by a reincarnated protagonist, whose tales record the story of exploitation, suppression, and colonial hegemony. The picaresque mode suits the historical narrative, and if read quickly, the three novels suggest a regression to the mode of *The Murder of Aziz Khan*. However, the carefully placed fabulosity and the metafictional comments alert the reader to the texture of the work, and the trilogy becomes both a retelling of history and a fictive construct. One of the major challenges of the trilogy is the elusiveness, its propensity to frustrate the reader's attempts to provide a convenient taxonomy that permits explication. The novels are very much in the tradition of modern picaresque in their fusion of verisimilitude and fabulosity, and the combination enables the author to deal with historical issues while constantly warning the reader of the status of history as a fictive construct. In some respects the trilogy is a colonial work written from a postcolonial perspective, and the complex narrative mode enables the author to preserve an admirable objectivity.

With the next collection of poems, *The Violent West* (1972), and his next novel, *Hulme's Investigations into the Bogart Script* (1981), Ghose moves into yet another phase, one that is less preoccupied with form and more with language. The issue of language and its complex relation to reality becomes the rationale for both the novel and his critical work *Hamlet, Prufrock and Language*. The novel, with its collection of nine scripts, can hardly be summarized, for apart from the names of characters, it provides very little basis for unity. The historical context is the United States, particularly the Southwest, but to foreground place would be to distort the effect of the novel. Essentially postmodern in its techniques, the novel is more important for its speculations on language, reality, and fiction than for its exploration of the native-alien experience.

The most recent phase includes one collection of poems entitled *A Memory of Asia* (1984) and three novels, *A New History of Torments* (1982), *Don Bueno* (1983), and *Figures of Enchantment* (1986). The novels are ostensibly set in Latin America, and appropriately enough they employ the magic realistic mode. Here the art is as much linear and causal as it is cyclical and mythical. The novels provide the illusion of referentiality while eschewing a recognizable underpinning of historical circumstance. Despite the portrayal of characters who have no ostensible relation to India or Pakistan, and despite the indeterminacy of historical circumstance, the novels are hardly solipsistic. By creating a structure in which the referential is both foregrounded and subverted, the author exploits the sense of immediacy that comes from recognition while forcing the reader to perceive complex synchronic structures. Issues of power, guilt, gender, nation, and history are thus explored in a manner that avoids both the snares of essentialism and the temptations of obscurity.

One of the most fascinating aspects of Ghose's writing is its open-endedness, its unceasing attempt to match form and language with content. His works are an important reminder that the position of liminality is infinitely complex, one that requires constant vigilance and experiment in order to avoid structures that enclose while claiming to liberate.

CRITICAL RECEPTION

The paucity of critical material on Ghose is a clear indication that he has not received the recognition he deserves. Significantly, the early works that are mimetic have been reviewed more favorably than his more experimental ones. Claire Tomalin, in a review of *The Murder of Aziz Khan*, comments that it "is written in the best manner of an English nineteenth-century novel" (27). Sometimes, as in the reviews of the Brazilian trilogy, Ghose has been praised for the wrong reasons, for writing historical novels that depict the cruelty of colonialism.

During the last few years, there has been a greater interest in the writings of Ghose. *Twentieth Century Literature* (summer 1986) published an interview with the author, and the *Review of Contemporary Fiction* (summer 1989) published a special issue on the works of Ghose and Milan Kundera. The section on Ghose includes comments by Thomas Berger, Wilson Harris, and several distinguished critics. The articles constitute a major attempt to assess the significance of Ghose's entire corpus, and they have helped in no small measure to establish Ghose as a major postcolonial and contemporary writer.

BIBLIOGRAPHY

Works by Zulfikar Ghose

"Redbrick Ritual." *Twentieth Century* (Oct. 1959): 275–79. (autobiography)
"Schooldays: In Bombay." *Twentieth Century* (Oct. 1960): 312–20. (autobiography)
"The Rough Ride." *Ambit* 16 (1963): 24–30. (short story)
The Loss of India. London: Routledge & Kegan Paul, 1964. (poetry)
Statement against Corpses. With B. S. Johnson. London: Constable, 1964. (short stories)
Confessions of a Native-Alien. London: Routledge & Kegan Paul, 1965. (autobiography)
The Contradictions. London: Macmillan, 1966. (novel)
Jet from Orange. London: Macmillan, 1967. (poetry)

The Murder of Aziz Khan. London: Macmillan, 1967; New York: John Day, 1969. (novel)

"The Absences." In *Winters Tales 14.* Ed. Kevin Crossley-Holland. London: Macmillan, 1968. 191–201.

"Ghose's London: A Valediction." *Hudson Review* 22 (1969): 374–88. (criticism)

"Poems, Poems, Everywhere, Nor Any Drop to Drink." *Guardian* (July 11, 1969). 28. (criticism)

"The Sounds of Cricket." In *Allsorts 2.* Ed. Ann Thwaite. London: Macmillan, 1969. 18–24. (short story)

"Tyrannical Situation in US English Teaching." *Times Higher Education Supplement* (Dec. 3, 1971): 9.

"Daniel Zwernemann's Flight." *Transatlantic Review* 41 (Winter–Spring 1972): 79–81. (short story)

The Incredible Brazilian: The Native. London: Macmillan, 1972; Herts: Panther, 1973; New York: Bantam, 1973; New York: Overlook Press, 1982. (novel)

The Violent West. London: Macmillan, 1972. (poetry)

"The Waxahachie Coincidence." *Transatlantic Review* 45 (Spring 1973): 86–94. (short story)

"The Language of Sports Reporting." In *Readings in the Aesthetics of Sport.* Ed. H.T.A. Whiting and D. W. Masterson. London: Lepus Books, 1974. 57–68. (criticism)

The Incredible Brazilian: The Beautiful Empire. London: Macmillan, 1975; New York: Overlook Press, 1984. (novel)

Crump's Terms. London: Macmillan, 1975. (novel)

Hamlet, Prufrock and Language. London: Macmillan, 1978; New York: St. Martin's Press, 1978. (criticism)

The Incredible Brazilian: A Different World. London: Macmillan, 1978; New York: Overlook Press, 1985. (novel)

"With Music by Dmitri Tiomkin." *New Quarterly* 3:1 (1978): 25–33. (short story)

"The One Comprehensive Vision." *Texas Studies in Literature and Language* 21 (1979): 260–79. (criticism)

Hulme's Investigations into the Bogart Script. Austin and New York: Curbstone Press, 1981. (novel)

A New History of Torments. London: Hutchinson, 1982; New York: Holt, Rinehart & Winston, 1982. (novel)

Don Bueno. London: Hutchinson, 1983; New York: Holt, Rinehart & Winston, 1984. (novel)

"Observations from a Correspondence: Letters from Thomas Berger." *Studies in American Humor* 2:1 (Spring 1983): 5–19. (criticism)

The Fiction of Reality. London: Macmillan, 1984. (criticism)

A Memory of Reality. Austin: Curbstone Press, 1984. (poetry)

"Bryan." *Review of Contemporary Fiction* 5:2 (1985): 23–34. (criticism)

"Lila of the Butterflies and Her Chronicler." *Latin American Literary Review* 13:25 (1985): 151–57. (short story)

"A Translator's Fiction." *Antaeus* (Fall 1985): 66–75. (short story)

Figures of Enchantment. London: Hutchinson, 1986; New York: Harper & Row, 1986. (novel)

Kanaganayakam, C. "Zulfikar Ghose: An Interview" (with "Zulfikar Ghose: A

Select Bibliography"). *Twentieth Century Literature* 32:2 (1986): 169–86. (interview and bibliography)

Vassanji, M. G. "A Conversation with Zulfikar Ghose." *Toronto South Asian Review* 4:3 (1986): 14–21. (interview)

"The Savage Mother of Desire." *Chelsea* 46 (1987): 279–90. (short story)

"The Sealed Light of Being." *Exile* 12:2 (1987): 89–93. (short story)

"Maggie's Orchard." *Journal of Indian Writing in English* 16:2 (1988): 191–209. (short story)

Masood, Hasan. "The Incredible Zulfikar Ghose." *Nation*, Lahore (Nov. 4, 11, 18, 1988). 16–17. (interview)

Dasenbrock, Reed Way, and Feroza Jussawalla. "A Conversation with Zulfikar Ghose." *Review of Contemporary Fiction* 9:2 (1989): 140–53. (interview)

"From The Triple Mirror of the Self" (novel in progress). *Review of Contemporary Fiction* 9:2 (1989): 121–34. (novel)

"Things That Appear." *Review of Contemporary Fiction* 9:2 (1989): 111–20. (criticism)

"Brazilian Beaches, Buenos Aires and Plaza Pakistan." *Toronto South Asian Review* 8:2 (1990): 3–10. (criticism)

"Going Home." *Toronto South Asian Review* 9:2 (1991): 15–22. (autobiography)

Studies of Zulfikar Ghose

Berger, Thomas. "A Selection of Letters." *Review of Contemporary Fiction* 9:2 (1989): 158–70.

Campbell, Ewing. "Encountering the Other in *The Fiction of Reality*." *Review of Contemporary Fiction* 9:2 (1989): 220–24.

Ferres, John F., and Martin Tucker. *Modern Commonwealth Literature*. New York: Frederick Ungar, 1977: 420–22.

Harris, Wilson. "A Note on Zulfikar Ghose's 'Nature Strategies.' " *Review of Contemporary Fiction* 9:2 (1989): 172–78.

Hashmi, Alamgir. "Tickling and Being Tickled à la Zulfikar Ghose." *Commonwealth Novel in English* 1:2 (1982): 156–65.

———. "Words, Words, Words: The Matter of a Weary Prince." *Explorations* 6:1 (1979): 65–69.

Hobsbaum, Philip. "Ghose Zulfikar." In *Contemporary Poets*. Ed. James Vinson. 3rd ed. London: Macmillan, 1980. 644–46.

———. "Ghose, Zulfikar." In *Contemporary Poets*. Ed. James Vinson and D. L. Kirkpatrick. 4th ed. New York: St. Martin's Press, 1985. 295–96.

Jussawalla, Feroza, and Reed Way Dasenbrock. "Introduction." *Review of Contemporary Fiction* 9:2 (1989): 108–11.

Kanaganayakam, C. "The Luminous Comprehension: From Realism to Counter-realism in the Writings of Zulfikar Ghose." *Review of Contemporary Fiction* 9:2 (1989): 225–35.

———. "Unreal Reel and the Unreeled Real: *Hulme's Investigations into the Bogart Script*." *Journal of Indian Writing in English* 16:2 (1988): 178–90.

———. "Zulfikar Ghose." In *World Authors 1980–85*. Ed. Vineta Colby. New York: St. Martin's Press, 1991. 234–36.

————. "Zulfikar Ghose: A Selected Bibliography." *Review of Contemporary Fiction* 9:2 (1989): 236–37.

King, Bruce. "From Twilight to Midnight: Muslim Novels of India and Pakistan." In *The Worlds of Muslim Imagination*. Ed. Alamgir Hashmi. Islamabad: Gulmohar Press, 1986. 243–59.

————. "Ghose's Criticism as Theory." *Review of Contemporary Fiction* 9:2 (1989): 204–8.

Kohli, Devendra. "Landscape and Poetry." *Journal of Commonwealth Literature* 13 (April 1979): 54–70.

Lim, Shirley Geok-lin. "A Poetics of Location: Reading Zulfikar Ghose." *Review of Contemporary Fiction* 9:2 (1989): 188–91.

Mukherjee, Meenakshi. "Ghose, Zulfikar." In *Contemporary Poets*. Ed. James Vinson. 2nd ed. London: St. James Press, 1975. 541–43.

New, W. H. "Ghose, Zulfikar." In *Contemporary Novelists*. Ed. James Vinson. 2nd ed. London: St. James Press, 1976. 511–13.

————. "Ghose, Zulfikar." In *Contemporary Novelists*. Ed. D. L. Kirkpatrick. 4th ed. London: St. James Press, 1986. 335–36.

————. "Structures of Uncertainty: Reading Ghose's 'The Zoo People.' " *Review of Contemporary Fiction* 9:2 (1989): 192–97.

Potts, Michael W. "Zulfikar Ghose—Only Pakistani Novelist to be Published in US." *India West* (April 8, 1983): 12, 21.

Rahman, Tariq. "Zulfikar Ghose and the Land of His Birth." *Review of Contemporary Fiction* 9:2 (1989): 179–87.

Ross, Robert. "*The Murder of Aziz Kahn*." *Review of Contemporary Fiction* 9:2 (1989): 198–203.

Scheick, William J. "Fictional Self and Mythical Art: *A New History of Torments* and *Don Bueno*." *Review of Contemporary Fiction* 9:2 (1989): 209–19.

Stoerk, Beatrice. "New Fiction by Zulfikar Ghose." In *Pakistani Literature: The Contemporary English Writers*. Ed. Alagmir Hashmi. 2nd ed. Islamabad: Gulmohar Press, 1987. 97–104.

Tomalin, Claire. "Unmotivated Raptures." *Observer* (Sept. 24, 1967): 27.

Warren, Bill. "Books." *Austin American-Statesman* (Dec. 17, 1972): 35, 38.

AMITAV GHOSH (1956–   )
Fakrul Alam

BIOGRAPHY

Amitav Ghosh was born in Calcutta but was raised in East Pakistan (now Bangladesh), Sri Lanka, Iran, and India. An anthropologist by training, he has studied at the Universities of Delhi, Alexandria, and Oxford. He has done fieldwork in ethnography in Egypt and has traveled extensively in the Middle East and North Africa. Currently in the Sociology Department of Delhi School of Economics, Ghosh has also taught at the University of Virginia and Columbia University.

Ghosh, in other words, has moved across four continents and has a personal as well as a professional interest in diasporas. Writing about the inhabitants of an Egyptian village in his short story, "The Imam and the Indian," for example, he notes how, like the grandparents and ancestors and relatives of the Egyptians, his relatives too had traveled and migrated across the Indian subcontinent and for similar reasons—"because of wars, or for money and jobs, or perhaps simply because they got tired of living in one place" (140). Professionally, and in his fiction, Ghosh has concerned himself with subjects such as emigration, exile, cultural displacement, and the stories that emanate from transnational cultural flows. These are among the themes of his work to date: "The Imam and the Indian" (1986); *The Circle of Reason* (1986); *The Shadow Lines* (1989); and the recent *Granta* piece, "An Egyptian in Baghdad" (1990).

MAJOR WORKS AND THEMES

Ghosh's short story "The Imam and the Indian" offers a convenient introduction to his themes. Published in *Granta*, this is the story of the sparks that fly or the bridges that are built when people from different backgrounds are suddenly thrown together. Ghosh's narrator notes, for instance, that the remote corner of Egypt in which he is doing his fieldwork has all "the busy restlessness of airline passengers in a transit lounge" (140). Migration and crosscultural encounters, he discovers, had always affected the lives of these villagers; the only difference was that the pace of transnational travel had picked up in recent years. We are all travelers, Ghosh seems to be saying, and there is always the possibility of displacement and confusion and tension when people from different cultures interact, but also of hybrid constructions and instant connections.

Traveling across continents and cultures is also a major subject of Ghosh's first novel, *The Circle of Reason*. This is the novel of a boy's adventures in three different parts of the world: rural Bengal, the mythical Middle Eastern "boom" city of al-Ghazira, and El-Oued, a desert town in Algeria. In his first appearance Alu is already a migrant, for he has come to stay in Lalpukur, a village not far from Calcutta, after his uncle Balaram adopts him. Balaram is an eccentric, a man with a very irrational belief in rationalism. Almost inevitably, Balaram's "rationalist" scheme, à la Pasteur, to purify the world of germs with carbolic acid backfires as it clashes with the ambitions of the local, and thoroughly unscrupulous, political boss, Bhudeb Roy. Exploiting his political connections, Roy has the Indian police shadow Balaram through an assistant superintendent of police, Jyoti Das, another zany who is more interested in watching birds than in pursuing human quarry. In the climax of the Lalpukur section of the novel, Balaram is blown up in a bizarre confrontation with Roy and the police, and Alu is forced to flee the village, with a reluctant Das being reassigned to track the fugitive through most of India.

The first section of the book contains a number of incidental observations on Indian migrations. Balaram's birth year, 1914, for example, reminds the narrator of crucial moments in the history of Indian emigration to the West, like the day when an American judge mulled over the "second-ever application by a Hindu for citizenship in the United States" and decided in favor of admitting the Aryan, or the day when Canada's colonial government decided not to admit "eight thousand Indians... after deciding that the ancient racial purity of Canada could not be endangered by Asiatic immigration" (39). Ghosh also provides several instances of internal diasporas in this part of the novel. The people of Lalpukur, for example, had been "vomited out of their native soil" in the carnage connected with the partition of India; within the narrative time of the novel they witness once again the spectacle of people being "dumped hundreds of miles away" because of the civil war that led to the emergence of Bangladesh (58).

But Ghosh's diasporic consciousness comes out most clearly in the central section of *The Circle of Reason* where Alu has to roam all over India and the Middle East. Within India, Alu moves first to Calcutta and then to the south, always just managing to elude the police and Das till he finally reaches Mahe, the southernmost part of India's west coast. Having reached land's end, Alu, still trying to evade the reach of the Indian police, takes the ultimate diasporic move—he leaves his country behind and sails over the Indian Ocean to al-Ghazira.

Alu's journey across the Indian Ocean on a mechanized boat allows Ghosh to depict the risks endured by thousands of Indians who leave their native land in search of a prosperous future. Illegal emigrants, they hazard their lives by voyaging on frail vessels. Alu's particular boat also bears witness to the wide range of social types who make the dangerous crossing in pursuit of economic security: among the passengers are a professor, a traveling salesman, and a madam and her girls, one of whom is even pregnant. Ghosh takes time out to emphasize the desperation and the dreams that move these people. The pregnant woman, for instance, has been lured to al-Ghazira by someone who has made her innumerable promises—"your child will be this, it'll be that, it'll have houses, and cars, and multi-storeyed buildings," it will be a Ghaziri by birth (177). As Zindi, the madam on board the boat, who also runs a lodging house, describes her success in attracting people to her establishment in al-Ghazira: "I can find any man a good job. And, as for women, why, when I go to India I don't have to do anything. These women find me and come running" (180). As the boat bearing this batch of hopefuls approaches the quintessential Middle Eastern boom city of al-Ghazira, Ghosh emphasizes the archetypal nature of its journey. It is doing what hundreds of other boats have been doing for a century and half: "carrying...an immense cargo of wanderers seeking their own destruction in giving flesh to the whims of capital" (189).

The al-Ghazira section of the book offers fresh evidence of Ghosh's fascination with the diasporic consciousness and the precarious lives led by migrant workers. This section begins with the description of Alu's burial in the rubble of a building that collapses due to faulty workmanship. However, the center of attention for much of the al-Ghazira section is the house of Zindi. It, and for that matter, the rest of al-Ghazira, is Ghosh's metaphor for a permanently unsettled world. Al-Ghazira, in fact, is a phenomenon of which Ghosh is one of the first chroniclers: the exodus of thousands of men and women of the Third World to the Middle East in search of an alternative, and viable, future. Looking at the oil town of al-Ghazira, for example, Nuri the Egyptian, one of Ghosh's displaced persons, observes an entire world: "Filipino faces, Indian faces, Egyptian faces, Pakistani faces, even a few Ghaziri faces, a whole world of faces" (260). Indeed, certain parts of al-Ghazira have the cosmopolitan hustle and bustle of a contemporary Vanity Fair. It is almost as "though half the world's haunts had been painted in miniature along the side of a single street of the city" (344). Although these faces and places have filled the desert spaces of the Middle East, they have not been able to make al-Ghazira into a home, because there were problems everywhere, no matter what you were paid, and because "foreign places are all alike in that they are not home. Nothing binds you there" (266).

Ghosh, adept at twisting and turning his narrative line, eventually climaxes the al-Ghazira section with a confrontation that will see Alu, an idealist like his uncle, being routed by the forces of capital. Alu's campaign to destroy the power of money which Alu has identified as the root of all evil, is crushed. However, Zindi manages to extricate Alu, herself, and Kulfi and Boss, two other members of her household, from the mess created by Alu's quixotic scheme, and eventually they all end up in the little town of El-Oued at the northeastern tip of the Algerian Sahara.

In El-Oued, the fugitives come across the Vermas, two Indian doctors who have taken up jobs in the Algerian desert. Mrs. Verma is delighted to see the fugitives, because Kulfi appears to be just the woman she was wanting to cast as the heroine of her production of a Bengali dance drama. Alu, on the other hand, is overjoyed to find in Mrs. Verma's library a present from Balaram to her father: *The Life of Pasteur*, the gift of one "rationalist" to another. But Das is present at the staging of the play, and that is enough to kill Kulfi in the third bizarre climax of *The Circle of Reason*. What Kulfi does not know, however, is that Das has dissociated himself from all security forces after the immigration officials of al-Ghazira had deported the members of Zindi's house who had survived the police assault on them. Witness to these migrant workers' deportation, he remembers vividly what one of them said at the moment of his forced departure: "how many people will you send away? The queue of hope [of Third World migrants] stretches long past infinity" (409).

In the desert town of El-Oued, the circle of reason is completed. Mrs. Verma, brisk and no-nonsensical, manages to disabuse Alu of the dream of a world purified by rational methods (it is pertinent here to remember that Ghosh is a disillusioned Marxist). The important thing, we learn, is to "try to be a better human being" (413). The only hope is "to make do with what we've got" (417). Not surprisingly, at the end of Ghosh's first novel, his major characters resume their travel again, disburdened of false dreams. Zindi and Alu head for "home" via Tangiers. Das joins them as he moves forward for a migrant's life in Germany. He will accompany Alu and Zindi till Tangiers, where migrating birds fill the sky as they make their annual flights between Europe and Africa, apt symbols of the universal tendency to leave behind "continents of defeat" and move toward "a world full of hope" (423).

The Circle of Reason, then, is an ambitious first novel, a sprawling work peopled with fascinating characters who move in exotic settings. It abounds in bizarre moments but is basically a serious attempt to deal with man's delusive quest for reason and with the contemporary diaspora that has taken countless Third World workers and professionals across continents in quest of a better life. Not that Ghosh's treatment of these themes is unfailingly interesting. At over four hundred pages, the book is bound to strike most readers as overlong and overwrought. Ghosh's focus is at times blurred, and he fails to sustain the narrative pace on more than one occasion.

Compared to *The Circle of Reason*, Ghosh's second novel, *The Shadow Lines*, is a much more accomplished and compelling work. Essentially a somber novel about the "shadow lines" that link people despite differences in space and in time, it is also a book about memory and desire, about the role of the creative imagination and the power of sympathy in human relationships. It is, in addition, a "rite of passage" novel, for in the course of the narrative, the nameless narrator is transformed from a gullible youngster spellbound by the stories told to him by his cosmopolitan relatives to a mature young man who has come to know much about himself and the way public events and private lives are interconnected. In the process, the narrator discovers his true vocation: with the growth in his power of perception, he will be a chronicler of the connections between people and places he had once seen as existing independently of each other and of the tragicomedy of life.

Although not directly a novel about the contemporary Indian diaspora, *The Shadow Lines* has much in it that shows Ghosh's continuing interest in this theme and the diasporic consciousness. The first part of the novel, for example, is titled "Going Away," and in the first sentence Ghosh indicates how a chain of events can be set in motion by one overseas trip. In 1939, thirteen years before the narrator's birth, his father's aunt, Mayadebi, left for England with her husband and their eight-year-old son, Tridib, and reestablished contact with the Prices, an English family that had made an Indian connection when Mrs. Price's father had settled down in Calcutta and had in the process come across Tridib's grandfather. As a result of the English trip, Tridib falls in love with Mrs. Price's daughter, May. Eventually May visits Tridib in Calcutta, where she stays with the narrator's family. She and Tridib then join Mayadebi and the narrator's grandmother as the Indian women fly to Dhaka, then the capital of East Pakistan, but once their home city before they left it in a mass exodus of Bengali Hindus to West Bengal. In Dhaka, Tridib is killed in a race riot after Mayadebi and the grandmother involve him and May in an expedition to bring away their uncle. Although May survives as do the two sisters, she is haunted by the nightmarish moment of the riot when she had inspired Tridib to an act of daring in front of an enraged mob. At the end of the novel, the narrator, on a year's research stint in England, meets May and has an affair with her as they try to come to terms with Tridib's death.

This brief outline of Ghosh's complicated plot indicates how he has woven a story based on people who are constantly traveling across frontiers and intermingling despite differences in race or nationality. The London scenes of the novel represent perfectly the cosmopolitan city created by a global diaspora. Ghosh's London is a megalopolis where one encounters Bangladeshi restaurants, retail shops run by South Asians, Muslim mosques, the smell of African or Caribbean curry, posters advertising the latest Hindi films, and "quick exchanges in a dozen dialects of Bengali" (98).

But the mass migration of Bengalis to England is of course only one aspect of the Indian diaspora. Within South Asia itself, recent history records several mass population movements of Hindu Bengalis from East to West Bengal, and of Muslim refugees from India's Bihar or Uttar Pradesh or West Bengal to Pakistan. Ghosh's *The Shadow Lines* offers glimpses into the lives led by these migrants. We get to hear also of Indian families scattering all over the world. While the narrator's grandmother's uncle had decided to stay in Dhaka, for example, his sons and daughters have either moved to Bangalore or Calcutta or the Middle East "or God knows where" (132).

With so much movement of people from one part of the world to another, what, precisely, constitutes a "home"? The narrator, for instance, can think of Calcutta as home, but for his grandmother the city can only be so in an invented sense. As the title of the second section of *The Shadow Lines*, "Coming Home," indicates, home to her really means Dhaka, but when she gets there the city is nothing like the birthplace she had known. In fact, among Ghosh's major themes in the novel are that in a permanently unsettled world, "home" is what we create only through a combination of memory and desire, and that in the contemporary world it is difficult to distinguish between "coming home" and "going away" when you are moving all the time.

Like *The Circle of Reason*, then, *The Shadow Lines*, is a novel of the movement of people across national borders and of traveling. But Ghosh's characters seem to yearn for a world without boundaries. Tridib, the man who had exerted a formative influence on the narrator's life, thus tells him the story of Tristan, a story of a hero who "was a man without a country, who fell in love with a woman-across-the-seas" (183). This, of course, is also Tridib's story, and the narrator's too. It is a story that expresses a nostalgia for a world where immigration and customs officials did not exist, where you did not cross into another country by flying over an imaginary line, where you did not give up your home because of political upheavals, or where you did not lose your faith in "the stillness of the earth" (200).

But, as the narrator of *The Shadow Lines* discovers, the people of India can no longer recognize a world without borders or a settled world, for diasporas have become their lot. They have, therefore, become fearful, aware "that normalcy is utterly contingent, that the spaces that surround one, the streets that one inhabits can become suddenly and without warning, as hostile as a desert in a flash flood" (200). That is why the uncle of the narrator's grandmother refuses to move from his home, for as far as he can see, "Once you start moving you never stop" (211).

Moving, however, has its compensations. For one thing, when you have "no home but in memory [you] learn to be very skilled in the art of recollection" (190). The narrator, for one, has become a master storyteller because of his experience of unsettled lives and his knowledge of the diasporic consciousness. He has also learned that people can become more, and not less, "closely bound to each other" after officials have drawn border lines, since these lines, paradoxically, lock them "into an irreversible symmetry" (228). At the end of the novel, therefore, Ghosh's narrator thinks more of linkages than of separations. He has had a glimpse into the "final redemptive mystery" of Tridib's death (246): Tridib had given up his life in an act of faith, an act that gives the lie to frontiers and suggests that shadow lines unite us despite the boundaries that disperse people and divide them.

Ghosh's most recent work, another *Granta* piece entitled "An Egyptian in Baghdad," once again comes back to his favorite subjects of dispersal, exile, and the exodus from impoverished Third World countries to the oil-rich nations of the Middle East. In this short piece, Ghosh is revisiting the corner of rural Egypt where he had once done fieldwork at the time of the Persian Gulf crisis. It is a difficult time for thousands of Egyptians, since so many of them had found jobs in Iraq and were now having to come back. One such Egyptian is his friend Nabeel, a man who had opted to remain in Iraq to make a little more money even when most of his countrymen had left the country as a result of the hostility being shown toward them during the crisis. At the end of "An Egyptian in Baghdad," Ghosh looks at a television news report on migrant workers stranded in Jordan, eagerly waiting for a way to get away from the war zone. To Ghosh, the scene of these men standing on a Red Sea beach "waiting for the waters to part" is reminiscent of the famous moment in the Bible; only, "Nabeel had vanished into the pages of the epic exodus" (193). It is a moment in history that obviously fascinates Ghosh: a moment that depicts a people caught in flight between borders, "diaspora culture," and the ongoing history of transnational cultural flows.

CRITICAL RECEPTION

Perhaps because Ghosh has only been publishing his work since 1986, he has not received much critical attention. Reviews of his two novels, however, have been mostly favorable. Thus even when critics found his first book, *The Circle of Reason*, overwritten and inadequately structured, they were willing to hail him as an exciting new writer with an original approach to fiction. Some early reviewers of the book also welcomed it because of its magic realism while other reviewers have noticed Ghosh's interest in cultural hybridity and migration. The *Economist* reviewer, for instance, lists "exile or restlessness" and "the nobility and pathos of people from an old world trying to cope with a new one" (16) as two of his major themes in the book. Although even the most appreciative critic of *The Circle of Reason* found the book overambitious, there has been near unanimity among reviewers about the artistic excellence of *The Shadow Lines*. Thus in an appreciative and insightful review, Edward Hower of the *New York Times Book Review* declares *The Shadow Lines* to be nothing less than "a stunning book— amusing, sad, wise and truly international in scope" (10). Writing in the *Times Literary Supplement*, Maria Cuoto applauds the assurance with which the second novel was written and observes: "in *The Shadow Lines*, Ghosh has found his own distinctive voice—polished and profound" (1212).

Readers interested in Ghosh as a writer of the Indian diaspora can get some help from James Clifford's *Times Literary Supplement* piece, "The Transit Lounge of Culture." To Clifford, a student of "comparative inter- cultural studies," Ghosh's story, "The Imam and the Indian," is "a prob- lematic parable" because it draws "attention to specific experiences of worldliness, complex roots and routes" and because it highlights not only cultural displacements but also inter-cultural connections" (8). Ghosh's de- piction of the encounter between the Indian ethnographer and some Egyp- tian villagers illustrates perfectly a postmodern phenomenon, "the brave new world of disorder, of rootless histories and selves." But the short story is important to Clifford also because it gives him an insight into another timeless feature of our existence: man's complex history "of dwelling and travelling, [of] discrepant cosmopolitanisms" (8). Clifford's brief piece, therefore, helps characterize Ghosh's work as both postmodern and timeless and underlines the novelist's interest in traveling as a metaphor of the human condition.

BIBLIOGRAPHY

Works by Amitav Ghosh

The Circle of Reason. New York: Viking Penguin, 1986; rpt. Penguin Books, 1990.
"The Imam and the Indian." *Granta* 20 (Winter 1986): 135–46.
The Shadow Lines. New York: Viking Penguin, 1989; rpt. Penguin Books, 1990.
"An Egyptian in Baghdad." *Granta* 34 (Autumn 1990): 173–93.

Studies of Amitav Ghosh

Anon. Review of *The Circle of Reason*. *Economist* 300:7457 (Aug. 2, 1986): 14, 16.
Bragg, Lois. Review of *The Circle of Reason*. *Best Sellers* 46:6 (Sept. 1986): 203.
Burgess, Anthony. Review of *The Circle of Reason*. *New York Times Book Review* (July 6, 1986): 6–7.
Clifford, James. "The Transit Lounge of Culture." *Times Literary Supplement*, no. 4596 (May 3, 1991): 7–8.
Cuoto, Maria. Review of *The Shadow Lines*. *Times Literary Supplement* no. 4465 (Oct. 28, 1988): 1212.

Guptara, Prabhu S. Review of *The Circle of Reason*. *British Book News* (April 1986): 240.

Heron, Liz. Review of *The Circle of Reason*. *New Statesman* 111:2866 (Feb. 26, 1986): 27.

Hower, Edward. Review of *The Shadow Lines*. *New York Times Book Review* (July 2, 1989): 10.

Klinkenborg, Verlyn. Review of *The Shadow Lines*. *New Republic* 201:37 (Aug. 7–14, 1989): 56.

Kureishi, Hanif. Review of *The Circle of Reason*. *New Republic* 195:5 (Aug. 4, 1986): 40–41.

Mellors, John. Review of *The Circle of Reason*. *London Magazine* 25:12 (March 1986): 98–101.

Nelson, Emmanuel. Review of *The Circle of Reason*. *Choice* (March 1987): 134.

Shack, Neville. Review of *The Circle of Reason*. *Times Literary Supplement* no. 4332 (April 11, 1986): 382.

PADMA HEJMADI (Padma Perera) (1939–   )

Gurleen Grewal

BIOGRAPHY

Padma Hejmadi, whose short stories have been published in India, Great Britain, and the United States under the last name Perera, was born in Madras, India, where her father worked in the Indian Civil Service. Her mother tongue, a version of Konkani, which has no script, engendered her interest in an oral tradition. Educated at the Universities of Madras and Delhi, with a master's in journalism and creative writing from the University of Michigan, Ann Arbor, she has taught creative writing for some years at the University of Colorado, Boulder, and offered seminars and readings at Vassar, the Rhode Island School of Design, the M.F.A. Program of Columbia University, New York, etc. A recipient of several writing fellowships, Hejmadi won the Hopwood Award for Major Fiction at Michigan. She now lives in Davis, California, with her husband, writer Peter Beagle; here she continues to write, and tends life as she does her wor(l)ds on the page: with artistry, care, and a sense of humor.

Believing in the aesthetic unity of all art, Hejmadi informs her writing by her practice of other arts. Trained as a child in the Manipuri style of classical Indian dance, she became aware of rhythms in prose; an accomplished photographer whose work, "Inscapes/Outscapes," was exhibited in Seattle in 1990, she found that photography clarified and confirmed for her the implications of perspective, both visual and verbal.

A seasoned writer, she has written several of her stories under contract for the *New Yorker*. Hejmadi has since gained recognition with the publication of *Birthday Deathday and Other Stories* (1985). Nine of the dozen short stories in *Birthday Deathday* (henceforth *BD*) comprised *Dr. Salaam and Other Stories of India* (1978), an American edition now out of print; many of these first appeared in a limited Indian edition, *Coigns of Vantage* (1972). Soon she expects to publish two works of nonfiction: *Ceremony and Sustenance* and *Sumi Spaces*. Her works of fiction and nonfiction reflect a poet's vision, one that strives to match shifting geographies with a corresponding "geography of the soul."

MAJOR WORKS AND THEMES

If a certain rootlessness is a condition of the diaspora, in her fiction cultural roots are transplanted and tended with skill. Aware of the difficult terrain of this literary (con)tending, Hejmadi has reviewed with great insight the "technical snags" facing both the Indian writer in English and the translator of regional Indian literature: "To cross different cultures is to be caught sometimes in the limbos that lie between what is known in one language and can't be expressed in another—not because a good translator doesn't know how to, but from a lack in the language itself, i.e., an absence of vocabulary and thought alike.... What might seem a mere matter of semantics [substituting "aunt" for a father's sister, for example] actually implies an entire spectrum of prescribed behavior, graded obligations of hierarchy... within the family or clan" ("The Challenge of Indian Fiction in English" 8). In her hands, English becomes a pliable medium of "tactful translation," and when it cannot, it gestures expressively: "But how to translate the untranslateable: exactly what it means to hear these languages sounding together again, plosive to fricative like clapper to bell: liquid Hindi phrases... harsh clatter of Marathi haggling in a market; pure classical Urdu ..." (BD 8).

Indian women of different classes and ages occupy the center of most stories, the pain of women's subjection a recurrent theme in *Birthday Deathday*. "Spaces of Decision, South India: 1890s to 1970s" is a monumental, exquisitely written tribute to the women in her family who, "permeated with traditional beliefs" (BD 174), resisted even as they complied: Radha-akka, the widowed storytelling great-aunt, who "won't be superannuated," and her sister Sita, of whom we are told "it is impossible to decipher the sentences of... and on... her life" (BD 173). The narrator hails these weathered freedom-fighters as her own "contemporaries across generations"; "one way or another," they have all been through fire (BD 174). "Too Late For Anger" reveals with sad ironies the circumscribed lives of four middle-class sisters, two of whom, having studied abroad, return home to find themselves overeducated for their own good. Commodities in the marriage market, they discover that they cannot afford to be "spoiled": no stigmas of body, mind, or character should attach to them or their families. In "Weather Report," the narrator, an Indian woman in the United States running away from her husband, finds herself journeying toward an unknown point of refuge, with a busload of Americans, a motley crew briefly united in their common predicament of pain. Journeying into awareness, the narrator realizes that her marriage was doomed from the start, being arranged by her father responding to an advertisement in *India Abroad*: "Pretty, fair, convent-educated virgin under 23, without spectacles, caste no bar, required for handsome rising electronic engineer, 5'9", residing in USA. High character, no habits. Widows and innocent divorcees, please excuse" (*BD* 148). In retrospect, the narrator sees the schism: "Our culture told us what to do, and we listened, but we were in another country" (*BD* 150).

Located at the juncture of East and West, Hejmadi is aware that she is writing for more than one audience. Even as she muses on the "unbearable statistics" of Indian women caught between "the neglect or sadism of husbands and the constant swarming venom of relatives," the narrator of "Monologue for Foreigners" adds: "Our people can be bound to suffocation by families; yours as ruthlessly torn apart" (*BD* 57). The stories carry a subtle critique of Western appropriations and definitions of the world. In "Weather Report," the narrator, taken to a football match by her husband, wonders "why something should be called The World series when no one else in the world, except possibly the Japanese, cared" (*BD* 151). In the short story "Letter," a female narrator writes from her retreat in a remote Himalayan village, informing her lover in the West about a momentous decision—i.e., to remain in India and *choose* the marriage arranged by her parents. Instrumental to this decision is an encounter with Tara, seven-year-old daughter of a nomadic tribeswoman whom the narrator wishes to educate. Uprooted by her sojourn in the West, a different kind of nomad, the narrator discovers in herself a need to re-route/root herself; the answer to her lover's offer of a life in the West is "no."

Impatience with the limitations and injustices of traditional Indian ways combines with a deep appreciation of the old culture casually "shuffling the centuries" like "a well-thumbed pack of cards" (*BD* 2). Conveying the moods and idioms of life in South India with insight and fond irreverence, short stories such as "Mauna," "Pilgrimage," and "The Schoolmaster" are finely crafted vignettes of the follies, cruelties, and comforts of the extended family and village life, while the hilarious "Appa-mam" taps the ambiguity and allowance at the heart of a culture in which a thief is also a saint. In "Birthday Deathday" the narrator, home from Europe and America, muses on her experience in the "temperate" and "compartmentalized" West: "[one] language at a time. One era at a time. One religion at a time... everything was pruned down to stay in its place, very tidy" (*BD* 9). Reflecting on her own passage through India she realizes: "Here one is thrown open with every window to every scrap and pain of life. To shut out, to soft-pedal, is to be lessened: not so lacerated, not so responsible, that much less alive" (*BD* 3).

In her work of the last decade, combining narrative and journal, Hejmadi makes the genre of the essay a creative medium for the exploration of a diasporic consciousness. Two exciting works of nonfiction, which include essays published in *Parabola, Horizon, Iowa Review* and elsewhere, currently await publication: *Ceremony and Sustenance: Views from a Portable Tradition* and *Sumi Spaces*, sketches of interior/exterior landscapes. Essays in *Ceremony* reckon with a "portable tradition," that which a diasporic consciousness comes to value after a process of sifting. Using a crosscultural idiom and drawing upon folk tale, festival, myth, Indian iconography, and the philosophy of the Vedanta, Hejmadi illuminates aspects of Indian culture in nimble, lucid prose. Inspired by the credo of the Japanese school of Sumi painting—"If you depict a bird in a scroll, give it space to fly"—the essays in *Sumi Spaces* constitute an innovative form of crosscultural cartography, tracking intimate social spaces: those of language, silence, and illiteracy; of work, music, and dance; of landscapes, journeys, and transitions. Acutely cognizant of the diasporic predicament, the essays register Hejmadi's paraphrased claim: "Have Roots, Will Travel." Collectively, they demonstrate that "trying to live a wise and examined life can perhaps require the greatest creativity of all" ("Witness Within," *Parabola* 68).

Hejmadi is currently working on an "Uncle Monkey" series; the short story "Uncle Monkey" (*Massachusetts Review*) employs a peripatetic ghost, who floats through time and continents, as a vehicle for crosscultural commentary. While the incongruity of cultures in collision is mirthful—between the ghost uncle and his niece, the diasporic narrator, the spirit of humor is alive—the story is also concerned with loss, as both ghost and narrator grieve for worlds left behind. Seemingly effortless, curving complex turns of thought into luminous prose, Hejmadi's writing upholds her belief that true art conceals art (*ars est celare artem*); however, for some readers the surface lyricism may obfuscate the stringency of the message.

CRITICAL RECEPTION

Reviewers have responded favorably to the short stories. Julia Older, reviewing *Dr. Salaam and Other Stories*, compares her "prose images [of] Madras and the surrounding countryside"—"sharp, intimate, and often spiritual"—to the cinematography of Satyajit Ray; she finds that the writer's special "gift" is "a prose that bridges cultures" (19). Detecting "a certain sentimentality" in these otherwise "solid stories, written in dense, rounded prose" about "sprawling [Indian] households," Isabel Raphael still believes in the characters' "agony," whether generated by prejudice or by the undermining of "long-held certainties" (13). Gillian Somerville-Large is "seduced by fine prose" and a "tropical green lushness" the stories "marvellously" describe (13), while Christopher Wordsworth takes note of the "cool visual quality of the writing" (9).

Hejmadi's comments in 1974 on the "exterior hurdles of marginality" facing the Indian writer in English are ironically prophetic ("The Challenge of Indian Fiction in English" 11). Though Hejmadi is internationally hailed as a brilliant new voice, her considerable talent awaits serious reckoning.

Perhaps this is so because Hejmadi's work, first published in the 1960s, lacked a sizable Indian audience that would recognize her work (the new Penguin edition of *Birthday Deathday*, released in India in 1992, should make her work more accessible to Indian audiences); on the other hand, the international audience that appreciated her work could not "place" her in any literary tradition. The concept of the Indian diaspora creates a significant space for this layered, multifaceted writing, which in turn illuminates what it means to be rooted when the ground itself shifts.

BIBLIOGRAPHY

Works by Padma Hejmadi (Padma Perera)

Coigns of Vantage. Calcutta: Writers Workshop Publication, 1972.
"The Challenge of Indian Fiction in English: Review of Recent Books." *Educational Resources Center Newsletter* 1:3 (Jan. 1974): 23 pp.
Dr. Salaam and Other Stories of India. Santa Barbara: Capra Press, 1978.
"Spaces of Illiteracy." *Iowa Review* 12:1 (Winter 1981): 121–34.
"Spaces of Intelligence." *Frontiers* 7:2 (1983): 56–60.
"Spaces of Work." *Extended Outlooks: The Iowa Review Collection of Contemporary Writing by Women*. Ed. Jane Cooper et al. New York: Macmillan, 1983.
"Ceremonies and Sustenance." *Parabola* 9:4 (Nov. 1984): 70–75.
"Guruji." *Parabola* 9:3 (Aug. 1984): 26–29.
Birthday Deathday and Other Stories. London: Women's Press, 1985.
"Flying in Your Own Food." [An essay on Gandhi/*Gandhi*, Attenborough's film] *Helicon Nine* 12 & 13, special issue on Peace (Summer 1985): 30–35.
"Smaran." *Parabola* 11:4 (Dec. 1986): 56–59.
"The Witness Within." *Parabola* 11:1 (Feb. 1986): 66–73.
"Uncle Monkey." *Massachusetts Review* 29:4, special issue on South Asian Expatriate Writing and Art (Winter 1988–89): 599–608.
"Dhyana: The Long, Pure Look." *Parabola* 15:2 (May 1990): 74–79.
"Geste et Ceremonie." *Initiations* 7 (Winter 1991–92): 67–71.

Studies of Padma Hejmadi (Padma Perera)

Older, Julia. "Indian Stories: Tradition on a Circular Track." Review of *Dr. Salaam and Other Stories*. *Christian Science Monitor* (July 9, 1979): 19.
Raphael, Isabel. Review of *Birthday Deathday and Other Stories*. *London Times* (Jan. 9, 1986): 13.
Somerville-Large, Gillian. Review of *Birthday Deathday*. *Irish Times* (Jan. 25, 1986): 13.
Wordsworth, Christopher. Review of *Birthday Deathday*. *Guardian* (Jan. 9, 1986): 8–9.

ISMITH KHAN (1925–   )
Anthony Boxill

BIOGRAPHY

Ismith Khan was born on March 16, 1925, into a Muslim family in Port of Spain, the capital of Trinidad. As most of the other Indians in Trinidad were Hindus and lived in rural areas, being a Muslim set him apart. Another difference was that his grandfather, Kale Khan, had not emigrated from India as an indentured laborer to work in the sugar plantations, but had come as a jeweller, a skilled craftsman. Kale Khan was much more militant and aggressive than the Hindus of his generation who were inclined to accept rather apathetically what fate had dealt them. These qualities seem to have had a profound influence on Ismith Khan, whose refusal to accept without question the status quo is very evident in his work.

Ismith Khan attended one of the most prestigious schools in Trinidad, Queen's Royal College, and, after leaving, worked for a while as a reporter for the *Trinidad Guardian*, the island's largest newspaper where Seepersad Naipaul, V. S. Naipaul's father, and Sam Selvon also worked. This stint provided him with the opportunity to learn more about his fellow islanders.

Khan then left Trinidad to study sociology in the United States, first at Michigan State University and then at the New School for Social Research in New York where he took his degree in 1954.

The next period of his life was spent in and around New York. Sometimes he was a full-time writer—his first two novels, *The Jumbie Bird* and *The Obeah Man*, appeared in 1961 and 1964 respectively—and at others he found work at such places as the New York Public Library; Cornell University, where he was a research assistant; and the New York School for Social Research and Johns Hopkins University, where he taught creative writing. He took a master's in creative writing at Johns Hopkins, and his thesis for this degree was to become his third published novel, *The Crucifixion*.

After leaving Johns Hopkins, Khan moved west to California and taught at various universities: at Berkeley (1970–71), at San Diego (1971–74), at the University of Southern California (1977), and at California State College, Long Beach (1978–81).

Khan moved back to New York, and in the 1980s he published *The Crucifixion* after a silence of more than twenty years. From his article "Dialect in West Indian Literature," it is clear that his career as a writer has been a prolonged struggle. The article suggests that he has often been pressured by publishers to modify and simplify his West Indian dialect to make it more accessible to American readers. To do this would alienate him from the very people he wants most to reach, and would deprive him of the language that permits him to "reach into the bowels of the Caribbean in search of itself" (160). On the other hand, because the West Indian "readership is not only small, but vastly indifferent to local works" (150), Khan cannot simply return to Trinidad and address himself to the people with whom he shares a language. His most recent novel, told in two voices, one standard English and the other dialect, reaches out and tries to reconcile two audiences. That Khan refuses to abandon one audience for the other is a measure of his integrity as an artist and of the strength of his determination to fight against the odds, a lesson learned from Kale Khan, his Pathan grandfather.

MAJOR WORKS AND THEMES

In his three novels, Khan investigates the attempts that people in the Caribbean make to define themselves, faced as they are with the erosion of their language and culture, and with the steady attack of the colonial process on their dignity.

In his first novel, this investigation is carried on in the microcosm of an Indian Muslim family in Port of Spain. *The Jumbie Bird* concentrates on three people: Kale Khan; his son, Rahim; and his grandson, Jamini. By interweaving their impressions, the author gives a picture of the past history of the Indian in Trinidad through the old man, Kale Khan; an idea of the present problems Indians face through Rahim; and a warning of what the future might be through the boy, Jamini. Kale Khan cannot accept Trinidad as his home and is nostalgic about India. He is the leader of a group of old men who yearn somewhat sentimentally for India, which they left as indentured laborers for the cane fields of Trinidad. Rahim has no nostalgia for India, but no strong attachment to Trinidad. His sense of displacement is easily capitalized on by the cunning, neo-colonialist Englishman, Hardaker. Khan, through Jamini, suggests one way in which the Indian can accommodate himself to his new home. He can attend an expensive school, accept its middle-class values, and suppress the pride in his race and culture instilled in him by his elders. He can change his manner of speaking so that he will sound less East Indian and more West Indian. Khan inserts two sketches of educated Indians, Dr. Gopal and Samuel Salwan, to indicate the pomposity and self-loathing that such a path can lead to. By contrast with the men, the women, Binti and Meena, are less sentimental and nostalgic and more practical and tough-minded. Instead of dreaming, they work and look to the future, not into the past. However, even though at the end Binti survives as the strong one after Kale Khan's death, Khan questions the use to which her hard-earned money is put to pay for Jamini's expensive school.

An atmosphere of death, symbolized by the calling of the jumbie bird, pervades the novel. There is no doubt that Kale Khan's death marks an end to a phase of Indian life in Trinidad. But the jumbie bird's call also means death to something vital and innocent in Jamini. Given this tone, the author's last-minute attempt at a happy ending rings false.

The vision of *The Obeah Man* is similarly bleak, and its ending similarly flawed. Here Khan, after wrestling with personal problems in his autobiographical first novel, moves on to explore similar problems of identity as they apply to all Trinidadians and to all humanity. For this reason many of the main characters of this novel are of mixed race. Its action takes place during carnival, when the people of Trinidad try to shed their identities to assume fantasy ones. Carnival is also a festival that is shared by Trinidadians of every race and religion. The main characters represent various aspects of the search for fulfillment in life. Massahood attempts to dominate others with his physical strength and his sexual prowess; Zolda equates fulfillment with sensual pleasure; Zampi, the obeah man, follows a spiritual path. Having abandoned the turmoil of the city for the peace of the country, he resolves not to misuse his powers as obeah man. His intuition and creativity correspond closely to those of an artist; an English painter comes closer to understanding Zampi's attitude to obeah than do his fellow countrymen, who merely want him to use his powers to benefit them materially. Given the selfishness of most of the characters and the confusion of the city at carnival, violence is inevitable, but it is not a violence that purges. Consequently, the reconciliation of Zampi, the spiritual, with Zolda, the sensual, seems contrived and at odds with the predominant vision of the book.

In *The Crucifixion*, the race of the characters is not significant. In the world of this novel, racial pride and cultural identity have so disintegrated that people cannot distinguish between true faith and mere superstition. The central character, Manko, is a preacher who self-righteously castigates those who offend him. Eventually, when he realizes that he has condemned an innocent person, his belief in his calling is so shaken that he climbs onto a cross and undergoes a parody of a crucifixion. The religion that he preaches is a mishmash of superstition and vehement words, the meaninglessness of which is underlined by the parrot that sits on Manko's shoulder and echoes his empty words. The action of the novel takes place in a squalid barracks yard and in various bars where people exist in a constant state of friction, and the narrative voice fluctuates between standard English and dialect to emphasize the profound confusion of the people's lives. Devoid of custom or culture or language, they are conscious of a sense of emptiness, but unaware of how to fill it.

Ismith Khan's fiction begins by describing his own separation from the values and institutions that gave his Indian ancestors strength; it goes on to recognize that this sense of loss is not peculiar to him or to his countrymen, but is a condition of the human race, which is symbolized powerfully by the cripple who recurs in the three novels.

CRITICAL RECEPTION

Critics who have written about Ismith Khan's work—and they are not many—share Rhonda Cobham's conviction that "there seems...to be no valid critical reason for his neglect" (240). Although the criticism so far implies that Khan's second novel, *The Obeah Man*, is his most successful, most of what has been written is devoted to his first, *The Jumbie Bird*. His third, *The Crucifixion*, is yet to be examined critically. Since it is generally recognized that *The Jumbie Bird* is an autobiographical novel in which Khan broaches many of the ideas and attitudes he develops in his later books, perhaps the critics feel that they must first come to terms with it to qualify themselves to comment on the other two.

Cobham, in her assessment of *The Jumbie Bird*, admires especially Khan's ability to use dialogue and dialect to place his characters socially: "For the practised ear, it is even possible to distinguish between various registers of speech, depending on the speaker's degree of remove from the Hindi language or his proximity to the creole spoken on the streets of Port of Spain" (245). Renu Juneja, on the other hand, examines the novel's treatment of history and finds that its "interpretation and clarification of historical experience is both true and emotionally persuasive" (27). Every commentary on *The Jumbie Bird* recognizes that it is structured around "three generations of East Indians in Trinidad, represented by Kale Khan, his son Rahim, and his grandson Jamini" (250), as Arthur Drayton puts it. The grandfather looks to the past with nostalgia; the grandson, to the future with misgiving; and Rahim, the son of the one and the father of the other, looks on the present with bewilderment. Each of them is symbolic of a stage in the East Indian community's search for itself in the wider Trinidadian environment. While most commend the symmetry of this structure, Barrie Davies finds that "the languid emphasis of Khan's rhythms betrays his interest and success in his analysis of the problem posed rather than the answer" (286).

The criticism of Khan's next book focuses on his use of characters as symbols: the following comment by Davies is quite representative: "In *The Obeah Man* there are really no people, but symbols which derive their special intensity and validity because they externalize the cross currents of the West

Indian past and present" (286). While R. M. Lacovia finds convincing Khan's use of the central character, Zampi, to represent intuition, and the use of Massahood to represent the physical and the manipulative, Kenneth Ramchand objects that "when the relationship between Zampi and Zolda is done in terms of aspiring spirit and voluptuous flesh, such a crude externalization does little justice to Khan's own intuitions" (53). Khan's sympathetic and nonstereotypical treatment of obeah and his vivid description of carnival have earned him the respect of those critics who have chosen to write about *The Obeah Man*.

Although the few commentaries on Khan's work have raised significant and interesting issues, implicit in the criticism is that all the novels would yield much more were they to be read and discussed more fully.

BIBLIOGRAPHY

Works by Ismith Khan

"In the Subway." In *New Voices 2: American Writing Today.* Ed. Don M. Wolfe. New York: Hendricks House, 1955. 451–54.

The Jumbie Bird. London: MacGibbon & Kee, 1961; New York: Obolensky, 1962; London: Longman, 1974, 1985.

"A Day in the Country." *Colorado Quarterly* (Autumn 1962): 121–35; *Cornhill Magazine* (Spring 1962); 52–55. In *From the Green Antilles.* Ed. B. Howes. New York: Macmillan, 1966. 48–62.

The Obeah Man. London: Hutchinson, 1964.

"The Red Ball." In *New Writing in the Caribbean.* Ed. A. J. Seymour. Georgetown, Guyana: Caribbean Festival of the Arts, 1972: 226–33. In *Caribbean Rhythms.* Ed. James T. Livingston. New York: Washington Square Press, 1974: 152–61. In *Caribbean Stories.* Ed. Michael Marland. London: Longman, 1979. Trans. into Tamil in *Manjari* (Madras, India) (April 1980). In *Short Story International* 18 (Feb. 1980): 18–27.

"Dialect in West Indian Literature." In *The Black Writer in Africa and the Americas.* Ed. Lloyd W. Brown. Los Angeles: Hennessey & Ingalls, 1973. 141–64.

"The Village Shop." In *Lambailey.* Ed. Ron Heapy and Anne Garside. London: Oxford University Press, 1979. 17–21.

The Crucifixion. Leeds: Peepal Tree Press, n.d.

Studies of Ismith Khan

Blundell, M. S. Review of *The Obeah Man. Caribbean Quarterly* 11 (March-June 1965): 95–97.

Brown, Stewart. Introduction. *The Jumbie Bird.* London: Longman, 1985.

Cobham, Rhonda. "*The Jumbie Bird* by Ismith Khan: A New Assessment." *Journal of Commonwealth Literature* 21 (1986): 240–49.

Davies, Barrie. "The Personal Sense of a Society—Minority View: Aspects of the

'East Indian' Novel in the West Indies." *Studies in the Novel* 4 (Summer 1972): 284–95.

Drayton, Arthur. "Ismith Khan." In *Fifty Caribbean Writers: A Bio-Bibliographical Critical Sourcebook.* Ed. Daryl Cumber Dance. New York: Greenwood Press, 1986. 246–54.

Jones, Joseph, and Johanna Jones. "Ismith Khan." In *Authors and Areas of the West Indies.* Austin, Texas: Steck-Vaughn, 1970. 30–31.

Juneja, Renu. "Representing History in *The Jumbie Bird.*" *World Literature Written in English* 30 (Spring 1990): 17–28.

Lacovia, R. M. "Ismith Khan and the Theory of Rasa." *Black Images* 1 (Autumn-Winter 1972): 23–27.

Ramchand, Kenneth. "Obeah and the Supernatural in West Indian Literature." *Jamaica Journal* 3 (June 1969): 52–54.

HANIF KUREISHI (1954–)
Alpana Sharma Knippling

BIOGRAPHY

Born in 1954 to an Indian father and a British mother in England, Hanif Kureishi has emerged as a leading voice of Asian, particularly Pakistani and Indian, immigrant cultures in that country. His father went to England for his education and, upon marrying an Englishwoman, chose to stay on there. Remaining members of the Kureishi family in Bombay, India, moved to Pakistan after the partition of Indian and Pakistan. It is no mistake, then, that Hanif Kureishi speaks with familiarity of the cultures of at least three countries: India, Pakistan, and Britain. But he considers himself primarily British: " 'People think I'm caught between two cultures, but I'm not. I'm British; I can make it in England. It's my father who's caught' " (Pally 53).

Growing up in a rather featureless suburb of London called Bromley, he witnessed with conflicting emotions his British friends' racist practice of "Paki-bashing." Initially ashamed, Kureishi would in the mid-1960s withdraw from these friends and begin to collect examples of racist language and ideas from the speeches of such politicians as Enoch Powell. The 1960s, a profoundly formative period in his life, introduced him to the work of James Baldwin and the tactics of the Black Panthers in the United States, and through them, to the possibility of a structured resistance to bigotry. It was during this time that Kureishi decided he was going to be a writer: " 'You can avenge yourself on the world by rearranging it in a way that suits you' " (Appleyard 44).

Kureishi studied at a technical college and, subsequently, made the move to London, where he studied for a degree in philosophy from King's College. Upon graduation, he began to write plays. Even before King's College, however, in 1976, Kureishi had submitted a play to the Royal Court Theatre (*Soaking Up the Heat*) and, as a result, was invited to watch rehearsals there. He continued to work at the Royal Court Theatre through his graduate years. If his philosophical leanings had been toward existentialism—Camus and Sartre—his influences in drama were no less radical: Peter Gill, Caryl Churchill, Max Stafford-Clark, and Bill Gaskill. Later, Kureishi was to eschew the idealistic politics of such left-wing directors and playwrights.

It was when the Soho Poly produced his play, *The King and Me*, in 1980, that Kureishi achieved some measure of success, culminating in a production at the Riverside Studio Company. This play, *The Mother Country*, won the Thames Television Playwright Award for 1980. In 1981, Kureishi became writer in residence at the Royal Court Theatre. In the same year, he won the George Devine Award for his next play, *Outskirts*, and then wrote two more plays, *Tomorrow—Today!* and *Borderline*.

Although his plays demonstrated a decided mastery of dramatic conventions, Kureishi still lacked a meaningful subject. By the mid-1980s, though, a subject—the Asian immigrant experience in Britain, dramatized with an attendant concern for imbrications of sexuality and politics—suggested itself to him in a crystallizing of events: the prior experience of having written *The Mother Country* and *Borderline*, the subsequent invitation by Channel 4 to write a film script, and a 1985 trip to Pakistan. Kureishi's work has since revelled in the particular ironies of the Asian (specifically Pakistani and Indian) immigrant culture in Britain. *The Mother Country* alerted him to the lack of attention he had paid to the entire subject of Asian life in Britain, while *Borderline* demonstrated his hesitant introduction to that hitherto missing subject; Channel 4's request to write about Asian immigrant life in Britain led him to the need to investigate native Pakistani culture; and his visit to Pakistan introduced him to the striking ironies involved in the articulation of a Pakistani temperament in both native and immigrant terms: native educated Pakistanis considered their immigrant counterparts to be Westernized traitors who "deserve whatever brutality they find in England because they are dirty and contemptible, while the white working classes in England disparage all Pakistanis—rich and poor" (Pally 50).

Kureishi began writing the script for his first major work, *My Beautiful Laundrette*, in Karachi, Pakistan, in 1985 and slid the completed draft under the door of the well-known British film director Stephen Frears. Frears recognized the freshness of the script, but neither Kureishi nor Frears was prepared for the eventual commercial success of the low-budget film, which was released first in Britain through Channel 4, and then in the United States through Orion Classics in 1986. Kureishi received an Oscar nomination for Best Screenplay for the script of *My Beautiful Laundrette*. He also published the screenplay of the film, along with an autobiographical companion, *The Rainbow Sign* (London and Boston: Faber and Faber, 1986).

The Kureishi-Frears partnership continued with their next film, *Sammy and Rosie Get Laid* (made in 1987 and released by the Cinecom Entertainment Group in 1988). Like *My Beautiful Laundrette*, this second film concerned itself with problematic aspects of Pakistani life in Britain, but was less universally celebrated than its predecessor. Its screenplay, coupled with Kureishi's diary, was also published in 1988, first by Faber and Faber in London and then by Penguin in London and the United States.

Having aspired all along to make his mark as a writer of fiction, Kureishi turned his attention to short stories such as "Esther" (*Atlantic* 263 [May 1989]). His most recent work comprises a provocative novel, *The Buddha of Suburbia*, which was published by Viking Penguin in 1990, and which received largely favorable reviews. Kureishi currently resides in West Kensington, London.

MAJOR WORKS AND THEMES

Hanif Kureishi's early one-act plays, such as *The King and Me* and *Tomorrow—Today!*, demonstrate thematic concerns that would surface again in his major work, such as the stagnation of family life, the violence of the decaying urban wilderness, and the now comic, now terrible, quirks in the lives of the rejected and marginalized. However, his characters were British and white. Kureishi's interest in the immigrant experience and ethnic conflict began to surface in 1981, when he was commissioned by Max Stafford-Clark to write about the Asian immigrant experience in Britain, in a collaborative workshop with the cast. This collaborative project eventually grew into the play *Borderline*. Initially, Kureishi was reluctant to venture outside his own experience for his material, and at one point during the workshop, he shouted, " 'It's impossible, I'll never be able to do it, write a play based on people I barely know, whose experiences I have never had, most of whom are from countries I've never visited' " ("Author's Note," *Borderline* 4). Perhaps Kureishi's salvation lay in conceiving the "immigrant experience" not as an isolated and self-contained issue, but, more importantly, as a perspective. Realizing this perspective, Kureishi wrote, "I realised that the issues of race, immigration, integration and the colonial legacy are closely connected to other issues and attitudes, they are like cracks in a wall through which you can view landscapes" ("Author's Note," *Borderline* 4).

With *Borderline*, Kureishi's scenes retain the quality of vignettes that had characterized his one-act efforts, but there is an increasingly broad perspective through which juxtaposition and montage take on a direction. Political unrest and quasi-organized violence in the streets emerge as a backdrop for interpersonal conflicts. Something like a sustained political debate between liberal, assimilationist, and radical positions or posturings also emerges, as immigrants with a faith in institutions confront active members of the Asian Youth Movement. The former group believes in slow progress, while the latter group reminds everyone that people are being burnt to death. In this manner, the actual heterogeneity of Asian immigrants is usefully enacted. At the same time, however, Kureishi's treatment is consistently bemused and epigrammatic. A question arises as to whether he achieves a trenchant treatment of politics, valuably foregrounding unde-cideability and indeterminacy, refusing the reductions of protest allegory or political treatise, or whether he raises issues for his own purposes only to abandon them with a wisecrack and a resigned shrug.

While the plays achieved local fame for Kureishi, his major work consists of the screenplays for *My Beautiful Laundrette* and *Sammy and Rosie Get Laid* as well as the novel, *The Buddha of Suburbia*. Viewed together, they enact an explosion of traditional Anglo-American literary and cultural con-ventions and concerns. While even what is traditional in literature in the United Kingdom and the United States has already been radicalized with the advent of hitherto marginalized cultures—mass or "popular," feminist, black, Asian, postcolonial, gay, and lesbian—Kureishi insists upon a more radical view of the discourse of radicalism itself, for he refuses for himself the persona of a writer of socially committed, politically correct causes. His writing may best be described as consisting of a particular tracing of the imbrications of race, sex, class, and politics that is willing to undo its own labor with an occasional deflating, comic-satirical, and ultimately subversive stroke. Thus, a montage in *Sammy and Rosie Get Laid* depicts, in quick succession, an exterior shot of policemen roping off a street, an interior shot in which a black mother in South London is brutally and mistakenly shot by one of the policemen, and a scene in which a white woman—Anna, the American photographer—is lying in bed with Sammy, revealing a tattoo of "W" on each of her buttocks (which, she explains, will spell "wow" when she bends over).

Kureishi's first film, *My Beautiful Laundrette*, interrogates the hitherto unobserved life of Pakistani immigrants in London. Focusing on the devel-oping romance between the young Omar (played by Gordon Warnecke) and his old cockney schoolfriend, Johnny (Daniel Day Lewis), the film manages to traverse the entire range of that vast, heterogeneous, immigrant life, from Omar's burnt-out alcoholic father to his extended family of upper-class Pakistani businessmen who are faring better than many of their British counterparts. Seething resentment on both the Pakistani immigrant and the native British sides erupts into increasingly violent racist confrontations, bringing the relationship between Omar and Johnny to crisis.

Early in the film, Omar is portrayed as a college-age man whose life is headed nowhere. When his uncle, Nasser (Saeed Jaffrey), offers him a job, Omar enlists the aid of his once-friend, Johnny, who is jobless at the time and who, along with his cockney friends, either hangs out or goes "Paki-bashing" in the seamy sections of London. Together, Omar and Johnny try to make a success out of Nasser's slummy laundromat, even as they discover a sexual passion between themselves. Their budding gay relationship is depicted by Kureishi sentimentally, romantically. Indeed, Kureishi has said that the script needed a love story, a "Romeo and Juliet," but that it couldn't represent an edgeless male friendship: " 'There had to be a passion between them to drive [the story]' " (Appleyard 44).

Eventually, Johnny's elevated economic status introduces intolerable ambivalences in his identity. He is already an outsider to Omar's family circle; but he is also an outsider to his own former community of socially underclass friends. Similar alienations turn up everywhere: Omar discovers the snobbery of his upper-class Pakistani family members, and his uncle, Nasser, agonizingly breaks off his ties to his longstanding British mistress upon his wife's vengeful voodoo assaults on the mistress's body. The film resolves the estranging distances caused by intense differences between classes, races, and sexes by a scene of brutal racial rioting, during which the laundromat is trashed by Johnny's friends and Omar and Johnny temporarily part ways.

My Beautiful Laundrette is a masterful film, not only because its project is ambitious in scope, but also because it disavows comfortable solutions to Britain's current multicultural, multiracial crisis in favor of a grim chronicling of unresolvable and irreconcilable tensions. When Johnny and Omar finally reconcile, they do not choose sides; they merely return to existences that have been touched by alienating cultural differences and, consequently, will never be the same. Further, the two sides, Pakistani and British, are portrayed as themselves deeply interdependent rather than separate and inviolable. In the era of late capitalism and postcolonialism in Britain, it is the Pakistani businessmen who have successful jobs and who are in the position of enlisting British labor: it is Omar who can better Johnny's economic status. This inverted situation is dramatized in the two men's feverishly clandestine sexual activity, in which who is pleasuring whom is unclear. But perhaps no character demonstrates more inexorably the predicament of living at the fringes of both the Pakistani and the British worlds than Nasser's daughter, Tania (Rita Wolf). Tania represents a new generation of Pakistanis in Britain for whom a return to the old ways is as absurd as the process of assimilation in contemporary mainstream British culture.

Kureishi's next film, *Sammy and Rosie Get Laid*, continues his investigation of the interrelations of race, class, sex, and politics against the backdrop of urban Pakistani life in Britain. As with the first film, we see a romantic couple that is marginalized in mainstream British life. The difference between the two films, however, is that here the love story centers around a *heterosexual* interracial couple, Sammy (Ayub Khan Din), the London-bred son of a Pakistani politician, and Rosie (Frances Barber), a British social worker. Beginning and ending with a slow overview shot of London slums and a voiceover of Margaret Thatcher describing the Tory plan to remedy problems of the inner city, the film only sporadically fulfills its promise of a scathing documentation of British politics in the metropolis.

After a glimpse of the rather self-righteously styled counterculture urban life of the married couple, we are introduced to Sammy's father, Rafi Rahman (Shashi Kapoor), a wealthy Pakistani politician and former freedom fighter, who has fled to England in the wake of several attempts on his life. England, as he envisions it, is the placid colonial landscape of civilized conversations over tea. But when he arrives in London, he finds it quite literally set afire with racial riots, its inner city streets populated with anarchic looters and squatters. Subsequent events unfold both Rafi's former history as a corrupt politician who ensured his power by systematic torture and his present desire to settle down in England with his ex-mistress, Alice (Claire Bloom), a middle-aged, genteel Englishwoman, once he has consolidated his son's future with a huge sum of money. Thanks to the fact-finding mission of Rosie's lesbian friends, who uncover the horrendous details of Rafi's past, and to a blood-sodden, bandaged specter of one of his past torture victims, Rafi's desire for an anonymous life of ease is rendered impossible, and he commits suicide. The film draws to a close with the picture of Sammy and Rosie locked in a despairing embrace and a scene of mass evacuation of squatters from London's inner city.

Like *My Beautiful Laundrette*, *Sammy and Rosie Get Laid* demystifies both Pakistani and British perspectives in the name of social and political critique rather than social and political reform, but it does so partially. Rosie's imagined radicalism unravels in the face of Rafi's decolonized position on history, while the diasporic space of the postcolonial occupied by Sammy (" 'Neither of us are English, we're Londoners you see' " [33]) foregrounds the actual—neither British nor Pakistani but metropolitan—immigrant worldview in Margaret Thatcher's Britain. But too many indeterminations afloat make for an intermittent, not ongoing, critique. It is unclear what is gained by Rosie's one-night stand with the black vagrant, Danny/"Victoria" (Roland Gift); the two lesbians, Vivia (Suzette Llewellyn) and Rani (Meera Syal), one black, the other Pakistani, seem to activate rather vacant ideological imperatives with their mightily overdone onscreen kissing. Hovering over *Sammy and Rosie Get Laid*, from Rosie's motto for her marriage, "freedom and commitment," to the scenes of hippies at play in the squatters' homes and communal get-togethers, is a kind of 1960s nostalgia, according to which the social order can be subverted if people only really *care* about each other. Such nostalgia is not only naive but also misplaced: the social order—in this case, Thatcher's Tory Britain—needs not an emotional response but a systematic intervention from its margins.

If, in *Sammy and Rosie Get Laid*, Kureishi's critique of British culture follows a sporadic path, in his next, and most recent, major work, *The Buddha of Suburbia*, it assumes a minor key. The novel marks Kureishi's break from screenwriting, which he currently views as involving less autonomy and free play of the imagination. A picaresque *bildungsroman* that follows the life and loves of Karim Amir, a half-Indian, half-British young man, *The Buddha of Suburbia* is a noteworthy, yet uneven, text. In it, Kureishi powerfully refines two functions already at work in his previous

writing: those of chronicling or documenting a life embroiled in the necessarily political issues of race, class, and sex and of satirizing those very
issues in a comic vein. But these two functions do not always work together,
as when the comic-satirical lapses to the level of a sexual farce.

Karim is the product of an interracial marriage between Haroon, the self-
styled Buddha of the book's title, who came to England from India in 1950
with his brother, Anwar, for his education and who preaches the art of
higher consciousness to his neighbors, and Margaret, an Englishwoman
whose roots are deeply entrenched in her hometown, Chislehurst, and for
whom World War II is still a live memory. Karim whiles away his teens
through a dedicated, if deliberate, immersion in the Rolling Stones, Norman
Mailer, various herbal tea combinations, and drugs. Frustrated by the boredom of the suburbs, where "security and safety were the reward of dullness"
(8), and his schoolboy crush on Chislehurst's latest rebel, Charlie, Karim
witnesses his parents' breakup, but he is only too pleased to move to
London—the city of unimaginably exciting possibilities—with his new family, consisting of his father, Eva, Charlie's mother, and Charlie himself.

Through a series of accidents, Karim lands the role of Mowgli in a second-
rate stageplay fashioned after Rudyard Kipling's *The Jungle Book*. With
brown paint rubbed over his body, he plays at being Kipling's Indian even
as he is disgusted by the part ("I resembled a turd in a bikini-bottom"
[146]). The role, however, enables him to invade certain avant-garde theater
circles in London. Their left-wing pretensions and hypocrisies are unveiled
by Karim, but his infiltration into their ranks makes possible a visit to the
United States, while on his tour with a stage production.

In the United States, Karim reunites with Charlie, who is now a famous
American rock-star, and stays on with him, doing nothing in particular.
The novel closes with Karim's return to London, following the prospect of
an important audition there. Defying the traditional structure of a novel
whose various voyages fully develop the main character's view of the world,
The Buddha of Suburbia eschews such character development: Karim comes
back with a more intense sense of what it meant to be British, but he is not
as much changed as he is changing. Nor is he always at the novel's center.
His feminist cousin's husband, Changez, forced on her by an arranged
marriage, embodies more pathetically and fully than any other immigrant
character the process of acculturation.

The novel is partially autobiographical. Karim's opening announcement
("I am often considered to be a funny kind of Englishman, a new breed, as
it were, having emerged from two old histories" [3]) represents the mixed
ancestry of Kureishi himself. Karim's hankering after the novelties of city
life while wasting away in a South London suburb is Kureishi's own former
predicament. The writer's exposure to London's theater scene becomes Karim's exposure. Even the punk rock-star, Charlie, is modeled after Kureishi's
own grade-school mate: Bill Broad, better known as Billy Idol. At some

point, however, the specificity of autobiographical correspondence gives itself over to the broader, more textured space in which numerous elements of a writer's life are mutatively written into his work.

Of these elements, no two are more insistent in Kureishi's case than his engagement with the politics of race, class, and sex, and his simultaneous distance from those very politics vis-à-vis his subversive, comic-satirical voice. An episode from the novel succinctly fuses the two—the comic-satirical vein and the political subject: Karim arrives at the run-down suburban house of a high school acquaintance, whom he wants to woo, but her cockney father not only forbids him to enter (his message replete with racist addresses such as "wog," "blackie," "coon," and "nigger"); he also lets loose after Karim his Great Dane, who promptly proceeds to masturbate on Karim's back. The scene is described funnily by Kureishi, but a scathing political critique of white working-class racist practice (which views the entire "black race," regardless of their class, as a threat) survives one's laughter. Similarly, Karim's Mowgli is hilarious, but it also poses the serious question of whether race is an absolute truth or whether it is a parodic performance and repetition in the postcolonial age.

Such political critique does not, however, inform several other scenes, which seem solely to service the reader's titillation. In these, critique is entertained in an incidental, by-the-way fashion, as an interesting proposition that is never quite fulfilled. Still, *The Buddha of Suburbia* consolidates Kureishi's status as Britain's newest, most engaging literary and diasporic voice.

CRITICAL RECEPTION

As yet, no full-length study of Hanif Kureishi's work has been published. His screenplays and novel have, however, received many reviews in leading newspapers and magazines, ranging from the *New York Times Book Review* and the *New Yorker* to the *New Republic* and the *Nation*. The ambivalence of many of these reviews reflects, in part, Kureishi's refusal to be a writer of causes, so that his writing fluctuates between political commentary and sometimes comic-satirical, sometimes farcical scenes.

My Beautiful Laundrette was unanimously received as a powerful film, particularly for its honesty toward the neither-black-nor-white issue of race, although, in the *New York Times Film Review* Vincent Canby noted in passing that some moments appear obscure and some characters behave implausibly (C8:5). *Sammy and Rosie Get Laid*, on the other hand, almost unanimously disappointed reviewers, who had come to see Kureishi as an exciting new screenwriter. Their chief complaint was that the film opted for a brilliance and dazzle which, finally, lacked depth. According to Pauline Kael, "the film suffers from the curse of the British: verbal facility, a terrible empty brilliance. I don't recall ever hearing so many failed epigrams in one movie" (142). Yet Stanley Kauffmann of the *New Republic* praised the film's obliqueness: "A new sidewise sophistication...is now the best way for art to approach ancient troubles" (24). For the most powerful defense of the film, see Gayatri Spivak's "In praise of *Sammy and Rosie Get Laid*," in which she considered it to be more of a "social text" than Kureishi's first film (80–88).

Critics' responses to *The Buddha of Suburbia* have been mixed, but the majority of them were generous, owing in part to Kureishi's status as a newcomer. Clark Blaise acknowledged the promise and freshness of the novel, while noting that the "book reads like three novellas flattened into one long narrative" (20). David Kim appreciated the novel's lack of preachiness (5), while Gilbert Adair called it a "multiracial artefact" that nevertheless appears rambling (34).

BIBLIOGRAPHY

Works by Hanif Kureishi

Borderline. London: Methuen/Royal Court Theatre, 1981.
Birds of Passage. Oxford: Amber Lane Press, 1983.
Outskirts, The King and Me, and Tomorrow—Today!. London: John Calder, 1983.
"Gentle Britain No More." *Harper's* 272 (May 1986): 22–23.
My Beautiful Laundrette. Dir. Stephen Frears. Orion Classics, 1986.
My Beautiful Laundrette and The Rainbow Sign. London and Boston: Faber and Faber, 1986.
"The Buddha of Suburbia." Excerpt. *Harper's* 274 (June 1987): 45–51.
Sammy and Rosie Get Laid. Dir. Stephen Frears. Cinecom Entertainment Group, 1987.
Sammy and Rosie Get Laid. Excerpts from screenplay. *Film Comment* 23 (Sept.–Oct. 1987): 70–74.
"Behind the Veils: Notes on Pakistan." *Utne Reader* (July–Aug. 1988): 84–90.
Sammy and Rosie Get Laid. New York: Penguin Books, 1988.
"Esther." *Atlantic* 263 (May 1989): 56–62.
The Buddha of Suburbia. New York: Viking Penguin, 1990.
"A Marriage of Convenience." *Mother Jones* 15 (April–May 1990): 77–78.

Studies of Hanif Kureishi

Adair, Gilbert. "The Skin Game." Review of *The Buddha of Suburbia*. *New Statesman and Society* 30 (Mar. 30, 1990): 34.
Appleyard, Brian. "The Boy from Bromley." Interview with Hanif Kureishi. *Sunday Times* (Mar. 25, 1990): 42–46.
Blaise, Clark. "A Guru by Night." Review of *The Buddha of Suburbia*. *New York Times Book Review* (May 6, 1990): 20.
Canby, Vincent. Review of *My Beautiful Laundrette*. *New York Times Film Review* (Mar. 7, 1986): C8:5.

————. "Chaotic London." Review of *Sammy and Rosie Get Laid. New York Times Film Review* (Oct. 30, 1987): C5:1.

Collins, Glenn. Interview with Hanif Kureishi. *New York Times* (24 May 1990): C17.

Glicksman, Marlaine. "Hanif Kureishi." *Rolling Stone* (Nov. 19, 1987): 33–34.

Hinson, Hal. "*Sammy and Rosie's* Brash Allure." Review of *Sammy and Rosie Get Laid. Washington Post* (Dec. 23, 1987): D1, D10.

Howe, Desson. "Sammy and Rosie Get Lost." Review of *Sammy and Rosie Get Laid. Washington Post* (Dec. 25, 1987): 27.

Jimenez, Felix. Review of *The Buddha of Suburbia. Nation* (July 9, 1990): 63–64.

Kael, Pauline. "The Current Cinema." Review of *Sammy and Rosie Get Laid. New Yorker* 63 (Nov. 16, 1987): 140–42.

Kauffmann, Stanley. "Stanley Kauffmann on Films." Review of *Sammy and Rosie Get Laid. New Republic* (Nov. 30, 1987): 24–26.

Kim, David D. Review of *The Buddha of Suburbia. Village Voice Literary Supplement* 86 (June 12, 1990): 5.

Ozer, Jerome, ed. Collected Reviews of *Sammy and Rosie Get Laid. Film Review Annual* (1988): 1320–32.

Pally, Marcia. "Kureishi Like a Fox." Interview with Hanif Kureishi. *Film Comment* 22 (Sept.–Oct. 1986): 50–55.

Spivak, Gayatri Chakravorty. "In Praise of *Sammy and Rosie Get Laid.*" *Critical Quarterly* 31 (Summer 1989): 80–88.

HAROLD SONNY LADOO
(1945–1973)
Srimati Mukherjee

BIOGRAPHY

Harold Sonny Ladoo was born in Couva, Trinidad, in 1945. The region he was most familiar with was the plantation area near McBean village, Trinidad, where he spent a large part of his life. Prior to his departure for Canada, Ladoo worked on the plantation fields and in boats, facts that, no doubt, enhance the realistic nature of his fictional delineation of plantation and water scenes. Ladoo, however, determined to move beyond the microcosmic island setting and left the West Indies for Toronto, Canada, in 1968. While pursuing a Bachelor of Arts degree in English at Erindale College, University of Toronto, Ladoo generally studied and wrote during the day and took up night jobs, such as dishwashing in restaurants, to support his wife and two children. In 1972 he graduated from Erindale College and then published his first novel, *No Pain Like This Body*. The following year, aided by a grant from the Canadian government, Ladoo returned to Trinidad with the intent of further research for his fiction. Ironically it was in Trinidad, the land that had inspired the milieu of his novels, that Ladoo was found brutally assaulted in a ditch, presumed to have been murdered. His second and last novel, *Yesterdays*, generally assumed to be incomplete, was published posthumously in 1974 as was his short story "The Quiet Peasant," in *Canada in Us Now*, in 1976. During his lifetime, Ladoo had won acknowledgment and support from writers Dennis Lee and Peter Such. At his death, Ladoo left behind manuscripts of poems, short stories, and several unfinished novels. According to Geoff Hancock, Ladoo had intended his novels "to form part of a Faulknerian cycle of up to 100 novels encompassing the history of the West Indies, his own biography, a history of Canada in the Caribbean, and slavery" (422).

MAJOR WORKS AND THEMES

What immediately strikes the reader of Harold Sonny Ladoo's first published novel, *No Pain Like This Body* (1972), is the sensuous, organic quality of the narrative. Apart from a profusion of onomatopoeic words, a large number of the similes used to depict human conditions repeatedly draw the reader into nature. Ladoo takes liberally from the elemental world to underscore the thin line between the human and the natural in this tale of cataclysmic ravage. The novel offers an unflinching presentation of a nature that both sustains and devastates. In a way, it seems appropriate that *No Pain Like This Body* is written from the child's point of view, a point of view that presents both the delights and the horrors inherent in the landscape, without any attempts at concealment. The authenticity of the child's point of view is reflected also in the nature of the similes, many of which stand out by virtue of their sheer simplicity and hence beauty. This is borne out by the following instance, "Ma felt grief; her grief was not as shallow as a basket, it was deeper than a river; deep like the sea; like a sea without fishes" (56). This simile, in fact, gets striking toward the end where the lack of movement or color in the water parallels, in the child's consciousness, the depth and uniform opaqueness of a sorrow that has nothing to redeem it. Further, the child's perspective imbues the narrative with an engaging freshness and with a delightful sense of wonder expressed at the simplest of things. Moreover, as characteristic of a child, there is a recounting of episodes with a clear focus on factual details. The novel primarily explores the miserable living conditions of a family of East Indian rice growers on Ladoo's imaginary "'Carib Island" in the West Indies. Written in dialect and in a sharply realistic vein, the narrative unfolds to show how this family of Pa, Ma, Balraj, Sunaree, Rama, and Panday is beset by raging storms, poverty, drunkenness, death, and insanity. The theme of man's puny struggles in the face of adverse elements and an inimical fate looms large in the novel. However, rare intimations of beauty do not escape the reader. The night scene in which rain falls, Nanny's long, bony fingers beat the goatskin drum, Sunaree plays the bamboo flute which produces music "sweeter than sugar," and Ma dances re-creates, in the West Indian setting, the ambience of a monsoon night in India and clearly brings to mind the music and dancing of Indian tribes such as the Santals. The feel of India is also present in Ladoo's deft descriptions of the rice fields and rice planting. Even while battling in a West Indian milieu, in moments of extreme stress, some of the characters are said to abandon the adopted English dialect and to communicate in the mother tongue (in this case Hindi). More transparent instances of the Indian influence are addresses such as "Sitaram," a continuing emphasis placed on caste distinctions by Indian locals, vignettes of lice picking prototypical of Indian villages, and a striking depiction of female drunkenness and bawdy humor, during the wake for Rama, reminiscent of group behavioral patterns of certain rural Indian women in equally grim situations.

If the diasporic consciousness manifests itself in scattered segments through *No Pain Like This Body*, in Ladoo's second novel, *Yesterdays* (1974), it becomes the agonized voice of loss that sounds ominously through the narrative. The novel is set in the Karan Settlement, once again in Carib Island, and one theme that rears its head repeatedly is that of lost territory. Separation from the motherland is loss too mammoth to forget, and several of the characters in *Yesterdays* are compulsive about new territorial acquisition. Apart from obvious instances of concern for property, such as Choonilal's fear of mortgaging his house, Ladoo frequently resorts to scatological and sexual metaphors to emphasize territorial interests and concepts of loss. Choonilal, one of the key characters in the novel, is denied the use of his own latrine and is compelled to seek out alternate places for defecating. This is clearly an analogy for the loss of one's home ground and a more veiled pointer to marking out new territory, even if that marking out is with excrement in a canine manner. The idea of branding property with excrement is reiterated in Choonilal's comment to his son, Poonwa: "Never forget boy dat you pee and shit fust touch dis earth in Karan Settlement. Didn't care where you livin in dis world, never forget home" (108). The concept of losing home ground is seen also in Sook, the village queer, who abandons his wife to practice sodomy with Poonwa in the Christian Church. The reader cannot but sense the implication that once legitimate territory is lost, new acquisitions can only be as unnatural as sex in God's house. Ladoo breaks down watertight compartmentalizations, as the scatological, the sexual, and the divine are frequently yoked together in this recounting of episodes at Karan Settlement. These at times unpleasant and often startling juxtapositions hint at the broader notion that in the immigrant consciousness, tenets of two diametrically opposed cultures often exist in a medley rather than in a patterned whole. Time barriers seem to be demolished as well, especially in the instance of Sook, who has an affair with Choonilal and later indiscriminately lusts after the latter's son, Poonwa. This loss of a sense of chronological progression can be linked to that part of the diasporic consciousness that is no longer grounded in the time of the motherland and is often out of touch with historical developments there. However, even if uprooted from or denied contact with India, many of the characters continue to think in uniquely Indian ways only and are unable to embrace the new culture to which they have migrated. This is exemplified in Pandit Puru's refusal to use local architects for the construction of a Hindu temple and in Choonilal's insistence that an indoor toilet is unholy. More of a compromise, albeit a sad one, is seen in Poonwa, who adopts tenets of the Western world without relinquishing a sense of his Indian identity, even if that identity is in jeopardy. In fact, even with Poonwa's raging and rather confused state of mind, the reader senses the sharp accuracy of statements such as "Today both Indian and Negro exist without culture. They are a lost people" (29). Poonwa empathizes with the dilemma of Indians who have moved away from home, especially with those who have been further subjected to missionary zeal. His avowal to go on a Hindu mission to Canada to teach Canadians "to mimic Indian ways" and to finally "let them go to exist without history" (78) characterizes his attempt to avenge Canadian missionary excesses arbitrarily inflicted on the Hindus in Carib Island. Poonwa's stance reveals the anger and the vengeance latent in the diasporic consciousness, but also an awareness of the ultimate rootlessness that sometimes results when one has no sense of being grounded in any one culture.

Ladoo's "The Quiet Peasant" (1976) once again shows the stubborn persistence of singularly Indian concepts and customs in the West Indies. There is mention of caste and dowry. In fact, the protagonist Gobinah's acquiescence to the demands of dowry for his daughter brings on his premature death as he labors rigorously to make the much needed money. In its portrayal of man striving in vain against a fate that cannot be beaten, the story draws close to *No Pain Like This Body*.

CRITICAL RECEPTION

Critics, in general, seem to be more favorably disposed to *No Pain Like This Body* than to *Yesterdays*. However, appreciation of the former work includes a greater eulogizing of technique rather than content. Speaking of noteworthy stylistic features in the novel, Clement Wyke refers to the author's use of "reduplication as a substitute for a grammatical intensifier" (45), a feature that points to Ladoo's familiarity with peculiarities found in creole forms of English. Wyke also notes Ladoo's competence in "exploring the cadences of dialogue" (45), as does Bruce Bailey, who refers to "the vitality and beauty of the dialect" in *No Pain Like This Body*, elements that help the novel to "survive plotlessness, as do Synge's dramas or Pinter's vignettes" ("No" 48). Bailey further compares Ladoo to a "Renaissance painter, applying only the warm hues to his work," for "Ladoo uses a simple vocabulary to fill out his latticework of subject-verb-objects, which is saved from monotony by periodic breaks from all syntax" ("No" 48). *Yesterdays* receives similar praise for style with critics such as Bailey noting the economy of Ladoo's flashbacks and the "hypnotic, engaging rhythm of the villagers' dialect" ("Yesterdays" 17). However, it is disquieting that several of the critics fail to see the significance of the scatological and sexual references scattered through the novel. This general lapse in recognizing such references as metaphorical of territorial loss or conquest results in observations such as "Ladoo hardly bothers to construct the links or even to allow subtle hints to fall in his scatological gallop through the novel" (Wyke 48). It is not difficult to find other comments of a similar tenor— "Ladoo loses himself in his descriptions of dialogue and everyday situations, so that incident follows incident as Ladoo plays out the variations on sex and shit" (Hatch 110). It is heartening, however, that even if critical reception has left the excremental/sexual mataphors in *Yesterdays* largely undeciphered, it has not failed to pinpoint the rage and pathos lurking beneath the comic facade of the work. Hence Wyke speaks of "the forces of rage and the years of cultural conflicts and evils" in the novel (41), and H. J. Rosengarten closes his review of *Yesterdays* by reminding the reader of the "deep and unappeasable anger" at the heart of the book (98).

BIBLIOGRAPHY

Works by Harold Sonny Ladoo

No Pain Like This Body. Toronto: Anansi, 1972; Caribbean Writers Series, London: Heinemann, 1987.
Yesterdays. Toronto: Anansi, 1974.
"The Quiet Peasant." *Canada in Us Now.* Ed. Harold Head. Toronto: nc, 1976.

Studies of Harold Sonny Ladoo

Bailey, Bruce F. Review of *No Pain Like This Body. Canadian Forum: An Independent Journal of Opinion and the Arts* 52 (1973): 48.
———. Review of *Yesterdays. Canadian Forum: An Independent Journal of Opinion and the Arts* 54 (1974): 17.
Bessai, Diane. Review of *No Pain Like This Body. Canadian Literature* 61 (1974): 108–9.
Birbalsingh, Frank. "*No Pain Like This Body.*" *Open Letter* 2 (1973): 106.
Gadpaille, Michelle. "Novels in English 1960 to 1982: Other Talents, Other Works 2." *The Oxford Companion to Canadian Literature.* Ed. William Toye. Toronto: Oxford University Press, 1983. 589–90.
Hancock, Geoff. "Ladoo, Harold Sonny." *The Oxford Companion to Canadian Literature.* Ed. William Toye. Toronto: Oxford University Press, 1983. 421–22.
Hatch, Ronald. Review of *Yesterdays. Canadian Fiction Magazine* 18 (1975): 109–10.
Naglin, Nancy. "The Tale of Poonwa, the Unofficial White." Review of *Yesterdays. Saturday Night* 89 (1974): 37.
Rosengarten, H. J. "The Walking Ghosts of Empire." Review of *Yesterdays. Canadian Literature* 63 (1975): 96–98.
Sarner, Mark. "*Yesterdays.*" *Books in Canada* 3 (1974): 16.
Story, Norah. "Fiction in English 4." *Supplement to The Oxford Companion to Canadian History and Literature.* Ed. William Toye. Toronto: Oxford University Press, 1973. 84–86.

Such, Peter. "Harold Lowry Ladoo—*Yesterdays.*" *Tamarack Review* 62 (1974): 78–
    80.
———. "The Short Life and Sudden Death of Harold Ladoo." *Saturday Night* 89
    (1974): 36.
Wyke, Clement H. "Harold Ladoo's Alternate Worlds: Canada and Carib Island."
    Canadian Literature 95 (1982): 39–49.

VIJAY LAKSHMI (1943–   )
Anne D. Ulrich

BIOGRAPHY

Today, Vijay Lakshmi lives on a quiet street in the college town of Glenside, Pennsylvania. She was born, however, in Srinagar, India, on April 25, 1943.

Lakshmi took two degrees at the University of Rajasthan in Jaipur. Her doctoral dissertation became the basis for her first book, *Virginia Woolf as Literary Critic*. In the late 1970s she left her teaching position at the university in Jaipur to do postdoctoral work in contemporary literary theories at Yale University as a Senior Fulbright Fellow. She had visited the United States twice before to read papers at the Modern Language Association conventions in New York and San Francisco.

In 1982, she returned to America on a more permanent basis, having married Pradyumna S. Chauhan, an English professor at Beaver College. Balancing the care of a home, the needs of a daughter and son, and the teaching duties at several colleges, she has managed to extend her writing beyond literary criticism to creative fiction.

MAJOR WORKS AND THEMES

Vijay Lakshmi explores the isolation that envelops immigrants who, in their adult years, leave behind their native security to follow a spouse or a dream to the United States. Climate, social conventions, and even manner of dress create barriers that threaten the newcomer's psychological well-being. In a chaotic land, having traveled halfway around the world from India where life was predictable and boundaries well established, immigrants attempt to negotiate a new territory. Inwardly, the newcomers struggle with both real and imagined fears, while outwardly they maintain aloof, serene facades that signal wholeness and security to the new community and often to the families as well. Without a social release or a personal promise of support, the souls of these Lakshmi characters are at risk. Lakshmi understands the emptiness and despair they face as the knowledge that they cannot go back first breaks upon their consciousness. It is of their acceptance, of their rejection, of this new world that Lakshmi writes.

Snow and ice typically lock the narrators inside their new houses upon their arrival in the alien land. Shadows of the past, however, dissolve the reality of the present setting, producing an inner screen on which is recast an Indian home-life in its ideal form. Sunny backyards, landscaped in bougainvillaea arches and jasmine and bela flowers, paint themselves over frosted window panes. Frost inevitably wins, invading the house, isolating the narrator from the husband and children whose outside adventures warm them in their adopted home.

Viewed from the streets, the public buildings stand harsh, blending with the sky in a "cold steel gray." Private dwellings are silhouettes. Although their windows cast light, no life appears within. Ivy seals the windows and doors as it clings and climbs ever higher.

With the exception of the young architect from "The Last Pavilion" (unpublished) all of Lakshmi's narrators are women, most of them mothers, who come to America with husbands skilled in the art of traveling, established in fulfilling careers, prepared to make the transition to Western life. Their children fall easily, too, into new patterns, delighting in snow, finding new friends, and learning school lessons and life lessons without skipping a beat. As if to distance the mother even more than by miles from her traditions, the children balk at her Indian meals and beg that she try Western apparel.

Husbands, tied to their careers and to a desire for worldly recognition, fail to respond to their wives' pleas for security. Not realizing that immersion in American society could soothe the women's fears, they reject the suggestion of work outside the home. More fears surface as the women over-imagine the beauty and competence of American women who work side by side with their men. Isolation becomes alienation when, at parties, Lakshmi's narrators struggle with introductions to people who have been simply names, with unidentifiable foods that recall religious restrictions, and with their own saris that confine their very steps. Uneasy in all settings, the transplanted women reach out tentative hands to sleeping husbands, only to draw them back in haste, not wishing to offend.

Going home to India in her fiction is both the covert and the overt desire of each woman. "We're not going back ... there's nothing to go back to. We'd be misfits there," the husbands tell them.

"We're aliens here," Anu argues for the rest.

"Better to be aliens here than strangers in your own country," Manish replies cryptically ("Distances" 51).

When the narrator in "Touchline" does return to gather her mother and possessions, the proximity of the juhi and the raat-ki-rani flowers cannot erase the reality of the crumbling walls, the barred windows, and the rats on the staircase of the old home. Mother and daughter argue at cross-purposes, and the narrator soon begins to long for her American "home." Even her brother, settled in the States, tells her to leave the mother behind. "The solution is to leave the past and go away" ("Touchline" 32). "Going away" signals acceptance of the Western world for Anu, for Gauri who leaves her lover, and even for Jayant, the architect, who renounces his engagement to a girl in India, sells the property of his dead mother, and returns to the United States then to be mugged as he protects the one bit of beauty he has uncovered.

Only one of Lakshmi's character fails to overcome the isolation, to make the transition. She, the oldest of the narrators, admits, "My world has got distorted, and the boundaries smudged" ("The Release"), as she submits to an intense religious experience and loses her focus.

Lakshmi's strengths as a writer of short stories lie in her first-person narrative, her imagery, and her handling of time. Each woman tells her own story, pulling the Western reader into a novel world of cultural nuances that loses its strangeness with the intimate unfolding of the narrator's isolation and despair. Lakshmi's narrators are at one with women everywhere. When their fears are greatest, horses thunder across the plains of the mind, against skies of liquid fire. When the moments are tender, the fragrance of jasmine and bela, which the narrator wants so much to pack in a box to carry to America, falls off hands "in tufts of cotton" and disappears ("Distances" 54). Time, Lakshmi's most wondrous trick, spans continents in milliseconds. In America, it is lightning, a clock that's going too fast, a mind "ticking furiously like a time bomb" (55). In India, it is the nets, cast by fishermen, that "catch flitting moments—slippery as little eels" ("Touchline" 30). One moment in America, the next in India, our minds lock with the narrator's, and we recognize the vastness of human geography.

Vijay Lakshmi joins such writers as Bharati Mukherjee and Maxine Hong Kingston as she examines the inner world of immigrants. Working and reworking their experiences, she creates characters whose isolation we understand because we are all partners in living. Though the distances we have traveled may not be as great, the insecurity, the alienation, are a part of the human condition.

CRITICAL RECEPTION

In "She Explores the Isolation of Immigration," Erin Kennedy notes that Vijay Lakshmi's success comes from writing "straight from the heart," using the first-person point of view to articulate the inarticulate feelings of others. Lakshmi called the use of "I" in the interview with Kennedy, "a kind of catharsis," which later freed her to achieve a detachment. American women become an area of focus in her later work, reports Kennedy, as Lakshmi explores their self-sufficiency and their ability to deal with their multiple roles.

G. S. Balarama Gupta, in "Vijay Lakshmi's 'Distances': An Appreciatory Note," calls "Distances" a "remarkably good story" and "a sensitive exploration into the problem of emigration." He goes on to say:

Even in the brief space of eight pages, Vijay Lakshmi has creditably succeeded in concretizing her abstract theme of identity crisis which involves such amorphous feelings and emotions as alienation, anguish, rootlessness, loneliness and despair, without ever slipping into the trap of gawky sentimentality or melodrama. Her handling of characters, her suggestive use of symbols and her restrained deployment of language—all these have contributed to the success of this haunting little story (68).

The same could be said of each of her short stories.

Chandra Agarwal chooses Vijay Lakshmi as one of four South Asian–American women writers whose work she examines in her paper "Enough to Manage Life: Humor in South Asian–American Women Writers," to challenge those who say there isn't much humor in South Asian women writers. By way of introduction to Lakshmi's work, she says, "All of her stories are carefully conceived and beautifully written with clever use of symbols, scenes, and feelings. However, her earlier stories are so charged with restrained emotions of the immigrant wife that they give me tears" (11). Instead of acting as, Agarwal says, Bharati Mukherjee's characters do, Lakshmi's female narrators reflect and narrate. Agarwal notes that Lakshmi's descriptions and, indeed, the stories are not long, "but they are so intense" (11). Lakshmi told Agarwal in an interview that she "writes straight from the heart—the heart of an Indian woman transplanted to America . . . from an intensely personal point of view" (11). Of that comment, Agarwal says, "Clearly such writing cannot have any humor because, as everybody knows, we can either laugh or mope" (11). However, in Lakshmi's recent stories, Agarwal says, "She has not become an observer of her own emotions. She has acquired 'a certain detachment.' In her words, 'I've learned to look at myself and yet be myself.' And this learning has colored the stories with quite an ironic stance, one that produces a low, pathetic humor" (12). To illustrate her claim Agarwal uses "Mannequins," the story of the pressured wife/mother who finally goes to a dress shop and, "after many pathetic adventures or humorous adventures, if you can laugh at her misery, buys a beautiful dress" (12), only to discover a family preoccupied by the television when she models her purchase for them. "The irony of the family's preoccupation with TV and of their neglect of the mother and the wife who has sold her soul in trying to please them by wearing an American dress is unmistakable. Equally unmistakable is the reader's snickering at the invincible naivete of the protagonist" (12). Lakshmi's detachment, Agarwal says, makes the stories "infinitely more valuable as a social document."

BIBLIOGRAPHY

Works by Vijay Lakshmi

Virginia Woolf as Literary Critic. New Delhi: Arnold-Heinemann, 1977.
"Smokescreen." *Femina* 23 April 1984: 61, 67.
"Distances." *Journal of Indian Writing in English* 13:2 (1985): 48–55.
"Touchline." *Orbis* 18 (1987): 30–34.
"Home." *Amelia* 4:1 (1990): 1–7.
"Mannequins." *Paris Transcontinental* (Fall 1991): 11–18.

Studies of Vijay Lakshmi

Agarwal, Chandra. "Enough to Manage Life: Humor in South Asian–American Women Writers." Unpublished manuscript.
Cheung, King-Kok, and Stan Yogi. *Asian American Literature: An Annotated Bibliography.* New York: The Modern Languages Association of America, 1988.
Gupta, G. S. Balarama. "Vijay Lakshmi's 'Distances': An Appreciatory Note." *Quest* I (March 1987): 66–69.
Kennedy, Erin. "She Explores the Isolation of Immigration." *Philadelphia Inquirer* Nov. 29, 1987: C6.

KAMALA MARKANDAYA
(1924–   )
Premila Paul

BIOGRAPHY

Kamala Markandaya is reluctant to speak about herself. The monosyllabic answers given to questions in the available interviews seem to direct the readers from the teller to the tale. She wants the works to speak for themselves. Hence the biographical information that the readers have of her is scarce.

Purnaiya Kamala Markandaya is a South Indian Brahmin from an upper middle class background. She was educated in intervals at various schools and at the Madras University. Her father worked for the railways and was an inveterate traveler. Her increasing interest in writing and travel stood in the way of her getting a degree in history. Her keen observation during the travels eventually encouraged her to take to creative writing. She gave up college studies and joined a weekly paper. Later she tried her hand in some clerical and liaison work for the army. After World War II, she attempted an experiment in rural living but soon returned to journalism. She worked in a solicitor's office for a while in London. She married an Englishman in 1948, and has been living in England writing novels ever since. Nine of her novels came out in quick succession between 1954 and 1977.

Kamala Markandaya's determined reticence about herself and her creative life for more than two decades has given rise to much speculation about the close connection between her works and her cultural background. Her novels deal with both Indian and British characters and the clash of Eastern and Western values. They are presented from a woman's point of view and there is conscious applause for the resilience, stoicism, and integrity of the women characters. This encouraged some critics to look for autobiographical elements in her novels. None of her novels could be labeled autobiographical. However, her interracial marriage just a year after India's independence and her residing in the land of the colonial power for decades have undoubtedly conditioned her creative consciousness.

Obsession with one's roots is an inevitable factor in the works of writers who have made a home in a land that is not theirs by birth. Such writers become intensely aware of the culture that they have left behind and there is a constant exploration of the past. Some writers, though they do not deny their past, reveal an eagerness to be assimilated in the adopted culture.

Kamala Markandaya's case is not just one of immigration. She has established an intimate relationship with the West and has made that relationship work. By being away she perceives more of India. As a member of the privileged class in India, she is probably more aware of the racial tension in and around her and of her own vulnerability as an immigrant. If the East-West encounter is a recurrent theme in her novels, it is because of her sustained interest in the complex issues involved in the Indo-British relationship and her perception perhaps is conditioned by her bicultural existence.

MAJOR WORKS AND THEMES

Kamala Markandaya shot into prominence in 1954 with the publication of her first novel, *Nectar in a Sieve* (a phrase from Coleridge), which was a Book-of-the-Month Club Selection. It has been translated into seventeen languages. Bookman's Manual (Fiction Catalogue, 1961) called *Nectar in a Sieve* "a simple unaffected story of human suffering, which more than a shelf of books on history and economics explains the people of India." Subtitled "A Novel of Rural India," *Nectar in a Sieve* explores the English industrialism and its sinister consequences that forcibly altered the life style of Indian villagers. A tannery, which is at the center of the novel, stands for all that is evil in capitalism and the imperial West, whereas a medical missionary, Dr. Kennington, popularly known as Kenny (reminiscent of de la Havre in Mulk Raj Anand's *Two Leaves and a Bud*), balances the picture with his medical services and altruism. In contrast to the thriving tannery, Kenny has to struggle to keep the hospital going. He tries his best to jolt the villagers out of apathy, ignorance, superstitiousness, and fatalism, but with little effect.

The novel presents in particular the plight of Rukmani and Nathan, victims of landlordism. The tannery uproots their peasant life. Nathan is evicted from the land he has been farming for thirty years and from the hut he had built with his own hands. Then it is the familiar pattern of moving to the city in pursuit of greener pastures and the disillusioned return. Nathan dies in the city. It is a horrible picture of human degradation where Iravadi, Rukmani's daughter, rejected by her husband as a barren woman, has to turn to prostitution to feed her dying brother, Kuti. The albino son born in the process has to be protected. Dr. Kenny could always be counted upon as a source of love and strength. Yet he always remains "a man half in shadow, half in light, defying knowledge" (90). Despite a long stay in India Kenny never understands the fatalism of the villagers: "I do not understand you. I never will." Rukmani's simple answer is "Our ways are not yours" (111). The understanding between them does not grow any further. Kenny longs to be treated as one of the villagers. Despite all familiarity and closeness, Rukmani returns gratitude for love and sees only a master and a benefactor in Kenny. Her casual remark that India can never be his country gives Kenny a painful awareness. He faces reality stripped of all illusions: "My country . . . sometimes I do not know which is my country. Until today I had thought perhaps it was this" (129).

An affirmative note in the novel is found in the strong familial love, the resilience and stoicism of Rukmani. The poor are always willing to help the fellow-poor. Even when faced with adversity, Rukmani does not hesitate to take in a leper boy, Puli. In the end the hospital is built, and Puli is healed. The novel glorifies underlying love and human interdependence.

Because of the glossary and the frequent authorial intervention to explain customs, rituals, taboos, and beliefs, one is tempted to believe that Kamala Markandaya has interpreted rural India for the Western readers.

The Independence Movement at its peak becomes the background in *Some Inner Fury* (1955). This largely nonviolent movement had its own sporadic violent outbursts. The novel exposes one such incident. The writer also explores the relationship between Mirabai and Richard, Premala and Hickey and the Western-educated Kitsamy, thus dealing with the East-West tension at both the political and personal levels.

Kit, who has felt the impact of Western education, has divided loyalties. Though he has modern views, the fact that Premala is traditional pleases him. In England he had a white girlfriend, but destroys her photo after he meets Premala. He marries Premala, but she finds the Westernized household stifling. Kit's parents, the so-called liberals, have two guest rooms, one for the Indian and the other for the English guests. Premala gets inhibited and nervous about Western etiquette, to the greatest disappointment of the stereotypical burra sahib, Kit. At the same time she feels perfectly secure and confident while assisting the British missionary, Hickey, on a village resettlement scheme. Kit's adopted brother, Govind, is a militant nationalist whose parochial Indian sentiments destroy the British school and also kill Premala, with whom he is in love. In the phase of political uprising, Mira and Richard become very aware of their racial disparity and find themselves naturally in opposite camps just by being themselves. There is just one way of seeing people—Indian or English, a nationalist or a government supporter. It is a situation where one's allegiance is put to the test, and taking sides becomes inevitable. Richard and Mira painfully realize that powerful forces keep them apart. Intimate relationships are possible only on equal terms, not between the colonizer and the colonized.

We are introduced to three kinds of Indians in this novel: Indians who are anti-British, those who cringe before the British, and the Western-educated liberals. There is, however, an obvious admiration of the ability to absorb the good in both cultures. Roshan, separated from her husband, is a self-sufficient journalist. It is said of her that "she belonged to the East too. Born in one world, educated in another, she entered both and moved in both with ease and nonchalance. It was a dual citizenship which few people had, which a few may have spurned, but many more envied, and which she herself simply took for granted, and curiously enough, both worlds were glad to welcome her in their midst" (128).

This novel ends in a tragic note. It is a case of the failure of personal relationship in the face of political allegiance. Kamala Markandaya has developed the relationship between Mira and Richard as a tender, ideal one. An ideal probably has to be the unrealizable, the impossible. The sudden realization of identities as "your people" and "my people" leads to the eventual separation of these two people. The fact that the political difference destroys what the racial difference does not, seems unconvincing.

A Silence of Desire (1960—the title is from Longfellow's sonnet "The Three Silences of Molinos") dramatizes the conflict between reason and faith. This is an age-old head-heart conflict. But rationalism is seen as the result of British influence. Dandekar has an English boss. When Dandekar ridicules his wife Sarojini's worship of the tulsi plant, she says, "you with your Western notions, your superior talk of ignorance and superstition . . . you don't know what lies beyond reason and you prefer not to find out" (87–88). The domestic harmony is totally shattered because of Sarojini's seeking the swami's help for a faith cure of the tumor in her womb. Sarojini neglects her household because of her obsession with the faith that is represented by the swami. And Dandekar, who stands for skepticism, does the same because he questions her loyalty to him. Even when he learns about her faith trips, he places reason above intuition. They impose some silence on themselves and fail to communicate. In the investigatory team, Chari represents an instinctive understanding of the relevance of the swami, whereas Ghose sees it all as superstition and even charlatanism. The swami leaves after advising Sarojini to undergo the operation. His departure is exactly what Dandekar had wanted. But when he actually leaves, Dandekar is left with feelings of guilt. Dandekar begins to see the salubrious side of the swami's presence. He cannot deny the swami's power to bring tranquility to those who surround him. He sees the effect of the swami's absence on the community, the needy, and the sick who are almost reduced to derelicts. Kamala Markandaya maintains perfect objectivity by keeping the novelist's attitude toward the swami ambiguous.

Possession (1963), set in England and India, raises issues of ownership. Here, a swami encourages and even inspires Valmiki, a shepherd boy, who paints Hindu gods and goddesses on rocks. Caroline Bell claims that he is her oriental cave discovery and transports him to England as an exotic object for exhibition. He becomes famous overnight. But, though he is delighted with his fame, he could never give up his values like strict vegetarianism. The suffering of the monkey affects him deeply. But under Caroline's influence the fame-drunk Valmiki (reduced to Val) eventually becomes callous toward his dying mother and does not go to see her.

Before long Val realizes his native pull, and has to return to his roots to continue to paint. Caroline, self-styled cultural patron, leaves no stone unturned to retain her prized possession. She produces fake letters from the swami and spoils his love relationship with younger women so that she can continue to be his lover. Eventually Valmiki severs all his ties with Caroline and returns to his caves with the help of Anasuya (the narrator), who is in England in connection with the publication of her novels. The independence gained signifies his moral and artistic salvation. Caroline could never admit defeat, and there is an assumption of future triumph in her Parthian shot that Val will eventually return to her. By trying to possess Val against all odds, she reduces him to a commodity. The human values are totally lost. The swami, on the other hand, makes no attempt to retain Val, as victory or defeat means nothing to him.

At one level the novel is the endless conflict between possession and detachment, materialism and spiritualism, represented by Caroline and the swami respectively. Caroline could never understand the spiritual urge behind Val's art. She could see them only as commodities that could fetch money and fame. At another level, Caroline's self-will, dominance, and possessiveness suggest a picture of colonialism, and of India struggling to free itself. The postcolonial love-hate relationship with the British is seen in Anasuya's attitude toward them. She admires and resents their hard work, their resolve, and the confidence born out of these qualities. Though the symbols are a little overdrawn, it is a powerful novel dealing with the psychological issues of ownership in relationships.

In *A Handful of Rice* (1966) Kamala Markandaya returns to the theme of hunger and social injustice. Here, unlike some other novels, the location is specified. Ravi Shanker leaves his village for Madras to eke out a living. The story presents his demoralizing experiences in the modern city. His son dies of meningitis. His wife, Nalini, is in a state of penury. His education is more a handicap than a help. Damodar and the underworld criminals offer to lead him in the path of prosperity, but are disgusted with his vacillation between their world and the world of his basic values. He joins the angry mob of rioters, but his raised hand manages neither to hurl a stone nor to grab a handful of rice.

The Coffer Dams (1969) introduces us to a coalition of the Indians and the British over the construction of a dam across a turbulent river in Malnad. Clinton, the head of a British firm, enlists tribal laborers and openly exploits them under the guise of developing a Third World country. His wife, Helen, establishes a rapport with the tribals effortlessly and is fascinated by the mystery of the jungle. The tribal chief helps her see the insensitiveness of the West and the exploitation of the Indians. Helen has an extramarital relationship with Bashiam, the tribal engineer. Racial tensions mount as the dam goes up.

Numerous accidents occur where the tribals are the main victims. Even Helen suspects her *tribe*, the British, when Bashiam is asked to operate a faulty crane that Smith refuses to operate. Clinton represents the indomitable will of the imperialistic West. He wants the dam completed at all costs. His mind is set on progress, and he has more concern for machines than for human beings. His steady move toward his goal has no place for ethical values. Tribals are uprooted from their land to provide housing facilities for the British engineers. A premature blast kills close to forty tribals.

The novel points out the double standards of the British in group relations. When Bailey and Wilkins die, work is suspended to give them "a decent, Christian burial" (81). But Clinton finds no reason to accommodate Indian sentiments and rescue the corpses of the Indians. They could form part of the basement if disposal of bodies was the concern. The tribals have a better understanding of the vagaries of nature than the British. The dam built against all odds faces a threat when there is heavy rain. Finally the water level falls, resolving the crisis.

We find here a clash of the native pride and the imperial arrogance that are working in close quarters. In some of Kamala Markandaya's earlier novels the natives are made to seem apathetic, used to being done out of their rights. But in *The Coffer Dams* they seem aware of their exploitation and even demand that their rights be given. With the constant complaint of hostile weather and fear of cobras, Rawlings wonders why the English insist on carrying the white man's burden even after delivering freedom on a plate to the Indians. While the British see India as "the vast sprawling enigma," the Indians consider the British fetish of privacy equally enigmatic.

The English women create a hierarchy even among the Europeans living in India. People from Russia and Sweden are considered inferior. Likewise the white women who have enjoyed the pre-independence days in India can never understand the ways and attitudes of their own younger generation. They could never belong in post-independent India as the reserved place was gone. Millie Rawlings, Mrs. Henderson, and Mrs. Galbirth, with their party and hunting interests, are all the colonial British stereotypes who distrust Indians and expect them to be grateful to the British for developing and mechanizing their country. The Indian characters in the novel admire the strength and determination of the English, but detest their imperial arrogance. The novel suggests the futility of progress when human values are sacrificed. This conclusion is presented not just in terms of race conflicts, but in terms of business attitudes versus human concerns, or in terms of the perception of nature's vagaries versus the scientific knowledge of nature.

In *The Nowhere Man* (1972) Kamala Markandaya deals with the problems of bicultural living faced by an Indian family in London. Srinivas, the protagonist, makes a futile attempt at acculturation. Each time he thinks he is close to integration, he is made aware of his Indianness and recognizes that he is a target of hostility. His wife, Vasantha, is in London not by choice, and so she wastes her life grieving. Their sons, Laxman and Seshu, become totally un-Indian, as the choice has been made for them. Seshu, who works as an ambulance driver during World War II, is killed by a German shell. Laxman, thoroughly anglicized, marries a British girl and repudiates all claims of Indian heritage. Laxman's excuse for not inviting his parents at the birth of his child—he has "no spare bedroom"—is a shattering experience for the Srinivases: their idea of privacy and familial closeness is very different from Laxman's. This experience gives them an awareness that their son is not Indian and therefore not theirs. Vasantha dies of tuberculosis, depriving Srinivas of the support and sustenance of his native culture. Some of the neighbors, though helpful, are not able to provide the support system Srinivas is used to. The relationship of Mrs. Pickering and Srinivas suggests a brief racial harmony, but is not indicative of a lasting bond. They do not manage to sustain each other emotionally. Mrs. Pickering does not come alive either in the relationship or in the novel.

When Srinivas contracts leprosy, considered an oriental disease, he is totally ostracized, and his outsider status is complete. It is ironic that Srinivas has to meet his end in a country that still suspects him, still oppresses him. After decades of stay in England and a son dying for that country, Srinivas dies not only as an outsider but also as "a nowhere man looking for a nowhere city." "One does not realise when one leaves one's country how much is chopped off and left behind too. The inconsiderables which one does not even think of at the time, which are in fact important" (70). The Srinivases were referred to as "people at No. 5 Ashcroft Avenue." After the World War at least their identity became "Srinivases." In the end the only identity that Srinivas has is that of an unwelcome intruder to be done away with. The novel is thus dominated by an atmosphere of pessimism regarding the future of race relations in England.

Savitri never entertains the idea of acculturation as the ultimate goal of racial interaction or survival. When she dies, her ashes are immersed in "alien waters," the Thames. For the British policeman, it was all "rubbish" polluting the river. Srinivas and Savitri believe that Christianity is inferior to Hinduism, and nonvegetarianism continues to bother them. However good Mrs. Pickering may be, she is after all the meat-eating kind. The Srinivases have problems with even eggs and cakes. Abdul of Zanzibar openly expresses hatred for the British and warns Srinivas against his liberal attitude. Even when Srinivas feels accepted, the acceptance is from the lower-class Londoners only. We see the liberal and the intolerant ones in the same family. Dr. Radcliffe, Mrs. Pickering, Mr. Glass, and Mrs. Fletcher are the few tolerant English. The younger generation—Mike, Joe, Bill, and Fred Fletcher—create an anti-Asian furor, as they believe that the economic pressure they experience is due to the inflow of Asian immigrants who occupy most places in the schools or hospitals. Mrs. Glass resents the success of Indians in different fields: "One day they're poor, living off the rates, the next they could buy us all up" (207). This novel, comparable to Farukh Dhondy's "Keep Britain White," has a tragic vision, the impossibility of harmonious race relations.

The recurrent conflicts like rural versus urban or Eastern values versus Western values find a place in Kamala Markandaya's *Two Virgins* (1973). But the novel certainly does not offer a fresh insight into resolving these conflicts. The different thematic strands are not well woven together. Kamala Markandaya's earlier novels have dealt with some of these themes in a more satisfactory manner. *Two Virgins* also deals with themes like initiation into adult awareness and escape from parental and rural restrictions. But the novelist does not manage to create an immediacy of the experience presented.

One of the two sisters, Lalitha, goes to the city with a movie producer, Gupta, to act in a documentary film but returns to her village pregnant. The abortion is done, but she is bent on returning to the city because she feels that the village stifles her talents and ambition. What seems to be of importance is that it is the Western-educated Miss Mendoza who puts Lalitha in touch with the Western-trained Gupta, and the corrupting influence can be traced back to the West. What follows predictably is an attack on urban society and materialism, a by-product of British influence. The novelist makes a number of generalizations on the British and their influence on the East. Alamelu, Lalitha's aunt, objects to Christianity's being taught to the young Hindu girls and considers her teaching of the Maypole dance ("May pole, bean pole, bamboo pole punk") shameful and contrary to the code of Hindu decorum. Gupta is a "Western punk" who has introduced the family members to tragedy. More than all this the British have created "a Western dream" that is detrimental to the happiness, peace, and progress of Indians.

Though the names of the two sisters, Lalitha and Saroja, sound South Indian, the vagueness of the location is maintained in this novel too. They are sisters, but their responses to situations are very different. This explodes certain stereotypical notions about Indian rural women. Lalitha's premarital relationship is attributed to the urban influence, but Saroja, who is village bound, is no less interested in sex. The difference between the two sisters is the structuring principle of the novel. But Saroja is able to resist temptations, partly because of the fear of the unknown, and partly because of the lack of opportunity to overcome that fear. She finds sexuality difficult to deal with outside the realm of fantasy. Saroja remains a virgin. In a certain sense she is pragmatic and does not want to be poor like Manikkam or without status like Alamelu. She is mature enough to see that there are problems in both village and city life, and she knows that sexuality can be different for different people. She returns to her village with a renewed perspective, able to meet all the problems she faces there. She could even accept Curly the homosexual as he is.

Unlike the other novels of Markandaya we find here a certain amount of exhibitionism. Even granting that the novel is based on adolescence and initiation, features such as lesbian tendencies or the sexual life of the parents do not seem to serve any purpose—artistic or moral.

The Golden Honeycomb (1977) has as its background the accession of princely states to India. There are Rajas, English tutors, legitimate and illegitimate princes and princesses, and brown sahibs all to suit the Western colonial tastes. The novel has the spirit of the old king and queen stories with the royal siblings developing a kinship with the working class. It contrasts the privileges of the rulers with those of the ruled through the growing consciousness of Rabi, a prince, who mingles freely with the servants' children. Both the mother and the grandmother encourage the spirit of nationalism in him. But the novel also presents the Indian royal folks as lackeys before the British. The rule of the illegitimate prince approved by the British viceroy is like a fragile golden honeycomb.

Rabi involves himself in demonstrations in support of the laborers. Here he is influenced particularly by women of the community: persons such as Janaki, Jaya, and Usha persuade him to support this cause. But Sophie (daughter of Sir Arthur Copeland), who starts out as a staunch supporter, slowly withdraws. Her presence certainly convinces Rabi of "the existence of secular heavens." He realizes that what stands between them is "her race," and her withdrawal is prompted by years of training in racial disparity. But with Usha he feels that "their lives interlocked at more than one level, with whom, it pleased him to feel, he could wait, or not, to come together. In their own country, in their own time . . ." (455).

We have here the attitude of three generations of Indians toward the British as rulers. Kamala Markandaya fails to give concrete particulars in the form of historical events while presenting the background. There is a frequent shift in the place of action, and this gives the novel an episodic effect.

In *Pleasure City* (1982), also published under the title *Shalimar*, Kamala Markandaya brings the British and the Indians together in a working relationship, as in *The Coffer Dams*. A holiday resort, Shalimar (the name of Emperor Jehangir's pleasure garden), is being built near a fishing village. With the contractors and caterers it is soon turned into a place of sheer commercialism. The project is undertaken by the Atlas International Development Corporation (AIDCORP). The chairman and the director of the project are English, the contractor, a Parsi, and the workers, Indians.

It is a familiar scene where the dominance of the British is easily contrasted with the passivity of the Indians, Western values with those of the East, spiritualism and acceptance with materialism and progress. But the novel has a positive outlook, as hope here lies in human relationships. The love between Srinivas and Mrs. Pickering, in *The Nowhere Man*, does not sustain their relationship through all their travails. But in *Pleasure City* the relationship between Rikki the young boy and Tully, the director at Shalimar, calls for admiration.

Rikki, an orphan, is well loved by his foster parents, and by the Brides, an English couple who run a school. He learns to speak English fluently because of this association. He works as a tea-boy at Shalimar after the death of the Brides. There he comes into contact with Tully, who encourages him to make a boat, and Tully's wife Corinna, who teaches him surfing. He adores Tully but has an ambivalent attitude toward Corinna. As one who has lived close to nature, he has an instinctive knowledge of the ways of the waters and manages to save Corinna from being drowned. This brings him close to Tully. "They shared a language that went beyond English, and was outside the scope of mere words" (340).

Though Markandaya glorifies this relationship, she is careful to point out the condescending attitude of the British who congratulate themselves for civilizing the natives. Rikki is adept at surfing but is unable to participate in a competition because of his Indian identity. The closeness of Rikki to the Tully family is frowned upon by some British who belief that a definite boundary has to be drawn between the blacks and whites, and it should not be crossed by either if the propriety of rank order is to be maintained.

However, the Rikki-Tully relationship has a redemptive hope for race relations. The usual conflicts do not develop into big events. The novel is devoid of bitterness. There is no impassioned attack against the British. Though some bemoan the loss of traditional values and the intrusion of the British in the form of urbanization, people are not blind to the brighter side that this urbanization brings. Though Rikki works under Tully, he is accepted on equal terms. This is definitely a progression here in Kamala Markandaya's vision, which has been tragic in many of her earlier novels. Here she seems to repudiate Rudyard Kipling's statement, "East is East, and West is West, and never the twain shall meet."

CRITICAL RECEPTION

Kamala Markandaya's novels usually evoke only two kinds of critical responses—one likes them or dislikes them. People like William Walsh, John Masters, A. V. Krishna Rao, Charles Larson, and Edwin Thumboo rave about her works and regard her as both the most gifted Indian woman writer and the best among those who write with India as the background.

But there are many who consider her fiction mediocre, most of whom are Indians likes Uma Parameswaran, Nissim Ezekiel, and P. Balaswamy.

Margaret Joseph's book is the first full-length study on Kamala Markandaya with a special focus on her tragic vision. S. Wali has made a detailed stylistic study of *Nectar in a Sieve*, which focuses on the language as it functions within the text, the linguistic patterns and lexical choices, and the way they contribute to the total impact of the novel. *Perspectives on Kamala Markandaya*, edited by Madhusudan Prasad, is a loosely strung collection of critical essays with no central principle governing them. *The Novels of Kamala Markandaya and Ruth Prawer Jhabvala*, by Rekha Jha, and *Cross-Cultural Interaction in Indian-English Fiction*, by Ramesh Chadha, explore the diasporic sensibility expressed in the novels of several writers including Kamala Markandaya.

Hundreds of articles on Kamala Markandaya have been published in various books and journals. But most of them decry the value of her work, as the critics think that she is out of touch with the Indian reality she writes about and has no sure grasp of the Indian sensibility. They argue that her novels present an alien and superficial perspective of India and Indians. Yet India is the main source of her creative inspiration.

Some of Kamala Markandaya's novels abound in sociological details and other matters of exotic interest. There is the eagerness of a tourist guide to interpret the social customs and beliefs for fear they will be lost on the readers. This makes one wonder whether she has developed this pattern as a conscious device to sell India abroad.

Feroza Jussawalla in her *Family Quarrels* enthusiastically and systematically defends Kamala Markandaya's dual perspective of her roots as seen in her novels. She refutes the sweeping, unfair remarks made by unsympathetic critics. The rejection of Kamala Markandaya by many Indian critics could perhaps be attributed to postcolonial Indian psychology. These critics probably see a trace of antinationalism and treachery in a willing immigrant turning to India for creative sustenance. Even while choosing to be away she lives in India. Her fictional attack on British racism or imperialism is seen as a self-defense and a way of convincing herself of her loyalty to her motherland. Sometimes critics tend to read unfair and nonexistent meanings into the perceptions and statements of Kamala Markandaya's characters. They lift them out of context and attribute them all to Markandaya and her long stay abroad.

Some critics complain that the earlier Indian writers in English could not internalize the alien language and therefore could not use it successfully for creative purposes. But when Kamala Markandaya could use English as "a British would, then the critics turned round and saw it as a sign of alienation" (Jussawalla 14). It has to be said to her credit that she has presented an authentic picture of Indian rural life, especially in her earlier novels, without adopting the flavor of vernacular idiom. This suggests that experimentation with the English language is not the only way to appropriate that language to the Indian sensibility. There is absolutely no self-consciousness in her use of English. Yet the rural picture comes alive.

Most educated Indians are products of a double culture even if they have not lived abroad. It is not impossible to assimilate both and accommodate the inherited and acquired values. It is a little disappointing that, though she calls her novels "literature of concern," Kamala Markandaya does not take a strong stand while discussing social issues, as Mulk Raj Anand and Bhabani Bhattacharya do. There is no bold all-out confrontation with the problems taken up for treatment. The hit-and-run tactics adopted, however, enable her to maintain a balanced outlook. She reveals both an involvement in her subjects and yet a certain detachment from them. She denies neither her roots nor the impact of the British influence on her. Time and again she returns to the same themes, raising the expectations of the readers. But it is often the same perception in a different cast. India and Indo-British race relations seem to be an obsessive concern with her.

There is a definite sense of security in the way Kamala Markandaya deals with India as a subject: no sentimental wailing to preserve her Indianness. Nor is there any desperate attempt to merge with the adopted culture, which is the way of the insecure. "The blessing and the bane of duality" offer the novelist the necessary security to perceive more and to maintain objectivity in her artistic endeavor. There is no total denigration of the white or glorification of the oppressed.

Kamala Markandaya's reticence about herself has encouraged a lot of biographical speculation on the part of critics. Though her crosscultural awareness is an extraliterary consideration, one cannot rule out the fact that this biographical detail gives a new dimension to critical reading. We have the right amount of information to see why she is obsessed with certain themes, but thankfully not enough to hunt for her biography in her fiction.

BIBLIOGRAPHY

Works by Kamala Markandaya

Nectar in a Sieve. Bombay: Jaico Publishing House, 1954.
Some Inner Fury. London: Putnam, 1955.
A Silence of Desire. London: Putnam, 1955.
Possession. Bombay: Jaico Publishing House, 1963.
A Handful of Rice. New Delhi: Hind Pocket Books, 1966.
The Coffer Dams. New Delhi: Hind Pocket Books, 1969.
The Nowhere Man. New Delhi: Orient Longman, 1972.
Two Virgins. New York: Signet, 1973.
The Golden Honeycomb. London: Chatto and Windus, 1977.
Pleasure City. London: Chatto and Windus, 1982.

Studies of Kamala Markandaya

Adkins, John F. "Kamala Markandaya: Indo-Anglian Conflict as Unity." *Journal of South Asian Literature* 10:1 (1974): 89–102.

Aithal, Krishnamoorthy, and Rishmi Aithal. "Indo-English Fictional Experiments with Interracial and Intercultural Relationship." *Alien Voice*. Ed. Avadhesh K. Srivastava. Lucknow: Print House, 1981. 84–100.

Aithal, S. K. "Indo-British Encounter in Kamala Markandaya's Novels." *Journal of South Asian Literature* 22:2 (1987): 49–59.

Anjanayulu, D. "Indian Writing in English from K. S. Venkataramani to Kamala Markandaya." *Triveni* 32 (1963): 19–28.

Appasamy, S. P. "*The Golden Honeycomb*: A Saga of Princely India by Kamala Markandaya." *Journal of Indian Writing in English* 6:2 (1978): 56–63.

Argyle, Barry. "Kamala Markandaya's *Nectar in a Sieve*." *Ariel* 4:1 (1973): 35–45.

Asnani, Shyam M. "Character and Technique in Kamala Markandaya's Novels." *Rajasthan University Studies in English* 9 (1978): 66–74.

———. "Contribution of Women in the Indo-English Novel." *Triveni* 44 (1975): 45–52.

———. "East and West Encounter in Kamala Markandaya's Later Novels." *Triveni* 48:4 (1980): 22–28.

———. "The Theme of Famine and Hunger: Bhabani Bhattacharya and Kamala Markandaya." *New Dimensions of Indian English Novel*. Delhi: Doaba House, 1987. 11–37.

Bai, K. Meera. "From Adolescence to Womanhood: Kamala Markandaya's *Two Virgins*, Ruth Jhabvala's *To Whom She Will* and Santha Rama Rau's *Remember the House*." *Indian Literature Since Independence*. Ed. K. Ayyappa Paniker. New Delhi: Indian Association for English Studies, 1991. 91–97.

Balaswamy, P. "The Distorted and Distortive Mirror of Kamala Markandaya." *Criticle* 4 (1977): 20–28.

Belliappa, Meena. "East-West Encounter: Indian Women Writers of Fiction in English." *Literary Criterion* 7:3 (1966): 18–27.

Bharathalakshmi, M. V., and S. K. Krishna Sarma. "The Brown British: A Study of Recent Immigrant Novels." *Literary Half-Yearly* 18:2 (1976): 53–70.

Chadha, Ramesh. *Cross-Cultural Interaction in Indian-English Fiction: An Analysis of the Novels of Ruth Jhabvala and Kamala Markandaya*. New Delhi: National Book Organization, 1988.

———. "Cross-Cultural Interaction in Markandaya's *Pleasure City*." *The New Indian Novel in English: A Study of the 1980s*. Ed. Viney Kirpal. New Delhi: Allied Publishers, 1990. 57–64.

———. "*Heat and Dust* and *The Coffer Dams*: A Comparative Study." *Comparative Literature*. Ed. R. K. Dhawan. New Delhi: Bahri Publications, 1987. 146–52.

Chandrasekhar, K. R. "East and West in the Novels of Kamala Markandaya." *Critical Essays on Indian Writing in English*. Ed. M. K. Naik et al. Dharwar: Karnatak University Publications, 1967. 320–43.

Chauhan, P. S. "Kamala Markandaya: Sense and Sensibility." *Literary Criterion* 12:2–3 (1976): 134–47.

Dale, James. "Kamala Markandaya and the Outsider." *Individual and Community in Commonwealth Literature*. Ed. Daniel Massa. Malta: University of Malta, 1979. 188–95.

Drum, Alice. "Kamala Markandaya's Modern Quest Tale." *World Literature Written in English* 20:2 (1983): 323–32.

Geetha, P. "Kamala Markandaya—An Interpretation." *Commonwealth Quarterly* 3:9 (1978): 96–109.

Gondal, Yogesh Chandra. "India and the West in the Novels of Kamala Markandaya." *Viswabharati Quarterly* 3 (1978): 96–109.

———. "Relationships and Dams." *Journal of Commonwealth Literature* 8:1 (1973): 134–35.

Gooneratne, Yasmine. "'Traditional Elements in the Fiction of Kamala Markandaya, R. K. Narayan and Ruth Prawar Jhabvala." *World Literature Written in English* 15:1 (1976): 121–34.

Goyal, S. Bhagwat. "Kamala Markandaya's *Nectar in a Sieve*: A Study." *Culture and Commitment: Aspects of Indian Literature in English*. Meerut: Shalabh Book House, 1984. 97–116.

Guruprasad, Thakkur. "And Never the Twain Shall Meet: Kamala Markandaya's *The Nowhere Man*." *Explorations in Modern Indo-English Fiction*. Ed. R. K. Dhawaan. New Delhi: Bahri Publications, 1982. 199–207.

Harrex, S. C. "A Sense of Identity: The Early Novels of Kamala Markandaya." *The Fire and the Offering: The English Language Novel of India 1937–70*. 2 vols. Calcutta: Writers Workshop, 1977. 1:245–60.

Indra, C. T. "The True Voice of Endurance: A Study of Rukmani in Markandaya's *Nectar in a Sieve*." *Feminism and Recent Fiction in English*. Ed. Sushila Singh. New Delhi: Prestige Books, 1991. 64–71.

Jain, Jasbir. "The Novels of Kamala Markandaya." *Indian Literature* 18:2 (1975): 36–43.

———. "Strangers in Enemy Territory: Expatriates and Exiles." *Littcrit* 4:2 (1978): 31–35.

Jain, N. K. "Kamala Markandaya: *Nectar in a Sieve*." *Major Indian Novels: An Evaluation*. Ed. N. S. Pradhan. New Delhi: Arnold-Heinemann, 1985. 74–87.

Jha, Rama. "Kamala Markandaya: An Overview." *Perspectives on Indian Fiction in English*. Ed. M. K. Naik. New Delhi: Abhina Publications, 1985. 161–73.

Jha, Rekha. *The Novels of Kamala Markandaya and Ruth Prawar Jhabbvala*. New Delhi: Prestige Books, 1990.

Joseph, Margaret P. *Kamala Markandaya*. New Delhi: Arnold-Heinemann, 1980.

Jussawalla, Feroza F. "The Twice Born Versus Those Who Have Crossed the Seven Seas: Thematic Concerns of Alienation and Expatriation." *Family Quarrels: Toward a Criticism of Indian Writing in English*. New York: Peter Lang, 1985. 133–56.

Kalinnikova, Elena J. "The Hindu Woman from London: Kamala Markandaya." *Indian English Literature: A Perspective*. Ghaziabad: Vimal Prakashan, 1982. 149–62.

Katamble, V. D. "*The Coffer Dams*: An Apology for Techno-Industrialisation of Rural India." *Vortex* 1 (1979): 8–14.

————. "Kamala Markandaya's *The Coffer Dams*." *Littcrit* 2:1–2 (1985): 54–62.

Krupakar, B. "Race Relations and *The Nowhere Man*." *Literary Endeavour* 2:2–3 (1980): 21–26.

Kumar, Prem. "Conflict and Resolution in the Novels of Kamala Markandaya." *World Literature Today* 60:1 (1986): 22–27.

Kumar, Shiv K. "Tradition and Change in the Novels of Kamala Markandaya." *Osmania Journal of English Studies* 7:1 (1969): 1–9.

Mahajan, Anita. "Tradition and Modernity in Markandaya's *A Silence of Desire*." *Indian Scholar* 5:1–2 (1983): 137–44.

Moktali, Laxmi R. "Experiments with Language in Kamala Markandaya's Novels: *Nectar in a Sieve* and *Some Inner Fury*." *Experimentation with Language in Indian Writing in English*. Ed. S. K. Desai. Kolhapur: Shivaji University, 1974. 129–43.

Mukherjee, Meenakshi. "Inside the Outsider." *The Awakened Conscience*. Ed. C. D. Narasimhaiah. New Delhi: Sterling Publishers, 1978. 86–91.

————. "The Theme of Displacement in Anita Desai and Kamala Markandaya." *World Literature Written in English* 17 (1978): 225–53.

————. *The Twice-Born Fiction: Themes and Techniques of the Indian Novel in English*. Delhi: Heinemann, 1971.

Nandakumar, Prema. "Swim against the Tide: Srinivas in *The Nowhere Man*." *Contemporary Indian Fiction in English*. Ed. K. Ayyappa Paniker. Trivandrum: University of Kerala Publications, n.d. 76–80.

Nelson, Emmanuel S. "Kamala Markandaya, Bharati Mukherjee, and the Indian Immigrant Experience." *Toronto South Asian Review* 9:2 (1991): 1–9.

Parameswaran, Uma. "India for the Western Reader: A Study of Kamala Markandaya's Novels." *Texas Quarterly* 11:2 (1968): 29–35.

————. "Native-Aliens and Expatriates—Kamala Markandaya and Balachandra Rajan." *A Study of Representative Indo-English Novelists*. New Delhi: Vikas Publishing House, 1976. 85–140.

————. "What Price Expatriation?" *The Commonwealth Writers Overseas: Themes of Exile and Expatriation*. Ed. Alastair Niven. Brussels: Librarie Marcel Didier, 1976. 41–52.

Pollard, Arthur. "Kamala Markandaya's *The Golden Honeycomb*." *Journal of Indian Writing in English* 8:1–2 (1980): 22–26.

Prasad, Hari Mohan. "The Quintessence of Kamala Markandaya's Art." *Commonwealth Quarterly* 3:9 (1978): 173–85.

Prasad, Madhusudan, ed. *Perspectives on Kamala Markandaya*. Ghaziabad: Vimal Prakashan, 1984.

Ramamurti, K. S. "The Indian Woman Novelist Writing in English." *Littcrit* 4:1 (1978): 33–42.

————. "Kamala Markandaya's *Two Virgins*: A Problem Novel." *Littcrit* 7:2 (1981): 36–45.

Rao, A. V. Krishna. *The Indo-Anglian Novel and the Changing Tradition: A Study of the Novels of Mulk Raj Anand, Kamala Markandaya, R. K. Narayan and Raja Rao—1930–1964*. Mysore: Rao and Raghavan, 1972.

Rao, E. Nageswara. "The Fertility Motif in Kamala Markandaya's *Nectar in a Sieve*." *Indian English Literature Since Independence*. Ed. K. Ayyappa Paniker. New Delhi: Indian Association for English Studies, 1991. 7–13.

Rao, K. S. Narayana. Rev. of *The Golden Honeycomb* by Kamala Markandaya. *World Literature Today* 52:2 (1978): 342.

———. "Kamala Markandaya as Craftsman." *Indian Writing Today* 3:8 (1969): 32–40.

———. "Kamala Markandaya: *A Silence of Desire*: A Note on the Title." *Indian P.E.N.* 35:12 (1969): 349–51.

———. "Kamala Markandaya: A Study." *Contemporary Indian Literature* 9:5 (1969): 8–11.

———. "Kamala Markandaya: A Study." *Contemporary Indian Literature* 9:6 (1969): 10–13.

———. "Love, Sex, Marriage and Morality in Kamala Markandaya's Novels." *Osmania Journal of English Studies* 10 (1973): 69–77.

———. Markandaya's *Possession* and the Idea of the Triumph of the Spirit." *Indian P.E.N.* 36:10–11 (1970): 292–96, 313–17.

———. "*Nectar in a Sieve*—A Footnote to the Title." *Indian P.E.N.* 35:11 (1969): 315–17.

———. "The Novels of Kamala Markandaya: A Contemporary Indo-Anglian Novelist." *Literature East and West* 15 (1971): 209–18.

———. "Religious Elements in Kamala Markandaya's Novels." *Ariel* 8:1 (1977): 35–50.

Rao, Susheela N. "England in the Novels of Kamala Markandaya." *Journal of Indian Writing in English* 15:1 (1987): 1–10.

Rao, Vimala. "The Achievement of the Indian Women Novelists." *Indian Literature of the Past Fifty Years 1917–1967*. Ed. C. D. Narasimhaiah. Mysore: University of Mysore, 1970. 213–24.

Reddy, P. Bayapa. "Rural Life Shaken to Its Roots: Kamala Markandaya's *Nectar in a Sieve*." *Studies in Indian Writing in English*. New Delhi: Prestige Books, 1990. 61–69.

Reddy, K. Venkata. "A Classic of the Hunger Theme: *Nectar in a Sieve*." *Major Indian Novelists*. New Delhi: Prestige Books, 1990. 78–86.

———. "A Tryst with Conscience: *A Handful of Rice*." *Major Indian Novelists*. New Delhi: Prestige Books, 1990. 87–96.

Rubenstein, Roberta. "Kamala Markandaya's *Two Virgins*." *World Literature Written in English* 13 (1973): 225–30.

Rubin, David. "Kamala Markandaya and the Novel of Reconciliation." *After the Raj: British Novels of India Since 1947*. Hanover, NH: University Press of New England, 1986. 157–71.

Sarma, S. Krishnan. "Two Recent Novels of Kamala Markandaya." *Triveni* 45:3 (1976): 28–35.

Sastry, Krishna L.S.R. "East-West Encounter in Indo-Anglian Fiction." *Essays and Studies* Ed G.V.L.N. Sarma. Machilipatnam: Triveni Publishers, 1977. 102–13.

Saxena, O. P. "The Bi-Cultural World of Kamala Markandaya's Novels." *Glimpses of Indo-English Fiction*. 3 vols. New Delhi: Jainsons Publications, 1985. 2:192–226.

Shimer, Dorothy Blair. "Sociological Imagery in the Novels of Kamala Markandaya." *World Literature Written in English* 14:2 (1975): 257–70.

Shirwadkar, Meena. *Image of Woman in the Indo-Anglian Novel.* New Delhi: Sterling Publishers, 1979.

Singh, Ram Sewak. "The Vision of Kamala Markandaya." *Vidya* 9 (1966): 45–55.

Srivastava, Nidhi. "The Image of India in the Novels of Kamala Markandaya." *Indian Scholar* 4:1–2 (1984): 13–24.

Srivastava, Ramesh K. "Limitations of Markandaya in *Nectar in a Sieve.*" *Six Indian Novelists in English.* Amritsar: Guru Nanak Dev University, 1986. 145–54.

———. "Love and Death in Kamala Markandaya's *Some Inner Fury.*" *Indian Literature Since Independence.* Ed. K. Ayyappa Paniker. New Delhi: Indian Association for English Studies, 1991. 14–26.

———. "Markandaya's *Nectar in a Sieve* as a Tragedy." *Indian Journal of English Studies* 19:4 (1983): 103–11.

———. "The Pattern of Hope and Fear in Markandaya's *Nectar in a Sieve.*" *Indian Journal of English Studies* 22:1 (1980): 125–32.

———. "Symbolism in *Nectar in a Sieve.*" *Indian Scholar* 1:2 (1979): 111–22.

———. "The Theme of Hunger in Bhattacharya and Markandaya." *Explorations in Modern Indo-English Fiction.* Ed. R. K. Dhawan. New Delhi: Bahri Publications, 1982. 172–83.

———. "A Village in Transition: *Nectar in a Sieve.*" *Commonwealth Fiction.* Ed. R. K. Dhawan. 3 vols. New Delhi: Classical Publishing Company, 1987. 1:211–27.

———. "Woman as Possessor: A Reflection of Markandaya's Anti-Patriarchal Rage and Divided Consciousness in *Possession.*" *Feminism and Recent Fiction in English.* Ed. Sushila Singh. New Delhi: Prestige Books, 1991. 72–88.

Thumboo, Edwin. "Kamala Markandaya's *A Silence of Desire.*" *Journal of Indian Writing in English* 8:1–2 (1980): 108–36.

Venkatachari, K. "Kamala Markandaya's *Nectar in a Sieve*: A Study in Romantic Realism." *Kakatiya Journal of English Studies* 3:1 (1978): 97–106.

———. "Sense of Life in Kamala Markandaya's *Nectar in a Sieve.*" *Osmania Journal of English Studies* 9:1 (1972): 55–59.

Venkateswaran, Shyamala. "The Language of Kamala Markandaya's Novels." *Literary Criterion* 9:3 (1970): 57–87.

Weir, Ann Lowry. "Worlds Apart: Feminine Consciousness in Markandaya's *Nectar in a Sieve* and *The Coffer Dams.*" *CIEFL Bulletin* 13:2 (1977): 71–85.

Williams. H. M. "Some Characters in Markandaya's Novels." *Galaxy of Indian Writing in English.* Delhi: Akshat Publications, 1987.

VED (PARKASH) MEHTA
(1934–   )
Joel Shatzky

BIOGRAPHY

Ved Mehta was born on March 21, 1934, in Lahore, India (now Pakistan). At the age of three, Mehta had a serious bout with meningitis, which left him blind. Many of his books reflect his childhood experiences in his native land. His parents' lives illustrated the split between the "Westernized" India of the Raj and the more traditional India. His father was educated as a doctor in England and became a distinguished practitioner in the Indian public health service. His mother, in contrast, was not educated, and after her son's blindness, attempted to restore his sight through faith-healing rituals.

At the age of five, Mehta was sent to Bombay's Dadar School for the Blind, which was so unsanitary that he contracted many infections including typhoid fever and malaria. After having experienced the trauma of the upheaval in India as a result of the 1947 partition, he was sent alone to the United States to the School for the Blind in Little Rock, Arkansas, when he was fifteen. A gifted scholar, Mehta continued his education in the United States, where he received his B.A. from Pomona College in California in 1956. Three years later he received a second B.A. degree from Balliol College, Oxford, an M.A. from Harvard University in 1961, and an M.A. from Balliol College, Oxford, in 1962.

At the age of twenty-three, in 1957, Mehta published his first autobiography, *Face to Face*. The book recorded his experiences growing up as a blind boy in India and at the school he attended in Arkansas as well as his subsequent life in college and university. It is clear from the tone of the book that there is no room for self-pity in Mehta's attitude toward his handicap. In fact, in much of his subsequent writings, he makes little or no reference to his blindness.

In 1961 he became a staff writer for the *New Yorker* and has continued to write regularly for it for the past thirty years. During this period he has lived for the most part in the United States with occasional return visits to India which he has recorded in a number of his books. In 1983 he married Linn Cary, an assistant program officer at the Ford Foundation. They have two children, Sage and Natasha.

Mehta has been quite successful in getting wide recognition for his work. He has received a number of Ford Foundation Travel Grants (1971–1976), two Guggenheim fellowships (1971–72; 1977–76), and a MacArthur Foundation fellowship (1982–87). Most of his work has been either autobiographical or reportorial with eighteen published books, many of which appeared serialized in the *New Yorker*. He has also taught literature at Bard College, 1985–86; Sarah Lawrence, 1988; Balliol College, Oxford, 1988–89; New York University 1989–90; and Yale University, 1990–

MAJOR WORKS AND THEMES

The critic and short fiction writer V. S. Pritchett once described the writer as "a man living on the other side of a frontier." This description well fits Mehta in two ways. As an Indian expatriate, he has returned numerous times to give his impressions of his homeland which, since his middle teens, he has visited as an exile by choice. As a man whose blindness occurred in his earliest childhood, he "sees" and describes the physical world around him remarkably well as if he were sighted. For as Herbert L. Matthews remarked in his review of *Walking in the Indian Streets*, "Mehta plays an extraordinary trick on his prospective readers and on anyone who does not know about him or has not read his previous book, *Face to Face*. . . . He has written [*Walking the Indian Streets*] about his return to India after ten years' absence as if he had normal vision" ("A Native's Homecoming," *New York Times Book Review*, August 21, 1960, p. 14).

Although he has written a novel, *Delinquent Chacha* (1976), Mehta's primary works may be divided into his ongoing autobiographical series, beginning with *Face to Face*, and his books of essays about India apart from his own personal experience, *Portrait of India* (1970) being the first of these.

Perhaps Mehta best expresses his feelings as a writer who lives apart from his native land when he says: "I don't belong to any single tradition. I am an amalgram of five cultures—Indian, British, American, blind and [the *New Yorker*]" (quoted in *Contemporary Authors*, New Revision Series, 23:274). This sense of a multiple influence on his life and work reflects Mehta's detachment, if not estrangement, from India as he vividly expresses:

Everywhere I went, I was assaulted by putrid odors rising from the streets, by flies relentlessly swarming around my face, by the octupus-like hands of a hundred scabrous, deformed beggars clutching at my hands and feet. My time in the West has spoiled me and I could now hardly wait to get back. (*Walking the Indian Streets,* quoted in *Contemporary Authors,* 273.)

After having written *Face to Face* and *Walking the Indian Streets* (1960), Mehta proceeded to write a series of autobiographical works which begin, in fact, before his own birth. *Daddyji* (1972) traces the life of his father from his youth until Mehta's departure from Lahore at age five to an American mission school for the blind in Bombay. This volume, which describes the Anglophilic allegiance of Mehta's paternal side of the family, contrasts sharply with his description of his mother's family in *Mamaji* (1979). The book depicts Mehta's mother, highly superstitious and convinced that Mehta's blindness could be lifted as if it were a spell, as devoted to her son, but her background, lack of education, and ignorance make her greatly different from her English-educated husband. The vast contrasts between his two parents serve the author as a metaphor for the cultural gaps between the two extremes of Indian culture: totally separate, yet both an integral part of the same "family." These and the rest of his autobiographical works he subsequently subtitled *Continents of Exile.*

Mamaji concludes with the author at age three being taken to a faith healer, and *Vedi* (1982), considered the most unusual of the autobiographies, begins with Mehta's arrival at age five at the School for the Blind in Dadar where his father sent him. The descriptions of this awful place—which might well have contributed to Mehta's later feelings of estrangement from India—are told from the point of view of a blind person, one of the few times since *Face to Face* that he describes his experiences from this perspective.

The Ledge between the Streams (1984) continues the narrative of Mehta's life from age nine, after he left Dadar and returned to his home. Although the first part of the book records the innocence of Mehta's youth, the second half is a vivid contrast in the author's description of the trauma that he and his family suffered as a result of the partition of India and the ensuing chaos in 1947. It concludes with Mehta's being admitted into the Arkansas School for the Blind in 1949, although there is no indication in the book that the experience will lead him into a new and different life as a permanent resident of the United States.

Mehta's experiences in Arkansas are recorded in *Sound-Shadows of the New World* (1986), which begins by revealing his ignorance of such basic customs as eating with a fork and knife and shows how he eventually became so well accepted by his fellow students that he was elected class president. His experience as editor of the school newspaper also led to his interest in becoming a journalist. The most recent volume in this series, *The Stolen Light* (1989), continues the narrative with Mehta's years at Pomona College.

Once more, he shows by his adventurous behavior that he conceded little to his handicap.

Throughout much of his autobiographical work, Mehta expresses a certain detachment from his direct experiences. There is no sentimentality or self-pity in his memories of his wretched life at the Dadar School. Certainly, the two major elements of his life, his blindness (although he is remarkable in concealing its effects on his work) and his separation from India, except as an occasional visitor, make him a prime example of a writer of the Indian diaspora.

Mehta's books about India begin with his *Portrait of India* (1970). It is a large book—520 pages—that attempts to give an impressionistic portrait of India, one in which the many contradictions of the country are captured through a collection of sketches. He reveals the religious intensity of the Hindu pilgrim to the Ganges, but also the shocking facts of the drownings of hundreds of pilgrims a dozen years before.

His other political books about India include *Mahatma Gandhi and His Apostles* (1977), *The New India* (1978), and *A Family Affair* (1983). The first of these is a critical account of the man most idolized by the Indian people. Mehta's approach to Gandhi illustrates again his detachment from his homeland. Instead of writing a hagiography, Mehta has attempted to "demythologize Gandhi," as he himself says in his preface to the book, and "to capture something of the nature of his influence on his followers." It is clear by the conclusion of the book that the high level of idealism embodied by Gandhi no longer survives among his disciples.

A Family Affair is about three Indian prime ministers, Morarji Desai, Charan Singh, and Indira Gandhi. Although he certainly finds a great deal of fault in Mrs. Gandhi, Mehta also grudgingly admires her skills as a leader as well as politician that makes her superior to her rivals. The book is less revealing than many of his others because of its straightforward reportage, but again it demonstrates Mehta's interest in India more as dispassionate observer than as apologist or uncritical admirer.

Because of his position as an essayist for the *New Yorker* for most of his creative life, Mehta's work has been somewhat limited by the formal demands of the *New Yorker* essay in terms of length and general approach. But, as his editor, William Shawn, once observed, "more than any other writer Mehta has educated Americans about India, illuminating that country with an insider's sensibility and an outsider's objectivity" (quoted in *Contemporary Authors*, p. 272).

Mehta's other books include *Fly and Fly-Bottle: Encounters with British Intellectuals* (1963), which involved his return to Balliol and interviews he conducted with some of his former professors; *The New Theologian* (1966), which included interviews with some of the more notable religious thinkers such as Karl Barth and Reinhold Niebuhr; and *Three Stories of the Raj* (1986), a collection of short fiction.

CRITICAL RECEPTION

Face to Face, Mehta's first book, was given a very positive critical reception. Even in this earliest of his works, his effort to control his tone is noted. Gerald W. Johnson, in the *New York Herald Tribune Book Review*, observed: "He writes of Pomona College and the rest of his American experience coolly, exactly, never hesitating to mention what he did not like, yet in all is the tension of strong emotion. It is a young man writing about his home" (August 18, 1957, p. 6). This last point illustrates Mehta's sense of allegiance to the country in which he was accepted after the terrors he experienced at the Bandar School for the Blind and the apparent rejection of his family during the deracinating times of the partition.

As alluded to earlier, Herbert L. Matthews was extremely impressed with Mehta's powers of description, considering his blindness, in *Walking the Indian Streets*. Mehta's detachment from India is apparent when Matthews observes: "[The book] is deliberately keyed to an almost frivolous and cynical gaiety, with the serious and genuine emotions the author experiences hidden under a veneer of indirection, understatement and mockery" ("A Native's Homecoming," in *New York Times Book Review*, August 21, 1960, p. 14).

Mehta's next major work, *Portrait of India*, received decidedly mixed reviews. Bernard Nossiter praised his "effortless prose" and his ability to create "a rare synthesis, an attitude that draws strength from both his heritage and the insights of his adopted culture" ("Whatever Can be Said of India, the Opposite Also is True," *Book World, Chicago Tribune*, May 10, 1970, p. 6). Mervyn Jones, however, regards the book as "boring," "significantly out of date," and says that "reaching the end, one has a curious sense of emptiness" ("Empty Canvas," *New Statesman*, September 25, 1970, p. 380). This contrast in reactions might be accounted for by the fact that Nossiter was fascinated by the intellectual content of the book, while Jones complained about the lack of information about rural India where a less stark contrast between classes exists. He senses, perhaps with some reason, that Mehta has a lack of "sympathy" for his native land (382), while Nossiter notes that Mehta is "troubled by Indians' lack of 'community sense,' a social discipline that is a prerequisite for development" (6).

It is the objectivity of the exile, however, that seems to come through most clearly in the critical reaction to Mehta's work. In his review of *Daddyji*, Paul Scott notes that "Mehta senior [is] affectionately but objectively observed" ("Lighting the Dark Landscape of Memory," *The Times*, London, October 19, 1972, p. 10). The critic adds that although "*Daddyji* is intimate, personal . . . [Mehta writes] in his especially tender and dispassionate way" (p. 10) about India.

In contrasting views of *Mahatma Gandhi and His Apostles*, Leonard A. Gordon finds Mehta's strengths in his interviews with Gandhi's former disciples but faults him for his lack of scholarship ("The Marginal View," *Nation*, July 2, 1977, pp. 26–28) whereas John Grigg finds that Mehta has omitted "nothing essential" from his account of Gandhi's life ("Across the Black Waters," *Listener*, August 18, 1977, pp. 220–21). But both reviewers remark on Mehta's far greater attention to the personal details of Gandhi's life than to his political activity. Mehta's more objective approach to the "Father of India" than is typical of books about Gandhi, either praising or faulting him, shows once more how the distance of time and exile have given the author a sense of objectivity.

In *The New India*, however, Pam Jablons takes Mehta to task for "his prejudices, which would be more palatable were they less insidiously couched" ("Trapped in the Past," *New Leader*, April 10, 1978, p. 23) in terms of his evaluation of Indira Gandhi during the time of the "Emergency" in India between 1975 and 1977 when the prime minister ruled without many of the legal checks of the Indian Constitution. Mehta reveals his distaste for the India of the present when he expresses his feeling that his native country had functioned best during the British Raj and that "the 'Indianization' of India that has been going on since independence is becoming a kind of regression to the days before the raj" (quoted in Jablons, p. 24).

Clearly, the warmest critical praise is for Mehta's autobiographical work. *Mamaji* demonstrates Mehta's "understanding of [Indian] culture" through the personal experiences of his mother, which he records in a "detached" tone (Clark Blaise, "Family Memoir," *New York Times Book Review*, October 21, 1979, p. 51). Janet Malcolm praises *Vedi* for its skill in conveying the world of blindness, fear, and confusion in which Mehta lived during his time at the Dadar school ("School of the Blind," *New York Review of Books*, October 7, 1982, pp. 2–4, 6). And Ainslie Embree praises *The Ledge between the Streams* as a "remarkable, perhaps even a unique, book," one of the few that succeed in conveying the "complexities and strengths of the Indian family system" ("Leaping Without Looking," *New York Times Book Review*, May 6, 1984, p. 14). Perhaps one of the most revealing statements, quoted in Ainslee's review, is an uncle's farewell when Mehta is about to leave India to attend the School for the Blind in Arkansas: "People who go to America nowadays never come back."

Finally, in Mehta's most recent work in his series of autobiographical books, *The Stolen Light*, Edward Blishen observes the singular importance of Mehta's writing about himself: that it not only served to record his life, "but may have preserved it" (*New Statesman*, May 18, 1989, p. 26).

Although Mehta has "returned" to India, both in person and in memory many times, his detachment from his homeland and his frank distaste for much of what it has become, reveal his basic estrangement. The fact that his most successful books, from a critical perspective, are his autobiographies rather than his repertorial essays reveals that he is more "at home" in the India of memory than the India of fact.

BIBLIOGRAPHY

Works by Ved Mehta

Face to Face: An Autobiography. Boston: Atlantic–Little, Brown, 1957.
Walking the Indian Streets. Boston: Atlantic–Little Brown, 1960.
Fly and the Fly-Bottle: Encounters with British Intellectuals. Boston: Atlantic–Little Brown, 1963.
The New Theologian. New York: Harper, 1966.
Delinquent Chacha. New York: Farrar, Straus and Giroux, 1970.
Daddyji. New York: Farrar, Straus and Giroux, 1972.
Mahatma Gandhi and His Apostles. New York: Viking, 1977.
The New India. New York: Viking, 1978.
Mamaji. New York: Oxford University Press, 1979.
A Family Affair: India under Three Prime Ministers. New York: Oxford University Press, 1982.
Vedi. New York: Oxford University Press, 1982.
The Ledge between the Streams. New York: Norton, 1984.
Sound-Shadows of the New World. New York: Norton, 1986.
The Stolen Light. New York: Norton, 1989.

Studies of Ved Mehta

Mehta, Ved. "Ved Mehta: A Bibliography." *Bulletin of Bibliography* 42:1 (March 1985): 19–25.
Philip, David Scott. "Perceiving India through the Works of Nirad C. Chaudhuri, R. K. Narayan and Ved Mehta." *Envoy* 47 (1986): 29–41.
Slatin, John M. "Blindness and Self-Perception: The Autobiographies of Ved Mehta." *Mosaic: A Journal for the Interdisciplinary Study of Literature* 19:4 (1986): 173–93.
Sontag, Frederick. "The Self-Centered Author." *New Quest* 76 (July–Aug. 1989): 229–33.

ROHINTON MISTRY (1952–   )
Amritjit Singh

BIOGRAPHY

Rohinton Mistry was born in Bombay on July 3, 1952, to Behram Mistry and Freny Jhaveri Mistry and migrated to Canada in 1975. Growing up in Bombay, he had many opportunities to observe the kind of Parsi enclaves he has evoked so powerfully in his two published works of fiction. He attended the Villa Theresa Primary School and St. Xavier High School, before finishing a bachelor's degree in science at St. Xavier's College, University of Bombay, in 1974. Upon leaving the university, he married Freny Elavia, and soon after their arrival in Toronto, he started working as a clerk at the Imperial Bank of Commerce. He studied English and philosophy part-time at the University of Toronto and completed a B.A. there in 1982. In 1983, he wrote his first short story, "One Sunday," which won the Hart House Prize that year in a literary contest at the University of Toronto. He won this award again in 1984, this time for "Auspicious Occasion." In 1985, the year in which he won the Annual Contributors' Prize from the *Canadian Fiction Magazine*, Mistry gave up his bank job to devote himself full-time to writing; he sometimes tells people curious about his last name that it means "craftsman" or "artisan" in India. The short stories he published in various Canadian magazines were well-received by many reviewers, including the *Toronto Star* critic Ken Adachi, who wrote most enthusiastically about the then unknown writer. In 1987, his collection of short stories, *Tales from Firozsha Baag*, was published by Penguin Canada and has since reappeared in Great Britain and the United States under the new title *Swimming Lessons and Other Stories from Firozsha Baag*. The book was very well reviewed in British and North American journals, and was short-listed for Canada's Governor-General's Award.

Mistry and his wife have lived in and around Toronto since their arrival there in 1975. But during 1986–87, they spent one year in Long Beach,

California, where she taught high school in a racially mixed, middle-class neighborhood. The gang violence they witnessed there has colored Mistry's views of American life in general: "I think I prefer [the Canadian] Multi-culturalism to the direct racism of the [American] Melting Pot because I'd rather be alive and face the subtle discrimination. The overt racism of the Melting Pot often leads to a violent end" (Hancock 145). So, Mistry likes it in Canada, and lives there in an unliterary, uninspiring Brampton—"a wasteland of subdivisions, shopping malls, light and heavy industry, and miles of franchise glitter," according to Hancock. He likes living in Brampton on a quiet street where he practices his craft most of the day in an almost vacant house, while his wife teaches in a local high school.

In 1991, Mistry's first novel, *Such a Long Journey* was nominated for Britain's prestigious Booker Prize and won the Governor-General's Literary Award for English-language fiction to general critical acclaim. At the post-awards luncheon in Toronto in December 1991, the grave and soft-spoken author dealt most patiently with long lines of admirers and told reporters that he had no special celebratory plans. "As soon as this is over, I'm going home to Brampton to write, basically," he said. (*Globe and Mail*, December 4, 1991, 18) In March 1992, *Such a Long Journey* also received the Smith Books/Books in Canada First Novel Award.

According to an interview he gave to Val Ross (*Globe and Mail*, November 30, 1991, 9), Mistry "begins work each day at 8.30 or 9 A.M. Although he loves classical music, he works in silence; he drinks tea before, but not while, he sits at his computer. He breaks for lunch at noon—'bread and cold cuts, Canadian food'—reads magazines for half an hour, and then works through the afternoon. He wrote his first novel in three drafts." He and his wife enjoy gardening and have a special interest in growing roses. He reads middle-brow magazines, *Time* and *Maclean's*. He does not want to talk about what he does not read. "I must be careful. This is how one makes enemies," he laughs gently. He speaks Gujarati, Hindi, and a bit of Marathi, but "English is technically my mother tongue." After telling the interviewer that his next book too will be set in Bombay, Mistry, now a Canadian citizen, adds, "I'll write a novel set in Canada if it comes to me. I have no policies on this." According to Mistry, his parents—father works in advertising and mother is a housewife—were "thrilled when I said I'd become a writer—they've always loved the arts." He emigrated to Canada, because his wife had family here. Also, in 1975, "Australia was racist, America was not too inviting with Vietnam and all that rubbish, and England wasn't England any more." The interviewer found Mistry "the soul of gravity," noting that it was "both improbable and inevitable [that] a rich novel with all its despairing, revolting, and glorious passages, should have been written by such a quiet, gentle man." Despite his apparent shyness and asceticism, Mistry claims that he is not uncomfortable with his new celebrity status and that he has "learned to love giving public readings" of his work.

MAJOR WORKS AND THEMES

Since 1983, Rohinton Mistry has established himself quite rapidly as an exciting new voice on the Canadian literary scene. His two published works of fiction are solid evidence of his prodigious talents as a writer and of the richness of language and texture he brings to his craft. He has wrestled with the issues that a diasporic writer of South Asian background must inevitably confront in his new homeland, Canada. In both his fiction and his interviews, he has addressed these issues with clarity and sharpness, with wit and humor, and especially with a strong sense of his artistic integrity and independence. As an immigrant writer, he has surely felt the pressure of the still nascent Canadian nationalism to write more about his new homeland, and as a person of non-French, non-English origins, he has probably been expected to incorporate reflections on multiculturalism into his works of fiction. He has admirably handled these expectations—more invidious than they appear on the surface—in asserting his artistic privilege in writing about what he feels best to write about, and rejecting implicitly the notion that every Canadian writer must by definition write about Canada alone and not someplace else. He has thus not fallen prey to the labels by which government agencies, journalists, reviewers, and scholars generally pigeonhole artists.

An immigrant writer's total experience is palimpsestically stored in his or her memory, and only the writer's own conscious choices and unconscious energies might regulate its artistic expression. By embracing in his fiction the many and not some selected few of the feelings, emotions, thoughts, and experiences that make up the continuum of an immigrant writer's personal history, Mistry has demolished by the brilliant example of his literary choices the false gods that his contemporary Bharati Mukherjee has idolized in her statements such as "Immigrant Writing: Give Us Your Maximalists" (*New York Times Book Review*, August 28, 1988). It is much less important to make a distinction between the expatriate writer and the immigrant writer, as Mukherjee does, than to examine what any particular writer has done with the materials chosen. Mukherjee does not acknowledge that the immigrant experience in literature could be as "dead and 'charming,' " or as exoticized, as the re-created experience of an ancestral land. Mistry's tales of his Bombay past are anything but "dead" and "charming"; in the richness of detail he manages to evoke with gentle irony, and in the resonance of his language and imagery, his narratives take a full measure of the human experience—a domain no less worthy of a new Canadian writer than of a Dickens or a George Eliot. For immigrant writers of color in North America, for example, self-definitions must emerge not from an easy, assimilationist surrender to labels supplied or inspired by others, but from their own individualistic ways of coming to terms with their specific backgrounds as they learn to accept their share of the burden of national histories they have embraced through their new citizenship.

The fictional world of Rohinton Mistry—as reflected in both the *Tales* and *Such a Long Journey*—centers on a lower middle class segment of the Parsi community of metropolitan Bombay. The world of the Khodadad Building in his new novel is but an extension of Firozsha Baag. Either of these two fictional locations forms a microcosm in itself—all its diverse cast of characters with their ordinary human struggles and their extraordinary range of eccentricities. This world is as richly suffused with the breath of contemporary Bombay as is Salman Rushdie's *Midnight Children* or Nissim Ezekiel's poetry. Firozsha Baag and Khodadad Building are at once part of the sprawling metropolis as well as a world apart, just as the Parsi community retains its distinctive ethos and culture in a predominantly Hindu India. Class and color distinctions made within the Parsi world are reinforced in both of Mistry's works by its close connection to the surrounding slums, and to the caste hierarchies of Indian life—"oozing the stench of bigotry," as a Mistry protagonist puts it. But the all-embracing humanity of Mistry's world is underscored even more by what happens to his characters and among them; in the moving moments of joy, despair, tenderness, and of temporary lucidities within the ever-present confusion, which each of them experiences alone or with others. In presenting his vast array of characters in their quiet dignity or subtle individuality, Mistry not only shows them resisting the societal pressures of conformity within India, but also de-exoticizes his ancestral land for Western readers for whom the whole Third World is often one large mass and most of whom rarely experience its many diverse parts in their specificity or full humanity.

Although a collection of eleven short stories, each of which might be read independently, *Tales from Firozsha Baag* achieves a unity of theme, tenor, and structure through the vital links between character and event from one story to the other. For example, while the lawyer Rustomji the Curmudgeon is a major character in the opening story, he is mentioned in several other tales, but especially in "Squatter" wherein the resident storyteller Nariman sits outside Rustomji's flat to entertain his young listeners, and in "The Paying Guests" where Rustomji's sister and her husband seek his advice on how to evict their subtenants. Each tale introduces new details (for example, about Kersi's Grandpa in "Swimming Lessons") or unknown facets of characters we already know. In the ways in which characters interact and operate beyond the confines of any single story, it is possible to read these tales together as a novel. In this respect, *Tales* is comparable with other twentieth-century texts such as Sherwood Anderson's *Winesburg, Ohio*, Jean Toomer's *Cane*, Ernest Hemingway's *In Our Time*, William Faulkner's *Go Down,*

Moses, and Gloria Naylor's *Women of Brewster Place*. The point of view varies from one tale to another, although a quickly shifting multifarious (omniscient?) narration is most frequently employed. At least three of the stories have the young Kersi's point of view, and two of them (including "Swimming Lessons") use a first-person narrative. Kersi, the young immigrant writer of "Swimming Lessons" who writes the Firozsha tales, comes as close to being Mistry's alter ego in his fiction as any character is allowed to.

Despite the shared locale and mood of the collection, each story is quite distinctive in the way it frames a slice of the human experience in all its Parsi specificity. "Auspicious Occasion" unfolds a series of disasters that take place on *behram roje*, a Parsi holiday, in the lives of the fifty-year-old Rustomji and his thirty-year-old wife, Mehroo. Mehroo's life is captured deftly in a single sentence: "Who, while trapped in the fervour of matchmaking at the height of the wedding season, could imagine a toothless gummy mouth, morning after morning, greeting a woman in her absolute prime? No one. Certainly not Mehroo" (3). But despite Rustomji's toothless mouth and his innocuous fantasizing about the voluptuous Gajra, the domestic help, Mehroo's life with him is not one of resentment or unfulfillment. She expects to squeeze joy and satisfaction out of every small gesture and ritual of this auspicious day. But nothing seems to go right from the moment in the morning when her constipated husband begins screaming about the leakage from the lavatory in the flat above theirs. In a manner quite characteristic of Mistry's short fiction, a central confrontation ensues in the story when Rustomji, dressed in impeccable white and on his way by bus to the fire-temple, is spat upon by a *paan*-eater on the second deck of the bus. When he turns his anger from the *paan*-eater to the taunting crowd that gathers quickly around him, he realizes that he faces the risk of sectarian violence (a "communal riot"). With his wits still around him, he manages to clown his way out of the situation by removing his dentures and presenting himself to the crowd as a helpless old man. But the *behram roje* has not gone well for Mehroo either. She comes home to report on much worse—Parsi has killed Parsi, the old priest at the temple killed by a temple worker. The link between the two scenes is suggested by Mehroo's startled reaction to Rustomji's *paan*-stained *dugli* and its momentary identification in her distraught mind with the priest's blood-stained one at the temple. So, the menaced quality of life derives not only from dangers lurking outside the community but also from the fissures within the group, hinted at earlier in Rustomji's refusal to go along with other tenants to pay for the painting of the flats. The story ends, however, on a note of tenderness, a shared ritual of tea-taking between Rustomji and Mehroo, who gets a "rare glimpse of the softness underneath" her husband's tough exterior and feels very close to him for the moment.

A deeper love finds expression in "Condolence Visit," which relates to

Daulat's grief over her husband Minocher's death after a prolonged illness. Born and brought up in Firozsha Baag, Daulat and Minocher "were the only childhood sweethearts [there] who had got married, all the others had gone their separate ways" (67). Mistry, who gives his erotic imagination free play in most of his other stories, refrains from doing so in this story of high love and remembrance. But as the title suggests, the story is even more about Daulat's dread at the rituals surrounding condolence visits and her fear that the visitors' prying questions would not allow her to "hold on the memory of those final blessed six days [of] spurious convalescence" (60). In arming herself for the expected stream of condoling friends and relatives, she wishes now that she had accepted the gift of a cassette player from her nephew, Sid-Sarosh—the central character in "Squatter"—and enjoys imagining the answers she would have recorded for them. But if the recording machine could not empower her against the meddling intruders, her late husband's handsome black *pugree*, the ceremonial wedding turban that adorns a glass case, comes to her rescue. Against the pious objections of a distant visiting cousin and her prying neighbor, Nijamai (the only resident of the Baag who owns a fridge), she gives the *pugree* to a Parsi young man who expects to have a traditional wedding soon. This action of hers privileges her desire to deal with her grief in her own way and not according to societal rules, an inclination already asserted in her refusal to let the bedside lamp go out after the conventional four days.

At one level, most of Mistry's fictions, including his novel, are about the patterns of empowerment in a world that denies the individuals their voices and exposes them to dangers in a wide variety of forms and controls: parental authority, class hierarchies, personal betrayal, political power and corruption, superstition and shamanism, physical or mental limitations. Jaakaylee, the Goan outsider who has served the Karani family as kitchen help for over forty years in "The Ghost of Firozsha Baag," enjoys the status she wins with her high-nosed mistress once the latter mistakes for a ghost the white sheet Jaakaylee wears as she stands on the balcony late one night. In the two stories that focus primarily on Jehangir, the sickly bookish boy who stands apart from other adolescents at the Baag apparently loses his battles for connection. In "The Collectors," his friendship with the gentle and sensitive Dr. Mody—who in his short life at the Baag wins universal respect for championing tenant rights—is betrayed by Mrs. Mody, who resents the fact that her husband finds time for Jehangir, but not for their own deviant son, Pesi the Fartmaker. In "Exercisers," whose title refers to his effete fascination with the big-muscled exercisers in the public park, Jehangir, now a college student, fails to win the freedom to resolve his own conflict between his love for Behroze and his parents' rejection of her. His failure is inevitable, once he accepts the intervention of Bhagwan Baba, the holy man who speaks in riddles and talks about life being a trap.

Mistry's loving attention to ordinary detail is a major element in the authenticity of his craft that belies false labels. In quick turns of phrase, he is able to capture the intricate details of a cricket bat that Kersi tries to repair in "One Sunday," or of grinding the *masala* or making goat curry that Jaakaylee weaves into her ghost tales. In "Of White Hairs and Cricket," almost like a clever painter, Mistry brings the morning scene at the Baag alive in a few verbal strokes. In "Lend Me Your Light," a tale imbued with social, even socialist, meanings, the legendary Bombay tiffin careers are pictured memorably; so is the skeletal coolie at the train station with several pieces of family luggage balanced on his head and hands, or the equally skeletal rickshaw-puller.

The pervasive erotic detail of all his fiction also serves many textual purposes. At one level, sexuality is Mistry's mode of seeing. But the erotic detail in his tales also establishes how the somewhat Victorian exterior of Indian life hides so well the rich and turbulent sexuality that underlies and shapes social life. As novelist Janet Turner Hospital notes, Mistry "evokes with sharp eye and gentle wit, the secret eroticism of a puritan culture: the innocent voyeurism of married men . . . and the fantasies of widowed women" (*Los Angeles Times Book Review*, March 5, 1989: C5). Patterns of repression and fantasy are brought to the surface and intermingle with the choices many Mistry characters face as they seek freedom and empowerment as individuals.

Such detail—erotic, scataological, cultural—is surely critical to the success of the two stories "Squatter" and "Swimming Lessons," which, along with "Lend Me Your Light," extend out from Firozsha Baag to Mistry's new homeland, Canada. The tales relate to two immigrants, one who feels compelled to relinquish his Canadian dream to return to India, and the other, who achieves a tentative peace with his new land as a young writer. Sarosh-Sid makes a sacred promise to his mother that he would return to India if he did not "become completely Canadian in exactly ten years" (155). The task of becoming "completely Canadian" (is this Mistry's satiric response to Canadian obsession with national identity?) includes getting used to Western-style toilets, something Sarosh fails to achieve until his final flight back to India is ready to take off. For Nariman the storyteller, the case of Sarosh-Sid provides an opportunity not only to reject the hypocrisy of both the American "melting pot" and Canadian multiculturalism, but also to suggest the Parsis' capacity to laugh at one of their own. Sid's story provides an important counterbalance to the other tales Nariman tells his young listeners about Parsi heroes, stories that border on ethnocentrism. In "Swimming Lessons," Kersi's first-person narrative relates to his unsuccessful attempts to learn swimming and his equally frustrated desire to view young female bodies in nudity in and around his apartment building. Other characters in this story only reinforce the microcosmic realities of Ferozsha Baag; the characters gathered at the Don Mills apartment building where Kersi lives now represent a diversity in age, social and ethnic background, national origin, or personal eccentricity, and certainly match the liveliness, if not the intricacy or subtlety, of the Baag denizens.

These two stories stand out in the collection for yet another reason. They are metafictional and include considerable commentary on the art of storytelling. In "Squatter," Jehangir, as the most bookish, sensitive listener, serves as a surrogate literary critic. He notices the care with which Nariman chooses his words and structures his sentences and the unpredictability that is the hallmark of his narratives. His listeners play a role in defining his stories—there are myriad gradations of tone and texture between "a funny incident [told] in a very serious way," and "a significant matter" expressed in "a light and playful manner" (147). In "Swimming Lessons," the "writerly text" takes the form of alternating narratives—the son in Canada writing stories out of his remembered past, and the old parents reading the stories and disagreeing about the creative energies at work in their son's art and in the choices he makes as well as the consequences these choices have for him and his readers, especially the Parsis. To the extent Mistry uses "Swimming Lessons" to answer some of his critics and reviewers, including those who would like him to write more about Canada, these juxtapositions are quite self-conscious. Not only is the humor of lines such as "water imagery in my life is recurring" (119) delightful, but it also contributes to the narrative cohesiveness of the tale.

Like his short stories, Mistry's multilayered novel too is about power and powerlessness, about the need for community in which the individual's voice is not muffled. *Such a Long Journey* is primarily the story of Gustad Noble, the little man who holds on to his dignity, strength, and humanity in a sweltering tide of disappointment, confusion, betrayal, and corruption. Forced to become a bank clerk because of his father's financial bungling at the family bookstore, he finds his life bounded by the workplace and the Khodadad Buildings, where he shares a small flat with his wife, Dilnawaz, his two sons, Sohrab and Darius, and his daughter, Roshan. Little annoyances in and around the lower middle class Parsi enclave include the wall outside the building that is used as a public urinal; too little space and too much noise in and around his apartment; and neighbors such as the "dogwalla idiot," who keeps a yapping Pomeranian, and the mysterious Miss Kutputia, who must be humored because she owns a phone. Gustad's vicarious search for liberation from his lower-class status and closing horizons ends abruptly when his elder son, Sohrab, relinquishes the opportunity to study engineering at a prestigious technology institute in favor of an ordinary B.A. Other problems follow—Roshan's recurring illness; the unexplained disappearance of his friend, Major Jimmie Bilimoria, whose letters from unknown locations gradually drag Gustad into a national plot of corruption and racketeering; and the death of his friend and bank colleague Dinshawji, who had for years hidden his bodily afflictions and his domestic anguish behind his clowning exterior. In lesser hands, such conditions of hardship and disillusionment in an Asian setting might have produced a sentimental, provincial, or exotic novel, but in Mistry's hands, these materials are treated with a rare economy of image and symbol, with wry humor, gentle irony, and tough-minded realism.

Mistry places these happenings in Gustad's life in the India of 1971, when Mrs. Indira Gandhi was at the height of her power and East Pakistan was getting ready to become Bangladesh. The events surrounding the life and death of Jimmie Bilimoria are clearly Mistry's fictional rendering of the notorious Nagarwala case: in May 1971, the chief cashier at the State Bank of India head office in New Delhi received a call, presumably from Prime Minister Indira Gandhi, instructing him to hand over 6 million rupees to a courier, Sohrab Nagarwala, for possible use in secret operations involving the Bangladeshi freedom movement. The chief cashier complied, but in a chain of events that has not been explained satisfactorily to this day, Mr. Nagarwala was arrested, given a hasty trial, and sentenced to four years in jail where he suddenly died the following year. Mistry uses this incident to bring together the personal and the political; the abuse of power and the corruption among the political elite reach out menacingly into the private lives of ordinary citizens. Helpless against the stupendous network of unseen forces, Gustad derives much satisfaction in the small victory he gains over excretory ugliness when he persuades a pavement artist to turn the compound wall "pisser-proof" by painting on it pictures of saints, gods, and goddesses from all religious traditions. When the wall is finally brought down by the municipality as part of urban improvement, the same artist suggests that "luck is the spit of gods and goddesses" (338). But Gustad can hold his head high, because of the moral fiber he shows in his many acts of courage and kindness—especially in the patience with which he understands the rapid and almost incoherent utterances of halfwit Tehmul and in the compassion with which he reconciles Tehmul's adult longings (making love to Roshan's doll) with his endearing childlike innocence.

Envied by most friends for his good health, the broad-shouldered Gustad adopts a tough and unsentimental stance in most situations that supersedes his physical personality. Turning bitter and ironic about son Sohrab's assertions of independence, he prefers total estrangement from Sohrab over appearing soft. He is touched by Dinshawji's death, but not moved to tears. When Dilnawaz suggests that it would be all right if "crying comes," Gustad lifts "his eyes defiantly to her face, so she could see them dry...." Although he travels to New Delhi to relieve Jimmie's loneliness in death, he does not shed a tear for him either. Like Okonkwo (another son of a failed father) in Chinua Achebe's *Things Fall Apart*, Gustad seems afraid to acknowledge for others the compassion and humanity he has always shown Tehmul. In the final scene of the novel, after a brick has fatally hit Tehmul in the riots that accompany the municipality's attempt to remove the wall, he cradles Tehmul's still-warm body in his arms "with a single mighty effort" (335). Like a tragic hero on a Shakespearean stage, watched in fear and admiration by Sohrab and others, "without a trace of his limp, without a fumble," Gustad carries the body to the bed in Tehmul's flat. As he prays over the dead body, tears begin "to well in his closed eyes" (335). Fully in contact with his humanity, he finally permits a free flow of "the salt water of his eyes, as much for himself as for Tehmul. As much for Tehmul as for Jimmie. And for Dinshawji, for Pappa and Mamma, for Grandpa and Grandma, all who had had to wait for so long . . . " (337). It is no surprise that he is reconciled in this very moment to his estranged son, who has waited motionless in the doorway through several cycles of prayers that Gustad says for Tehmul.

CRITICAL RECEPTION

There are few scholarly studies of Mistry's fiction so far, but he will definitely receive more attention in the academy once his prize-winning novel becomes more easily accessible for classroom adoption. In an essay entitled "Insider/Outsider Views on Belonging: The Short Stories of Bharati Mukherjee and Rohinton Mistry," Amin Malak contrasts Mukherjee's "satirical style (à la Naipaul)" with Mistry's "gentle and penetrating irony," which is reminiscent of Joyce. However, Malak recognizes the similarity in the two writers' subject matter. Both deal, in his view, with "frightened beleaguered minorities"—in Mistry, "Parsis enclosed by a predominantly Hindu culture," and in Mukherjee, "Indians transplanted into a North American setting." While darkness and defeat mark Mukherjee's treatment of her characters, Mistry's humorous rendition of a traditional community precludes "his condemning or disowning his culture in its entirety" (189).

Mistry's two books have been widely reviewed in Canada, Britain, the United States, and India. Most of the reviewers have praised his books for their realistic but humorous portrayal of Bombay Parsi life and recognized his control and craftsmanship. He has been especially credited with powerful characterization and for the economy of his images and symbols—for example, the wall outside Khodadad Building, and his humorous but effective use of differing toilet habits as an icon of nearly insurmountable cultural differences. His fictional world has been compared in its microcosmic quality to R. K. Narayan's Malgudi novels; for its realism, to Anita Desai's fiction; for the elegance of his writing, to V. S. Naipaul; for its tragicomic quality to Charles Dickens; for its epic grandeur to Salman Rushdie.

In reviewing *Swimming Lessons and Other Stories* in the *New York Times Book Review* (March 8, 1989), Hope Cooke praised the book for its "compression" and Mistry's ability to make the sad lives of tenants in an all-Parsi enclave "life-affirming, even ebullient." Roshan Shahani in *The Indian Post* (October 27, 1987) suggested that the ribald and scatological humor of some of Mistry's stories placed them "on par with the best of Robert Kroetsch or Mordecai Richler, Mistry's better-known Jewish counterparts." Janet Hamilton praised the stories for their unusual structure: "They are tales rather than conventional short stories, meandering through the terrain . . . by association and episode" (*Quill & Quire*, June 1987). In her review (already cited), Janet Turner Hospital observes a blind spot in the story's narrator, "an unintentional one, I suspect, on the author's part. The swimmer alludes . . . to racist gestures and remarks made by others in the locker room; but he himself frequently makes extremely sexist observations about women and seems unaware of the parallel insult."

Such a Long Journey too has been reviewed widely and hailed as a great success. Reviewing the book in *India Abroad* (November 21, 1991), Rochelle D'Souza marvels at the "photographic memory" that serves Mistry so well in furnishing "a wealth of tiny details that flesh out the thinnest possible plot and endows the writing with the laughter, sadness, anecdote, character, and speech patterns of which memorable novels are made." In the *New York Times Book Review* (July 7, 1991), David Ray highlights the "vivid picture of India" Mistry provides in his novel and notes his gift for "erotic satire." Not only does Mistry catch "the unsettling effects on everyday life of the many upheavals afflicting India in the 1960's and 1970's," he also provides "sharp, affectionate sketches of Indian family life," and "fascinating" portraits of Bombay's crowded precincts. But Ray does not find Gustad "a convincing figure . . . , [who] never seems more than a kind of suffering drudge, a bepuzzled gull drawn into a world he does not understand." David Townsend, reviewing the book in *Quill & Quire* (March 1991), praises *Such a Long Journey* as a "brilliantly controlled novel [which] combines the interest of compelling subject matter with depth of characterization and symbolic density."

BIBLIOGRAPHY

Works by Rohinton Mistry

Swimming Lessons and Other Stories from Firozsha Baag. Boston: Houghton Mifflin, 1989. (Originally published in 1987 by Penguin Books Canada Limited as *Tales of Ferozsha Baag.*)

Such a Long Journey. London: Faber and Faber, 1991; Toronto: McClelland and Stewart, 1991; New York: Alfred A. Knopf, 1991.

Studies of Rohinton Mistry

Adams, Phoebe-Lou. Review of *Such a Long Journey. Atlantic* 267 (May 1991): 124.

Carey, Glenn O. Review of *Such a Long Journey. Library Journal* 116 (Apr. 15, 1991): 27.

Cryer, Dan. Review of *Swimming Lessons and Other Stories from Firozsha Baag. New York Newsday* (June 2, 1989): 18.

Dwyer, Victor. Review of *Such a Long Journey*. *Maclean's* 104 (May 27, 1991): 67.

Hakutani, Michiko. Review of *Swimming Lessons and Other Stories from Firozsha Baag*. *New York Times* (Feb. 3, 1989): 8.

Hancock, Geoff. "An Interview with Rohinton Mistry." *Canadian Fiction Magazine* 65 (1989): 143–50.

Iyer, Pico. Review of *Such a Long Journey*. *Time* 137 (Apr. 8, 1991): 76.

Malak, Amin. "Insider/Outsider Views on Belonging: The Short Stories of Bharati Mukherjee and Rohinton Mistry." In *Short Stories in the New Literatures in English: Proceedings of the Nice Conference of the European Association for Commonwealth Literature and Language Studies*. Ed. Jacqueiline Bardolph. Nice: Faculté des Lettres et Sciences Humaines de Nice, 1989: 189–96.

Miller, Lucasta. Review of *Such a Long Journey*. *New Statesman and Society* 4 (Mar. 22, 1991): 46.

Mukherjee, Arun. "Narrating India." *Toronto South Asian Review* 10: 2 (1992): 82–91.

Novak, Dagmar. "Interview." In *Other Solitudes: Canadian Multicultural Fictions*. Ed. Linda Hutcheon and Mario Richmond. Toronto: Oxford University Press, 1990: 255–62.

Oza, Rajesh C. Review of *Such a Long Journey*. *India Currents* (San Jose, CA) 5: 10 (Jan. 1992): 54.

Russell, Judith. Review of *Swimming Lessons and Other Stories from Firozsha Baag*. *Whig Standard* Kingston, Ontario (June 13, 1987): 7.

Shostak, Elizabeth. Review of *Swimming Lessons and Other Stories from Firozsha Baag*. *Wilson Library Bulletin* 63 (May 1989): 128.

Steinberg, Sybil. Review of *Swimming Lessons and Other Stories from Firozsha Baag*. *Publishers Weekly* 234 (Dec. 9, 1988): 43.

Steinberg, Sybil. Review of *Such a Long Journey*. *Publishers Weekly* 238 (Mar. 8, 1991): 66.

Wigston, Nancy. Review of *Swimming Lessons and Other Stories from Firozsha Baag*. *Globe and Mail* Toronto (May 2, 1987): 12.

PRAFULLA MOHANTI
(1936–   )
Asa Briggs

BIOGRAPHY

Prafulla Mohanti is the youngest son of Bipra Charan Mohanty and Srimati Rama Devi, both now dead. He was born in the Cuttack District of Orissa in the village of Nanpur. In his childhood the village was totally isolated; there were no roads, no electricity, no cinema, no radio or television. Epidemics were common. His eldest brother died of diphtheria in infancy.

The traditional occupation of the Karan caste into which Mohanti was born was writing and accountancy, and he was brought up in an atmosphere where learning was respected. His mother tongue is Oriya, but he had taught himself to read and write in English and Bengali before attending the village primary school. His father could read and write in simple English, but his mother could only sign her name in Oriya and read the printed holy texts. Many times she pawned her gold bracelets, part of her dowry, to pay his fees.

Arts and crafts were an integral part of village life, and Mohanti helped his mother to decorate the mud walls of their house with rice paste for religious ceremonies. Soon other villagers were inviting him to decorate their homes. His interest in literature developed by listening to stories told by his mother, grandmother, and professional storytellers. He produced plays and wrote short stories, poems, and essays in Oriya, which he published in the school magazine that he edited and wrote in his own hand. It was natural for him to treat all the arts as interrelated.

Until Mohanti was fifteen the village was his world—with occasional visits to the forests to stay with his father, who worked as a ranger. There, in close touch with nature, he would nurse wounded animals and birds that his father brought back from hunting. He decided that he would like to be a doctor, but found that science did not appeal to him, and after failing to secure entry to a medical school he won a scholarship in architecture at

Bombay University, which he had read about in an advertisement, not then knowing what an architect was.

Bombay was 1500 miles away and took three days to reach by train. Mohanti was now a migrant in his own country, and for five years he experienced city life. Everything there was different—language, customs, and culture. The method of teaching was Western, and he was taught that everything British was superior to everything Indian. It again seemed natural for him, therefore, to travel to London in 1960, after graduation, to continue his studies. The number of Indians living in England then was small, but he was made to feel inferior at once. His degree in architecture was not recognized, and he was handicapped by the color of his skin. He worked in several architects' offices in London, however, and his first job was to design lavatories for London Airport.

Disenchanted with architectural practice, Mohanti decided to study town planning, and once again became a migrant, moving in 1962 to Leeds, a northern industrial city. There he reflected on life in village India, comparing it with life in the West and thereby establishing his own sense of identity. Having completed his courses, he was anxious to return home and devote his time to the development of village India, but he had no political or financial backing, and after explaining his plans to the authorities in India he was frustrated when his voice remained unheard.

In 1965 Mohanti took a decision that was to influence the rest of his life: to stay on in London and work for the Greater London Council, designing new towns. He got to know London well, living at first in the working-class East End and later in the very different western district of Pimlico. After four years he left the Greater London Council and began experimenting with painting, dancing, and music. While painting, he felt he was dancing too: his hands were moving to express his feeling. While writing, he was painting pictures in words.

He established his reputation as a painter, and has subsequently held a large number of one-man exhibitions in Europe and Japan as well as in England and India. His work now figures in major collections, including the Museum of Modern Art, Berkeley, California, and the National Gallery of Modern Art, New Delhi. His paintings are abstract and draw imaginatively on the shapes and colors of his village, to which he regularly returns for several months each year. His circles recall the three circles his teacher taught him to draw at his first lesson in the nursery school.

In 1971 Mohanti's village was almost destroyed by a cyclone, and it was when he was planning to return to help his fellow villagers that an English publisher, Reg Davis-Poynter, commissioned him to write *My Village, My Life*, the first book on village life written by a villager and the first to deal not with people of wealth or power but with unknown Indians.

Almost all his later books, illustrated by him with sketches of people and places, deal with village life, and in 1990 he started a center in Nanpur where artists, craftsmen, and writers can experience village life.

MAJOR WORKS AND THEMES

Through Brown Eyes is not a straight autobiography. It describes how and why Mohanti became both a painter and a writer and how through loneliness and suffering in a distant land he found his identity as an artist both in words and in pictures. When he first arrived in England (Bilayat), he had great expectations. Slowly, faced as he was with racial discrimination, subtle and violent, disillusionment set in. He felt himself a stranger. Meanwhile, the number of Indians living in England greatly increased.

Through Brown Eyes is far more than a catalog of prejudice and discrimination. It charts Mohanti's discovery of the villagers of Nanpur, with whom he knew that he belonged, as well as his discovery of himself. It was because of his separation from his village that he saw its people more clearly than if he had stayed at home. Likewise, he saw the place. Like his earlier writings, *Through Brown Eyes* evokes a particularly strong sense of place— from busy Bombay to squalid Wapping, where one night he was physically attacked by a group of white thugs outside the underground station and left lying unconscious in a pool of blood in a deserted street. Ever since then he has suffered in body as well as in mind. *Through Brown Eyes* dwells on lost innocence, not on success as an artist.

Mohanti's first book, *My Village, My Life* (1973), was dedicated to his parents and to his village. In no sense is it a piece of sociological writing, although sociologists find it interesting and helpful. There Mohanti sees the village from inside, having contemplated it from outside, and in presenting his galaxy of characters he allows them to speak freely for themselves in a way they would never have done to any outsider.

All aspects of village life are explored. One chapter—and the chapters are deliberately not numbered—is called "A Child Is Born," another, "Disasters and Death." Much of the fascination of the book lies in the detail, but Mohanti insists throughout that villages like Nanpur are India, and he begins by quoting Mahatma Gandhi, "Go to the villages; . . . therein lies the soul of India."

In *Changing Village, Changing Life* (1990) Mohanti takes his readers back to Nanpur nearly twenty years later. His book describes the disturbing changes that have taken place in his village and lead him to reflect more generally on the fragilities as well as the strengths of village life. There are many cross references also to England, where there have been even more disturbing changes. All these he had registered in his chosen exile.

His book begins with a transcript of a lecture delivered to students at a university in Delhi. It makes points about villages that the students question, but the questions make Mohanti feel it essential to get back to his village as quickly as he can. A vivid description of his journey comes next, and this is followed by a return to the source, a chapter on his family. Once again, the villagers talk about themselves in their own language, explaining both what has happened to them and how they view the future. Much in the book is depressing, yet the last sentence describes the villagers dancing for joy.

Songs are still part of oral village culture. So too are stories, some of which Mohanti told simply and beautifully in *Indian Village Tales* (1975) at a time when he already feared that the storytelling tradition was dying out. The stories themselves are timeless. They are not strict translations, but their authenticity, like that of his illustrations, is never in doubt. Some of the stories Mohanti had heard from his mother: some were enacted in the village with puppets. Like much else in his writing, they carry with them a sense of fate. The village astrologer is never far away. He had forecast that Mohanti was destined to travel far.

CRITICAL RECEPTION

Mohanti's published writings have been widely acclaimed for their deceptively simple prose and their directness of vision. *My Village, My Life*, widely reviewed for a first book, was praised by many for its ability to paint pictures with words. Indian critics, however, had less to say about it than might have been expected. Yet it has been translated into several languages—Danish, Japanese, and Norwegian are among them—and reading it has persuaded many people to travel to Nanpur. Those who did not go, a London reviewer observed, could feel India's heart beating merely by reading the book.

Reviewers of *Indian Village Tales* make much of the charming simplicity of the tales and of Mohanti's gifts as a storyteller. The tales have been welcomed in schools, especially in British schools with large numbers of students of Indian origin, many born in Britain.

Through Brown Eyes, not surprisingly, inspired or provoked more reviews than any other of Mohanti's books both in India and in Britain. Racism, the difficulty of "being brown in Britain" (Murphy 13), was the aspect that most critics picked out. Other critics chose, however, to concentrate on the consequences for an artist of living between two cultural worlds. A few British critics have responded defensively and negatively to the book's relentless critique of racism in contemporary Britain. But reviewers such as Hanif Kureishi—himself an important writer in the Indian diaspora—have praised Mohanti's narrative precisely for its uncompromising exposure of British racism.

Mohanti's most recent work, *Changing Village, Changing Life*, was less widely reviewed in Britain than in India. But its universal message was highlighted by the BBC World Service, which featured it prominently in its program "Arena," and by the Third World Network program "Features."

BIBLIOGRAPHY

Works by Prafulla Mohanti

My Village, My Life. London: Davis-Poynter, 1973; New York: Praeger Publishers, 1974; London: Corgi Books, 1975; Tokyo: Heinbonshe Ltd., 1975.
Indian Village Tales. London: Davis-Poynter, 1975.
Through Brown Eyes. New York: Oxford University Press, 1985; New York: Penguin, 1988.
Changing Village, Changing Life. London: Viking, 1990; New York: Penguin, 1991.

Studies of Prafulla Mohanti

Jack, Ian. "Welcome to Britain." *Sunday Times* (London) (Oct. 27, 1985): 21.
Kureishi, Hanif. "A Different World." *Times Literary Supplement* (Dec. 20, 1985): 3.
Mishra, Ganeswar. "How Does an Indian Village Speak?: A Study of the Form of Prafulla Mohanti's *My Village, My Life.*" *Autobiographical and Biographical Writing in the Commonwealth.* Ed. Doreen MacDermott. Barcelona: University of Barcelona Press, 1985. 25–38.
Murphy, Dervla. "Being Brown in Britain." *Irish Times* (Dublin) (Oct. 26, 1985): 13.

ROOPLALL MONAR (1947–   )
P. Rudi Mattai

BIOGRAPHY

Rooplall Monar was born in 1947 in the County of Demerara in the Republic of Guyana, South America. He grew up in Lusignan Estate, one of the sugar estates in what was then largely a plantation society. His parents were laborers on the sugar estate, and Monar grew up in poverty.

Details of his childhood and schooling remain sketchy. As a young adult he worked as a bookkeeper at the estate where his parents worked; later he worked as a teacher and practiced folk medicine. He lives in Guyana, where he has gained considerable recognition as a writer; in fact, his poems and short stories are broadcast on the Guyana Broadcasting Service, a government-owned radio station. Abroad, however, his work has received practically no attention.

MAJOR WORKS AND THEMES

Much of Monar's work remains unpublished, largely because of the absence of a viable publishing industry in Guyana. As the introductory essay in his only published work, *Backdam People*, contends, "There is little alternative but to engage in the neo-colonial business of metropolitan publication and then re-export Guyana's own talents back home" (6). Fortunately, however, *Backdam People* is brilliantly representative of the author's talent; though it is Monar's only published work to date, it is significant enough to make him a major Indo-Guyanese writer.

Backdam People is a collection of eleven unpretentious short stories that focus on the lives of Indo-Guyanese plantation workers. The estate communities of the 1940s and 1950s provide the setting, and Monar, with ironic detachment and unsparing realism, chronicles the complex struggles of Indian indentured laborers and their families attempting to maintain their cultural identity in an alien context. Perhaps the most noteworthy feature of the stories is Monar's magnificent use of the creolized language of his characters. His accurate rendition of the rhythms and cadences of the Indo-Guyanese speech has the effect of authenticating his narratives.

In "Bully Boy," one of the stories in *Backdam People*, Monar explores the nature of violence in a colonized culture. The narrative centers around Bully Boy, a barber, who terrorizes his entire community with his brute force and general lawlessness. But the members of the community—a community that is made up of indentured workers on a white-owned plantation—have so hopelessly internalized the structures of hierarchy imposed by colonial management that they offer little resistance. Only after Bully Boy is severely beaten and permanently disabled by someone from a neighboring village do the people begin to articulate their frustrations.

In "Hakim," another story in the volume, Monar again explores the apparent resignation of the colonized to abusive colonial power, but his treatment of the relationship between the powerful and the powerless is more ambivalent here. The setting of the story is a typical sugar plantation where abuse of power by the functionaries is commonplace. Since the estate provides the only opportunity for economic survival, the workers offer little opposition. Hakim, the main character in the story and a midlevel manager on the plantation, demands sexual favors from the women in the cane fields. His demands are met because the women know that "Hakim is one powerful driver, and too beside, how life going you can't tell, when Hakim could help you with Big Manager whenever trouble meet you" (61). The unseen but aggressive presence of the "Big Manager"—the white colonial plantation owner—clearly points to the license for authoritarianism and abuse inherent in the various levels of colonial hierarchy. At the end the husband of one of Hakim's victims stabs him several times in the abdomen and leaves him permanently weak and impotent. The "Big Manager," however, is still safe and in control.

Some of the other stories in the volume adopt a comic tone in their presentation of Indo-Guyanese mores. "Sukul," for example, offers a comic yet sympathetic examination of the belief among rural Indo-Guyanese in *jumbie* (ghosts, often associated with whites). In "Bahadur," the principal character wears a white sheet and pretends to be a jumbie in order to scare away the security personnel detailed to guard a barn. Even the bravest of the security men, upon seeing the jumbie, flees: "O Gawd Mutton, is a Dutchman. . . . And me hear Dutchman is bad-bad. . . . To hell wid cowpen. Me ain't want Dutchman kill me tonight" (72).

The stories in *Backdam People* collectively offer a memorable and poignant picture of embattled Indian diasporic rural families in Guyana prior to the dismantlement of the estate communities that occurred during the late 1950s.

CRITICAL RECEPTION

Backdam People has received little critical recognition. The only major critical commentary available is the introductory essay that accompanies the volume. The writer of the introduction, who for some reason remains anonymous, does justice to Monar's work and sums up the stories as being invaluable "not only because of what they say but [because] of the way they say it" (10). On the back cover of the book is the following comment by Peter Nazareth, another writer of the Indian diaspora: "We see people who have their own world and their own world view ... but the author places their fate within a wider economic context, extending all the way to the heart of the colonial empire." Monar's inclusion in this sourcebook on the writers of the Indian diaspora perhaps will generate scholarly interest in his work.

BIBLIOGRAPHY

Works by Rooplall Monar

Backdam People. Leeds, England: Peepal Tree Press, 1987.

DOM MORAES (1938–   )
Kamakshi P. Murti

BIOGRAPHY

Dom Moraes was born on July 19, 1938, in the city of Bombay—a city that would continue to haunt his sensibility as a writer long after he had severed the umbilical cord. Although he calls Bombay gritty and impossible, it remains an unforgettable place: "When I was a child in Bombay, I was continually aware that we were surrounded by water," suggesting a symbiotic relationship that cannot be dissolved without anguish (*Bombay* 5). His parents were highly educated—father Frank Moraes was literary editor on the *Times of India* and mother Beryl Moraes a doctor in the tradition of her family, a pathologist who worked in a large hospital half the week and in a research laboratory the other half, as Dom Moraes mentions in his autobiography *My Son's Father* (6).

His father represented the anchor in his life and offered him easy means of identification as a role model, the only fixed point he had ever had in his life (*My Son's Father* 165). His relationship with his mother was much more complex and served more often than not to irritate and confuse him, because, as he himself admits, she offered him a responsibility of love that he did not want to accept (*My Son's Father* 41). Even before he left for England at age seventeen, this relationship became intolerable because of her slowly deteriorating mind with moments of unbearably selfless love. He traveled a great deal as a child with his parents—to Sri Lanka, Australia, New Zealand, Singapore, Vietnam, Thailand, Burma. Possibly this is the beginning of a wanderlust that does not leave him again, as his extensive travels around the world document.

He began to write poetry at the age of twelve. In his opinion he wrote verse nearly all the time, but perceived every new attempt as being a similar kind of failure; this was his conclusion at age thirteen (*My Son's Father* 75), hardly an age warranting such scathingly destructive self-criticism! Soon after, he went to hear W. H. Auden and Stephen Spender read from their works in Bombay. When his father introduced him to Spender, he blurted out that he wanted to be a poet, upon which Spender remarked gently: "Perhaps you are one" (*My Son's Father* 76). As Moraes confesses, in this innocent remark he saw "a recognition of one poet by another, transcending all barriers" (*My Son's Father* 76). His first real moment of promise as a poet came when Nissim Ezekiel, the assistant editor of the *Illustrated Weekly of India*, remarked that although his attempts did not seem to be poetry yet, they held promise of talent. Soon afterwards, the poem "French Lesson" elicited a more enthusiastic response from Ezekiel, who congratulated him on what he called a good poem. "It's the first poem you've ever written," he said (*My Son's Father* 91). For a sixteen-year-old, this was high praise indeed. Spender published his poems in *Encounter*, and Karl Shapiro did so in *Poetry Chicago*. His first book of poems, *A Beginning*, won the Hawthornden Prize for the best work of the imagination in 1958. He remains the first non-English person to win this prize, also the youngest.

In 1960 his second book of verse, *Poems*, became the Autumn Choice of the Poetry Book Society. In 1965 his third book of verse, *John Nobody*, appeared. Apart from these three volumes, he published a pamphlet of verse, *Beldam & Others*, in 1967. Since then, Moraes has not published any poetry except a privately printed book, *Absences*, produced in Bombay in 1983. He has, however, edited magazines in London, Hong Kong, and New York, been a correspondent in various wars, and an official of a UN agency. While on his various assignments he has written twenty-three prose books, including the autobiography *My Son's Father* and a biography of Indira Gandhi. He has also scripted and partially directed over twenty television documentaries from England, India, Cuba, and Israel for the BBC and ITV.

Dom Moraes has a son, Francis, by his first marriage to Judith Ann, an Englishwoman. He now lives in Bombay with his second wife, the Indian actress Leela Naidu.

MAJOR WORKS AND THEMES

As a Christian in the predominantly Hindu state of India, Dom Moraes must have grown up with an increasingly bewildering sense of belonging to two cultures that were mutually exclusive, mainly because one of these was shared by the race that had colonized India till 1947. The reality of the West as the colonial master was indubitably and irreconcilably connected with Judaeo-Christian tradition, and Indian Christians as well as Anglo-Indians were confronted by the fact that they had to constantly choose between two not merely different but openly antagonistic cultures. This marginalized group of Christians was thus a diaspora in its own right, further confounding Moraes's diasporic consciousness. Such a double-edged diasporic consciousness—one emanating from India and the other stemming from Britain and the West—created an ambivalence that is ubiquitous in Moraes's themes and language.

Moraes's poetry seems to reflect only one side of this consciousness: it identifies, almost unconsciously, with the white Anglo-Saxon, Christian world; perhaps it is "his apparent refusal or inability to acknowledge roots anywhere except in literature" (*Modern Fiction Studies* 30 [1984]:463). Until he was twenty-one, at which age he came down from Oxford, Moraes's entire life seemed to focus on the manipulation of words, as he admits in the foreword to *Collected Poems 1957–1987*—"an attempt to break down language till the words on the page have become the only words language has left for your purpose" (xi). His first three attempts at poetry—*A Beginning* (1957), *Poems* (1960), and *John Nobody* (1965)—revealed a steady journey away from the world of an aesthete, of pure imagination, to that of a painful but healing encounter with reality, the reality of his biculturalism. Again, in his foreword to *Collected Poems 1957–1987*, he writes "Suddenly what had haunted me on this trip became explicit. My mother and my father had nothing to do with India itself: they were simply themselves, as I was myself, and our relationship had to be worked out independent of where we were. But the colours and smells of India, the emotions I had at Kanheri, the painful sort of affection I had for Kutthalingam all pulled me one way, and the new life I led abroad, with friends and work and a milieu I understood, more than I did India, pulled me the other" (ii–iii). But although his poetry received critical acclaim both in Britain and in India, this was obviously not the mode of creativity that would sustain him for long and express the doubts and concerns of the split in him.

It is in his nonfictional work that one finds the true measure of his Janus-like diasporic consciousness. His book *From East and West*, published in 1971, exemplifies this ambiguity perfectly. In this collection of essays the first section deals with problems in Britain from a British point of view. One of them, "The Lost Tribes of Kenya," talks about the misery of people of Indian descent who had been resident in Kenya and have now fled to Britain on the strength of their British passports. Moraes says: "During these days . . . I suddenly realized how much I was a product of the British Empire. . . . The historical accident of British rule in India worked on my family, so that it lived an English life there and spoke no Indian languages" (*From East and West* 27–28). It was not until the Kenyan controversy blew up that he had a sudden sense of how false his own insulation from the reality of race must be (*From East and West* 28). In the second section Moraes seems to project India as a *geographical* entity, but proceeds to appropriate this space as the closed construct he wishes it to be.

Most of his nonfictional work has usually been commissioned by government agencies in India or other countries. But the degree of fictionality within each work is what marks the diasporic consciousness in him. In 1976 he wrote *The Open Eyes—A Journey through Karnataka*, typically weaving a Mowghli-like narrative, although he begins to distance himself from his earlier tendency to derive the East from his Western education. Sentences like "He had obviously had breakfast recently, since he kept belching" remind one of Rana Kabbani's admonition, while discussing V. S. Naipaul's *An Area of Darkness*, about the danger of adhering to the archetypal native of the Western imagination "engrossed in his revolting habits." As Kabbani points out, no contemporary European writer would risk such a description. One photograph illustrating the Hindu custom of creating statuettes of gods and goddesses displays only nude plaster-of-Paris *female* models from the front in all their voluptuous eroticism. Although Moraes states that such workshops are open to onlookers, his penetrating, almost rapacious gaze is clearly different from theirs. Thus Moraes seems at times to be using his Indian origin to abuse it. Nevertheless, he makes an attempt to get away from the perception of Indian culture as a static one. The Indians—professional and nonprofessional—who accompany him on his various travels represent efforts at progress on various levels. Moraes shows great sensitivity toward these guides into the diversity that is India. The thumbnail sketch he provides for each one is at once graphic and poetic. *Answered by Flutes: Reflections from Madhya Pradesh* from the year 1983 provides yet another facet of Indian life: the tribal peoples. Moraes fashions out of his encounters with the tribals an intensely passionate image of racial memories. There is a sympathy here, a willingness to understand and to mediate that brings Moraes closer to the possibility of a synthesis between his two warring diasporic consciousnesses.

Looking back from the year 1986 at his first three poetic excursions and exertions, Moraes remarks: "I chased Äthe Museü for 17 years, writing poems or trying to, and I was stopped by time, circumstances, and my own technique, which in my first three books was of tight, rhymed verse. In 1982 something happened to me which I cannot account for. I not only started to write poetry once more, but a new style seemed to come to me without my ever trying to master it" (*Collected Poems* xii). In 1982 he was forty-five years old and had perhaps come to terms with his dual identity, having assimilated to the best possible extent the Western and the Indian. In his introduction to *Voices for Life* (1975), a collection of essays by eminent people from all walks of life voicing a deep concern for the improvement of the human condition, he may have begun to discern this "new style." This encompasses "a care for humanity, a care uncommon among most people in the world today, a delicate, a particular, a necessary care" (*Voices for Life* xvi). It is a level beyond the Indian or any other diasporic consciousness, a level of attainment well within the reach of this writer. Like V. S. Naipaul, "he is no longer obsessed with parts of the world relevant to his ancestry, but the whole world is now relevant to him" (*Modern Fiction Studies* 30 [1984]:464).

CRITICAL RECEPTION

When I asked him in July 1991 what his own reactions were to a critical appraisal of his works, he replied in a rather tired voice that he was not in the habit of keeping track of such reviews. As an afterthought, however, he mentioned Bruce King's *Three Indian Poets*, which had just appeared, remarking that King's analysis of his poetry seemed "quite comprehensive." King finds in Moraes's early poetry an "intensity of concern with the self and its immediate world." In *Poems* (1960) there is "that curious combination of mythologized autobiography and Caroline love lyric." *John Nobody* (1965) shows greater density of thought and a debunking of the earlier romantic and heroic writings. "Loss is central to *John Nobody*," says King. *Collected Poems* (1987) presents the entire gamut of Moraes's poetic endeavors. Several are "concerned with ... the excitements of sexual desire, the passing of time and hopes and other personal matters." But the most significant pieces in the latter half of the *Collected Poems* are "dramatic monologues, characters and character descriptions through which Moraes can project and yet distance himself by use of someone else" (31–33). King feels that some of Moraes's best poetry has appeared since 1988, albeit in magazines and newspapers. This is significant given Moraes's lethargic attitude toward a reception of his works, which I had sensed in talking to him.

More than any other prose he has written, however, Dom Moraes aroused the critical interest of the international community when his biography *Indira Gandhi* was published in 1980. The theme challenges to the utmost Moraes's understanding of his cultural identity. Kurt Lewin, the social anthropologist, explains that a person belonging to a marginalized group is condemned to feel not sufficiently rooted in either group to be clear and confident about his personal relations with either side. But it is this ambiguity that lends this particular work by Moraes a multi-voicedness. Moraes the narrator effaces himself, submitting to Moraes the admirer of Mrs. Gandhi. There is also inscribed in the text a sense of identity with Mrs. Gandhi and the latter's own isolated childhood—aristocratic and in a grand Anglo-Indian style, as was Moraes's own childhood. According to one critic, Moraes's biography of Mrs. Gandhi presents a creature of flesh and blood (Sterling 6). Another critic finds precisely this intensely personal statement insufficient. According to him, it is a fine portrait of a woman, but hardly a judicial assessment of a statesman. He sees Mrs. Gandhi's importance as a politician being underestimated and sidetracked in favor of the private person. And since her political perspicacity had enabled her to govern a country with such a vast population and tremendous diversity for the fourth time, a personal account ran the danger of distorting and weakening the charismatic qualities that characterized her (Mason 1054). It is precisely this "personal" note that is so characteristic of Moraes's writing. Bruce King's remark sums this up succinctly: "the emotions in Moraes' poetry"— and prose—"are universal" (33).

BIBLIOGRAPHY

Works by Dom Moraes

My Son's Father. London: Macmillan, 1968.
From East and West. New Delhi: Vikas Publications, 1971.
A Matter of People. New York: Praeger Publishers, 1974.
The Open Eyes—A Journey through Karnataka. Bangalore: Director of Information and Publicity, Government of Karnataka, 1976.
Bombay. Amsterdam: Time-Life International, 1979.
Indira Gandhi. Boston: Little, Brown, 1980.
Answered by Flutes: Reflections from Madhya Pradesh. Bombay: Asia Publishing House, 1983.
Collected Poems 1957–1987. New Delhi: Penguin Books, 1987.

Studies of Dom Moraes

King, Bruce. *Three Indian Poets*. Madras: Oxford University Press, 1991.
Mason, Philip. "Between Tyranny and Chaos." Review of *Indira Gandhi*. *Times Literary Supplement* (Feb. 18, 1980):1054.
Sterling, Claire. Review of *Indira Gandhi*. *New York Times Book Review* 85 (1980):6.

BHARATI MUKHERJEE
(1940–   )
Gita Rajan

BIOGRAPHY

Bharati Mukherjee, born in Calcutta, India, on July 27, 1940, is the daughter of Sudhir Lal and Bina (Barrerjee) Mukherjee. Growing up as an upper middle-class Brahmin girl of educated parents, Mukherjee had the privilege of traveling to Europe (England and Switzerland) in her early life, and attending Loreto Convent, an exclusive all-girls high school in Calcutta. She graduated with honors in English literature from Calcutta University in 1959, got her master's degree from Baroda University in 1961, and came to the United States for postgraduate work. Mukherjee joined the M.F.A. program, attended the Writer's Workshop at the University of Iowa, and got her creative writing degree in 1963. While at Iowa, she married Clark Blaise (Canadian-American writer) in September of 1963. Mukherjee completed her doctoral degree also from the University of Iowa in 1966, and joined McGill University in Montreal as an assistant professor. In 1978, she moved as a full professor from McGill to Skidmore College in Saratoga Springs, New York. Next, she taught creative writing at Columbia University and City University of New York, and moved to San Francisco to teach writing at the University of California at Berkeley in 1988. Mukherjee won the Canada Arts Council Award in 1973–74 and 1977, the Shastri Indo-Canadian Award in 1976–77, a Guggenheim Foundation Grant in 1978–79, and the National Book Critics Circle Award in 1988. Bharati Mukherjee has two sons, Bart and Bernard, the latter named after Bernard Malamud, a celebrated writer and valued friend to whom she dedicated *Darkness*.

MAJOR WORKS AND THEMES

Bharati Mukherjee's oeuvre comprises novels, short stories, nonfiction prose, sociopolitical commentaries, and journal articles and interviews. In chronological order they are *The Tiger's Daughter* (novel, 1972), *Wife* (novel, 1975), *Days and Nights in Calcutta* (with Blaise, travel memoirs, 1977), "Response: American Fiction" in *Salmagundi* (journal article, 1980–81), "An Invisible Woman" in *Saturday Night* (political prose, 1981), *Darkness* (short stories, 1985), *The Sorrow and the Terror: The Haunting Legacy of the Air India Tragedy* (with Blaise, nonfiction, 1987), *The Middleman and Other Stories* (short stories, 1988), and *Jasmine* (novel, 1989).

The Tiger's Daughter deals with Tara Banerjee Cartwright, a 22-year-old girl, who revisits India after a seven-year stay in the United States. Tara, a product of Vassar, married to an American writer, feels strangely at a loss in her native Calcutta. Ironically, the fragmentation in Brahminical and Westernized selves in this new Tara allows her to see the naïveté and viciousness of her elite, super-refined friends. The privileges that she had taken for granted, such as her circle of convent-educated, giddy, sophisticated friends, her luxurious surroundings, her aestheticized sensibilities, elaborate dances and picnics, seem incomprehensible and ineffectual in understanding Calcutta as "home" again. The squalor of Calcutta and the callousness and corruption of her friends make her doubt her benevolent Brahmin heritage. Idealistically, even predictably, she yearns for an old-fashioned riot, a blood-letting almost, that will cathartically restore the purity of her homeland. Ironically, simultaneous with this desire to see India restored to its romanticized glory, is her desire to distance herself from India, and go back to the safety of David's (her husband's) American heritage. This gaping fissure in Tara's sense of self is seamed together through the intervention of McDowell, an American visitor to her home. This, however, is merely the denouement, not the conclusion of the novel, for McDowell turns out to be a black revolutionary, with an outlandish Afro hairdo. The incongruity of the final scene with the escalating unfamiliarity and fear becomes wedded in the figure of Tara, who as an unwitting agent becomes the eye of the storm. Locked in her car, in the middle of a streetfull of angry rioters, she sees her husband's view of Calcutta as apocalyptic: "the collective future in which garbage, disease, and stagnation are man's estate" (190).

If *The Tiger's Daughter* is read as a nostalgic journey "back" home, *Wife* can be read as its sequel, a fantastic voyage to a new land. However, both center on the debilitating, corrosive influence of an alien (and alienating) culture on a fragile self. In *Wife*, Dimple Dasgupta is nurtured on a staple diet of girlish fantasies and impossible expectations. Reading *The Doctrine of Passive Resistance* for her university exams, Dimple conjures up visions of a romantic husband, and her plan to keep him enthralled through passive resistance, i.e., withholding her love as a way to ensure his continued passion. Like so many confused adolescents, Dimple's sense of self is predicated on representations of that self in society. Her father manages to marry her off to Amit Basu, a consulting engineer, about to emigrate to the United States. Thus, in her sudden transportation from Calcutta to New York,

Dimple goes into future shock. Unable to cope with the trauma of leaving home, both in the literal and figurative sense, Dimple creates an alternate reality—the world of American television. Her husband, caught in the grimy business of life, is unable to fathom her anguish and terror in such a dislocation, and denies it by calling it "culture shock." Slowly, Dimple's identity is being shattered, detonated by a raw and alien reality. Yet she manages to fight back through her meaningless acts of cruelty; she learns to lie and deceive; she torments and kills a mouse; she even flushes a goldfish down the toilet—her interaction is through violence that ripples in small concentric circles. The final scene of the novel, where Dimple kills her husband with a kitchen knife, is an ultimate gesture of fragmentation and desperation. In fact, Dimple's powerlessness and helplessness transcend the boundaries of the text and the new culture to become a sinister reminder of the devastation of women living in an alien, patriarchal world.

Darkness, dedicated to Malamud, is a collection of vignettes of immigrant experiences, which do justice to both Mukherjee and Malamud. Jonathan Raban writes that in such a dedication, "she was both saluting an old friend and bedding herself down in a tradition" (Raban, *New York Times Book Review* June 19, 1988: 1, 22–23). This remark, with its strange, psychosexual ring, is countered by Anita Desai, the *other* Indian, who also comments on this unlikely alliance: "Malamud's characters have enriched American literature [with] new sounds and resonances; the Indian tongue as reproduced by Mukherjee is unlikely to do anything like that for the American language—it may distort, bend, and mispronounce...but it cannot be said to have enriched" (Desai, "Outcasts," *London Magazine* 25: 9–10 [Dec. 1985–Jan. 1986]: 143–46). Lest Desai be quoted out of context, it is imperative to point out that she indeed praises Mukherjee for maintaining her difference from Malamud and concludes her review by congratulating Mukherjee for an admirable job, "done with honesty, with clearsightedness, and with remarkable distinction" (146). It is this very trope of difference that Mukherjee plays out in *Darkness*, drawing from a repository of psychological and emotional energy that motors all immigrants. In fact, she writes in the introduction to *Darkness* that "for a writer, energy is aggression; urgency colliding with confidence" (3), and goes on to make the subtle, yet vital distinction between expatriation and immigration, between V. S. Naipaul (her model) and herself. While both writers employ irony, Mukherjee's art is more self-reflexive in its use, revealing "the moment away from aloofness of expatriation to the exuberance of immigration" (3).

"The World According to Hsü" and "Isolated Incidents" won major Canadian journalism awards, and "Angela" was included in *The Best American Short Stories 1985* (all in *Darkness*). Most critics note the strong Naipaul tone that emanates from *Darkness*, yet there is a stronger tone of disappointment and disillusionment with Canada that persists in the work. This in turn has earned her criticism from the Canadian reviewers. "Tamurlane" (which invokes Timur the Lame from Indian history, the crippled but fierce warrior) recounts the tragedy of a mutilated, illegal immigrant chef, Gupta. Assaulted physically (by being pushed in the path of a Toronto subway train) and psychologically (by Canadian authorities), Gupta finds himself balanced precariously against his kitchen counter braving the Mounted Police in the final scenes of the story. It is a battle of wills, and the grotesque scene culminates in a mockery of Gupta's inexplicable desire to remain in an unyielding land. In "The World According to Hsü" too there is the same fear and bittersweet irony toward Canada, where Ratna recounts that "an eight-year-old Punjabi boy was struck down by a car with a bumper sticker that read 'Keep Canada Green—Paint a Paki Red' " (23). Another character in "Isolated Incidents" remarks "Canadians are mean as hell," to which the human rights official responds, "I don't know about that... if this had happened in New York, you'd be left for dead." The victim's lawyer intervenes: "if this had happened in New York, he'd have been mugged for his money, not racially assaulted" (70). The last story in the collection, "Courtly Vision," which is a reading of a Mogul painting, serves as a metaphor for Mukherjee's own miniaturist style of writing. Like the painting, which captures resplendent Fatehpur Sikri, a dream of a city that hoped to celebrate Hindu-Muslim solidarity, the story signals diasporic desire metaphorically; it wishes to wed Indo-Canadian communality. What critics call the "two-dimensional" surface of "Courtly Visions" and its miniaturist texture could also be read as Janus-faced. It can be argued that Mukherjee is stylizing the reader's gaze; like the Mogul emperor who is glancing back into treachery and deceit and forward into an exquisitely ordered world, so too the immigrant can walk away from disillusionment and look forward with hope into the new future-land.

Days and Nights in Calcutta and *The Sorrow and the Terror* are works that Mukherjee coauthored with her husband. Both are nonfiction texts, structured coaxially on the dislocation of the immigrant self and the disinterestedness of a racist political milieu. While *Days* is nostalgic and documentary in tone, *The Sorrow* hammers away unceasingly at structural, governmental bigotry. In the introduction to *The Sorrow*, the authors sum up the Air India plane crash: "politically, the tragedy was 'unhoused' in that Canada wished to see it as an Indian event sadly visited on these shores by uncontrollable fanatics, and India was happy to treat it as an 'overseas incident' with containable, financial implications" (2).

The Middleman and Other Stories explores the nuances of diasporic consciousness from varying countries like India, Afghanistan, Vietnam, Lebanon, the Philippines, Sri Lanka, Italy, and the Caribbean. The title story, "The Middleman," is about Al Judah, a Jew from Baghdad who is caught on the other side of the border from Texas in the jungles of South America. Al finds himself prostituted at the nexus of impossible situations—illegal arms dealers, Contras, Sandinistas, Mexican Indians, and his host's voluptuous wife. Al is able to act, yet not have any agency behind these actions; thus, he is only a middleman. In "Fathering" a veteran sends for his Vietnamese love-child, Eng, to mediate between himself and his new girlfriend. Even more interesting than this enforced family situation is Eng's rhetorical repertoire. She shuttles between perfectly normal, American use of the English language and curses/war slang in Vietnamese. This vacillation in Eng's language usage also reveals her position between two cultures and her splintered psyche. When Eng becomes sick (she believes it is the result of a curse), she assures her father that she can cure herself by digging American quarters into her arms—a combination of witchcraft and G. I. Joe magic. Once again, Mukherjee straddles the cultural boundaries and interrogates the trauma of enforced dislocation. "Angela," "Jasmine," and "Saints" carry a faint but clear trace of irony, i.e., Mukherjee's signature—the fragile and fractured self—where immigrants do not merely assimilate, they change the land as much as the land changes them. The last story, "The Management of Grief," is clearly a docudrama of the Air India plane crash in which hundreds of Indo-Canadian citizens were killed by Sikh terrorists. In a span of about twenty pages, Mukherjee encapsulates the hypocrisy behind Canadian gestures of goodwill.

Jasmine is the story of Jyoti, born to impoverished parents in Hasnapur, India, who with no formal education or patron arrives in America with neither money nor passport. Yet Mukherjee's narrative cannot be read as merely another thematic record of illegal transportation; it is a rich experiment in semiotic narrativity. Jasmine is fashioned and read through her body, her clothes, and her gestures from "illegal immigrant" to stable, American resident. Patricia Holt accurately picks up Jyoti's fate in the new land through "her Hasnapuri sidle, a mincing, hunched-over walk that immigration officials see as a dead giveaway of an 'illegal' without a green card" (1–2). This novel is perhaps Mukherjee's strongest feminist statement in that she reads Jasmine's body as text. By suggesting that Jasmine can shed her Karma (God-given destiny), along with her Hasnapuri sidle, that she can fashion her own destiny and stride purposefully across America, Mukherjee proves what she once claimed in an interview—that Indianness is a metaphoric precondition of her fictional selves. While Karma, with its restrictive gender politics, predicted "widowhood and exile" for Jyoti, America guarantees Jase/Jane the security of conjugal bliss with a midwestern banker. The impossible transformations in the female protagonist always occur at a gestural/semiotic level and become slowly encoded in her psychic memory.

CRITICAL RECEPTION

At first glance, the list of Mukherjee's works looks like the haphazard offerings of an energetic and prolific writer. But, on closer scrutiny, it becomes apparent that all of Mukherjee's creativity is focused with razor-sharp precision on a diasporic imagination and the politico-cultural implications of this very imagination. The trope of diaspora, of dislocation, transcends the rhetorical dimension of the text and becomes the material core of Mukherjee's narrativity. From the point of initial, critical evaluation, Mukherjee's works have been recognized as recounting the nuances of her diasporic experiences. Mukherjee has fascinated readers with varying portraits of the immigrant self. *Wife, The Middleman and Other Stories,* which won the National Book Critics Circle Award, and more recently, *Jasmine,* all recapture and reiterate the experiences of immigrants to the United States from Asia, Europe, and the Caribbean. While readers and critics can glean tracings of autobiographical instances in all her works, it is perhaps more important to acknowledge the imprint of alternate (*and* alternating) selves, in dislocated (*and* dislocating) cultural topographies in her narratives. Martin Levine in remarking of Tara, the heroine of *The Tiger's Daughter,* as being "perfect for recording the mutations of her time: sensitive, observant, and almost spongelike in relation to experience ... is a better barometer ... than most of the alleged non-fiction pouring from the presses," could very well be categorizing Mukherjee herself (*New York Times Book Review* Jan. 2, 1972: 16). The traditional distance between author, text, and reader is constantly breached in Mukherjee's fiction, such that one is always haunted by Mukherjee's shadow behind her characters, and ghosts of her characters behind her "realistic" prose. Thus, while, as some Canadian critics have pointed out, Mukherjee's fiction is repetitive of her diasporic predicament, it is equally true that each of her works and characters is balanced just a little differently on the abyss of dislocation. It is for this reason then that each text is wrought at a different angle of experience, each the same yet not the same, each valid, and each equally terrifying. She can be read as a psychoanalyst of culture and a champion of the voiceless, and each of her characters serves as a model of representation of human caprice caught in a moment of self-preservation glimpsing the horror of difference. Since current critical debate is focused on issues of postcoloniality and multiculturalism (a word that Mukherjee abhors for its duplicitous connotations of sociopolitical egalitarianism), the need to recognize and legitimize difference, particularly experiential difference, is central to understanding the thematic cohesion of Mukherjee's oeuvre.

Most critics accurately note Mukherjee's eye for detail, her understated irony, and the repeated unpredictability of her central characters when their sense of identify is shattered. Critics have compared Mukherjee to V. S. Naipaul, to Anton Chekov, and/or to Bernard Malamud. While these are connections worth noting in literary heritage, particularly in a woman who is writing of an unfamiliar diasporic imagination, it is equally important to trace her Victorian, intertextual repertoire. In the worlding of her narratives, particularly *The Tiger's Daughter,* or *Wife,* or even *The Middleman,* she seems to replicate the techniques of Charles Dickens, or William Makepeace Thackeray, or Thomas Hardy in coordinating character motives and actions. There is a marked similarity between the ways in which Mukherjee's characters balance interiority/exteriority, self/society, and most importantly, anarchy/culture. In this context, like the narratives of Dickens, Thackeray, or Hardy, Mukherjee's narratives function as ironic commentaries of contemporary culture and society. Other critics, not focusing on literary technique per se, question Mukherjee's complete rejection of Canada for its "overt" racist politics and think her exuberance in embracing the American dream rather naive. It is at this point, they argue, that her irony seems artificial. But, with her experiences in the two countries, she admits that she finds it easier to function in America, and manifests this sentiment with a certain understated gentleness while situating her characters in the United States. Yet when charged with being an assimilationist, she said to Patricia Holt of the *San Francisco Chronicle*: "The complexion of America has already changed. Let's admit it, let's deal with it instead of pretending that the white Anglo model still holds for everybody. Each of us, mainstream or minority, is having to change. It's a two-way metamorphosis" (2). While this sentiment appears theoretical in the light of contemporary critical focus on postcoloniality and Third World politics, it is essential to point out that all of Mukherjee's fictions have consistently hammered home this message. Framed thus, within discourse theory and postmodern fiction, it is fitting to sum up Mukherjee's oeuvre as problematic. Of course, problematic has layers of signification, most of which demand a sustained inquiry by the reader into the issues that Mukherjee raises—personal, sociopolitical, and cultural.

BIBLIOGRAPHY

Works by Bharati Mukherjee

The Tiger's Daughter. Boston: Houghton Mifflin, 1972; London: Chatto & Windus, 1973.

Wife. Boston: Houghton Mifflin, 1975.

Days and Nights in Calcutta. With Clark Blaise. Garden City: Doubleday, 1977; revised and enlarged, Markham, Ontario: Viking-Penguin, 1986.

"Response: American Fiction." *Salmagundi* 50–51 (Fall 1980–Winter 1981): 151–57.

"An Invisible Woman." *Saturday Night* 96 (March 1981): 36–40.

"A Conversation with V. S. Naipaul." With Robert Boyer. *Iowa Review* 54 (Fall 1981): 4–22.

Darkness. Markham, Ontario; Harmondsworth, U.K.; and New York: Penguin, 1985.

The Sorrow and the Terror: The Haunting Legacy of the Air India Tragedy (with Clark Blaise). Markham, Ontario: Viking, 1987.

The Middleman and Other Stories. New York: Grove Press, 1988.
Jasmine. New York: Grove Weidenfeld, 1989.
"Prophet and Loss: Salman Rushdie's Migration of Souls." *Village Voice Literary Supplement* 72 (March 1989): 9–12.
Mukherjee, Bharati, and Clark Blaise. "After the Fatwa: The Satanic Verse Controversy." *Mother Jones* 15:3 (1990): 28–31.

Studies of Bharati Mukherjee

Bradbury, Patricia. "Mukherjee Draws Tales from Fear in the Streets in Toronto." *Quill and Quire* 51:8 (Aug. 1985): 43.
Carb, Alison B. "An Interview with Bharati Mukherjee." *Massachusetts Review* 29 (Winter 1988): 645–54.
Chua, C. L. "Passages from India: Migrating to America in the Fiction of V. S. Naipaul and Bharati Mukherjee." *Reworlding: The Literature of the Indian Diaspora.* Ed. Emmanuel S. Nelson. Westport, Conn.: Greenwood Press, 1992. 51–62.
Desai, Anita. "Indian Fiction Today." *Daedalus* (Fall 1989): 206–27.
Foster, Douglas. "Rushdie Wars." *Mother Jones* 15 (Sept.-Oct. 1990): 21.
Frakes, J. R. Review of *The Tiger's Daughter* in *Book World—The Washington Post* (Jan. 9, 1972): 2.
Healy, Barth. "Mosaic vs. Melting Pot." *New York Times Book Review* (June 19, 1988): 22.
Holt, Patricia. "Mukherjee's Vision of America." *San Francisco Sunday Examiner and Chronicle* (Feb. 17, 1991): 1–2.
Nelson, Emmanuel. "Kamala Markandaya, Bharati Mukherjee, and the Indian Immigrant Experience." *Toronto South Asian Review* 9:2 (Winter 1991): 1–9.
———. Ed. *Bharati Mukherjee: Critical Perspectives.* New York: Garland Publishing, 1993.
Rostomji-Kerns, Roshni. "Expatriates, Immigrants, and Literature: Three South Asian Women." *Massachusetts Review* (Winter 1988): 655–65.
Srivaramkrishna, M. "Bharati Mukherjee." *Indian English Novelists.* Ed. Madhusudan Prasad. New Delhi: Sterling, 1982: 71–86.
Steinberg, Sybil. "A Biography." *Publishers Weekly* 236 (Aug. 1989): 46–48.
Vaid, Krishna Baldev. Review of *Wife. Fiction International* 4/5 (1975): 155–57.

ANAND MULLOO (1936–   )
Viney Kirpal

BIOGRAPHY

Anand Sawant Mulloo was born on January 14, 1936, in Beau-Bassin in Mauritius, then an English colony. His father, Jayeram, a third-generation migrant from India, after experiencing the degradation of indentured labor in Alma, came to Beau-Bassin to try out his fortune as a tailor. Anand Mulloo was brought up in extreme poverty. Even as a child, he was determined to get out of the wretched life. His iron will is mirrored in Harry Pingley, the protagonist of his historical novel, *Watch Them Go Down*. Mulloo acquired his intense commitment to educational, social, and political reforms from his father. From his mother, Sayabai, he inherited his small build, his qualities of leadership, his strong character, and the will to serve society.

His primary schooling was haphazard. He attended a small private school in a *baitaka* run by G. Kooraram, who taught once in a while as he had to cope with all the classes single-handedly. Mulloo jumped from Standard III to Standard VI after he had wasted two years learning practically nothing. After completing his schooling, he taught English and history in New Eton College (London) alongside reading for a B.A. degree.

Since 1963, he has held a number of posts, dabbling with a variety of occupations and interests. He has been a teacher of history, education officer, director of studies, college principal, and political activist. He is now a researcher in Mahatma Gandhi Institute in Mauritius.

The socialist ideas of British and Mauritian intellectuals, the ideals of Mahatma Gandhi, and *The Gita* have had a profound impact on his life and writings.

Anand started writing when he was in Form III. He wrote stories about ordinary people. As a young man, he rebelled against social inequality and injustice. In his novel, *Watch Them Go Down*, he daringly predicted the downfall of the colonial regime. Besides creative writing, he enjoys interpreting Mauritian culture, which he sees as a blend of British socialism and democratic institutions, French manners, Indian culture and philosophy, and Chinese practical commonsense. (Information supplied by Mulloo to Viney Kirpal.)

MAJOR WORKS AND THEMES

Anand Mulloo is a writer-activist. Unlike the typical writer in the West, he is not interested in creating literary works as aesthetic artifacts but for raising the consciousness of his readers to grasp social and political inequities and prejudices. It would be facile to dismiss him as a "committed" writer because his works have shown the capacity to survive even after the issues the works had examined have died. That is the mark of good art. Mulloo, however, did not plan his literary career in a systematic way until very recently. As a consequence, not too many outside Mauritius have read this writer of the Indian diaspora. He was actively involved in the political activities in his country until 1979. It was only after his disenchantment with the Mauritius Militant Movement (MMM) that he turned away from politics toward creative writing as a career.

His two principal published literary works are *Watch Them Go Down* (1967), a novel, and *Dust of Time* (1970), a book of poems. Several short stories written during his early years as a writer and poems protesting the emergency (1972–76) have remained unpublished. His novel *Nalini*, announced many years ago, is being completed presently. Also under completion is his novel *Across the Seven Seas*, a book about the search by immigrants for ancestral roots. In 1981, Mulloo visited India and, in particular, his ancestral Konkan to do research for this novel. Also about to go to press is an autobiographical novel, *Give Me Back My Son*. It is about Mulloo's moving experiences as a political activist and his painful growth to maturity as a human being. When published, it should prove to be a prominent work, so sensitively have the theme and the technique been handled. But these qualities were in evidence in his first work, *Watch Them Go Down*, as well.

Watch Them Go Down is a political novel. It can be described as Mauritius's novel of decolonization just as is George Lamming's *In the Castle of My Skin* (1953) in the Caribbean context. The novel depicts the way in which the brutally oppressed estate people conquer their fears and expel the white planters. The process is never easy, the novel shows, as it means evolving from a fear-stricken, demoralized people into self-respecting human beings demanding their rights. The novel invites comparison with Raja Rao's *Kanthapura* (1938), but with one difference. In *Kanthapura*, the political consciousness of the estate people is raised by Moorthy's efforts, but the people are unable to oust the planters. In *Watch Them Go Down*, the struggle is more successful. As Harry Pingley leads the laborers in rebellion, the planters are driven out of the country while the British government is compelled to give the Mauritians a representation on the council. The movement is also supported and assisted by a number of Western-educated Mauritian intellectuals, inspired by the ideals of British democracy and Gandhi's freedom struggle, who are able to mobilize the people and to articulate their aspirations to the colonizers, thus paving the path to ultimate independence. The novel captures in short, staccato sentences the tension, pressure, and nervousness that the collective defiance of the "masses" creates in the colonizers—the planters, the administration, the police:

The Meline crowd was marching on towards the capital. But they were to meet other crowds. One huge crowd composed of six hundred laborers joined their ranks on the way. Laborers from three different estates had formed one big party. They carried rum, sticks, stones and made bonfire of the cane fields. They threw stones at sugar mills and the planters, overturned truckloads of sugarcane, stopped lorries and persuaded all laborers they met to follow them. The party trudged on, brushing aside the scared-looking policemen who preferred to avoid them. . . . (125)

Harry Pingley, the protagonist of the novel, is one of the most remarkable heroes in Third World writing. Although a common laborer, he has the elemental strength and passion of the gods in him. When first introduced in the novel, he is described as "a caged lion" who longs to break through the stranglehold of the planters' tyranny but who does not know how to do it. The laborers, including Harry's father, have always accepted their condition passively and timidly and have submitted to savage treatment by their oppressors. To be framed on false charges and then to be flogged by the white masters was common practice. Harry, too, is punished by Mr. Garot (10), and he is described as taking the flogging with "clenched fists." However, toward the end of the novel, not only Harry but also the laborers learn to conquer their fears and to defy their persecutors (125).

The phenomenon of oppression is such that for its continuance it needs the compliance of the oppressed. But once the estate people revolt against the planters, nothing, not even guns, can keep the people repressed, and so, victory is theirs. This is the point of the novel: that freedom is a psychological state of the mind.

In the novel, Mulloo is also keen to depict Mauritian culture. He highlights the multiracial character of Mauritian society. Descriptions of the Chinese way of mourning their dead, the singing of the *siga*, an African song, the fighting of wrestling matches during the Ghoon festival, the conduct of Hindu religious meetings, all crisscross through the narrative and form the cultural grid in the lives of the people.

Watch Them Go Down—the title refers to the downfall of the oppressors—remains a powerful novel though Mauritius gained independence in

1968. The novel has been translated into Hindi (1968), Russian (1975), and Marathi (1985). It is now going into its second edition and is also being dramatized in Hindi and Marathi.

Although Mulloo identifies himself completely with the destiny of Mauritius, the theme of exile, the idea that an immigrant is a divided person is the subject of a poem in his collection, *Dust of Time*. The poem is titled "The Outcast" (27) and captures the split cultural self and the anxieties that such a person experiences. Bound to three continents—Asia, Africa, Europe—the poet wonders if he can murder his ethnic self or be totally Western. Bravely, he concludes that he is a citizen of the world. But the feeling of rootlessness persists in the poem.

The poems in this collection are not only about exile but also about poverty and hunger. In 1968, Mulloo had visited India and been profoundly shocked by the sight of poverty. The poems express his sorrow and guilt at witnessing human debasement in its most naked form. For example, the poem "Hunger" uses stark, skeletal, bare imagery to bring out the opposition between the stomach that aches with hunger and the thwarted efforts of the starving to find food. The poem "Wardha" conveys the contradiction that in the village where once Gandhi had tried to uplift depressed humanity the poor are still being demeaned every day. The rickshawman, who pedals and pants like an animal, the famished girl with "diseased skin" lurching toward "slow death"—are all victims of that new, grim political reality that is independent India. *Dust of Time* mirrors the felt social concern of the writer who, in his personal life, has paid a heavy price to oppose social and political injustice in his own country.

In *Give Me Back My Son*, his forthcoming novel, he depicts his disenchantment with Marxism, but he also brings out the utterly human qualities of Mulloo, the political novice, capable of making mistakes and misjudgments and indulging in self-deception. The following extract, where he describes his discovery that the MMM was a ruthless, totalitarian party that would not hesitate to "finish" him off, is typical of his style in the novel:

Unable to fight back in open Council debates, one evening, soon after Council meeting, I saw L'Estrac charging on me and [sic] pushed me to the wall savagely. Then he muttered between his lips in a most threatening manner, thrusting his fingers into my throat and eyes: "You shut up, you little man or else I break your bones. You're nothing here. I'll finish you...."

That night and the following nights, I could not sleep. The stinging words and threats of de L'Estrac had pierced into my heart like red hot iron. During those sleepless nights, I began to search into my conscious and I kept hearing my father's voice with his gentle advice and warnings: "Know who are your real friends and your enemies," he had told me. And I clearly saw that I could count more enemies inside the MMM than outside and that all the fiery words about ideology, proletarian revolution were but empty words to conceal their dark intentions. (From the manuscript)

The passage conveys in direct, concrete, vivid language the shock and pain of Mulloo's humiliation and degradation at the hands of those for whom he had sacrificed his best years. There is no attempt at sentimentalization as the writer describes the feelings of Mulloo, the character. The power to move through distancing is the hallmark of all his works.

CRITICAL RECEPTION

There are no published studies on Anand Mulloo. What is available are a few excerpts from reviews by fellow writers on the back cover of his novel *Watch Them Go Down*. For example, a reviewer, J. Tsang Mang Kin, quoted there describes *Watch* as "the first serious attempt at an English novel [in Mauritius]." Another, Jay Narain Roy, a playwright, finds the descriptions "beautiful," the language "racy," and the novel "a laudable first venture." Frank Richard, a professor of English, commends the novel for its portrayal of the freedom struggle and the Mauritian heritage.

There is an unpublished paper by Professor Michel Fabre that he had presented at the Indian Ocean Island Writers' Workshop held in Moka, Mauritius, in 1980. In contrast with the above reviews, Professor Fabre's evaluation is subdued. While he concedes that *Watch* is "the first authentically Mauritian novel in English" (page 8 of his manuscript), he also notes that the narrative is "somewhat didactic" and the depiction of the people's struggle "more allegorical than realistic." By his tone, these appear to be defects.

Again, commenting on *Dust of Time*, Professor Fabre notes the poem "Hurricane" for its vivid evocation of scenes. He also describes the poem "Africa" as successful. That is all. No detailed analysis of the writer's work has been published so far. The fact stresses the need to undertake one on this interesting writer of the Indian diaspora.

BIBLIOGRAPHY

Works by Anand Mulloo

Watch Them Go Down. St. Port Louis: Mauritius Writers' Association, 1967.
Dust of Time. Published by the author. 1970.

TIMERI MURARI (1941–   )
Alpana Sharma Knippling

BIOGRAPHY

Timeri Murari was born in 1941 in Madras, India. Growing up in the 1940s and 1950s in an India that was first occupied by the British and then beset by the period of decolonization, Murari was later to consistently represent India as irrevocably tied to the British and Western influence. At the age of eighteen, he went to England to study electronics, but after two years, he grew dissatisfied with the subject, switching to a bachelor's program in political science and history at McGill University in Montreal, Canada. The degree incomplete, Murari started writing articles for the *Kingston Whig-Standard* in Kingston, Montreal, in 1965. In 1966, he moved to London, where he worked as a subeditor for the *London Guardian*, during which time he also started to write some fiction and nonfiction: the novel *The Marriage* (1973) and the journalistic study *The New Savages: Children of the Liverpool Streets* (1975).

In 1975, curious to investigate American culture and politics, Murari moved to the United States. He remained there until 1987. During this time, he wrote several works: the novels *Lovers Are Not People* (1977), *The Oblivion Tapes* (1978), *The Field of Honour* (1981), *Taj* (1985), and *The Shooter* (1986). Of these, *Taj* achieved European success: it was translated into nine European languages, including French, Italian, German, and Portuguese, and it came out in paperback in 1986. Murari also wrote a documentary trilogy for Thames Television entitled *Only in America* and a nonfiction text, *Goin' Home: A Black Family Returns South* (1980). His next novel, *The Imperial Agent* (1987), written as a sequel to Rudyard Kipling's *Kim*, brought him some measure of status in Anglo-America, as did its sequel, *The Last Victory*, published in 1990 by St. Martin's Press. Murari has also written three stage plays, *Grenade*, *Lovers Are Not People*, and *The Inquisitor*.

Timeri Murari's most recent novel, *Enduring Affairs*, was published in 1991 by Viking Penguin. He is currently engaged in writing the screenplay for a film based on *The Field of Honour*, coproduced with Ashok Amritraj. Murari presently divides his time between London and New York.

MAJOR WORKS AND THEMES

With a writer as prolific as Timeri Murari, whose career spans not only the writing of fiction, but newspaper articles, nonfiction, television documentary, and, most recently, film, it becomes difficult to single out some works as more representative than others. Murari brings to his fiction the historicized vein of the journalist, while at the same time actively inserting himself into his nonfiction. In the nonfictional *Goin' Home: A Black Family Returns South*, Murari reports firsthand, in a New Journalistic style, on a young African-American couple's experience of "remigration," of moving back to the South after having come North. Murari researches this episode from something like an ideal position: English-speaking but not Western; dark-skinned but not American. The book succinctly captures the silent apprehension and dread that settle over the couple, Arthur and Alma Stanford, as they stop for a meal and are treated with naked, ominous contempt by everyone in the restaurant. But it sometimes falls short of insight into the systematic logic of racial oppression.

A similarly historicized view dictates a common strain, an abiding concern, in all of Murari's fiction. Three novels, *The Field of Honour*, *The Imperial Agent*, and *The Last Victory*, can be seen as comprising Murari's major accomplishments. For it is in these novels that Murari seems to coalesce and concentrate his historical vision of India's colonial past and its impingement on India's contemporary social, political, and cultural present. In Murari's view, the attempt of many Indians to "wipe out the past and two hundred years of oppression" ignores the "reality of British influence" (telephone interview, June 3, 1991), amply evidenced in the numerous ways in which the English language and culture have radically structured India's own government, administration, and education.

However, not only do we repeatedly read of Britain's colonial legacy in India; we also witness some of the ways in which the West (specifically Britain and the United States) finds itself changed as a result of the colonization of India. As an Indian writer who was born before India became independent of the British and who has made his home in both Britain and the United States, Murari seems most interested in India's points of overlap with the West.

In *The Field of Honour*, for instance, Murari chooses to write from the perspective of an American man, the ex-boxer "Gunboat" Jack, who comes to India and, because of lack of funds, remains there, getting by on a part-ownership of a bar with his friend, Johnny (the Brahmin, Jaganathan Swaminathan). His life changes when he is employed by the Rajah of a princely state, Tandhapur, to teach the Rajah's son, Nicky (Nataraj), how to box. The novel subsequently uncovers the larger, more historical significance of a high school boxing match, in which Nicky fights the son of Mrs. Hobbs, the power-hungry British mistress of the Rajah, who has appointed herself as manager of Tandhapur.

The novel is set in 1948. By no mistake, this year signifies the moment of decolonization in which India is being hurtled into a modern industrial future even as it clings to feudalism and the belief in an idealized pre-colonial past. Also by no mistake, the process of decolonization is made to affect not an Indian town or city, but a princely state, the last vestige of quasi-Victorian royalty that is the least willing of Indian centers to break from the British even though it, too, participated, at times willingly, at others reluctantly, in India's Freedom Movement. This particular transitional period finds itself articulated in most of its problematic multiplicity, from the modern young Nicky and his sister, who has to choose between Western education and an arranged marriage, to Johnny, the Brahmin who recites mantras and avoids contamination by untouchables, but drinks alcohol and espouses socialist views (" 'Nehru is the biggest Maharajah of them all. But one day his time will come too. We need to change faster' " [40]).

The choice of the American, Gunboat Jack, as a main character reflects Murari's belief that the United States replaced Britain as a world power which, in India's period of decolonization, inundated it with American influences. It is not surprising, in this context, that Gunboat Jack's quintessentially American sensibility is itself being restructured by Indian influences: he speaks in an American dialect, eats *dosas* while longing for a hot dog, drinks local brew while pining for a "Bud," and is in love with an Anglo-Indian girl.

Two subsequent novels, *The Imperial Agent: A Sequel to Rudyard Kipling's "Kim"* and *The Last Victory*, pursue themes already at work in Murari's fiction: those of an India opening itself to the West through colonialism and those of a West finding itself changed in the process. The main character in both novels (together constituting a sequel to *Kim*) is Kipling's Kimball O'Hara, the Indian-born son of British parents who is left to the care of his guardian, Colonel Creighton, and who, in these novels, grows in maturity in India's colonial period as he discovers where his actual allegiances lie. Employed as a British spy by Colonel Creighton in *The Imperial Agent*, Kim sets out to hunt down two Indian men, whom Creighton believes to be Freedom activists, only to fall in love with an Indian girl, Parvati. Parvati is fleeing from her husband, an upper-class Indian in cahoots with Creighton himself. She is separated from Kim, and in his search for her, he voyages literally and spiritually through India. By the end of the novel, Kim discovers that Creighton's real intent is to use him ruthlessly in order to ensure his own, and Britain's, continued presence in India. *The Last Victory* picks up where its predecessor left off. It opens in 1910 in North India and ends in 1919 with the historical Jhallianwalla Bagh massacre in Amritsar, in which General Dyer ordered his troops to fire on a large and peaceful gathering of Indians. In the interim, Kim escapes Creighton along with Parvati; their escape is plagued by Parvati's mother-in-law's diabolic sorcery, which they fight back with the assistance of Hindu deities.

In his author's note to *The Imperial Agent*, Murari fondly remembers Kim from his intense adolescent reading of Rudyard Kipling, noting that he was disappointed with Kipling's ending to *Kim*. He states there that he wrote *The Imperial Agent* fired by the conviction that Kim was truly Indian. Murari initially presents Kim as an ambivalent character in terms of his partly Indian, partly Western identity. Like Gunboat Jack of *The Field of Honour*, he is split between these two contestatory fronts. But, more emphatically than Gunboat Jack, Kim embodies the changes wrought by Indian influences when, by the end of *The Last Victory*, in 1919, he is on the side of the Indians in the Freedom Movement against the British.

Murari does not make as his subject the grim contradictions involved in the articulation of a split identity, especially those contradictions that get formulated when a formerly colonized country takes stock of its colonial legacy. Conversely, he does not pose the question of exactly how Kim can be truly Indian when he is, in fact, British and, indeed, complicit with the actual British machinery of imperialism. Rendering his colonial characters as uniformly evil, he delineates Kim as essentially good and Indian at that. But while *The Imperial Agent* and *The Last Victory* do not forcefully foreground these kinds of difficulties, they usefully enact the risk-ridden implications of a postcolonial, diasporic appropriation of a colonial text such as *Kim*. Viewed from this perspective, Murari's rewriting of Kipling itself enacts the passage of Indian writing from a local literature to a global presence.

Timeri Murari's most recent novel, *Enduring Affairs*, continues his exploration of relationships between the West and India, as the novel moves between two time frames and histories: the United States in the 1960s and India in the 1990s.

CRITICAL RECEPTION

The critical reception to Timeri Murari's work consists of miscellaneous book reviews. Generally, reviewers have expressed a mixed response to his work. According to readers of *Goin' Home*, for instance, the nonfictional study was both thought-provoking and interesting. Murari's novel *The Shooter*, an experimental crime fiction set in the Bronx, on the other hand, was reviewed unfavorably by John Mutter. Readers appreciative of the art of storytelling have read *The Imperial Agent* and *The Last Victory* and praised Murari's ability to move the narrative while displaying "[c]olorful characters, romance, intrigue, and vivid descriptions of India" (Scarinci

148). Others found themselves drawn to "the emotional complexity of deeply entangled British-Indian relationships" (Steinberg 43). Yet others decried an overcrowded cast of characters only tangential to the plot (Buck 18) or a tendency toward melodrama (Steinberg 43).

BIBLIOGRAPHY

Works by Timeri Murari

The Marriage. London: Macmillan, 1973.
The New Savages: Children of the Liverpool Streets. London: Macmillan, 1975.
Lovers Are Not People. London: Methuen; New York: Morrow, 1977.
The Evil Within, ed. London, Melbourne, and New York: Quartet Books, 1978.
The Oblivion Tapes. London: Methuen; New York: G. P. Putnam's Sons, 1978.
Goin' Home: A Black Family Returns South. New York: G. P. Putnam's Sons, 1980.
The Field of Honour. London: Methuen; New York: Simon and Schuster, 1981.
Taj. London: New English Library, 1985.
The Shooter. London: New English Library; New York: Dell, 1986.
The Imperial Agent: A Sequel to Rudyard Kipling's "Kim." New York: St. Martin's Press, 1987.
The Last Victory. New York: St. Martin's Press, 1990.
Enduring Affairs. New Delhi: Viking Penguin, 1991.

Studies of Timeri Murari

Buck, Mason. Review of *The Imperial Agent. New York Times Book Review* (Aug. 6, 1989): 18.
Mutter, John. Review of *The Shooter. Publishers Weekly* (Nov. 14, 1986): 480.
Nandakum, P. Review of *The Last Victory. Indian Literature* 32 (1989): 36.
Scarinci, Florence. Review of *The Imperial Agent. Library Journal* (June 1, 1989): 148.
Schenck, William. Review of *Goin' Home. Library Journal* (April 15, 1980): 994.
Steinberg, Sybil. Review of *The Imperial Agent. Publishers Weekly* (May 26, 1989): 55.
———. Review of *The Last Victory. Publishers Weekly* (Feb. 9, 1990): 43.
Waller, J. M. Review of *Goin' Home. Southern Literary Journal* 27 (Summer 1980): 101.

SEEPERSAD NAIPAUL
(1906–1953)
Harold Barratt

BIOGRAPHY

Seepersad Naipaul, father of V. S. Naipaul and descendant of Indian indentured workers from eastern Uttar Pradesh and the ancient town of Ayodhya, was born in Longdenville, Trinidad.

Of his father's three children Seepersad was chosen to become a pundit; but this failed, and Seepersad became a sign painter after having attended different church schools. Sign painting brought him to Chaguanas, the heart of Trinidad's sugarcane area and home of many indentured Indians. At Chaguanas's Lion House—the model for Hanuman House of V. S. Naipaul's *A House for Mr. Biswas*—he met Bropatie of the powerful and wealthy Capildeo family. He married Bropatie in 1929, and in that year he began writing on Indian topics for the *Trinidad Guardian*.

He also did a variety of jobs, including a stint with the government; but it was his spasmodic and stressful career in journalism that had a profound and lasting effect on his life. His congenial relationship with Gault MacGowan, the English editor of the *Guardian*, brought out the creative and imaginative writer in him. Encouraged by MacGowan, Seepersad Naipaul wrote energetically, and not without some mischievousness, about village feuds, family vendettas, crime, election battles, and eccentric characters; in other words, the prime stuff of sparkling fiction. Meanwhile, he contributed short fiction to Henry Swanzy's seminal BBC program "Caribbean Voices." It was during this time, V. S. Naipaul believes, that his father found his voice as a writer.

Other factors played crucial roles in Seepersad Naipaul's growing consciousness. Of these his economic dependence upon his wife's family and that of a wealthy uncle, both of whom pulled his strings for most of his life, was important. And so too was his rootlessness—he lived in several places and never owned a house for thirteen years, a source of considerable strain—in a crumbling Hindu society in a neglected British crown colony.

Seepersad Naipaul's father also played an important role in his son's emotional development. His father, evidently, was a thoroughly repellent man, and his cruelty—it is an important issue in the story "They Named Him Mohun"—became Seepersad's obsession for the rest of his life. Another shaping influence was his fascination with Hinduism, which he seemed to have studied with some diligence. When Hindu reformist missionaries from India arrived in Trinidad in the 1920s, he championed the cause of reform, which had become a rather volatile issue in Trinidad's isolated Hindu community. This too is treated in "The Adventures of Gurudeva."

Seepersad Naipaul's espousal of reform, however, was not without peril. In 1933, after severely criticizing a Kali sacrificial ceremony and receiving a death threat, he was forced to sacrifice a goat to appease the goddess. The humiliation was profound, and it seems to have brought about his emotional, even mental, collapse. The scars of his humiliation remained with him for several years.

In 1943 the Guardian Commercial Printery published Seepersad Naipaul's only collection of short fiction, *Gurudeva and Other Indian Tales*. Few copies have survived; but, fortunately, the original collection was edited by his son and republished in 1976. Seepersad Naipaul lived for only ten years after his 1943 success. They were years of anxiety and strain, and he died under distressful circumstances.

MAJOR WORKS AND THEMES

Scholars have examined *The Adventures of Gurudeva and Other Stories* as source material for V. S. Naipaul's fiction; but the intrinsic value of the stories has not been sufficiently studied. The stories are important for several reasons, not the least of which is Seepersad Naipaul's candid and—given the time of composition—daring treatment of male-female relations in Trinidad's closed Hindu society of the thirties and forties. The plight of the Hindu woman, wife or daughter, is pervasive in the stories, and the ideal Hindu woman is depicted as an unobtrusive shadow or appendage of the male. Although he is only fourteen, Gurudeva instinctively enforces his wife's subordination by frequent beatings, which he regards as his privilege and prerogative as a husband. In other stories, "My Uncle Dalloo," for instance, the female is kept in her subordinate place by less violent, but equally humiliating, methods such as the threat of being reborn as a snake or scorpion as punishment for disobedience. In "The Wedding Came" Lalta, who is ferociously Hindu and traditional, rebels against educating his daughter even though he has been living in Trinidad's melting pot for thirty years; and in "The Engagement" the ideal bride is described as a cow, "gentle, long-suffering, the giver of plenty" (184).

The double standard, furthermore, is firmly rooted in the society Seepersad Naipaul knows so intimately: the female is required to be like Sita; but the male does not resemble Rama. The tone of the stories, one feels, is not so much an angry condemnation of the treatment of the Hindu female as it is a candid and accurate recording of a society cut off forever from its roots in India and struggling at all costs to maintain its Indian ethos in an alien and at times hostile society. Seepersad Naipaul's achievement is his lively evocation of this society and sensitive delineation of Indian peasants who, wrenched from Mother India, come together rather defensively, and with noticeable pride, in a polyglot society.

While the predominantly Christian, self-serving colonial society sees only illiterate Indian peasants and their alien rites and culture, Naipaul sees individuals whose impoverished and severely circumscribed lives are worthy of serious literary treatment. Sanyasi of "The Gratuity" is a case in point. The theme of the story is Sanyasi's quest for self-respect and integrity. The gratuity he seeks after fifteen years of strenuous labor is the material equivalent of his value. But he receives only a pittance, and when he squanders it entertaining his friends, he is showing, without being fully aware of it, his contempt for a system in which he has little value.

Under different circumstances, certainly a less harassed life, Seepersad Naipaul would have undoubtedly become a writer of some distinction. The signs are unmistakable. There is, for example, his gift for characterization and vivid evocation of a story's setting. Many of his characters, such as Uncle Dalloo, who is described to the life by an observant and imaginative first-person narrator, are carefully drawn in sparse but effective strokes. Using concrete and arresting detail, Naipaul can call up vivid pictures of unforgettable characters. For instance, Bhakhiran's collarbones resemble "rusty iron rings held under taut elastic" ("The Adventures of Gurudeva" 39).

But while Seepersad Naipaul writes sympathetically and sensitively about the Indian men and women transplanted in foreign soil, he is always aware of their failings, and indeed uses strong, sometimes overwritten, satire. The ironic voice of Mr. Sohun, the cynical schoolteacher of the title story, is at times Seepersad Naipaul's. One notices this, for instance, in Naipaul's strong criticism of the caste system, which the exigencies of the diaspora have not undermined. The satirical voice can also be heard in the amiable, but uncompromising, exposure of Gurudeva, the self-serving, artificial Hindu who, notwithstanding his strenuous attempts at sincerity, is a charlatan, the sort of picaro that would later become a recurring and thoroughly engaging figure in V. S. Naipaul's work.

The Adventures of Gurudeva and Other Stories contains early and remarkably penetrating sketches of largely illiterate Indian peasants deceived by the promise of fulfillment in the New World and set adrift after the expiration of their contracts in a colonial society that treats them like second-class citizens. It is their rootlessness, their struggle to maintain their distinctive Indianness that give Seepersad Naipaul's characters their compelling appeal. Lost in the colonial void, Seepersad Naipaul's displaced Indians will lose all connection with Mother India and become assimilated West Indians.

CRITICAL RECEPTION

In his "Prologue to an Autobiography," the first section of *Finding the Centre*, V. S. Naipaul writes perceptively of his father's stressful life and the extent to which this contributed to his own vocation as a writer. In his foreword to *The Adventures of Gurudeva and Other Stories* Naipaul changes his focus and writes with equal perception of his father's fiction which, he says, shares some of the characteristics of Nikolai Gogol's Ukrainian stories. Both writers, he explains, share a fine eye for landscape, dwellings, and people; and their focus on detail is particularly compelling. V. S. Naipaul also describes his father's stories as a valuable part of West Indian literature since they are a unique record of the Indian community in Trinidad in the first fifty years of the century (Foreword 19).

In *V. S. Naipaul: A Critical Introduction* Landeg White examines the son's literary debt to the father's writing. From his father, White says, "the young V. S. Naipaul must have learned a great deal . . . about how to shape a story" (32), to say nothing of his appreciation of eccentric characters. The most important effect of Seepersad Naipaul's stories, White claims, was to teach V. S. Naipaul the value of his local material. Naipaul's brilliant evocation of the world of indentured Indian workers in *A House for Mr. Biswas* "draws extensively" on his father's fiction (35). But White cautions that it would be a mistake to regard the stories as merely source material. He points to their value as "early attempts to define Trinidad in fictional terms" (37–38), and he praises Seepersad Naipaul's effective use of dialogue, arguing that the father's "ear for dialog is as finely attuned as his son's" (40).

In "V. S. Naipaul's Starting Point" Anthony Boxill maintains that the themes of Seepersad Naipaul's stories are "entrapment and escape" (2). But the focus of the essay is on V. S. Naipaul's debt to his father. Boxill points out that the Gurudeva persona reappears frequently in V. S. Naipaul's work, and he describes as remarkable the extent to which Seepersad Naipaul's work foreshadows V. S. Naipaul's fiction in "tone, in sentence structure, and even in vocabulary" (8). Boxill also claims that father and son share a love-hate relationship with Hindu customs.

BIBLIOGRAPHY

Works by Seepersad Naipaul

The Adventures of Gurudeva and Other Stories. 1943. London: Andre Deutsch, 1976.

Studies of Seepersad Naipaul

Boxill, Anthony. *V. S. Naipaul's Fiction: In Quest of the Enemy.* Fredericton: York Press, 1983.

——. "V. S. Naipaul's Starting Point." *Journal of Commonwealth Literature* 10:1 (1975): 1–9.

Naipaul, V. S. *Finding the Centre.* London: Andre Deutsch, 1984.

——. Foreword. *The Adventures of Gurudeva and Other Stories.* By Seepersad Naipaul. London: Andre Deutsch, 1976.

White, Landeg. *V. S. Naipaul: A Critical Introduction.* London: Macmillan, 1975.

SHIVA NAIPAUL (1945–1985)
David Racker

BIOGRAPHY

Before his death of a heart attack at the age of forty, Shiva Naipaul was considered one of the most talented writers of his generation in Britain. He had published three novels, the first two of which had garnered four literary awards between them; he had written two books of nonfiction, both a mixture of journalism, travel writing, and autobiography; and he had collected his short stories and articles into a book entitled *Beyond the Dragon's Mouth*. After his death on August 13, 1985, several eulogies appeared in the British press that testified to Naipaul's intensity, sincerity, and warmth.

In all of his nonfiction works, Naipaul writes of his ambivalent attitude toward his native country of Trinidad. Born on February 25, 1945, in Port of Spain, he was, as he says, "brought up by and among women": his mother and his five sisters (*Unfinished* 23). His father, the Indian journalist and short story writer Seepersad Naipaul, died when Shiva was seven, and his older brother, the novelist V. S. Naipaul, was, in Shiva's childhood, a dim, distant figure living in London. Although at one point Naipaul describes his childhood as "a happy innocence" (*Journey* 27), he came to see it in retrospect as a time when, in both his mother's and father's extended families, his Indian heritage began to erode and he was left with a sense of personal fragmentation. When he left Trinidad, armed like his brother before him with a scholarship to Oxford, Naipaul was in his own opinion "haphazardly cobbled together from bits and pieces taken from everywhere and anywhere" (*North* 104). At Oxford, he studied Chinese and graduated in 1968 with a Third Class. In 1967 he married Jenny Stuart, with whom he later had a son, Tarun. In his final year at university he began his first novel, *Fireflies*, which he published three years later in 1971 and for which he received the John Llewellyn-Rhys Memorial Prize, the Winifred Holtby Memorial Prize, and the Jock Campbell *New Statesman* Award. His next novel,

The Chip-Chip Gatherers, won the Whitbread Literary Award for 1973. In addition to publishing four more books—*North of South: An African Journey* (1978), *Journey to Nowhere: A New World Tragedy* (1980) (originally published in Great Britain as *Black and White* [1980]), *Love and Death in a Hot Country* (1984) (originally published in Great Britain as *A Hot Country* [1983]), and *Beyond the Dragon's Mouth* (1984)—Naipaul taught for a year at Aarhus University in Denmark. His last book, *An Unfinished Journey,* was published posthumously in 1986.

MAJOR WORKS AND THEMES

Naipaul's two early novels are set in Trinidad and deal with the conflicts of second- and third-generation immigrants within or against their Indian communities. *Fireflies* is the saga of the Khojas, an extended Indian family living in Port of Spain. The novel is ambivalent toward the hierarchical structure of the Indian family which, on the one hand, provides each of its members with a clearly defined identity within the hierarchy but which, on the other hand, subordinates young to old, poor to rich, and women to men. Much of the novel ridicules Govind Khoja, the family patriarch, for the niggardliness with which he carries out his familial responsibilities and for the self-importance with which he presides over Hindu rituals. But in its sympathetic portrayal of the Lutchmans, distant and poorer relatives of the Khojas, *Fireflies* examines the loss of the cultural and ethnic identity that goes along with the break away from the traditional Indian family. With their arranged marriages and *pujas,* the Khojas are the means by which Baby Lutchman remains rooted in Indian and particularly Hindu customs and beliefs. But Baby's husband Ram and their two sons Bhaskar and Romesh see the Khojas' preservation of Indian tradition as a hypocritical justification for maintaining their privileges over their poorer relations. By rejecting their position within the Khoja hierarchy, however, the Lutchman men also reject their Indian heritage. Ram throws himself into the more modern but also in his case more faddish pastimes of gardening and photography, while Romesh turns to the cinema and models his personality after the protagonists in American gangster films. Only Bhaskar fully contemplates the emptiness that results from his loss of faith in the culture in which his mother stakes her beliefs and ambitions. Like Naipaul himself, Bhaskar escapes the sterility of his deracinated existence by leaving Trinidad and sailing for England.

"All travel," writes Naipaul, "is a form of gradual self-extinction" (*Unfinished* 65), and throughout his fiction characters recur who try, through travel or other means, to extinguish their selves, which have been cast into and circumscribed by the Indian community. Either like Bhaskar they question the righteousness of a hierarchy that subordinates them to elders who are selfish and ignorant, or like Ashok Ramsaran in *The Chip-Chip Gath-*

erers they see their Indianness as a drawback to their economic success in the wider colonial society. Ashok, for example, changes his name to Egbert and converts to Presbyterianism as part of his campaign to be taken seriously as a Trinidadian entrepreneur. His name change and conversion, however, are less signs of his self-extinction than indications of his ability to forge a new identity through sheer force of will. In fact, as an alternative to the hierarchically determined identities that the characters in *Fireflies* must either accept or reject, *The Chip-Chip Gatherers* entertains the possibility of generating a self out of the currents of human vitality. Egbert and his mistress Sushila are the dynamo and virgin. The former's manner and energy in acquiring a fortune overawes his fellow Indians, while the latter's sexuality overawes the men of her community, particularly Egbert. In both cases, the vitality, one entrepreneurial and the other sexual, is placed in opposition to the enervating poverty, ignorance, and brutality of the rural Indian community in which both Egbert and Sushila grow up. In the end, however, Egbert and Sushila become the victims of their own capitalist ventures. Egbert is dehumanized by the years of struggle and ruthlessness that prove necessary to build up his transport company, and Sushila's sanity unravels as she realizes that age is deteriorating the trading value of her beauty. Egbert's son Wilbert inherits his father's cruelty without his father's sense of purpose, while Sushila's daughter Sita inherits her mother's alienation from the Indian community without her mother's faith in the force of an individual will. Like Bhaskar before her, Sita neither is rooted in an Indian tradition nor has the faith in her ability to transcend her present circumstances.

With *North of South* and *Journey to Nowhere* Naipaul widens his scope of observation and takes into account the social and political situation of Indians in postcolonial East Africa and Guyana. What he finds are Indians who are, at best, marginalized in the countries in which many of them were born or, at worst, objects of black vengeance. Both the socialism of Tanzania and the antipathy of Kenyan blacks toward Indians are, in Naipaul's analysis, responses to the colonial exploitation of Africans. However, Tanzanian socialism is vitiated by its ties to a discourse that is grounded in abstractions and textbook Marxism rather than in material reality. And in Kenya, Naipaul sees black racism against Indians as a displacement of the Kenyans' resentment of their former white colonizers. While he does not absolve the Indians of racism, he argues that such racism springs from their "tightly wrapped bundle of caste and group loyalties" (*North* 117). The Indian in Africa, argues Naipaul, is not so much a "racist" as he is a "communalist" (*North* 118).

Although the main interest of *Journey to Nowhere* is its investigation into the causes of the mass suicide of Jim Jones and his followers at Jonestown, Guyana, in 1978, Naipaul's sidelight into Guyanese politics presents a portrait of a mostly Indian population under the control of a black supremacist regime. Naipaul's characterization of the Guyanese prime minister, Forbes Burnham, is that of an opportunist who cynically veils his power grabs and his anti-Indian racism behind the outward signs of both African socialism and the American Black Power Movement. The Guyanese opposition party, composed mainly of Indians, is itself powerless to stop Burnham because it places its faith in a brand of socialism whose "bankrupt formulas" bear no resemblance to Guyanese reality (94). Like Burnham's ruling party, the opposition avoids what Naipaul calls the "one abiding issue of Guyanese politics": the racial polarization of blacks and Indians (85).

In *Love and Death in a Hot Country*, Naipaul portrays Cuyama, a fictional country whose social and political characteristics are based on his experiences in Africa and Guyana. The heroine of the novel, Dina Mallingham, suffers from the same cultural deracination as the characters in Naipaul's early novels, but Dina's consciousness, imploded by racial tension and a history of colonial and postcolonial exploitation, is psychologically more complex than the consciousness of the characters in *Fireflies* or *The Chip-Chip Gatherers*. Although no reason is given for her grandfather's change of name from Mahalingam to Mallingham or for his conversion from Hinduism to Presbyterianism, the motives for such transformations are made clear in the case of Dina's father. Indians, or Hindustanis as they are called in Cuyama, are ridiculed for their names, their food, their customs, and their gods and goddesses. Even Dina's mother, who has "a modicum of Portuguese blood flowing in her veins," taunts her husband with his "coolie relations" (107). Through his construction of a Christian identity, Dina's father attempts to distance himself from his Hindustani cousins and to create new ties with Cuyama's European colonizers. In one sense, he succeeds when Dina marries Aubrey St. Pierre, the son of a former land- and slave-owning family. But in another sense, he fails when the color of his skin bars him from the inner sanctum of a whites-only hotel and prompts from him the defiant but pained remark that he "wasn't going to run after anybody begging to be admitted to the human race" (183). Dina's realizations that her father had spent his entire life begging for just such an admittance and that he had associated humanity with whiteness comes as a shock to her. For Dina, white and black have been, until her epiphany at the end of *Love and Death*, matters of indifference. While Aubrey, through his albeit naive and pedestrian acts of philanthropy, tries to atone for the cruelty of his colonial ancestors, Dina's lack of a past has made her indifferent to her fate and the fate of her country. While Aubrey makes ineffectual protests against Cuyama's slide into totalitarianism, Dina remains indifferent to the "[b]anditry, cynicism and lies" of Cuyama's postcolonial black regime (59). Yet at the end of *Love and Death*, Dina realizes that her malaise and the impending violence of Cuyama's black rulers are different effects of the same cause. Like her "they had been cheated out of . . . selves, souls" (184): she, by the deliberate suppression of her ancestry; they, by a colonial history of slavery and second-class citizenship. The result of her lack of self is a moral torpor; the result of theirs is the desire to wreak vengeance.

Beyond the Dragon's Mouth and *An Unfinished Journey* span Naipaul's entire career as journalist, traveler, and short story writer. The Indians of his short stories, all of which appear in *Beyond*, are for the most part comic figures whose comedy stems from their encounters in Trinidad with other cultures, American and African, Christian and obeah. In the nineteen articles of *Beyond* and the six articles and section of a book collected in *An Unfinished Journey*, Naipaul chronicles the problems of identity, race, and the relationship between rich and poor that he sees as vital threads in the fabric of developing countries. The title essay of *Beyond* recounts Naipaul's childhood in Trinidad, many of the events of which also appear in his fiction. "Living in Earls Court" tells of Naipaul's efforts to rent a room in 1960s London and registers his surprise that, as a Trinidadian of Indian extraction, he is counted among the "Kolored Pipple" who "Need Not Apply" for bedsits advertised in Earls Court newsagents (*Beyond* 209). In "Passports to Dependence" Naipaul visits a refugee camp of Ugandan Asians who in 1972 were expelled *en masse* from Uganda by Idi Amin. As he does with the Kenyan Indians in *North of South*, Naipaul criticizes the Ugandan Asians for narrowly pursuing their economic interests while remaining apathetic to the political and social changes of their country. The Asians are in part to blame for their expulsion, says Naipaul, because they were unwilling to defend their economic security in the Ugandan political arena. The four essays about India that appear in *Beyond* as well as the two Indian essays in *An Unfinished Journey* provide a glimpse into the tensions of India and the Indian diasporic consciousness. For India's poor, the only hope of relief from their poverty as well as from the overcrowding and from the caste and communal violence of India is through escape to such labor-intensive regions as the Persian Gulf. For India's educated, staying at home means being torn between loyalty to their country and living with the knowledge that their talent and expertise would earn them much larger incomes as exiles in Britain or the United States. And for India's well-to-do, money means not help for India but an eager consumption of Western goods, fads, and ideas.

In "The Illusion of the Third World," Naipaul pulls back from his focus on countries such as India, Sri Lanka, and Grenada in order to express his distaste for the concept that lumps these countries together. The term "the Third World" says Naipaul, is an artificial and overly simplifying concept that the richer nations impose on the poorer ones, and in London, at least, "the Third World" is being reduced to a synonym for "Blackness." It is now "fashionably radical," to insist that immigrants from India, Pakistan, and Cyprus group themselves, "for the sake of solidarity," with England's black immigrants and that for simplicity's sake all four groups place themselves under the rubric of "Blackness." Such a "travesty" of understanding, according to Naipaul, "unites the Far Left and the Far Right" of London (*Unfinished* 40–41).

CRITICAL RECEPTION

All of Naipaul's books have received mixed reviews, and only two, *North of South* and *Love and Death*, have been the subject of critical essays. Although most critics do not question Naipaul's abilities as a writer, several question his aesthetic choices or the political perspective from which he writes. The debate over *Fireflies* and *The Chip-Chip Gatherers*, for example, centers on the relevancy of the social novel to late twentieth-century readers. Naipaul's British reviewers find his two early novels comparable in breadth and tone to Dickens's large novels and argue that Naipaul needs plenty of space in which to explain the "local and peculiar relationships and institutions" of a little-known minority in a Commonwealth country ("Shades" 1437). Annette Grant, on the other hand, finds that *Fireflies* raises the "uncomfortable question" of why "family sagas are so unappealing these days." Her own answer is that *Fireflies* lacks a psychological texture and is more memorable for its characters' habits and rituals than for their internal conflicts and relationships (6). Critics agree, however, that *Fireflies* is more successful than *The Chip-Chip Gatherers*, which they find gloomier and less well-organized.

North of South is perhaps Naipaul's most heavily condemned work. Critics argue that it is more a projection of Naipaul's prejudices than an accurate and representative portrait of East Africa (Darnton 14, 24; Beatty 38–39; Oliver 124). In "The Naipauls on Africa: An African View," Adewale Maja-Pearce argues that *North of South* exemplifies Naipaul's passionate hatred of Africans (111). Maja-Pearce and Lewis Nkosi attack both of the Naipaul brothers for judging Africa by "European" or "metropolitan" standards, and Maja-Pearce argues that the Naipauls' "slavish worship" of such standards has made them insensitive to the suffering of Africans (117). J. U. Jacobs, on the other hand, argues that in *North of South* the younger Naipaul, at least, writes from neither a European nor an African position but from a position of "tacit marginality" ("Writing" 57).

Critics have generally applauded Naipaul's next work, *A Journey to Nowhere*, for its subtle and thorough analysis of the causes behind the mass suicide at Jonestown. However, Jeremy Poynting finds that Naipaul gives only a diminished portrait of the political opposition in Guyana, an opposition that is, in fact, not limited to the Indian-dominated People's Progressive Party but extends to "all sections of society" (196, 198).

Love and Death, however, is the main subject of Poynting's essay, and his article, along with two critical essays by J. U. Jacobs, constitutes the most in-depth analysis of Naipaul's work. Poynting finds a glimmer of psychological complexity in the character of Dina but argues that Naipaul suppresses any attempts at psychological exploration under an "ideology of futility" the main components of which are "an extreme environmental and historical determinism" and "an outright racism" (175, 194). Poynting also finds that much of *Love and Death* is a regurgitation of themes and approaches from V. S. Naipaul's novels (173). In "Writing in the Margin: Shiva Naipaul's *A Hot Country*," Jacobs observes that, as a novel having its "origin in the travel journal," namely *North of South* (55), *Love and Death* does not emanate from but rather is a work about the Third World (57). Naipaul projects onto his material his own feelings of "being unstuck from his native land" (64), and what in *North of South* had been a "tacitly marginal stance" becomes in *Love and Death* an "explicit narrative attitude" (58). The predominance of such an attitude of marginality gives *Love and Death* the air of a "*roman à thèse*" in which Naipaul skillfully applies "his grid" to bring into being the "palimpsest" country of Cuyama over any actual country of the Third World (58, 64). Jacobs concludes that Naipaul's analysis of Cuyama's "metaphysics" is "virtually formulaic" and Cuyama is less a portrait of a Third World country than Naipaul's "hot country of the self" (58, 65). In a later essay, "The Colonial Mind in a State of Fear: The Psychosis of Terror in the Contemporary South African Novel," Jacobs has a different perspective on *Love and Death*. Here he sees Dina's "imploded intelligence" and Aubrey's "compulsion to expiate the sins of his slave-owning forefathers" as symptoms of a "colonialist disease" that he calls a "psychosis of terror." Such a psychosis, according to Jacobs, is most readily apparent in contemporary novels on the South African situation that depict "the Janus-relationship between on the one hand the apparatus of state terror and individual fear, and on the other, state fearfulness and acts of revolutionary terrorism" (25). Jacobs suggests that the high level of anxiety produced by such terror and fear is not limited to South Africans but is a paradigm of "a late-colonial, pre-revolutionary society," and he points to Aubrey and Dina as examples of how, even in newly independent societies, such anxiety can infect both the colonizer and the colonized (29–30).

Jim Crace and John Krich praise the short stories of *Beyond the Dragon's Mouth* for their verisimilitude and warmth, but each differs in his assessment of Naipaul's nonfiction. Their differences of opinion center on the relationship of Naipaul's persona and tone to his subject matter, a relationship that John F. Avedon also focuses on in his review of *An Unfinished Journey*. While Avedon argues that Naipaul's persona of a culturally fragmented and deracinated observer makes his works in *An Unfinished Journey* "passionate" and "often brilliant...laments" for developing nations (26), Krich argues that, in *Beyond*, Naipaul's obsession with his own physical and emotional dislocation has made him insensitive to others in the same predicament (13). Crace falls somewhere in between in that he finds the overall tone of both books to be misanthropic yet praises Naipaul for presenting tough and "disquieting arguments" (996).

BIBLIOGRAPHY

Works by Shiva Naipaul

Fireflies. New York: Knopf, 1971.
The Chip-Chip Gatherers. New York: Knopf, 1973.
North of South: An African Journey. New York: Simon, 1978.
Journey to Nowhere: A New World Tragedy. New York: Simon, 1980. Originally published as *Black and White*. London: Hamilton, 1980.
Love and Death in a Hot Country. New York: Viking, 1984. Originally published as *A Hot Country*. London: Hamilton, 1983.
Beyond the Dragon's Mouth: Stories and Pieces, London: Hamilton, 1984.
An Unfinished Journey. London: Hamilton, 1986.

Studies of Shiva Naipaul

Amis, Martin. "Educated Monsters." Review of *The Chip-Chip Gatherers*. *New Statesman* (Apr. 20, 1973): 586.
Avedon, John F. "A Magnet for Lost Strangers." Review of *An Unfinished Journey*. *New York Times Book Review* (Mar. 22, 1987): 26.
Beatty, Jack. Review of *North of South*. *New Republic* (June 9, 1979): 38–39.
Berger, Peter L. "Revolutionary Suicide." Review of *Journey to Nowhere*. *New York Times Book Review* (July 5, 1981): 8 + .
Bose, Mihir. "A Tour of Naipauland." *Literary Review* [Edinburgh] 57 (1983): 19–21.
Crace, Jim. "Misanthropy Abroad." Review of *An Unfinished Journey* and *Beyond the Dragon's Mouth*. *Times Literary Supplement* (Sept. 12, 1986): 996.
D'Arcy, David. "Lost in a Landscape of Neglect." Review of *Love and Death*. *New Leader* (May 28, 1984): 20–21.
Darnton, John. "Black and White and Middleman." Review of *North of South*. *New York Times Book Review* (May 6, 1979): 14 + .
Enright, D. J. "The Opium of the People." Review of *Black and White*. *Times Literary Supplement* (Oct. 30, 1980): 1218.
Grant, Annette. "Hindus Coming Apart in Trinidad." Review of *Fireflies*. *New York Times Book Review* (Feb. 7, 1971): 6.
Hess, Linda. Review of *Fireflies*. *Saturday Review* (Mar. 20, 1971): 37.
Jacobs, J. U. "The Colonial Mind in a State of Fear: The Psychosis of Terror in the Contemporary South African Novel." *North Dakota Quarterly* 57:3 (1989): 24–43.
———. "Writing in the Margin: Shiva Naipaul's *A Hot Country*." *Theoria: A Journal of Studies in the Arts, Humanities and Social Sciences* 70 (1987): 55–65.
King, Francis. "Potent." Review of *A Hot Country*. *Spectator* (Oct. 1, 1983): 22.

Krich, John. "Laureate of Cultural Confusions." Review of *Beyond the Dragon's Mouth*. *New York Times Book Review* (Mar. 24, 1985): 13.

Maja-Pearce, Adewale. "The Naipauls on Africa: An African View." *Journal of Commonwealth Literature* 20:1 (1985): 111–17.

Nkosi, Lewis. "Panning Africa." Review of *North of South*. *Times Literary Supplement* (Sept. 29, 1978): 1076.

Oliver, Roland. "Ujamaa." Review of *North of South*. *New Statesman* (July 28, 1978): 124.

Poynting, Jeremy. "A Struggling Imagination and the Ideology of Futility." *New Voices* [Trinidad and Tobago] 15 (1987): 172–99.

"Shades of Black and White." Review of *Fireflies*. *Times Literary Supplement* (Dec. 11, 1970): 1437.

Stuart, Douglas. Introduction. *An Unfinished Journey* by Shiva Naipaul. London: Hamilton, 1986.

Thorpe, Michael. "Laws of Life." Review of *Fireflies*. *Encounter* (June 1972): 71.

Walters, Ray. Review of *Journey to Nowhere*. *New York Times Book Review* (July 4, 1982): 5.

"Wasting Away." Review of *The Chip-Chip Gatherers*. *Times Literary Supplement* (Apr. 13, 1973): 409.

Yglesias, Jose. "Would Dictatorship Make a Difference?" Review of *Love and Death*. *New York Times Book Review* (Aug. 12, 1984): 26.

V. S. NAIPAUL (1932–   )

Maya Manju Sharma and Frank Palmer Purcell

BIOGRAPHY

Vidyadhar Surajprasad Naipaul was born in 1932 in Chaguanas, on the island of Trinidad, in the British colony of Trinidad and Tobago. Chaguanas was an Indian village re-created by indentured laborers brought over to work the fields and by their descendants, some of whom had become rich and powerful. His mother's family was among the latter; his father was not. In Chaguanas and later in Port of Spain Vidya and his mother lived as part of the extended family of her mother, whose husband, he would learn much later, had gone back to India with another woman.

Naipaul's extended family was ruled by his grandmother's sons-in-law; among these his father was odd man out. A poor boy brought up to be a pundit, he was attracted to the reformist Arya Samaj, married above himself, and earned a precarious living as a sign painter and journalist. His public stand in favor of religious enlightenment, child labor laws, and public health measures infuriated his in-laws. Threatened with death, he accepted the humiliation of sacrificing a goat to Kali, the symbol of all he loathed, and suffered a mental breakdown. This was the end of his career as the Chaguanas correspondent of the *Trinidad Guardian*, though later, in Port of Spain, he would work as an anonymous reporter for the same paper.

Chaguanas was village India, Port of Spain a kaleidoscope of races, languages, and cultures. Here Naipaul got to know his father, first through the old newspaper columns in a scrapbook, then the man himself. At this point in his life the elder Naipaul was turning to fiction to express himself in a way that his newspaper work did not permit, and as he learned his craft he would read draft after draft to his enchanted son. In this intense bond with the long-absent father the young writer's vocation was forged. Vidya's little brother Shiva would become a writer too, but he was not born until 1945, and lost his father to death when he was still a boy: Shiva did not experience those hours of intimacy or the remorse of having separated himself from him to make a life of his own in England and the world.

In Port of Spain V. S. Naipaul had opportunities for formal education his father had lacked, and he took advantage of them. Queen's Royal College was somewhat behind the times, and Naipaul emerged—as the founding fathers of the United States had emerged from their colonial colleges—feeling more like a citizen of ancient Rome than an inferior subject of the British Crown. Even in this he followed his father who, in distress, would call for his Epictetus or Marcus Aurelius to comfort him. In 1948 he won a full government scholarship, and in 1950 went up to University College, Oxford, to study English literature.

After Oxford, Naipaul went to London, where he worked as a free-lance broadcast journalist for the BBC's Caribbean Service. In this transplanted West Indian milieu he began to write. *Miguel Street* evoked the Port of Spain of his boyhood and youth, and *A House for Mr. Biswas*, the legacy of his father's life, confirmed an already solid reputation as a man of letters. His first published novel, *The Mystic Masseur*, had won critical acclaim when it appeared in 1957, and by 1958 he was a regular contributor to the *New Statesman*. Naipaul's literary success soon enabled him to undertake the journeys of exploration into history and culture, which it would be unjust to characterize as mere travel books.

Eric Williams, the prime minister of Trinidad, took notice of Naipaul's achievement in fiction, and suggested he write a book-length essay on his native region. So, in *The Middle Passage* (1962) Naipaul returned to the West Indies, but found no home for him there. *An Area of Darkness* (1964) recounts a similar disappointment with ancestral India. Working on his historical book of Trinidad, *The Loss of El Dorado* (1969), he began to feel the pull of his native island, but the book was a failure with its intended publisher. Trinidad society was coming apart in racial animosity, and his own health took a turn for the worse. He returned to England, and England remained his home. His writings reflect extensive travel in Africa, India, the Muslim world, and the United States.

After beginning *The Loss of El Dorado*, Naipaul did not keep up the steady pace of publication that had marked his earlier years. *A Flag on the Island* (1967) was a collection of short stories including juvenilia, outtakes from *Miguel Street*, and later tales, of varying quality, with little unity of theme or tone. *In a Free State* (1971) took the unusual form of two short stories and a long one preceded and followed by selections from a travel journal. *"The Overcrowded Barracoon" and Other Articles* (1972) was a collection of nonfiction. Naipaul continued to support himself as a writer, and journalistic assignments in Uganda, Trinidad, and Zaire set the scene for *In a Free State* (1971), *Guerrillas* (1975), and *A Bend in the River* (1979). Journalism provided more than the background—it involved him deeply in the moral and historical perplexities the later fiction seeks to explicate. The very complexity of his moral insight into postcolonial societies has estranged him from a number of critics and scholars who find his general tendency politically perverse.

Though living in England, Naipaul grew to have a special relationship with the United States, publishing in the *New Yorker* and with the house of Knopf, and serving as writer-in-residence at Wesleyan University in Connecticut. In 1984 he went to cover the Republican convention in Dallas, but found no book in it. Nevertheless, in some obscure way this Texas expedition provoked the extended meditation on England and his own past that became *The Enigma of Arrival* (1987), and inspired the American journey recorded in *A Turn in the South* (1989), a book dedicated "in ever renewed homage" to his father.

MAJOR WORKS AND THEMES

Early Fiction

Although well worth reading in their own right, the three early novels can also be seen as a preparation for *A House for Mr. Biswas*. *Miguel Street* (1959), a loosely unified group of stories, has added interest as the first mature book Naipaul wrote. Indeed, the "Prologue to an Autobiography" in *Finding the Center* crystallizes around the act of writing the first of these stories and describes, among many other things, his tracking down of the model of its protagonist much later in life. *Miguel Street* is more than a collection of short stories, but their unity is a function of the speaker's voice and tone rather than of any narrative drive. The same voice can be recognized in the narrator of *The Mystic Masseur*. Indeed, the last story of *Miguel Street* introduces the former masseur himself. It tells how the speaker's mother took him to Ganesh Pundit, now a government minister, for help with a scholarship to study abroad.

The dramatic emergence of colonies into nationhood, though more peaceful in the British Empire than in others, created sudden opportunities for men (and less frequently women) of ability, whose horizons had been, until then, severely restricted. The protagonist of *The Mystic Masseur* (1957) is one such. Born Ganesh Ramsumair, he is successively schoolteacher, masseur, psychic healer, New Age guru, colonial politician, and elder statesman G. Ramsay Muir, Esq., M.B.E. A failure as a teacher and masseur, Ganesh combines mumbo jumbo with modern psychology to cure a case of hysteria, and finds that the similarly afflicted flock to him. He turns to politics to foil his father-in-law's campaign of defamation and is elected to Trinidad's lower house, where he is something of a rabble-rouser. Flexibility is his great gift, and when the crowd turns on him in a labor dispute, he turns to anticommunism and imperialism, and is appointed to the upper house by a grateful government. Having acted the part of a Hindu holy man for a couple of years, he ends up as a professional Englishman.

Unlike *Miguel Street* and *The Mystic Masseur*, *The Suffrage of Elvira* (1958) is told in an impersonal voice and, unlike *A House for Mr. Biswas*, depicts its central character from an external point of view. It is the comedy of a rural Trinidad election of the colonial period. Politics of this sort had been a major preoccupation of Naipaul's mother's family, and had involved his father in painful and even tragic conflict with them, an experience the more fortunate Biswas would be spared. If Ganesh Pundit made a success in politics without really trying, Surujpat Harbans, Hindu candidate for the district of Elvira, earns his election the old-fashioned way: he buys it. The locals turn out to be shrewd horse traders, and he winds up paying much more than he bargained for. Still, it is to be assumed that the income from bribes will cover the expense, and that his suppliants will get value for their money.

A House for Mr. Biswas

A House for Mr. Biswas, published in 1961, is acknowledged as Naipaul's early masterpiece. Naipaul took the outline of his story from his own father's struggle to make a place for himself in a small world dominated by his powerful in-laws. Like Seepersad Naipaul, Mohun Biswas seeks to escape the constraints of Trinidad Indian society, but he is not fully happy or confident in a more cosmopolitan setting. Naipaul's irony is affectionate and compassionate, though his little brother Shiva felt he was unjust to their mother's family, as if the novel were not a work of fiction.

The prologue gives us Mohun Biswas, dismissed from his reporter's job for ill health, worried about the mortgage he sees no way of paying off. The body of the work shows him, ill at ease, in the houses of his mother-in-law. In the epilogue he dies, having held off debt and disaster long enough for his children to grow up and his daughter to take over. His son Anand, who has a good bit of Naipaul in him, remains estranged.

Mohun Biswas is a born loser. He comes into the world with an extra finger which, fortunately, falls off. He is asked to watch a neighbor's calf, loses it, and hides under the bed. Looking for him, his father dives into a pool and drowns. The family breaks up in a dispute over the father's non-existent money, and he and his mother are taken in by relatives. He is sent to live with a pundit to study Hinduism, but unable to make it to a latrine, he defiles a sacred tree and is sent back.

Biswas is employed in various ways by a wealthy and powerful family, and eventually marries into it without improving his status much. He can't stand to live with his in-laws, and the houses he builds for himself on their land fall down or go up in smoke. His break comes when he takes off for Port of Spain and eventually talks his way into a job as a reporter. He has an eye for the grotesque and a certain flair for language, and proves to be the apt pupil of a good editor, though when the editor is fired, he finds the job less rewarding, and even works for a time for the Welfare Department. Still, at the end he has a house and a car. He paid too much for the house and may not live to pay it off, but at last he has a place of his own.

At the end of his life Mr. Biswas has a house. He also has four children, among them the boy Anand who, like Naipaul himself, suffers from asthma, does well at college, and wins a scholarship to England. The relationship between father and son is one of the foci of the latter part of the novel. Biswas can hardly be expected to be a model father, having hardly known his own. Moreover, he is moody, irascible, and generally neurotic. Nevertheless, he really loves the boy and is genuinely pleased with his success. Anand is himself moody and withdrawn, but the two manage to get on after a fashion. Biswas is hospitalized for the last time while Anand is still abroad, and the young man doesn't know how to respond. He wants to come home, but changes his mind after Biswas offers to borrow the money to bring him back. It is his sister Savi who returns, and just as Biswas's severance pay runs out finds a better job of her own and saves the day. Biswas dies content—his last letter to Anand is a happy one—and his house remains in the family.

Throughout the long book Mr. Biswas is referred to as Mr. Biswas, even when his birth is described. The authorial voice is not putting any ironic distance between his subject on the one hand, and himself and his readers on the other. Rather, he is identifying himself, and helping his reader identify with the self-deprecating and mock boastful irony that is Mohun's chief defense mechanism and successful survival strategy. This stance of Mohun's is quintessentially Trinidadian, of the soul of Calypso bared in the very names of its chief avatars, from Sir Launcelot and the Mighty Sparrow to Lord Nelson and the Mighty Wonder. This style is behind Naipaul's own public persona, easily misread as that of the British schoolmaster calling his colonial pupils to order.

Nonfiction

A House for Mr. Biswas was the crowning achievement of Naipaul's early period. His next book, published the following year, marks a new beginning as an observer, historian, and critic of culture. *The Middle Passage: Impressions of Five Societies—British, French and Dutch—in the West Indies and South America* (1962) places the region in a much more comprehensive perspective, in which even the British Commonwealth is seen as only one of several colonialisms. *The Loss of El Dorado: A History* (1969) is more narrowly focused on Trinidad and Port of Spain, with an epic narrative sweep. Fiction was Naipaul's first way of defining himself in relation to his early milieu; in his historical, cultural, and social writing he found another.

In *An Area of Darkness* (1964) Naipaul began his often painful confrontation with the civilization that nurtured him in his earliest years, to which he became alien, and which has yet marked him as a kind of resident alien in the West. Just as his own family found *Biswas* unfair and hurtful, the Indian community abroad, ever preoccupied with public relations, has been similarly upset by his books on India, especially the second. *An Area of Darkness* was frankly personal, but *India: A Wounded Civilization* (1977) was more ambitious. In it he attempted, using the then unpublished theories of the neo-Freudian Sudhir Kakar, to psychoanalyze a subcontinent. Such an attempt was bound to fail, to infuriate, and to titillate. Still, it was an important step forward in his understanding of his South Asian heritage, and the emphasis on family structure surely paved the way for his later essays in autobiography. By the time of *India: A Million Mutinies Now* (1990), he had become able to capture in anecdote a wonderfully nuanced sense of a great land and its various communities in the grip of historical processes highly uncertain in their outcome.

It is only fair that *India: A Wounded Civilization* infuriated many Indians and liberal "friends of India," because Naipaul was furious with India for not shaping up, writing in hot disappointment rather than frigid disdain. For Naipaul the legacy of Mahatma Gandhi was a revolting sham covering up frivolousness and ineptitude. Surely the Indian national character must be dangerously warped; perhaps Kakar's theories suggest why Indian men can't act like grown-ups. Hard words, these, but blurted out in a lovers' quarrel.

In 1978 Naipaul did not yet appreciate the intractable nature of the tensions he would explore so well later. He has never shown any grasp of the geopolitical constraints under which the Indian leadership has had to labor. Threatened by China and Pakistan, both seemingly backed to some degree by the United States, India had little choice but to be a kind of client state of the Soviet Union. Only with the decline of Soviet power and Marxian orthodoxy were Indian leaders free to experiment with sensible domestic policies. Gandhianism was a figleaf designed to cover up the reality of a new and temporarily necessary form of colonialism. In hindsight, Naipaul's anger at the politicians appears distinctly shortsighted. At the time it was all the more unforgivable because neither Naipaul nor his critics were prepared to acknowledge the global political realities behind India's predicament. By 1990 the world had changed, India had changed, even Naipaul had changed, and *India: A Million Mutinies Now* is as generous in its sympathies as it is judicious in its assessments.

For a thousand years Hindu civilization has defined itself in opposition to Islam, which is also the greatest contemporary challenge to the Western secularism with which Naipaul identifies himself. It is significant that before his third and most successful expedition to India Naipaul made a similar survey of the Muslim world. *Among the Believers: An Islamic Journey*

(1981) was the result. In it Naipaul gives a strong impression of the unity of Islam and the diversity of Muslims and Muslim cultures. His portrait of Islam is not the menacing juggernaut of Western fears, but the way of life of intelligent and decent people (among others) of many kinds, though he feels that it has little to offer the rest of us as a faith. The combination of empathy and critical distance that emerged in the course of his Islamic adventure is displayed to fullest effect in *A Turn in the South* (1989). In this book he explores an exquisitely painful subject: race relations in the southern United States, getting southerners of all characters and persuasions to open their minds and hearts to him and reveal the tragedy of their condition. He does not theorize, but reflects on his own experiences of life in other societies as they are recalled to him by what he hears and sees. This is the method that would prove so fruitful in his third book on India.

Later Fiction

Naipaul never gave up fiction, though the novels of his middle period have attracted less attention than those that came before and after, or the works of nonfiction. *Mr. Stone and the Knights Companion* (1963) is a quiet story of an aging Englishman who marries for the first time and comes up with a creative idea for his company. The public relations man spoils the idea somewhat, but Mr. Stone has become a little more human, capable of kindness to cats though he fears and detests them. *The Mimic Man* (1967) is in the form of the reminiscences of a Caribbean politician of Indian descent exiled in poverty to the England that has always been more real to him than his native island. *A Flag on the Island* (1967) is a collection of stories, and *In a Free State*, a triptych of stories framed by sections of a travel journal. Of another author these might have been acknowledged as major works, but they did not come up to the master of *A House for Mr. Biswas* and were soon eclipsed by the powerful and controversial *Guerrillas* and *A Bend in the River*.

Guerrillas (1975) concerns a Black Power movement in a place very much like Trinidad. The movement is led by the son of a Chinese shopkeeper whose ambition had been to go to China and offer his services to Chairman Mao until he was taken up by London whites as a black militant. He has no feeling for the people he purports to lead and thrives on the attention of Europeans. The protagonist is an Englishwoman infatuated with the idea of revolution, who embarks on a sexual relationship with the leader without realizing what a psychopath he is. He finally humiliates her in an anal rape and gives her to his boy lover to be horribly done to death. The brutality of the conclusion still has power to shock. If the book is read as a black comedy in which the fatuous liberal gets what's coming to her, the author appears to be moved by a sadistic contempt for what the woman represents, and a fear and loathing for the revolutionaries. This misreading of the book has haunted Naipaul. As ideological passions cool, it is possible to read it as a tragedy involving real understanding for the protagonist and an authentic catharsis of pity and fear.

Guerrillas is not a tract attacking black aspirations, much less black people as such. The racial demagogue who works the mischief is half Chinese, and motivated as much by self-hatred as by anything else. This does not make him a figure of farce but a vivid reminder that in our miscegenated world racial chauvinism is a dangerous delusion indeed. Naipaul's truths were painful ones, especially for the 1970s, but expressing them does not make him an enemy of the Afro-Caribbean peoples or an Asian toady of white imperialism.

A Bend in the River (1979) is the story of an Indian merchant struggling to survive in the chaos of postcolonial Africa. It is Naipaul's epic of the Indian diaspora, and there is more of him in it than in any previous work of fiction. When the narrator describes the shock of seeing the dhows he takes for granted in his home on the Indian Ocean depicted on British postage stamps as icons of quaintness, we can be sure that Naipaul is acknowledging a similar shock in his own consciousness. The European and African characters in the story are neither stupid nor wicked, at least no more so than the rest of the species, but are carried along by a historical process beyond their control. The vision is almost Tolstoyan, but without the mystical epiphanies. The Indian characters have no place in the new Africa and must reconcile themselves to making a place in London or the United States, where they are at least tolerated and have established a kind of network.

Autobiography

Naipaul's nonfiction is full of personal feeling, reaction, and reminiscence, and his early fiction mirrors the milieu of his boyhood. *In a Free State* juxtaposes fact and fiction by placing three stories between the covers of passages of a travel journal. The first part of *Finding the Center*, "Prologue to an Autobiography," is an extended meditation, musical rather than narrative in structure, on autobiographical themes. In it Naipaul describes the moment he found his voice as a writer in a story about a distant relative who lived down the street. He speaks of tracking this man down on his return to the Caribbean, and piecing together the story of his family and the tragedy of his father, who had been a model for Mr. Biswas and his own model as a writer. *The Enigma of Arrival* (1987) is officially designated a novel, but there is no doubt that the novelist-narrator is a man who has lived Naipaul's life. Perhaps all autobiography, even all narrative, is fiction. To acknowledge this gives an author the license to omit, to alter, to shade as he wishes. This license enables him to bring out the truth behind the fact and to guard his privacy and that of others in his life. Without a doubt

Naipaul is an intensely private man, loyal to his friends and scrupulous about telling the truth. But the truths he needs to tell are impersonal ones, though they come to him through his personal experience. This is what gives his writing its unique authority. Nevertheless, as a biographical source, *The Enigma of Arrival* remains an enigma.

Major Themes

Gustav Mahler used to say that he was three times an exile: a Bohemian in Austria, an Austrian in Germany, and a Jew in the world. V. S. Naipaul has him beat—as an Indian in Trinidad, a West Indian in England, a Westerner in India, and a bemused man of Hindu culture in the material universe. Mahler was the first great master of international modernism in music; Naipaul is a recent master of international modernism in English prose. Arguably, modernism is the typical product of the diasporic sensibility, of the struggle to express in a language you must re-create, however subtly, to make your own.

We tend to forget to what extent twentieth-century literature in English is the fruit of the colonial struggle to master the tongue of an alien overlord. James Joyce and his compatriots were most conscious of this circumstance, but the theme is there in the Welsh writers Dylan Thomas, Vernon Watkins, and David Jones, as well as the Northumbrian Basil Bunting. Virginia Woolf's attempt to make her language true to a woman's sensibility and experience of the world is somewhat analogous. Various expatriated Americans present themselves, with varying degrees of success, as colonials returned to the motherland, a motherland they had to construct for themselves.

Such is the recent history of the language in which Naipaul writes. It is a history in which Coomaraswamy and Tambimuttu had a profound if hidden influence, and because of which the prose of Nirad C. Chaudhuri and the poetry of Jayanta Mahapatra can be integrally Indian and still in the mainstream of English letters. Winston Churchill's phrase about the "English-speaking peoples" has a resonance now that the old curmudgeon could hardly have imagined, and this language of ours has proved uniquely suited to Naipaul's exploration of multiracial society and multicultural consciousness.

Cultural pluralism and a certain cosmopolitan syncretism are characteristic of great empires in their maturity and decline. Diasporic communities, such as those of the Jews of the Roman world, must live their lives in the constant epistemological tension of having to take three reality systems into account—their own and that of their scattered brethren, that of the people around them, and that of the imperium that gives them protection. Such was the condition of Indians and Chinese, and to a lesser degree even Scots and Irish, in the British Empire. To the extent that the United States is more like an empire than like a nation-state, such may be the condition of American ethnic groups today. Naipaul's work is a classic delineation of diasporic consciousness.

Mohun Biswas may well be taken as emblematic of diaspora. He has lost his earliest home, where he was happy with his mother, where his umbilical cord is buried along with his deciduous sixth finger. When he goes back to the place there is no sign of it, as diasporic pilgrims to India often find no trace of the home their parents or grandparents left behind. Mohun is never Mohun even, indeed, especially to himself. He is always Mr. Biswas. Though he seldom meets an Englishman, his very identity is impersonally British. His son Anand breaks through to authentic consciousness and his vocation as a writer by being faithful to the experience of nearly drowning, rather than writing the conventional essay on a happy seaside holiday. One reason Naipaul's earlier nonfiction is so profoundly disturbing is that it gives a powerful feeling of drowning, of being nearly overwhelmed by a flood of impressions, memories, and reflections that knock the solid ground out from under his feet.

Naipaul's fictional protagonists present important variations on his own experience. The narrator of *The Mystic Masseur* remarks that if Ganesh had been born earlier he would (like Mohun Biswas and Seepersad Naipaul) not have attended the college in Port of Spain; a man born later would have gone on (like Ralph Singh and V. S. Naipaul) to a university abroad. Singh represents the danger of diaspora into which some critics wrongly believe Naipaul himself has fallen. Ralph has never been moved by, much less moved to, the Calypso rhythms of *Miguel Street*, and fancies himself the Roman administrator of some barbarous province until events force him to take up the life of an English man of letters.

V. S. Naipaul's diasporic sensibility is a complex feature. He is deeply committed to the core values of Western civilization, especially rational discourse and respect for the human person. He takes these for universal, and his fictional portraits of Third World dictators and would-be dictators are as unsparing as his depictions of European imperialism in *The Loss of El Dorado*. If *Among the Believers* has a moral, it is that irrational beliefs lead to deplorable actions even with the best of intentions; this is also his attitude toward the Southern mystique of the Lost Cause, which he explicitly compares to the Shia myth of Muslim history.

As firmly as Naipaul holds to that core of Western values he takes for universal, he cannot deny that much of what the Englishman takes for granted—William Wordsworth's daffodils and Charles Dickens's slums—was utterly alien to his young experience. Though English was his first language, he studied English literature as a foreign literature, and always kept the ironic detachment that prevented him from joining the ranks of the "mimic men." His first book set in England, *Mr. Stone and the Knights Companion*, took enormous labor, and his second, *The Enigma of Arrival*, years of patient and sympathetic observation.

As a man of the diaspora, Naipaul cannot simply be of the time and place in which he was born. To be sure, he was steeped in the urban folk culture of Trinidad and did not feel stigmatized by his Indian heritage. Still, he felt a double pull, toward the imperial metropolis and toward ancestral India. The one was the future, the other, the past. Unlike his less appealing characters, he could not simply turn his back on the past, on his father's suffering and whatever family history lay behind it, despite their separation. Much as India distressed him at first, he couldn't keep himself from wringing his hands and offering unwanted advice.

Alongside or underneath Naipaul's espousal of the core values of the West, his sensibility may rest on a hard core of Hindu bedrock that he doesn't explicitly avow. There is the deep conviction that our consciousness is but a partial thing, that we are all mired in illusion. There is also the hope of some kind of transcendence, of a vision, however fleeting, going beyond partial views and material interests. This hope, if it is not itself illusion, must rest on an unconquerable determination to control the mind so as to see things as they are and not as we wish them to be. This would seem to be Naipaul's creed as a writer; it is not so far from the ancient idea of yoga.

CRITICAL RECEPTION

Naipaul's own literary production has itself been dwarfed by the productivity of his scholars and critics. The Modern Language Association has catalogued 179 books and articles on his work appearing between 1981 and 1991, and it probably missed a few. It is therefore only possible to give the most general survey of what has been written.

Of all the general introductions and critical appreciations of Naipaul, that of Paul Theroux (1972) has the double distinction of being written by a friend who is himself a writer of merit. Being written so early in the careers of both men, it only takes us up to *In a Free State*. Fortunately, in 1984 *Modern Fiction Studies* gave Theroux a chance to bring his reflections up to date.

Of the briefer introductory surveys, the pioneering study by Robert Hammer in Twayne's World Authors Series (1973) is worth consulting on the earlier works. Michael Thorpe's survey for the British Council (1976) covers the same ground, with a postscript on *Guerrillas*. Thorpe's reaction shows how this new departure surprised critics who felt, with some justification, that Naipaul had worked his fictional vein to the point of exhaustion. Peter Hughes (1988) takes the reader through *The Enigma of Arrival*. The virtue of Hughes is to situate Naipaul in the mainstream of English and world literature, beginning with a comparison of Naipaul's vision with that of Edward Gibbon and ending with a moving evocation of Hermann Broch's *Death of Virgil*. A decade and a half earlier it had taken a writer of Theroux's stature to see that Naipaul was more than just a regional storyteller who had made good as a highbrow journalist. *Guerrillas* made it clear that his moral imagination is engaged with the fundamental questions of human life, and by the end of the 1980s he was seen as a major figure indeed.

The West Indian response to Naipaul, often hostile, sometimes bitterly so, was exhaustively discussed by Dolly Zulakha Hassan (1989). Hassan, herself an expatriated Indian Muslim from Guyana, mustered a remarkable sympathy both for the sometimes tortured and tactless persona of the younger Naipaul and for the rage he provoked. Sudha Rai (1982) gave an Indian response to Naipaul's animadversions on Gandhianism and the Indian character in his first two India books, and was particularly insightful in pointing out the limitations of Naipaul's use of Sudhir Kakar's theories in *India: A Wounded Civilization*. The Marxist theoretician Selwyn Cudjoe (1988) accepted Naipaul as a great writer through *The Mimic Men*. Cudjoe claimed he later became successful as an apologist for Western racism and imperialism in works that would be quickly forgotten after the inevitable defeat of the West. Cudjoe's reading of Naipaul was more nuanced than his frank declaration of allegiance might lead one to expect, and his partial legitimation of Naipaul was important in American academe, where Cudjoe's authority had great weight in departments of Third World and multicultural studies.

As we have seen, diaspora is a phenomenon of empire, and Naipaul has chronicled the suffering of diasporized minorities in the breakup of empire. Most critics acknowledge that this does not make him an imperialist. More troubling to many is his conviction that the rational and ethical values of Western civilization have universal validity, that they are somehow appropriate to human nature as such. It is hard not to see this stance as a rejection of cultural relativism and an affirmation of the Natural Law tradition. Larry David Nachman quotes Naipaul's preference for the West over against India, and comments:

When and where have we in the West heard such a voice and last received such a summons to get on with our historical work? Besides its clarity of purpose and confidence in the power of human reason to illuminate and thereby give grace to human affairs, the figure of the western intellectual gone native—from Jung to Sartre—seems more than a little bit puny and pathetic. Mister Kurtz has nothing more to say to us; perhaps he never did.

...From the time of the Stoics through the Enlightenment, the West has kept alive—against every historical reality—the ideal of a cosmopolis of the wise, a republic of letters. V. S. Naipaul is now one of its best citizens. (76)

Writing (significantly) in the *New Criterion*, Joseph Epstein has a similar assessment:

Everything Naipaul writes has the quality that used to be called gravity, which derives in part from the subjects he writes about, his themes, and his inexorable manner of pursuing them. In part, too, it derives from his almost sovereign authority. *Sui generis*, he is a writer above nationality, above received opinions, above (apparently) normal attachments and loyalties. He is "a being organized for literature," as Henry James once described himself, but a being that not even Henry James, in all the richness of his imagination, could have anticipated. (6)

Epstein warmly praises Naipaul's "conservative temperament":

Civilization, for Naipaul, is a fragile thing, always in peril. Rural England, in his reading, is rather like Trinidad, or East Africa, or India; without the authority of tradition, it is, like every other place in the world, under siege by rot and at the mercy of rotters. In Naipaul's writing generally, there is a great, not ever fully expressed, longing for a society where he can cease the struggle, come to rest, feel at home. Although a British citizen, he remains, spiritually, a stateless soul, yearning for a society that the modern world just may not be able to provide. It is one of Naipaul's great themes, and perhaps the principal sadness of his life. (15)

Unfortunately, perhaps, the longings of the conservative temperament are not universally admired, still less Naipaul's rage when things don't measure up. For Eugene Goodheart, Naipaul's attitude of unrelenting criticism of all he surveys is as problematic as it is crucial:

What is the appeal of this virtuoso of the negative? Every scene in V. S. Naipaul's work is the occasion for mandarin scorn. It doesn't matter whether the scene is the half-developed or "mimic" societies of the Caribbean or the abysmal material squalor of India or the cruel places in Africa where revolutions are being made or, for that matter, the advanced societies of the West. Naipaul encounters one and all with a cold-eyed contempt. ("V. S. Naipaul's Mandarin Sensibility" 244)

In the end, Goodheart recognizes Naipaul's stance of negation as related to traditional Indian spirituality:

In Naipaul, the "No" has its ultimate metaphysical source in a vision of the abysmal nothingness of life. The vision is not to be confused, however, with continental versions of the abyss, whose chief sponsorship has been existentialism. Naipaul's "nothingness" is an agnostic version of Hinduism, without the promise of reincarnation. Unlike existentialism, for which the abyss is an occasion for a creative leap, Naipaul's nothingness is an ultimate condition. And to the extent that it forms his sensibility, it provides a perspective on the futility of all created things. This feeling for metaphysical nothingness is, I suspect, a source of great strength in Naipaul. It gives his vision equanimity. It permits him to gaze at the created forms of life without illusion—that is, with a knowledge of their final destiny. ("V. S. Naipaul's Mandarin Sensibility" 256)

Goodheart's account can be accepted, with certain qualifications. Not all existentialism involves the same sort of "creative leap," and Naipaul's bleak vision bears some resemblance to the Heidegger of *Sein und Zeit*. And the Naipaul described by Goodheart has affinities, not with any orthodox Hindu system, but rather with Buddhism. Buddhist, too, is that fierce, unsentimental compassion, unremarked by Goodheart, which moves Naipaul to write what he writes. It is curious indeed that Naipaul's travels have not yet taken him to the Buddhist cultures of East Asia, which have successfully assimilated so much of what the West has to offer without losing their identities.

Salman Rushdie, the Indian English author with an Iranian price on his head, entertains a low opinion of Naipaul, except for the early comedies. He claims that the first visit to India, the one recorded in *An Area of Darkness*, demoralized Naipaul to the point that he threw his lot in with the West, losing something of his integrity in the process. It is ironic that Rushdie has now made himself a kind of martyr to Western values. Naipaul has not commented publicly on Rushdie's *Satanic Verses* or the Islamic death sentence pronounced by the Ayatollahs against him for it. It is likely that he feels enough solidarity with a fellow writer in trouble for telling the truth as best he knew how, not to want to expose the ironies of his predicament (Gorra 375).

Naipaul's reputation has grown along with his work. He has been recognized successively as a Commonwealth writer, a world traveler, a controversial novelist of Third World turmoils, a voice of the Indian diaspora, and a literary figure of world significance. Younger writers like Rushdie might attempt to forge a multicultural consciousness by deconstructing each of the cultures he is in dialogue with, but Naipaul chose a harder path. For Naipaul the diasporic experience has been a key to the modern condition, the sense of alienation from one's roots and one's fellows, the yearning to find some meaning in one's origins. It is the vocation of India in exile, as represented by V. S. Naipaul, to bring the present age of humanity to consciousness itself. It is therefore entirely fitting that Joseph Epstein should look to an Indian of the diaspora for moral authority:

Whatever he does next I take to be of the most serious consequence, for this man, the grandson of an indentured laborer, the son of an unsuccessful island journalist, is far and away the most talented, the most truthful, the most honorable writer of his generation. (15)

BIBLIOGRAPHY

Works by V. S. Naipaul

The Mystic Masseur. London: André Deutsch, 1957; rpt. Harmondsworth: Penguin, 1964.

The Suffrage of Elvira. London: André Deutsch, 1958; rpt. Harmondsworth: Penguin, 1969.

Miguel Street. London: André Deutsch, 1959; rpt. Harmondsworth: Penguin, 1971.

A House for Mr. Biswas. London: André Deutsch, 1961; rpt. Harmondsworth: Penguin, 1969.

The Middle Passage: Impressions of Five Societies—British, French and Dutch—In the West Indies and South America. London: André Deutsch, 1962; rpt. New York: Vintage, 1981.

Mr. Stone and the Knights Companion. London: André Deutsch, 1963; rpt. Harmondsworth: Penguin, 1973.

An Area of Darkness. London: André Deutsch, 1964; rpt. New York: Vintage, 1981.

A Flag on the Island. London: André Deutsch, 1967; rpt. Harmondsworth: Penguin, 1969.

The Mimic Men. London: André Deutsch, 1967; rpt. Harmondsworth: Penguin, 1969.

The Loss of El Dorado: A History. London: André Deutsch, 1969; rpt. Harmondsworth: Penguin, 1973.

In a Free State. London: André Deutsch, 1971; rpt. Harmondsworth: Penguin, 1973.

"The Overcrowded Barracoon" and Other Articles. London: André Deutsch, 1972; rpt. Harmondsworth: Penguin, 1976.

Guerrillas. London: André Deutsch, 1975; rpt. Harmondsworth: Penguin, 1980.

India: A Wounded Civilization. New York: Alfred A. Knopf, 1977; rpt. New York: Vintage, 1978.

A Bend in the River. New York: Alfred A. Knopf, 1979; rpt. New York: Vintage, 1980.

"The Return of Eva Perón" with "The Killings in Trinidad." New York: Alfred A. Knopf, 1980; rpt. New York: Vintage, 1981.

Among the Believers: An Islamic Journey. New York: Alfred A. Knopf, 1981; rpt. New York: Vintage, 1982.

"A Note on a Borrowing by Conrad." *New York Review of Books* 16 Dec. 1982: 37–38.

"Writing 'A House for Mr. Biswas.' " *New York Review of Books* 24 Nov. 1983: 22–23.

"Among the Republicans." *New York Review of Books* 25 Oct. 1984: 5 + .

Finding the Centre: Two Narratives. London: André Deutsch, 1984; rpt. New York: Alfred A. Knopf, 1984. (Includes "Prologue to an Autobiography" and "The Crocodiles of Yamoussoukro.")

"An Island Betrayed." *Harper's* Mar. 1984: 61–72.

The Enigma of Arrival. New York: Alfred A. Knopf, 1987.

"Some Thoughts on Being a Writer." *Chronicles: A Magazine of American Culture* 11 (May 1987): 13–15.

A Turn in the South. New York: Alfred A. Knopf, 1989.

India: A Million Mutinies Now. New York: Alfred A. Knopf, 1990.

Studies of V. S. Naipaul

Anderson, Linda R. "Ideas of Identity and Freedom in V. S. Naipaul and Joseph Conrad." *English Studies* 59 (1978): 510–17.

Angrosino, M. B. "V. S. Naipaul and the Colonial Image." *Caribbean Quarterly* 21:3 (1975): 1–11.

Belitt, Ben. "The Heraldry of Accommodation: A House for Mr. Naipaul." *Salmagundi* 54 (1981): 23–42.

Blaise, Clark. "The Commonwealth Writer and His Material." *Awakened Conscience: Studies in Commonwealth Literature.* Ed. C. D. Narasimhaiah. New Delhi: Sterling, 1978. 118–26.

Boxill, Anthony. "The Little Bastard Worlds of V. S. Naipaul's *The Mimic Men* and *A Flag on the Island.*" *International Fiction Review* 3 (1976): 12–19.

———. "The Paradox of Freedom: V. S. Naipaul's *In a Free State.*" *Critique: Studies in Modern Fiction* 18:1 (1976): 81–91.

———. *V. S. Naipaul's Fiction: In Quest of the Enemy.* Fredericton, New Brunswick: York, 1983.

Boyers, Robert. "Confronting the Present." *Salmagundi* 54 (1981): 77–97.

Campbell, Elaine. "A Refinement of Rage: V. S. Naipaul's *A Bend in the River.*" *World Literature Written in English* 18 (1979): 394–406.

Carnegie, Jenipher R. *Critics on West Indian Literature: A Selected Bibliography.* Barbados: University of West Indies Press, 1980.

Cooke, John. "A Vision of the Land: V. S. Naipaul's Later Novels." *Caribbean Quarterly* 25:4 (1979): 31–47.

Cooke, Michael G. "Rational Despair and the Fatality of Revolution in West Indian Literature." *Yale Review* 71:1 (1981): 28–38.

Cudjoe, Selwyn R. *Resistance and Caribbean Literature.* Athens: Ohio University Press, 1980. 70, 71, 178, 232–44, 271, 272.

———. "Revolutionary Struggle and the Novel." *Caribbean Quarterly* 25:4 (1979): 1–30.

———. *V. S. Naipaul: A Materialist Reading.* Amherst: University of Massachusetts Press, 1988.

Dunwoodie, Peter. "Commitment and Confinement: Two West Indian Visions." *Caribbean Quarterly* 21:3 (1975): 15–26.

Epstein, Joseph. "A Cottage for Mr. Naipaul." *New Criterion* (Oct. 1987): 6–15.

Eyre, M. Banning. "Naipaul at Wesleyan." *South Carolina Review* 14 (Spring 1982): 34–47.

Figueroa, John J. "Introduction—V. S. Naipaul: A Panel Discussion." *Revista/Review Interamericana* 6 (1976–77): 554–63.

Goodheart, Eugene. "Naipaul and the Voices of Negation." *Salmagundi* 54 (1981): 44–58.

———. "V. S. Naipaul's Mandarin Sensibility." *Partisan Review* 50 (1983): 244–56.

Gorra, Michael. "Naipaul or Rushdie." *Southwestern Review* (Summer 1991): 374–89.

Gottfried, Leon. "A Skeptical Pilgrimage." *Modern Fiction Studies* 30 (1984): 567–71.

Gottfried, Leon, and Shaun F. D. Hughes, eds. Special Issue: V. S. Naipaul. *Modern Fiction Studies* 30:3 (1984).

Guinness, Gerald. "Naipaul's Four Early Trinidad Novels." *Revista/Review Interamericana* 6 (1976–77): 564–73.

Gurr, Andrew. "The Freedom of Exile in Naipaul and Doris Lessing." *Ariel* 13:4 (1982): 7–18.

Hamner, Robert D., ed. *Critical Perspectives on V. S. Naipaul.* Washington, D.C.: Three Continents, 1977.

Hassan, Dolly Zulakha. *V. S. Naipaul and the West Indies.* New York: Lang, 1989.

Hemenway, Robert. "Sex and Politics in V. S. Naipaul." *Studies in the Novel* 14:2 (1982): 189–202.

Jama, Virginia. "The Image of the African Leader in Recent Western Fiction." *Horn of Africa* 3:1 (1980): 43–45.

Jarvis, Kelvin. *V. S. Naipaul: A Selective Bibliography with Annotations, 1957–1987.* Stamford, Conn.: Scarecrow Press, 1989.

Kachru, Braj B., ed. *The Other Tongue: English across Cultures.* Urbana: University of Illinois Press, 1982.

Kelly, Richard. *V. S. Naipaul.* New York: Continuum, 1989.

King, Bruce. *The New English Literatures—Cultural Nationalism in a Changing World.* New York: St. Martin's Press, 1980. 98–117, 221–23.

———. "Recent Commonwealth Fiction." *Sewanee Review* 85 (1977): 126–34.

———. "V. S. Naipaul." *West Indian Literature.* Ed. Bruce King. London: Macmillan, 1979. 161–78.

McSweeney, Kerry. *Four Contemporary Novelists: Angus Wilson, Brian Moore, John Fowles, V. S. Naipaul.* Montreal: McGill-Queen's University Press, 1983.

———. "V. S. Naipaul: Sensibility and Schemata." *Critical Quarterly* 18:3 (1976): 73–79.

Mahood, M. M. "The Dispossessed: Naipaul's *The Mimic Men.*" *The Colonial Encounter: A Reading of Six Novels.* London: Collings, 1977. 142–65.

Mann, Harveen Sachdeva. "Variations on the Theme of Mimicry: Naipaul's *The Mystic Masseur* and *The Suffrage of Elvira.*" *Modern Fiction Studies* 30 (1984): 467–85.

Mishra, Vijay. "Mythic Fabulation: Naipaul's India." *New Literature Review* 4 (1978): 59–65.

Mukherjee, Bharati, and Robert Boyers. "A Conversation with V. S. Naipaul." *Salmagundi* 54 (1981): 4–22.

Nachman, Larry David. "The Worlds of V. S. Naipaul." *Salmagundi* 54 (1981): 59–76.

Nandan, Satendra, ed. *Language and Literature in Multicultural Contexts.* Suva, Fiji: University of South Pacific Press, 1983.

Nazareth, Peter. "Out of Darkness: Conrad and Other Third World Writers." *Conradiana* 14:3 (1982): 173–87.

Nightingale, Peggy. *Journey through Darkness: The Writings of V. S. Naipaul.* New York: University of Queensland Press, 1987.

Niven, Alastair. "Crossing the Black Waters: N. C. Chaudhuri's *A Passage to England* and V. S. Naipaul's *An Area of Darkness.*" *Ariel* 9:3 (1978): 21–36.

Noel, J. "Historicity and Homelessness in Naipaul." *Caribbean Studies* 11:3 (1971): 83–87.

Nunez-Harrell, Elizabeth. "Lamming and Naipaul: Some Criteria for Evaluating the Third-World Novel." *Contemporary Literature* 19:1 (1978): 26–47.

Padhi, Bibhu. "Naipaul on Naipaul and the Novel." *Modern Fiction Studies* 30 (1984): 455–65.

Parrinder, Patrick. "V. S. Naipaul and the Uses of Literacy." *Critical Quarterly* 21:2 (1979): 5–13.

Pyne-Timothy, Helen. "Women and Sexuality in the Later Novels of V. S. Naipaul." *World Literature Written in English* 25 (1985): 298–306.

Raghavacharyulu, D.V.K. "Beyond Exile and Homecoming: A Preliminary Note." *Alien Voice: Perspectives on Commonwealth Literature.* Ed. Avadhesh K. Srivastava. Lucknow, India: Print House, 1981; Atlantic Highlands, N.J.: Humanities Press, 1982. 31–39.

Rai, Sudha. *V. S. Naipaul: A Study in Expatriate Sensibility.* Atlantic Highlands, N.J.: Humanities Press, 1982.

Rao, K. I. Madhusudana. "The Complex Fate: Naipaul's View of Human Development." *Alien Voice: Perspectives on Commonwealth Literature.* Ed. Avadhesh K. Srivastava. Lucknow, India: Print House, 1981; Atlantic Highlands, N.J.: Humanities Press, 1982. 194–209.

Rao, K. I. Madhusudana. "V. S. Naipaul's *Guerrillas*: A Fable of Political Innocence and Experience." *Journal of Commonwealth Literature* 14:1 (1979): 90–99.

Rothfork, John. "V. S. Naipaul and the Third World." *Research Studies* [Pullman, Wash.] 49:3 (1981): 183–92.

St. Omer, Garth. "The Writer as Naive Colonial: V. S. Naipaul and *Miguel Street*." *Carib* [Kingston] 1 (1979): 7–17.

Sandall, Roger. " 'Colonia' According to Naipaul." *Commentary* (Dec. 1983): 77–81.

———. "Two Naipauls: Father and Son: *Journey through Darkness*." *Quadrant* 31:6 (June 1987): 62–65.

Sederberg, Peter C. "Faulkner, Naipaul, and Zola: Violence and the Novel." *The Artist and Political Vision.* Ed. Benjamin R. Barber and Michael J. Gargas McGrath. New Brunswick, N.J.: Transaction, 1982. 291–315.

Simpson, Louis. "Disorder and Escape in the Fiction of V. S. Naipaul." *Hudson Review* 37 (1984): 571–77.

Subramani. "The Historical Consciousness in V. S. Naipaul." *Commonwealth Quarterly* 4:13 (1979): 3–22.

Suleri, Sara. "Naipaul's Arrival." *Yale Journal of Criticism* 2:1 (1988): 25–50.

Swinden, Patrick. *The English Novel of History and Society, 1940–80: Richard Hughes, Henry Green, Anthony Powell, Angus Wilson, Kingsley Amis, V. S. Naipaul.* New York: St. Martin's Press, 1984. 210–52.

Theroux, Paul. "V. S. Naipaul." *Modern Fiction Studies* 30 (1984): 445–54.

Thieme, John. "Authorial Voice in Naipaul's *Middle Passage*." *Prose Studies* 5:1 (1982): 139–50.

Thieme, John. "Naipaul's English Fable: *Mr. Stone and the Knights Companion*." *Modern Fiction Studies* 30 (1984): 497–503.

Thieme, John. *The Web of Tradition: Uses of Allusion in V. S. Naipaul's Fiction.* n.p.: Hansib, 1987.

Wilson-Tagoe, Nana. "No Place: V. S. Naipaul's Vision of Home in the Caribbean." *Caribbean Review* 10:2 (1980): 37–41.

Winser, Leigh. "Naipaul's Painters and Their Pictures." *Critique: Studies in Modern Fiction* 18:1 (1976): 67–80.

Woodcock, George. "Two Great Commonwealth Novelists: R. K. Narayan and V. S. Naipaul." *Sewanee Review* 87 (1979): 1–28.

———. "V. S. Naipaul and the Politics of Fiction." *Queen's Quarterly* 87 (1980): 679–92.

SUNITI NAMJOSHI (1941–)
Diane McGifford

BIOGRAPHY

Suniti Namjoshi was born in Bombay, India, in 1941. As a young adult, she joined the Indian Administrative Service (1964), but was "bored" once she "figured out how to stay out of trouble." Four years later (1968), on leave from the IAS, she did a Master's degree in public administration at the University of Missouri (Columbia, Missouri). In 1969 she resigned from the Administrative Service and moved to Montreal to do a Ph.D. at McGill University. After completing her degree and dissertation ("Ezra Pound and Reality: The Metaphysics of the Cantos," 1972), she accepted a teaching position at Scarborough College, University of Toronto. Namjoshi's first sabbatical (1978–79), spent in London and Cambridge, was a period of political development and political transformation. A few years later, in May of 1987, Namjoshi moved to Devon, England, and in October 1988, she resigned from the University of Toronto. Life as a teacher meant writing between classes and semesters: in Devon, where she presently lives and writes, Namjoshi has both the freedom to write poetry and the burden of living on a poet's income.

Even this cursory sketch of "important" dates manifests Namjoshi's courage, her willingness to abandon comfortable, prestigious positions and make dramatic life changes in order to facilitate personal and artistic growth. One senses a personality who views life as process and discovery and who lives accordingly. As well, courage, braced by self-scrutiny, incisive analysis, and rare frankness, characterizes her political development. Namjoshi has bravely, assiduously deconstructed her social assumptions and named them as privilege, an insight that stimulated her politicization as a feminist and a lesbian. "Coming out," becoming an activist, and the open-mindedness, energy, and commitment that these decisions imply, permeate Namjoshi's highly unorthodox writing, particularly her play with perspectives, her quest for alternate forms, and her fabulist material. As well, feminism and lesbianism make it impossible for her to be a poet of impersonality; indeed, her private, public, intellectual, and poetic lives irreverently intertwine, and any discussion of her life quite naturally spills over into a discussion of her art and ideas. For Namjoshi's art, this policy—the rejection of impersonality and the integration of her various selves into her work—is a sound one, since it has given birth to a genuine poetic voice.

MAJOR WORKS AND THEMES

Suniti Namjoshi's first book of poetry, *Poems*, was published in 1967; still, *Because of India* (Onlywomen Press, 1989), published twenty-two years later, is both a better starting point for a discussion of her writing and an excellent guide to her books. In *Because of India* Namjoshi retrospectively explores the interrelatedness of her life and her work. She combines personal openness with respect for privacy as she explains the development of her sexual politics; critical insight with inside knowledge as she assesses the roles that nationality, family, geography, class, and culture occupy in her art. *Because of India* is structured chronologically and divided into ten sections; each includes poems and/or prose fables from a specific work, and the author's comments on these pieces and on her own life while she was writing them. Sound structure, editorial acuity, and excerpts from all the major works, except *The Mother of Maya Diip*, ensure that all her central themes and their evolution emerge. Even the title and publisher of this book have implications for the body of her writing: India has shaped her perspective and consciousness, but her lesbian-feminist politics are hers, part of her individuality, and her signature on her cultural heritage. She publishes with a women's press because she's a woman and a feminist; she writes as she does "because of India" and because of her sexual politics.

Namjoshi wrote *The Jackass and the Lady* (Calcutta, 1980), in Canada from 1972 to 1976 and revised it in 1980 after her "political" sabbatical in England; from 1976 to 1978 she wrote *The Authentic Lie* (Canada, 1982), her first book published outside India. The revised manuscript of *The Jackass* reflects Namjoshi's political awakening, clear in poems like "And She Wrote Her Poems," "I Give Her the Rose," and "Homage to Circe." *The Authentic Lie*, which struggles with death and the impact of death on a child, is understandably less political. Namjoshi's father was killed in a plane crash when she was eleven, and *The Authentic Lie* is a mature reconsideration of childhood grief, though it includes poems about other aspects of death and the dead.

Neither book examines the immigrant experience or directly addresses the themes one associates with the Indian diaspora. Yet, consciousness and voice in *The Jackass*, particularly the identification with the wholeness of creation, including the world of animals, tie these poems to the culture and traditions of Hinduism, not to the patriarchal thinking of Western Christianity. To date, however, it remains safe to say that Namjoshi exhibits little of the cultural dissociation one expects in the writings of immigrants and that she rarely writes of immigrant experience, though she has, in succession, immigrated to the United States, Canada, and Britain. Judging from published work, the central biographical facts in the production of Namjoshi's art are not the racial discrimination and alienation from culture that haunt so many Indians of the diaspora, but gender, sexual orientation, and politics. Her marginality, her sense of "otherness," springs from her life, in a male-centered society, as a woman, a feminist, and a lesbian.

Feminist Fables (1981) and *The Conversations of Cow* (1985), prose works rather than poetry, propose different perspectives from and alternate realities to those usually sanctioned by Western humanism. In *Feminist Fables* Namjoshi extends the traditional form of the fable, for though her fables teach and have animals as teachers, her lessons usurp the status quo to endorse feminist thought. This combination of formal innovation and radical content generates fresh perspectives and exposes closed systems: her pithy, feminist fables speak with a new voice and coax the reader to the inevitable conclusion that women have been silenced and men have not. *The Conversations of Cow*, less satirical and more fabulation than fable, continues this work. Here the main conversationalist is a goddess who first becomes a cow and then a human with the skill to switch sexes at will. Greenpeace memberships outrank bank cards; scotch-drinking, lesbian cows wonder if they are really like men or more like women. Reality and identity are rearranged to suggest life's possibilities, while the reshaping and reinventing of form—the mixing of novel, fantasy, science fiction, and fable—stress the point that feminist art needs new forms.

Namjoshi's scholarly training, Hindu background, and feminist-lesbian consciousness are all apparent in *From the Bedside Book of Nightmares* (1984). Again the themes one tends to associate with writings of the diaspora—a sense of cultural and social isolation and alienation, the shock and violence of racism, yearnings for the homeland, the difference between expectation and reality—are absent. Namjoshi's response to Western society and culture is her evolving awareness that this patriarchal world prizes white males and regards women, along with the rest of creation, as "other." Like many Indian immigrants to North America, she has resisted the seductive appeal of assimilation into the mainstream in order to give voices to these "others," and while her voices may differ from those of most Indian immigrant writers, she writes in the voices that she hears.

In *From the Bedside Book of Nightmares* Namjoshi hears several voices: in the book's first section, Baby F of "From Baby F with Much Love"; in the middle section, "The Creature," a variety of voices, those of victims and victimizers, observers and participants, women from myth and from contemporary society; and in the final sequence of poems, "Snapshots of

Caliban," those of Caliban, Miranda, and Prospero. The title itself, *The Bedside Book of Nightmares*, is an index to thematic content: here Namjoshi writes of what she calls in *Because of India* "the bloodier aspects of gay and women's liberation" (2), and includes a concomitant theme, the ferocity of human ego. Many of these poems brim with savagery, linking them more to nightmare than reality, and yet in their extremity they comment on what it means to be human and on the social institutions we humans have constructed.

In "From Baby F with Much Love," Baby F, a kind of female Frankenstein, though certainly human enough, views the family from the female perspective. She loves and hates intensely, unrestrainedly, as she strives for her place in an institution that has wounded her, that has demanded girls and women be self-effacing and passive. Eventually Baby's ego subsides and she is reconciled to her mother. This reconciliation is mostly on Baby's terms, an important fact because Namjoshi never denies the necessity of ego; she even implies that Baby's tremendous ego fuels her campaign for individuality and keeps her from becoming another faceless, nameless female. Like "From Baby F with Much Love," "Snapshots of Caliban" reevaluates power politics in the family, examines the struggle between combative egos, and serves as a telling comment on *The Tempest*. Namjoshi's Caliban is female and writes a journal, recording her grief, love, and suspicions; Miranda is sadistic and jealous—one has trouble telling the monster from the maiden. And Prospero, the creator of both Miranda and Caliban, is no wise and benevolent sage, but a doddering, manipulative egotist, disgusted with his unruly daughters and puzzled when they become "sisters." His patriarchal perspective prevents him from understanding their reunion. Family life on this island is mostly nightmare and warfare, and though at times egos declare a truce and share a joke, a hug, even love and a common purpose, the curtain always falls and the nightmare always comes again. Family life is power politics.

Despite the political implications of *The Bedside Book of Nightmares* these poems are neither didactic nor ideologically overbearing, because Namjoshi works through indirection and innuendo, spices her poems with wit and humor, and roots them in specific circumstances—the classical, the literary, the everyday. In "The Reformed Antigone" Antigone's decision to save her own life rather than to bury her brother becomes the basis for revising the old myth and exposing its sexist implications. In "Archetypes" Penelope's nightly unravelling of her day's weaving is neither love, duty, nor virtue; it is healthy rage. Namjoshi assures us that "Virtuous women punish themselves" (20), intimating that Western civilization encourages women to internalize anger, rendering their rage invisible, useless, and personally destructive. But Namjoshi's Penelope is not one of these icons of virtue. A born survivor, she undoes her weaving instead of herself, and so retains her sanity. Once again feminist dissatisfaction with the old myth invites the reader to examine its implications and then consider Namjoshi's alternate myth, one written from Penelope's perspective, with woman at the center rather than in the margin. In *From the Bedside Book of Nightmares*, the revision of myth and the delineation of theme are sustained by Namjoshi's sound craft, exemplified by her control of line, manipulation of punctuation and various kinds of print, intermingling of prose and poetry, and succinct language—all enriched by her germane literary allusions, her wit, and her dexterity with tone. Namjoshi has always written well-crafted poems, and here her accomplished poetics illuminate her political, cultural, and literary perspicacity.

In 1986 Suniti Namjoshi and Gillian Hanscombe jointly published their *Flesh and Paper*, a poetic dialogue, designed to voice lesbian reality and experience in lyrical poetry. *Flesh and Paper* does not distinguish between Namjoshi's poems and Hanscombe's, so a thematic discussion of Namjoshi's work in this text is not possible. Clearly Namjoshi and Hanscombe challenge our notions of writing by breaking with the sacrosanct tradition of individual authorship and by posing the complex question of how one writes liberating verse when using the language of the oppressor. As well, the book shows that Namjoshi's feminist-lesbian perspective is at the heart of her creativity. There is congruency between her life and art. She cannot write lesbian poetry and conceal her sexual orientation; nor can she live as a lesbian and write "straight" poems.

The Blue Donkey Fables (1988), a book of fables, fabulation, and poetry, is populated mostly by animals, tigers, robins, magpies, rabbits, pigs, cats, and monkeys, but dominated by the blue donkey, a clever, companionable beast who writes poems, tells stories, and chats with animals and people. Through her wise, feminist donkey Namjoshi pokes fun at human pretensions, stupidities, and frailties, while her combination of fables written in prose and various poetic forms—most notably the sonnet—produces a stylistically sound and thematically lively work. Her wit spares few of us. Poets, feminists, literary critics, readers, and patriarchs—Namjoshi, as the blue donkey, castigates all of these, some more severely than others. She wants us to reform. In promoting her reformation, she banks on irony and satire, and so moves us to laugh at ourselves, partly to agree with Parrot and Tortoise of "The Creation: Plan B." The animals negotiate a new creation and live happily ever after because their world has no people.

Namjoshi's *The Mothers of Maya Diip* (1989) is a work of prose fiction, stylistically akin to *The Conversations of Cow* in that it combines elements of myth, fable, the novel, science fiction, and fantasy, and reminiscent of *Gulliver's Travels* because it is satirical. Yet while *The Mothers of Maya Diip* mixes various genres and, like its possible prototype, *Gulliver's Travels*, features a medley of satirical devices, the delicacy of Namjoshi's blend produces a new, integrated form, just the brace required in a book where nothing is sacred and where the rules are made up as the narrative proceeds.

In *The Mothers of Maya Diip*, Namjoshi takes issue with at least one facet of contemporary feminism—the dream that a matriarchal world would be a paradise of sisterhood, peace, and goodwill. The world of Maya Diip turns out to be the patriarchy turned upside down; woman is at the center with everything else consigned to the margins, regarded as "other." Male children are milked for their semen and then abandoned under the Tree of Death; those who manage to survive commit suicide in their teens. The matriarchy falls just shy of infanticide, but clearly it, like the patriarchy, depends on the devaluation and suppression of one sex in order to exalt and privilege the other. And distressingly, Maya Diip, like any other state, is intolerant of those deemed deviants. Children, as long as they are female, must be idolized; motherhood is a sacred calling with its own system of hierarchy. The State will brook no questioning of these "self-evident" truths. To question State-sanctioned truth is heresy, and heretics are banished and excommunicated. Maya Diip even has its ruthless, power-hungry sisters: a coup d'état led by the Ranisaheb's daughter provides the backdrop to this study of matriarchy.

Though the pipe dream of a matriarchal Nirvana bears the brunt of Namjoshi's satire, she freely castigates other ideologies and institutions. For example, Valerie, an American expatriate, describes the cultural, political, and personal relationship between the sexes in her homeland, unintentionally explaining why she favors exile in Maya Diip to repatriation. A group of American commandos, who come to rescue Valerie whether or not she wants to be rescued, turn out to be androids whose behavior is disturbingly like that of "normal" men. Paradise in this world is an island populated by adults or "gallants" who worship mothers, but motherhood is a risky business since the cost of adulation is the heavy baggage of romantic adoration. In Paradise nobody wants this responsibility. Still, all is not lost. The name "Maya Diip" has negative and positive meanings, and the "mothers" have some correctives for the intemperate human heart. The abdicating matriarch urges her daughters to go where they are needed and do what they must; she understands that power corrupts all and that even women must square their ideals with reality. In the end we see that community and individuality, common good and individual need are the beginnings of a better society. Here Suniti Namjoshi weds Western feminism to Eastern community, deciding that mix and compromise is our only possible starting point and that the only possible leader is the woman who least wants the job.

CRITICAL RECEPTION

To date the critical response to Suniti Namjoshi's work has been limited to reviews of her books and references to them in broadly based articles on Indians of the diaspora. Reviewers invariably comment on the excellence and elegance of her craft, her stylistic and formal innovations, her feminist-lesbian politics and thought, her psychological insights, her literary allusions, and her deconstruction of tradition. Few note that she is an Indian of the diaspora, and no one has considered the implications this dislocation has for her work.

BIBLIOGRAPHY

Works by Suniti Namjoshi

Poems. Calcutta: Writers Workshop, 1967.
Cyclone in Pakistan. Calcutta: Writers Workshop, 1971.
More Poems. Calcutta: Writers Workshop, 1971.
The Jackass and the Lady. Calcutta: Writers Workshop, 1980.
Feminist Fables. London: Sheba Feminist Publishers, 1981.
The Authentic Lie. University of New Brunswick: Fiddlehead/Goose Lane Press, 1982.
From the Bedside Book of Nightmares. University of New Brunswick: Fiddlehead/Goose Lane Press, 1984.
The Conversations of Cow. London: Women's Press, 1985.
Aditi and the One-Eyed Monkey. London: Sheba Feminist Publishers, 1986.
Flesh and Paper with Gillian Hanscombe. Seaton, England: Jezebel Tapes and Books, 1986: Charlottetown, Canada: Ragweed Press, 1986.
The Blue Donkey Fables. London: Women's Press, 1988.
Because of India: Selected Poems and Fables. London: Onlywoman Press, 1989.
The Mothers of Maya Diip. London: Women's Press, 1989.

Studies of Suniti Namjoshi

Lane, M. Travis. "I and My Creature: Three Versions of the Human." *Fiddlehead* 145 (Autumn 1985): 94–100.
Sawton, Ian. "Pastoral Lines." *Canadian Literature* 97 (Summer 1938): 124–26.
York, Lorraine. "Monsters Within." *Canadian Literature* 105 (Summer 1985): 190–92.
———. "Fluent Shadows." *Canadian Literature* 116 (Spring 1988): 185–87.

PETER NAZARETH (1940–)

John Scheckter

BIOGRAPHY

Peter Nazareth, of Goan ancestry, was born in Kampala, Uganda, on April 27, 1940. His father was born in Goa, and his mother had been born in Malaya to Goan parents: the topics of multiple removes and layered identities figure strongly in Nazareth's writing. He studied in Kampala and at the London School of Economics, and rose rapidly as a finance officer in the Ugandan government. The expulsion of Asians by Idi Amin in 1972 carried exceptional threat for government insiders such as Nazareth, who at the time was a senior finance officer with responsibility for the state lottery. Enduring this personal terror as well as the general hardships of stripped citizenship and invalidated passports, Nazareth was eventually able to leave Uganda with his wife and two children and to take up a fellowship at Yale University. From there, he moved to the University of Iowa to serve in the International Writing Program established by Paul Engle; he has remained in Iowa City, where he is currently professor of English, chair of the African-American World Studies Program, and advisor to the International Writing Program.

Published only nine days before Amin's expulsion order, Nazareth's first novel, *In a Brown Mantle*, directly addresses the quest of Goan identity in Africa (as well as predicting the author's own exile). Nazareth's first-person narrator clearly admires the nationalist, pan-Africanist, socialist definitions of the character Pius Cota; such notions include Asian ancestry among the types of background in the fictional country of Damibia, so that Goans have an automatic definitional inclusion within continental and national identities. Cota's death, however, forces the narrator to recognize that such structures of respect are extremely fragile and that most of the alternative views propose narrow, more divisive definitions of individual and collective identity. Cota's political antithesis, Robert Kyeyune, successfully manipulates ethnic and affiliational loyalties and rises to power in the resulting confusion and violence. By the end of the novel, President Kyeyune has forced Asians into a separatist isolation that he can then exploit as disloyalty; Nazareth's fiction became public policy within a week and a half.

Having experienced the worst misuses of group identification, Nazareth defines himself as an African of Goan ancestry. This description, not lightly undertaken, carries several meanings simultaneously and sometimes contradictorily. The Goan community in Kampala had obvious distinctions from other Ugandans, but had also distanced itself from metropolitan Goa: in the story "The Institute," Nazareth describes how a character sent to Goa for secondary schooling is surprised to discover that Goa embraces a variety of social and economic conditions, that Goans are not inherently middle class. Further, Nazareth's Goan Africans are regarded with suspicion by native Goans, so that a return to past identities seems impossible and self-identification as African becomes a matter of realistic psychological progression. Thus, as in "The Confessor," the diasporic Goan can—but also must—forge an identity not out of historical circumstances but out of current situations. Nor is this condition, the freedom and necessity to claim the precedence of personal negotiation, a presupposition exclusive to the modern diaspora: "The Confessor" and *In a Brown Mantle* claim that Goan history is itself a continuing shift and negotiation of identity, brought about by the Portuguese invasion, promoting Catholicism and *assimilado*, by the Indian takeover, prompting realignments of loyalty and assimilation, and by the wars of Pakistan and China against India, provoking new demonstrations of militance and violence. Thus, identity shifts as Goa itself changes; in the daily round of work and responsibility, of friendship and entertainment, offshore Goans may note resemblances to other former Portuguese colonials, or to their neighbors, more strongly than the pull of a distant speculation upon nationality and ethnicity. In the accounting of these layers of individual circumstance, with the attendant personal responsibility for sorting and reasserting, and in the utter rejection of univocal identifications of group, such as those made by the Ugandan expulsion order, personal identity remains a matter of personal choice. It is not for Idi Amin, then, to determine for Peter Nazareth the relationship between his Goan ancestry and his African nativity. Being African, Nazareth says, is now a matter of claim, taking ancestry into account along with all other factors—including, paradoxically, the recognition that the opportunity to perform his best work as a Goan and as an African is presented while living in the United States.

Foremost among the expanded opportunities of Nazareth's relocation is his work as a teacher and administrator in the International Writing Program (IWP). Unlike the more common workshops in creative writing, the IWP gathers authors who have already achieved some recognition in their home countries, offering residencies of six months to several years for mutual exchange and critical dialogue. The political, social, and cultural benefits of the ongoing convocation are obvious, but participation has several difficult consequences as well: working in an international situation, explaining themselves to an audience that does not necessarily share their assumptions and experiences, posits for the writers an additional problematic layer, a new factor to negotiate within an individual identity. Nazareth, familiar with the many conditions of diaspora, dislocation, and conflicted definition, is central to the ongoing success of the program. Bearing responsibility for facilitating the exchange in all its aspects, he adds a further dimension to the idea of a literary life.

MAJOR WORKS AND THEMES

Despite its high degree of social insight, Nazareth's early critical work, *An African View of Literature*, appears to be an unconnected collection of essays; commentaries on Wole Soyinka and Ngugi wa Thiong'o are among the expected topics, while essays on *Othello* and Jean Anouilh's *Antigone* are refreshingly interrogatory (especially in dealing with Ismene, the survivor of social carnage in *Antigone*). The appearance of disconnection is dispelled, however, when the collection is viewed along with Nazareth's more recent criticism. In such essays as "Bibliyongraphy, or Six Tabans in Search of an Author" and "The Second Homecoming: Multiple Ngugis in *Petals of Blood*," Nazareth finds great value in multiple layerings of voice, synchronous expressions of a variety of psychological and affiliational identities. In the works of Ngugi and Taban lo Liyang, in those of Cyprian Ekwensi, Meja Mwangi, and Bharati Mukhejee, Nazareth as a critic characteristically locates and particularizes the multiplicity of viewpoints that propel the authors' complicated personalities into artistry. The task of the writer, he says, is to trace the frequently unresolvable sources and products of individual and social tension, rather than to indicate monopolar solutions or— having been thus victimized—to find a scapegoat for the world's ills. Literary work is exploratory, tentative, and inconclusive: like the notion of diasporic identity that acknowledges continuing dislocation, a work of literature celebrates not its permanence, its appeal to universality, but the utility of its momentary stance, its crucial ability to engage the moment of its coincidence with an audience.

The concern for multiple and simultaneous layers of meaning is likewise the strongest characteristic of Nazareth's fiction. In "The Institute," characters wonder about their decision to admit African members to the local Goan Institute; obviously, their thinking goes both ways, as they implicitly ponder the degree to which they have been "admitted" to Africa. "Eccentric Ferns" climaxes when the nonconformist Horace Fernandes barges into a Goan Catholic church and delivers a sermon on property and humility. His action is at once that of an odd individual and that of a community in diaspora breaking ties with the rigidities of the home culture; tonally, the story is both troubled and deeply funny. Likewise, in "The Confessor," the storyteller Uncle Ramos describes how he had revenge upon a priest by confessing to a murder—and then confessing to lying. The story is told as a joke during a bout of drinking; again, however, the narrator speculates seriously upon the ways that historical "accidents," such as Portuguese interest in Goa, influence entire realms of thinking, for Ramos acts as a lapsed Catholic and not as the Hindu or Muslim he might otherwise have been.

The first-person narrator of *In a Brown Mantle*, P. D. Joseph D'Sousa, is caught between the broad vision of Pius Cota, attractive but airy, and the cynical confidence of Robert Kyeyune, threatening but attractive. Much of the novel follows a *bildungsroman* pattern, so that D'Sousa's early inquiries into politics and social insight seem as much a part of his growth as his other intellectual and sexual emergences. Political reality—the factor of violence underneath the surface of Kyeyune's speeches—makes futile D'Sousa's attempt to amalgamate the two directions of his attraction: Kyeyune becomes the first president of "Damibia," and D'Sousa, convinced that Asians in Africa have no security except for the immediate favor of the government, chooses exile: " 'Goodbye, Mother Africa,' I said, as the plane lifted off. 'Your bastard son loved you' " (150). His terms indicate closeness and distance, love and heartbreak, urgency and cynicism, all at once and without resolution.

The problems of postindependence Damibia also form the conflict of *The General Is Up*, Nazareth's second novel. Rather than predicting the expulsion as *In a Brown Mantle* does, *The General Is Up* treats it after the fact, describing more concretely and speculating more sharply upon what had become autobiographical material. When, for example, the protagonist, David D'Costa, waits overnight in a long queue to learn whether he has lost his citizenship, his vision works ceaselessly upon the panorama of the street. He ruminates, as the line passes an automobile showroom, upon the subculture of *wabenzi*, the middle classes so eager to acquire and display Benz cars and other trappings of Western materialism; he wonders whether the recent victims have miscalculated the resentment building against them and whether they have in part brought trouble upon themselves. That may be so, but the trouble quickly moves beyond the redress of inequality: the sequence ends with D'Costa overhearing the story of a friend's murder, the proof being that a police official now drives the man's car. D'Costa also wonders about his own part, whether his love for Damibia and his loyalty to the government are merely manifestations of self-interest (he concludes that they are not); he worries that Indians, having spread so widely, are now condemned to be the most visible remnant of colonialism after the Europeans have departed. Finally at the end of the line, "wordlessly" informed that he is now stateless, D'Costa marvels at the human capacity for cruelty and, at the same time, at the converse capacity for survival.

The General Is Up was published in a limited form by the Writers Workshop of Calcutta in 1984; it was republished in 1991. Several chapters have appeared in journals, and several have been translated widely: the work appears to shed light upon the nature of dictatorship and political repression in a wide variety of forms and locations.

CRITICAL RECEPTION

While Nazareth's works have not received critical focus on their own—a situation that will change with the wider publication of *The General Is Up*—they form a consistent part of critical surveys of East African and Indian diasporic writing. O. R. Dathorne, for example, includes Nazareth among a group of writers he considers "optimistic"; Jeremy Poynting, in unpublished remarks, is more specific in placing *In a Brown Mantle* among novels that do not rely upon racial distinctions to formulate their social criticisms.

Nazareth's own statements offer the best explanation of his work to date. The most extensive of these is the national survey "Waiting for Amin" in G. D. Killam's *The Writing of East and Central Africa*. *In a Brown Mantle*, Nazareth notes, so accurately described the interplay of social forces in Uganda that it appeared to predict both the coup that brought Amin to power and the later expulsion of Asians. Prominent among these forces is the failure of the general population to recognize the actual motives of the rulers—urges for power and wealth—which lie beneath their rhetorics of invidious nationalism and ethnocentrism. "The novel ends as it begins, with an assassination and coup attempt to protect certain business interests inside and outside the country" (14). In this context, *The General Is Up* continues the analysis, tracing the economics of colonial and postcolonial exploitation "back to all its homes (including England and the United States)" (25), but reserving much of the blame for African leaders who rush to ingratiate themselves with international business interests at the expense of serving their people.

Martin Tucker's encyclopedia entry quotes at length from a correspondence with Nazareth, in which the author relates his publishing history and reaffirms his African identity.

BIBLIOGRAPHY

Works by Peter Nazareth

An African View of Literature. Evanston: Northwestern University Press, 1974. First published as *Literature and Society in Modern Africa*. Nairobi: East African Literature Bureau, 1972.

In a Brown Mantle. Nairobi: East African Literature Bureau, 1972.

"The Institute." *Dhana* 4:1 (1974): 65–69.

The General Is Up. Calcutta: Writers Workshop, 1984; revised edition, Toronto: Toronto South Asian Books, 1991. Chapters 11–12 in *Pacific Quarterly Moana* 4:2 (1979): 159–66.

"Eccentric Ferns." *Short Story International* 19 (1980): 127–32.

"The Confessor." *Short Story International* 28 (1981): 151–57.

"Bibliyongraphy, or Six Tabans in Search of an Author." *The Writing of East and Central Africa*. Ed. G. D. Killam. London: Heinemann, 1984. 159–76.

"Waiting for Amin: Two Decades of Ugandan Literature." *The Writing of East and Central Africa*. Ed. G. D. Killam. London: Heinemann, 1984. 7–35.

"The Second Homecoming: Multiple Ngugis in *Petals of Blood*." *Marxism and African Literature*. Ed. Georg M. Gugelberger. Trenton: Africa World Press, 1985. 118–29.

Studies of Peter Nazareth

Dathorne, O. R. *African Literature in the Twentieth Century*. Minneapolis: University of Minnesota Press, 1975.

Elder, Arlene A. "Indian Writing in East and South Africa: Multiple Approaches to Colonialism and Apartheid." *Reworlding: The Literature of the Indian Diaspora*. Ed. Emmanuel S. Nelson. Westport, Conn.: Greenwood Press, 1992. 115–39.

Tucker, Martin. "Peter Nazareth." *Literary Exile in the Twentieth Century*. Ed. Martin Tucker. Westport, Conn.: Greenwood Press, 1991. 508–10.

UMA PARAMESWARAN
(1941?–   )
Diane McGifford

BIOGRAPHY

Uma Parameswaran was born in Madras but raised in Nagpur and Jabalpur in India. She attended schools and universities in India, but in 1963 when she was awarded a Smith-Mundt Fulbright Fellowship, she traveled to the United States in order to study American literature at Indiana University. She completed her M. A. degree, with a thesis in creative writing in 1964, and this same year began doctoral studies at Michigan State University. In 1972 she was awarded her Ph.D. from Michigan State. Uma Parameswaran moved to Winnipeg, Canada, in 1966 and the following year joined the Department of English at the University of Winnipeg, where she continues to write and teach. Her special teaching interests are Commonwealth literature and creative writing. She has, as well, worked to develop the Women's Studies Program at the University of Winnipeg and has a reputation in both the academic and the broader community as an advocate of women's rights and equality.

Uma Parameswaran is a scholar and a creative writer. In addition to numerous scholarly articles, she has published three books of literary criticism, *A Study of Representative Indo-English Novelists*, *Cyclical Hope Cyclical Pain*, and *The Perforated Sheet: Essays on Salman Rushdie's Art*. Her poems, stories, and plays have appeared in several journals, magazines, and anthologies, and in her two books, *Trishanku* (1988) and *The Door I Shut Behind Me* (1990). Her literary plan for the future include the publication of a collection of poems, provisionally titled *Of Women, I Sing*. Uma Parameswaran's commitment to poetry and women is exemplified by her membership in the editorial collective of *Contemporary Verse II*, a feminist poetry journal. Her commitments to multiculturalism and to her Indian heritage are exemplified in her community activities, particularly her role as founder, producer, and host of the weekly television program PALI (Performing Arts and Literature of India).

MAJOR WORKS AND THEMES

Uma Parameswaran's writing is, in one sense, a reaction to the Indian diaspora, particularly the experiences of South Asian Indians in Canada, and more specifically in Winnipeg, the city where she has lived since 1966. Her play *Rootless But Green Are the Boulevard Trees*, first published in 1979 and reprinted in *The Door I Shut Behind Me* (1990), and her sequence of poems, *Trishanku* (1988), are both set in Winnipeg, and a seasoned Winnipegger certainly senses Winnipeg in the title story of the collection *The Door I Shut Behind Me*. These three explore the lives and experiences of Indian immigrants as they struggle with the painful and bewildering task of adjusting to and claiming their new land. Most Canadians are immigrants and, therefore, the themes and motifs of Uma Parameswaran's work are no surprise to students of Canadian literature. As an immigrant she is profoundly Canadian. Yet Parameswaran writes of these same events with important, necessary, and delightful difference, a difference that has its origins in the rich cultures and traditions of her homeland.

"The Door I Shut Behind Me" (a short story that won the 1967 Lady Eaton Award) introduces Uma Parameswaran's saga of thematically related, intergenerational and intertextual immigrant experience. The story begins in "The Door" with Chander's departure from India, moves through a crisis in the communal lives of the Bhave family from *Rootless But Green Are the Boulevard Trees*, and ends in *Trishanku* when Savitri Bhave, briefly joined by her husband Sharad, is suspended above her city, becoming a kind of mystical purveyor, a Trishanku, caught upside down between heaven and earth. *Trishanku* concludes in quiet triumph, with Sharad assuring Savitri that their children, all the immigrant children, will be "okay." The parents may be suspended between past and present, between homeland and country of adoption, but the children will be free to claim Canada as their own. They can wear Canadian clothes and speak Canadian English without accents; India is not their home but a place to discover things about themselves; they may be pulled but they will not be torn. In *Rootless But Green* Jayant, of an age when young men repudiate their fathers' values, mocks Sharad Bhave's hopes that Canada will give his children the environment necessary for dignity and spirituality. *Trishanku* implies that Jayant was wrong to laugh and Sharad right to dream. By the end of this long poem the family and community trees are beginning to take root in Winnipeg, and the reader cognizant of "shut doors," now sees that new ones are open. This theme of reconciliation is enriched by Uma Parameswaran's adeptness in transforming the everyday voice into poetry and ordinary activities into mythic experiences. She pushes the reader to see that time and space are artificial constructs that can be overcome when we carry our gods within us. Like the characters in *Trishanku*, the reader comes to understand why a Hindu Temple can arise at the confluence of Red and Assiniboine rivers and how the Ganga can be brought here. *Trishanku* assures us that when the sacred infuses the profane, all times and spaces are equal.

One of the obvious strengths of Uma Parameswaran's writing is her ability to blend modern experience with traditional myths and stories. Not only does this conflation of sacred and secular bring power and conviction to her work and elucidate her beliefs, but, as well, the incision of Hindu myth broadens the literary map of Canada by allowing this mythology to join with Norse, Greek, Roman, and, of course, Christian. All become part of the Canadian mosaic. Uma Parameswaran is a firm believer in multicultur-alism, in the theory of unity through diversity; she envisions a day when the reader will take references to Krishna and Shakti in stride and find them as unnerving as those to Jesus and Mary. Uma Parameswaran insists on her cultural heritage, not because she disavows the one she found here, but because it is hers; because she trusts that a union of Eastern and Western traditions will reconcile her people to Canadian society and enhance its culture.

Uma Parameswaran's two major works, *Rootless But Green Are the Boulevard Trees* and *Trishanku*, share themes and certain characters. The former focuses on a single family and the latter widens the focus to embrace a range of characters—an entire immigrant community—and to explore its varying responses to expatriation and its stages of adaptation to the new homeland. *Rootless But Green*'s primary interest is the younger generation, the Bhave children, and their struggles: the complexities of interracial re-lationships, especially those between men and women; the painful reality of racism; the sense of feeling rootless, caught between parents and main-stream culture. Different characters have different perspectives and register different ideas. One believes that romantic love will overcome cultural di-vergence and send racism packing; she seems to change her mind as the play proceeds. One angry young man would fight bigotry with fire, while another outwardly ridicules his father's values and inwardly hungers for the traditions that his family has left in India. The light shines on the younger generation; still, one of the adults, Veejala Moghe, precipitates the play's central crisis. Veejala, a gifted astronomer, is fed up with the low academic standards and the various bigotries of Canadian universities. Her decision to abandon her family and return to India where she will receive respect from colleagues and the challenge of worthy academic research shocks her family-loving brother for one reason and the complacent Canadian for another. This nice bit of irony does exactly what Uma Parameswaran in-tends: raises the consciousness of Canadians by telling them that immigrants, far from coming empty-handed, bring intelligence, education, and expertise with them.

At the end of the play conflict and tension are temporarily put to rest as the Bhaves share a meal with their sister-in-law Veejala and her soon-to-be-deserted children. Veejala is not much of a cook, but she does the best she can and orders pizza for everyone. As the extended family sit down to eat—they are planning to do this as the final curtain falls—one sees eating together as communion, as being together, as confirmation of family solidarity. Throughout the play Savitri and Sharad Bhave have nurtured and sustained their children, their children's friends, and Veejala's brood. Savitri and Sharad love one another, and their love makes their home a refuge and a haven for their personal and communal families. Uma Parameswaran suggests that the mainstay of the younger generation, its source of strength and renewal, is that most traditional and most valued of Indian institutions, the family. Furthermore, this modern family, Eastern but also informed by Western ideas, will support *all* family members, even those who forsake traditional roles in pursuit of individual goals. When Veejala leaves for India, she will carry Savitri's blessing with her.

In *Trishanku* Uma Parameswaran adds a number of characters in order to flesh out the extended Bhave family and construct a representative East Indian–Canadian community, one that includes immigrants of both sexes, of all ages, of varying periods of time in Canada, from many professions and vocations, at different stages in the process of adaptation, and from different backgrounds and cultures in the mother country. By developing the character of the community more than individual character or characters, Uma Parameswaran makes the community her protagonist. Here community outweighs individuality or, to put it another way, individuality is possible only in a strong community. Yet Uma Parameswaran does not abandon the individual. In fact, her method and structure in *Trishanku* are perfect vehicles for articulating individual memory, experience, and desire. *Trishanku* is a series of monologues, spoken by different characters; some voices recur, others do not; all gather richness and meaning from each other; each monologue is a poem in itself; each is part of *Trishanku*. This pastiche of voices is a celebration of the community's human resources and its individual manifestations. Structure and form, then, suggest the interrelatedness of community and individual life. And we hear these voices as authentic because Uma Parameswaran has almost a faultless ear for idiom.

The range of experience that Uma Parameswaran addresses in *Trishanku* is extensive, and it too suggests the interdependence of individual and community. Childbirth and child-rearing, education, love, marriage and family, death, even poetry: these experiences are made concrete, brought to life by the individuality of the speakers. Nor do these experiences fall on deaf ears; they are made real because the community—the listeners inside and outside the long poem—hears the voices. Perhaps Uma Parameswaran's finest achievement is this: she ends the isolation and silence of her immigrant people by giving them a place and voice in Canadian literature.

Trishanku, with its epic questions, invocation of the muse, gods and mythic qualities, shares much with the epic, including the epic's final note of arrival and reconciliation. At the end of *Trishanku* one senses that Uma Parameswaran has blessed her people and now she will let them go. Transplantation is complete; cross-fertilization is a distinct possibility. Uma Parameswaran's promise to publish a second collection of poems, *Of Women, I Sing*, marks a new stage in her artistic development. Judging from works like the haunting elegy "Vigilance," her voice will continue as passionate, as intense, as unifying as the flame that lights that poem.

CRITICAL RECEPTION

Uma Parameswaran's writing has been widely reviewed and discussed in India, but though she has a coterie of supporters in Canada, Canadian critics have not yet given her work the attention it merits. Her writing has been studied in broadly based critical articles on the writings of the diaspora or the work of South Asian Canadians, and *Trishanku* has received positive reviews in Canada. As South Asian Canadian writing continues to blossom, one hopes that academic and popular critics will broaden their focus and give serious critical attention to writers who, like Uma Parameswaran, are members of this minority group. It is time to acknowledge their contribution to Canadian literature.

BIBLIOGRAPHY

Works by Uma Parameswaran

Trishanku. Toronto: Toronto South Asian Review (TSAR), 1988.
The Door I Shut Behind Me: Selected Fiction, Poetry and Drama. New Delhi, Madras, Bangalore, Hyderabad: Affiliated East-West Press, 1990.

Studies of Uma Parameswaran

Rustomji, Roshni. "Travelers Between Cultures," *TSAR* 7:2 (Winter 1989): 86–92.

RAJAGOPAL PARTHASARATHY
(1934–   )
Terence Diggory

BIOGRAPHY

Rajagopal Parthasarathy was born August 20, 1934, in Tirupparitturai, Tiruchirapalli District, Tamil Nadu. He learned Tamil as his mother tongue, Sanskrit as the sacred language of his Brahmin caste, and English as the privileged code of his social class. For a while he attended a Hindi school in Bombay, where his family had moved, but for the most part his early schooling was in English, at Don Bosco High School (1944–51), where the English and Irish priests also inspired in him a love of English literature. World War II interrupted Parthasarathy's education at Don Bosco, and he returned to Tamil Nadu to live with his grandmother. Here he began his formal study of Tamil in a *pātacālai*, or traditional school, and cemented his attachment to legendary features of the southern Indian landscape, including the river Kaveri, which surrounds the island of Srirangam where he lived. Parthasarathy looks back on this period of his life as "Edenic" ("Whoring" 65). "You cannot stop thinking of Srirangam" is the first line of a recent poem.

After taking degrees in English literature at Bombay University (B.A., 1957; M.A., 1959), where his writing was encouraged by the Marathi poet Vinda Karandikar, Parthasarathy remained in Bombay as lecturer in English at Ismail Yusuf College (1959–62) and Mithibai College (1962–63), the latter also the employer of the Indian poet Nissim Ezekiel. Since 1956 Parthasarathy's poems had been appearing in such journals as *Quest, Miscellany*, and *Literary Half-Yearly*, with a breakthrough occurring in 1962, when both the *Times Literary Supplement* and the *Review of English Studies* printed his work.

The next year brought a turning point in Parthasarathy's relation to the English language, when he traveled to England as a British Council Scholar and discovered to his chagrin that he must remain an outsider to the nuances of the language as it was spoken in its native environment. England itself seemed lacking in the romantic aura that Parthasarathy's reading had attached to it. Nevertheless, he remained for the year to complete a postgraduate diploma in English studies at Leeds University, writing "A Linguistic Study of the Poetry of Dylan Thomas" under the direction of the English poet Geoffrey Hill. Returning to India in 1964, Parthasarathy took up a series of positions in teaching and publishing, married in 1969, and sought to reorient himself to his Tamil heritage in the light of his disenchantment with England. He was aided in this quest by an assignment to Madras as regional editor of Oxford University Press–India from 1971–1978, after which a promotion to the position of editor removed him to New Delhi.

A major focus of Parthasarathy's quest for self-definition was the attempt to assemble his poems into a book. As he began this project, he found encouragement in the appearance of Nissim Ezekiel's *The Exact Name* (1965) and A. K. Ramanujan's *The Striders* (1966). As Parthasarathy recalls, "Poems like 'Night of the Scorpion' [Ezekiel] and 'Small-Scale Reflections on a Great House' [Ramanujan], by their vision of an everyday Indian reality expressed in an unobtrusive personal voice, stood out in the reader's mind as signposts indicating the direction [Indian] poetry in English was likely to take in the future" ("Whoring" 74). Parthasarathy contributed to the charting of that direction through influential prose statements such as "Whoring after English Gods" (1970) and the introduction to his anthology *Ten Twentieth-Century Indian Poets* (1976). Finally, Parthasarathy found a satisfactory shape for his poetry by combining his previous work into one long poem, *Rough Passage* (1977). That book, a runner-up for the Commonwealth Poetry Prize, has gone through four printings.

In 1982 Parthasarathy left India for the United States, where he had previously spent a year (1978–79) as writer in residence at the International Writing Program of the University of Iowa, Iowa City. The occasion for the later journey was Parthasarathy's entrance into the Ph.D. program at the University of Texas at Austin. His dissertation, completed in 1987, was a study and translation of the Tamil "Epic of the Anklet," the *Cilappatikāram*, since revised for publication. Residence in Austin enabled Parthasarathy to continue his association with the novelist Raja Rao, an important practitioner in prose of the "Indianization" of English that Parthasarathy has sought to achieve in verse. In 1986 Parthasarathy joined the English Department of Skidmore College in Saratoga Springs, New York, where he currently lives with his wife and two sons.

MAJOR WORKS AND THEMES

Rough Passage is unquestionably Parthasarathy's major work, and exile is its dominant theme. In the published version, the book is divided into three parts headed "Exile," "Trial," and "Homecoming." Each part consists of eight or more sections, most of which Parthasarathy has published elsewhere as separate poems under individual titles. In *Rough Passage* however, they are identified only by number. The various forms in which the poems originally appeared have been altered to accord with the uniform pattern of *Rough Passage*: a loose line of two to four beats; unrhymed stanzas of three lines each; anywhere from two to fourteen stanzas grouped together to form a section. This uniformity reinforces Parthasarathy's assertion, in his brief preface, that *Rough Passage* "should be considered and read as one poem." It promises to grow along with the poet's experience. Two sections ("Trial" 15 and "Homecoming" 15) were added to the second impression (1979), and a major new revision is currently in preparation.

"Exile," written between 1963 and 1967, announces the book's theme by exploring the disillusionment Parthasarathy felt during his sojourn in England. The title of Parthasarathy's essay "Whoring after English Gods," expressing his bitter reaction against his previous infatuation with things English, is a phrase from one of the sections in this part ("Exile" 2). Other sections reflect Parthsarathy's wanderings through various cities—Bombay, Old Goa, Madras, Calcutta—upon his return to India. The sense of alienation remains. The colonizers seem to have left their mark everywhere, not only on the landscape, but also on the very consciousness of those represented by the poem's persona: "that uneasy class of Anglicised Indians," as Parthasarathy calls them, in whom colonialism has fostered values foreign to their cultural inheritance ("Whoring" 698). As specific as this condition is, Parthasarathy manages also to universalize the alienation he depicts by pointing to similarities in his experience of cities, whether English or Indian. Collectively they form an image of the "Unreal City" evoked as a sign of the modern condition by T. S. Eliot in *The Waste Land* (1922).

The subsequent parts of *Rough Passage* respond in several ways to the problem set forth in "Exile." "Trial," which includes the earliest work and spans the longest period of composition (1961–74), dwells intimately on relations between men and women, as if to reaffirm the human bonds threatened by the impersonality of the city. On another level, "Trial" works toward the goal announced by Parthasarathy in "Whoring after English Gods": to renounce his love affair with the English language and devote himself to Tamil as his bride ("Whoring" 71). Although still written in English, "Trial" reflects a tradition of erotic poetry in Tamil, a tradition ancient and distinctive enough to be traceable as an influence in the Song of Songs in the Hebrew Bible, according to the scholar Chaim Rabin. "Homecoming," written in Tamil Nadu between 1971 and 1978, imports "the essence of Tamil mores" ("The Exile as Writer" 9) into English-language poetry by other means: by evoking places central to Tamil culture, like the city of Madurai and the river Vaikai; by weaving the dense network of family relationships typical of southern India; and even by imitating certain syntactical structures common in Tamil—though this last strategy is less insistent than it is in other experiments such as Raja Rao's embedding of Kannada syntax in the English of *Kanthapura* (1938). A final device that Parthasarathy avowedly takes over from Tamil literature is its typically ironic voice, which in "Homecoming" he turns against Tamil culture itself. The language has been debased by the popular film industry, and the Vaikai, like the Passaic River in William Carlos Williams's *Paterson*, has been reduced to a sewer. If the end of *Rough Passage* celebrates a "Homecoming," Parthasarathy has no illusions that his house is in order.

To the extent that *Rough Passage* is linked to its author's life history, its further evolution has been considerably complicated by Parthasarathy's decision during the 1980s to take up residence in the United States. Though he would seem to have gone back into exile, he told an audience in Saratoga Springs that "I feel more at home here than I ever did in England. The Adirondack is a distant cousin of the Himalaya, and everytime I step into Lake George it is the waters of the Kaveri I hold in the palm of my hand. The English language here has a more pungent flavor contributed by languages as remote from one another as Armenian and Zuni. The Americans, unlike their English cousins, are innocent of the nostalgia of empire, and have altogether done away with history" (Reading at Skidmore College, February 20, 1991), whereas in England, "history caught up with me" ("Whoring" 66).

The assertion that Americans have done away with history needs to be taken with a healthy dose of Tamil irony, but as a statement of Parthasarathy's goal, it may be taken at face value. While as a Tamil Parthasarathy seeks to reexamine history, to sink roots deep into his culture's past, he also understands that, as a writer, "it is in exile that [he] is most at home" ("The Exile as Writer" 2). In the revised version of *Rough Passage* now in preparation, the third part, now simply called "Book Three" rather than "Homecoming," moves toward conclusion by recalling a conversation in Austin, Texas, with Raja Rao and the Caribbean novelist Wilson Harris. The moral for writers is that "the word must absolve the object" in order to free the mind from time. That freedom, a state of metaphysical withdrawal such as Indian ascetics have traditionally sought, is imaged in the next section by the snows of Saratoga, whose cleansing power eventually, in the last two sections of the poem, flows into the waters of the Kaveri and the Ganga. Through such dissolves of imagery, Parthasarathy once again broadens the meaning of exile and discovers a home within it.

CRITICAL RECEPTION

Most of the abundant criticism of Parthasarathy's work falls within a domain defined by Parthasarathy himself, both in his poetry and in his own critical statements in prose. The possibility and desirability of Indian verse in English are central issues in most discussions. Critics point to the accomplished craftsmanship of Parthasarathy's verse as indisputable evidence that it is possible for an Indian poet to master English as his medium. On the other hand, Parthasarathy's "Whoring after English Gods" has frequently been read as questioning whether the poet who seeks such mastery only exacerbates his alienation from his native culture. Parthasarathy has since denied that he intended his declared commitment to Tamil to entail a complete renunciation of English (Paniker 10), which has remained his primary language of composition, the bulk of his work with Tamil being confined to translation. Finally, some critics have questioned whether the poet's choice of language is a problem to the extent that Parthasarathy claims. Especially for the generation of Indian writers born since independence, English can be accepted as "just one of the languages in which they happen to be proficient," not peculiarly as the language of the colonizer (Deshpande 28).

The introduction to Parthasarathy's anthology *Ten Twentieth-Century Indian Poets* has aroused lively debate centering on two related claims, that "poetry should from the beginning aspire to the condition of silence" (11) and that lack of verbal resonance is an advantage for the Indian poet writing in English (9). Both of these claims reflect the ascetic project that critics of *Rough Passage* have tended to overlook, since it emerges more clearly in the as yet unpublished revision of *Rough Passage* as well as in Parthasarathy's recent essays on Raja Rao. Arvind K. Mehrotra, a poet of a younger generation, argues against Parthasarathy in favor of another direction, toward greater engagement with rather than a self-conscious distancing from the particulars of experience. Ujjal Dutta and Bijay Kumar Das warn against the aspiration to silence as in the undoing of Parthasarathy's practice unless he broadens the scope of his verse. Brijraj Singh finds it ironical that Parthasarathy would maintain the ideal of a language without resonance while his poetry itself resonates in the work of other writers of Indian English verse. Because of his role in shaping that tradition, Singh argues, "R. Parthasarathy is one of the most significant of contemporary Indian English poets, not only for what he has written, but also for what he represents" (49).

BIBLIOGRAPHY

Works by Rajagopal Parthasarathy

Ed., with J. J. Healy. *Poetry from Leeds.* Calcutta: Writers Workshop, 1968.
"Whoring after English Gods." *Perspectives.* Ed. S. P. Bhagwat. Bombay: Popular Prakashan, 1970. 43–60. Rpt., rev.: *Writers in East-West Encounter: New Cultural Bearings.* Ed. Guy Amirthanayagam. London: Macmillan, 1982. 64–84.

Ed. *Ten Twentieth-Century Indian Posts*. Delhi: Oxford University Press 1976; 11th imp., 1990.

Rough Passage. Delhi: Oxford University Press, 1977; 4th imp., 1989.

"Tradition and Creativity: Stylistic Innovations in Raja Rao." *Discourse Across Cultures: Strategies in World Englishes*. Ed. Larry E. Smith. New York: Prentice Hall, 1987. 157–65.

"*The Chessmaster and His Moves*: The Novel as Metaphysics." *World Literature Today* 60:4 (1988): 561–66.

"The Exile as Writer: On Being an Indian Writer in English." *Journal of Commonwealth Literature* 24:1 (1989): 1–11.

Studies of Rajagopal Parthasarathy

Das, Bijay Kumar. *Perspectives on the Poetry of R. Parthasarathy*. Bareilly, Uttar Pradesh: Prakash Book Depot, 1983.

Deshpande, Gauri. "R. Parthasarathy." *Contemporary Indian Poetry in English*. Ed. Saleem Peeradina. Bombay: Macmillan, 1972. 21–36.

Devi, G. N. "The Two Faces of Alienation: The Poetry of A. K. Ramanujan and R. Parthasarathy." M.A. thesis, Leeds University, 1979.

Dutta, Ujjal. "Tension into Poetry: R. Parthsarathy." *Indian Literature* (New Delhi) 26:1 (1983): 88–95.

Iredale, R. O. "R. Parthasarathy: Images of a Poet." *tenor* (Hyderabad) 1 (1978): 84–92.

Jussawalla, Adil. "The New Poetry." *Readings in Commonwealth Literature*. Ed. William Walsh. Oxford: Oxford University Press, 1973.

King, Bruce. "And Return: Parthasarathy and Jussawalla." In King, *Modern Indian Poetry in English*. 2nd ed. Delhi: Oxford University Press, 1989.

Mehrotra, Arvind K. "The Emperor Has No Clothes." *Chandrabhāga* (Cuttack) 3 (1980): 12–28; and 7 (1982): 1–32.

Nagarajan, S. "R. Parthasarathy." *Contemporary Poets*. Ed. James Vinson and D. L. Kirkpatrick. 5th ed. New York: St. Martin's Press, 1988.

Paniker, K. Ayyappa. "The Parthasarathy Passage: An Interview with the Poet." *tenor* (Hyderabad) 2 (1979): 6–24.

Singh, Brijraj. "The Achievement of R. Parthasarathy." *Chandrabhāga* (Cuttack) 3 (1980): 49–74.

Sivaramkrishna, M. " 'That Last Refinement of Speech': The Poetry of R. Parthasarathy." *Contemporary Indian English Verse: An Evaluation*. Ed. Chirantan Kulshrestha. New Delhi: Arnold-Heinemann, 1980. 250–71.

Walsh, William. "Poetry: Ezekiel, Parthasarathy, Kolatkar, Ramanujan and Others." In Walsh, *Indian Literature in English*. London: Longman, 1990. 125–158.

ESSOP PATEL (1943–   )

Cecil A. Abrahams

BIOGRAPHY

Essop Patel was born in 1943 in Germiston, South Africa, an industrial town close to Johannesburg. Patel observes that his birth was "near a gold mine dump . . . in a room at the back of my grandfather's shop" (Interview with Jane Wilkinson, University of Rome, 1989). Patel recalls, "I spent many school holidays at my grandparents' home often on a fig tree by the loo. I also explored the ridges and contours of the gold mine dumps and I was fascinated by the headlamps of the miners emerging from the darkness of the earth covered in yellow dust" (Interview with Jane Wilkinson).

Patel's paternal grandfather came from India and worked as a dishwasher and hawker before returning to India to seek a wife. On his return to South Africa, he established a small business in Germiston and later Van Reenan, a town on the border of Natal and the Orange Free State. Patel's father later inherited the Van Reenen shop. Patel received his first schooling in Germiston and soon learned about the cruelties of apartheid. As he says: "Elsewhere a child is socialised at a tender age but in South Africa a child of colour is politicised whilst he is sucking lollies" (Interview with Wilkinson). Later, Patel was transferred to Ladysmith, where he boarded with friends of his parents. It was in this tiny village that he explored the lush, green hills and cool mountain streams, and collected ferns from the black soil. As he says, "It made me aware of the splendour and beauty of my country" (Interview with Wilkinson).

After completing high school, Patel deliberately chose not to attend an apartheid postsecondary institution but moved to England in 1962. Here he lived and worked for many years until he pursued an honors law degree at the University of London. While in London, he befriended the exiled South African writer and journalist Nat Nakasa, and later collected this writer's work in the book *The World of Nat Nakasa* (Raven Press, 1975).

Patel did the same for the work of Can Themba (Raven Press, 1985), another well-known South African writer, and with Tim Couzens he coedited *The Return of the Amasi Bird* (Raven Press, 1982), a collection of poems by black South African writers.

Patel began his own writing while he lived in London. His early poems were published in journals such as the *Classic, New Classic, Staffrider,* and *Ophir.* Patel's first collection of poems, *They Came at Dawn,* was published in 1980. This was followed by *Fragments in the Sun* (1985), and *The Bullet and the Bronze Lady* (1987). Essop Patel lives in Johannesburg, where he practices law and is an active participant in the work of the Congress of South African Writers. He is married and has two children.

MAJOR WORKS AND THEMES

Essop Patel's living experiences both in South Africa and England reflect strongly in his themes. As a member of the oppressed black population he has to contend with the suffocating and all-embracing reality of apartheid. Because he sees himself to be at the center of apartheid's draconian laws and has the articulate and imaginative gift of being able to interpret his people's suffering, much of his poetry deals with the brutality of racism. His first major work, *They Came at Dawn,* is dedicated to the oppressed who are struggling against their oppressors to seek their liberation. Hence, in a poem like "How Long," the poet wonders when "the black-green-gold sunrise" (the colors of the African National Congress and liberation) will appear. In "The Earth Speaks Our Thoughts," Patel laments the unbearable pain of ugliness and destruction that the Earth must suffer because of the cruel dislocations of people. A poet brought up in the soft, green verdant hills of Ladysmith, Patel is always caught up in observing the Earth and being jarred by the ugly presences that have been created artificially. This power of observing nature shows itself well in poems such as "Barbed Wire Silence."

Patel's work is largely concerned with people, sometimes individuals, who have been brutalized by racism but who have nevertheless refused to cower to the tyrants. A poem such as "Behold the Pain, Brother" emphasizes the fact that life emerges painfully; this pain becomes a necessary element in the oppressed learning that only they can liberate themselves. A theme that can lend itself easily to sentimentality is handled with astute poetic sensibility. The poet understates rather than boldly declares, and even when he uses the hounding image of the hog, he quickly reins it in to concentrate on his chief image of enchainment.

Patel is never morbid or one-track minded. With the glint of his mischievous eye, he thrives on the stupidity of racism. Thus his poems on Haanetjie not only realize his aim to be critical of the "master race," but show up the silly and stupid behavior of the Afrikaners. Using the peculiar

South African dialogue of mixed English and Afrikaans, Patel pokes fun at Haanetjie's rural background and her inability to function in the more sophisticated city. Regardless of her boorishness, Haanetjie is convinced that being white is the only thing that matters.

Patel's roving eye, like a social worker, takes him through the various ghettos of South Africa. In one poem he concentrates on a lady with a red saree in Durban. The lady fascinates the poet because she appears daily to drop a coin in the old beggar's can, and then she disappears in her arabesque loveliness only to return the next day. There is no mystery in the behavior of the "Bronze Lady of Vrededorp." She is a prostitute, but she trades her wares with grace and her beauty is not merely physical.

Patel thrives in his use of depressing imagery and thought juxtaposed with hopeful images and declarations. What strikes him about "Limehill," one of the depressing areas to which blacks have been removed, is the side-by-side presence of graceful flowers and rotten fruits, hungry dogs and tired children. In this hell of a place the children are using the barbed wire to make armored cars and the rotting planks to carve guns.

In the title poem of the collection, "They Came at Dawn," Patel makes reference to the all-too-common scene in apartheid South Africa of the fascist security police rudely awakening suspected inhabitants in the early morning hours to search their homes and to arrest them. This poem is peopled with uniformed police in trucks who, after asking questions, leave with "the flimsy evidence of poetry written on a dry leaf." South Africa's fascist system shows through clearly when the police recognize that the pen is mightier than the gun. But Patel juxtaposes this depressing thought with "The Universal Song" of hope that the children of tomorrow will indeed succeed in creating a free and democratic South Africa.

The collection *They Came at Dawn* contains several poems that were written while Patel lived in England. But even in these poems his status as an exile in a foreign land is underscored. In Brockwell Park, London, he ignores the landscape around him and thinks nostalgically of his home south of Johannesburg. And even when dreaming, Patel traverses new territories, nursing his nostalgia for home. Not only does the poet sustain his interest in his homeland, but the same fervor and beliefs that Patel holds for South Africa are displayed when he attacks the Americans for violating the Vietnamese people.

Patel's second collection of poems, *Fragments in the Sun*, contains both poems by Patel and a performance text compiled by Patel, Bhekizizwe Peterson, and Benjy Francis. The poems in this collection are directed in a very focused way at the struggle for the liberation of the South African people. There are some wonderfully conceived images and metaphors propelling the ideas of lament and hope. The section titled "At the End of the Night" is especially significant. After the long journey of pointing to the struggle and humiliation of the oppressed, Patel's feelings culminate in shouts of joy. Whether in romantic or patriotic love the bruised hand of the lover is prepared to take the "Dark Rose" and break the curfew of unjust laws so as to enjoy the love of a woman and of a country. For, as Patel points out, beyond the dehumanizing walls of apartheid lies hope. Convinced that liberation will come at dawn, after the long night of struggle, Patel can hear the cry of freedom everywhere.

As if to sum up all his feelings and thoughts regarding oppression inside and outside South Africa, Patel dedicates five poems, "Sand in the Eleventh Hour Glass," to the great Cuban revolutionary Che Guevera. These poems must rank among the best and maturest poems Patel has written, and they help to establish him as an important writer in South Africa. The poems combine deep feeling with forthright thought, and the direct statements regarding injustice and oppression throughout the world do not ring false. Moreover, Patel demonstrates clearly that his final aim is not black consciousness but human consciousness. In his short lifetime, Guevera lived a life of revolutionary fervor that captured the imagination of all oppressed people. In the eleventh hour, Patel recounts the history of human oppression where the powerful people have labelled the oppressed people "coolies coons kaffirs calibanis" and have for centuries deceived and distorted the truth. In a cry of battle, Patel calls upon the oppressed to reject all the lies.

In characteristic fashion, this poem of rejection is followed by a poem of love. Patel sees himself to be a preacher of love. He claims that even as he writes about hateful happenings, the other side of the coin is to love those who do not understand their behavior. In remembering the many incidents of hate levied against the oppressed, Patel mentions the anguish of displaced Palestinians; the children blown to pieces in a church in Birmingham, Alabama; the global conspiracy in Biafra; and killings in Bangladesh, Sharpeville, and Soweto. It is against all of these brutal incidents that Che Guevera rose and rallied the oppressed. His message then, and now, is that this is not the hour for tears and regrets. This is, in fact, the moment of resistance that will birth a new dawn.

No matter how far Patel's mind and emotion traverse, his final thoughts are always on his own homeland. In the powerfully apt and vivid images of sound and light Patel sees vividly the birth pangs of a new day all over the world, but especially in Angola, Zimbabwe, and Namibia. The last shooting stars of freedom are reserved for South Africa; in the final section of the collection, Patel joins two other creators to sing songs of liberation and to create dances and visual images of freedom.

Essop Patel's third collection of poetry, *The Bullet and the Bronze Lady*, was published in 1987. For many of Patel's admirers this is his most important collection to date. Since the collection contains poems dating back to 1968, we have here a veritable journey of the poet's mind. Thus, for example, in the poem "Exile's Return," the poet, in a Wordsworthian copy, nostalgically travels across his land. After seven years away from his homeland, he still finds himself at the end of the poem "weeping for" the destruction of his country. Hence in a 1979 poem in memory of the Soweto uprising of 1976, Patel recollects the bullets that maimed and killed children.

The themes of defiance and liberation that have preoccupied Patel in his earlier collections continue but somewhat less stridently in his third volume. In "Tormentors of our Dreams," he calls upon the oppressed not to be afraid of the police who terrorize them at night in their own homes. In the poem "On the Green Hill," Patel does not lament the unnatural death in detention of Imam Haroon. Instead, he foresees the day when all the prisoners held on the notorious Robben Island will be set free, and then the Imam, who fought against oppression, will be buried on the hill amid the eternally blooming roses. And Patel returns again to the prediction that the struggle will end, and children of the future age will live a life of hope and freedom.

The section "Poetic Miscarriage" continues Patel's criticism of the functioning of the apartheid society. However, here he is less declaratory and more ironic. This more relaxed focus extends Patel's poetic ability. The themes are, of course, more localized, but the observations will hold the attention of the South African audience. In the two poems "Who-Zhit Elections" and "The Right Honourable Abuselingumjie Speaks," Patel deals with the absurdity of Indian and "Coloured" elections and those who seek election to a segregated parliament. He demonstrates clearly that such representatives are interested in their own gain and that they have no difficulty in supporting the apartheid system.

In this collection Patel returns to his Haanetjie poems. Haanetjie, as we discovered before, is an Afrikaner girl wrapped up in the cloak of apartheid's stupidity and brutality. Although Haanetjie has a "spoorweg" (railway) mentality, she is white and she votes for the ruling party. In several of the poems on the Haanetjie theme, Patel pokes fun at the girl's naïveté and her loyalty to practices she has not tried to understand. Although there are parts that are comical, the Haanetjie poems are on the whole weak and irrelevant.

The Bullet and the Bronze Lady is the most experimental of the collections. Since the poems span almost two decades in time, there is less unity in this collection. Many of the poems are impressions of visits or facile studies of individual concerns. Patel does best when he writes seriously about the struggle for liberation. His need to seek comic relief in a furnace-hot country is laudable. However he seldom manages to convey that sense of lightheartedness and comedy to his readers.

Patel's chief theme in his work is the struggle of oppressed South Africans to free themselves of the shackles of apartheid and to envision a new dawn free of racism. Although South Africa has undergone some important change in the past year, the road to a new dawn is filled with obstruction. It is this road, peopled with the discarded and disadvantaged of society, that must continue to interest Patel. For it is here that his significance as a poet in South Africa will be sorely needed.

CRITICAL RECEPTION

When Essop Patel published his first collection of poetry in 1980, *They Came at Dawn*, James Matthews, a well-known South African writer, hailed Patel as "a new voice" (1) in the chorus of poets (Foreword, *They Came at Dawn*). Later in the same "Foreword," Matthews argues that although Patel's poetry may be termed "protest poetry," "it is never cliche-ridden"(3). After Patel published his second collection in 1985, *Fragments in the Sun*, his book received an honorable mention in the NOMA awards competition. For the last few years Patel has read from his work both at conferences overseas and at gatherings inside South Africa. All of this should indicate that Patel's work is quickly being paid attention to. It is predictable that, with the sophisticated progress Patel has made as a poet, his writings will in the not too distant future become the object of critical study.

BIBLIOGRAPHY

Works by Essop Patel

They Came at Dawn. Athlone: Blac Publishing House, 1980.
Fragments in the Sun. Johannesburg: Afrika Cultural Centre, 1985.
The Bullet and the Bronze Lady. Johannesburg: Skotaville Publishers, 1987.

Studies of Essop Patel

"Creativity Itself Is an Act of Life." *Fragments in the Sun*. Johannesburg: Afrika Cultural Centre, 1985; vi–viii.
Matthews, James. Foreword. *They Came at Dawn*. Athlone: Blac Publishing House, 1980, v.
Wilkinson, Jane. "Essop Patel." London: University of London School of Oriental and African Studies, (unpublished manuscript) 1989: 1–37.

RAYMOND C. PILLAI (1942–)
Srimati Mukherjee

BIOGRAPHY

Born on August 30, 1942, Raymond C. Pillai hails from an Indo-Fijian family of schoolteachers, a family that came to Fiji during indenture. Pillai spent his childhood years in Fiji, and in the early 1960s his comic sketches were published in *Tharunka* in Sidney. Toward the end of the sixties, Pillai played a key role in fostering the development of creative literature in the South Pacific. The late 1960s saw several promoters of creative literature at the University of the South Pacific (USP). Pillai led the *Unispac* (the student newspaper at USP) group with Ata Ma'ai'i and Vanessa Griffen. He contributed fiction to *Unispac* in the late sixties and early seventies. In 1971, in an article in *Unispac*, "Individual Development vs. National Development: Creativity vs. Utility," fourteen undergraduate students, inclusive of Pillai and Griffen, critiqued the current educational policy at USP. Claiming that the English curriculum tended to be utilitarian, they called for the promotion of creativity. Eight years later, in his paper "Prose Fiction in Fiji—A Question of Direction," presented in Adelaide, Pillai indicated that the USP's attempts at promoting creative writing had been, at best, half-hearted. In 1973, Pillai became a member of the South Pacific Creative Arts Society and subsequently published several works in *Mana* magazine. Graduating with a bachelor's from the University of the South Pacific, Pillai worked on his master's at Southern Illinois University, Carbondale. His master's thesis, entitled "Fiji Hindi as a Creole Language," was submitted to the Department of Linguistics at Southern Illinois University, and Pillai graduated with a master's degree in 1975. Returning to Fiji, he coedited, with Ruth Finnegan, the collection *Essays on Pacific Literature*, which was published in 1978. In 1980, Pillai's *The Celebration: Collection of Short Stories* was published by Mana and the South Pacific Creative Arts Society.

Pillai coauthored, with Jeff Siegel, the experimental play *Adhura Sapna* (1988) in Fiji Hindi. Following the military coup in Fiji in 1987, Pillai left Fiji and currently resides in New Zealand.

MAJOR WORKS AND THEMES

Raymond Pillai has to his credit some early poems, namely "Labourer's Lament" and "To My Foster Mother," published in 1974 and 1976 respectively. The former voices the apprehensions of the Indian in Fiji, a figure who, Pillai believes, is discriminated against as an alien. The latter reiterates the theme of discrimination, closing with the possibility of violent retaliation by Indians.

Soon after the publication of this early poetry, the focus of Pillai's interest shifted to prose, resulting in *Essays on Pacific Literature* (1978). This collection, edited by Ruth Finnegan and Raymond Pillai, comprises essays written by students at the University of the South Pacific as part of their regular course work. As the introduction to the volume points out, the essays collectively emphasize that our understanding of the word "literature" should include its oral manifestations and its noncanonical components. The essays engage in discussions of both oral and written literary forms in the South Pacific. The introduction further notes that the essays are marked by the authenticity of the insider's viewpoint, the authors generally having addressed the literatures of their respective cultures. However, these same authors exhibit the power of detached analysis, a skill fostered by their university studies (2). According to the introduction, the contributors highlight the contemporary relevance of older literary forms. In accord with the essayists on this issue of current relevance, the editors refer to the enactment of the Indian drama described in the essay by Shaista Shameem, suggesting that the performances of such "dramatized myths" in Fiji "explain and remind people of their original Indian heritage—their ancient Indian culture, their gods and their religion" (6). In the essay "The Performance of an Ancient Indian Drama on the Night before the Fire-Walking Ceremony at the Howell Road Temple, Suva," Shameem speaks of the dramatization of an episode from *The Ramayana*, a dramatization that originally occurred in India. However, the author also states how the drama has incorporated local elements to enhance its appeal for a Fijian audience (53). This idea of the preservation and modification of heritage, in a diasporic context, becomes the major theme of Pillai's *The Celebration: Collection of Short Stories* (1980).

The pieces in *The Celebration* address, in varying degrees, the general persistence of Indian practices and beliefs in transplanted contexts. However, in a few stories, Pillai does not hesitate to show how dogmatic notions can be quickly outgrown and stereotypical thought patterns reversed, frequently with exposure to highly Westernized cultures such as Australia or the United States. The dynamics of the collection is enhanced by the fact that even while a few Pillai characters lament the forfeiting of elements of the native Indian culture, the author himself indicates how some of these elements have lost their validity in non-native environments. The collection, therefore, becomes, in its entirety, an expression of a mind capable of presenting the many-faceted nature of the diasporic experience.

The survival of Indian customs is seen in "Brief Skirmish," a story set in Fiji, which mentions the perpetuation of Indian festivities such as Rakshabandhan and Diwali and depicts the heroine's acquiescence to the tradition of arranged marriages. In a second story, "Muni Deo's Devil," which again has Indian characters but Fiji as milieu, Moti Lal and Ragini's marriage is preceded by implications of interregional tension characteristic of India, the tension being a consequence of the fact that the bride and groom are from the south and north of India respectively. At the opening of "A Matter of Conscience," apprehension about whites seems limited to the Indian protagonist's elderly mother, but by the close of the story, this prejudice has manifested itself in the young, educated hero, thereby showing the stubborn, deep-rooted nature of these beliefs.

The theme of arranged marriages, only touched upon in "Brief Skirmish," receives more extended and complex treatment in "To Market, To Market ...," a tale that once again dramatizes the enduring of Indian practices in Fiji. At the end of the story, the mother, Mrs. Kundaswami, implies through her comment that the family will be unable to find husbands for the two younger daughters after it has been revealed that the eldest daughter, Meena, has entered her arranged marriage carrying the child of a lover who has abandoned her. Mrs. Kundaswami says to her husband, who seems averse to condemning Meena and is, therefore, in his wife's understanding, insensitive to the implications of the situation, " 'It isn't easy to arrange a decent marriage nowadays. You can't treat your daughters like cattle to be sold in the market. We women have our pride too, you know' " (43). The comment, which is ironic to say the least, boomerangs on the mother, for it is not the father who treats the daughters like salable commodities. The father sees no point in persecuting Meena, a victim of male infidelity and the repressive system of arranged marriage. Rather, it is the mother who seems oblivious to Meena's pain and is concerned only with upholding this Indian institution of marriage and the supposed propriety associated with it.

The tenacity with which Indian immigrants or their descendants cling to native customs is depicted also in the title story, "The Celebration," in which Rama's attempt to flout the conventional abstinences associated with mourning is met with almost unqualified resistance from his family. A later story in the collection, "Laxmi," addresses the persistence of Indian notions in a foreign setting albeit not with grim overtones as in the above-mentioned two stories. The story indicates that even if material well-being for Raju, the hero, has not resulted from the yearly lighting of the lamps at Deepawali in homage to the goddess Laxmi, the marital happiness of Raju and his wife is a consequence of the presence of the goddess in their house. The story closes with a characteristic Indian suggestion of divine presence and benediction.

However, even if numerous pieces in *The Celebration* illustrate the continuing prevalence of traditional Indian thought patterns and practices in Fiji, a few stories portray how these native beliefs and customs lose their significance in transplanted environments. In "The Funeral," for instance, the incongruity of certain Indian burial rites in a non-native milieu strikes Edward, the grandson who has flown in from Sidney to attend his grandmother's funeral in Fiji. Pillai records the impressions as they register themselves on Edward's consciousness. Edward says of his grandmother, "She lay there, an odd improbable figure, decked out as a bride in accordance with some old Malayalam Christian custom" (24). For Edward, this old funeral rite has lost its efficacy, not only because he is of a different generation, but because he is aware of the vacuity and meaninglessness that often pervade native customs in foreign contexts. The above quote implies that the custom is unfamiliar to Edward, that, in fact, it has lost its currency from general neglect and stands out more as a singularity than as the norm. Hence, for Edward, it creates dissonance rather than adding to the significance of the funeral process, as does the attempt of the Irish priest to say the Lord's Prayer in Hindi during the burial. The English script distorts the Hindi pronunciation, detracts from the intensity of the prayer, and adds to the incongruity of the situation. "The Funeral" underscores that the uncompromising perpetuation of these Indian customs, out of their native habitat, only builds an atmosphere of discomfort. Yet older generations of Indians attempt to preserve their culture in a foreign land.

In a story such as "Preliminary Inspection," the heroine Savitri's father, who is a resident of Fiji, mourns the neglect of the Indian culture by the younger generation. A felt sense of loss emerges in his conversation with Gopal, his daughter's suitor. Yet his tone is also caustic as he feels educated young Indians are indifferent to this loss. However, "When in Rome..." clearly demonstrates the inaccuracy of such generalizations, simultaneously showing how deeply embedded notions must occasionally yield to the demands of expediency and adaptability. In the story, the Fiji-Indian student, Ray, holds apparently unwavering notions about sexual liberty between couples and is initially amazed and affronted by the promiscuity and permissiveness he notices among American students in Illinois. He tries to uphold the inherent Indian beliefs about sexual reserve, but ultimately capitulates to Peggy, a liberated American. He moves in with Peggy and finally decides to marry her. Hence Pillai presents a story that illustrates the deep significance of native values, but one that also dramatizes how such values must occasionally undergo modifications in new, and very changed, circumstances. To a certain degree, "When in Rome..." burlesques extreme ideological stances in transplanted contexts. For instance, toward the middle of the story, Ray's dismay and unreasonable anger at realizing that he has spent the night in a drunken stupor in Peggy's apartment seem disproportionate to the actual seriousness of the event. The situation is perfectly acceptable in most Western cultures, and Peggy's laughter seems more in place than Ray's outrage.

A more concentrated emphasis on interculturalization is evident in "Bride of Dakuwaqa," one of the later pieces in *The Celebration*. The story's Fiji-Indian protagonist, Madhawan, is a refreshing departure from Indian males, in earlier mentioned stories such as "A Matter of Conscience," who have been inoculated with stereotpyical myths about the heartlessness of Western women. Reflecting on the severance of emotional ties with his Australian friend Holly, Madhawan feels, "How civilized they were, these white folks! They could enter into the most intensely personal relationships, and then retreat without recriminations. So refreshingly different from Indian women who went all lachrymose and hysterical" (101–2). For Madhawan, therefore, the diasporic experience is not a rigid adherence to inherent native beliefs, but an opportunity for exposure to other modes of thought, action, and reaction. Madhawan shows a heartening readiness to know the options afforded to him by cultural diversity and to evaluate those options rather than be blindly judgmental. As a result, he acquires the unprejudiced largeness of vision that enables him to see the maudlin and the melodramatic in his countrywomen, just as it empowers him to recognize the strengths of their Western counterparts.

However, the movement toward inter-exploration of cultures can also be noticed on a far more implicit level in "Bride of Dakuwaqa." The title of the story refers to a Fijian oral myth in which Dakuwaqa, the shark god, falls in love with a Fijian girl who spurns him. In anger, Dakuwaqa kills the girl but then, the legend goes, periodically returns to a spot near the banks of the Sigatoka River, driven by the desire to be reunited with his lost beloved. Pillai's story reenacts this myth, and through the figure of Holly unites its original orality with the more contemporary literateness of Holly's culture. In a masterful climax, Holly, who has spent a considerable part of her professional life in attending conferences and befriending poets, gives herself up to a deadly shark at exactly the spot where Dakuwaqa is said to periodically return. Thus, Pillai figuratively suggests that a large degree of self-effacement by the literate may be necessary before it can appreciate the merits of orality. With the shark's consuming of Holly, "Bride of Dakuwaqa" ends with the symbolic triumph of the oral, the story being a strong artistic manifestation of current and increasingly emergent emphases on marginal forms of literature.

CRITICAL RECEPTION

Critics have responded to Pillai's writings in ways that seem sharply divergent, and this lack of general critical consensus may be partly exemplified by positing the views of Shaista Shameem against those of Stan Atherton. In her feminist critique of some Indo-Fijian short fiction, Shameem, speaking of *The Celebration*, refers to Pillai's "limited perceptions" of women (34). This, according to Shameem, results in inauthentic women characters and the perpetuation of a "male supremacist ideology" (35), as in "Muni Deo's Devil." In contrast to this view may be presented Atherton's praise of Pillai's portrayal of women in *The Celebration:* " 'Muni Deo's Devil' and 'The Celebration' sensitively explore the difficulties of a woman's position in a male-dominated society" (73). Shameem, addressing Pillai's "To Market, To Market . . . " and the system of arranged marriage delineated in it, further writes, "the unfortunate reality is that while the bartering of women is presented as fact, as indeed it is, Pillai's approval of this state of affairs is obvious" (36). At the close of the above story, however, Pillai's satirical tone renders it impossible to ignore his strong denouncing of "the bartering of women," and one would tend to agree with a critic such as Atherton, who notes Pillai's sensitive depiction of women. Atherton, however, does not fail to point out that *The Celebration* being a first collection, "some of the stories are contrived and even occasionally clichéd" (73). One of Pillai's fellow Fiji-Indian authors, Subramani, however, underscores that this contrivance may be partly intentional. According to Subramani, Pillai's characters generally move in a "relatively unambiguous moral universe in which there seldom are dilemmas of moral choice" (10). His characters are "reasonable human beings, seldom given to excess," and "when they err there is the author's irony which works towards reconciliation" (10). Speaking of recurrent patterns of conclusion in Pillai's stories, Subramani rightly notes that the narratives invariably "end with an adage or ironic comment that has the effect of giving them the rounded impression of the *exempla*" (10). Even while recognizing the deliberate crafting in Pillai's fiction, however, Subramani regrets the fact that Pillai "continues to work with the already exhausted forms of the *fabliau* and the *exemplum* without any apparent shift towards the regeneration of these forms" (13). But Vijay C. Mishra, claiming that Pillai's writings represent an endeavor to move beyond the pain and fragmentation endured by Indians during indenture in Fiji (402), argues the relevance of such formalistic repetitiveness. Speaking of Pillai's persistent use of the form and style of the fable, Mishra writes, "given the strong allegorical potentiality of the Fable, these stories, in their overall structural organization, tend to suggest that such a narrative technique is itself an attempt on the part of the Indo-Fijian writer to impose meaning over chaos" (403). However, ultimately it is left to Pillai's reader to weigh the merits of such therapeutic repetitiveness against the possibility of structural monotony.

BIBLIOGRAPHY

Works by Raymond C. Pillai

"Labourer's Lament." *Some Modern Poetry from Fiji*. Ed. Albert Wendt. Suva: Mana, 1974. 10.

"To My Foster Mother." *Mana Review* 1 (1976): 17.

Finnegan, Ruth, and Raymond Pillai, eds. *Essays on Pacific Literature*. Fiji Museum Oral Tradition Series 2. Suva: Fiji Museum, 1978.

The Celebration: Collection of Short Stories. Suva: Mana and South Pacific Creative Arts Society, 1980.

Pillai, Raymond, and Jeff Siegel. *Adhura Sapna: A Play in Fiji Hindi. Language Transplanted: The Development of Overseas Hindi*. Ed. Richard K. Barz and Jeff Siegel. Wiesbaden: Harrassowitz, 1988. 221–25.

Studies of Raymond C. Pillai

Atherton, Stan. Review of *The Celebration*. *International Fiction Review* 8 (1981): 73.

Manoa, Pio. "Across the Fence." *The Indo-Fijian Experience*. Ed. Subramani. St. Lucia: University of Queensland Press, 1979. 184–207.

Mishra, Vijay C. "Indo-Fijian Fiction: Towards an Interpretation." *World Literature Written in English* 16 (1977): 395–408.

———. "Rama's Banishment: A Theoretical Footnote to Indo-Fijian Writing." *World Literature Written in English* 19 (1980): 242–56.

Shameem, Shaista. "The Art of Raymond Pillai, Subramani and Prem Banfal: A Feminist Critique of the Indo-Fijian Short Story." *SPAN: Journal of the South Pacific Association for Commonwealth Literature and Language Studies* 20 (1985): 29–46.

Subramani. "Short Fiction in the South Pacific." *New Literature Review* 9 (1981): 7–15.

BALACHANDRA RAJAN
(1920–   )
Uma Parameswaran

BIOGRAPHY

Balachandra Rajan was born to Arunachala and Visalam Thyagarajan on March 24, 1920, in Toungoo, Burma. His father (who abbreviated his name to A. T. Rajan) was a member of the civil service which, at the time, spanned Burma as well as undivided India. Balachandra Rajan was educated at Presidency College, Madras, and, like Krishnan, the hero of his first novel, continued his studies in England. He was an exceptionally bright student at Trinity College, Cambridge, where he was the first Indian to receive a fellowship in English. He received his B.A. in 1941, M.A. in 1944, and Ph.D. in 1946, and continued at Cambridge as lecturer in modern poetry. From 1948 to 1961 he was a member of the Indian Foreign Service. As a diplomat he had various postings; among the more significant were his tenure in New York as advisor to the Permanent Mission of India to the United Nations and as chairman of the Executive Board of UNICEF (1955–57), and in Vienna as the resident representative of India to the International Atomic Energy Agency (1957–59). Subsequently, he reversed the sequence of careers that he charts out for Krishnan and turned from diplomatic service to an academic career. He was on the faculty of Delhi University from 1961 to 1964, during which time he was dean of arts for a year (1963–64). For a year after that he was visiting professor at the Institute for Research in the Humanities, University of Wisconsin. In 1966, he joined the faculty of the University of Western Ontario in Canada, and has been there ever since.

Rajan is primarily an eminent scholar and literary critic. He is the author of several acclaimed books of literary criticism including *Paradise Lost and the Seventeenth Century Reader* (1947); *W. B. Yeats: A Critical Introduction* (1965); *The Lofty Rhyme: A Study of Milton's Major Poetry* (1976); and *The Form of the Unfinished: English Poetics from Spenser to Pound*

(1985). He is the founder and editor of *Focus* and editor of three collections of essays on Milton.

He has received numerous honors and awards, including citation as Honored Scholar of the Milton Society in 1979, Chauveau Medalist of the Royal Society of Canada in 1983, and fellowship in the Royal Society of Canada. He has been professor emeritus since 1985, and continues to teach graduate courses. His reading list for the course "Discourse and Dominance: India in English Literature" shows his emphasis on integrating a historical sense (but not mere chronicling) into any study of literature. His view of literary sensibility is comprehensive and eclectic, as seen in the inclusion not only of literary and historical texts but also philosophical texts in his reading list.

Rajan has published two novels, *The Dark Dancer* (1958) and *Too Long in the West* (1961). *The Dark Dancer* has been translated into German, Swedish, and Yugoslavian.

He married Chandra Seshadri Sarma on August 29, 1946: Chandra is a poet and translator; they have a daughter, Tilottama, who is a professor of English. In person, Rajan is soft-spoken; the restraint and intense introspection that characterize V. S. Krishnan in *The Dark Dancer* are noticeable in the author. Krishnan returns home to India a day earlier than scheduled because he "was anxious to avoid the clusterings and the insanities" (*DD* 2). So also with Professor Rajan. Students are somewhat awed by his monumental scholarship. An expatriate most of his life, he has captured the highs and lows of this experience in his novels. One wishes he would turn again to fiction and write a novel in Canada as "cold and passionate as the dawn," to adapt William Butler Yeats's words, as *The Dark Dancer* is in its Indian setting.

MAJOR WORKS AND THEMES

Rajan has written only two novels but together they show the potential range of his expertise. *Too Long in the West* is a hilarious comedy, a spoof of the absurdities in Indian and American social codes, and of the foibles and eccentricities of individuals. Everyone and everything is caricatured and made an occasion for laughter. *The Dark Dancer*, on the other hand, is an intense story of the self-division and maturation of an individual and of a nation, of the cyclic phenomenon of fratricidal war.

In light of more recent Indo-English fiction, in its parallel plotting of an individual's life and a nation's life, *The Dark Dancer* develops a motif that has since been used by Salman Rushdie in *Midnight's Children* (1981) and Shashi Tharoor in *The Great Indian Novel* (1989). Whereas Rajan ends his novel with a reference to the epic battle of Kurukshetra, Tharoor uses the epic as a structural device for retelling India's recent history. Whereas Tharoor highlights the treacheries and bloodshed of the fratricidal war and says there was no glorious victory at Kurukshetra, Rajan sees its message transmitted in the blood consciousness of a people—that Kurukshetra was not and never shall be fought in vain.

India's historical moments parallel key moments in Krishnan's life. The day in Delhi that he meets Cynthia, with whom he has been in love during his stay in England, is the day of the Rawalpindi carnage, a day of foreboding that sets a pall of inevitability. The battle of Kurukshetra is waged within Krishnan with the same intensity and destructiveness as it was being waged in the country moving toward independence. After his wife Kamala dies while doing volunteer work in the strife-torn village of Shantipur, Krishnan reaches a metaphysical understanding of the philosophy propounded in the *Bhagavad Gita* that one should pursue righteous action for its own sake and not for the fruits thereof. The novel ends with Krishnan walking "back slowly to the strength of his beginning" (*DD* 308), as did India toward freedom and a new birth.

The predominant images in the novel are the *gopuram* and the Dark Dancer. Just as the diaspora of scholars fleeing from the Turkish onslaught of Constantinople carried literary treasures that gave rise to the European renaissance, the Indian diaspora has carried into English literature the central symbols of Hinduism. The dancer is Nataraja, lord of dance, who in Hindu iconography wears a snake (coils of Time) and stands with his right foot on demon ignorance, and his left foot and arms raised in the dance of creation and dissolution, "all that infinite power of destruction drawn back into the bronze circle of repose" (*DD* 28). The *gopuram* is the four-sided pyramid built above the gates of temples and above the inner sanctum. For Rajan, it symbolizes lonely but steadfast defiance. It is symbolic of man, for each human being at the core is a thrust of earth in an alien and unfriendly environment, "however blunted...upheld unyieldingly from the obstinate earth, the blunted thrust giving aspiration, solidity and earthiness" (*DD* 166). The stress of the blunted top, unlike the pointed spire of Western architecture, is significant. The enmity of the sky and environment exerts ceaseless pressure on the lonely, upthrust (a favorite word with Rajan) tower, but a *gopuram*-like individual resists the pressures and stands on, lonely, defiant, beautiful.

Such a person is Kamala. Whereas Krishnan's commitment to Cynthia is made and stays at the physical level, his commitment to Kamala is made at a spiritual-sensual level. The bronze figure of Nataraja that Kamala carries away with her to Shantipur is symbolic of the essence of the Dance; Krishnan's affair with Cynthia thereafter becomes a blind alley. He follows Kamala to Shantipur and once again sees the Dancer, who as he watches, raises him "to the mystery's center" (*DD* 225). Through the ensuing trauma of communal bloodshed, sacrifice, and bereavement, Krishnan slowly becomes aware of his Brahmin heritage; through Kamala's silent strength, he learns something about Indianness and the sense of belonging for which he has yearned all his life.

The yearning to belong recurs time and again in the writings of the diaspora. Earlier Indian critics often spoke about not-belonging as something that came with the territory for all those who chose to write in English rather than a regional language. Of this controversy, Rajan has said, "Though the writer in English is taunted with having chosen exile, there is a turbulence that all of us must move through in order to move anywhere" (in *Literatures of the World in English*, ed. Bruce King, 81).

Too Long in the West, in tone and theme, is the opposite of the first novel. It is a combination of Stephen Leacock and Mark Twain and P. G. Wodehouse: funny, lighthearted, and mildly satirical. The novel is a fantasia woven around an assemblage of parents, suitors, and rustics, set in a monstrosity of a house in the remote recesses of a range of barren hills. For nine months of the year, the father, Sambasivan, is a potbellied, henpecked professor who has long emptied his rooms and his mind to their bare essentials; but every summer he becomes a minor god ruling benevolently over the rustics of Mudalur. The four suitors who come in response to his matrimonial advertisement for his daughter, Nalini, are also eccentric, each in a different way. Through them, Rajan satirizes not only the rigmarole of a system where marriages are arranged by parents, but he also satirizes different kinds of people, and Indian-English quirks such as omitting articles or having a superabundance of them. One of the suitors speaks in babu offcialese: "You are author of advertisement in Hindu of fourteenth ultimo? Indicating availability of daughter, presumably virgin?" (*TLW* 27). An American joins the race for Nalini's hand because, being American, he just cannot pass up a chance for competition. While Rajan satirizes American consumerism, he extols American education. Nalini, during her sojourn at Columbia University, learns to speak in her own voice, unlike one of the suitors who has made it his life's purpose to imitate the great masters.

Both novels show protagonists who have lived a long time in the West, but not too long. They are the richer for having lived in the West, for their sojourn has helped them gain a better appreciation of their own heritage.

CRITICAL RECEPTION

The Dark Dancer was received very favorably in Britain and the United States. It was the first book by an Indian to be made the Book Society's choice of the month (Markandaya's *Nectar in a Sieve* and Malgonkar's *The Princes* came later). However, literary critics in India were unbelievably harsh.

It is interesting to note that Rajan's hallmark of scintillating prose has come under fire more often than any other quality of his writing. Frederic

Morton calls his "lyric way with words" "an uncertain blessing" (6). David McCutchion is surprised that the critic of *Paradise Lost* and editor of *Focus* would publish the novel under his own name "because of the astonishing insensitivity to language that it reveals" (21). C. D. Narasimhaiah calls his prose style "mannered," "a wash basin in one's flat" rather than the river (15). Such negative criticism has come only from his Indian critics, perhaps because he is compared to R. K. Narayan, who excels in the simplicity of everyday speech, and to Raja Rao, whose prose style is like a river in flood. The fact is that Rajan's prose style is consistent with his characters. Krishnan is a very sensitive, intellectual, and snobbish individual, and he speaks like one.

Too Long in the West was hardly noticed within or outside India. This neglect, I have reason to believe, is what has dissuaded Rajan from continuing as a novelist.

Balachandra Rajan's name is recognized in the annals of Milton and Eliot scholarship, but his contribution to the literature of the Indian diaspora remains unacknowledged.

BIBLIOGRAPHY

Novels by Balachandra Rajan

The Dark Dancer. New York: Simon and Schuster, 1958.
Too Long in the West. London: Heinemann, 1961.

Studies of Balachandra Rajan

McCutchion, David. "Le Style C'est L'Homme." *Writers Workshop* (May–June 1961): 20–21.
Morton, Frederick. "New Truth, Old Values." *New York Times Book Review* (June 29, 1958): 6.
Nandakumar, Prema. "The Achievement of the Indo-Anglian Novelist." *Literary Criterion* (Winter 1961): 18–27.
Narasimhaiah, C. D. "Why This Animus?" *Literary Criterion* (Summer 1966): 15–16.
Parameswaran, Uma. Chapter IV of *A Study of Representative Indo-English Novelists.* Delhi: Vikas, 1976.

RAVINDER RANDHAWA
(1952–   )
Jogamaya Bayer

BIOGRAPHY

Ravinder Randhawa was born in India in 1952 of Sikh parents. Her father had left for England soon after she was born, and the family joined him there when she was seven. Relatives on both sides had emigrated, and the concept of migration had always been a part of the context in which she grew up.

Randhawa received a degree in English in 1973 from the Polytechnic in London. From 1975 to 1976 she worked as a teacher, and from 1976 to 1977 for the civil service. Until 1984 she was a development worker for an Asian women community workers' group that set up refuges and resource centers for Asian women. Currently, Randhawa is married and lives in London. After the birth of her two children, she took a break from writing. Now she has taken up writing again and considers herself to be at the beginning of her literary career. Randhawa's first published work, a short story called "India," was published in the anthology *More to Life Than Mr. Right* in 1985. In 1987 her short story "Sunni" came out in *A Girl's Best Friend*. In the same year her first novel, *A Wicked Old Woman*, was published and has since been translated into Italian and Spanish. In 1988 four short stories appeared in the anthology *Right of Way*, which was edited by the Asian Women Writers' Collective. Randhawa was a founder member of this London-based group that was established in 1984, originally on the initiative of Randhawa herself, who also gathered financial support.

MAJOR WORKS AND THEMES

Having grown up reading books and watching films in which the Asian/ black characters always played demeaning roles, Randhawa decided to make her main characters Indian because she thinks that they are the most interesting. She also makes them women because they have to contend with sexism in addition to racism. However, she believes that it is not enough to show the characters merely as victims. So in her depiction of women growing up in a hybrid culture, her characters strive constantly for new values and for a new way of life. In some of Randhawa's writing, adolescent immigrant women play the key roles. Their experience of restrictions in the family and also in the community is an important feature of her work. Randhawa shows that the imposition of a moral code on young immigrant women—a moral code that has no contextual validity—could lead to emotional disruption.

Randhawa's first short story "India" describes the first love of an Indian schoolgirl for a boy in her community. As the boy, a son of rich parents, accepts the arranged marriage with another Indian woman, likewise from a rich house, she feels deceived. In her naïveté she trusted his promises and concealed her relationship with him from her parents, who would not have allowed it. When at the end of the story a white boy with racial prejudices makes clumsy attempts to attract her, she knows how to resist his provocation. This first short story of Randhawa contains her ideological stance on race, class, and gender, which she develops further in the course of her writing.

The story "Sunni," published in the anthology *A Girl's Best Friend*, also deals with the fragmented psyche of a young immigrant woman, the title character. Her love for a young political activist, Firoz, whom she comes to know through community work for women, remains unfulfilled. After being injured in a demonstration against the National Front, Firoz leaves her for political reasons. Although her attempts to hold him are futile, she still adores him for his courage and sacrifice. Sunni's disillusionment in love and the man's cold detachment can be seen as a consequence of the place and situation in which this love has developed. In the immigrant culture the relationship between man and woman is influenced by the everyday experience of intolerance in a racist host society.

The first story of the anthology *Right of Way*, "Pedal Push," likewise describes the emotional disruption of a young immigrant woman whose boyfriend leaves her. However, the protagonist here has appropriated a new attitude. She wants to be independent and therefore refuses to marry before finishing her studies and lets him go. Randhawa foregrounds the aspirations of this woman while at the same time focusing our attention on the issue of living in the midst of an alien culture. In the text the young woman is thoughtful when she listens to the plan of her parents to go back to India in their old age. She cannot imagine going back as her parents want to. "She would be a stranger all over again, more of a stranger than here. What were they going to do? All the black people who were young like her but who would soon be old like their parents?" (10).

In the next story, "The Heera" ("The Diamond"), Randhawa endows her protagonist, Surinder, with unusual courage and physical strength. Surinder has to fulfill the mission of rescuing a legendary diamond from a robbery. A long time ago, this diamond was presented by an African chief to an Indian princess as a sign of deep love. Now it is the property of an Indian family and the protagonist, its designated inheritor. This diamond has been stolen, and Surinder wins it back through cunning and feats of courage. Once she has it, she has it cut into pieces and sells it to support an African women's organization. Through a mixture of humor and tension Randhawa creates a female version of a sort of James Bond. In opposition to the conventional model of a passive little Asian woman, Randhawa presents a radically new alternative. Indeed she asserts that Indian women have often been portrayed stereotypically, either as submissive or as overly academic. She therefore makes it a point to portray them in a more realistic way—as sharp, witty, fun-loving, subversive.

The short story "War of Worlds" in the same anthology presents a pair of Punjabi teenage twin sisters who show precisely these traits. While describing confrontations with their community concerning restrictions imposed on women, Randhawa provokes the reader to consider the issue of imported customs on the immigrants that have lost their contexuality. However, the story also cautions women from being trapped in the illusion that seeking refuge in white society would be the alternative. In the text one of the sisters says: "They'll want us to change to their ways." So the other sister's conclusion: "I guess it's a case of Here to Stay—Here to Fight" (162).

The ideological stance of Randhawa, as developed in the short stories, is articulated even more insistently in her novel A Wicked Old Woman. It is the story of a subversive woman, Kulwant or Kuli, who was brought from India to England when she was still very young. Several other characters appear in the scenario, which enables the reader to get insight into the problems of the immigrant women. These are, for example, Shanti, who could not open her eyes until her runaway daughter returns; Rani, Shanti's daughter, who leaves home in search of a different way of life; Maya, the myopic academic woman, and others. The main story itself is shaped by the experiences of the protagonist Kuli as a young girl, later as wife and mother. The actual thread of action is always interwoven with Kuli's memories and daydreams. Shabbily dressed and leaning on a stick, although she does not really need it, Kuli, when seen from above, looks like a three-legged insect. She spends her time visiting her grown-up sons, the Asian center, and her white girlfriend Caroline, with whom she shares school-day memories: memories of the white boyfriend Michael, who wanted to marry her. She declined the proposal because she could not defy her parents. She had to give in to an arranged marriage that ended in separation because Kuli could not return her husband's love. Caught in the conflict between two different value systems, Kuli lives in permanent fragmentation of her self. An affair with a white socialist, Karm/Mark, whom she knew from party meetings, gave her what she missed in her marriage: sharing dreams or ideological love. However, when she became disillusioned by the party and gave up politics, she left Mark as well.

While portraying Kuli as a fallen woman, cherishing a love affair outside marriage, Randhawa brings up the issue of love, morality, and marriage. She leaves the reader with the aporia concerning the significance of conventional moral values. Kuli's desire to give birth to a daughter, who would have all the chances she herself had missed, remains unfulfilled. Because of this, the ideal woman, in terms of Kuli's projections, remains absent. But even if she had had a daughter, this woman would not have been able to fulfill her ideal in a phallocentric marginal culture. It is interesting that in the story Kuli leaves Mark, whom she equates with the Labour party, but does not break up with Caroline, who is also a party activist. As Kuli, full of rage and depression, spends days in bed, Caroline comes to give her new hope. Her attempt to establish a bond of solidarity between them as women cannot be disregarded by Kuli. Caroline's sympathy for Kuli's isolation and displacement is of special significance. The same bond of solidarity among women in the community with which the novel ends foregrounds the importance of sisterhood in the feminist movement. Both Caroline and Kuli are in search of a new way of life. In spite of the similarity in their situations, Kuli is conscious of the difference: "Women weren't women only, they were also their colours and their national fears" (49). In her search for identity, Caroline finds in Kuli "the other." Without involvement with this other, Caroline cannot find her own true self.

Randhawa urges Western women to have this involvement with the immigrant black women and give up their self-centeredness. The form of feminism found here deviates substantially from a feminist movement that confines itself to the removal of certain institutional barriers of sexism. It asks the more fundamental question about a discourse on gender relations in connection with race and class. For the immigrant culture itself, the novel gives a hint that it could occlude its disintegration by recognizing the serious intention of women to map out their own way to self-realization, instead of imposing on them a code of values that have no contextuality. In order to achieve this "right of way," Asian women should choose sisterhood and start to look at each other "horizontally" instead of looking hierarchically through their own patriarchal family structures. In this way, they could come out of the impasse generated by the binary oppositions between the genders and the races.

CRITICAL RECEPTION

Though Randhawa is still at the beginning of her career, her works have found positive reactions from critics. In writing about some Asian women novelists in Britain who have recently created a new genre, Sharbani Basu in a review in *Sunday* includes Randhawa in that group. Caught in a hybrid culture and not able to feel as if they belong to either of the two, the members of this group have taken refuge in writing (76). According to Basu, Randhawa's writing is largely autobiographical, her immigrant experience being the most important source of inspiration. She contends that Randhawa does not like to be categorized either as a feminist or as an Asian writer. In a brief book notice, Maria Couto says that the novel *A Wicked Old Woman* works as a social document about the Asian community that gives details concerning the daily life and the cultural conflicts, but that the portrayal of the protagonist suffers from certain inconsistencies. The review of Lyn Innes is more detailed. She considers Randhawa's novel as "one of the most promising first novels to have been published in 1987" (32). What might sometimes be seen as weaknesses in a conventional novel contributes to the strength of this one. The structure, although it might appear rambling and difficult to follow, promotes the novel's complex development.

BIBLIOGRAPHY

Works by Ravinder Randhawa

"India." *More to Life Than Mr. Right: Stories for Young Feminists*. Ed. Rosemary Stones. London: Piccadilly Press, 1985. 11–29.
"Sunni." *A Girl's Best Friend*. Ed. Christina Dunhill. London: Women's Press, 1987. 126–36.
A Wicked Old Woman. London: Women's Press, 1987.
"Games." *Right of Way*. Ed. Asian Women Writers' Workshop. London: Women's Press, 1988. 120–30.
"The Heera." *Right of Way*. Ed. Asian Women Writers' Workshop. London: Women's Press, 1988. 70–83.
"Pedal Push." *Right of Way*. Ed. Asian Women Writers' Workshop. London: Women's Press, 1988. 7–13.
"War of the Worlds." *Right of Way*. Ed. Asian Women Writers' Workshop. London: Women's Press, 1988. 155–62.

Studies of Ravinder Randhawa

Basu, Sharbani, "The Native Writes Back." *Sunday* 8 (Oct. 14, 1989): 76–77.
Couto, Maria. "In Divided Times." *Times Literary Supplement* 435 (Apr. 1–7, 1988): 363.
Gupta, Vineeta. "Asian Women Take Up Their Pens." *An Indian Bookworm's Journal* (Summer 1988): 21.
Innes, C. Lyn. Review of *A Wicked Old Woman*. *Wasafiri* 8 (Spring 1988): 32–34.

RAJA RAO (1908–   )

Anindyo Roy

BIOGRAPHY

Raja Rao was born on November 8, 1908, in Hassan, Mysore State, to a Brahmin land-owning family. Influenced in his early years by his grand-father, a man steeped in Brahminical spirituality, Raja Rao went to an all-Muslim *Madras-e-Aliya* in Hyderabad in 1915 for his primary and second-ary education. Graduating in 1925, he entered Aligarh Muslim University in the erstwhile United Provinces in North India where he studied English with Eric Dickinson and French with Jack Hill. From 1926 to 1929, he attended Nizam's College, Hyderabad, from where he graduated with a B.A. in English and history. In 1929, he traveled to France to attend the University of Montpellier on receiving the Asiatic Scholarship for study abroad awarded by the government of Hyderabad. His travel to France inspired his early writing in Kannada, his native tongue, and he began publishing in the periodical *Jaya Karnatak*. During this time, he also studied under Louis Cazamian, the literary historian, and conducted his research on the Indian influence on Irish literature. From 1932 to 1937, he held the position of member of the editorial board of *Mercure de France* (Paris), the same period when he came in close contact with Romain Rolland. He returned to India for a brief visit in 1933 to live in Pandit Taranath's ashram in Tungabhadra, Madras constituency. In 1937 he married Camille Mouly in France, and between 1933 and 1938, he published a series of short stories including the French versions of "Javni" in *Europe* (Paris), "Akkayya" in *Cahiers du Sud* (Paris), "A Client" in *Mercure de France* (Paris), and "In Khandesh" (written in English) in *Adelphi* (London). It was during this time that he came under the influence of socialist thought that was sweeping much of Europe. He established himself as a novelist in 1938 with the publication of *Kanthapura*. The author's foreword to *Kanthapura* contained what was to be later regarded as the new credo of Indian writing in

English. Claiming that "we cannot write like the English . . . [but] only as Indians," he urged Indian writers to develop a mode that "will someday prove to be as distinctive and colourful as the Irish and the Americans. (vii)"

The same year saw the publication of the short story "The Cow of the Barricades" in *Asia*. Raja Rao returned to India in 1939, when the threat of Nazi Germany was spreading throughout Europe. From 1939 to 1948, he lived at various ashrams including Sri Aurobindo's in Pondicherry, Ramana Maharishi's in Tiruvannanmalai, and Gandhi's Sevagram in Central India. He also met in 1943, in Trivandrum, Sri Atmananda Guru, the person whose influence on the aesthetic and spiritual outlook of the young writer was to develop and mature in years that followed. Despite this interest in Hindu spiritualism, he also committed himself to the cause for national independence, joining Gandhi's Quit India Movement (1942), and also participating in the underground activities of the young socialist leaders who were part of the national movement. In 1946, he joined the cultural organization *Chetna* (literally, "awakening"), founded by a group of intellectuals belonging to the Indian National Congress. In 1948 he returned to France. He visited the United States in 1950. In 1958, he traveled to India with André Malraux, De Gaulle's emissary to Nehru's India. "The Cat" was published in 1959 in the *Chelsea Review* (New York), followed by *The Serpent and the Rope* in 1960 (London). "The Policeman and the Rose" was published in 1963, along with the American editions of *The Serpent* and *Kathapura*.

In 1964, he was awarded the prestigious Sahitya Akademi Award (National Academy of Letters) by the government of India for *The Serpent and the Rope*. In 1965 he published *The Cat and Shakespeare* and the French version of *Comrade Kirillov*. In 1959 he accepted an invitation to teach philosophy at the University of Texas, a position he held till his retirement as professor emeritus in 1980. In 1969, he received the Padma Bhushan (The Order of the Lotus) from the government of India for outstanding contribution to the field of literature. In 1972 he was made Fellow of Woodrow Wilson International Center, Washington, D.C. *Comrade Kirillov* was published in English in 1976. The Modern Language Association of America elected him an Honorary Fellow in 1984. In 1988 he published *The Chessmaster and His Moves* in New Delhi, and was awarded the Tenth Neustadt International Prize for Literature the same year. Raja Rao currently lives in Austin, Texas.

MAJOR WORKS AND THEMES

The Cow of the Barricades and Other Stories, the first collection of short stories by the author, was published in 1947, though most of the stories in it were written in the 1930s. Rural life in south India during the early phase of Gandhi's noncooperation movement provides the general setting for these stories, though they also evoke an acute sense of the timelessness of rural life, as it is lived in the midst of legend, gossip, and superstition. Rao develops narrative strategies that are clearly derived from traditions of local story-telling, incorporating not only themes from local myths, but also imitating the patterns and rhythms of local speech. Legends about serpents and mir-acles, the belief in rebirth and karma, the early effects of Gandhi's grass-roots political movement, the relationship between members of upper and lower castes, the decline of village trade in the face of British imperialism— all form part of the fabric of these stories. These elements are often fused together or are represented at two levels—the private and the public. "The Cow of the Barricades" blends together the theme of Indian nationalism with the religious and the mythological represented by the common Hindu belief of the cow as goddess Gauri. In this story, the cow protects the lives of innocents in the village in the face of an attack by British soldiers by sacrificially offering herself as their protector. "Javin" exemplifies the writ-er's larger public concern for social justice in its presentation of the personal lives of two widows—from two separate classes—who are joined together in a common fate of suffering and misery caused by a social system that oppresses women as much as the marginals. The incorporation of serpent legends in stories like "Kanakapala" and "Companions" reflects Raja Rao's concern with developing a form of moral symbolism that is deeply steeped in the south Indian storytelling tradition. In a land where history and legend are fused together in the myth-laden memories of its people, real historical events often acquire mythic dimensions. Like "The Cow of the Barricades," "Narasinga" and "In Khandesh" portray the emergence and growth of a national consciousness in the minds of people through the projection of ancient myth and legend into the present history of nationalism and political change.

Though he avoids the typical stylistic approaches of social realism, there is a sense in these stories of outrage at deprivation, social injustice, poverty, and inequality caused by centuries of social stratification and British colon-ialism. Yet Raja Rao almost never steps into the arena of the overtly political, preferring to delineate in more sober terms the complexity and mystery of Indian rural life in the 1920s and 1930s. Thus the prevalence of belief in the laws of transmigration, karma, and rebirth—common to Indian rural society during that time—are quite dealt with on the same level as the social problems of rural India caused by ignorance, poverty, and superstition. Moreover, his concern in these stories seems to be directed more toward the aesthetic than the overtly political. He develops a style and narrative techniques that imitate and highlight the rhythms and tone of local speech, as well as embody the force and vibrancy of verbal storytelling. Repetitions and similes and idioms adapted from their native use add a special flavor to the language, helping to create a sense of both a lived present and a timeless reality. Much of this will go into the fashioning of his second work, his first novel, *Kanthapura*.

Kanthapura is a story of a small south Indian village caught in the political unrest of Gandhi's noncooperation movement in the 1930s. The village represents a microcosm of India's past, including its social stratification, its agricultural life, and the collective memory of its people embodied in the timelessness of its rituals and legends. Subjected to the drastic and sudden changes of history, the village gradually loses its "innocence," and the lives of its villagers are suddenly thrown into chaos and disarray. The novel begins with the young protagonist Moorthy, the Gandhian, bringing the message of nationalism and social change to the villagers. Moorthy's task is not easy but gradually the villagers respond to his message. Not only do they become aware of their own oppressive social system, but they also learn to question the authority of their British masters, which had always seemed too remote from their daily experience of life. Moorthy is a resourceful man. Realizing that his revolutionary message goes against many of the traditional mores of the village, he presents it in the easily recognizable form of Hindu tales taken from the Upanishads—stories of divine intervention and of struggle between good and evil. Perhaps the most moving aspect of the novel is the effect of Moorthy's message on the women of Kanthapura. Caught between the traditional bonds of family honor and the bondage of illiteracy, and the desire to break free from oppression, they dramatize the spirit of an old village gradually and painfully awakening to the changes of history. Moorthy himself commits the final act of transgression by entering the house of an untouchable, thus challenging a centuries-old custom of caste segregation. Moorthy's enemies recognize the threat he poses; the moneylender sees his authority challenged by the presence of the young revolutionary. Moorthy is arrested and then released, but the spirit of Gandhi's revolutionary fire has caught on. The people are ready to suffer and, in fact, undergo a kind of spiritual transformation in their desire to fight against the injustice of their colonial rulers. In the confrontation between the villagers and the police, the village is devastated. The novel ends with the final ruin of the village, and the complete dispersion of the villagers. *Kanthapura*'s theme of social awakening combines aspects of Greek tragedy uniquely adapted to record one of the most significant moments in modern Indian history. Written in the French Alps, the novel reflects the diasporic consciousness of a writer yearning to capture the reawakened spirit of a real India, striving to establish its modern identity. Its narrative technique is largely borrowed from the Puranic stories, which accounts for the seeming formlessness of the novel and its multiple digressions. The syntax and rhythms of Indian speech are captured in the descriptions, and the literal translation of Kannada phrases into English adds a distinctive dimension to a language attempting to establish a new aesthetic ethos for Indian writing in English.

Usually regarded as the first of Raja Rao's "philosophical novels" that deals with the complexity of the Indian "Brahmin" psyche, *The Serpent* also demonstrates many of the striking characteristics of a diasporic consciousness as it comes to be defined within the new context of India's postindependence optimism. Autobiographical in many significant ways, the novel is about the experience of an expatriate, Ramaswamy, who leaves his native south India for France to study history at a French university, eventually to marry a Frenchwoman, Madeleine, herself a scholar of history. After Ramaswamy's return from his first visit home to attend the funeral of his dead father, the couple find themselves drifting apart. Affected by his experiences in India, both within the family and from his trip to Benaras, Ramaswamy finds himself unable to relate to his French wife. His altered sense of reality finds its expression in his growing fascination for Savithri, whom he meets first in India and subsequently in Cambridge. Savithri, a rebel and an intellectual, comes to represent for the protagonist all that Indian womanhood embodies, in spiritual and intellectual terms, something that Madeleine cannot live up to, even when she converts to Buddhism.

This is a kind of a postcolonial *bildunsgroman* built around the theme of spiritual growth and suffering undergone by a male Brahmin as he strives to define his social and spiritual identity. Therefore, the use of this specific genre by the author allows us to explore issues that are particularly relevant to the understanding of a diasporic consciousness. First, the East-West encounter embodied in the relationship between Ramaswamy and Madeleine is worked out in "spiritual" terms on a plane that is as metaphysical as it is cultural. Ramaswamy's encounter with his own stepmother widow, "Little Mother," her daughter, and Savithri allow the emotionally confused expatriate to gradually recognize the essential spirituality of Indian womanhood as well as his own potential for a new spiritual and cultural awakening. Second, this spiritual dimension is extended into the realm of philosophical ideas derived from Vedantic philosophy, a gesture that in many ways represents the expatriate's search for an essential unity and identity of cultural origin. In this context, the conflict of "reality" and "illusion" is played out in terms of the Self's relation with the Absolute and the male/female (Shiva/ Shakti) dynamics of Vedantic spirituality. Such philosophical concerns are projected and dramatized in many significant sections in the novel—in Ramaswamy's introspective jottings in his diary, in his metaphysical conversations with Madeleine, and in his symbolic marriage with Savithri. In fact, the mythical story of Savithri, the subject of Sri Aurobindo's spiritual poem by that name, serves as a thematic and formal construct reflecting the spiritual quest that Ramaswamy is engaged in. In more historical terms, Ramaswamy's sense of home and homelessness, as evoked in his emotional relationship with the West, becomes clear in the way England and France get defined in this novel. While France's Roman Catholicism (represented by his French wife) seems adequate to the kind of quest for spiritual understanding that is Ramaswamy's obsession, England—as the former colonial power—is evoked in more positive terms. The possibility of a new spiritual relationship between the two nations serves to transcend the history of two centuries of colonization, and is represented by Ramaswamy's reflections on the queen's coronation in 1948, soon after India's independence. Important influences on the form and themes of this novel include Paul Valery's works, Rainer Maria Rilke's *The Notebook of Malte Laurids Brigge*, Charles Morgan's *The Voyage*, Walter Pater's *Marius the Epicurean*, as well as the Indian epics, the *Ramayana* and the *Mahabharata*, the *Brihadaranyaka Upanished*, and the *Puranas*. Raja Rao's preoccupation with the spiritual and the metaphysical gains new prominence in his next work, *The Cat and Shakespeare*, originally published as "The Cat" in the *Chelsea Review* in New York.

At once intimidating and fascinating, *The Cat and Shakespeare* brings together within its "metaphysical" mold the heterogenous strands of Rabelaisian comedy, Shakespearean tragedy, beast fable, Sanskrit's "kavya," and Vedantic meditation. At the level of narrative, the novel focuses on a series of "adventures" revolving around the lives of the main protagonist, Govinda Nair—a kind of a rogue figure (see Naik, *Raja Rao* 15–42), who represents the philosophical core of the novel, and his naive friend, Ramakrishna Pai, an ordinary clerk in a revenue office. The seeming unconnectedness of their adventures serves the larger purpose of delineating one of the philosophical messages of this novel—that the world of "cause" and "effect" has no basis in the world of "higher reality." The adventures of Govinda often exceed the limits of credulity in their "comic extravanganza" (Naik, *Raja Rao* 118); disguised in the form of practical jokes and buffoonery, they often represent the inverted world of a "higher meaning" that undergirds Rao's philosophical purpose. Govinda Nair's belief in the "Mother Cat," dramatized in many different ways in the novel, is derived from the nondualistic philosophy of Ramanuja where the Cat is the feminine principle that holds the Universe together. Nair uses "Mother Cat" to philosophize and explain the significance of human as well as nonhuman actions in terms of the inclusiveness and unity of creation, the potential for achieving higher selfhood and the true perception of the Absolute.

The Cat, despite its heavy philosophical machinery, does offer an interesting picture of India's rising bourgeois culture. Pai, as a government clerk married with two children and bored with years of middle-class domestication, can only dream of building a house and of keeping his extramarital affair with Shantha alive. Shantha is an independent-minded and headstrong woman, belonging to the matriarchal Nair community, who is not ashamed of her affair with a married man. Pai's office is a microcosm of India's postindependent middle class, with members from all of India's major religions—Islam, Christianity, and Hinduism. The world of "ration cards" and supervisors, of corruption, nepotism, and bribery, the little aspirations of city clerks in the world of rising commercialism all point to India's postindependent realities. The novel is thus both an insider's and an outsider's look at postindependent India: outside, because it still attempts to see "India" from an originary philosophical position, as representing a certain state of mind in its relation with the Absolute, and inside because, as a comedy of manners, it offers a penetrating look at the Indian middle-class mind.

Comrade Kirillov, a novella that deals with the conflict between Vedanta and Marxism, is a another example of Rao's agonistic style developed in *The Serpent and the Rope*. The work presents an interesting view of modern Indian nationalism as it emerged historically from the conflicting ideologies of Gandhism and communism. Set in Europe during the war, the novel deals with the relation between the narrator, "R," and the protagonist, Kirillov (whose real name is Padmanabha Iyer), a Brahmin south Indian Marxist and expatriate. Throughout the story the narrator (who is the author's persona) maintains an ironic distance from the views of Kirillov, even subjecting them to the harshest of criticisms. Rao's own philosophic position stands in sharp contrast to the seeming materialist determinism of Kirillov's philosophy. Kirillov is portrayed as a man of contradictions and raging rigidity, an ideologically bent materialist, and his viewpoints are often presented in the form of "ideological harangues" (Powers 611), which dehumanize him and make him into a one-dimensional figure. For Raja Rao, Kirillov also represents the communist expatriate whose historical allegiance with Stalin during the period of Indian independence and the war makes him the antagonist of Gandhi and the Vedantic revolutionary spirit that he embodied. As a metaphysical novel with a strong argumentative core, the novel is also patterned around the internal adventure and the growth of the psyche, a form that characterizes much of Rao's diasporic fiction. Approaching the structure of a novella, or an extended short story with three characters, the novel is more restricted in its scope than his other novels.

In "The Policeman and the Rose," Rao develops a narrative that is essentially based on the mystical quest motif of the Self as the Absolute. Appropriating the symbol of the red rose from the Western medieval romance tradition, Rao blends it with the white rose of Travancore that represents, according to S. C. Harrex, the "ascetic Indian corollary of an Indian ideal of love, or beauty, or truth" (Harrex,*"Raja Rao's Experiments"* 593). Representing the duality of truth and illusion, the narrator "I" and its other, "the policeman," dramatize the condition of the ego in its separation from and its yearning for the Absolute. In a sense, as C. D. Narasimhaiah contends, the action of the policeman represents the law of Karma, because "when it 'arrests' you, you become 'free,' for it must work itself out" (*Raja Roa* 137). By developing a symbolic and surreal narrative, Rao is further able to explore the dimension of the philosophical within the context of an aesthetics of modern fiction.

The Chessmaster and His Moves, a monolithic work of nearly 700-odd pages, is Rao's most recent venture in developing and perfecting the philosophical novel. The narrative is interspersed with major segments on discourses from Advaita Vedanta. Set in India, France, and England, its diasporic characters hail from countries like Greece, Israel, and Senegal. Interestingly, this kind of diasporic "internationalism" (Thumboo 567) serves to foreground the intrinsic Indianness of Rao's vision, which is manifested in the way in which individual relationships are dramatized in the novel. Through the multiple narratives, and in the interactions between Sivarama, the mathematician; Michel, the Holocaust survivor; Jean-Pierre, the "half-Greek and half-Senegalais" whose personal identity is part of a mythic vision that he carries with him; and the women Suzanne, Uma, Jayalaksmi, and Mireille, Rao explores the dilemma of personal relationships as well as the cultural and historical forces that have shaped their individual philosophies. Often, however, their philosophies are judged against the background of the nondualistic philosophy of Advaita Vedanta that has been part of Rao's developing intellectual and aesthetic vision. The dialogic form of the work is demonstrated in sections like "The Brahmin and the Rabbi" (the final book of the novel), which brings together the multifaceted concerns about life, politics, art, and history within the philosophical framework of the novel. The theme of home and origin is also part of the intensely meditative nature of this work, as are the questions of personal identity, tradition, and cultural ethos that mark the condition of the expatriate.

CRITICAL RECEPTION

The critical reception of Raja Rao's work extends from full-length studies of his fiction, to scholarly essays published in journals, to reviews, and to poems dedicated to his vision and aesthetics. On receiving the Neustadt Award for Literature in 1988, *World Literature Today* dedicated an entire issue (vol. 62, Autumn 1988) to the scholarship on his works. In addition to a select bibliography of his fiction and critical essays on his works, the issue carries a list of books edited by Rao, contributions to books, interviews, and dissertations on Rao's fiction. The issue also includes selected texts by the author that were formerly published in journals and newspapers.

The number of books, essays, and reviews of Rao's works published in India, Great Britain, and the United States exceeds 120. Although much of the available criticism focuses on the metaphysical themes in Rao's fiction, a large number of the essays deal with comparative studies (comparing Rao with other Indo-Anglian writers, or writers from the British Commonwealth, as well as French writers of the twentieth century), linguistic and stylistic analysis, formal and structural approaches, Rao as a social writer, and the significance of his contribution to the growth of an artistic ethos for Indian writing in English.

SELECT BIBLIOGRAPHY

Fiction by Raja Rao

Kanthapura. London: Allen & Unwin, 1938; Bombay: Oxford University Press, 1947; New York: New Directions, 1963; Westport, Conn.: Greenwood Press, 1977.

The Cow of the Barricades and Other Stories. Madras: Oxford University Press, 1947.

The Serpent and the Rope. London: Murray, 1960; New York: Pantheon, 1963; Delhi: Oxford University Press, 1978; New York: Overlook, 1986.

The Cat and Shakespeare: A Tale of India. New York: Macmillan, 1965; Delhi: Hind, 1971.

Comrade Kirillov. New Delhi: Vision Books, 1976.

The Policeman and the Rose: Stories. Delhi: Oxford University Press, 1978.

The Chessmaster and His Moves. New Delhi: Vision Books, 1988.

Select Studies of Raja Rao

Agnihotri, G. N. *Indian Life and Problems in the Novels of Mulk Raj Anand, Raja Rao and R. K. Narayan*. Meerut: Shalabh Book House, 1984. 61–82.

Aithal, S. Krishnamoorthy, and Rashmi Aithal. "Interracial and Intercultural Relationships in Raja Rao's *The Serpent and the Rope*." *International Fiction Review* 7:2 (Summer 1980): 94–98.

Ali, Ahmed. "Illusion and Reality: The Art and Philosophy of Raja Rao." *Journal of Commonwealth Literature* 5 (July 1968): 16–28.

Belliappa, K. C. "The Question of Form in Raja Rao's *The Serpent and the Rope*." *World Literature Written in English* (Guelph, Ont.) 24:2 (Autumn 1984): 407–16.

Bhalla, Brij M. "Quest for Identity in Raja Rao's *The Serpent and the Rope*." *Ariel* (London) 4:4 (1973): 95–105.

Bhattacharya, P. C. *Indo-Anglian Literature and the Works of Raja Rao*. Delhi: Atma Ram, 1983.

Birje-Patil, J. "*Kanthapura* from an African Perspective." In *Commonwealth Literature: Problems of Response*. Ed. C. D. Narasimhaiah. Madras: Macmillan, 1981. 102–6.

Curtis, Chantal. "Raja Rao and France." *World Literature Today* 62:4 (Autumn 1988): 595–97.

Das, Elizabeth. "The Choric Element in *Kanthapura*." *Punjab University Research Bulletin (Arts)* (Chandigarh) 15:1 (April 1984): 53–58.

Davies, M. Bryn. "Raja Rao's *The Serpent and the Rope: A New Literary Genre?*" In *The Commonwealth Writer Overseas: Themes of Exile and Expatriation*. Ed. Alastair Niven. Brussels: Didier, 1976. 265–69.

Dayal, P. "The Image of Woman in the Novels of Raja Rao." *Punjab University Research Bulletin (Arts)* (Chandigarh) 16:1 (April 1985): 45–53.

Desai, S. K. "Transplantation of English: Raja Rao's Experimentation with English in his Works of Fiction." In *Experimentation with Language in Indian Writing in English (Fiction)*. Ed. S. K. Desai. Kolhapur, India: Shivaji University Department of English, 1974. 1–32.

Dissanayake, Wimal. "Questing Self: The Four Voices in *The Serpent and the Rope*." *World Literature Today* 62:4 (Autumn 1988): 598–602.

Eng, Ooi Boo. "Making Initial Sense of *The Serpent and the Rope*." *Journal of Indian Writing in English* (Gulbarga) 8:1–2 (Jan.-July 1980): 53–62.

Gemmill, Janet Powers. "Dualities and Non-Duality in Raja Rao's *The Serpent and the Rope*." *World Literature Written in English* (Arlington, Tex.) 12:2 (Nov. 1973): 247–59.

———. "Elements of Folktale in Raja Rao's *The Cow of the Barricades*." *World Literature Written in English* (Guelph, Ont.) 20:1 (Spring 1981): 149–61.

———. "*Kanthapura*: India en Route to Independence." *CEA Critic* (College Station, Tex.) 44:4 (May 1982): 30–38.

———. "Rhythm in *The Cat and Shakespeare*." *Literature East & West* (Austin, Tex.) 13:1–2 (June 1969): 27–42.

———. "The Transcreation of Spoken Kannada in Raja Rao's *Kanthapura*." *Literature East & West* (Austin, Tex.) 18:2–4 (March 1974): 191–202.

Gorlier, Claudio. " 'See What I Am': The Figure of Beatrice." *World Literature Today*. 62:4 (Autumn 198): 606–8.

Gowda, H. H. Anniah. "Phenomenal Tradition: The Case of Raja Rao and Wilson Harris." *Bulletin of the Association for Commonwealth Literature and Language Studies* 9 (1972): 28–48.

Guzman, Richard R. "The Saint and the Sage: The Fiction of Raja Rao." *Virginia Quarterly Review* 56:1 (Winter 1980): 32–50.

Harrex, S. C. "Raja Rao's Experiments in Short Story." *World Literature Today* 62:4 (Autumn 1988): 591–94.

———. *The Fire and the Offering: The English Language Novel of India 1935–70*. 2 vols. Calcutta: Writers Workshop, 1977, 1979.

Harris, Wilson. "Raja Rao's Inimitable Style and Art of Fiction." *World Literature Today* 62:4 (Autumn 1988): 587–90.

Hemenway, Stephen Ignatius. *The Novel in India*. Vol. 2: *The Indo-Anglian Novel*. Calcutta: Writers Workshop, 1975. 71–109.

Iyengar, K. R. Srinivasa. *Indian Writing in English*. Bombay: Asia Publishing House, 1973. 302–20.

Jamkhandi, S. R. "*The Cat and Shakespeare*: Narrator, Audience and Message." *Journal of Indian Writing in English* (Annalmalinagar) 7:2 (1979): 24–41.

Kachru, Braj. "Toward Expanding the English Canon: Raja Rao's 1938 Credo for Creativity." *World Literature Today* 62:4 (Autumn 1988): 582–86.

Kalinnikova, Elena J. *Indian-English Literature: A Perspective*. Ghaziabad: Vimal, 1982. 133–49.

Kantak, V. Y. "The Language of *Kanthapura*." *Indian Literary Review* (New Delhi) 3 (April 1985): 15–24.

Kaul, R. K. "*The Serpent and the Rope* as a Philosophical Novel." *Literary Criterion* (Mysore) 15:2 (1980): 32–43.

Krishna Rao, A. V. *The Indo-Anglian Novel and the Changing Tradition: A Study of the Novels of Mulk Raj Anand, Kamala Markandaya, R. K. Narayan and Raja Rao, 1930–64.* Mysore: Rao and Raghavan 1972.

———. "Raja Rao." *Triveni* 36 (Jan. 1968): 16–30.

Larson, Charles R. "Revolt and Rebirth, Cultural Renewal: Raja Rao's *Kanthapura* and Kamala Markandaya's *Two Virgins*." In *The Novel and the Third World.* Ed. Charles R. Larson. Washington, D.C.: Inscape, 1976. 131–51.

Lehmann, W. P. "The Quality of Presence." *World Literature Today* 62:4 (Autumn 1988): 578–81.

Lewis, Robin Jared. "National Identity and Social Consciousness in Modern Indian Literature." In *Problems in National Literary Identity and the Writer as Social Critic.* Ed. Anne Paolucci. Whitestone, N.Y.: Griffon House, 1980. 38–42.

McCutchion, David. *Indian Writing in English.* Calcutta: Writers Workshop, 1973. 83–98.

Maini, D. S. "Raja Rao's Vision, Values and Aesthetic." In *Commonwealth Literature: Problems of Response.* Ed. C. D. Narasimhaiah, Madras: Macmillan, 1981. 64–89.

Mani, Laxmi. "Voice and Vision in Raja Rao's Fiction." *South Asian Review* (Jacksonville, Fla.) 4 (1980): 1–11.

Mathur, O. P. "The East-West Theme in *Comrade Kirillov*." *New Literature Review* (Armidale, N.S.W.) 4 (1978): 25–29.

Mukherjee, Meenakshi. "Raja Rao's Shorter Fiction." *Indian Literature* 10:3 (1967): 66–76.

Muller, Ulrich, and William C. McDonald. "Tristan in Deep Structure: Raja Rao's *The Serpent and the Rope* (1960)—A Paradigmatic Case of Intercultural Relations." *Tristania: A Journal Devoted to Tristan Studies* (Chattanooga) 12:1–2 (Autumn-Spring 1986–87): 44–47.

Nagarajan, S. "Little Mother in *The Serpent and the Rope*." *World Literature Today* 62:4 (Autumn 198): 609–10.

Naik, M. K. *A History of Indian English Literature.* New Delhi: Sahitya Akademi, 1982. 166–75.

———. "*Kanthapura*: The Indo-Anglian Novel as a Legendary History." *Karnatak University Journal* 10 (1966): 26–39.

———. "*The Cow of the Barricades and Other Stories*: Raja Rao as a Short Story Writer." *Books Abroad* (Autumn 1966): 392–96.

———. "*The Serpent and the Rope*: The Indo-Anglian Novel as Epic Legend." *Critical Essays on Indian Writing in English.* Ed. M. K. Naik, et al. Dharwar: Karnatak University Press, 1968. 14–49.

———. "The Short Story as Metaphysical Parable: *The Policeman and the Rose*." *Explorations in Modern Indo-English Fiction.* Ed. R. K. Dhawan. New Delhi: Bahri Publications, 1982. 110–22.

———. *Raja Rao.* New York: Twayne, 1972; rev. ed., Bombay: Blackie, 1982.

Narasimhaiah, C. D. "National Identity in Literature and Language: Its Range and Depth in the Novels of Raja Rao." In *National Identity.* Ed. K. L. Goodwin. London: Heinemann Educational Books, 1970. 153–68.

———. *Raja Rao.* New Delhi: Arnold-Heinemann, 1973.

———. "Raja Rao's *Kanthapura*: An Analysis." In *Critical Essays on Indian Writing in English*. Ed. M. K. Naik et al. Dharwar: Karnatak University Pres, 1961. 270–96.

———. *"The Cat and Shakespeare." Literary Criterion* 8 (Winter 1968): 65–95.

———. *"The Serpent and the Rope*: A Study." *Literary Criterion* 3 (Summer 1963): 62–89.

———. *Raja Rao*. New Delhi: Arnold-Heinemann, n.d.

Narayan, Shyamala A. "Ramaswamy's Erudition: A Note on Raja Rao's *The Serpent and the Rope.*" *Ariel* (Calgary) 14:4 (Oct. 1983): 6–15.

Narayana Rao, K. S. "The Untranslated Translation and Aesthetic Consequences: Indian Fiction in English." *Southern Review* (Adelaide) 8:3 (1975): 189–204.

Niranjan, Shiva. "The Nature and Extent of Gandhi's Impact on the Early Novels of Mulk Raj Anand and Raja Rao." *Commonwealth Quarterly* (Mysore) 3:11 (1979): 36–46.

———. *Raja Rao: Novelist as Sadhaka*. Ghaziabad: Vimal, 1985.

———. "An Interview with Raja Rao." *Indian Writing in English*. Ed. K. N. Sinha. New Delhi: Heritage Publishers, 1979. 19–28.

Niven, Alastair. *Truth within Fiction: A Study of Raja Rao's "The Serpent and the Rope."* Calcutta: Writers Workshop, 1987.

Paniker, K. Ayayappa. "Man and God in Indian and African Fiction: A Study Based on *Kanthapura, Arrow of God* and *Mookaji's Vision.*" In *Commonwealth Literature: Problems of Response*. Ed. C. D. Narasimhaiah. Madras: Macmillan, 1981. 107–16.

Parameswaran, Uma. "Karma at Work: The Allegory in Raja Rao's *The Cat and Shakespeare." Journal of Commonwealth Literature* (London) 7 (July 1969): 107–15.

———. "Shiva and Shakti in Raja Rao's Novels." *World Literature Today* 62:4 (Autumn 1988): 574–77.

———. *A Study of Representative Indo-English Novelists*. New Delhi: Vikas Publishing House, 1976. 141–70.

Parthasarathy, R. *"The Chessmaster and His Moves*: The Novel as Metaphysics." *World Literature Today* 62:4 (Autumn 1988): 561–66.

———. "Tradition and Creativity: Stylistic Innovations in Raja Rao." In *Discourse Across Cultures: Strategies in World Englishes*. Ed. Larry E. Smith. London: Prentice-Hall, 1987. 157–65.

Powers, Janet M. "Initiate Meets Guru: *The Cat and Shakespeare* and *Comrade Kirillov." World Literature Today* 62:4 (Autumn 198): 611–16.

Prasad, Baidya Nath. "The Language of Raja Rao's *The Serpent and the Rope.*" In *Indian Writing in English*. Ed. K. N. Sinha. New Delhi: Heritage Publishers, 1979. 29–41.

Raine, Kathleen. "On *The Serpent and the Rope.*" *World Literature Today* 62:4 (Autumn 1988): 603–5.

Raizada, Harish C. "Literature as 'Sadhana': The Progress of Raja Rao from *Kanthapura* to *The Serpent and the Rope.*" In *Indo-English Literature: A Collection of Critical Essays*. Ed. K. K. Sharma. Ghaziabad, India: Vimal, 1977. 157–75.

Ram, Atma. "Peasant Sensibility in *Kanthapura.*" In *Indo-English Literature: A*

Collection of Critical Essays. Ed. K. K. Sharma. Ghaziabad, India: Vimal, 1977. 193–200.

Rama Moorthy, P. "Death in Raja Rao's *The Policeman and the Rose* and Witilhimaera's *pounamu pounamu.*" In *Commonwealth Literature: Problems of Response.* Ed. C. D. Narasimhaiah. Madras: Macmillan, 1981. 127–36.

Ramaswamy, S. "Self and Society in Raja Rao's *The Serpent and the Rope.*" *Aspects of Indian Writing in English.* Ed. M. K. Naik. Madras: Macmillan, 1979. 199–208.

Ranchan, Som P. "Ramaswamy's Dilemma: An Analytical Interpretation of *The Serpent and the Rope.*" In *Explorations in Modern Indo-English Fiction.* Ed. R. K. Dhawan. New Delhi: Bahri Publications, 1982. 101–9.

Rao, A. Ramakrishna. "Kirillov in the First Circle." *Literary Encounter* (Nizamabad) 6:1–4 (1958): 45–54.

Rao, K. R. *The Fiction of Raja Rao.* Aurangabad: Parimal, 1980.

Reddy, K. Venkata. "An Approach to Raja Rao's *The Cat and Shakespeare.*" *World Literature Written in English* (Guelph, Ont.) 20:2 (Autumn 1981): 337–43.

Sarachchandra, Ediriwira. "Illusion and Reality: Raja Rao as Novelist." In *Only Connect: Literary Perspectives East and West.* Ed. Guy Amirthanayagam and S. C. Harrex. Adelaide/Honolulu: Centre for Research in the New Literatures/East West Center, 1981. 107–7.

Seshachari, Candadai. "The Gandhian Dimension: Revolution and Tragedy in *Kanthapura.*" *South Asian Review* 5:2 (July 1981): 82–87.

Shahane, Vasant A. "Raja Rao's *The Serpent and the Rope* and Patrick White's *The Solid Mandala*: A Comparative Appraisal." In *The Laurel Bough: Essays Presented in Honour of Professor M. V. Rama Sarma.* Ed. G. Nageswara Rao. Bombay: Blackie, 1983. 177–89.

Sharma, J. P. *Raja Rao: A Visionary.* Meerut: Shalabh Book House, 1980.

Sharma, Jatindra K. "Response to Alien Culture in Henry James and Raja Rao: Comprative Observations on *The American* and *The Serpent and the Rope.*" *Punjab University Research Bulletin (Arts)* 15:1 (April 1984): 11–25.

Sharma, K. K., ed. *Perspectives on Raja Rao: An Anthology of Critical Essays* Ghaziabad: Vimal, 1980.

Sharma, Som P. "Raja Rao's Search for the Feminine." *Journal of South Asian Literature* 12:3 (1977): 95–101.

Sharrad, Paul. "A Sense of Place in Raja Rao's *The Serpent and the Rope.*" In *A Sense of Place in the New Literatures in English.* Ed. Peggy Nightingale. St. Lucia: University of Queensland Press, 1986. 86–96.

———. "Aspects of Mythic Form and Style in Raja Rao's *The Serpent and the Rope.*" *Journal of Indian Writing in English* 12:2 (July 1984): 82–95.

———. *Raja Rao and Cultural Tradition.* New Delhi: Sterling, 1987.

Shepherd, R. "Raja Rao: Symbolism in *The Cat and Shakespeare.*" *World Literature Written in English* (Arlington, Tex.) 14:2 (Nov. 1975): 347–56.

———. "Symbolic Organization in *The Serpent and the Rope.*" *Southern Review: An Australian Journal of Literary Studies* 6 (1973): 93–107.

———. "The Character of Ramaswamy in Raja Rao's *The Serpent and the Rope.*" *New Literature Review* 4 (1978): 17–24.

Singh, R. S. *Indian Novel in English.* New Delhi: Arnold-Heinemann, 1977. 73–95.

Srivastava, Narsingh. *The Mind and Art of Raja Rao*. Bareilly: Prakash Book Depot, 1980.

Taranath, Rajeev. "A Note on the Problem of Simplication." In *Fiction and the Reading Public in India*. Ed. C. D. Narasimhaiah. Mysore: University of Mysore Press, 1967. 205–12.

Thumboo, Edwin. "Raja Rao: *The Chessmaster and His Moves*." *World Literature Today* 62:4 (Autumn 1988): 567–73.

Tiffin, Helen. "The Word and the House: Colonial Motifs in *The Double Hook* and *The Cat and Shakespeare*." *Literary Criterion* 20:1 (1985): 204–26.

Verghese, C. Paul. "Raja Rao, Mulk Raj Anand, R. K. Narayan and Others." *Indian Writing Today* 3:1 (Jan.-Mar. 1969): 31–38.

———. *Problems of the Indian Creative Writers in English*. Bombay: Somaiya Publications, 1971. 142–54.

Westbook, Perry D. "Comrade Kirillov: Marxism and Vedanta." *World Literature Today* 62:4 (Autumn 1988): 617–20.

———. "Theme and Inaction in Raja Rao's *The Serpent and the Rope*." *World Literature Written in English* 1:4 (1975): 385–98.

White, Ray Lewis. "Raja Rao's *The Cat and Shakespeare* in the U.S.A." *Journal of Indian Writing in English* 7:1 (1979): 24–29.

Williams, Haydn Moore. "Raja Rao's *The Serpent and the Rope* and the Idea of India." In *Rule, Protest, Identity: Aspects of Modern South Asia*. Ed. Peter G. Robb and David D. Taylor. London: Curzon, 1978. 206–12.

SANTHA RAMA RAU (1923–   )
Ann O. Gebhard

BIOGRAPHY

Born in Madras on January 24, 1923, Santha Rama Rau lived in India during her childhood but was educated in England and in the United States. With roots in both the East and West, she has been characterized as a "link and interpreter between the Occident and Orient" ((Webb 718). Although best known as a travel writer, she has made notable contributions as a novelist, biographer, and dramatist. Much of her work is imbued with the personal perspective of autobiography.

During her childhood her Cambridge-educated father, Sir Benegal Rama Rau, one of the architects of Indian independence, was posted as a civil administrator to districts ranging from primitive rural areas to the cosmopolitan capital of New Delhi. He eventually served as Indian ambassador to South Africa, Japan, and the United States, and at the time of his death in 1969 was governor of the Federal Reserve Bank of India. Her mother, Dhanvanthi Handoo, was the first daughter of a Kashmiri Brahmin family to attend college, and subsequently, became a pioneer of family planning and health care in India. Throughout their marriage her parents spoke to each other in English, their only common tongue. The writer later claimed that the two strong influences of her childhood were "the shifting life of district touring and the strong universe of family" (*Gifts* 6). In her writing an appreciation for family tradition and Indian diversity are consistent themes.

Because of a diplomatic assignment of her father's, at six she and her family moved to England. She was educated in primary school in Weybridge, Surrey, and at St. Paul's School, London. In 1938, the family traveled to South Africa, where her father served as Indian High Commissioner. In South Africa she felt for the first time the injustice of colonialism. She saw signs reading, "Indians, natives, and dogs not allowed" (*Home* 3) and realized that she and her sister could go to a public movie house only when her father used his diplomatic privilege on their behalf.

When war broke out, Rama Rau, her mother, and sister returned to India to live in Bombay in a traditional Hindu household dominated by her conservative grandmother. In both households of her grandparents, "the great, complex system of family and religion and custom that produced the old India still operated" (*Gifts* 3). After two years, she decided to go to the United States for college education and enrolled at Wellesley in Massachusetts.

At Wellesley, Rama Rau majored in English and during summer vacations worked as a writer for the Office of War Information. Of her youthful American experience, she writes, "It was a strange time for me—half in love with America, with its driving energy, its earnestness, its kindness, and its extraordinary beauty, half deploring its ignorance of conditions in the rest of the world, its smug self-righteousness, and its assumption of privilege" (*Gifts* 27). Realizing that she wanted to be a writer, she began her first book, the best-selling *Home to India*, published in 1945, a year after her graduation from college.

Returning to India, she took a position on a magazine, despite a strong family tradition that forbade a young woman to work for pay. In 1947 she left once again; this time to serve as hostess for her father, who had been appointed the first ambassador of free India to Japan. In devastated postwar Japan she took a teaching job at Miss Hani's progressive Freedom School. In arranging a field trip for her students to a kabuki theater, an art form in which she has a keen interest, she met Faubion Bowers, an American working as a censor for the Occupation. Later, with Bowers and two other friends, she toured Asia, visiting, among other places, remote, communist-threatened northern China and newly liberated Indonesia. An account of her travels became her second book, *East of Home*, published in 1950.

She and Bowers, also a writer, were married in France on October 24, 1952. The couple honeymooned in Spain and continued to travel throughout Europe but returned to India the following year for the birth of their son, Jai Peter. In 1956 she published *Remember the House*, a coming-of-age novel set in India.

Throughout the fifties Rama Rau traveled, generally on assignment for *Holiday* magazine, to Africa, again to Asia, and to Russia, returning periodically to New York City, where she made her home, and to India. Three travel books, *This Is India* (1954), *View to the Southeast* (1957), and *My Russian Journey* (1959), were based on articles she had written for *Holiday*. She also wrote other travel sketches, personal essays, and occasional short stories, most frequently for the *New Yorker* and the *Reporter*, but also for a wide variety of popular magazines such as *Redbook, New York Times Magazine, Vogue, House and Garden*, and *Good Housekeeping*. Her autobiographical *Gifts of Passage* is largely based on previously published magazine pieces.

In 1957 Rama Rau met novelist E. M. Forster for the first time and noted "the immutable reality that his characters, invented or not, had for him" ("Remembering" 101). She had written a dramatization of his *Passage to India*, one that he warmly approved, which was successfully staged in London and New York. This meeting led to a collaborative friendship that lasted until Forster's death.

In 1970 Rama Rau published *The Adventurers*, her last major creative work to date. In that year, also, having divorced Bowers, she married Gurdon Wallace Wattles, an American international lawyer with the United Nations. She presently resides in Amenia, New York.

MAJOR WORKS AND THEMES

With the publication of *Home to India* Santha Rama Rau cast for herself a dramatic persona, one that has served her well throughout her writing career. As a Western-educated Asian, born early in the century, she seeks to integrate the two strains of her background, the pragmatism of the West and the traditionalism of India. *Home to India* opens with her grandmother's greeting, a question directed to a sixteen-year-old who has spent her last ten years living abroad: "My dear child, where in India will we find a husband tall enough for you?" (1). Thereafter, much of the book details the culture shock of its author.

Most vividly representative of traditional India in her writing is the life of her grandmothers, one living in Bombay and the other in Kashmir, both devout Hindus and strong matriarchs, willing servants of a conservative male-oriented society. As in *Home to India*, her most serious creative works, the novel *Remember the House* and the autobiography *Gifts of Passage*, thematically address the conflict between Western and traditional Indian values.

Baba, the Western-educated heroine of *Remember the House*, enjoys the social whirl of upper-class Bombay. It is the year India achieves its independence, but Baba is preoccupied with personal concerns: should she marry the man that her family has decided is suitable or seek out a Western ideal of romantic love, as exemplified in the relationship of two American friends? On a visit to southern India, Baba listens to her grandmother's recollections. By the novel's end, acknowledging the superficiality of the American view of life and the authenticity of her grandmother's perspective, she accepts an arranged marriage. A sensitive coming-of-age story, the novel deftly explores alterations in the consciousness of a young girl. Through its descriptions of life in spartan rural India and in the glittering, upper-class Bombay of the last days of British rule, it also subtly reveals contrast and changes in the life of a nation.

In her own life Rama Rau reconciled the two strains of her background by becoming that quintessential expatriate—the travel writer. Originally published in popular American magazines, much of her travel writing is standard for its genre. But in *East of Home* and *View to the Southwest* Rama Rau's growing understanding of herself as an Asian is manifest. Her most consistent theme in these books is anticolonialism, a theme also evident in *Gifts of Passage*. Sometimes her view of the consequences of colonialism in Asia is humorous, as in the narrative of two "England-returned" young professionals in "Who Cares?," and sometimes rueful, as in her description of the fearful isolation of "The Missionary," but it is always imbued with an understanding of the harmful results to Asia of foreign domination. Despite this interest and although the chronology of her reports of the Orient coincides with three decades of unparalleled revolutionary turmoil there, her writing manifests little interest in or sympathy for social movements. She is critical of the stultifying uniformity of communist Russia and compares life in that country unfavorably with the richness and variety of life in India. Her accounts of India deal largely with its picturesque scenery and customs and the life of its privileged classes. In a characteristically vivid, somewhat confused image, she describes this group as a layer that lies "thin as the skin on boiled milk over the daunting poverty of the mass of Indians" (7). Her appreciation of the pageantry and romance of the Raj are fully evident in *A Princess Remembers*, a collaboration with Gayatri Devi that is a gracefully written, nostalgic account of the life of a former maharani of Jaipur.

Customarily, her writings are notable for their particularized human interest. This is especially true of *Gifts of Passage*, which includes some of her best magazine pieces loosely linked together by personal narrative. Because in each section a vivid vignette illustrates and expands upon the autobiographical narrative, the work tests the boundaries between fiction and autobiography. "Who Cares?," for instance, originally appeared as a short story in *Good Housekeeping*, but is offered as autobiography in this work.

"The Adventurers" is a carefully observed picaresque tale of a stateless oriental heroine who exploits the gullibility of an American officer of the occupation and a wealthy Philippino woman but ultimately finds security as the wife of a British flyer. Like many of her travel writings, it seems clearly aimed at a popular market.

Rama Rau undertook to dramatize E. M. Forster's *A Passage to India* as a literary exercise and reported herself "dazed and incredulous" when the author strongly endorsed her efforts ("Remembering" 101). The dramatization was successfully received in London and New York and became the basis of the 1984 film version of Forster's well-known novel of cultural conflict.

CRITICAL RECEPTION

Given the nature of the popular magazine genre in which she has chosen to work, critical attention to Santha Rama Rau has been largely limited to reviews of her book-length works. For the most part, this criticism has been positive, especially for the literary quality of *Remember the House* and *Gifts of Passage*.

In a *New Yorker* review of *Remember the House* Anthony West claims that the novel "is a brilliant success in its daringly chosen field" (164) and goes on to compare its form and style favorably to that of E. M. Forster. A *Time* reviewer made similar comparisons, noting that the novel "faithfully endorses Forster's strong plea for simple human contact" ("Coming" 118). One critic remarked upon "its documentary quality," saying that "as a picture of a particular stream of Indian society, the Bombay smart set, uneasy despite independence, it is vivid and instructive" (Webb 718). Other critics had reservations, as they did in regard to her second novel. Writing in the *New York Times Book Review*, W. G. Rogers admired *The Adventurers* for "its entertaining combination of Western shape, Eastern character and fictional hocus-pocus" but indicated that it "was not quite her best" (50).

Critics more uniformly applauded *Gifts of Passage*, apparently particularly impressed by the quality of the stories that accompanied the autobiographical narrative. Orville Prescott noted Rama Rau's "conscious artistry, carefully omitting the unessential so that the quality of an individual or the significance of an incident can be emphasized properly" (33). Rumer Godden similarly praised these pieces as "unmistakably true, beaming with wit" and admired the work's "likable humanity balanced between the coolness of observation and a warmth of understanding" (5).

Beginning with *Home to India*, reviewers have typically found her travel books noteworthy as much for their revelation of the author's life and attitudes as for their literary merit. Critics commented on the "young and gay" (Webb 718) quality of her first book and on its youthful author.

Rama Rau's dramatization of Forster's *Passage to India* has been frequently commended. Mollie Painter-Downes found it "one of those rare dramatizations of novels which give almost complete satisfaction to everyone" (184). In a program note Forster praised her as "an Indian writer of celebrity and distinction" and applauded her "excellent and sensitive" dramatic version ("Theater" 53).

In critic Roshni Rostomji-Kerns's terms, Rama Rau is "a perceptive and compassionate narrator of the expatriate experience" (655), while one *Time* writer more glowingly remarked that she "writes English with the flourish of conquest" ("Coming" 114).

BIBLIOGRAPHY

Selected Works of Santha Rama Rau

Home to India. New York: Harper and Brothers, 1945.
East of Home. New York: Harper and Brothers, 1950.
"Who Cares?" *Good Housekeeping* June 1953: 146 +.
This Is India. New York: Harper and Brothers, 1954.
Remember the House. New York: Harper and Brothers, 1956.
View to the Southeast. New York: Harper and Brothers, 1957.
My Russian Journey. New York: Harper and Brothers, 1959.
Gifts of Passage. New York: Harper and Brothers, 1961.
A Passage to India: A Play. New York: Harcourt Brace, 1961.
"Speaking of Books: Well, What Happened Afterwards." *New York Times Book Review* (Aug. 1, 1965): 2.
Recipes: The Cooking of India. New York: Time-Life Books, 1969.
The Adventurers. New York: Harper and Row, 1970.
A Princess Remembers: The Memoirs of the Maharani of Jaipur. London: Century Publishing, 1976 (with Gayatri Devi).
"Remembering E. M. Forster." *Grand Street* 5:4 (1986): 99–119.

Studies of Santha Rama Rau

"Coming of Age." *Time* (April 16, 1956): 114 +.
Godden, Rumer. "A Life at Large." *New York Times Book Review* (May 7, 1961): 5.
Mehta, N. "Profiles," *New Yorker* (Sept. 15, 1962): 85.
Painter-Downes, Mollie. "Letter from London." *New Yorker* (May 14, 1960): 184.
Prescott, Orville. "Books of the Times." *New York Times* (May 8, 1961): 33.
Ramachandra, Ragini. "The Imagination of Fact." *Commonwealth Quarterly* 9 (1978): 204–23.
Rogers, W. G. "Like Becky Sharp, Kay Was Fast on Her Feet." *New York Times Book Review* (Oct. 18, 1970): 50.
Rostomji-Kerns, Roshni. "Expatriates, Immigrants, and Literature: Three South Asian Women Writers." *Massachusetts Review* (Winter 1988–89): 655–65.
"Santha Rama Rau." *Current Biography.* Ed. Anna Rothe. New York: H. W. Wilson, 1945.
"Theater Abroad: Passage to the Stage." *Time* (Feb. 1, 1960): 53.
Webb, Margaret. "Santha Rama Rau." *Wilson Library Bulletin* 33 (1959): 718.
West, Anthony. "East Is East." *New Yorker* (Apr. 14, 1956): 164–66.

SALMAN RUSHDIE (1947–   )
Anuradha Dingwaney

BIOGRAPHY

Salman Rushdie was born into an affluent Muslim family in Bombay on June 19, 1947, almost two months before India won her independence from Britain. Bombay, the "most cosmopolitan, most hybrid, most hotch potch of Indian cities," Rushdie recalls, exerted a tremendous pull on him, and became one of the major settings for his novel about India's birth, *Midnight's Children*. An only son (Rushdie has three sisters), and the eldest child in an Indian family, he grew up thinking that the world revolved around him.

Starting his education at Cathedral School in Bombay, at age fourteen Rushdie left for England to pursue his studies at Rugby, an exclusive British "public" school. Although he departed without any serious apprehensions about going so far away from his family and home ("I think I had actually wanted to go," he says, "I was groomed for it"), Rugby (and England) turned out to be quite different from what he had expected. Made to feel like an "Indian" for the first time, Rushdie had his first taste of racial bigotry when he found one of the boys, who shared his study, scrawling "wogs go home" on the wall over his chair (Glendenning 38). His experience at Rugby made him reluctant to return to England.

In 1967, his parents moved to Pakistan. Rushdie notes that his parents were not of the "Pakistani persuasion," belonging to that group of Muslims who stayed back in India after the partition of the subcontinent (Kaufman 22). But over a couple of decades, they changed their minds; and Rushdie recalls (via Saleem in *Midnight's Children*) that he never forgave them for moving. After spending some time in Pakistan, on his return from Rugby, he was persuaded to go to King's College, Cambridge, where he took a degree in history. He stayed on in England, working first in the fringe theater, and then as a copywriter in an advertising agency.

Meantime, he was also working at becoming a writer, a role and a profession he had aspired to from his youthful days. Rushdie describes how he grew up surrounded by books because his was a family of writers and storytellers. His paternal grandfather was a "good Urdu poet"; his father, a student of Arabic and Persian literature and Western literature, and his mother, "the keeper of family stories," were themselves "gifted story-tellers" (Kaufman 22). For his father, however, writing did not count as a "real job" (Glendenning 38).

Liz Calder, an editor at Gollancz, and later Rushdie's agent till Andrew Wylie wooed him away, was a lodger at the Rushdie home in Victoria. She encouraged Rushdie to submit *Grimus* for a science-fiction contest Gollancz was organizing. *Grimus* did not win in the contest, but Calder persuaded Gollancz to publish it anyway. Critics savaged the book. While Rushdie took the rejection badly, he soon recovered and decided to write an "epic" novel about India, embodying its past, present, and (possibly) its future. In preparation for this ambitious undertaking, Rushdie and his wife embarked on an extended trip to India. Rushdie had made several visits to his family in Pakistan; but this was his first visit to India in ten years.

In "The Indian Writer in England," Rushdie recalls how, on revisiting his house in Bombay, he was "gripped by the conviction that I, too, had a city and a history to reclaim"; at that moment, *Midnight's Children* "was really born" (75). Published in 1981, this novel was a runaway success; it went on to win the prestigious Booker Prize, which with its award of £10,000 finally gave him the freedom to write full-time; it also made him a celebrity, lionized by the media in England, and then in India, where huge crowds turned out to hear his readings and lectures.

Shame (1983), his novel set in and about Pakistan, followed two years later, and was also enthusiastically received, garnering much critical acclaim. It was banned in Pakistan, but smuggled copies allowed it to be read by several members of the intelligentsia.

Around this time, and especially between the years 1981–1985, Rushdie wrote a series of essays where he reflected both on his location as an "author from three countries," and on that of emigrant/expatriate writers, in general, pointing to the net gains and losses that accrue from being situated, as it were, between two or more cultures. He noted how "three places have more or less an equal claim on me . . . England . . . where I live, India . . . where I was born, Pakistan . . . where my family lives" (Kaufman 22). Each of these places, he says, can be, and is, legitimately a subject of his writing. He describes those who would confine him to his Indian identity alone as invoking an "imperial" notion about how writers from the West can write about any place and anything in the world, while Third World writers are confined to the places (and cultures) of their "origins" (In interview by Brooks 66–67). At the same time, in a scathing critique of the Raj revival in the recent spate of films and novels about India—*Gandhi, The Far Pavillions, Jewel in the Crown, A Passage to India*—Rushdie, in "Outside the

Whale," wrote vociferously against both the attempt to revive imperial values and the political quietism that allowed this to happen. During this time, Rushdie also expressed his anger over Britain's imperial adventure in the Falkland Islands, which, he said, released "an atavistic, jingoistic patriotism," and he vehemently criticized British racism, by writing about the "empire within Britain" (123–24).

In July 1986, Rushdie traveled to Nicaragua as a guest of the Sandinista Association of Cultural Workers. During his three-week stay there, he spent most of his time with fellow writers, and in traveling throughout the country. From this visit emerged a travelogue of sorts, and Rushdie's fourth book. *The Jaguar Smile: A Nicaraguan Journey* (1987).

Over the years, Rushdie was thinking about and mapping what was to become his most controversial novel, *The Satanic Verses*, another ambitious undertaking. He wished in this work "to treat directly" the "position ... [of] being at one and the same time an insider and outsider in society" ("A Dangerous Art Form" 3), by turning to and making central his interest in recording the migrant's vision. Set in Margaret Thatcher's Britain, it would cover the Indian subcontinent as well, and embody his attitudes toward Islam, toward issues of religious faith and skepticism. When Rushdie finished writing *The Satanic Verses*, he is reported to have said: "This is the first time that I have managed to write a book from the whole of myself. It was written from my entire sense of being in the world" (Quoted in Weatherby 108). Even before it hit the market, Rushdie's book caused a stir in the publishing world by receiving a huge advance. While the book was much discussed, and received favorably by British reviewers, it wasn't until India banned it, a week after its publication in Britain, that it began to be seen as a political and controversial work. Soon Pakistan, Saudi Arabia, Egypt, Indonesia, South Africa, and countries with large Muslim populations also banned it. Its (and Rushdie's) fate was sealed, however, when, a little under five months after its publication, Ayatollah Khomeini announced his "fatwa" against Rushdie, calling upon "zealous Muslims" to execute him quickly. The rest, as they say, is history. Rushdie went into, and till today remains in, hiding.

While in hiding, he has written a "children's" book, *Haroun and the Sea of Stories* (1991), that he had promised to write for his son, Zafar. He continues to review books, and has recently put together a collection of his essays, written between 1981 and 1991, entitled, not inappropriately, *Imaginary Homelands*.

MAJOR WORKS AND THEMES

Despite variations in form and subject matter in his various fictional works, Rushdie displays remarkable consistency when it comes to certain ideas, certain literary and philosophical preoccupations; and these appear and reappear in his works. His nonfictional essays explicitly articulate some of these ideas and, thus, function as a veritable gloss on his fiction. Rushdie can be (and is) a very personal writer, drawing upon his own experiences or of those he knows, fashioning (and transforming) them into images and events of haunting power. Not surprisingly, one of the most significant ideas, addressed in his essays, and informing his fiction, springs from his own location as an expatriate or migrant.

In "The Indian Writer in England," while defining his (and other migrants') identity as plural and partial, at once straddling two cultures and distanced from both, Rushdie speculates about the competing claims of wholesale assimilation to or wholesale rejection of dominant (English) values. For him, neither alternative is acceptable on its own; rather he recommends that the migrant negotiate the values of both cultures—"native" and "adopted"—strategically drawing upon each to create a "new," hybrid entity (81).

Inevitably, he turns to what these and other pressures might mean for the migrant writer who chooses to write about the "native" culture he or she has left behind, but not forgotten. Here, as an Indian expatriate writer, his "physical alienation" from India means that he cannot reclaim "precisely the thing that was lost" and is "obliged to deal in fragments," to create "imaginary homelands; Indias of the mind" (76). However, in a characteristic Rushdian move, the migrant writer's "long, geographical distance" from the culture he writes about and his access to "imaginative" and "partial" truth are turned into strengths only the migrant writer possesses. First, insofar as he defines the role of a writer as a principled opponent or adversary of the ruling myths and self-presentations a culture propogates about itself, Rushdie is primarily interested in the truths these myths suppress. In this regard, then, a migrant writer like him, who is both *inside* (therefore intimately knowledgeable about the "native" culture he represents) and *outside* (therefore not invested in its dominant ideologies), is best able to excavate such "suppressed truths" and offer a critically self-conscious portrait of that culture: "To see things plainly, you have to cross a frontier" ("Location of Brazil" 53). Furthermore, the writer, any writer, but most especially the migrant writer, through his access to "imaginative truth," can "draw new and better maps of reality" ("Outside the Whale" 137). He can, in other words, write alternate accounts of reality, which may include those suppressed by the people in power. Finally, the migrant writer, insofar as he depends upon fragmentary, partial memories about all he left behind, highlights the contingent nature of his "truths."

Despite his emphasis on the "imaginative" and "created" nature of the migrant's vision, the words "reality" and "world" appear constantly in his reflections on the writer's tasks. He is careful, for example, to distinguish between imaginative visions that remain hermetically sealed within the pages of a book and those that constantly spill outside, establishing and reestablishing their ties with the world; he prefers the latter.

Grimus, Rushdie's first foray into fiction writing, was a failed novel; few readers of Rushdie refer to it; even fewer may have actually read it. But Timothy Brennan makes a persuasive case for it as exemplifying "most clearly what Rushdie was up to in [his] later work" (*Salman Rushdie* 70). The hero, Flapping Eagle, is an American *Indian* (my emphasis), in search of his lost sister, whom he finds on a Mediterranean island under the control of Grimus, an expatriate European magician. (The Mediterranean exists midway between the West and the "Orient"; thus, Rushdie's choice of locale is not accidental.) Flapping Eagle leaves home because he has to: he is an outcast (or "outsider") from his birth, because his mother dies bearing him; he and his sister are shunned by their community, which is defined by antiquarian values and religious bigotry, for going against its laws against seeking contact with the outside world. To reach Grimus, and thereby find his sister, Flapping Eagle has to scale Mountain Calf, which task Brennan identifies with the "act of climbing the ranks of British opportunity" (*Salman Rushdie* 72). What seems to be at stake here are Rushdie's initial thoughts on a figure arriving in a "new" country and culture, an immigrant, as it were, who then tries to (uncritically) assimilate the values of this new culture. The terms used to characterize this process will resonate, in a more critically self-aware manner, in Rushdie's later comments, in "The Indian Writer in England." It is instructive to keep in mind that in the latter, the problematic of assimilation and/or rejection will be framed through questions, and will be formulated as a productive tension between the two; in the following passage from *Grimus*, however, only one pole of the problematic appears:

Stripped of his past, forsaking the language of his ancestor for the languages of the archipelagoes of the world, forsaking the ways of his ancestors for those of the places he drifted to, forsaking any hopes of ideals in the face of the changing and contradictory ideals he encountered, he lived, doing what he was given to do, thinking what he was instructed to think, being what it was most desirable to be. (36)

A "chameleon, changeling, all things to all men" (36), Flapping Eagle's "problems" are those of rootlessness, which represent only one element in the dialectic of assimilation and estrangement that Rushdie identifies as making up the "hybrid" identity of the migrant or expatriate. More than anything else, perhaps, *Grimus* is valuable insofar as it foregrounds Rushdie's attempt to find "a suitable voice to speak in" (36), which also entails articulating a series of concerns that best demonstrates the competing claims of "native home" versus "adopted home" for the migrant/expatriate.

In his interview with *Third World Book Review*, entitled "A Dangerous

Art Form," Rushdie responds to the problem that he lives in England, writes in English, but his two major books are about the Indian subcontinent by stating: "I'd say that the main problem [in writing *Midnight's Children* and *Shame*] was that I absolutely did not want to write an outsider-novel. This meant that the imaginative leap required was larger than it would have been ... " (3). Of course, in *Shame* the narrator (like Rushdie) is an expatriate who has returned to Pakistan for an extended visit; as such, his account proceeds explicitly from the perspective of a migrant, who is at one and the same time an *outsider* and an *insider* in the culture he writes about. *Midnight's Children* is another matter. Nowhere *within* the text are there any markers showing that this is the work of an expatriate. And yet people know that Rushdie is an expatriate and has participated only partially in the postindependence life of India. How, then, does Rushdie circumvent doubts about his being an "outsider"? Through what strategies does he establish his credibility as a recorder of India's "history"—past, present, and even future? Answers to these questions are significant not only because his ambition is to encompass so much of India's life, but also because his account is, for the most part, a bitter exposé of what, despite all its youthful promise, this nation has become.

By far the most important strategy he deploys is the one through which he places his hero-narrator, Saleem Sinai, *inside* and at the *center* of India's history. Born at the moment India won formal independence from the British, Saleem is a child "*of the time*: fathered, you understand, by history" (139). Saleem's life (and identity) is represented as a product of and continuous with the life of postindependence India, but he also *creates* this life. Thus, at the same time as his life coincides with his nation's (Jawaharlal Nehru's letter to "Baby Saleem" predicts: "Your life will be, in a sense, a mirror of our own" [143]), Saleem also initiates (and is the cause of) major events in the political life of India: he triggers the language riots in Bombay in one instance and plots Ayub Khan's coup in another, by moving "pepperpots," "mustard-jars," and "bowls of chutney" on Uncle Zulfikar's dinner table to shape things to come (348). But it is clearly not enough to establish Saleem's credibility alone, for that does not necessarily establish Rushdie's. Thus, Rushdie creates the "assumption of autobiography" ("*Midnight's Children* and *Shame*" 12), drawing upon key events of his own life to structure Saleem's, whose life can, then, be read as continuous with Rushdie's. Not surprisingly, several readers have read *Midnight's Children* as if it were an autobiography.

Among the key moments Saleem/Rushdie selects to narrate in his "history" of India are the much-written-about massacre at Jallianwala Bagh in Amritsar in 1919; the partition of the subcontinent in 1947 (though, as Tariq Ali notes, this episode "is almost muted" in the book, which is also curiously reticent about "the personal conflicts and political contradictions that traumatized the bulk of the middle-class families" [89]); Nehru's First

Five-Year Plan in 1956; Ayub Khan's coup in 1958; the Indo-Chinese war of 1962; the Indo-Pakistani wars of 1965 and 1971, when Bangladesh was created; and the Indian Emergency of 1975 when Indira Gandhi suspended all civil rights and jailed her political opponents.

Inevitably, selection proceeds on the basis of inclusion as much as exclusion. Among the experiences excluded from Saleem's/Rushdie's narrative is an account of Gandhi's national movement, which, says Timothy Brennan, is "impertinently excised" so that the "story of Indian nationalism is erased from the book that documents its sad outcome" (*Salman Rushdie* 84). Tariq Ali, who finds *Midnight's Children* enormously important and predicts its great impact, nevertheless notes that Rushdie "has been able to recreate his subject only partially" (94). Yet "partial" or "fragmentary" vision, with its ability to highlight the contingent status of narratives, including narratives of nation-forming, is, for Rushdie, the hallmark of "modernism" within which he places his own work. Moreover, for Rushdie, it also defines the condition, and, thus, the perspective of migrants who, as culturally displaced subjects, have had to accept "the provisional nature of all truths, all certainties" ("The Indian Writer in England" 77). The migrant's vision, then, is silently insinuated into the perspective that informs *Midnight's Children*, even though it is never explicitly addressed, as it is in *Shame*, within the work itself.

In a curious and paradoxical way, Saleem's/Rushdie's narrative of India's "history" vies for *representative*, "truthful" (even a totalizing) status, at the same time as it undermines this status by bringing us back to the perspective of a single narrator, whose own quirks, especially his desire to impose form on and wrest meaning from the chaos of his life and that of his nation's, are highlighted in the narrative itself.

Several of Rushdie's abiding interests are in evidence in this work, presented to us via a series of narratives that nest within the larger narrative composing Saleem's life. Through Saleem's account of his grandfather's return from Germany, his conversations with Tai, the ancient Kashmiri boatman, about religious faith and doubt, and his marriage to Naseem, the conflict between modernity and tradition is illustrated. Through an account of his parents' move to Methwold's estate, with Methwold insisting that everything be retained in the houses he sells, Saleem demonstrates the colonial formation of the Indian elite. Through his account of the "Land of the Pure," religious bigotry is exposed. Of course, all this and more come to us via the perspectives defined by Saleem's "plural" and "partial" identity(ies). Saleem is, after all, the son of a departing English sahib and an Indian woman married to a street singer, switched at birth with Ameena Sinai's real son, Shiva, and brought up in a Muslim household in cosmopolitan Bombay. Moreover, Saleem's historical (re)construction of events in Indian "history" is structured through photographs and newspaper clippings; a willful mixing of "fairy tale style . . . court evidence, school essay, public speech, and other variations of the narrative mode" (Bader, "The Indian Tin Drum" 76). And Bombay cinema—that most ubiquitous icon of Indian popular culture—is invoked in the form and content of the book, just as Rushdie/Saleem uses the vocabulary of filmmaking to comment on his narrative strategies.

The trajectory of Saleem's life seems deeply pessimistic: castrated and prematurely old at thirty-one, his body cracking up into a million pieces, neither he nor the nation whose trajectory he embodies seems to be at all a fulfillment of the hopes invoked at the moment of their birth. Rushdie, however, denies the charge of pessimism, pointing toward his representation of "India's talent for non-stop self-regeneration," exhibited via the plenitude/excess of narratives in his work as the essential counterweight ("The Indian Writer in England" 80). *Shame*'s pessimism, on the other hand, cannot be argued against, even if one sees the final apocalyptic pages, with everything going up in flames, as a "clearing of the stables" before a new order can begin.

The difference between *Midnight's Children* and *Shame* goes deeper, arising from Rushdie's radically different perceptions about the "imagined communities"—Benedict Anderson's luminous definition about the process of nation-forming—each nation, India and Pakistan, represents. About India Rushdie says: "Its existence as a political entity was a fiction invented by the British in 1947. Even the British had never ruled over more than 60 percent of India. But it was a dream that everyone agreed to dream. And now I think there actually is a country called India" (Glendenning 38). In *Midnight's Children*, Saleem says: "India, the new myth—a collective fiction in which *anything was possible*..." (129; emphasis added). By contrast, "Pakistan... may be best described as the failure of the dreaming mind.... perhaps the place was just *insufficiently imagined*" (*Shame* 92; emphasis in original). Rushdie's narrative focus also is narrower: instead of narrating the nation, Rushdie has settled for a more restricted portrait of the ruling elite, especially its corruption and shamelessness.

More than anything else, *Shame* is a long meditation on various embodiments of shame as they exhibit themselves both in the domestic sphere and on the spiritual level. His reflections about the former are directed primarily at the management of (women's) sexuality. Thus, for example, after a night of carousing, when one of the Shakil sisters becomes pregnant by an "Imperial Sahib," all of them don the garments of their patriarchal culture and retreat into the seclusion of their mansion, their only contact with the world being through an old maidservant who must travel in a dumbwaiter and through intricate security arrangements. Similarly, in Bariamma's household, husbands must steal into their wives' beds like "the forty thieves," because matters dealing with human sexuality must not be seen or heard. Bilquis Hyder lays the blame for her inability to bear sons on this unnatural arrangement. In the male-dominated society of the subcontinent, for a woman to participate in the public sphere entails that she, like Arjumand Harrappa, "rise above her gender," that she quite literally transform herself into a man: "When her breasts begin to swell, she will bind them tightly in linen bandages, so fiercely that she blushes with pain. She will come to enjoy the war against her body..." (136). Naveed "Good News" Hyder wills herself to become beautiful so she can attract men and get married, but realizes that to her husband she is just a "vegetable patch" to be planted with his "seed" annually; she understands "there was no hope for women in the world" (228).

In such a world, women either go crazy (Bilquis), or kill themselves (Naveed), or turn into figures of violent vengefulness (Sufiya Zinobia). Sufiya is the titular heroine of this book without a clear center (except that provided by the idea of shame, or, intermittently, by the rivalry between Iskander Harrappa and Raza Hyder). A "miracle-gone-wrong, a family's shame made flesh" (150), she is the firstborn daughter who should have been a son. Pure herself, she absorbs the unspoken, suppressed, unrealized shame of those around her, until such time as she is transformed into nothing but shame—pure, violent, unadulterated. She exemplifies one of the more striking moves Rushdie makes in his fictions whereby a metaphor is made literal: her blushes don't just look like flame, they *actually burn* like flame.

At the national level, shame is the shamelessness, greed, and violence of the ruling elite; it is the defining condition of Pakistan's public and political life: "Wherever I turn," says the narrator, "there is something of which to be ashamed" (22). The way to the top, as the careers of Iskander and Raza illustrate, is through the murderous and sleazy exercise of power. The cast of characters, in this national tragedy played out as farce, are a bunch of small, squalid actors whose actions are at odds with what should be the scale of Pakistan's history if it is to become a viable nation.

The two levels of shame, enacted in the domestic and national spheres, are not mutually exclusive; indeed they overlap significantly, with repression ("the seamless garment" [189]) serving as a bridge between the two. As Anthony Barnett notes, Sufiya, who is at one and the same time "the family's shame made flesh" and a repository of national shame, "can be said to 'stand for' the necessary violent reaction of women against patriarchy and of the people against dictatorship, that the fantastic Pakistan of this novel seems to provoke." (96).

If repression entails suppressing alternate values/visions, then, in a patriarchal society, women can become the source of alternative values, alternate histories. But in *Shame*, as in *Midnight's Children*, alternate histories are not accounts of what a new order should be, but rather are exposés of what's suppressed. Thus, the Rani's eighteen shawls of memory expose "The Shamelessness of Iskander the Great" (210). Similarly, the expatriate narrator, through indirection ("My story, my fictional country exist, like myself, at a slight angle to reality.... My view is that I am not only writing about Pakistan" [24]), exposes the shoddy history of nation-building in *Shame*.

The narratives of *Shame* come to us through "the characters of the narrators.... some of whom ... are serious fellows, reflective and mature; others querulous or coy, or sometimes mannered...; some again... breathlessly enthusiastic..." (Edgar 126); primarily, however, it is the voice of the reflective expatriate writer who sees himself as part of the fray, but only as the occasional participant distanced from the action as well. His perspective is that of a "translated man," mediating between two cultures, exasperated sometimes that "shame" is not as resonant as the word it translates, *sharam*, which contains "Encyclopaedias." Nevertheless, he insists that much is to be gained through translation. Presumably, since the expatriate narrator is a translated man, much is to be gained from his perspective as well, although, as in translation, the process is inevitably open to distortions and dislocations.

Among the interests Rushdie identifies as central to his most controversial work, *The Satanic Verses*, he mentions (1) the desire to "give voice and fictional flesh to the immigrant culture" ("The Book Burning" 26), which entails an examination of the metamorphoses immigrants undergo, the divided selves that result from negotiating two or more cultures simultaneously; (2) an attempt to explore the nature of divine revelation from the perspective of a secular person, which entails, in turn, an examination of religious faith versus religious doubt. He chose to focus on Islam, from its birth to its more contemporary manifestations, because it is the religion he knows most about.

The book opens with its two heroes, Saladin Chamcha and Gibreel Farishta, hurtling through the sky as they plunge into the English Channel—an image that represents, for Rushdie, the "most spectacular act of immigration [he] could imagine" (Quoted in Weatherby 103). *The Verses'* exploration of immigrant experience is situated in a very specific context, dealing with the life of immigrants from formerly colonized Third World countries to Britain—Margaret Thatcher's Britain. The novel unpacks this experience(s) through individuals and through groups, sketching in their living and lived spaces, as it were. The novel recognizes that immigrations compel radical change: when Gibreel and Saladin land in a Sussex swamp, the former acquires an angel's halo, the latter sprouts horns, grows goat's hooves, and begins to display an immense erection. In almost all instances, immigrants are called upon to adapt, even to remake or reinvent themselves, to which they respond with varying degrees of complexity: the most single-minded either absolutely refuse or agree too willingly, too completely, to their transformation.

Simply transplanting one's native culture in an "alien" soil can be variously unrealistic, perverse, politically reactionary, unacceptable, or unworkable. There's something unrealistic about Hind's (the proprietess of Shaandaar Cafe) refusal to step out, her decision to let her "real world" be defined entirely by "the endless supply of Bengali and Hindi movies on VCR" and by "her ever-increasing hoard of Indian movie magazines" (250). Hind's nativism (which is the privileging of one's native culture by reviving and preserving it; it is premised on the notion of the native and native culture as an immutable essence that is somehow transhistorical and transcendent) can be best cast as an unexamined nostalgia for the home she has left behind. Much more extreme, indeed downright perverse, is the exiled Imam's willful seclusion from the "alien" nation (206) in the hope of keeping himself "unsullied, unaltered, pure" (207). Equally perverse is his desire to simulate the "dry heat of Desh" in his London mansion by turning on the "central-heating full blast" and keeping the "windows tightly shut" (208).

By the same token, remaking oneself completely in the image of the adopted country/culture (which, here, also happens to be that of one's former colonizer) simply reverses the nativist position. Saladin Chamcha, a deracinated Indian who had striven to be English even before he left Bombay, who feels "contempt for his kind" (45) and presumes he's marrying "bloody Britannia" when he marries Pamela of the aristocratic English voice (175), is, until his fall from the sky, a mirror image of the Imam in his fanatical devotion to *Englishness*. His remaking flies in the face of historical reality, for, in a race-conscious Britain, his face is still the wrong color. When, after his landing on a Sussex swamp, the police arrest him for entering the country illegally, the repressive apparatus of the British state is directed against him: he is beaten senseless by the police in the back of a Black Maria and forced to eat his own feces. (Through these and other passages, Rushdie provides a devastating critique of the overt racism of "Mrs. Torture's" Britain.)

Transformed into the veritable image of the devil ("Shaitan"), forced to find refuge among his own kind, for whom he feels contempt, Chamcha undergoes yet another transformation: he comes to signify the visible face of resistance when the black community's opposition to dominant British values and representations about nonwhite peoples takes the form of accepting the devil's role assigned to them, thus, embodying a strategy that turns "insults into strengths" (98). If, as Rushdie has said, part of his concern was to show how we learn to be human (Meer 37), then Chamcha's attempt to become human is fundamentally linked to his acknowledgment of the ties that bind him to his family, his people, and his (Indian) past. Thus, a process that begins with his sojourn in Brickhall is completed, as it were, when Chamcha returns to Bombay to be reunited with his dying, until now estranged, father. And it ends with Zeeny Vakil's injunction: "If you're serious about shaking off your foreignness, Salad baba, then don't fall into some kind of rootless limbo.... We're all here. We're right in front of you. You should really try to make an adult acquaintance with this place, this time" (541).

Several readers of *The Verses* have remarked that it is a deeply Islamic work, "a work," notes Sara Suleri, "of meticulous religious attentiveness" (606). Rushdie himself observes that the Prophet "insisted throughout his life on his simple humanity" ("The Book Burning" 26). This humanity Rushdie sets out to explore via his account of "Mahound's" career and of "the satanic verses," both of which are presented as part of Gibreel's hallucinatory dreams. "The Satanic Verses" of the title refers to an incident in the life of the Prophet, recorded by early Arab historians, when he accepted that the worship of three female deities, Al-Lat, Al-Uzza, and Al-Manat, was permissible within the bounds of Islamic doctrine; he later repudiated this as an act inspired by the devil. Here Rushdie is interested in interrogating the status of religious belief versus "modern" skepticism, and the status of religious revelation: "Centrally my book is about a dispute between ... the sacred and the profane ideas of what a book is. The book whose legitimization comes simply as an act of the imagination—and these other kinds that are supposed to be handed down from another place" (Rushdie in Meer 36).

While identifying the taboos against which his book transgresses, Rushdie mentions his attempt to write about the "place of women in Islamic society and in the Koran" ("The Book Burning" 26). This project seems to be most evident in the "Ayesha" episode that, according to Suleri, "retells the tale of the Satanic Verses in a contemporary cultural context" and attempts "to locate an idiom for the feminization of Islam" (615). The episode is based on an incident that really happened: "The Hawkes Bay Case," in which a young woman persuaded a village to make a pilgrimage to the sacred site of Karbala and the waters would part. Here the figure of the Prophet as woman enables Rushdie to explore the nature of religious belief through this "most extraordinary image of faith that [he had] come across in years" (Rushdie in Meer 35). It is crucial that in his retelling of this incident, his account shuttles between doubt and faith: several pilgrims drown; but those who survive claim they saw the sea part.

His most recent work of fiction, *Haroun and the Sea of Stories*, reworks, this time ostensibly for children, some of Rushdie's favorite concerns: his "faith" in the value of imaginative truth; his interest in storytelling as an instance of such imaginative truth. Its wry fantasy, wordplay, and fantastic characters are vintage Rushdie. But it is also written in the shadow of his current predicament, which it embodies through setting up the conflict between the claims of the human imagination versus the forces that would silence the imagination.

CRITICAL RECEPTION

Rushdie's *Midnight's Children* put the Indo-English novel on the map in a way that had not been done before: "No other novel about India has had such an impact" (Ali 95). It also made Rushdie, at age thirty-four, into a major literary figure. Critical praise showered on the work characterized it variously as "an outstanding achievement" (Nazareth), "a novel of international importance" (Chaudhuri), a work that "sounds like a continent finding its voice" (Blaise), enormously creative in its "fecundity, extravagance, and scope" (Towers). Rushdie's exuberant comic gift, imaginative boldness, big talent, prodigious powers of storytelling, debt to Gabriel Garcia Marquez, Gunter Grass, Laurence Sterne—all became part of the vocabulary of critical acclaim that greeted *Midnight's Children*. Nor was this praise articulated by Western reviewers alone. Anita Desai, recognizing it as a book "of major interest to Indian readers," went on to characterize it as "a great tour de force, a dazzling exhibition of the gifts of a new writer with courage, impressive strength, the power of both imagination and control, and sheer stylistic brilliance" (13). In the Indian subcontinent, the book garnered other favorable reviews as well. Its impact, in the subcontinent and the West, can perhaps be best gauged through the fact that the book's characterization of the generation of Indians born after independence as "midnight's children," and its naming of Indira Gandhi as "the Widow," have become part of the common vocabulary of people when they speak about India. In England, it was awarded the prestigious Booker Prize. Its critical reception more than made up for Rushdie's disappointment over *Grimus*, which was panned by the critics.

Shame also opened to largely favorable reviews. Some reviewers in fact found it better than *Midnight's Children*. Both Anthony Barnett, reviewing it for *Race and Class*, and Michael Hollington, for *Meanjin Quarterly*, found the "successor . . . superior to its predecessor" (Hollington 403), "tauter, harder, cleverer even" (Barnett 91). For others, however, it didn't work as well: Timothy Hyman described it as "a smaller book for a meaner world" (93). Nevertheless, as with *Midnight's Children*, the vocabulary of praise for *Shame* isolated Rushdie's dazzling gifts of storytelling, linguistic innovation, and juxtaposition of the fantastic with the real. *Shame* too was short-listed for the Booker Prize, but it did not win the prize.

The Satanic Verses, which became available in British bookstores in September 1988, was also praised by British reviewers in terms that had by now become familiar to Rushdie's readers. But the features that were to make the novel so controversial for Muslims the world over were largely ignored in the early reviews in the West. *India Today* and *Sunday*, two magazines from India, were among the first to key in to its political and controversial aspects; both predicted the protests that soon followed. The Indian government quickly banned the book, and similar bans soon followed in other parts of the world with large Muslim populations. *The Verses* became available in the United States after all the furor and controversy had already begun. Thus, several reviewers in the United States inevitably referred to the controversy, even when they went on (as most did) to praise it for its literary merits.

With regard to more extended commentaries on his works and on Rushdie himself, one has to begin, perhaps, with the only full-length critical study on Rushdie, Timothy's Brennan's *Salman Rushdie and the Third World: Myths of the Nation*. In addition to offering very insightful readings of each of Rushdie's fictional works and his nonfictional *The Jaguar Smile*, Brennan's terms for discussing Rushdie ("cosmopolitan writer" versus "frontline fighter"; "anti-colonial liberalism" versus "nationalism," to name some) provide an illuminating context within which Rushdie's oeuvre can be read and understood. Brennan's analysis is especially useful for studying Rushdie's diasporic sensibility because the "master" term that organizes his study is that of the "cosmopolitan writer." For Brennan, "cosmopolitan" writers are writers attached to specific locales in the "third" world who mediate, interpret, and translate this world for "first" world/metropolitan readers. Their success depends upon their being simultaneously "alien" and "familiar"—their being able, that is, to offer an "insider's" view of "third" world cultures and peoples, while complying with their metropolitan readers' tastes, which requires, most importantly, an entrenched skepticism toward, even revulsion of, nationalism.

Among the essays on Rushdie's *Midnight's Children* and/or *Shame*, the most interesting, theoretically informed pieces worth mentioning are Rustom Barucha's "Rushdie's Whale," which looks closely at Rushdie's linguistic innovations and wordplay to make the point that "Rushdie has added a new dimension to . . . English by being idiosyncratically true to the sounds of his birth and youth" (222). Inderpal Grewal's "Salman Rushdie: Marginality, Women, and *Shame*" critiques the "feminist project of the novel" by arguing that "there is a disjunction between the mode of inclusion in which the narrative is written and the authoritative stance of the writer suggested in the novel, a stance that breaks down a coalition between the writer and women" (25). Kum Kum Sangari's "The Politics of the Possible," a wide-ranging comparative analysis of Garcia Marquez and Rushdie, examines how Western readers appropriate the "magical realist" narratives of the two writers under the terms of postmodernism, thereby displacing (or erasing) the politics implicit and explicit in the work of these writers.

A great deal of the extended commentary on *The Verses* has been not so much about the work itself as it has been about the broader social, political, and cultural implications of both Rushdie's book and Ayatollah Khomeini's "fatwa" for an understanding of Islam and its place in a "modern" world. Thus, for example, Akeel Bilgrami, in his essay "Rushdie and the Reform of Islam," through "a . . . more historically contextual argument" attempts to "convey why it so crucial today that there should be a growing body of Muslim opinion which, despite acknowledging and regretting the book's effect on devoted Muslims, must all the same stand behind Rushdie" (173). Why? For one, the book, according to Bilgrami, has started a valuable debate about "the nature and role of Islam" (181), which will enable the reform of Islam and help the Islamic world to join the "international community of modern and progressive nations" (176).

From a quite different perspective, Talal Asad, in "Multiculturalism and British Identity in the Wake of the Rushdie affair," examines the British government's response to the crisis precipitated in Britain's Muslim communities in the wake of the publication of *The Verses.* According to Asad, the government's response was affected by and arose from a "perceived threat to a particular ideological structure, a cultural hierarchy organized around an essential *Englishness,* which defines British identity" (457).

Sara Suleri's "Contraband Histories: Salman Rushdie, and the Embodiment of Blasphemy" is, perhaps, apart from Brennan's in his book, one of the more stimulating readings of the work itself, even as it contextualizes the work in terms of Islamic culture in which it is clearly embedded. She attempts to show that Rushdie has written a "deeply Islamic book," which performs an "archaic act of devotion to the cultural system that it must both desecrate and renew.... a gesture of wrenching loyalty, [the work] suggests[s] that blasphemy can only be articulated within the compass of belief" (606).

BIBLIOGRAPHY

Works by Salman Rushdie

Grimus. London: Overlook Press, 1979. (fiction)
"Calvino." *London Review of Books* (Sept. 17–30, 1981): 16–17. (review)
Midnight's Children. New York: Knopf, 1981. (fiction)
"Prophet's Hair." *Atlantic* (June 1981): 23–29. (short story)
"The Dean's December." *New Statesman* (Apr. 2, 1982): 22. (essay)
"The Empire Writes Back with a Vengeance." *(London) Times* (July 3, 1982): 8. (essay)
"The Golden Bough." *Granta* 7 (1982): 47–51. (essay)
"Imaginary Homelands." *London Review of Books* (Oct. 1982): 18–19. (review)
"The New Empire within Britain." *New Society* (Dec. 9, 1982): 34–37. (essay)
"Yorick." *Encounter* (Sept.-Oct. 1982): 3–8. (essay)
"Free Radio." *Atlantic* (June 1983): 75–78. (short story)
Dharker, Rani. "An Interview with Salman Rushdie." *New Quest* 42 (Nov.-Dec. 1983): 351–60. (interview)
"I Borrowed My Expressions from the East." *Muslim Magazine* (Islamabad) (Nov. 18, 1983): 1. (essay)

"The Indian Writer in England." *The Eye of the Beholder: Indian Writing in English.* Ed. Maggie Butcher. London: Commonwealth Institute, 1983. 75–83. (essay)

Kaufman, Michael. "Author from Three Countries." *New York Times Book Review* (Nov. 13, 1983): 3, 22–23. (interview)

"Outside the Whale." *Granta* 11 (1983): 123–41. (essay)

"Raggedy Gandhi." *Movies* (July 1983): 14. (review)

"A Dangerous Art Form." *Third World Book Review* 1 (1984): 3–5. (interview)

"Dynasty and Democracy." *New Republic* (Nov. 26, 1984): 17–19. (essay)

Foreword. *An Indian Dynasty: The Story of the Nehru-Gandhi Family.* By Tariq Ali. New York: Putnam, 1984. (essay)

Introduction. *Home Front.* By Derek Bishton and John Reardon. London: Jonathan Cape, 1984. (essay)

"Peruvian Master." *New Republic* (Oct. 8, 1984): 25–28. (essay)

Shame. New York. Vintage/Aventura, 1984. (fiction)

Brooks, David. "Salman Rushdie." *Helix* 19–20 (1985): 55–69. (interview)

"The Location of Brazil." *American Film* 10 (Sept. 1985): 50–53. (essay)

"*Midnight's Children* and *Shame.*" *Kunapipi* 8:1 (1985): 1–19. (essay)

"On Gunter Grass." *Granta* 15 (1985): 180–85. (essay)

"Adventures and Epics." *New York Times Magazine* (Mar. 16, 1986): S26–S28. (essay)

"Goodness—The American Neurosis." *Nation* (Mar. 22, 1986): 344–46. (essay)

"On Palestinian Identity: A Conversation" (with Edward W. Said). *New Left Review* (Nov.-Dec. 1986): 63–81. (essay)

"The Press: International Viewpoint." *Times Literary Supplement* (Feb. 17, 1986): 90. (essay)

"After Midnight." *Vanity Fair* (Sept. 1987): 88–94. (essay)

"Good Advice Is Rarer Than Rubies." *New Yorker* (June 22, 1987): 26–29. (short story)

The Jaguar Smile: A Nicaraguan Journey. New York: Viking-Penguin, 1987. (nonfiction)

"Dear Mill." *New York Times Book Review* (Nov. 13, 1988): 39. (review)

"Song Doesn't Know the Score." *Black Film British Cinema.* ICA Documents 7. London: Institute of Contemporary Arts, 1988. 16–17 (essay)

"Untime of the Imam." *Harper's Magazine* (Dec. 1988): 53–59. (short story)

"Zia Unmourned." *Nation* (Sept. 19, 1988): 188–89. (essay)

"The Book Burning." *New York Review of Books* (Mar. 2, 1989): 26. (essay)

"Clandestine in Chile." *Times Literary Supplement* (Oct. 6, 1989): 1088. (essay)

"A Clash of Faiths." *Maclean's* (Feb. 27, 1989): 24. (essay).

Meer, Amina. "Salman Rushdie." *Bomb* 27 (Spring 1989): 35–37. (interview)

"My Book Speaks for Itself." *New York Times* (Feb. 17, 1989): 23. (essay)

The Satanic Verses. New York: Viking-Penguin, 1989. (fiction)

"Big Deal: One Year as a Professional Poker Player." *Times Literary Supplement* (Nov. 16, 1990): 1239. (essay)

"In Good Faith." *Newsweek* (Feb. 12, 1990): 52–57. (essay)

"The Oxford Guide to Card Games." *Times Literary Supplement* (Nov. 16, 1990): 1239. (essay)

"Vineland." *New York Times Book Review* (Jan. 14, 1990): 1. (essay)

"Christopher Columbus and Queen Isabella of Spain Consummate Their Relationship, Santa Fe, 1492." *New Yorker* (June 17, 1991): 32–35. (short story)
Haroun and the Sea of Stories. New York: Viking-Penguin, 1991. (fiction)
Imaginary Homelands: Essays and Criticism. New York: Granta Books, 1991. (nonfiction)
"Is Nothing Sacred?" *New Perspectives Quarterly* 8:2 (Spring 1991): 8–24. (essay)

Studies of Salman Rushdie

Al-Azmeh, Aziz. "The Satanic Flame." *New Statesman and Society* (Jan. 20, 1989): 16–17.

Albertazzi, Silvia. "In the Skin of the Whale: Salman Rushdie's 'Responsibility for the Story.' " *Commonwealth Essays and Studies* 12 (Autumn 1989): 11–18.

Ali, Agha Shahid. "*The Satanic Verses*: A Secular Muslim's Response." *Yale Journal of Criticism* 4 (Fall 1990): 295–300.

Ali, Tariq. "*Midnight's Children.*" *New Left Review* 136 (Nov.-Dec. 1982): 87–95.

Allison, Lincoln. "Race, Reason, and Mr. Rushdie." *New Society* (Jan. 13, 1983): 53–54.

Alter, Robert. "The Novel and the Sense of the Past." *Salmagundi* 68–69 (1985–86): 91–106.

Amanuddin, Syed. "The Novels of Salman Rushdie: Mediated Reality as Fantasy." *World Literature Today* 63 (Winter 1989): 42–45.

Appignanesi, Lisa, and Sara Maitland. *The Rushdie File.* Syracuse: Syracuse University Press, 1991.

Aravamudan, Srinivas. " 'Being God's Postman Is No Fun, Yaar': Salman Rushdie's *The Satanic Verses.*" *Diacritics* 19 (Summer 1989): 3–20.

Arguello, Xavier. "The Writer as Tourist." *New Republic* (Apr. 29, 1987: 30–34).

Asad, Talal. "Multiculturalism and British Identity in the Wake of the Rushdie Affair." *Politics and Society* 18 (Dec. 1990): 456–80.

Bader, Rudolf. "The Indian Tin Drum." *International Fiction Review* 11 (Winter 1985): 75–83.

———. "On Blood and Blushing: Bipolarity in Salman Rushdie's *Shame.*" *International Fiction Review* 15 (Winter 1988): 30–33.

Bardolf, Jacqueline. "Language Is Courage: *The Satanic Verses.*" *Commonwealth Essays and Studies* 12 (Autumn 1989): 1–10.

Barnett, Anthony. "Salman Rushdie: A Review Article." *Race and Class* (Winter 1989): 91–98.

Barucha, Rustom. "Rushdie's Whale." *Massachusetts Review* (Summer 1986): 221–36.

Batty, Nancy. "The Art of Suspense: Salman Rushdie's 1001 (Mid-)Nights." *Ariel* 18 (1987): 49–65.

Bilgrami, Akeel. "Rushdie and the Reform of Islam." *Grand Street* 8 (Summer 1989): 170–84.

———. "Rushdie, Islam, and Post-Colonial Defensiveness." *Yale Journal of Criticism* 4 (Fall 1990): 301–311.

Blaise, Clark. "A Novel of India's Coming of Age." *New York Times Book Review.* April 19, 1981: 1, 18–19.

Brennan, Timothy A. *Salman Rushdie and the Third World: Myths of the Nation.* New York: St. Martin's Press, 1989.

———. "India, Nationalism, and Other Failures." *South Atlantic Quarterly* 87 (Winter 1988): 131–46.

Campbell, Elaine. "Beyond Controversy: Vidia Naipaul and Salman Rushdie." *Literary Half-Yearly* 27 (July 1986): 42–49.

Chaudhuri, Una. "Writing the Raj Away." *Turnstile* 2 (1990): 26–35.

———. "Imaginative Maps." *Turnstile* 2 (1990): 36–47.

Close, Anthony. "The Empirical Author: Salman Rushdie's *Satanic Verses.*" *Philosophy and Literature* 14 (Oct. 1990): 248–67.

Corcoran, Marlena S. "Salman Rushdie's Satanic Narration." *Iowa Review* 20 (Winter 1990): 155–67.

Couto, Maria. "Midnight's Children and Parents: The Search for Indo-British Identity." *Encounter* 58 (Feb. 1982): 61–66.

Cronin, Richard. "The Indian English Novel: *Kim* and *Midnight's Children.*" *Modern Fiction Studies* 33 (Summer 1987): 201–13.

Cunningham, Valentine. "Nosing Out the Indian Reality." *Times Literary Supplement* May 15, 1981: 38.

Decter, Midge. "The Rushdiad." *Commentary* 87 (June 1989): 18–23.

Desai, Anita. "Where Cultures Clash by Night." *Book World-Washington Post.* March 15, 1981: 1, 13.

Dingwaney, Anuradha. "Author(iz)ing *Midnight's Children* and *Shame*: Salman Rushdie's Constructions of Authority." *Reworlding: The Literature of the Indian Diaspora.* Ed. Emmanuel S. Nelson. Westport, Conn.: Greenwood Press, 1992. 157–168.

Dissanayake, Wimal. "Towards a Decolonized English: South Asian Creativity in Fiction." *World Englishes* 2 (1985): 233–42.

Dossa, Shiraz. "*The Satanic Verses*: Imagination and Its Political Context." *Cross-Currents: A Yearbook of Central European Culture* 39 (Summer 1989): 204–12.

During, Simon. "Postmodernism or Post-Colonialism Today." *Textual Practice* 1 (Spring 1987): 32–47.

Durix, Jean-Pierre. "Magic Realism in *Midnight's Children.*" *Commonwealth Essays and Studies* 8 (Autumn 1985): 57–63.

———. "The Artistic Journey in Salman Rushdie's *Shame.*" *World Literature Written in English* 23 (Spring 1984): 451–63.

Edgar, David. "The Migrant's Vision." *New Left Review* 144 (March-April 1984): 124–28.

Enright, D. J. "So and Not So." *New York Review of Books* (Mar. 2, 1989): 25–26.

Fletcher, M. D. "Rushdie's *Shame* as Apologue." *Journal of Commonwealth Literature* 21 (1986): 120–32.

Fokemma, Aleid. "English Ideas of Indianness: The Reception of Salman Rushdie." *Crisis and Creativity in the New Literatures in English.* Ed. Geoffrey V. Davis et al. Amsterdam: Rodopi, 1990. 355–68.

Fuentes, Carlos. "Words for Salman Rushdie." *New York Times Book Review* (Mar. 12, 1989): 28–29.

Glendenning, Victoria. "A Novelist in the Country of the Mind." *Sunday Times* (Oct. 25, 1981): 38.

Graham, Peter S. "Free Speech, Salman Rushdie and Research Libraries." *Journal of the Rutgers University Libraries* 51 (June 1989): 1–8.

Grewal, Inderpal. "Salman Rushdie: Marginality, Women, and *Shame*." *Genders* 3 (Nov. 1980): 24–42.

Grove, Lloyd. "Salman Rushdie: Caught Between Two Worlds." *International Herald Tribune* (May 27, 1986): 37.

Harrison, James. "Reconstructing *Midnight's Children* and *Shame*." *University of Toronto Quarterly* 59 (Spring 1990): 399–412.

Herd, E. W. "Tin Drum and Snake-Charmer's Flute: Salman Rushdie's Debt to Gunter Grass." *New Comparisons: A Journal of Comparative and General Literary Studies* 6 (Autumn 1988): 205–18.

Hewson, Kelly. "Opening Up the Universe a Little More: Salman Rushdie and the Migrant as Story-teller." *SPAN: Journal of the South Pacific Association of the Commonwealth Literature and Language Studies* 29 (Oct. 1989): 82–93.

Hoggart, Simon. "Rushdie to Judgement." *New Society* (Feb. 17, 1983): 267.

Hollington, Michael. "Salman Rushdie's *Shame*." *Meanjin Quarterly* 43 (Sept. 1984): 403–7.

Howells, Carol Ann. "Rudy Wiebe's *The Temptations of Big Bear* and Salman Rushdie's *Midnight's Children*." *Literary Criterion* 20 (1985): 191–203.

Hyman, Timothy. "Fairy-Tale Agitprop." *London Magazine* (Oct. 1983): 40.

Irving, T. B. "The Rushdie Confrontation: A Clash in Values." *Iowa Review* 20 (Winter 1990): 175–84.

Johansen, Ib. "The Flight from the Enchanter: Reflections on Salman Rushdie's *Grimus*." *Kunapipi* 8 (1985): 53–61.

Karamcheti, Indira. "Salman Rushdie's *Midnight's Children* as an Alternate Genesis." *Pacific Coast Philosophy* 21 (Nov. 1986): 81–84.

King, Bruce. "Who Wrote *The Satanic Verses*?" *World Literature Today* 63 (Summer 1989): 433–35.

McLaren, John. "The Power of the Word: Salman Rushdie and *The Satanic Verses*." *Westerly* 35 (Mar. 1990): 61–65.

Malak, Amin. "Reading the Crisis: The Polemics of Rushdie's *The Satanic Verses*." *Ariel* 20 (Oct. 1989): 176–86.

Mars-Jones, Adam. "A Marriage of Two Minds." *Times Literary Supplement* 9 (Sept. 1986): 949.

Marzoratti, Gerald. "Fiction's Embattled Infidel." *New York Times Magazine* (Jan. 29, 1989): 24–25, 27, 44–45, 47–48, 100.

———. "Rushdie in Hiding." *New York Times Magazine* (Nov. 4, 1990): 31–33, 68, 78, 84–85.

Massing, Michael. "Snap Books." *New Republic* (May 4, 1987): 21–25.

Mazrui, Ali K. "Is *The Satanic Verses* a Satanic Novel? Moral Dilemmas of the Rushdie Affair." *Michigan Quarterly Review* 35 (Mar. 1989): 347–71.

Merrivale, Patricia. "Saleem Fathered by Oskar: Intertextual Strategies in *Midnight's Children* and *The Tin Drum*." *Ariel* 21 (July 1990): 5–21.

Mishra, D. S. "Narrative Techniques of Salman Rushdie's *Shame*." *Punjab University Research Bulletin (Arts)* 18 (Apr. 1987): 37–44.

Mojatabi, A. G. "Magical Mystery Pilgrimage." *New York Times Book Review* (Jan. 29, 1989): 3, 37.

Moore, Susan. "Comic Novels about India: Neglected Masters and Others." *Quadrant* 29 (Sept. 1985): 76–79.

Mufti, Aamir. "In the Realm of the Censors." *Voice Literary Supplement* (Mar. 1989): 13.

Mukherjee, Bharati. "Prophet and Loss." *Voice Literary Supplement* (Mar. 1989): 9–12.

Naik, M. K. "A Life of Fragments: The Fate of Identity in *Midnight's Children*." *Indian Literary Review* 3 (Oct. 1985): 63–68.

Nandy, Ashish. "Satyajit Ray's Secret Guide." *East-West Film Journal* 4 (June 1990): 114–37.

Narayan, Shyamala. "*Midnight's Children*." *Literary Criterion* 18 (1983): 23–32.

Nazareth, Peter. "Rushdie Wo/manichean Novel." *Iowa Review* 20 (Winter 1990): 168–74.

———. "Salman Rushdie's *Midnight's Children*." *World Literature Written in English* 21 (Spring 1982): 169–71.

Needham, Anuradha Dingwaney. "The Politics of Post-Colonial Identity in Salman Rushdie." *Massachusetts Review* 29 (Winter 1988–89): 609–24.

Ommen, Susan. "Fictional Intent in Rushdie's *Shame*." *Literary Criterion* 20 (1985): 36–41.

Pai, Sudha. "Expatriate Concerns in Salman Rushdie's *Midnight's Children*." *Literary Criterion* 23 (1988): 36–47.

Parameswaran, Uma. "Autobiography as History: Saleem Sinai and India in Rushdie's *Midnight's Children*." *Toronto South Asia Review* 1 (Summer 1982): 27–34.

———. "Handcuffed to History: Salman Rushdie's Art." *Ariel* 14 (Oct. 1983): 34–45.

———. " 'Lest He Returning Chide': Saleem Sinai's Inaction in Salman Rushdie's *Midnight's Children*." *Literary Criterion* 18 (1983): 57–66.

———. "Salman Rushdie in Indo-English Literature." *Journal of Indian Writing in English* 12 (1984): 15–25.

Phillips, K. J. "Salman Rushdie's *Midnight's Children*: Models for Story-Telling." *Comparative Literature East and West: Traditions and Trends*. Eds. Cornelia N. Morre and Raymond A. Moody. Honolulu: University of Hawaii Press, 1989. 202–7.

Pipes, Daniel. "The Ayatollah, the Novelist, and the West." *Commentary* 87 (June 1989): 9–17.

Rajkowska, Barbara Ozieblo. "The Reality of the Alien: An Exploration of Salman Rushdie's Novels." *Revista Canaria de Estudios Ingeleses* 13–14 (Apr. 1987): 9–27.

Ram, N. " 'My Book Being Put in Jail': Rushdie." *Hindu* (Oct. 1988): 2.

Rao. M. Madhusudana. "Quest for Identity: A Study of the Narrative in Rushdie's *Midnight's Children*." *Literary Criterion* 25 (1990): 31–42.

Rienmenschneider, Dieter. "History and the Individual in Anita Desai's *Clear Light of Day* and Salman Rushdie's *Midnight's Children*." *World Literature Written in English* 23 (Winter 1984): 196–207.

Sangari, Kum Kum. "The Politics of the Possible." *Cultural Critique* 7 (Fall 1987): 157–86.

Sanghi, Malavika Rajbans. " 'You Fight to Like Where You Live.' " *Indian Express Magazine* (Mar. 20, 1983): 1.

Sethi, Sunil. "After Midnight." *India Today* (Apr. 15, 1983): 21–23.

———. "An Indian Scheherazade." *India Today* (May 16, 1981): 126–27.

Shephard, Ron. "Growing Up: A Central Metaphor in Some Recent Novels." *The Writer's Sense of the Contemporary: Papers in South East Asia and Australian Literature.* Ed. Bruce Bennett et al. Nedlands: Center for Studies in Australian Literature, University of Western Australia, 1982. 48–61.

Simawe, Saadi A. "Rushdie's *The Satanic Verses* and Heretical Literature in Islam." *Iowa Review* 20 (Winter 1990): 185–98.

Singh, Sushila. "Salman Rushdie's *Midnight's Children*: Rethinking the Life and Times of Modern India." *Punjab University Research Bulletin (Arts)* 16 (Apr. 1985): 55–67.

Smith, Colin. "The Unbearable Lightness of Salman Rushdie." *Critical Approaches to the New Literatures in English.* Ed. Dieter Riemenschneider. Essen: Blaue Eule, 1989. 104–115.

Srivastava, Aruna. " 'The Empire Writes Back': Language and History in *Shame* and *Midnight's Children.*" *Ariel* (Oct. 1989): 67–78.

Stephens, John. "*Midnight's Children*: Parody of an Indian Novel." *SPAN* 21 (Oct. 1985): 184–208.

Suleri, Sara. "Contraband Histories: Salman Rushdie and the Embodiment of Blasphemy." *Yale Review* 78 (Summer 1989): 604–24.

Swann, Joseph. " 'East Is East and West Is West'? Salman Rushdie's *Midnight's Children* as an Indian Novel." *World Literature Written in English* 26 (Autumn 1986): 353–62.

Towers, Robert. "Review of *Midnight's Children.*" *New York Times Review of Books* (Sept. 24, 1981): 30.

Tyssens, Stephane. "*Midnight's Children: Or, the Ambiguity of Impotence.*" *Commonwealth Essays and Studies* 12 (Fall 1989): 19–29.

Veerstraete, Beert C. "Classical References and Themes in Salman Rushdie's *The Satanic Verses.*" *Classical and Modern Literature: A Quarterly* 10 (Summer 1990): 327–34.

Watson-Williams, Helen. "Finding a Father: A Reading of Salman Rushdie's *The Satanic Verses.*" *Westerly* 35 (Mar. 1990): 66–71.

Weatherby, W. J. *Salman Rushdie: Sentenced to Death.* New York: Carroll and Graf, 1990.

West, Richard. "Rushdie and the Raj." *Spectator* (Apr. 7, 1984): 18–19.

Wheatcroft, Geoffrey. "Writers and Comparisons: Salman Rushdie and Shiva Naipaul." *Encounter* 75 (Sept. 1990): 38–40.

Wilson, Keith. "*Midnight's Children* and Reader Responsibility." *Critical Quarterly* 26 (Autumn 1984): 23–37.

I. ALLAN SEALY (1951–   )
Linda Conrad

BIOGRAPHY

I. Allan Sealy (born Allahabad, India) describes his background as "Anglo-Indian, lower middle class"; his father was a police officer, his mother a schoolteacher. His schooling was at La Martinere College, Lucknow, the city where the fictional Nakhlau of his first novel, *The Trotter-Nama*, was largely created and on which it is based. After studying at St. Stephen's College, Delhi University, Sealy was awarded a master's degree in Asian studies at Western Michigan University, which had offered him an exchange scholarship. When Sealy's parents migrated to Australia (they later returned to India), he tutored in government at Sydney University. The University of British Columbia awarded him a doctorate; his thesis was on Wilson Harris, the Guyanese novelist, whose work and friendship he highly values.

While writing *The Trotter-Nama*, Sealy did "the usual odd jobs: grocery shops, shoe works at Sydney Tech, etc." and is now a full-time writer. He also paints "sporadically—and cathartically" and illustrated the jackets of *The Trotter-Nama* and the Indian edition of *Hero*, his second novel. Sealy is still technically an Australian resident and has a "special feeling for the Australian landscape." He lives with his New Zealand wife in Christchurch, dividing his time between New Zealand and India.

Sealy is currently writing a travel book and plans a third novel. He has said that his novels are "part of a larger project . . . to revise the canons of fiction writing so as to accommodate an 'Oriental mode of production', i.e., to play by Asiatic, or at any rate Indian, rules." His first novel, though influenced by European forms, was based on the *nama* (chronicle) of court historians in the Moghul Empire. "*Hero* used another peculiarly Indian form, the Bombay movie," and his "next novel (after the travelogue) will explore the raga form in Indian music." (Quotations from Sealy are taken from interview with the author, July 3, 1991.)

Sealy writes "for an international audience" but "especially values the attention of the Indian reader" (Matuz 84).

MAJOR WORKS AND THEMES

The Trotter-Nama (1988) and *Hero* (1990) are set in India. The first chronicles an Anglo-Indian (Eurasian) clan's experiences from the eighteenth century onwards, and centers on the "home rule" of the Trotter family home of Sans Souci, which ends with independence. *Hero* focuses on home rule of another kind. *The Trotter-Nama*'s magic realism, with all its ebullience and complexity, gives a marginalized community an etiological myth and a fictional voice. The more sober, brusque, ascetic *Hero* highlights the vicissitudes of a postcolonial country adapting to Westminster democracy. Sophisticated wordplay, interpolated set pieces, and imaginative visual imagery are the hallmarks of Sealy's style, which is, like a meal in *The Trotter-Nama*, "so rich you had to embezzle it" (9).

The locale for *The Trotter-Nama* is almost exclusively one *place*—Sans Souci, the Trotter estate—but *displacement* is the major preoccupation of the novel. Justin, the Great Trotter (originally Trottoire), is himself displaced, "Fate having cast my lot in three separate lands of Europe, America and Asia (four if the Africa of my getting be counted) and brought me at last to this place which I have come to consider my home" (178). But characters do not have to leave their country: the Great Trotter's wives are displaced from their homes to be virtually imprisoned in Sans Souci. Farida finds living at her husband's house "like being in another country" (130–31), and Justin Trotter sees that she is "inhabiting as much as I do a new world" (134).

The imagery of the novel is ubiquitously transitional or bidirectional. The Seventh Trotter Eugene carries his manuscript (the *Trotter-Nama* itself) with him in a frequently replaced paper bag, inscribed with his current impermanent address. The "icelight" described early in the novel is the period between light and darkness that "freezes time, or rather it traps it at that tremulous point just short of freezing when time is neither solid nor liquid" (4). The book opens with Eugene Trotter in an airplane, between and above lands. The indigo dye manufactured by the Trotters turns cloth blue only after exposure to the sun; "the secret, it seemed, was neither in the dye nor in the cloth but in a third place" (33). The recurring family feature of one eye blue and the other brown, looking in two directions, toward past and future, and the conflicting advice of Eugene's ancestors, one of whom says "paint" and the other "write" (9), further locate the characters as in or floating above two worlds.

The lavish praise of corpulence suggests that the body is one's only home and that body fat is an expandable and portable border. The First Trotter Justin, the Seventh Trotter Eugene, and his great-grandmother Victoria, who resembles a spouting whale when she bathes, delight in their hugeness; and the narrator applies a dazzling array of epithets to the skinny. Fatness is related to the leitmotif of sweets (gulab jamuns, sweet tea, sweet wine, peppermints). The distinctive taste of gulab jamuns cannot be translated to other countries, but "sugar is constant across all borders, like carbon or hydrogen" (3) and even in mango-fool "the sugar is invariable" (68).

The antique miniatures that the Seventh Trotter forges find a correlative in the novel itself. *The Trotter-Nama* suggests historical and spatial scope through the heaping of detail upon detail, avoiding the perspective that imitates the real. In the miniaturized landscape, the colonial presence in India is dwarfed; India is not so much colonized as absorbing and transforming all that enters it. Colonialism is, however, pervasive. Justin is aware that the "nearer I approach this land the further I am driven back into my already formed ideas . . . —not India but Europe, or Europe's India, which is the same thing" (134).

After reading *The Trotter-Nama*, taking up *Hero* is like moving to another country—or from a richly painted landscape to a pen-and-ink sketch of a stage set. The intermeshed worlds of Indian politics and the Indian movie industry are the focus of *Hero*, the scenario of the rise and fall of a film star turned politician. As Zero, the writer of the script within the novel, observes: "We have more film stars-turned-politicians than any country on earth" (15), and three of the four major characters at some time play an explicitly political role. Zero's script follows the movie formula of the vibrant Bombay Mix and tells of the rise and fall of a film star and political leader.

Throughout the book the links between politics and the screen are highlighted. The political leader Hero is a former star who creates media portfolios: a Minister for Truth, a Minister of Laughter, a State Minister of Screens. Zero's final assassination of Hero is in the genre of the film thriller. Scriptwriter Zero in his action-packed melodrama considers his slavish feelings about Hero; the nature of leaders and followers; truth, lies and film; class and caste differences; Hero's ideas of Karmascope ("For the price of a film ticket you can have a new soul," 67); and the new god of India, television.

As in *The Trotter-Nama*, notions of home are crucial to *Hero*. The character Hero is haunted by thoughts of the home he has left in Kanyakumari, "at the cape where India ends, or, as he liked to think of it, begins" (39). This suggests a sense of displacement, but the true displacement is that of the real by the reel. The "family" is the cast—the leader Hero, the villain Nero, the sidekick or flunky Zero, and the love interest, U. D. (a common Indian pronunciation of "eau de") Cologne.

Despite their differences, *Hero* and *The Trotter-Nama* have common elements. Color and its gradations are thematized in both novels. Central to both novels is the question of what India really is. In *The Trotter-Nama*,

Justin finds that India is "a thousand shifting surfaces which enamour the newcomer and then swallow him up . . . obliging him to accept a single rigid function, that of conqueror. The very divisiveness that allowed him in enmeshes him. How is he to grasp what cannot be held—what in fact holds him fast?" (134). While quintessentially Indian, the film genre that is the basis of *Hero* nevertheless has characteristics of Hollywood and Paris; and *Hero*, loved for his Indianness, dies wearing a pair of Hollywood-style imported Ray-Bans.

Sealy has the postmodern preoccupation with narrators and writers, but with an emphasis on this displacement. The urbane narrative voice in *The Trotter-Nama* is displaced in the epilogue by the colloquial voices of a remnant of the Anglo-Indian community. Two narrative voices speak in *Hero*: first the narrator, who identifies himself as the author of *The Trotter-Nama* and *Hero*, and then Zero, who tells the story through what is loosely a script for a film called "Star." Eugene, displaced from *The Trotter-Nama*, appears as a minor character in *Hero*. At the end of *Hero*, Zero displaces the author, announcing a "coup—a *coup de theatre*" to oust the "tyrant author" (311).

A coup of another kind—against Western rule of writing in English—is suggested in a formula for the survival of the colonized person, articulated by the librarian and writer Munshi Nishan Chand in *The Trotter-Nama*: "study the . . . barbarian; learn his roughcast languages, school yourself in his childish arts . . . until that day when you are more skilled in his arts than he. Then overwhelm him . . . " (53).

CRITICAL RECEPTION

The Trotter-Nama was winner of the Best First Book Section (Eurasia) of the 1989 Commonwealth Writers' Prize. There has been too little time for considered critical articles to appear, but most reviews are highly favorable. Sealy's work has been particularly welcomed by reviewers in Indian newspapers and journals, some of which, however, are either not indexed or not easily accessible in Western libraries. Sealy observes that *The Trotter-Nama* "was not widely reviewed outside India" and believes that the novel might well be "outside the ken of the Western reviewer" (Interview with the author, July 3, 1991).

New York Times book reviewer Timothy Mo declares that Sealy "often writes prose supremely well" but dismisses the superlative set pieces in *The Trotter-Nama* as "a set of gambits in search of a novel," giving a "purely cosmetic and always redundant semblance of sophistication" (14). Mo also points to what he sees as a lack of success in "making people live on the page" (14), but this comment is of questionable appropriateness to the stylized, extravagant genre in which Sealy writes and to his focus on communities rather than individuals. Australian reviewer Michael Wilding sees

Sealy's work as excessive, with little substance. However, James Idema, the *Chicago Tribune*'s reviewer, recognizes Sealy as "unique, imaginative and challenging" (7), and the *Guardian* reviewer Maya Jaggi sees him as funny, inventive, and profound (27). Indian reviewers are not uniformly admiring. Bharati Mukherjee assesses *The Trotter-Nama* as "a tiresome, show-offy, obese book" (4). But most reviewers recognize that Sealy is attempting new, clearly Indian forms with resounding success. Mukul Kesavan of the *Hindustan Times* finds the Nama "easily the best novel you are likely to read this year" (19); Abraham Eraly finds it a "true world classic, undeniably the greatest novel in English written by an Indian" (21); and several reviewers take pains to assert Sealy's superiority to Salman Rushdie, with whom he is often compared. Many reviewers place Sealy among the most promising new postmodern writers and in the august company of Rabelais, Dostoevsky, Faulkner, Fielding, Cervantes, and Garcia Marquez.

BIBLIOGRAPHY

Works by I. Allan Sealy

The Trotter-Nama: A Chronicle 1977–1984. New York: Alfred A. Knopf, 1988; London: Viking, 1988; Penguin Group (New York; Ringwood, Victoria, Australia; Markham, Ontario, Canada; Auckland, NZ), 1990.
Hero: A Fable. London: Secker and Warburg, 1991.

Studies of I. Allan Sealy

Bajpai, Kanti. "A Stellar Performance." Review of *Hero. Indian Express Sunday Magazine* (June 17, 1990): 18.
Eraly, Abraham. "At Last, an Indian Genius." Review of *The Trotter-Nama. Aside* (Feb. 15, 1989): 21–22.
Idema, James. "Witty Novel Chronicles Family's Fall." Review of *The Trotter-Nama. Chicago Tribune* (Mar. 6, 1988): sec. 14, p. 7.
Jaggi, Maya. "Bollywood Hole." Review of *Hero. Guardian* (Feb. 7, 1991): 27.
Joshi, Rita. "A Spoof on History." Review of *The Trotter-Nama.* Sunday *Observer* (India) (Feb. 19, 1989): 9.
Kesavan, Mukul. "A Glittering Anglo-Indian Odyssey." Review of *The Trotter-Nama. Hindustan Times Sunday Magazine* (June 19, 1988): 19.
Matuz, Roger, ed. "I. Allan Sealy." *Contemporary Literary Criticism: Yearbook 1988.* vol. 55. New York: Gale Research, 78–84.
Mo, Timothy. "From the Mines of Curry Powder." Review of *The Trotter-Nama. New York Times Book Review* (Feb. 28, 1988): sec. 7, p. 14.
Moraes, Dom. "An Indian-Nama." Review of *Hero.* Sunday *Independent* (Bombay) (May 20, 1990): 111.
Mukherjee, Bharati. "An Anglo-Indian Family Caught between Two Worlds." Review of *The Trotter-Nama. Washington Post Book World* (April 3, 1988): 4.

Panwar, Purabi. "Stars and Political Stripes." Review of *Hero*. Sunday *Financial Express* (New Delhi) (May 27, 1990): 5.

Sen, Rehanna. "A Man of Many Parts." Inset on author with review of *Hero*, *Indian Express Sunday Magazine* (June 17, 1990): 16.

Singh, Khushwant. "Of Curries and Custard: A Sensitive Saga of an Anglo-Indian Family." Review of *The Trotter-Nama*. *India Today*, International edition (Sept. 15, 1988): 100.

Wilding, Michael. "Playing Tricks with History." Review of *The Trotter-Nama* and others. *Weekend Australian* (Feb. 10, 1990): 10.

SAMUEL DICKSON SELVON
(1923–   )
Frank Birbalsingh

BIOGRAPHY

Samuel Dickson Selvon was born on May 20, 1923, in San Fernando, Trinidad. His father was a Tamil from Madras, India, who worked in a dry goods shop on the High Street in San Fernando. His mother was half Indian, her father being a Scotsman who worked as an overseer on a coconut estate in an Indian village. Probably as a result of interaction with the villagers among whom she grew up, Selvon's mother spoke Hindi fluently, and he remembers her conversing in Hindi with Indian street vendors and farmers who came to their home to sell vegetables.

Despite his ancestry and environment (in the south of Trinidad), which were Indian, Selvon's upbringing appears to have been culturally cosmopolitan. He claims to have been creolized at an early age, by which he means that he and his family did not observe exclusively ethnic (Indian) cultural customs and practices. Having lost their religious inheritance from India, his family were members of the Canadian Presbyterian Mission Church, and he attended Naparima High School, which was run by the same church. Selvon joined the Scout movement, which provided a wider social experience, eventually becoming a king's scout. Scouting, Christianity, grace before meals, and a piano in the home where all marks of Selvon's creolization.

After high school, Selvon joined the Royal Navy Reserve which, by patrolling the seas between Trinidad and Venezuela during World War II, protected convoys of ships taking Venezuelan oil to Europe. Being able to help his parents financially, after his father had lost his job, increased the young Selvon's sense of maturity. More importantly, the job provided a feeling of security, and enough free time in which to write. Selvon began to compose both prose and poetry.

At the end of the war, Selvon pursued his interest in writing by getting a job as a reporter on the *Trinidad Guardian*, the main daily newspaper in the capital city, Port of Spain. Some of his poems were broadcast on "Caribbean Voices," the literary program produced by the British Broadcasting Corporation (BBC) in London. Acceptance by the BBC served as a powerful boost to Selvon's literary ambition. When he moved from reporting to working as subeditor and editorialist on the *Trinidad Guardian*, the more practical approach of concentrating on the actual craft of writing greatly improved the technical aspects of his writing.

More and more of his pieces were published in Trinidad in the Barbadian literary journal *Bim*, and in the *West Indian Review*, edited by Esther Chapman in Jamaica. His contacts with the *Trinidad Guardian* led him to subedit a weekly magazine, the *Guardian Weekly*, that published short stories and poems. This opened the way for him to meet some of the aspiring local writers—Errol Hill, Joseph Penko, Cecil Grey, Barnabas Ramon Fortune, Alfred Mendes, Cecil Herbert, Ian Roach, and Clifford Sealey. One can gauge the scale of Selvon's achievement by the fact that although these writers had varying success, none was able to build up an oeuvre of similar size and quality to his.

At that stage of his career, Selvon's prospects were favorable: he had a good job, he was married (to a woman from Guyana), and he was writing with some success locally. He was also reading a lot, for instance, Richard Jefferies's work on the English countryside, and Will Durant's *The Study of Philosophy*, which he read several times. But his wife went back to Guyana, and his horizons in Trinidad took on a more limiting appearance: he saw only beach parties and complacency ahead. So in 1950, armed with an encouraging letter from Henry Swanzy, the editor of *Caribbean Voices*, he left for England. That he and George Lamming sailed on the same boat to London was pure coincidence.

Selvon wrote *A Brighter Sun* while he was employed at India House in London. To evade the India House rule that manuscripts of employees should be vetted by a civil service official, he claimed that he had brought the novel with him from Trinidad. Thus, by innocent subterfuge came into being one of the most influential novels in West Indian literature. Excellent reviews, both in Britain and America, encouraged Selvon to start on his second novel; but the process was delayed by tuberculosis and a consequent operation, which proved to be successful. After he returned to work at India House, he received a Guggenheim Fellowship for one year. About the same time, *Lilliput* magazine accepted one of his pieces and paid him thirty guineas. With his career going so well, Selvon decided to take the plunge into writing full-time.

The years immediately following his illness and the Guggenheim Fellowship were the most productive in Selvon's career. Three books came out quickly—*The Lonely Londoners* (1956), *Ways of Sunlight* (1957), and *Turn*

Again Tiger (1958). While he was on the fellowship at the MacDowell Colony for writers in New Hampshire, Selvon began writing *The Lonely Londoners* in standard English, with only the dialogue in dialect, but he was dissatisfied with the drafts. It suddenly dawned on him that the entire narrative should be in what he calls "the Trinidadian form of the Caribbean language." Then everything flowed. When the novel was published, it created an impact as the first full-length narrative in Caribbean dialect to attract international readers. Meanwhile, Selvon's wife had rejoined him in England; but the marriage broke down and they were divorced.

During the 1960s, Selvon produced three more novels, together with other writings. In 1975 he wrote *Moses Ascending*, in which the chief character was Moses Aloetta, who had first appeared in *The Lonely Londoners*. *Moses Migrating*, in 1983, completed a trilogy of novels about Moses, and meanwhile Selvon had written other books. But in 1978 he emigrated to Calgary, Canada, where he now lives with his second wife and family. He has continued writing in Calgary, while spending periods as writer-in-residence at various universities and colleges. He gives frequent public readings from his work, and often appears on panel discussions at literary conferences. So far, Selvon has written ten novels, one volume of short stories, and three children's books, apart from other stories, essays, poems, film scripts, and plays. He has also given several talks and interviews.

MAJOR WORKS AND THEMES

A Brighter Sun re-creates rural Trinidad in the 1940s. It was composed at a time when Selvon's memories—of people, places, the sea, the building of roads in Trinidad—were all fresh. The chief characters, Tiger and his wife Urmilla, are Indian, and their unsophisticated way of life is the core of the novel. After marriage, Tiger and Urmilla move from their estate surroundings to the urban village of Barataria. This allows the author to contrast their former, rural agricultural and Indian milieu with a more culturally mixed, multiracial, and urbanized part of Trinidad. The contrast illustrates both the social diversity of Trinidad and its implications for an evolving sense of nationality.

Perhaps some of the concerns raised in *A Brighter Sun* have now been superseded by more urgent postindependence realities in contemporary West Indian literature (Trinidad became independent in 1962); but it is important to realize that Selvon was writing about a British colony whose social formation was the product of centuries of slavery, indenture, and exploitation. In the two decades preceding independence, nationality and national identity were considered urgent realities in Trinidad. This is why Selvon brings Tiger and Urmilla into close association with Afro-Trinidadians like Joe and Rita, and into closer contact with city life, the influence of American technology, and other facets of Trinidadian experience. The idea was to consider whether nationhood could emerge out of such diversity.

Because of his own creolized preferences, Selvon appears to advance the desirability of a national creole culture in *A Brighter Sun*. But the final episode in the novel, where Tiger seeks urgent medical services only to be rebuffed by Trinidadian doctors, suggests that the process of creolization has not taken sufficient root in Trinidad. In *Turn Again Tiger*, the sequel to *A Brighter Sun* (although it is Selvon's fourth novel), Tiger and Urmilla return to their Indian origins. The novel is centered overwhelmingly on Tiger's maturing consciousness as it struggles to come to grips with his status as a Trinidadian whose peasant Indian roots tend to set him apart from changing cultural modes and the processes of westernization going on around him. As he struggles to find himself, Tiger comes into fierce physical conflict with his father. He also burns his books, and sleeps with a white woman, wife of a white supervisor on the estate. These challenges to established authority are supposed to reconcile Tiger to his situation, but as in *A Brighter Sun*, Selvon is more successful in his exposition of Tiger's problems than in their solution. Tiger's psychic regeneration appears sound in theory, but rather melodramatic in action. Where *Turn Again Tiger* succeeds is in its sensitive descriptions of Trinidad, and true-to-life portraits of minor characters like Babolal, Soylo, Otto, and More Lazy, who match Sookdeo, Tall Boy, and Deen of *A Brighter Sun*.

Selvon's second novel, *An Island Is a World*, considers wider terms than *A Brighter Sun* by focusing on a Trinidadian nationality that embraces all the West Indian territories. In the 1950s, the subject of a West Indian political federation was a topic of absorbing interest, until it became a reality in 1958. Although the federation seemed theoretically sound as a whole structure, it dissolved soon afterwards, probably because it did not fully recognize the interests of its individual units. In *An Island Is a World*, two brothers, Rufus and Foster, are on a quest for self-knowledge that leads them abroad, Rufus to America, and Foster to England. They gain wider perspectives abroad, but return home with an awareness that Trinidad is their world and that their national identity links them inescapably not only to Trinidad, but to the West Indies. Again, this new awareness is as theoretical and tentative as Tiger's sense of maturity and nationality, and one does not feel that Rufus and Foster have fully succeeded in resolving their problems.

Selvon's third novel, *The Lonely Londoners*, is a watershed in his career, partly because it is written entirely in dialect. The main theme may still be West Indian nationality, but in *The Lonely Londoners* it now includes the experience of West Indians in the diaspora, in this case in England. The characters in *The Lonely Londoners* are essentially innocents abroad, West Indians whose free and easy ways come into sharp contrast with more rigid British customs. Selvon reaps a rich harvest of comedy out of this contrast, as Sir Galahad, Bart, Lewis, Cap, Big City, Five-past-twelve, Tolroy, Tanty, and others show (by their names alone) how ill-equipped they are to face up to an alien English setting. The novel is a series of loosely connected sketches in which these characters come and go freely. It is a flexible format that allows them to mix with each other and discuss their thoughts and feelings in their own language. For it is their language that expresses any sense of nationality they might have, and it is the effectiveness of that language in accurately expressing West Indian personality and character that constitutes Selvon's main achievement as a writer.

Selvon's language is a variation of Trinidad dialect skillfully adapted to register the consciousness of all West Indians. It is astonishingly accurate with respect to semantics, intonation, stress patterns, vocabulary, and rhythm. As employed by Selvon, it is basically an oral medium with all the spontaneity of speech and its capacity to improvise. It is packed with wit that is sometimes irreverent, often playful though not trivial. It directs irony both at the lonely Londoners, fresh from the Caribbean, and at indigenous Londoners whose frosty reception causes their Caribbean visitors to feel lonely.

Moses Ascending is written nearly twenty years after *The Lonely Londoners*. This long lapse suggests that the second novel was an afterthought, made necessary by continued living, for both the author and his characters, in the diaspora. The characters in *The Lonely Londoners* are mere transients whose concerns are coping with the weather, finding their way about London, and getting jobs, food, and shelter in a strange environment; in *Moses Ascending*, however, Moses Aloetta, whose flat had been a meeting place for fellow immigrants in *The Lonely Londoners*, has put down roots in England and has become, so he fancies, part of the English social establishment. He is now a landlord, worried about Black Panther militants and illegal Pakistani immigrants infiltrating his house and getting him into trouble with the police. This is a complete reversal of the role of friend, host, and comforter that Moses played to fellow immigrants in *The Lonely Londoners*.

Moses Ascending follows the conflict between Moses and his fellow immigrants, alienated social misfits who pursue strategies to relieve their alienation, even using Moses's house for revolutionary activities. The structure of the novel, and its language, operate through a series of reversals. In the first place, Moses—a black man—plays the role of Robinson Crusoe, while Bob is his illiterate, white Man Friday. Initially, Moses lives in the highest room, and keeps Bob in a basement room. This situation is reversed in the end, while Moses is left plotting to have it changed yet again, thus incorporating flexibility within a firm narrative structure.

Second, the style of the memoirist adopted by Moses in retirement parodies the classical English tradition of writing memoirs. The clichés and satirical touches employed by Moses at least detract from, even if they do not totally reverse, the solemnity and seriousness of this tradition. *Moses*

Migrating sustains this pattern of ironic reversals as Moses continues his odyssey in his new role of a black Englishman. With his English friends Bob and Jeannie as his servants, he returns to Trinidad not as a member of the diaspora longing for contact with home, but as a representative of British culture, playing the role of Britannia in carnival.

Although *A Brighter Sun* remains an important pioneering work that defines and probes basic elements of West Indian nationality, the Moses trilogy must be acknowledged as Selvon's most important contribution to West Indian fiction. These three books reflect the course of Selvon's own career in leaving Trinidad and becoming an exile, someone who lives "permanently" in the diaspora. This in turn is a reflection of contemporary history, since large West Indian communities have now become established abroad, particularly in Britain, Canada, and the United States. The Moses books broaden the definition of West Indian nationality given in Selvon's earliest writing, to include West Indians who live abroad. Some, like Moses in *Moses Migrating*, have adopted other loyalties in the course of long residence abroad; others have been born abroad. For these people nationality may be a matter of ambivalence, perhaps of self-contradiction and confusion. Selvon's advocacy of Britannia's virtues in *Moses Migrating* might appear harmlessly comic or pointedly ironic to the extent that it mocks these virtues, but the fact that Moses flaunts Britannia's virtues among people who may still flock to Britannia's fold in spite of their misgivings, gives their sense of West Indian nationality a peculiar touch of flexibility and adaptability.

In terms of form, the episodic nature of Selvon's novels implies a liking for short fiction. This is confirmed by the fact that some of his best comic and ironic effects are achieved in the form of the short story. It is a form that stimulates his skills, no matter how slender the incident, how trivial the scene, or how uninteresting the character. Selvon's stories abound with invention and variety, and those in dialect are especially successful in communicating nuances of character, shades of meaning, and insights of all kinds. These qualities are evident in *Ways of Sunlight*, Selvon's only collection of stories. As in the rest of his fiction, the stories in this collection deal with experience both in the Caribbean and in England. In fact, in the powerful last story, "My Girl and the City," immigrant experience is described with such feelings as to make London look like home.

A proper estimate of Selvon's fiction should consider his vision of West Indian nationality, his preoccupation with the West Indian diaspora, and his original use of dialect or creole forms of speech. Prevailing critical opinion appears to be most interested in Selvon's linguistic performance and tends to downplay his interest specifically in social or political issues. But Selvon's essential preoccupation is always with the condition of being West Indian, whether in *A Brighter Sun* or any of the later books. There is no evidence that Selvon intended to leave Trinidad for good in 1950. Like most

West Indian immigrants, although he probably went abroad with the intention of making his fortune and returning home, he did not return home to live. His fiction reflects these changed expectations, in particular the collapse of the West Indian Federation in the early 1960s and the consequences that ensued. This is partly why nationality, as enunciated in *A Brighter Sun* and *An Island Is a World*, is not uppermost in the later books, which deal more and more with the immigrant or diasporic West Indian experience. The implication is that to be West Indian nowadays increasingly means displacement and exile, and the feelings and attitudes that flow out of life in the diaspora.

As a writer who belongs to the Indian diaspora, Selvon is peculiar for his lack of interest in experience that is exclusively Indian or ethnic. This type of experience is evident mainly in his early novels and stories set in Trinidad. The Indianness of this early writing is perhaps not as fully acknowledged as it deserves to be. This is no doubt because of Selvon's preoccupation with creole social values and his explicit attempt to promote them in his fiction. These values flourish particularly in Selvon's works that deal with the diaspora. In this context, they are seen to influence his characters in positive as well as negative ways, always helping them to survive.

CRITICAL RECEPTION

Selvon has been regarded as a major West Indian novelist and author since his first novel appeared in 1952. Especially in the 1950s, his books were warmly welcomed, and his use of West Indian dialect was regarded as original, inspired, and authentic. His work has received the attention of critics within the Caribbean, as well as international critics such as Michel Fabre, Peter Nazareth, Bruce MacDonald, and Jeremy Poynting. Most of the criticism is in the form of reviews and essays. There are also some interviews.

One of the most influential assessments of Selvon's work was made by Edward Brathwaite in his essay "Sir Galahad and the Islands." Brathwaite emphasized the value of writing based on the "folk," and this has remained a standard approach to Selvon's fiction—seeing it as representing a "folk sensibility."

Other influential critics have been Gordon Rohlehr and Michel Fabre. In "The Folk in Caribbean Literature," Rohlehr relates Selvon's writing to oral traditions such as calypso, "ole talk," and "picong." Fabre, a French critic who has written authoritative studies of African-American writers, also reacts sensitively to Selvon's language and its oral antecedents.

Two essays by Kenneth Ramchand are notable. "*A Brighter Sun*" compares Selvon's novel to Edgar Mittelholzer's *Corentyne Thunder*, which deals with Indian peasant experience in Guyana, while "*The Lonely Lon-*

doners as a Literary Work" points to Selvon's skill in creating a special language that is broadly representative of West Indian sensibility.

Edward Baugh compares *Moses Ascending* with Austin Clarke's novel *The Bigger Light* in an essay called "Friday in Crusoe's City: The Question of Language in Two West Indian Novels of Exile." But the most comprehensive critique of Selvon's work is *Critical Perspectives on Sam Selvon*, edited and compiled by Susheila Nasta. This study consists mainly of critical articles and reviews on most of Selvon's books. It gives a good sense of the chronological development both of Selvon as a writer and of critical reaction to his work.

BIBLIOGRAPHY

Works by Samuel Selvon

A Brighter Sun. London: Wingate, 1952; London: Longman, 1971.

An Island Is a World. London: Wingate, 1955.

The Lonely Londoners. London: Wingate, 1956; London: Longman, 1972.

Ways of Sunlight. London: MacGibbon & Kee, 1957; London: Longman, 1973.

Turn Again Tiger. London: MacGibbon & Kee, 1958; London: Longman, 1978; London: Heinemann, 1979.

I Hear Thunder. London: MacGibbon & Kee, 1963.

The Housing Lark. London: MacGibbon & Kee, 1965.

A Drink of Water. London: Nelson, 1968.

The Plains of Caroni. London: MacGibbon & Kee, 1970.

Those Who Eat the Cascadura. London: Davis Poynter, 1972.

Moses Ascending. London: Davis Poynter, 1975.

Moses Migrating. London: Longman, 1983.

Studies of Samuel Selvon

Barratt, Harold. "Sam Selvon's Tiger: In Search of Self-Awareness." *Reworlding: The Literature of the Indian Diaspora.* Ed. Emmanuel S. Nelson. Westport, Conn.: Greenwood Press, 1992. 105–14.

Baugh, Edward. "Friday in Crusoe's City: The Question of Language in Two West Indian Novels of Exile." *ACLALS Bulletin*, 5th series, 3 (1980): 1–12.

Birbalsingh, Frank. "Samuel Selvon and the West Indian Literary Renaissance." *Ariel: A Review of International English Literature* 8 (July 1977): 5–22.

Brathwaite, Edward. "Jazz and the West Indian Novel." *Bim* 11 (Jan.-June 1967), 275–84; 12 (July-Dec. 1967), 39–51; 12 (Jan.-June 1968): 115–26.

———. "The New West Indian Novelists: Part One." *Bim* 8 (July-Dec. 1960): 208–10.

———. "Roots." *Bim* 10 (July-Dec. 1963): 10–21.

———. "Sir Galahad and the Islands." *Bim* 7 (July-Dec. 1957): 8–16.

Davies, Barrie. "The Sense of Abroad: Aspects of the West Indian Novel in England." *World Literature Written in English* 11 (Nov. 1972): 67–80.

Fabre, Michel. "From Trinidad to London: Tone and Language in Samuel Selvon's Novels." *Literary Half Yearly* 20 (Jan. 1979): 71–80.

———. "Moses and the Queen's English: Dialect and Narrative Voice in Samuel Selvon's London Novels." *World Literature Written in English* 21 (Summer 1982): 385–92.

———. "The Queen's Calypso: Linguistic and Narrative Strategies in the Fiction of Samuel Selvon." *Caribbean Essays and Studies* 3 (1977–78): 69–76.

MacDonald, Bruce F. "Language and Consciousness in Samuel Selvon's *A Brighter Sun*." *English Studies in Canada* 5 (Summer 1979): 202–15.

Nasta, Susheila. *Critical Perspectives on Sam Selvon.* Washington, D.C.: Three Continents Press, 1988.

Nazareth, Peter. "The Clown in the Slave Ship." *Caribbean Quarterly* 23 (June-Sept. 1977): 24–30.

———. "Interview with Sam Selvon." *World Literature Written in English* 18 (Nov. 1979): 420–37.

Paquet, Sandra Pouchet. Introduction to *Turn Again Tiger.* London: Heinemann, 1979.

Ramchand, Kenneth. "*A Brighter Sun*." *An Introduction to the Study of West Indian Literature.* London: Nelson Publishing, 1976. 58–72.

———. "*The Lonely Londoners* as a Literary Work." *World Literature Written in English* 21 (Autumn 1982): 644–84.

———. "Sam Selvon Talking: A Conversation with Kenneth Ramchand." *Canadian Literature* 95 (Winter 1982): 56–64.

Rohlehr, F. Gordon. "The Folk in Caribbean Literature." *Tapia* 2 (Dec. 17, 1972): 7–8, 13–15; 2 (Dec. 24, 1972): 8–9.

Warner-Lewis, Maureen. "Samuel Selvon's Linguistic Extravaganza: *Moses Ascending*." *Critical Issues in West Indian Literature.* Ed. Erica Sollish Smilowitz and Roberta Quarles Knowles. Parkersburg, Iowa: Caribbean Books, 1984. 101–111.

VIKRAM SETH (1952–   )
C. Vijayasree

BIOGRAPHY

Vikram Seth was born on June 20, 1952, in Calcutta, India. He lived in India till he was seventeen, when he went to England for higher studies. He took his first degree from Corpus Christi, Oxford. In 1975, he moved to California and graduated in economics from Stanford University. He worked on the economic demography of seven villages in China for his doctoral thesis and spent a couple of years at Nanjing University, China, in pursuit of this project. Seth thus came into close contact with four cultures: his native India, England, California, and communist China. His interest in these cultures is not that of an observer with an eye for the exotic, but that of a studious learner bent on apprehending the essence of them all. His work reveals the response of an expansive Indian sensibility to the richness of varied cultures outside: he does not resist influences, reject the possibilities of alternative points of view, or disapprove of divergences. On the other hand, he absorbs a wealth of influences, never losing his own Indian identity.

Seth always had a keen interest in literature though he never liked the idea of studying literature for a university degree. The sustaining support for this young graduate with a flair for writing and an urge for creativity came from Timothy Steele, a teacher at the University of California. The association between Seth and Steele began rather curiously when Seth, prevented from taking a course in creative writing at Stanford, visited the latter's office seeking an informal mentor. This association soon developed into a fruitful literary collaboration, and Steele became the guiding force behind Seth's major work, *The Golden Gate*.

Vikram Seth is firm about his priorities as a literary artist. He places clarity and intelligibility above experimentation and novelty. He believes that literature should be, first and foremost, accessible to the common reader (quoted in Leslie 2). To Seth, the world around him is real and worth observing. Steele, who has known him intimately, observes, "He [Seth] is more interested in the world outside of himself than he is in himself" (quoted in Leslie 5). Seth's work bears a testimony to the truth of this statement.

MAJOR WORKS AND THEMES

Vikram Seth started his career as a poet with the publication of a collection of poems, *Mappings*, in 1980. However, it is with the publication of his second book, a travel diary, *From Heaven Lake: Travels through Sinkiang and Tibet* (1983), that he attracted the attention of international readership. This book won him the prestigious Thomas Cook Travel Book Award. Another collection of Seth's poems, *The Humble Administrator's Garden*, appeared in 1985. His major work to date, the much acclaimed *The Golden Gate*, a novel in verse, was published in the following year. In 1990, Seth brought out yet another collection of poems, *All You Who Sleep Tonight*.

The single unifying theme that runs through all his works is the plea for human camaraderie cutting across political, national, and cultural barriers. Moving between New Delhi and London, Nanjing and California, Seth has learned to look for "the Commonalty of all mankind" (*From Heaven Lake*, p. 76). Seth explains his quest explicitly when he says:

... to learn about another great culture is to enrich one's life, to understand one's own country better, to feel more at home in the world, and indirectly to add to that reservoir of individual goodwill that may, generations from now, temper the cynical use of national power. (178)

In his travel book, *From Heaven Lake*, Seth enumerates the travails and experiences of his journey from Nanjing to New Delhi. His work is different from the conventional travel diaries because he avoids organized ways of traveling and hitchhikes through Chinese towns and Tibetan villages. This gives him and the reader tremendous advantage: they get to see the place at close quarters, and know the people more intimately. Along with the picturesque descriptions of people and places, there are reflections on sociopolitical issues such as the cultural revolution in China, destruction of Tibetan temples, rigidity of the bureaucracy in China, and Indo-China political relationship. At the end of it all, Seth makes the readers see that there is a need for greater understanding between the two great culture zones of India and China which, after all, are parts of the same land mass.

Seth continues to elaborate his dream of a humane and harmonious world in his verse collection, *The Humble Administrator's Garden*. The book is divided into three sections: "Wutong," "Neem," and "Live-oak," named after the principal trees of China, India, and California respectively. As Seth's imaginative eye traverses across these three different sceneries, he discovers in nature the bonds of kinship that bind all men together. All the poems here are as a rule lucid and are splendidly evocative and sensuous. He summons from the hinterland of memory certain buried moments of surprise, sensuous pleasure, or pathos and turns them into vivid poems.

Seth's *The Golden Gate* was a striking success and elicited enthusiastic response from readers and critics alike. The novel is set in present-day San Francisco. The authenticity of the Californian life presented here seems to be a matter of consensus among critics. It has been described as an up-to-date tale of San Franciscan "Yuppiedom" (Ionnone 54), and hailed as "The Great California novel" (Gore Vidal on dust jacket). What really makes Seth's portrayal of California complete is his capacity to be inside and outside this locale at the same time. The Californian life with its billboards, personal ads, and pet psychologists is intimately known to the author; yet he responds with freshness to certain aspects of this life that a native would either overlook or take for granted. He observes the place and its quaintness, partakes of it, and transcreates it in his work, looking at it alternatively with mild amusement and fondness, genuine sympathy and an urgent sense of concern.

Another aspect of Seth's work that made it an astonishing success is its technical virtuosity. *The Golden Gate* is a rare technical achievement—all of it, including acknowledgments, dedication, and table of contents, is written in intricately patterned sonnets numbering 593, strictly measured and rhymed. As Seth himself declares in the text, the inspiration for this work came from Charles Johnston's 1977 translation of Pushkin's masterpiece *Eugene Onegin* (1833), which had stirred his brain like champagne (*Golden Gate* 5:5).

However, what has been overlooked by critics hitherto is the fact that the text is not so much a celebration of yuppiedom as a discerning analysis of the malaise of modern times, for which Seth prescribes love as the only cure. The golden gate to happiness is love, the genuine reaching out between individuals. The novel traces the growth of a set of young Californians into an awareness of this truth.

The narrative begins with John Brown, a young, well-placed computer scientist, complaining of boredom and loneliness. John's predicament is symptomatic of a general disorder found in the computerized world, where files take precedence over friends and almighty "Chip" replaces God. His Asian friend Janet Hayakawa promptly diagnoses his illness: "You need a lover, John" (*Golden Gate* 1:23). She tells him to seek a fuller vision of life (*Golden Gate* 1:24). John's progress toward a more complete vision is beset with hazards, but he takes the first step forward as he realizes that true love is giving and forgiving, not demanding and exacting. In fact, all the characters in the novel—Liz, Phil, Ed, and the possessive tabby Charlemagne—move toward a greater ambience of love and friendship, compassion and companionship through the narrative. Seth's message of love comes across unequivocally. Within this framework, Seth fits in his plea for nuclear disarmament and world peace as well.

Most of the verses in Seth's recent collection *All You Who Sleep Tonight* are based either on the poet's personal experience or documentary evidence of the real-life experience of some historical personages. The major concerns of the poet remain unaltered, but the focus shifts from individual loneliness to a sense of insecurity experienced by the modern man faced with the threat of war and violence. There is greater pain and agony in these verses, but there is greater hope too. Memory is an important device employed here. The poet recalls incidents either from his own experience or from a commonly shared historical past, and re-creates the emotions associated with these experiences through powerful images. The diction comes closer to the conversational idiom, and the occasional awkwardness of phrase seen in the earlier verses is totally absent. The poet still keeps to the conventional stanzaic form, but it does not impede the flow of thought anywhere.

CRITICAL RECEPTION

Seth received favorable reviews for all his works and enthusiastic critical response for his *Golden Gate*. All the reviewers of this book, including Carl Ionnone, Patrick Parrinder, and John Hollander, give him unreserved praise for his poetic dexterity and metrical skill. Seth's mastery of metrical forms is undoubtedly a rare merit in this age of free verse. However, equally significant is the vision of life embodied in his works. Because of the casual matter-of-factness of tone and the posture of playfulness he adopts, critics are sometimes misled to take Seth's work rather lightly. For instance, Patrick Parrinder, reviewing *Golden Gate* for the *London Review of Books*, considers it "morally" "simplistic" (8). But on a closer reading of Seth's work, one discovers that a holistic view of life, one that underscores the essential oneness of all human existence, clearly emerges through his writing. This needs to be further explored for a better understanding of Seth's work.

BIBLIOGRAPHY

Works by Vikram Seth

Mappings. Calcutta: Writers Workshop, 1980.
From Heaven Lake: Travels through Sinkiang and Tibet. London: Chatto and Windus, 1983.
The Humble Administrator's Garden. Manchester: Carcenet Press, 1985.
The Golden Gate. London: Faber and Faber, 1986.
All You Who Sleep Tonight. New Delhi: Penguin Books, 1990.

Studies of Vikram Seth

Hollander, John. "Yuppie Time, In Rhyme." *New Republic* 194 (Apr. 21, 1986): 32–34.

Ionnone, Carl. "Yuppies in Rhyme." *Commentary* 182 (Sept. 1986): 54–56.

Leslie, Jaques. "Rhyme and Reason." *SPAN* (Nov. 1986): 2–7.

Paranjape, Makarand. "*The Golden Gate* and the Quest for Self-Realization." *ACLALS Bulletin*, 8th Series, no. 1. Contemporary Commonwealth Fiction. Aarhus: 1989. 58–73. Special issue.

Parrinder, Patrick. "Games Playing." *London Review of Books* 8:14 (Aug. 7, 1986): 8.

Robinson, Andrew. Review of *From Heaven Lake: Travels Through Sinkiang and Tibet. British Book News* (Sept. 1985): 559.

SHARAN-JEET SHAN (1945–   )
Rosemary Marangoly George

BIOGRAPHY

In *In My Own Name*, the fictional autobiography that shot her into fame, Sharan-Jeet writes of taking on the pseudonym Shan for its meaning: "I adopted the name Shan, . . . a word meaning grace, dignity and pride" (162). It is the search for these attributes in her personal life that led to the transformation of an unhappy young immigrant mother and housewife to a dynamic teacher and writer.

Shan was born in 1945 to Sikh parents in the village of Dhootkalan in Punjab, India. She was educated in New Delhi where her father, a middle-ranking army officer, was stationed during her youth. After finishing high school in 1961, Shan attended medical school in Delhi from 1961 to 1965. At Maulana Azad Medical College, Shan met and fell in love with a fellow medical student who happened to be Muslim. Given the strict prohibition of interreligious marriage even in the most liberal Indian families at the time, and given the very fresh memory of Sikh/Muslim animosity in the traumatic partition years (around 1947), what Sharan-Jeet and her young Muslim lover had done amounted to a grievous crime in the eyes of the elders in her family. Shan was rudely pulled out of medical school halfway through her training and compelled to agree to a hastily arranged marriage with a suitable young man of the community who was visiting from England. Shan works this traumatic personal experience into the central event in the narrative of *In My Own Name*.

Coming to England at the age of twenty, Shan was forced to abandon her ambition of pursuing a medical career. However, after an initial period of despair over the losses and changes in her young life, she obtained her teacher's certificate in 1971 from Newland Park College of Education at Chalfont St. Giles, Bucks. Since then she has taught in various capacities in local schools in the area. In 1985, after her divorce and the subsequent death of her ex-husband, Shan published *In My Own Name*, a fictionalized account of her life. The narrative covers growing up as a female child in a patriarchal society, her early rebellions against an autocratic father, the horrific account of the cruel punishments the young girl was subjected to by her father for having fallen in love with a Muslim man—beatings, torture, starvation, and finally being pushed into a forced and unhappy marriage to a stranger in a strange country.

In My Own Name was written as an attempt to put a traumatic past to rest, a cathartic act of writing to ease the mind of its burden of painful memories. "Suicide," writes Shan in the preface, "would have been the only other alternative. In writing my story, in reliving the past, the healing process has begun" (n.p.). Her other purpose, she writes in this preface, is served "if my book awakens awareness in just one woman's heart, that inside all of us there lies a latent courage, a whole host of inner resources" (n.p.). It is not an exaggeration to say that the publication of Shan's book caused a furor in the Asian community in England. Very soon after its publication, Shan found herself and her two young children ostracized from her immediate family, from friends, and from the Asian community in England. The book was also read with interest by white readers of mixed political persuasions for the picture it painted of the lives of young Asian women immigrants in urban England.

The publication of this book was followed by a flurry of writing by Shan on the racism and sexism in the school curriculum in contemporary England. While some of this writing has been included in the selected bibliography that follows, much of it comprises various scholarly conference presentations as well as position papers on curricular reform. In June 1990, Trentham books published *Multiple Factors: Classroom Math for Equality and Justice*, a book on racial stereotyping in math classrooms and textbooks that Shan co-authored with Peter Bailey. More recently, she team-wrote, with a group of nine other teachers, a book entitled *Race, Equality, and Science Teaching*.

In a recent phone interview (January 2, 1992) Shan stated that despite the success of *In My Own Name*, she sees herself as a teacher first and then as a writer. In the course of the interview Shan stated that her interests had shifted somewhat from the focus on women's oppression as dealt with in *In My Own Name* to considerations of the impact of racism and inequality on young children. In 1990 Shan received a master's degree in social science from Birmingham University. Since April 1990 she has been working as a general advisor to the Sandwell Education Authority in the West Mildlands and writing in her spare time. At present Shan is working on a fictional/autobiographical account of the impact of single-parent upbringing on immigrant children in England.

Shan currently lives in Birmingham, England, with her two sons. She remarried in October 1991 and is delighted with her discovery that personal and professional fulfillment can blossom in a marriage between equals.

MAJOR WORKS AND THEMES

Shan's major theme in *In My Own Name* as well as in her other writing is her belief in the need to work toward equality and toward providing all persons, regardless of race and gender, with opportunities to thrive.

While *In My Own Name* is mainly autobiographical, it is written in the manner of realist fiction. The book can be compared to the Nigerian writer Buchi Emecheta's *Second-Class Citizen* (1975), another partly autobiographical account of an immigrant mother's story of breaking out of an abusive marriage and bringing up her children single-handedly in a hostile England.

In My Own Name unflinchingly plots out a story that is riveting in its stark account of the violence with which daughters, wives, and mothers are made docile, subservient figures. The pivotal turns in the narrative come when the reader finds that though the heroine's spirit is broken repeatedly, it mends. The narrative begins at the end of one unhappy phase in the life of the protagonist and at the threshold of another, possibly more fulfilling phase. But before the second phase can begin, the "ghosts of the past must be put to rest," and this requires the telling of the entire history of the narrator (4). *In My Own Name* proceeds in the manner of the *bildungsroman*: tracing the moral development of a child over the years of growing up. However, instead of the conventional ending with the falling in love of the young protagonist, and of her/his love triumphing over all odds, we have an explosion of the genre. When the heroine falls in love, her life falls apart. Later in the narrative, Shan avoids another avenue for a traditional happy ending by refusing to let the almost miraculous reunion of the old lovers proceed beyond a brief time of togetherness.

Shan has been read by Asian as well as British readers as being unequivocally against Indian social traditions such as "arranged" marriages. In the preface to the second edition of her book, she insists that she is not condemning the arranged marriage system—but only a tyrannical enforcement of such systems on unwilling participants. And as one reads the text, one finds that the critique is definitely more far-ranging and more devastating. From the perspective of a woman who has suffered great brutality, we get an examination and rejection of the "comforts" offered by community, family, religion, marriage, and even friendship.

The very first sentence of the preface of *In My Own Name* proclaims, "I am not a writer by the furthest stretch of imagination" (n.p.). In the interview of January 2, 1992, Shan said that she had always thought of writers as persons of almost mythological stature. And yet she also believes that writers are born out of the specific life histories of ordinary people. Shan's deliberate, straightforward narrative style is indeed noteworthy. The sensational aspects of the story are somewhat subdued by this narrative style, which eschews any literary adornment. But by the end of the book there is no doubt that what Shan has produced is a sparse and therefore effective tale of oppressive circumstances that can choke a woman's self-esteem but that can also be overcome by a woman of courage.

CRITICAL RECEPTION

In My Own Name has been read for the most part as representational fiction that mirrors the very difficult life of young Asian immigrant women in contemporary England. The book received a great deal of attention right after publication. It was widely reviewed by mainstream as well as academic media.

Perhaps the greatest recognition came from the writer Fay Weldon's inclusion of Shan's book in a top ten fiction list that she compiled for *Women's Review*. Interestingly, Weldon categorizes *In My Own Name* as an "immediate" book, by which she means to imply "the kind [of book] I recommend to friends and family, saying you must read this, it's so interesting, it will change the way you think, and so forth" (15). Weldon goes on to note that such "immediate" books are frequently published by Virago or the Women's Press.

Like Weldon, other white feminists have seen in Shan's text an account of the "terrifying world of contemporary immigrant Britain," as Weldon phrases it, and especially of the life of young Indian women in India and in England (15). Critics of Asian origin who have commented on this book inevitably assess Shan's work in a positive light but almost always caution that her text must be read as no more than *one* account of being an Asian woman.

Marion Gastonbury compares her response to *In My Own Name* to Virginia Woolf's response to *Maternity* (the collected correspondence of the Co-operative Women's Guild 1915). Gastonbury quotes Woolf as assessing *Maternity* as "Not like a book at all" (Weldon 15). Other critics share this inclination to see *In My Own Name* as more than fiction as well as more than autobiography. The writer's and narrator's courage and fortitude draw unanimous admiration from all readers.

In 1991, *In My Own Name* was selected a recommended textbook for high school students in England and was republished by Cambridge University Press for this purpose. Shan has been approached for a movie contract, and negotiations are underway.

BIBLIOGRAPHY

Works by Sharan-Jeet Shan

In My Own Name. London: Women's Press, 1985; 2nd ed., 1986; New Delhi: Rupa Press, 1991; Cambridge: Cambridge University Press, 1991.

"Racism & Science: A Black Perspective." *Multicultural Review* 7 (Summer 1987): 6–9.

Multiple Factors: Classroom Math for Equality and Justice. With Peter Bailey. London: Trentham Books, 1991.

Race, Equality, and Science Teaching. With Steve Thorpe et al. London: Association of Science Education, 1992.

Studies of Sharan-Jeet Shan

Brown, Reva. Review of *In My Own Name. British Book News* (Dec. 1985): 719.

Chatterji, Bobby. "On Behalf of Womankind." *Savvy* (Feb. 1986): 83–88.

Cutter, Mary. "Not Just Saris and Samosas." *Arts Report* (July-Aug. 1986): 17.

Gellner, Sarah. "Culture Shock." *Spare Rib* (Jan. 1986): 27.

———. "In Her Own Name." *Monochrome* (Nov.-Dec. 1985): 9.

Hennessey, Val. "Marriage of Inconvenience." *Times* [London] (Oct. 23, 1985): 15.

Jones, D.A.N. "Not Fair Enough." *New Society* (Nov. 1985): 251–52.

Khan, Naseem. "Rare Pleasures." *Chartist* (Apr. 1986): 36.

Kumrai, Rajni. Review of *In My Own Name. Working with Girls* 33 (May-June 1986): 1.

Verma, Asha. Review of *In My Own Name. Dialogue* 2 (Summer 1986): 50.

Weldon, Fay. "Top Ten." *Women's Review* 8 (Dec. 1985): 15.

KIRPAL SINGH (1949–   )

Rajeev Patke

BIOGRAPHY

Kirpal Singh was born in Singapore, in March 1949. His father was a Sikh, a champion athlete, and a champion boxer. His mother was a Scottish Jew. They divorced and remarried shortly after his birth. From 1955 he was brought up by his paternal grandmother and uncle, the primary formative influences of his early life. He grew up in a cosmopolitan atmosphere, among a community comprising Indians, Chinese, and Malays. Though not strictly orthodox, he continues with the traditional observances of the Sikh faith he was brought up in.

Kirpal began publishing and editing early. His school poems appeared in *Lines Not for Squares* (1968). The same year he edited a miscellany, *Singapore Pot-Pourri* (published 1970), and in 1971, *Sex Yesterday and Today*, which created a certain furor. His early days were a period of struggle, self-sacrifice, and hard work. Getting educated had to be combined with giving support at home. While completing National Service he went up to university in 1969, also teaching at the Singapore Adult Education Board. He did his B.A. honors in English literature under teachers like D. J. Enright and Edwin Thumboo, whom he came to admire. As an undergraduate he published poems in the university newspaper and in the journal of the Literary Society.

Since his undergraduate days Kirpal's many activities have made him what he calls "a very small public figure . . . invited constantly to various organizations and institutions to address them and give speeches, and to appear on panels and things like that . . . this . . . is important because it continues my ever abiding sense of public responsibility" (De Berg Tapes, National Library of Australia). In 1975 this led to *The Community Touch* and *Together Toward Greater Responsibility*. He edited his first anthology of Singaporean poetry, *Articulations* (1972), while still an undergraduate. After getting an M.A. with his thesis "Technology and the Modern Novel," in 1973 he became lecturer in what was then Singapore University, now the National University of Singapore. In 1976 he was in Adelaide on a scholarship, working on Aldous Huxley for a Ph.D. During his two years abroad he became acquainted with literary circles in Australia and in New Zealand, taking part in many poetry readings, getting published in successive volumes of the *Friendly Street Poetry Reader* (1976, 1977, 1978), interviewed on several radio stations, and represented at home in Edwin Thumboo's influential anthology, *The Second Tongue* (1976).

In Singapore he resumed his literary activities, and was a founder-editor of the journal *Singa*. From 1980 to 1983 he edited the Poetry Corner in the *Sunday Times*. It attracted many contributions and some hostile notice. During 1982–83 he went on secondment to the University of Papua New Guinea, where he edited a similar feature. Apart from brief periods as visiting fellow and writer-in-residence at Geelong College (1978), University of Wollongong (1987), University of Western Australia (1989), and Curtin University (1991–92), Kirpal has continued teaching at the National University of Singapore, where he is a senior lecturer. He is consultant to the Three Continents Press, Dangaroo Press, Solidaridad Press, and Peter Lang. He is on the editorial board of *Kunapipi* and *Studies in World Literature*. He also reports on Southeast Asia for *Year's Work in English Studies*, and is regional editor for Routledge's *Encyclopaedia of Commonwealth Literature*. He has been involved with a number of writers' workshops and reading festivals, locally, in Europe, and in America.

MAJOR WORKS AND THEMES

Kirpal Singh is the kind of literary individual whose work is better seen as all of a kind, not as an activity split up into writing poems, short stories, plays, criticism, or scholarship. He engages in all these (and now concentrates more on his own writing), but above all he has compiled and edited, devoted, in the sense of entrepreneur and agent provocateur, to making room and creating a role not only for himself but for the type of the "new" or "third world" writer looking for a sense of vocation, a style, and an audience from the perspective of his time and place. Hence his almost obsessive interest in the conditions and viability of creative writing in Singapore, and his work as editor, reviewer, and critic of new literatures in English (as, for example, on Ee Tiang Hong, Edwin Thumboo and Chandran Nair, Patrick White, Indian writing in English, and Catherine Lim).

The 1960s were the years when Singapore became independent and set about the task of defining for itself a sense of identity motivated by a commitment to a future based on the economics of an industrialized and technologically oriented society, with a cultural life synthesized from its historical links to the mores of its Chinese, Malaysian, Indian, and Eurasian communities. The public quality of Kirpal's writing, its sense that every feature of the communal life is directly relevant to the personal, is shared with contemporaries like Robert Yeo. This concurrence between the formation of the writer's sensibility and the growth of the nation explains even better than the events of his personal life the momentum and direction of his work. It also explains his zeal for science fiction. The history of modern Singapore may be said to be the very real predication of a very speculative fiction about nation building. What could be more appropriate for Kirpal than science fiction's extrapolation into the realms of the possible, its concern for how science and technology shape man's physical and cultural environment. Paradoxically then, science fiction interests Kirpal because it is a form of realism.

The stories show the full extent of this attachment to realism. The issues dramatized are public and generic: the role of the writer in contemporary Singapore ("The Interview," "Ruminations"), the ethics of the teaching profession ("One Day in the Life of Dr. X", "A Revelatory Experience"), integrity in public affairs ("Hullabaloo over Television"), the choice between idealism and pragmatism ("Julie," "Love/Hate"). The thinly fictionalized characters and situations dramatize representative issues of moral choice. The satire and condemnation ("In order to love you must hate") stem from an idealized morality of a very straightforward kind. One supposes that the Kirpal who championed popular creativity in the Poetry Corner has little use for subtlety and sophistication lest they lead to preciousness, obliquity, and an elitism that might lose the general audience he seeks. The style is functional, its realism hospitable to local idiom ("Little Sister Writes Home"), drawn to the racy and the earthy. The issues are specifically Singaporean ("A Play in Two Acts"). "Monologue" handles personal experiences in a striking manner rare in his work. It appears to confess to the strain of trying to write in a willed way, while tapping a deeply troubling private memory that tortures recollection. For the most part, however, his fiction does not accommodate a private realm that does not also implicate the public.

The poetry essays a more personal note. "I am that half-gone, angry young man who fell asleep and is now awake / To the haunting magic of your bellbones" ("Alternative"). It is forceful in utterance and belief, direct in manner, rhythmic rather than visual in orientation, focused exclusively on the human landscape, exhorting moral responsibility. "O my partner what have we done? What have our fire and water brought to life?" asks "A Vision." The first volume shows a sobriety, even somberness, which finds more adequate expression in the shorter poems. Those with an Australian setting express personal loneliness, a side not too often exposed. Many of the later poems ("Two Voices") are experiments with Singaporean English, like Arthur Yap's, or Nissim Ezekiel's Indian English poems. The recent poetry is more meditative, reflecting feelingly on individuals, occasions, and memories that matter.

CRITICAL RECEPTION

Apart from Krishna Rao's essay in practical criticism (devoted to "Palm Readings," which he finds "quizzical, though not cynical"), critical reaction to Kirpal Singh's poetry is mainly in the form of reviews. Xuan Xong singles out irony as his chief strength, and "A Four Month Invitation" (from *Articulations*) as "the author at his best—economical . . . spare, terse" (22). Ee Tiang Hong finds that most of the *Twenty Poems* show up "the discrepancy between intention and act, word and deed in various personal relationships." He finds that their characteristic pattern "is one where an idea stated directly, or an image presented at the beginning, is developed with little ceremony until the ending, which rephrases the original line, extending the associations or giving it an ironic thrust" (52). For Ee Tiang Hong the experiments of the second volume have the interest of exploring the creative possibilities of "Singlish." Anne Brewster finds that the second book, *Palm Readings*, "marks a radical shift from earlier work" (104). Many of the new poems engage in a dialogue where a persona "speaks from a position outside or marginal to the dominant discourses he addresses" (105), discourses (like those of region or race) which seek to marginalize that persona. She too, like other reviewers, singles out irony and ambiguity as general characteristics of the poetry.

BIBLIOGRAPHY

Works by Kirpal Singh

Ed. *Articulations: An Anthology of Poems*. Singapore: Club Adconmeli, 1972.

Twenty Poems. Calcutta: Writers Workshop, 1978.

Ed., with R. Shephard. *Patrick White: A Critical Symposium*. Adelaide: Centre for Research in the New Literatures in English (CRNLE), 1978.

Ed. *Singapore and Malaysian Literature*. Hamilton: Outrigger Publications, 1979.

Wonder and Awe: The World of Science Fiction. Singapore: Chopmen Publishers, 1980.

Ed., with M. Tolley. *The Stellar Gauge: Essays on Science Fiction Writers*. Melbourne: Nostrilia Press, 1980.

Ed., with R. S. Bathal and D. de Souza. *Singapore Science Fiction*. Singapore: Singapore Science Centre, 1980.

Ed. *Through Different Eyes: Foreign Responses to Indian Writing in English*. Calcutta: Writers Workshop, 1984.

Palm Readings. Singapore: Graham Brash Pte Ltd., 1986.

Ed. *Critical Engagements: Singapore Poems in Focus*. Singapore: Heinemann Asia, 1986.

Notes on Catherine Lim's "Little Ironies." With Anne Brewster. Singapore: Heinemann Asia, 1987.

Ed. *The Writer's Sense of the Past: Essays in Southeast Asian and Australian Literature.* Singapore: Singapore University Press, 1987.

Poetry for You—Book 1. With Geoffrey Hall. London: Macmillan, 1988.

Ed. *Stories from Asia and the Pacific.* Singapore: Federal Publications, 1988.

Why Make Love Twice: Collected Short Stories. Forthcoming, 1993.

Studies of Kirpal Singh

Brewster, Anne. Review of *Palm Reading. SPAN* 26 (1988): 104–6.

Churches, Christine. Review of *Twenty Poems. Pacific Quarterly Moana* 4:1 (Jan. 1979): 103–4.

Janadas, Devan. Review of *Twenty Poems. Commentary* 3:1 (Sept. 1978): 54–57.

Ee Tiang Hong. Review of *Twenty Poems. Asia Week* 4:25 (June 1978): 52.

Rao, A. V. Krishna. "Kirpal Singh." In *Critical Engagements.* Ed. Kirpal Singh. Singapore: Heinemann Asia, 1986. 69–74.

Xuan Xong. Review of *Twenty Poems. Sunday Nation* (Aug. 20, 1978): 22.

SUBRAMANI (1943–   )
Srimati Mukherjee

BIOGRAPHY

Subramani, one of the most dynamic contemporary Indo-Fijian writers, was born on June 20, 1943, in Labasa, Fiji. His father came to Fiji from India as an indentured laborer, and Subramani grew up in Fiji, attending high school in that country. He attained his bachelor's degree in English from the University of Canterbury, New Zealand, in 1966 and his master's from the University of New Brunswick, Canada, in 1972 with his thesis entitled "Search for a Country: A Study of V. S. Naipaul's Fiction and Non-fiction Writings." His doctoral studies were conducted at the University of the South Pacific, Fiji, and he received his Ph.D. in 1981 for his thesis, "From Myth to Fabulation: Emerging South Pacific Literature." From 1985 to 1986, he pursued postdoctoral studies at the University of Birmingham, England, as a recipient of the Association of Commonwealth Universities' Post Doctoral Award. Subramani has been teaching at the University of the South Pacific since 1974 and is currently a professor there in the Literature and Language Department. From 1980 to 1983, he was dean of academic affairs and subsequently a pro vice-chancellor at the University of the South Pacific. An active promoter of creative literature in the South Pacific, he edited the journal *Mana* from 1976 to 1978. At the present time, he edits the periodical *South Pacific Literature*. Subramani's publications include *The Indo-Fijian Experience* (1979)—a collection of which he is the editor, *South Pacific Literature: From Myth to Fabulation* (1985), and *The Fantasy Eaters: Stories from Fiji* (1988). His second and more recent edited collection is *After Narrative: The Pursuit of Reality and Fiction* (1990). Subramani has to his credit a number of critical essays such as the longish article *The Mythical Quest: Literary Response to the South Seas*. Of several awards and laurels that Subramani has won for his fiction may be mentioned the Japan Foundation Award in 1988 for his short story "Marigolds." In 1991, he was awarded a Fulbright Scholarship and consequently spent five months in the United States at Johns Hopkins University. Following the military coup in Fiji, Subramani was arrested by the army in 1988 and later released from custody. Despite such incidents, however, he chooses to remain in Fiji and continues to play a pivotal role in supporting literary endeavor in that country.

MAJOR WORKS AND THEMES

The Indo-Fijian Experience (1979), published precisely a hundred years after the first indentured Indians began arriving in Fiji in 1879, is a centennial collection edited by Subramani. It comprises both historical and critical essays, short stories, and poems and endeavors to "provide a glimpse into the historically evolving character of the Indo-Fijian" (xi). In some of Subramani's short stories included in the collection, the diasporic consciousness manifests itself as one that is tortured and alienated in the new land (Fiji), clinging to tenuous vestiges of its Indian past to combat the harsh reverses suffered in the land of migration. This depiction of the diasporic consciousness holds true for "Sautu," in which the life of Dhanpat, the central character, is pervaded by loss and desolation. Dhanpat lives in Fiji with a few paltry belongings from his Indian past only to lose even these in a fire. The narrative closes with Dhanpat's lone wanderings through the village of Sautu and his ultimate removal from the village following the villagers' conjecturing his insanity. "Tell Me Where the Train Goes" spawns an atmosphere of terror and brutality in the Fijian barracks where the Indian laborers are concentrated. Manu, the child protagonist, attempts to flee the vituperation and latent nihilism of the barracks by escaping to a local cave termed "Kailas" or "home of Shiva" by his late father. In that Manu's central point of refuge, the cave, is linked to India through association, Subramani privileges the legends of the land left behind over the reality of the Fijian present. However, as in "Sautu," the present proves too pervasive to be kept at bay with meager icons of a forsaken India. Manu, who is finally witness to the laborers' assault of the sahib (his mother's lover), is ravaged at the end of the story, till he senses once again the nurturing by his mother after a period of emotional distancing. This reader may be forgiven if she sees in this restored nurturing Subramani's implied imperative for the revitalization of bonds with India. In fact, the intermittent presence of a taunting mother adds to the agony of Chetram, the protagonist in "Marigolds." Subramani's fictional schema often calls for unqualified maternal sustenance and, by analogical extension, an unbroken link with the motherland. The absence of the latter leads, in "Marigolds," to Chetram's reiterative and ominous dream of being placed before a "stone altar under a crumbling thatch, smelling of goat droppings on the sides" where he is subjected to "reproaches from the shadow" (136). Fragmented presences of Indian icons in Chetram's mind only accentuate his displacement in a story about interpersonal and cultural estrangement.

In *South Pacific Literature: From Myth to Fabulation* (1985), Subramani focuses on the literature of the Cook Islands, Fiji, Kiribati, Nauru, Niue, Solomon Islands, Tokelau, Tonga, Tuvalu, Western Samoa, and Vanuatu and attempts to "interpret the genesis of this new literature in English and explicate its artistic accomplishment" (Preface ix). He addresses the span of this literature—from accumulation, recording, and translation of myths to its metafictional manifestation in the writings of Albert Wendt. In tracing the origins of this literature, Subramani gives credit to missionary activities in the colonial period of the above countries, activities that fostered reading and writing among the converts, initially in local languages and subsequently in English. Addressing a more holistic development of this new South Pacific literature, however, the author notes its concurrence with the desire for political independence, the literature drawing "sustenance from wide-spread anti-colonial sentiments in the region" (6). Referring to contemporary South Pacific literature, Subramani draws a connection between creativity and the diasporic consciousness, asserting that for some writers, the Indo-Fijians, for example, writing is a means of identifying with the Pacific environment. Even if Indo-Fijian writing has no explicit connections with South Pacific oral tradition, it shares with the new South Pacific literature the dominant themes of colonialism, cultural divisiveness, personal and racial identity. Speaking of the genres, Subramani notes that South Pacific poetry is in a formative state in contrast to which short fiction appears to have attained a greater measure of success. He refers to the paucity of written plays, commenting that the South Pacific offers the playwright limited opportunities to acquire the skills of "stage craft, visual and auditory effects, and the requirements of continuous performance" (68). He addresses a noteworthy development in the literature of the South Pacific—an interexploration of cultures, the beginnings of which are evident in virtually all the literary genres. He speaks of the literary development of Albert Wendt as dramatizing remarkably the interplay between the personal and social roles of the creative artist. Subramani is heartened by fabulation in Wendt's fiction, feeling that the technique is suggestive of "an ontological movement, a serious reaching towards the unformulated, indeterminate ideas, a desire for the unattainable" (157).

A close examination of some of the stories in Subramani's *The Fantasy Eaters* (1988) reveals a thematic progression in the area of diasporic experiences and consciousness. Subramani moves from deft depictions of craving for one's motherland to situations of quasi-identification with the land of immigration to an underscoring of the undeniable bond occasionally formed with the new land to tales in which separation from the motherland has been so long imposed that memories of the motherland remain only nebulously in the realm of one's reveries. "Groundlings," stand at one end

of this spectrum, embodies the yearning for things Indian and in this particular case, the craving for popular Indian films in Fiji. The story dramatizes
the protagonist's viewing of one such film, and shows how in spite of the
crass stupidity of the presentation, the indulgence of the production in sheer
fantasy, and the discomfort caused by the stifling crowds, the craving for
things Indian remains unshaken. Even if a distinction is made between the
gullible sections of the film's audience (most of whom are concentrated on
the ground floor of the theater and hence are "groundlings") and the discerning narrator, the clear implication is that the latter too cannot escape
the lure of visual representations of the motherland. The story's irony is
heightened at its close when the narrator, by booking "upstairs" for the
next film, effects merely an artificially imposed, physical separation from
the groundlings. In a story such as "Tropical Traumas," the tourist resort
the narrator escapes to as a refuge from the city of Suva becomes a microcosm for the new country the immigrant moves to. Even in a brief time
span, the traveler/narrator establishes a many-faceted relationship with the
resort. He partakes of its pleasures and diversions, but is also deeply moved
by the indignities hurled on the land. The reader is left with the sense that
the resort/new land molds, to a certain extent, the personality of the traveler/
narrator, so that his leaving is, in some senses, a loss. However, the narrator
feels inclined to wrench himself away as a deep involvement with this new
land is about to start. If "Tropical Traumas" is a metaphoric manifestation
of the diasporic experience, then at its close, Subramani underscores the
evading of commitment to the new country, an escapism that could very
well be characteristic of the traveler who has already suffered one estrangement from his motherland and is intent on avoiding similar involvement
and pain. "Dear Primitive" shows a further progression in the theme of
identification with the new country in that it is a story in which the immigrant (Elaine) identifies more with the natives in Fiji than with her own
people. It is a tale of becoming synonymous with the spirit of the new land
to the extent that natural phenomena of the land are humanized in Elaine's
imagination and reach out to her in a virtually spine-tingling manner.
Elaine's brief affair with Ronnie, who is not a native Fijian, is pervaded by
a strain of tension as, ironically, in Elaine's mind, Ronnie becomes the
intruder who has no comprehension of her bonding with the land. Hence,
at the end of "Dear Primitive," Elaine craves not Ronnie's return, but the
drowned Senibulu's—a native girl who had initiated her into the beauties,
mysteries, and legends of the land. Through a powerful dream image at the
close of "Dear Primitive," Subramani points to the submerging of Elaine's
consciousness by the primal forces of the new land. In that none of the
main characters in the above story is Indian, Subramani leans toward the
universalization of the diasporic experience. In "Gamalian's Woman," memories of Indian luxuries, such as the palanquin, or of elaborately detailed
Indian myths remain only in the nebulous zone of Mrs. Gamalian's dreams,

while her reality in the land of indenture (Fiji) is fraught with great hardship. In the recounting of Mrs. Gamalian's sufferings on the sugarcane plantations (labor colonies) in Fiji and of the debacles of most of her marriage, this story provides objective correlatives of the unfulfilled dream—the dream of the promised land initially held out by indenture. Yet it is this stark Fijian reality that prevails, while the Indian memories lose their vividness and eventually appear "faded like leaves in a compost" (60). In that Mrs. Gamalian is dead at the beginning and dead at the end of the story, that her life, when lived, had been an amalgam of denied dreams and withered hope, and that yet, Subramani, through fiction, wishes to re-create that life, the reader senses an emergent connection between writer and protagonist. This bonding is made all the more explicit as Mrs. Gamalian is initially presented as a teller of tales (like her creator), but one whose narrative powers progressively dwindle. By rendering Mrs. Gamalian a victim of the fraudulent nature of dreams held out by indenture and a victim of the receding powers of creativity, Subramani draws together the experiences of indenture and art, signaling the possibilities of betrayal in both.

CRITICAL RECEPTION

Negative criticism of Subramani's work, despite being minimal, is evidenced in Shaista Shameem, who regards the writer's women characters as being subordinates to his fleshed-out males (38). Yet such critiques may be countered by commentaries, such as that offered by Trixie Te Arama Menzies, which make pointed references to Subramani's widely divergent women protagonists. Irrespective of his characters' sexual identities, Subramani emerges a master of negative capability, and Menzies, addressing his representation of a Fijian youth in "No Man's Land," notes, "there would be few Pakeha New Zealand writers who could write with such insight and familiarity from the point of view of an ahi kaa radical" (100). Menzies makes the singular point that notwithstanding Subramani's "anti-utopian approach," the prevailing impact is one of "teeming life, an existential celebration of survival" (100). However, her observation on Subramani's "anti-utopian approach" finds greater critical validation than her comment on the carnivalesque in the writer. A case in point is Uma Parameswaran who, even while commending the editor and publishers of *The Indo-Fijian Experience* for their initiative and taste, recognizes that Subramani's characters people a wasteland in which the possibilities of rain are void (257). Yet Pio Manoa regards this severe fictive landscape as acclamatory, for indenture figures very much as a historical reality for Subramani (201), who does not see imaginative escape from that reality as a panacea for the Fiji Indians (203). Manoa hails Subramani as a writer sensitive enough to apprehend the impasse created by the absent presence of indenture, yet one who perceives the impasse as a possible "threshold situation" (203). In fact,

Vijay C. Mishra emphasizes that "Subramani has performed, structurally, the linguistic act necessary for the change in direction of Indo-Fijian fiction" ("Rama's" 252). Instead of precluding indenture from his fiction or addressing it as an objective phenomenon from the past, Subramani's oeuvre has presented indenture as a "dynamic process," a sociopersonal reality that persists in haunting the author (251–52). By virtue of this process orientation, and indeed by virtue of the ironic undertones and plurality of signification inherent in his work, Subramani has written, in Barthesque terms, *scriptible* texts, texts that other "fictions can be related" to and ones that can be constantly "rewritten by the artist[s]" (251–52).

BIBLIOGRAPHY

Works by Subramani

The Mythical Quest: Literary Response to the South Seas. Mysore: University of Mysore, 1977.
Ed. and introd. *The Indo-Fijian Experience.* St. Lucia: University of Queensland Press, 1979.
South Pacific Literature: From Myth to Fabulation. Suva: University of the South Pacific, 1985.
The Fantasy Eaters: Stories from Fiji. Washington, D.C.: Three Continents, 1988.
Ed. *After Narrative: The Pursuit of Reality and Fiction.* Suva: University of the South Pacific, 1990.

Studies of Subramani

Manoa, Pio. "Across the Fence." *The Indo-Fijian Experience.* Ed. and introd. Subramani. St. Lucia: University of Queensland Press, 1979. 184–207.
Menzies, Trixie Te Arama. Review of *The Fantasy Eaters: Stories from Fiji. Landfall: A New Zealand Quarterly* 44 (1990): 99–101.
Mishra, Vijay C. "Indo-Fijian Fiction and the *Girmit* Ideology." *The Indo-Fijian Experience.* Ed. and introd. Subramani. St. Lucia: University of Queensland Press, 1979. 171–83.
———. "Rama's Banishment: A Theoretical Footnote to Indo-Fijian Writing." *World Literature Written in English* 19 (1980): 242–56.
———. "The Girmit Ideology Revisited: Fiji Indian Literature." *Reworlding: The Literature of the Indian Diaspora.* Ed. Emmanuel S. Nelson. Westport, Conn.: Greenwood Press, 1992. 1–12.
Parameswaran, Uma. "The Indo-Fijian Experience." Review of *The Indo-Fijian Experience. World Literature Written in English* 19 (1980): 256–59.
Shameem, Shaista. "The Art of Raymond Pillai, Subramani and Prem Banfal: A Feminist Critique of the Indo-Fijian Short Story." *SPAN: Journal of the South Pacific Association for Commonwealth Literature and Language Studies* 20 (1985): 29–46.

BAHADUR TEJANI (1942–)
Arlene A. Elder

BIOGRAPHY

Bahadur Tejani's literary genres are creative, cultural, and scholarly, all of his work reflecting the ethnic diversity of his heritage, place of birth, travels, and immigrations. A Ugandan citizen, Tejani was born in Kenya, East Africa, on March 9, 1942, of Gujrati heritage. The writer's education reflects the former interdependence of the three countries of the East African Economic Community, as well as their Commonwealth status with Britain. He attended primary school in Tanzania (then Tanganyika), secondary school in Uganda, and received his B.A. in 1964 from Makerere University, Kampala, in English and African literature and history.

Tejani's creative potential was recognized early; in November 1966, critic David Cook read and analyzed his story "Emergence" on "Black and White," Radio Uganda's monthly program introducing new writers in East Africa, and chose the story for inclusion in a collection of works from the radio show published in 1976 by the East Africa Literature Bureau. The following year, the young writer completed an M.A. at Cambridge University, England, in English and European literature and saw his play, "Babalola," about political and generation conflict in Nigeria, staged and broadcast that spring by the BBC Theatre Group in London. He continued experimenting with short fiction and published the story "The Writer" in the *East Africa Journal* in Nairobi in 1967, as well. Traveling to India for the first time, he taught there from 1967 to 1969 and published a collection of poems expressing his responses to this country of his ancestors, *The Rape of Literature and Other Poems* (1969). Tejani's short story "The Chowkidar in Our Mohalla" appeared the same year in the Delhi journal *Thought*.

Returning to East Africa in 1970, Tejani accepted a teaching position at the University of Nairobi. From this time, his poetry was anthologized in influential collections such as *Poems from East Africa* (Cook and Rubadiri,

1971) and *Poems from Black Africa* (Soyinka, 1974) as well as in local journals and newspapers. He received tenure at the University of Nairobi in 1972, where he both taught and took classes. Tejani's greatest professional triumph to date occurred the following year, 1973, with the publication of his well-known novel *Day after Tomorrow*; however, he was forced to leave Africa in 1974 after his protest against the military takeover of Uganda. Tejani and his wife, Yasmin, emigrated to Vancouver, Canada, encouraged by letters from one of his sisters who had already settled there. In 1974 *Transition* published "Farewell Uganda," an account of his personal and political feelings at this turbulent time for Afro-Asians. The piece resonates with a sense of nostalgia: "We Asians are true heirs of the dead East Africa. Long before self-government, we children knew of Nairobi, Dar and Kampala and had been to them" (65). Rather than despair at the subsequent disruption of his and his East African countrymen's lives, Tejani was characteristically upbeat in an interview in the Nairobi *Daily Nation* of June 1974: "What am I going to do in Canada? I hope to publish a volume of poems and do as much writing as possible" (17).

Nevertheless, he soon focused upon the confusion and disillusionment of trying to adjust to the racism of Western society in "The New Canadians: Afro-Indo Reflections on the West End," printed in the Vancouver *West End Courier* in 1975, the same year that the University of Nairobi awarded him his Ph.D. in African literature. The following year, 1976, brought professional success in his new environment, as well; he saw the production at the Vancouver Public Library and Langara College of his satiric play "The Other Side of the Coin," written two years earlier, with Gandhi and Churchill as the main characters, the first Indo-Canadian play in English. In 1976, Tejani's growing recognition as an important African voice was attested to by an interview with Lee Nichols on Voice of America, subsequently included in Nichols's *African Writers at the Microphone* (1984). This interview capped a number of media appearances in London and Africa, dating back to a poetry reading in the fall of 1969 on Radio Uganda.

In an "attempt to reconnect" with his homeland, Tejani settled in West Africa, teaching at Sokoto University, Nigeria, from 1977 to 1981 (telephone interview, June 18, 1991). His return from West Africa to the United States was to another academic institution, Medgar Evers College, City University of New York (CUNY), where he was an assistant professor from 1983 to 1988. This most recent relocation was appropriately marked by his essay "A Very New Yorker" that appeared in 1985, in the CUNY *Community Review*, the journal that published a selection of his poetry the same year and an essay, "Nourishing Traditions from an African Village," in 1987. Also in 1987 his parody, "Alice in Yankeeland," appeared in the *Toronto South Asian Review*.

Tejani has published more than fifteen scholarly articles and has delivered a comparable number of papers at literature conferences and in other academic settings. A recent article, "Cultural Continuity in Ancient and Modern Africa," published in *Présence Africaine* in 1988, reflects his continuing scholarly as well as creative involvement with his homeland. Tejani's scholarly achievement was recognized by a National Endowment for the Humanities Fellowship in 1987 to work at Columbia University on African-American autobiographies, a congenial relationship that led to the deposit of his books and manuscripts at Columbia. The writer has held teaching appointments at Fordham University from 1988 to 1989 and at New York University from 1989 to 1990. In 1988, his interest in multicultural education led to an appointment as a consultant on global perspectives on literature for the New Jersey Teachers Workshop, Montclair State College. Most recently, in 1990, Tejani expanded the reading audience for his creative work by allowing a story, "Freedom Star," to be adapted for the *Seedling Series*, a quarterly intended for young people ten to twelve years of age. "The Writer" was accepted for reprinting in *Short Story International*, and "Black Cosmos," a satire on the possibility and political implications of African space travel, was published in the Autumn 1990 issue of *Wasafiri*. His recent work "experiments with the creation of positive images of African and Asian cultures in art and literature" (telephone interview, June 18, 1991). Bahadur Tejani presently resides in Freeport, New York, with his wife, Yasmin, and sons, Nabyl and Nafees, and is an associate professor of Asian and African literatures at the State University of New York (SUNY) at Old Westbury, New York.

MAJOR WORKS AND THEMES

Bahadur Tejani's best-known work is *Day after Tomorrow* (1971); this novel and his collection of poetry, *The Rape of Literature* (1969), reveal both the complexities and strengths of his multicultural heritage and many relocations and the solutions he judges necessary for personal and communal success in the postcolonial world of the Indian diaspora. Tejani's repeated plea is for understanding and for recognizing unity among all peoples, regardless of cultural background or class.

Most of the poems in *The Rape of Literature* were written while the poet was living in India from 1967 to 1969. These poems present Tejani's sense of unity with those apparently very different from himself and his insistence that the reality of a country is mirrored in its least fortunate. "The Child Beggar," "The Analogy," "Calcutta," and "In The Orthopaedic Ward" ironically reflect this theme of personal and national connection. Another persistent motif in both *The Rape of Literature* and *Day after Tomorrow* is criticism of the Indian community for an insular rejection of difference and fear of the Other that leads to the selfishness and indifference to suffering shown in "The Alternative to Communism" where it is turned against one of its own. In his foreword, Tejani complains against the Indian bourgeoisie who show a virulent dislike of other successful Indians born abroad. It is the self-destructive consequence of social, national, and class separation plus a smug materialism that particularly concerns the poet. Additionally, as in his novel, he focuses in "Lines for a Hindi Poet" on what he judges an exaggerated asceticism and squeamishness about sex he finds in Indian custom that lead to sexism and distorted, emotionally sterile relationships between men and women. "Leaving the Country" expresses Tejani's depression at the dislocation his move represents and his muted solace that he shares his sadness with many others who have made the same kind of exodus from a homeland.

Day after Tomorrow, set in Uganda right after independence, focuses again upon characteristics of the Asian community that the author finds both self-destructive and limiting emotionally and politically. Samsher, the young protagonist, is a rebel from his Asian society, the prototype of a new African of universal sensibilities, incorporating the best in both Indian and African cultures. The novel presents a community still stinging from the cynical colonial manipulation of the Indians as buffers between white power and black labor. Tejani's concern is not only with imperialist exploitation, however, but with traditional weaknesses within the Asian community itself, especially its anti-intellectualism, sexual repression, materialism, conservatism, isolation, and fear of anything or anyone different.

This social problem is reflected in the narrative in the tension between Samsher and his merchant father, representative of the conservative Indian response to life. Like his father, before him, Samsher works from dawn to dusk in his small shop, waiting on African customers whom he mistrusts and is contemptuous of, stopping this routine only to instruct his son in the methods of sharp trading. In the village where the protagonist grows up, the Asian community is strong, but its cohesiveness is born out of fear. We are told that the Asian traders are obsessed with the Africans around them but only as objects of trade or sources of fear, certainly not as fellow victims. Samsher's rejection of his parents' racism and/or fear and apathy is complemented by his growing appreciation of the world of the Africans that he judges more natural, hence more humane and fulfilling. Significantly, he comes to sexual awareness while observing the delicate touching and wordplay of an African couple. It is no surprise, then, that he marries the outspoken, self-confident African woman Nanziri, who herself has had to weigh the warnings against racial intermingling angrily presented by her friend Jane. Jane's negative characterization of Asians, although Nanziri does not allow it to affect her love for Samsher, reminds the reader of their fate in Uganda, during Idi Amin's version of Africanization. The solution Tejani posits for both political and social/racial conflict is intermarriage between blacks and Asians, thereby creating a new culture, children who can forge a new civilization.

CRITICAL RECEPTION

The responses to both *The Rape of Literature* and *Day after Tomorrow* have been generally favorable. The reviewer of *The Rape of Literature* in the Nairobi *Sunday Nation* responds both to the poet's fulfilling a traditional artistic study to warn society about self-destructive practices and to his "freshness of observation" and "powerful imagery" (21). Moreover, the reviewer judges the collection "a powerful contribution that comes at an opportune time in the East African Literary scene when so much that is being published [is] a trifle frivolous" (22). Ashok K. Gupta in *Thought* appreciates Tejani's free verse form, his "vividly concrete" imagery, and what Gupta terms his "realistic-surrealistic" mode: "In these poems we find no self-indulgence, only the poet's deep concern with Indian life in its various aspects" (18).

Day after Tomorrow has been well received as well, although some critics find its solution to racism too idealistic. The timeliness of the novel is noted in the Nairobi *East Africa Standard*. After praising Tejani's "bold and original approach to the problem of the helplessness of the Asian youth of East Africa," the reviewer also notes that the book "tries to deal with the effects of industrialization on the present, in a predominantly agricultural land, an idea which strikes at the urgent theme of man and machine in East Africa" (12). Samsher's idealism for an interracial solution that the *Standard*'s reviewer appreciates, however, is a flaw in the novel, according to Margaret Marshment in a review in the Nairobi *Sunday Nation*. Marshment considers the book "a young man's novel" and faults Tejani for uncritically accepting his protagonist's views, "resulting in an uneasy tension between the harshly critical analysis of the Asian community and idealisation of the African" (29). While classifying the novel as "not essentially a realistic one," she, nevertheless, judges it as "very readable . . . there are some fine scenes; particularly those showing the child's vulnerability, intensified here by racial divisions" (30). In an unpublished study of diasporic South Asian literature, Jeremy Poynting agrees with Marshment's general mistrust of Samsher's interracial solution to political problems; in retrospect, he comments, "History has not dealt kindly with Tejani's idealism." More pointedly, Charles Sarvan of the University of Zambia remarks in "Ethnicity and Alienation: The African Asian and His Response to Africa." "It is ironic that [*Day after Tomorrow*] was published in the year Idi Amin seized power. The day after tomorrow brought indignity, expulsion, and exile, even to the Samshers of Uganda" (103). Perhaps the last word should be Tejani's. While he may be recognized as idealistic, no one could accuse him of naïveté. In "Farewell Uganda," the article published three years following *Day after Tomorrow*, he comments, "We were a generation betrayed by our elders who never understood nor tried to interpret Obote's leftist radicalism or Amin's coldly calculated Asian Census. Many I am sure would have been praying for the General to have dreams anew for a better tomorrow" (66). The harsh realities of East African postcolonial life that sparked Samsher's youthful idealism and the wish-fulfillment of Tejani's solution through biracial marriage ultimately led the writer to confront the challenge of adjusting to life as an immigrant in Canada and the United States.

BIBLIOGRAPHY

Works by Bahadur Tejani

"The Writer" (story). *East Africa Journal* [Nairobi, Kenya] (Jan. 1967): 1–9. Reprinted, *Short Story International*. Ed. Sylvia Tankel. Vol. 16, no. 91. 118–33.
"The Chowkidar in Our Mohalla" (story). *Thought* [Delhi, India] (Feb. 15, 1969): 19–25.
The Rape of Literature and Other Poems. Delhi, India: Falcon Poetry Society, 1969.
"Finites," "End of Saturday Dance," and "Back on Trains" (poems). *East Africa Journal* (July 1970): 3–5.
Day after Tomorrow. Nairobi: East African Literature Bureau, 1971. Reprinted in 1977.
"Wild Horses of Serengeti" and "On Top of Africa." *Poems from East Africa*. Ed. David Cook and David Rubadiri. London: Heinemann, 1971.
"Lines for a Hindi Poet" and "The Analogy." *Poems from Black Africa*. Ed. Wole Soyinka. London: Secker and Warburg, 1974. Reprinted, London: Heinemann, 1975, 1978.
"Farewell Uganda" (essay). *Transition* 45 (1974): 64–66.
"The New Canadians, Afro-Indo Reflections on the West End" (essay). *West End Courier* [Vancouver, Canada] (Jan. 16, 1975): B2.
"Emergence" (story). *Black and White*. Ed. David Cook. Nairobi: East African Literature Bureau, 1976. 41–50.
"The Sea's Complaint" and "The Mid-Year Rain" (poems). *Sunday Nation* [Nairobi] (Sept. 20, 1978): 7.
"A Very New Yorker" (essay). *CUNY Community Review* (1985): 38–41.
"Alice in Yankeeland" (story). *Toronto South Asian Review* 6, no. 3 (1987): 51–55.
"Black Cosmos" (story). *Wasafiri* 12 (1990): 19–24.
"Song of the City" (poem). Ufahamu 9, no. 1 (1991): 95–97.

Studies of Bahadur Tejani

Botham, Holly. "Socio-Political Soccer." Review of "The Other Side of the Coin." *West End Courier* [Vancouver, Canada] (Jan. 21, 1976): B4.
Elder, Arlene A. "Indian Writing in East Africa: Multiple Approaches to Colonialism and Apartheid." *Reworlding: The Literature of the Indian Diaspora*. Ed. Emmanuel S. Nelson. Westport, Conn.: Greenwood Press, 1992. 115–39.

Gupta, Ashok K. Review of *The Rape of Literature and Other Poems*. *Thought* [Delhi, India] (Nov. 1, 1969): 18–20.

Janmohamed, Karim. "Reflections on Tejani's Novel." *Africa Ismaili* [Nairobi, Kenya] (May 1972): 28–32.

Koshi, Annie. "The Afro-Asian and American Dreams of Race Relations in Bahadur Tejani's *Day after Tomorrow*." *Wasafiri* 3 (1991): 11–13.

Marshment, Margaret. "An Idyllic Love Story That Shuns Reality." Review of *Day after Tomorrow*. *Sunday Nation* [Nairobi, Kenya] (May 1970): 29–30.

Review of *Day after Tomorrow*. *East Africa Standard* [Nairobi, Kenya] (November 1971): 12.

Review of *The Rape of Literature and Other Poems*. *Sunday Nation* [Nairobi, Kenya] (Dec. 1969): 21–23.

Sarvan, Charles Ponnuthurai. "Ethnicity and Alienation: The African Asian and His Response to Africa." *Journal of Commonwealth Literature* 20:4 (1985): 103–10.

"Ugandan Author Interviewed." *The Nationalist* [Lagos, Nigeria] May 13, 1979.

SHASHI THAROOR (1956–   )
Uma Parameswaran

BIOGRAPHY

Shashi Tharoor was born in England to Chandra and Lila Tharoor on March 9, 1956. His father was in the Foreign Service, and as Shashi says in his interview with *The World & I,* from childhood on he was groomed "for a career in government or administration" (351), while unofficially, he relentlessly prepared to be a writer. He was educated at Campion School, Bombay, and St. Xavier's Collegiate High School, Calcutta; he graduated from St. Stephen's College, Delhi, in 1975 and later took his master's and doctoral degrees from the Fletcher School of Law and Diplomacy, Tufts University. His graduate studies led to his book *Reasons of State* (Vikas, 1982). He started working at the United Nations in 1978, and has worked extensively with refugee settlement and UN peacekeeping activities.

He started writing very early in life, modeling his adventure stories on those of Enid Blyton, the author whose works have been familiar to generations of the Indian diaspora across the world. He has won awards for journalistic and creative writing, including the Rajika Kripalani Young Journalist Award in 1976 and the Hindustan Times/Federation of Indian Publishers' Literary Award and Commonwealth Writers' Prize in 1991.

Shashi Tharoor is an articulate, handsome man, and during the afternoon I had lunch at his New York apartment, he and his wife, Tilottama, ranged over a wide variety of topics that periodically returned to two themes—the vast journalistic potential in India and the Indian diasporic life in North America. Tilottama is a writer of nonfiction and is working on her Ph.D. at New York University; they have two sons, Ishan and Kanishk, born in 1984.

MAJOR WORKS AND THEMES

There is a story that at a writers' convention dinner, an overbearing woman condescendingly made conversation with the quiet woman seated next to her. "And how many books have you published?" she patronizingly asked the quiet woman, who answered, "Just one. *Gone with the Wind.*" Even if Shashi Tharoor does not publish anything in the future, his place both in India and in the diaspora is assured by virtue of *The Great Indian Novel.*

The Great Indian Novel is a significant work of literature. It retells the history of contemporary India. Like Salman Rushdie's *Midnight's Children,* it uses major events of the last nine decades; unlike other Indo-English novelists (Manohar Malgonkar, Chaman Nahal, Balachandra Rajan, Santha Rama Rau, Salman Rushdie, Khushwant Singh) who have used a central participating character to retell history, Tharoor uses the ancient epic device of a nonparticipating narrator. He uses an ingenious structure for his narration: instead of using central metaphors or frequent allusions, he retells the *Mahabharata* itself as a political allegory.

The Hindu epic *Mahabharata* ("the great Indian story" would be its literal translation) is a saga in about 100,000 couplets composed by Veda Vyasa; it tells the story of the Pandava-Kuru dynasty: the rivalry between cousins, the political and matrimonial alliances forged between rulers, conspiracies and battles, ending in the battle of Kurukshetra, which destroyed everyone except the five Pandavas and their wife, Druapadi. These survivors take solace in the philosophy that they are agents in the periodic dissolution of the world that must take place, a part of the pattern of cosmic purification and regeneration.

Tharoor is far more politically engaged than most other Indo-English novelists. His fictionalization is transparent, and the figures onstage are easily identifiable political giants of the last fifty years. The epic is so wide ranging and has so many secondary stories that an astute writer can select episodes that form the pattern he would like to trace. Even so, it is rather surprising that the epic should lend itself so aptly to being an allegory of recent history and contemporary politics. Gangaji (Bheeshma, son of Ganga in the epic), mentor to the Pandavas and the Kauravas from childhood on, is Gandhi. The blind king Dhritarashtra is Jawaharlal Nehru; the epic patriarch's hundred sons are compressed into one daughter, Duryodhani; Pandu, who loves pleasures of the flesh and of battle, is Subhash Chandra Bose, the leader of the Indian National Army, who wanted to use terrorist tactics to oust the British but was restrained by Gandhi's philosophy of nonviolence.

Tharoor identifies others even more obviously by transmuting epic names—Mohammad Ali Karna for Mohammad Ali Jinnah, leader of the

Muslim League that insisted on the creation of Pakistan; Jayaprakash Drona for Jayaprakash Narayan; Kanika Menon for Krishna Menon, etc. One of the main characters is Priya Duryodhani, who is unmistakably identified with Indira Priyadarshini Gandhi, India's third prime minister who led the country from 1964 to 1984 except for a brief period between 1977 and 1979. Tharoor selects episodes from the epic in which Duryodhana indulges in plots and treacheries to disenfranchise or kill his cousins. These closely parallel political plots attributed to Indira Gandhi, including the stripping of all rivals through the Kamraj plan whereby senior congressmen "voluntarily" stepped down to make way for "new blood," and a plot related to the murder of a railway minister. These are but two examples of Tharoor's eminently successful method of simultaneously allegorizing epic and modern history. Such a method allows not only for the reinterpretation of modern history through epic but for the reinterpretation of epic through modern history.

The tone, language, and allusions used by Tharoor are influenced by and directed toward a particular literary tradition that might be called standard Indo-English; this is the tradition of Indians educated in private schools who are equally conversant with Indian history and English/American literary allusions. The titles of Tharoor's chapters exemplify this: "A Raj Quartet," "The Son Also Rises," "Midnight's Parents," "Passages through India," etc.

The Great Indian Novel, like Balachandra Rajan's novels, is by a member of the diaspora but not about the diaspora. (Tharoor, unlike Rajan, is an Indian citizen but has lived outside India for the greater part of his life.) It is set wholly in India, and all the Indian characters are Indians and not hyphenated immigrants such as Indo-Canadians. There are several non-Indian characters, such as Sir Richard (Winston Churchill) and his assistant Heaslop (from E. M. Forster's *Passage to India*) and Viscount and Viscountess Drewpad (Lord and Lady Mountbatten.)

One of the few episodes in which the novel differs significantly from the epic is in the birth of Draupadi. In the novel, Draupadi is the daughter of Dhritarashtra and Georgina Drewpad. She is called Draupadi D. Mokrasi, one of Tharoor's many atrocious puns. Thus democracy is made the child of India and Britain, just as Saleem Sinai in Rushdie's *Midnight's Children* is the bastard child of an Englishman and an Indian woman. However, as in the epic, Draupadi is married to five husbands concurrently; the five husbands can be seen as allegorical representations of India's major religions, or as India's diverse regional cultures, or as the five arms of government—jurisprudence, defense, media, external, and national affairs.

Tharoor satirizes India and the course of Indian political history. His final note, like Rushdie's in *Midnight's Children*, is of qualified optimism, but his degree of optimism is greater. There are many truths, many ways of telling the same story. Democracy *will* survive, even as India moves "chaotically" into the twenty-first century.

The Five-Dollar Smile (1990) is a collection of Tharoor's earlier stories and a play. The fourteen stories were written in Tharoor's teens and early twenties. The foreword and authorial prefaces to each piece are unduly apologetic, but they also give useful annotations. The title story's inspiration clearly comes from the posters pasted on billboards and bulletin boards across the world asking the public to donate to charitable missions that try to bring a smile to a child's face. Just as T. S. Eliot's "Journey of the Magi" retells the Christmas card story from the point of view of one of the Wise Men, this story explores the feelings of the recipient of charity who is represented in familiar posters. Twelve-year-old Joseph Kumaran, on a flight to the United States, remembers how he was catapulted to dubious fame by a photographer visiting an orphanage in India for a suitable subject. "Get him away from that food, Sister.... We want a hungry child, not a feeding one" (15), says the photographer; the nuns bully the poor boy into posing, and he forfeits the one delicacy that is occasionally served the orphans, *pappadam*, a crisp rice or lentil flour wafer that is fried in oil. The message that comes out of this fairy-tale situation of maneuvering his adoptive parents into sponsoring his visit to the States is ambiguous; while Kumaran suffers systemic abuse for his vulnerability and shyness all the way through, including on the plane where the hostess overlooks his needs, the story can also be read to mean that the five-dollar-smile poster campaign has been effective in making an orphan nurture his talent and resourcefulness to make a bid for a better life.

Several stories are set against the backdrop of college life. "Friends" is an episode that captures the spirit of campus life where youthful idealism and youthful competition to impress the opposite sex find expression in elaborate wordplay. Some of the puns are trite and others incorrigible, but Tharoor's language rings true.

Indira Gandhi's Emergency Rule of 1975–77 has inspired several pieces, including the two-act play "Twenty Two Months in the Life of a Dog." Adapting the plot of Mikhail Bulgakov's novella "Dog's Heart," the play satirizes political figures such as Sanjay Gandhi, who is called "The Rising Son," and various ministers who unscrupulously use their power to line their pockets or indulge in excesses. The main plot centers around a professor of genetic experimentation who grafts a human brain onto a dog with a plan to combat the increasing number of animal-like humans with humanized animals. One can only say H. G. Wells was far more effective in his *Island of Dr. Moreau.*

CRITICAL RECEPTION

Both of Tharoor's books are still too new to have received much critical analysis. *The Great Indian Novel*, however, has been widely reviewed in

India, Britain, and the United States. In general, Western reviewers tend to be more enthusiastic than their Indian counterparts. The reason for the discrepancy could be that the Westerners find Tharoor's device of paralleling ancient epic and modern politics innovative, whereas Indians know that it is used very often in Indian political plays and cartoons. P. Lal, writing in the *Telegraph*, argues that *The Great Indian Novel* deserves "unreserved kudos" (12). Kushwant Singh, a distinguished Indian journalist and author, declares that it is "perhaps the best work of fiction written by an Indian in recent years" (36). Clark Blaise, however, expresses disappointment: writing in *The World & I*, he says that *The Great Indian Novel* is "not a novel at all" and that it has merely recast "twentieth century characters in Vedic drag" (349).

BIBLIOGRAPHY

Works by Shashi Tharoor

The Great Indian Novel. New York: Little, Brown, 1989.
The Five-Dollar Smile: Fourteen Early Stories and a Farce in Two Acts. New Delhi: Vikas, 1990.

Studies of Shashi Tharoor

Blaise, Clark. "Passages from India." *The World & I* (July 1991): 343–49.
Lal, P. Review of *The Great Indian Novel. Telegraph* (Jan. 4, 1990): 12.
Parameswaran, Uma. "Finding the Epic Center." *The World & I* (July 1991): 351–61.
Singh, Kushwant. Review of *The Great Indian Novel. All Asia Review of Books* 31 (Feb. 1990): 36.

EDWIN THUMBOO (1933–   )
Koh Buck Song

BIOGRAPHY

Edwin Nadason Thumboo was born on November 22, 1933, in Singapore. His early home was in Mandai, in the middle of the island's central catchment area. His father, a primary schoolteacher, owned a wooden bungalow with an attap roof, at the foot of Mandai Hill, amid lush tropical rainforest.

The young Thumboo grew up in surroundings of natural beauty, something hard to find in modern Singapore, with the hectic pace of urban development in the city-state. In the shadow of Mandai Mountain, he was once chased by a cobra, and was quite comfortable with toads and green snakes nearby and the constant chirp of crickets at night.

Thumboo denies that he yearns for lost nature (interview at the National University of Singapore, July 1991), and he is much more than a nature poet, but the influence of nature's rhythms can be seen in Thumboo's lyrical poetic sensibility. To him, such experiences "open the doors of our perception" and equip one with a certain mechanism of response to nature and urban life alike.

His father, an upper-class Tamil who was an Anglicized Protestant, moved to Singapore from Muar in southern Malaysia, where he used to hunt boar and deer. Thumboo recalls his colonial demeanor, often dressed in white, with silver buttons glinting and patent leather boots shining. His mother was a Chinese Teochew housewife, and he has five sisters and two brothers.

After his early education at Victoria School and graduation with a B.A. honors degree from the then University of Malaya in Singapore in 1957, he worked as an assistant secretary in the Singapore Telephone Board until 1966. He then joined the University of Singapore as an assistant lecturer and completed his Ph.D. there in 1970. He rose to become a full professor in the Department of English Language and Literature in 1979, serving also as dean of the Faculty of Arts and Social Sciences until late 1991.

He started writing poetry as an undergraduate in the 1950s, and has published three volumes: *Rib of Earth* (1956), *Gods Can Die* (1977), and *Ulysses by the Merlion* (1979). He won the National Book Development Council of Singapore Award for poetry in 1978 and 1980, the Southeast Asia Write Award in 1979, the Cultural Medallion for Literature in Singapore in 1980, and the Asean Cultural Award in 1987. His works have also been published in numerous journals, newspapers, and anthologies. He has edited and coedited several anthologies of poetry from Singapore and Malaysia, including *The Flowering Tree* (1970), *Seven Poets* (1973), *The Second Tongue* (1976), the Asean Literatures series (in the 1980s), and *Words for the 25th* (1991).

Thumboo lives in Singapore with his Chinese wife, Swee Chin, and two children, Julian and Claire.

MAJOR WORKS AND THEMES

Edwin Thumboo made his considerable reputation as a poet with two monumental volumes in the late 1970s. He is perhaps best known for his statements of social and political importance in verse such as *Gods Can Die* and the two "9th of August" poems. But the private voice that probes the subtler nuances of personal relationships and reflections is just as important a part of Thumboo's most significant poetic utterances.

This voice was most prominent, as is only to be expected, in his first volume, *Rib of Earth* (1956), published when he was still an undergraduate. The marks of a youthful pen are distinct yet indelible, pondering the nostalgia of youth with borrowed echoes of T. S. Eliot and John Keats.

The inspiration also springs from early experience of home and hearth. In the poem "Yesterday," for instance, he refers to the area where he grew up, where he promises to show a "sleeping secret stream" (2) in the shadow of Mandai Mountain.

Although it is true that Thumboo is not, strictly speaking, a nature poet, the sense of nature as a necessary if not sufficient condition for a healthy urban ecosystem shows throughout his work, even in a late piece such as "Scene" (in *Singa: Journal of Literature and the Arts* [Singapore] 20 [June 1990]: 28), in which he notes that the city would be "a strange invention" without "a sigh upon the leaf, the drifting wind."

Adopting a similar tone of the poet as revealer of nature's essence, the poem "East Wind" in *Rib of Earth* recalls the reverie of the drowsy speaker of Keats's "Ode to a Nightingale." This stance of the poet as guide to the mysteries and felt significances to be drawn from the world of the senses was to be sustained and savored as the poet matured.

But even with maturity, the shadow of the past continues to be cast over the present, as in the poem "Father" in the anthology *Words for the 25th*

(1991), apparently musing on memories of a father's influence, which can still "change mystery into wonder" (144).

Another major characteristic already evident here is Thumboo's judicious blending of the cultural, philosophical, intellectual, and spiritual inputs that go into making him what he is. For example, Confucius' works, *The Analects*, figure in "East Wind" just as naturally as the Greek mythology of Zeus and the Olympians does in "Elixir" (8).

And Thumboo continues to indulge this penchant even in his more recent poetry, such as "Evening by Batok Town" (in *Singa* 16 [June 1988]: 31), which incorporates Ne Zha, the spirit boy of Chinese mythology and the Krishna and Arjuna of Indian thought into a context of modern Singapore, in a scene with a radar station, four-point blocks, mass rapid transit, and passing couples in love.

But these inputs are not mere ornamentation. They are always weaved significantly into the Singapore context, thereby infusing the present with the rejuvenating, invigorating resonances of the past. And this can work, even if the past is perceived to play an increasingly reduced role at the conscious level. In the poem "Singapore River," an image on a timeless lacquer tray, somewhat like Keats's Grecian urn, can tell a story of old China, "forgotten, forgotten by the boatman" (24).

Where the personal has begun to establish its voice in *Rib of Earth*, and does a commendable job of it, it is the public persona that undoubtedly steals the limelight in *Gods Can Die* (1977).

In poems like "9th of August—I," the desire to form an identity of Singapore as an independent nation, and Singaporeans as a separate people, makes itself heard. At the same time, suggestions of an anti-imperialist voice also begin to sound, as in the opening lines of this poem, which are mildly sarcastic in their use of the adjective "gently colonial" in reference to the proclamation that "Singapore shall forever be..." (26).

Such lines show evidence of deep memories of the colonial experience, which surface perhaps most strongly in the poem "May 1954" from *Ulysses by the Merlion* (1979), which has the stark, somewhat disturbing refrain "Depart white man" (16).

Also making a mark in *Gods Can Die* is Thumboo's urge to articulate the unseen ironies of destiny, often seen in the uneasy dilemmas that man puts himself into by his own lack of foresight, now having to wait "for the years to bring back commonsense" (26).

In the companion piece, "9th of August—II," in the line "Forgetting his crying eyes meant much" (27), Thumboo alludes to the anguish of a prime minister finding himself in the unusual situation of leading a nation having had independence thrust upon it. This instance illustrates another feature of Thumboo's verse: his uncanny ability to see social and historical significance in private acts, and his acute poet's sensitivity to the feelings of others, especially those dear to him.

This instructive communion between the private and the political is more often than not in Thumboo's writing subtle and suggested, as in the poems "For Peter Wee" (10) and "Louise" (15). It can also come to the fore overtly, as in the poem "A Brother (in Nairobi)," in which he states that the African can be his brother best "when he is most himself," without deference to colonialism. Here, Thumboo states, more blatantly than elsewhere, one of his strongest beliefs: that the way forward is not to cling to the outmoded ways of old but to forge one's own path according to one's own nature.

But that way too is fraught with uncertainties. One of these is the very transience of life. And this is made all the more poignant by the lack of enduring faith in oneself, a point made with most brutal honesty in the poem "Cremation."

Yes, time changes all things. But the worst eventuality must surely be the erosion of personal integrity, a course of nature made all the more tragic by willing cooperation in the process of decay, as the poem "Gods Can Die" makes clear: when "we gain uncertain statesmen: many lose a friend" (63).

Despite such strident notes struck in his mature poetry, Thumboo never really loses touch with the reasons for an optimistic outlook in his verse.

In *Ulysses by the Merlion* (1979), he is nostalgic for a unspoiled past yet hopeful for the future, largely because of the human capacity to adapt to change. In the poem "Island" he notes that the body emerging into a new historical situation can learn "this other song" (16).

This song is one of harmony, as in the poem "Ulysses by the Merlion"— in which he imagines the Greek hero contemplating the meaning of city-state's image of itself embodied in a statue of a lion with a fish's tail at the waterfront. He sees the people try to "explore the edges of harmony, search for a centre" even though they have "unequal ways" (19).

As his multiracial people explore the edges of harmony and find common ground despite their different landscapes of heritage and worldview, Thumboo the poet must feel that his role is partly satisfied. In seeking to share his personal response to private situations and those in public life, the poet himself has come closer to finding his own center. Hopefully, his audience has also taken a few more steps in the right direction.

CRITICAL RECEPTION

By all accounts, Edwin Thumboo is the unofficial poet laureate of Singapore. Since the early 1970s, he has had greater influence over the direction and development of Singapore poetry and writing than anyone else. In his own verse, he has captured some of the most crucial times and moods of the nation, including its early, uncertain years of independence. As an academic, editor, organizer, mover, and mentor, he has helped nurture many young poets and writers.

And they have benefited from his energy and enthusiasm. As Peter-John Lewis of Macquarie University, Australia, has said: "Has there been a significant literary publication from Singapore appearing in the past 30 years which has not contained the seen or unseen presence of Edwin Thumboo?" (73).

The consensus among critics and reviewers has been that Thumboo's work is essential reading for anyone seeking an understanding of Singapore literature. Ban Kah Choon and Lee Tzu Pheng consider his work "poetry (that) must be rated as among the most important of local works." They note also that he "successfully articulates the need for a continuity whose meaning must be found not only in the personal but the larger purpose of a society." His other strengths mentioned include a "sensitivity to language" and his adeptness at "reconstituting history, reorganising it into a typography more significant to him" (190–91).

Geraldine Heng sees him as "the most Singaporean of all Singapore poets" because he "registers on the counter of his consciousness the emotional tenor of the society in its phases of transition through the past thirty years, in an individual, yet paradoxically generalised distillation." In the final analysis, Heng rates Thumboo's beautifully wrought poems, with their brutal honesty, delicately balanced emotions, and social and political nuances of the age, "of their kind, superior to almost all the poetry written by other Singaporean poets on the same subjects." Interestingly, too, she notes that Thumboo's later verse, such as "RELC," a poem on the country's Regional English Language Centre, are what one might call "a Poet Laureate's poems" (27–28).

BIBLIOGRAPHY

Works by Edwin Thumboo

Rib of Earth. Singapore: Lloyd Fernando, 1956.
The Flowering Tree. Singapore: Educational Publications Bureau, 1970.
Child's Delight. Singapore: Federal Publications, 1972.
Gods Can Die. Singapore: Heinemann Educational Books, 1977.
Ulysses by the Merlion. Singapore: Heinemann Educational Books, 1979.
Words for the 25th. Singapore: Unipress, 1991.

Studies of Edwin Thumboo

Ban Kah Choon and Lee Tzu Pheng. "Only Connect: Quest and Response in Singapore—Malayan Poetry." *The English Language in Singapore*. Ed. William Crewe. Singapore: Eastern University Press, 1977. 189–207.
deSouza, Dudley. "Edwin Thumboo: Conversation with My Friend." *Critical Engagements: Singapore Poems in Focus*. Ed. Kirpal Singh. Singapore: Heinemann Educational Books, 1982. 17–24.

Gooneratne, Yasmin. "Edwin Thumboo: *Ulysses by the Merlion.*" *Critical Engagements: Singapore Poems in Focus.* Ed. Kirpal Singh. Singapore: Heinemann Educational Books, 1982: 7–16.

Harrex, Syd, and Sudesh Mishra. "Interview with Edwin Thumboo." *CRNLE Review Journal* 1 & 2 (1988): 1–8.

Heng, Geraldine. "Measure of Grace: The Poetry of Edwin Thumboo." *Commentary* 4:2 (1980): 18–28.

Kwan-Terry, John. Review of *Gods Can Die. World Literature Today* 52 (Summer 1978): 524.

Lewis, Peter-John. "Interrogating Singapore." *CRNLE Review Journal* 1 (1991): 73.

Lim, Shirley. "Edwin Thumboo: A Study of the Influence in the Literary History of Singapore." *The Writer's Sense of the Contemporary.* Ed. Bruce Bennett et al. Nedlands: University of Western Australia Press, 1982. 30–34.

Nazareth, Peter. "Interview with Edwin Thumboo." *World Literature Written in English* 18:1 (1979): 151–71.

O'Sullivan, Vincent. "Edwin Thumboo: *Gods Can Die.*" *Critical Engagements: Singapore Poems in Focus.* Ed. Kirpal Singh. Singapore: Heinemann Educational Books, 1982. 1–6.

Singh, Kirpal. "Edwin Thumboo, *Gods Can Die*: A People's Poet." *World Literature Written in English* 17:2 (1978): 598–603.

———. "Towards a Singapore Classic: Edwin Thumboo's *Ulysses by the Merlion.*" *Literary Criterion* 15:2 (1980): 74–87.

——— and Ooi Boo Eng. "The Poetry of Edwin Thumboo: A Study in Development." *World Literature Written in English* 24:2 (1984): 454–59.

M. G. VASSANJI (1950–   )
Harold Barratt

BIOGRAPHY

M. G. Vassanji was born in Nairobi, Kenya, but he grew up in Dar es Salaam, Tanzania, as a member of the small Muslim Shamsi sect. The arrival in Junapur, India, of Shamas, the sect's founder, together with the community divisiveness his proselytizing spawned, is mentioned in *The Gunny Sack*.

The early expatriate Shamsi community was not educated, and indeed Vassanji's generation was the first to successfully complete the British system of A levels in Dar es Salaam. After what appears to be an altogether unrewarding period as a conscript in Tanzania's National Service, Vassanji fled the country for London and later America, where he studied physics and earned the Ph.D. from Massachusetts Institute of Technology (MIT). He also studied Sanskrit, medieval Indian language and literature, as well as old Gujarati, avocations that he uses to delineate the character of Sona in *The Gunny Sack*.

The study of physics and Sanskrit opened the door to literature and writing for Vassanji. Both disciplines stimulated and enhanced his intellectual curiosity and his sense of discovery; and these in turn increased his desire to explore his family's remarkable past in East Africa. Meanwhile his admiration of Ngugi Wa Thiong'o, the brilliant Kenyan novelist, gave Vassanji the incentive to write about his past. Vassanji was particularly impressed by Ngugi's efforts to recreate the Kikuyus' rich culture, and he is convinced that if the peoples of the Third World are to achieve self-respect, they and their compellingly complex pasts and cultures must be mythologized through art and literature.

M. G. Vassanji has been writer-in-residence at the University of Iowa and research associate and lecturer at the University of Toronto. He is currently teaching and writing in Toronto.

MAJOR WORKS AND THEMES

The Gunny Sack, which was awarded a Commonwealth Literature Regional First Novel prize in 1990 and has recently been published in a German translation, is an invigorating union of thematic material and structural dynamic. The novel's large theme may be regarded as the volatile union of Africa and expatriate India from which is produced a being—Salim, the novel's central intelligence, is in many ways the embodiment of this being—who "forever stalks the forest in search of himself" (39–40). Every aspect of the novel, including its episodic structure, turns around this hub. Although there is an instantaneous antagonism between the Indian Salim and the African Amina, their union, which is a repetition of Salim's great-grandfather Dhanji's cohabitation with an African slave, is inevitable. The exhilarating tension at the heart of the novel comes from the clash between these two powerful cultures, personalities, and modes of thought.

The gunny sack, which is of course the novel's central metaphor, miraculously resists destruction because it is the rich repository of Salim's past. It is in this gunny-womb that Salim is conceived. Salim is who he is, what he is because of the volatile mixture of Africa and India. From this mixture ebullient and sometimes eccentric men and women emerge. One of Vassanji's most notable achievements in his first novel is the creation of these fully embodied, vivacious characters. His women are particularly engaging. Intelligent, buoyant, and sometimes earthy, they are determined to succeed in the ferociously masculine world of coastal East Africa.

The episodic structure of *The Gunny Sack* has been misunderstood. The memories released from the gunny resemble "asynchronous images projected on multiple cinema screens" (112). These images mirror the incoherent, chaotic, and turbulent nature of exile, displacement, and the struggle to put down roots in what is at times inhospitable soil, in an area of dramatic and sudden change, political uncertainty, and instability. The episodic structure, we may say, reflects the simultaneity of these diverse forces as well as the amorphousness of East Africa. Moreover, the mosaic of seemingly independent episodes is held together by the durability and resilience of Vassanji's charismatic characters who must survive and thrive in the explosive mixture of European, Indian, and African cultures.

While Vassanji's displaced Indians have severed their roots in India—a dislocation begun when Dhanji set sail from Porbander for Zanzibar in 1885 in quest of his fortune—they work strenuously to maintain their distinctive Indianness. This is not to say that they reject Africa. They have indeed become an integral part of Africa; but Dhanji and his numerous descendants resist being taken back into Africa's womb, resist obliteration, a fate that befalls Huseni, Dhanji's feckless, half-Indian, half-African son. The monumental struggle to maintain an Indian identity in a continent that threatens to swallow them is driven home in Dhanji's relentless efforts, including the illegal use of the community's funds, to find Huseni and, as it were, reclaim him for India.

The Gunny Sack shows evidence of a substantial, but not altogether finely tuned, talent at work. The novel re-creates the East Africa of immigrant Indians from the end of the last century through the harrowing first decades of this century in concrete, at times pungent, detail and with compelling vividness. Vassanji's prose is arresting and energetic. It is not a prose of understatement; it is muscular and of a piece with the sensual and stimulating characters who people the African communities he describes with such verve.

Like all good writers, Vassanji also has a sharply observant eye and sensitive ear. He can focus upon a character's unique trait or appearance quickly, economically, and with telling accuracy; and the novel's dialogue is obviously the recording of an attentive and sensitive listener.

In *No New Land*, which is set in Don Mills, a Toronto suburb, Vassanji explores the power of the Shamsi past to shape and mold character. This time his central character, the ineffective Nurdin Falani, is a man without a strong identity. Vassanji has described him as one of those individuals who feels that he does "not belong anywhere" (Kirchhoff E2). Immigration to Canada promises fulfillment; but Nurdin and his family's transplantation in inhospitable Canadian soil does not take. Nurdin, furthermore, is hobbled by his failure to find a fulfilling job as well as by the sudden, and certainly perplexing, confrontation between the unfamiliar Canadian ethos and his rigidly orthodox Shamsi and colonial nurturing. And his insecurity is exacerbated when he is unjustly accused of sexually assaulting a white Canadian girl. Although it is not without some dramatic tension, the "assault" episode is not a particularly effective method of forcing a crisis. Nurdin's offer of assistance to the girl, who appears to be ill or distressed, is so palpably genuine, and the girl's hysteria is so obviously racist, that together they impart to the episode a rather contrived and gratuitous atmosphere, the sort of gratuitousness Vassanji avoids in the more effective subway scene when Esmail, Nurdin's friend, is attacked by three white louts.

Nurdin remains an uncommonly introspective and tentative person until the end of the novel. For Nurdin the journey that began with the diaspora ends when he discovers how to exorcise his past yet incorporate it with the exigencies of the present and the bright promise of the future.

Vassanji's second novel again shows his gift for creating compelling characters; but the novel lacks its predecessor's effervescence and engaging rhythms.

The world of *Uhuru Street* (formerly Kichwele Street of Dar es Salaam), Vassanji's most recent work, reminds one of the bizarre and compelling world of V. S. Naipaul's *Miguel Street*. Eccentric, severely flawed, pathetic men and women, many of whom long to escape their circumscribed world, live on both streets. Vassanji describes a world of humor and joy, brutality and gratuitous cruelty, and political corruption.

Uhuru Street, however, lacks the coherent device of *Miguel Street*—a unifying central intelligence through whose shifting and growing perceptions the stories unfold. Vassanji focuses instead on the child or young adult whose experiences, many of which take him into the disconcerting world of reality, dominate more than half of the sixteen stories. Vassanji's use of the first-person point of view is carefully controlled. The narrative voices, whether they are children or adults, are true and authentic. Throughout the collection these voices draw readers into an engaging intimacy and introduce us to the disingenuous, self-serving, lusty, arrogant, honest, courageous, displaced men and women, some of whom are fetching derivatives of the more fully developed characters of *The Gunny Sack*.

CRITICAL RECEPTION

To date critical assessments of Vassanji's work have been confined to reviews that have largely emphasized *The Gunny Sack*'s strong features. Some reviews have been either slight and superficial or intemperate and hyperbolic; but others are a judicious reading of the novel. Although he praises Vassanji's ability to create vibrant characters, Keith Garebian criticizes Vassanji's use of too many characters as well as the novel's episodic method which, he argues, blurs the novel's central focus. He also praises Vassanji's evocation of East Africa, but claims that Vassanji's "reach has exceeded his grasp" (29).

Nazneen Sadiq discusses Vassanji's humor and pathos as well as his treatment of colonialism which, she claims, shows much tolerance. The novel, she also says, conveys the African-Asian experience as if it were a voyage. Michael Thorpe, another reviewer, stresses *The Gunny Sack*'s irony which, he remarks, surpasses V. S. Naipaul's since "it does not yield passages which . . . could be labelled anti-black" (10). Although he criticizes the first part of the novel, which he considers "clogged and difficult" (130), Peter Nazareth stresses Vassanji's treatment of themes such as syncretism, moral choice, and the importance of one's inheritance.

Other commentators, Ahmad Harb, for instance, focus on the symbolism of the gunny sack. Harb interprets the gunny as "the feminine principle, representing its various associations of the feminine protection, the womb, and hence rebirth" (39). Harb also believes that *The Gunny Sack* ensures its author a secure place among contemporary African novelists.

In his review of *No New Land* Clark Blaise draws attention to the novel's balance and clarity, and he points out that the minor changes in Nurdin's life are actually "transformations of history" (E1). In an unsympathetic review Stan Persky dismisses *Uhuru Street* as a collection suffering from "the reek of reminiscence." Readers, Persky claims, "know too much more about what lies beyond the ocean where Uhuru Street ends" (C8).

BIBLIOGRAPHY

Works by M. G. Vassanji

The Gunny Sack. London: Heinemann International, 1989.
No New Land. Toronto: McClelland and Stewart, 1991.
Uhuru Street. Toronto: McClelland and Stewart, 1992.

Studies of M. G. Vassanji

Blaise, Clark. "Voyages of Discovery." Review of *Such a Long Journey*, by Rohinton Mistry, and *No New Land*, by M. G. Vassanji. *Globe and Mail* (May 4, 1991): E1.

Garebian, Keith. Review of *The Gunny Sack*, by M. G. Vassanji. *Quill and Quire* 56:6 (June 1990): 29.

Harb, Ahmad. "A Novel of Wanderlust." Review of *The Gunny Sack*, by M. G. Vassanji. *Weekly Review* (Mar. 30, 1990): 39–40.

Jansen, Ann. Review of *No New Land*, by M. G. Vassanji. *Quill and Quire* 32 (Feb. 1991): 32.

Killam, G. D. Review of *The Gunny Sack*, by M. G. Vassanji. Toronto South Asian Review (*TSAR*) *Book Reviews* 8:2 (Winter 1990): 84–87.

Kirchhoff, H. J. "Figuring That Words Are the Way To Go." *Globe and Mail* (May 4, 1991): E2.

Marshall, Joyce. Review of *The Gunny Sack*, by M. G. Vassanji. *Books in Canada* (Mar. 1990): 48.

Nazareth, Peter. "The First Tanzanian/Asian Novel." Review of *The Gunny Sack*, by M. G. Vassanji. *Research in African Literatures* 21:4 (Winter 1990): 129–33.

Persky, Stan. "*Uhuru Street* Is a Little Quaint for the Times." Review of *Uhuru Street*, by M. G. Vassanji. *Globe and Mail* (April 11, 1992): C8.

Rajab, Ahmed. "A Sack Full of History." *Africa Events* (Jan. 1991): 52–53.

Roberts, Paul William. "Everyman's Concern." Review of *The Gunny Sack*, by M. G. Vassanji. *Toronto Star* (May 12, 1990): M16.

Sadiq, Nazneen. "Life in the Bag." Review of *The Gunny Sack*, by M. G. Vassanji. *Globe and Mail* (Feb. 3, 1990): C17.

Thorpe, Michael. Review of *The Gunny Sack*, by M. G. Vassanji. *University of Toronto Quarterly* 60:1 (Nov. 1990): 9–10.

Versi, Anver. "An African Sheherazade." Review of *The Gunny Sack*, by M. G. Vassanji. *New African* (Dec. 1990): 44.

APPENDIX: DOMICILE AND THE DIASPORIC WRITERS

The following list offers the reader a guide to the geographic dispersal of the writers of the Indian diaspora. Parenthetically placed next to each writer's name is the name of the country in which he or she was born; it is followed by the names of countries in which he or she has lived for extended periods of time; the last item in the series identifies the country in which the writer currently resides (or resided at the time of death).

It should be noted, however, that some writers live bicontinentally: for example, Anita Desai divides her time between the United States and India; Timeri Murari divides his time between New York and London.

Also, the dismemberment of the Indian subcontinent in 1947 and again in 1971 has rendered problematic the "national origin" of certain writers. For example, Zulfikar Ghose was born in 1935 in Sialkot, which at that time was in India but is currently part of Pakistan. Similarly, Nirad Chaudhuri's hometown, Kishoreganj, was part of India at the time of his birth in 1897, but it is now a city in Bangladesh.

Meena Alexander (India, Sudan, Britain, USA)

Agha Shahid Ali (India, USA)

Deepchand C. Beeharry (Mauritius, India, Mauritius)

Sujata Bhatt (India, USA, Germany)

Neil Bissoondath (Trinidad, Canada)

Sasthi Brata (India, Britain)

Nirad Chandra Chaudhuri (India, Britain)

Saros Cowasjee (India, Britain, Canada)

Rienzi Crusz (Sri Lanka, Britain, Canada)

Cyril Dabydeen (Guyana, Canada)

David Dabydeen (Guyana, Britain)

Mahadai Das (Guyana, USA, Guyana)

Anita Desai (India, USA/India)

G. V. Desani (Kenya, Britain, India, USA)

Leena Dhingra (India, Britain)

Farrukh Dhondy (India, Britain)

Indira Ganesan (India, USA)

Sudhin N. Ghose (India, Britain)

Zulfikar Ghose (India/Pakistan, Britain, USA)

Amitav Ghosh (India/Bangladesh, Egypt, Britain, India/USA)

Padma Hejmadi [also Padma Perera] (India, USA)

Ismith Khan (Trinidad, USA)

Hanif Kureishi (Britain)

Harold Sonny Ladoo (Trinidad, Canada, Trinidad)

Vijay Lakshmi (India, USA)

Kamala Markandaya (India, Britain)

Ved (Parkash) Mehta (India, USA)

Rohinton Mistry (India, Canada)

Prafulla Mohanti (India, Britain)

Rooplall Monar (Guyana)

Dom Moraes (India, USA, Britain/India)

Bharati Mukherjee (India, Canada, USA)

Anand Mulloo (Mauritius)

Timeri Murari (India, Canada, Britain/USA)

Seepersad Naipaul (Trinidad)

Shiva Naipaul (Trinidad, Britain)

V. S. Naipaul (Trinidad, Britain)

Suniti Namjoshi (India, USA, Canada, Britain)

Peter Nazareth (Uganda, USA)

Uma Parameswaran (India, USA, Canada)

Rajagopal Parthasarathy (India, Britain, USA)

Essop Patel (South Africa, Britain, South Africa)

Raymond C. Pillai (Fiji, USA, New Zealand)

Balachandra Rajan (India, Britain, USA, Canada)

Ravinder Randhawa (India, Britain)

Raja Rao (India, France, USA)

Santha Rama Rau (India, Britain, South Africa, USA)

Salman Rushdie (India, Pakistan, Britain)

I. Allan Sealy (India, New Zealand)
Samuel Dickson Selvon (Trinidad, Britain, Canada)
Vikram Seth (India, Britain, USA)
Sharan-Jeet Shan (India, Britain)
Kirpal Singh (Singapore, Australia, Singapore)
Subramani (Fiji)
Bahadur Tejani (Kenya, Uganda, Britain, India, Canada, USA)
Shashi Tharoor (Britain, India, USA)
Edwin Thumboo (Singapore)
M. G. Vassanji (Kenya, Tanzania, USA, Canada)

SELECTED BIBLIOGRAPHY

Since the application of the diasporic paradigm to the study of Indian literary and cultural productions outside the Indian center is a relatively recent scholarly phenomenon, there are only a few critical studies that directly engage the diasporic issues. The following critical works offer the most useful discussions available so far.

Brennan, Timothy. *Salman Rushdie and the Third World: Myths of the Nation.* New York: St. Martin's Press, 1989.

Katrak, Ketu H., and R. Radhakrishnan, eds. *Desh-Videsh: South Asian Expatriate Writers and Artists. Massachusetts Review* 29: 4 (1988). This special issue has creative works by, as well as critical studies of, South Asian writers in the diaspora.

Mishra, Vijay. "Indo-Fijian Fiction: Towards an Interpretation." *World Literature Written in English* 16 (1977): 395–408.

———. "Rama's Banishment: A Theoretical Footnote to Indo-Fijian Writing." *World Literature Written in English* 19 (1980): 242–56.

Mukherjee, Arun. *Towards an Aesthetics of Opposition: Essays on Literature, Criticism and Cultural Imperialism.* Stratford, Ontario: Williams-Wallace, 1988. Five chapters in this volume focus on South Asian writers in Canada.

Mukherjee, Bharati. "Prophet and Loss: Salman Rushdie's Migration of Souls." *Village Voice Literary Supplement* 72 (March 1989): 9–12.

Nelson, Emmanuel S. "Kamala Markandaya, Bharati Mukherjee, and the Indian Immigrant Experience." *Toronto South Asian Review* 9 (Winter 1991): 1–9.

———. *Reworlding: the Literature of the India Diaspora.* Westport, Conn.: Greenwood Press, 1992. A collection of fourteen critical essays, this volume covers all major geographical areas of the Indian diasporic dispersal and discusses the works of all representative writers of the diaspora.

Nixon, Rob. "London Calling: V. S. Naipaul and the License of Exile." *South Atlantic Quarterly* 87 (Winter 1988): 1–38.

Poynting, Jeremy. "East Indian Women in the Caribbean: Experience, Image, and Voice." *Journal of South Asian Literature* 1 (Winter/Spring 1986): 8–18.

———. " 'You Want to be a Coolie Woman?': Gender and Ethnic Identity in Indo-Caribbean Women's Writing." *Caribbean Women Writers.* Ed. Selwyn R. Cudjoe. Wellesley, Mass.: Calaloux, 1990. 98–105.

Sarvan, Charles Ponnuthurai. "Ethnicity and Alienation: The African Asian and His Response to Africa." *Journal of Commonwealth Literature* 20: 4 (1985): 101–10.

Sugunasiri, Suwanda. "Realism and Symbolism in the South Asian Canadian Short Story." *World Literature Written in English* 26: 1 (1986): 98–107.

Thieme, John. "A Hindu Castaway: Ralph Singh's Journey in *The Mimic Men.*" *Modern Fiction Studies* 30: 3 (Autumn 1984): 505–18.

———. "V. S. Naipaul and the Hindu Killer." *Journey of Indian Writing in English* 9: 2 (July 1981): 70–86.

INDEX

ABOUT THE CONTRIBUTORS

CECIL A. ABRAHAMS, who grew up in South Africa, is Dean of the Faculty of Humanities at Brock University in Ontario, Canada.

HENA AHMAD is a doctoral candidate in English at the University of Massachusetts at Amherst.

FAKRUL ALAM is associate professor of English at the University of Dakha, Bangladesh. He is currently writing a book on Bharati Mukherjee's immigrant narratives for Twayne Publishers.

HAROLD BARRATT, a specialist in Caribbean and other postcolonial literatures, teaches at the University College of Cape Breton in Nova Scotia, Canada.

JOGAMAYA BAYER is a doctoral candidate in English at the University of Aachen, Germany.

FRANK BIRBALSINGH, associate professor of English at York University, Canada, is the author of *Passion and Exile: Essays in West Indian Literature* (1988) and editor of *Indenture and Exile: The Indo-Caribbean Experience*.

ANTHONY BOXILL teaches at the University of New Brunswick, Canada; he is the author of *V. S. Naipaul's Fiction: In Quest of the Enemy* and numerous articles on Caribbean literature.

ASA BRIGGS, a social and cultural historian, was Vice-Chancellor of the University of Sussex, England, from 1967 to 1976. He is a frequent visitor to India.

JANE CARDUCCI, who received her Ph.D. from the University of Nevada, is associate professor of English at Winona State University, Minnesota. A specialist in Shakespearean drama, she has published several articles on Renaissance English literature.

LINDA CONRAD received her doctorate in American literature from the University of Queensland, Australia. She lives in Brisbane.

TERENCE DIGGORY, author of books on William Carlos Williams and William Butler Yeats, is professor of English at Skidmore College, New York.

ANURADHA DINGWANEY is assistant professor of English at Oberlin College, Ohio, where she teaches courses in anglophone postcolonial literatures.

ARLENE A. ELDER, a specialist in African and African-American literatures, is professor of English at the University of Cincinnati. Her publications include *"The Hindered Hand": Cultural Implications of Early Afro-American Fiction* (Greenwood Press, 1979).

BARRY FRUCHTER received his doctorate in English from SUNY-Stony Brook; he currently teaches at Nassau Community College.

ANN O. GEBHARD received her Ph.D. in English Education from Syracuse University. She is currently professor of English at SUNY-Cortland; her research interests are in composition theory and multicultural literature.

ROSEMARY MARANGOLY GEORGE is assistant professor of English at the University of California at San Diego.

GURLEEN GREWAL received her Ph.D. in English from the University of California at Davis in 1991; she is now assistant professor of Women's Studies at the University of South Florida.

CHELVA KANAGANAYAKAM received his doctorate from the University of British Columbia. A specialist in postcolonial writing, he is currently assistant professor of English at the University of Toronto.

VINEY KIRPAL, author of *The Third World Novel of Expatriation* (1989), is professor of English at the Indian Institute of Technology, Bombay.

DENISE KNIGHT is assistant professor of English at SUNY-Cortland. Editor of books on Cotton Mather and Charlotte Perkins Gilman, she is currently coediting a volume titled *Contemporary Lesbian Writers of the United States*, scheduled for publication in 1993 by Greenwood Press.

ALPANA SHARMA KNIPPLING, assistant professor of English at the University of Delaware at Newark, is a specialist in multicultural literature and critical theory.

KOH BUCK SONG, a graduate of Cambridge University, is the literary editor for *The Straits Times* in Singapore.

DIANE McGIFFORD has taught English at the University of Manitoba and at the University of Winnipeg; one of her recent books is *Shakti's Words: An Anthology of South Asian Canadian Women's Poetry* (1989).

A. L. McLEOD received his undergraduate education in Australia and his doctorate from Pennsylvania State University. Professor of English at Ryder College, New Jersey, he has published several articles on postcolonial literatures.

P. RUDI MATTAI is professor of Education at SUNY College at Buffalo.

SRILATA MUKHERJEE is a doctoral candidate in English at the University of Texas at Austin.

SRIMATI MUKHERJEE teaches at the University of New Orleans. Her most recent article appears in *Mark Twain Encyclopedia*.

KAMAKSHI P. MURTI is assistant professor of German at Arizona State University, Tuscon.

DENISE deCAIRES NARAIN is a doctoral candidate in English at the University of Sussex.

NALINI NATARAJAN holds a doctorate in English from Aberdeen University, Scotland; she is currently associate professor at the University of Puerto Rico at Rio Piedras.

LAWRENCE D. NEEDHAM teaches at Oberlin College, Ohio. He is at work on a book that explores British Romanticism and the rise of imperialist ideologies.

EMMANUEL S. NELSON is associate professor of English at SUNY–Cortland. He is the editor of *Connections: Essays on Black Literatures* (1988), *Reworlding: The Literature of Indian Diaspora* (Greenwood Press, 1992), *AIDS: The Literary Response* (1992), *Bharati Mukherjee: Critical Perspectives* (1993), and *Contemporary Gay American Novelists: A Bio-Bibliographical Critical Sourcebook* (Greenwood Press, 1993), and has published numerous articles on ethnic, postcolonial, and gay literatures.

VARA NEVEROW-TURK teaches at Southern Connecticut State University; among her areas of teaching and research interest are women's writing and critical theory.

UMA PARAMESWARAN—a poet, playwright, and critic—is professor of English at the University of Winnipeg.

RAJEEV PATKE teaches at the National University of Singapore.

PREMILA PAUL is senior lecturer in English at American College, India. Author of a book on Mulk Raj Anand, she has published several articles on Indian women writers.

FRANK PALMER PURCELL holds a doctorate from Columbia University in Philosophy; he is currently employed by the New York City Board of Education.

DAVID RACKER is a doctoral candidate in English at Tulane University.

GITA RAJAN is assistant professor of English at the University of New Orleans, where she teaches courses in British literature, feminist theory, and postcolonial writing.

VICTOR J. RAMRAJ, author of a book on Mordecai Richler and numerous articles on postcolonial literatures, is professor of English at the University of Calgary.

ANINDYO ROY is a lecturer in English at the Southern Methodist University, Texas.

CHAMAN L. SAHNI is professor of English at Boise State University. He is the author of *E. M. Forster's "A Passage to India": The Religious Dimension*, in addition to several articles on Indian writing in English.

DAIZAL R. SAMAD is assistant professor of English at St. Thomas University, Fredericton, Canada.

JOHN SCHECKTER teaches at Long Island University; he has published several articles on ethnic American and postcolonial literatures.

MAYA MANJU SHARMA is assistant professor of English at Hostos Community College (CUNY) in the Bronx. She received her doctorate in English from Columbia University.

JOEL SHATZKY, editor of *Hitler's Gift to the Jews: Theresienstadt in the Words and Pictures of Norbert Troller* (1991), has published several articles on modern drama. He is professor of English at SUNY-Cortland.

AMRITJIT SINGH is professor of English at Rhode Island College, Providence. He has published widely on the literature of the Harlem Renaissance as well as on Indian writing in English. At present he is at work on a biography of Richard Wright.

ANNE D. ULRICH is a recent graduate of Beaver College, Pennsylvania.

C. VIJAYASREE teaches at the Osmania University in Hyderabad, India. She holds a doctorate in postcolonial writing.

MARILOU BRIGGS WRIGHT received her Ph.D. in English from SUNY-Binghamton. Author of several articles on contemporary women writers, she is currently executive assistant to the president of SUNY-Cortland.

DATE			